PRAISE FO
GOD'S PROPHETIC SYMBOLISM

CH00684163

God's Prophetic Symbolism in Everyday Life will help you hear, see, and recognize the voice of God in everyday occurrences, natural incidents, pictures, symbols, and so-called "coincidences." After reading this book, you are going to start hearing God's voice with a new, supernatural clarity that will lead you into your destiny-defining moments!

SID ROTH
Host, *It's Supernatural!*
New York Times bestselling author of *Heaven is Beyond Your Wildest Expectations*

The Holy Spirit raises up specialists in different fields of ministry and gifting. He has done that with Adam Thompson and Adrian Beale from Australia. These men are dream decoders and revelatory interpretive specialists with their new book, *God's Prophetic Symbolism.* It is a joy to commend these teaching materials to you to help fill in the gaps of the growing library of tools the Holy Spirit is releasing in these days.

JAMES W GOLL
Founder of God Encounters Ministries
Author of *The Seer, Dream Language*, The Discerner and many others

In this new book, God's Prophetic Symbolism in Everyday Life, Adam F. Thompson and Adrian Beale tells the reader, that, among other things, "We open our hearts to hearing God's voice through natural occurrences." This book is long overdue and is very needed in the Body of Christ. Few teachers really know how to train people to hear God's voice through "natural occurrences, signs and wonders, and divine appointments." As this fresh book teaches, many feel they never hear from God, but that is simply not true. God is speaking all the time to all His Children. Sometimes God uses words—but far beyond words, are the myriad of clues God gives us every day to "make our path straight!" If you're one who feels you want to hear God's voice, or you just want to hear God's voice better, this book is a divine appointment for you! Please get your copy and while you're at it, why not get a copy for a friend who needs this!

STEVE SHULTZ,
The Elijah List

What a resource God has given us, being "wired" to hear God's voice. He speaks to us in so many ways, even natural events that take place all around us. Adam F. Thompson and Adrian Beale have written a handbook for us to decipher and discern God's multifaceted voice. Expect to be stunned as you turn the pages of this book. Full of Biblical references and supernatural activity, *God's Prophetic Symbolism in Everyday Life* will enlighten your mind and fill your heart with expectancy. The metaphor dictionary included at the end is worth the price of the book itself. Get ready to grow in your prophetic understanding through reading this new installment of *The Divinity Code* series.

BRIAN SIMMONS
Stairway Ministries

The Passion Translation Project *God's Prophetic Symbolism in Everyday Life* by Adam Thompson and Adrian Beale is a phenomenal addition and continuation of revelatory terminology that will unlock the mysteries of the Holy Spirit's language for all who read it.

Adam and Adrian are cutting-edge vision and dream interpreters. I view them as 21st-century spiritual language articulators that have been able to unlock the understanding and knowledge of signs, symbols, and dream language for the Body of Christ like very few I know. The late Bob Jones was my spiritual papa and he was the master of it. Adam and Adrian have taken this to a whole new level. I highly recommend this new book for all who are looking to understand how the Holy Spirit communicates in everyday life through visions, signs, symbols, pictures, and supernatural occurences.

JEFF JANSEN
Global Fire Ministries International
Senior Leader, Global Fire Church
Author of *Glory Rising* and *Furious Sound of Glory*

God's Prophetic Symbolism in Everyday Life is the key to a closed door you have been just waiting to open. Within these pages are secrets and mysteries revealed, unlocking the Biblical understanding of the connection between the natural and spiritual realms. Adam F Thompson and Adrian Beale have done it again! What the Divinity Code was for Dream Language, this book is for Prophetic Language. This resource is essential for your growth in the supernatural and will activate you in interpreting prophetic events in your own life.

CHARLIE & BRYNN SHAMP
International Speaker, Revivalist and Prophetic Voice
Founders, Destiny Encounters International
www.destinyencounters.com

In their book, *God's Prophetic Symbolism in Everyday Life*, Adam Thompson and Adrian Beale open up a prophetic world of discerning and hearing the voice of God through everyday life. You will discover the many ways God communicates with you, not only through His word and by the Person of the Holy Spirit, but also through the natural world around you including events, names, numbers, music, nature, and so much more. As you glean from Adam and Adrian's prophetic life experience and knowledge of Scripture, you will grow deeper in hearing, deciphering, and interpreting the voice of God for your own life.

MATT SORGER
International Speaker, Author, and Prophetic Healing Minister
mattsorger.com

Adam Thompson and Adrian Beale are passionate about hearing from Heaven in every way possible. In *God's Prophetic Symbolism in Everyday Life,* they show us how God speaks not only through dream and vision, but also nature, numbers and news stories. We heartily agree when they say, "the observable...arena is but a shadow of that which is above it, namely, the spirit realm." Indeed, the spiritual dimension is the true eternal reality, the one Paul exhorted us to live to (2 Cor. 4:18). In their latest book we find remarkable examples and testimonies of what living to the Kingdom of Heaven on a daily basis can look like, and most importantly, inspiration and encouragement to do the same.

DR. MARK VIRKLER and DR. CHARITY VIRKLER KAYEMBE
Authors, *Hearing God Through Your Dreams—*
Understanding the Language God Speaks at Night

I am so excited about Adam and Adrian's new book! This follow-up to *The Divinity Code* is a much needed resource to help people listen for the voice of God in their everyday world. With rich biblical insights, Adam and Adrian share their prophetic experience in interpreting natural events and phenomena, equipping the reader to be more alert to God's communication. I believe this book is a resource for the awakening that is beginning in the church right now. Take your time to read and absorb the revelations within and enjoy the fascinating insights this book brings. *God's Prophetic Symbolism in Everyday Life* truly is a gift to the Body of Christ.

KATHERINE RUONALA
Author, *Living in the Miraculous: How God's Love is Expressed Through the Supernatural,*
Wilderness to Wonders: Embracing the Power of Process, and
Life with the Holy Spirit: Enjoying Intimacy with the Spirit of God
Senior Leader of Glory City Church, Brisbane, Australia
Host of Katherine Ruonala's Glory City TV
www.katherineruonala.com

God's Prophetic Symbolism in Everyday Life is a deep well of revelation that will greatly assist you on your journey of hearing, understanding, and discerning the voice of God in your daily life. I know that as you journey through the pages, a whole new world of encountering His heart and understanding the language of the Holy Spirit will open up to you. The beautiful revelation of Scripture contained in this book, alongside the practical stories and keys of insight gleaned by Adam F. Thompson and Adrian Beale, will leave you in awe all over again of our beautiful God and the creative ways that He speaks every day. I believe that the fire in you for deeper intimacy with Him and to have "eyes to see" and "ears to hear" will be ignited in you in greater ways than ever before through this timely resource. The metaphor dictionary at the back of the book is worth its weight in gold and will be a constant "go-to". I believe this book not only holds a depth of revelation but an impartation of joy, for you as the reader, the joy of growing in recognizing how He is intimately involved and present in your day-to-day life to communicate His heart. What a gift and precious tool we have been given in this wonderful book for such a time as this!

LANA VAWSER
International Prophetic Voice, Speaker, and Author
www.lanavawser.com

God is speaking to us multi-dimensionally and in ways we've never imagined! Too often we fail to recognize His voice because we don't yet know how to identify it let alone understand the signs and symbols He uses. Adam Thompson and Adrian Beale provide an excellent resource to help us distinguish the voice of God in deeper and more unusual ways while expanding our spiritual vocabulary for signs, symbols, and metaphors. I know without a doubt that after you've read *God's Prophetic Symbolism in Everyday Life*, your eyes will be opened and your hearts will expand to embrace God's voice more creatively.

JENNIFER EIVAZ
Executive Pastor, Harvest Christian Center, Turlock, CA
Founder, Harvest Ministries International
Author, *The Intercessors Handbook* and *Seeing The Supernatural*

There is an active and definite desire rising within the Body of Christ to discern and understand the heart of God for the hour in which we live.

In answer to this desire, God is raising up prophetic voices like Adam Thompson and Adrian Beale to enable His people to see that we are children of a Father who is constantly communicating to us. *God's Prophetic Symbolism in Everyday Life* is set to be a profound spiritual guide that will equip and enable believers to discover how God uses natural events to convey spiritual realities. I believe as you read this book there will be a fresh spiritual awakening in your heart and a newfound sensitivity to the ways of God. Your Heavenly Father loves to speak to you, so get ready for daily encounters!

ANDREW MAGRATH
Hope City Church, Melbourne Australia
Author: *The Gospel according to Noah* and *Finding Peace in Troubled Times.*

The Divinity Code has widely become the "go-to" reference and manual for dream interpretation and wisdom on understanding prophetic symbols, allegory, and words. Our personal copy is a very well-worn book and one of our most used ministry resources. We are excited by this follow up volume, *God's Prophetic Symbolism in Everyday Life*, and we believe that it will also have a significant impact globally as a key piece in furthering the increasing prophetic maturity of the Body of Christ.

BEN and JODIE HUGHES
Senior Leaders, Pour It Out Church and Revival Centre
Hosts of the *Pineapple Revival*
www.pouritout.org

GOD'S
PROPHETIC SYMBOLISM
IN EVERYDAY LIFE

GOD'S
PROPHETIC SYMBOLISM
IN EVERYDAY LIFE

The Divinity Code to Hearing God's Voice Through
Natural Events and Divine Occurrences

ADAM F THOMPSON   ADRIAN BEALE

DESTINY IMAGE® PUBLISHERS, INC.
P.O. Box 310, Shippensburg, PA 17257-0310
"Promoting Inspired Lives."

This book and all other Destiny Image and Destiny Image Fiction books are available at Christian bookstores and distributors worldwide.

Cover design by Bethel Media
Interior design by Terry Clifton

For more information on foreign distributors, call 717-532-3040.
Or reach us on the Internet: www.destinyimage.com.

ISBN 13 TP: 978-0-7684-1589-6
ISBN 13 EBook: 978-0-7684-1590-2
HC ISBN: 978-0-7684-1640-4
LP ISBN: 978-0-7684-1641-1

For Worldwide Distribution, Printed in the U.S.A.
1 2 3 4 5 6 / 20 19 18 17

CONTENTS

INTRODUCTION

Surely the Lord God will do nothing,
but He reveals His secret unto His servants the prophets.
—AMOS 3:7 AKJV

The above verse declares that God is committed to letting His people know ahead of time His plans and purposes. As well as being received through the normal channels of revelation, such as the written word and dreams and visions, these are also often communicated to those with "ears to hear" on the world stage through what Jesus called *"the signs of the times"* (Matt. 16:3).

This book is about opening the ears and eyes of God's people to His voice in these everyday prophetic incidents and natural events so that we—His people—know His purposes and can take action in accordance with what He is doing. God is still committed to His people being *"the head, and not the tail"* (Deut. 28:13) and He is ever-prepared to lead those who meditatively consider His word (however it comes) into prosperity and success (see Josh. 1:8). While this book is not focused on financial gain, just imagine how wonderful it would be to know ahead of time the next change of government, the next global financial crisis, or what will be the next boom commodity so that you are positioned accordingly. Having said that, this text takes a broader approach so that individuals can grow to see the spiritual "lay of the land" and seek wisdom to make contextually appropriate personal decisions and actions.

Although prophetic incidents occur on a regular basis, for the most part they go unnoticed by the general populace. One such catastrophic sign was recently relayed in the 2017 Oscars presentation, where the whole of the Western world witnessed the gaffe made during the announcement of the year's best picture. As you are likely aware, the film *La La Land* was announced as the winner of the best picture category, and accordingly, its cast and crew made their way forward to receive the award, only to find out that somehow the wrong card had been handed to the presenters. So, while they were gathered on the podium anticipating their prize, the scene suddenly turned awkward as the correct winner—*Moonlight*—was announced. "How was this embarrassing public blunder a prophetic sign or statement?" you may ask. The scene was a prophetic reenactment of the earlier presidential election, where elements of mainstream media and voices within the entertainment industry, which promote the growth and develoment of fantasy, were forecasting and projecting an unrealistic win for their preferred nominee. How did the eventual winner, *Moonlight*, fit into this scenario? Moonlight, as the reflection of the sun's glory, is symbolic of the Bride of Christ rising in prayer to depose anti-Christ spiritual forces having influence over a darkened world. (Please Note: this prophetic sign only relates to the titles of the two movies not their content or subject matter.)

> *And he dreamed yet another dream, and told it his brethren, and said, Behold, I have dreamed a dream more; and, behold, the sun and the moon and the eleven stars made obeisance to me. And he told it to his father, and to his brethren: and his father rebuked him, and said unto him, What is this dream that thou hast dreamed? Shall I and thy mother and thy brethren indeed come to bow down ourselves to thee to the earth?* (Genesis 37:9-10 KJV).

> *But unto you that fear My name shall the Sun of righteousness arise with healing in His wings; and ye shall go forth, and grow up as calves of the stall* (Malachi 4:2 KJV).

Why would God allow the orchestration of such a mistake? Firstly, to remind us of His sovereignty, that indeed nothing happens on the world stage that cannot be redeemed according to His knowledge and purpose as mentioned in Daniel 2:21:

*And He changes the times and the seasons: He removes kings, and sets up kings:
He gives wisdom to the wise, and knowledge to them that know understanding.*

This prophetic scene also reminds us and our duly elected president that he has a mission to restore righteousness in the nation. *"Righteousness exalts a nation: but sin is a reproach to any people"* (Prov. 14:34 KJV). It also reminds the Church that she has authority when united and exercised in prayer. Finally, it says that the "best picture" will always be that which is revealed by God and delivered and exercised on a spiritual plain. This prophetic sign is not about political agendas. It is a sign to show how powerful the church can be when it rises up and is united in prayer.

Welcome to Supernatural Phenomena

As modern-day prophets, we are called to hear God's voice and to gain understanding of His revelations. There are so many experiences and circumstances that we are involved in each day that we naturally write off as being normal, but God's voice may be embedded within those experiences. In the life of the believer, there needs to be a fine balance for hearing the rhema voice of God that imparts faith and the need for applying the logos—the written Word of God—to one's daily life. God often speaks through signs and symbols, through numbers and names, and through natural means that reveal larger spiritual principles and applications, thus drawing us into greater intimacy with Him.

It is imperative not to seek out omens and "force" the voice of God; this book is a guide on how to recognize when these supernatural phenomena keep coming up in our daily lives and how to attune our hearts and minds to hear what God may be saying. For example, we don't try to search for specific numbers and see what God may be saying to us; rather, as we go about our day-to-day business, God will often speak through certain situations, circumstances, and even numbers. Once we have recognized these recurring incidents as coming from God, then we are to study and interpret what God may be saying to us through those occurrences.

Our walk with God goes deeper than just listening to His voice. We are called to be intimate with God. Understanding the multifaceted ways God speaks is not just about hearing His voice as much as it is about developing a personal relationship and greater intimacy with Him. People can have a prophetic gift and understand mysteries, but without intimacy those revelations will lack true fruit and will not be sustained for any length of time. Furthermore, spiritual insight doesn't come to impart more knowledge to us; it comes to be applied to our lives.

The aim of *The Divinity Code to Hearing God's Voice through Prophetic Incidents and Natural Events* is to encourage every believer that you too can hear the voice of God through recurring circumstances and/or events in your life. This is not some mystical occurrence for the prophets of the Bible or a select few during our time here on earth. This book has been designed to provide easy-to-understand teachings on the way God speaks to us and the importance of hearing His voice. Interspersed throughout it are testimonies of how God has spoken to the authors and others through supernatural phenomena and the resulting impact on their lives. It concludes by providing practical application for how to interpret the signs that God may be using to speak to one's heart through Scripture and with the addition of a metaphor dictionary.

Part I

DISCOVERING PROPHETIC INCIDENTS AND NATURAL EVENTS

Chapter One

THE VOICE OF THE SPIRIT

ADRIAN BEALE

Often believers will question whether God still speaks to us in this day and age. When this question arises, they are often referring to the audible voice of God. God can speak to us audibly if He so chooses; however, when it comes to hearing God's voice outside the traditionally accepted means, my experience has been that it is typically through something that gains your attention because it is unusual or out of character. We are not cookie-cutter Christians; we are unique beings, and therefore God will speak to us in ways that are unique to our spiritual makeup. God does not speak the same way to each of us. Sometimes His words come as a natural incident or event that is a revelation to you. This is not an invitation for us to go looking for omens, but if something is a little freaky, jumps out at you, or is regularly repeated, then take the time to get God's perspective on it by looking at it through the lens of Scripture.

I would like to start off this chapter by highlighting a supernatural event that occurred on November 6, 2016. An eleven-mile stretch of Russian coastline was covered in snowballs ranging from the size of a tennis ball to three feet in diameter. Locals in Nyda, a small village on the Yamal Peninsula, said they had never seen anything like it before. The snowballs reportedly were the result of a rare environmental process where a piece of ice is rolled by the wind, turning the water crystals into giant snowballs. What I find interesting about this natural phenomenon is that it occurred one day after the US presidential election, with all its speculated Russian interference. Could this event communicate something more than that it was cold, wet, and windy outside?

This book is dedicated to exploring the link between supernatural events and incidents in the natural world and their possible spiritual meaning. Unlike the happening described above, which potentially is telegraphing either a message of renewed relationship between Russia and the United States, the readiness to launch cold words, or a warning of something "snowballing" out of control, most natural phenomena are communicating on a more congregational and personal level. Which of the three options above becomes reality is dependent on our prayers. We are called to pray for our leaders because it works into our spiritual enemy's agenda to sour international relations. Therefore, it is most timely that today there is an awakening of believers, who, unlike those Jesus described as dull of heart (see Matt. 13:15), are emerging to corporately pick up the mantle of Elijah and embrace a new level of sensitivity to the voice of the Spirit.

A Call for Balance

It needs to be emphasized at the very outset when considering the potential prophetic meaning of natural events and incidents that a balanced outlook is essential. Therefore, we need to be aware and honest about bias within our own hearts. This is because there are many whose default setting is to think the worst when a loved one is late coming home, and there are others who, because of their background and upbringing, are prone to negativity when interpreting. Jesus Himself explained that every world event is not the result of spiritual forces arrayed against us when He stated that the falling of a tower that killed eighteen men was not the result of their personal sin: *"Or those eighteen on whom the tower in Siloam fell and killed them, do you think that they were worse sinners than all other men who dwelt in Jerusalem?"* (Luke 13:4 NKJV).

To correct any faulty foundation, it is essential to keep before us that God is good. The Hebrew word for "good" is *tov*. *Tov* is made up of three letters: *tet* (surround), *vav* (nail), and *bet* (house). Together the meaning of the letters is "good is that which surrounds and is inside the house." In other words, what you see on the outside comes from what is on the inside. There is no deception, no hypocrisy in God. He is and does what He says. Not only does "good" describe His being, it also describes His faithfulness. This means His goodness surrounds us as His living temples. His favor is always toward us as sons of God.

Reinforcing the need for balance is the fact that Scripture paints both sides of the coin. God acts with judgment with earthquakes, storms, and fire in Isaiah 29:6, but First Kings 19:11-12 emphasizes that God was not speaking to Elijah through earthquakes, wind, and fire.

> *Thou shalt be visited of the Lord of hosts with thunder, and with earthquake, and great noise, with storm and tempest, and the flame of devouring fire* (Isaiah 29:6 KJV).

> *And he said, Go forth, and stand upon the mount before the Lord. And, behold, the Lord passed by, and a great and strong wind rent the mountains, and brake in pieces the rocks before the Lord; but the Lord was not in the wind: and after the wind an earthquake; but the Lord was not in the earthquake: and after the earthquake a fire; but the Lord was not in the fire: and after the fire a still small voice* (1 Kings 19:11-12 KJV).

Elijah, who, it may be reasoned, was accustomed to God speaking through natural phenomena, was on this occasion being directed to greater intimacy—to hear the still small voice of God's Spirit. Therefore, as we open our hearts to hearing God's voice through natural occurrences, let's not negate times of intimacy with Him, which are the real marks of maturity in Christ.

Speaking Without Words

The rhema word is the spoken word, or the living voice of the Spirit. The Bible says, *"...faith comes by hearing, and hearing by the word* [rhema] *of God"* (Rom. 10:17). It is the rhema word and not the logos, or written word, that strengthens the heart with faith. However, the rhema word can be spoken out of the logos. When the Bible speaks of *"the sword of the Spirit, which is the word of God,"* it is talking about the rhema word (Eph. 6:17). Now it is important to understand that God is able to convey the rhema word to us by means beyond those that are either written or spoken, providing direct communication to our heart rather than to our head.

The rhema word may be thought of as coming to us as a "wheel within a wheel." Just as the rim of a wheel has no beginning and no end and therefore can be a depiction of a spirit (which is likewise eternal), so the living voice of the Spirit of God is often "couched in" or "conveyed out of" another setting. When Jesus taught using parables, it wasn't the story itself, but the hidden message within the story, that conveyed what the Spirit was saying. The rhema word may be conveyed and received through God's creation (the natural world), an expression, a dream, a vision, an enactment, an annual celebration, a quickened Scripture, or in any other of a multitude of ways. It is effectively the recognition and understanding of "a voice within a voice." In fact, God will speak to you in whatever way you are primed and prepared to listen.

Think about it: when Elijah cast his mantle on Elisha as his replacement, he initially conveyed that message without saying a thing. Subsequently, in time, Elisha picked up the same mantle and struck the waters of the Jordan with it. The river was divided, and he was able to walk across on dry ground. According to the New Testament, it is the Word of God that divides:

> *For the word of God is quick, and powerful, and sharper than any two-edged sword, piercing even to the dividing asunder of soul and spirit, and of the joints and marrow, and is a discerner of the thoughts and intents of the heart* (Hebrews 4:12).

So the mantle thrown over Elisha, and thereafter used to divide the Jordan was God's Word—and yet, unspoken!

When Jesus met the disciples after His resurrection in Galilee, there was a miracle catch of 153 fish. That's a pretty specific number, wouldn't you say? I find it interesting that Peter, who was initially called with a miracle catch of fish, is also reinstated with one. The two incidents are landmarks to reinforce his life's calling, which was to be the evangelist (fisher of men) who began the harvest of believers. So why was God so specific in numbering the fish? The reason is because that number was an unspoken message. Many people write off the number as incidental and of no importance, but I asked God why there were specifically 153 fish, and a still small voice told me to break it down. So how do you break down the number 153? A Western mind might say "100, 50, and 3." However, looking at it from God's perspective, let's consider 120, 30, and 3. What does that combination spell out for us? Well, 120 is the number of disciples "waiting" in the upper room (see Acts 1:15). It also appears that Noah was building his ark for 120 years (see Gen. 6:3). So, the number represents a period of waiting. Now, what about the number thirty?

Consider how old Joseph and David were when they came to reign, and Jesus, too, when He started His ministry. All of them were thirty years of age (see Gen. 41:46; 2 Sam. 5:4; Luke 3:23). So, thirty represents the right time to reign. Finally, what about the number three? Among other things, the number three speaks of resurrection. It also may speak of witness, fullness, or the Holy Spirit. Putting it all together produces a period of waiting, for the right time to reign, in the resurrection power and fullness of the Holy Spirit! God had a perfect timing to bring the outpouring of the Holy Spirit on the Day of Pentecost. Even though it looked like nothing was happening, the disciples were being assured that God was at work.

That God speaks outside of Scripture is supported by Solomon, who spoke three thousand proverbs relating the wisdom to be found in insects, birds, fauna, and flora:

> *And he spoke three thousand proverbs: and his songs were a thousand and five. And he spoke of trees, from the cedar tree that is in Lebanon even unto the hyssop that springs out of the wall: he spoke also of beasts, and of fowl, and of creeping things, and of fishes. And there came of all people to hear the wisdom of Solomon, from all kings of the earth, which had heard of his wisdom* (1 Kings 4:32-34).

This notion is reiterated by prophets who enacted God's message (see Isa. 20:3; Ezek. 4:12-13; Hosea 1:2); by the Magi, who were led by a star (see Matt. 2:2); by a potter whose actions spoke to Jeremiah (see Jer. 18:2); and by Jesus Himself, who quoted the proverbial adage, "Red sky at night, shepherd delight..." as one of the most commonly recognized examples of God's voice in creation (see Matt. 16:2-3; cf. Rom. 1:20).

Signs and Symbols

A number of years ago, I was battling mentally with some health issues. I was experiencing chest pains, I could hear the pulse of my heart in my head when I lay down at night, and the enemy was in my ear about my physical health and the prospect of death. There were times when I would get up at night and study and meditate in the Scriptures for hours because I couldn't sleep. So that you can appreciate the gravity of the situation, this incident led me to adjust and finalize my last will and testament at that time. However, it was no coincidence that this attack came just days before a scheduled period of extended ministry both interstate and overseas. So together with a good friend, I headed into the Australian Outback with some basic camping equipment for a few days, planning to fast and seek God for the situation to be resolved. On the second day, I had gone out into the bush and was sitting in a camp chair reading my Bible when I came across the following verse:

> *He that finds his life will lose it: and he that loses his life for My sake will find it* (Matthew 10:39).

The second part of the verse jumped out of the page at me and caused me to make a resolution. I said, "I don't care if I die, and if I die, I'm going to do it preaching the Gospel!" Above me the sky was a mixture of moving clouds and open sky, when almost on cue, a massive cloud in the shape of a dragon came into center screen. When I saw it, I pointed at it and rebuked it. It held its shape, almost in slow motion, as if to test me, while the other formations around it were morphing into other configurations. There was no one around me, so I repeated over and over what I had resolved, but now making it a loud verbal declaration. As I did so, the dragon broke up and its components dissipated, and then immediately a cloud in the shape of a man on a cross slid into its place. As a reasonably sane and intelligent person, I have not told this story openly in many churches, but believe it or not, that's what happened. As the Master Artist, God sculpted and spoke through the clouds in my world that day to confirm His word and strengthen my spirit. As a side note, I have found that whenever you are about to step into the Kingdom—bringing Heaven to earth by engaging in a God-given assignment with its associated provision and authority—the enemy mounts pressure against you. If what you carry is in your heart and not merely in your head, and you hold on to it, it is the enemy that yields.

At another time, while traveling from one city to another by car, I heard what sounded like my cell phone text tone. I opened my phone, but there was no text, and I knew from experience that God was going to speak to me. The driver's iPod was playing, and we were listening to the testimony of Smith Wigglesworth. Within a minute of the text signal, the orator shared that there was a time when Smith had backslidden in his Christian walk. That was a revelation to me, having never heard that part of his story before. Now, I had been told earlier that one of the churches I was scheduled to speak in that day was pastored by a woman whose son-in-law had not been to church for a long time. The text message signal, followed by the revelation of Smith's backslidden state, along with my natural knowledge, alerted me that God wanted me to weave Smith's testimony into my preaching. I did just that, and at the end I invited forward those who related to what had been shared. A number of people responded. The first, a woman in her seventies, was an ex-nun who came to rededicate her life to Christ after being defrocked by her order. The next person, also a woman but young with multicolored hair, told me she had just come out of a lesbian relationship and wanted to rededicate her life. And so it continued down the line, which included the pastor's son-in-law. How good is our God! God had alerted me with that text signal just in time to hear the voice of His Spirit in Smith Wigglesworth's testimony so He could minister reconciliation to all those who came forward.

One time, I was just coming into a town where I was to speak when out of the corner of my eye I noticed pigeons huddling together under a roof overhang. It could have been nothing, but it is my understanding from Scripture that a poor man's offering is two turtledoves or two pigeons:

> *And if he be not able to bring a lamb, then he shall bring for his trespass, which he hath committed, two turtledoves, or two young pigeons, unto the Lord; one for a sin offering, and the other for a burnt offering* (Leviticus 5:7 KJV).

I wondered whether the pigeons were symbolic of the state of the town's people. Sure enough, in the process of sharing God's Word, interpreting dreams, and ministering, the characteristics of the poverty spirit were openly recognized and confessed by congregational members. This enabled us to teach on the characteristics of the spirit of poverty and proclaim the opposite over the people.

Driving through the Australian Blue Mountains on another occasion, I was wondering about the future. As we descended along the narrow roads, three or four long-horned Highland cattle scooted off the road and down a laneway ahead of us. They are truly magnificent-looking creatures, with shaggy fur and massive horns about four feet across from point to point. I suddenly realized they conveyed a spiritual encouragement to me. The word *Highland* declares they were Heaven sent. Horns in Scripture are symbolic of strength (see Ps. 18:2; 89:17), so their being "long-horned" was a picture of enduring strength. In addition, cattle are representative of God's provision (see Ps. 50:10). I knew that God was telling me that not only would He provide financially for my family, but He would also do it on an ongoing basis. Sure enough, it was on that particular ministry trip that a young couple, recognizing I live by faith, became the first to support me on an ongoing basis.

In Summary

Some believers can bemoan that God does not communicate with them, but as we have read, God is always talking to us. The beauty of the ways God communicates with us is that they are tailored to our unique design and the level of intimacy we have with

Him. God's Words are purposeful; they are used for correction, for guidance, to bring hope, and to draw us ever closer into His loving arms.

By opening our hearts and coming to God with an understanding that He only wants what is best for us, it becomes easier to still our minds and hear the voice of His Spirit. God can speak to us through His written word, and as we meditate upon the Scriptures He will bring forth His rhema word that will speak to our heart. God can bring revelation through dreams, visions, and expressions, and sometimes God will use the natural world to express His rhema word; this can be through natural events, signs, symbols, and recurring numbers.

I would like to close this chapter with an encouragement from Scripture that God does indeed speak to us. This is confirmed in Hebrews 1:1-2: *"God, who at various times and in various ways spoke in time past to the fathers by the prophets, has in these last days spoken to us by His Son, whom He has appointed heir of all things, through whom also He made the worlds"* (NKJV). And as mentioned in John 10:27, you too can hear the voice of God: *"My sheep hear My voice, and I know them, and they follow Me."*

Chapter Two

NATURAL SIGNS WITH PROPHETIC MEANINGS

ADAM F. THOMPSON

If you have read our first book, *The Divinity Code to Understanding Your Dreams and Visions*, you will know that God can speak to us through signs in our dreams and visions. He can also speak to us through signs occurring in the natural. The Lord releases words through prophetic signs that will help us in our daily walk with Him and in ministering to those around us. This book is not about looking for omens or believing that every little thing has a deeper meaning. It is about understanding what God is telling us through a natural incident or revelatory experience. The signs to which we usually have to pay attention are the ones where the incident is out of the ordinary. It might be something you haven't seen for a long time, or it could be something that is so freaky to have occurred in the natural that you may question if you actually saw it at all.

As believers, we are called to walk in and embrace the prophetic. We are called to see with our spiritual eyes beyond this natural realm. The Word of God throughout the Scriptures is so profound that you will not be able to gain full understanding of it if you are just viewing it through your natural mind. How many times have you heard unbelievers say, "I tried to read the Bible, but I just don't get it! It doesn't make any sense"? Even believers can have trouble understanding the Bible. This is because they are reading it with their natural eyes or hearing it with their natural ears instead of with their spiritual senses. When you become born again, God gives you a new heart, the old one is taken away—never to return—and this new heart contains a spiritual understanding. God tells us to renew our minds so that this spiritual understanding develops (see Rom. 12:2; Eph. 4:23). The Bible was written for this new spiritual heart and not the head. It is with the heart that we understand the Bible, which in turn challenges and changes the natural thoughts of the mind.

The Nile Turning into Blood

As we mature and devote our time to study and prayer, we will become more aware of recognizing when God is talking to us and we will have a greater understanding of what He is trying to convey. Oftentimes God will speak to us through a natural incident, but it will have a spiritual meaning. This is mentioned in the Bible. First Corinthians 15:46 says:

> However, the spiritual is not first, but that which is natural, and afterward the spiritual.

There are layers of revelation to this passage of Scripture, but I do believe that at the base of every outstanding natural incident there is a spiritual underlay that, when understood, opens God's message to us.

One example is in the Book of Exodus when the Lord turned the River Nile into blood. The Nile was one of the first signs God used to harden Pharaoh's heart toward God and His people. That was not a party trick. It was a major natural incident that physically took place as one of the first signs of judgment to come upon Egypt. Scientists have tried to bring some evidence to explain why the Nile turned to blood, but the reality is that it was a supernatural event that occurred in the physical world. It was a prophetic sign to remove principalities over Egypt before major judgment would come upon the whole nation.

I believe that the river turning to blood was actually a sign of the blood of Jesus, the coming Messiah. Jesus is the same yesterday, today, and forever. He is eternal, and this prophetic sign was showing how the blood of Jesus would wash away hardness of hearts and also dismantle any principalities or powers operating over people's lives. When the Nile was turned to blood, the principalities over Egypt were dismantled. Ezekiel 32:2 says:

> *Son of man, take up a lamentation for Pharaoh king of Egypt, and say to him: "You are like a young lion among the nations, and you are like a monster in the seas, coming forth in your rivers, troubling the waters with your feet, and fouling their rivers"* (NKJV).

And verses 12 and 13:

> *...They shall plunder the pomp of Egypt, and all its multitude shall be destroyed. Also I will destroy all its animals from beside its great waters; the foot of man shall muddy them no more, nor shall the hooves of animals muddy them* (NKJV).

Pharaoh was being controlled by a water spirit. Water spirits are mentioned in the Bible, with the most notorious one being Leviathan. Isaiah 27:1 mentions:

> *In that day the Lord with His severe sword, great and strong, will punish Leviathan the fleeing serpent, Leviathan that twisted serpent; and He will slay the reptile that is in the sea* (NKJV).

There are references to Leviathan in the books of Job, Psalms, and Revelation. There is also a water spirit behind Rahab (a metaphor for Egypt), but some versions of the Bible have translated *Rahab* into the word "proud."

> *You rule the raging of the sea; when its waves rise, You still them. You have broken Rahab in pieces, as one who is slain; You have scattered Your enemies with Your mighty arm* (Psalms 89:9-10 NKJV).

It is believed that Revelation 13:1 is speaking of satan himself and thus some deduce that his power is based in the waters: *"Then I stood on the sand of the sea. And I saw a beast rising up out of the sea, having seven heads and ten horns, and on his horns ten crowns, and on his heads a blasphemous name"* (NKJV).

Even to this day there are certain ethnic and religious groups who worship and are controlled by water spirits. A few examples of where these practices are rife can be found in African countries like Nigeria and Liberia; here witchdoctors summon up the powers of the beasts below the waters and use those powers to control their villagers. Voodoo powers are often sought with the gift of tokens from a waterfall in Haiti, and rituals and various sacrifices are performed in the River Ganges of India.

In ancient Egyptian religion, the god Hapi was worshiped to bring the annual flooding of the Nile, which in turn brought fertile soil. It can be surmised that Pharaoh was worshiping the water spirits because in Exodus 7:15, God instructed Moses to go see Pharaoh at the water's edge in the morning:

> *Go to Pharaoh in the morning, when he goes out to the water, and you shall stand by the river's bank to meet him; and the rod which was turned to a serpent you shall take in your hand* (NKJV).

The teachings on water spirits are beyond the scope of this book, but to return to our example of a supernatural incident occurring in the natural, this demon principality that controlled the waters of the River Nile and Pharaoh caused much confusion. The "muddying of the waters" mentioned in Ezekiel 32 means that confusion can come and block people from the truth (see Ezek. 32:13). Pharaoh could not see the truth because of his hardened heart and because of the principality operating through him. The River Nile turning into blood completely dismantled that demon, and this made the way for God to bring complete judgment upon Egypt.

Hosea's Life Example

Another example is Hosea. His life itself was a prophetic sign. He portrayed naturally a truth that applied spiritually. The Lord called Hosea to marry a prostitute named Gomer. This was unorthodox, and when you read the Book of Hosea, you may find yourself questioning why the Lord would tell him to do such a thing. At that time, Israel was in a mess. The nation had turned away from God, and it was not uncommon for women to turn to prostitution. God told Hosea to take Gomer as his wife and to have children with her. Hosea 1:2 explains:

When the Lord began to speak by Hosea, the Lord said to Hosea: "Go, take yourself a wife of harlotry and children of harlotry, for the land has committed great harlotry by departing from the Lord" (NKJV).

After marrying Hosea and having children, Gomer returned to prostitution. Hosea was angry and felt betrayed by his wife lusting after other men.

Bring charges against your mother, bring charges; for she is not My wife, nor am I her Husband! Let her put away her harlotries from her sight, and her adulteries from between her breasts; lest I strip her naked and expose her, as in the day she was born, and make her like a wilderness, and set her like a dry land, and slay her with thirst. I will not have mercy on her children, for they are the children of harlotry. For their mother has played the harlot; she who conceived them has behaved shamefully. For she said, "I will go after my lovers, who give me my bread and my water, my wool and my linen, my oil and my drink" (Hosea 2:2-5 NKJV).

Gomer had slid to such a low point that she was actually on the market to be sold as a slave.

Chapter 2 alternates between describing Hosea's relationship to Gomer and detailing its symbolic representation of God's relation to Israel. God's anger at His people is portrayed in Hosea 2:13:

> *"I will punish her for the days of the Baals to which she burned incense. She decked herself with her earrings and jewelry, and went after her lovers; but Me she forgot," says the Lord* (NKJV).

But God showed mercy upon His people in Hosea 2:23:

> *Then I will sow her for Myself in the earth, and I will have mercy on her who had not obtained mercy; then I will say to those who were not My people, "You are My people!" And they shall say, "You are my God!"* (NKJV).

Ultimately, Hosea receives a revelation of the love of God and in doing so buys his wife back.

> *Then the Lord said to me, "Go again, love a woman who is loved by a lover and is committing adultery, just like the love of the Lord for the children of Israel, who look to other gods and love the raisin cakes of the pagans." So I bought her for myself for fifteen shekels of silver, and one and one-half homers of barley. And I said to her, "You shall stay with me many days; you shall not play the harlot, nor shall you have a man—so, too, will I be toward you"* (Hosea 3:1-3 NKJV).

Hosea displayed real grace and forgave his wife and restored her to her rightful place as his beloved bride. While this story happened in the natural, spiritually speaking it was a prophetic sign of how the Lord was feeling toward Israel. Israel was metaphorically the wife of the Eternal God. She turned from God and lusted after other idols. This brought anger, but it also brought God's mercy upon the whole nation. In Hosea 1:10, God speaks of Israel's restoration:

> *Yet the number of the children of Israel shall be as the sand of the sea, which cannot be measured or numbered. And it shall come to pass in the place where it was said to them, "You are not My people," there it shall be said to them, "You are sons of the living God"* (NKJV).

And in Hosea 3:4-5, Israel's return to God is prophesied:

> *For the children of Israel shall abide many days without king or prince, without sacrifice or sacred pillar, without ephod or teraphim. Afterward the children of Israel shall return and seek the Lord their God and David their king. They shall fear the Lord and His goodness in the latter days* (NKJV).

The Gospels and the revelation of Jesus Christ can also be seen throughout the Book of Hosea. Just as the Lord pursued Israel with relentless love despite her backslidings, He has similarly followed close after our affection in the death of His Son for our sins.

The Ladybug Angel

As an iterant minister, I often get to travel and minister internationally with Adrian. The schedules are tight, with little to no downtime between meetings, and this, in the addition to my pastoral work, can often leave me feeling exhausted. For those in ministry, it is good to be aware of the warning signs of doing too much in your own strength. Exhaustion or burnout may cause you to stop caring about your role. It's also important not to allow exhaustion to lead you into sin or cause any personal issues to arise in your life. Being in a place of not caring is dangerous; you are more susceptible to having a moral fall. The Lord has warned me about exhaustion and has told me that I need to be refreshed continually. It is imperative to remain intimate with the Lord, take breaks, and even have sabbaticals.

Here is an example of when the Lord has used a prophetic sign or a prophetic message through a natural incident to speak to me about my level of exhaustion: After a particular trip, I arrived home feeling completely exhausted. Pastor Todd, who is the co-founder of our church, Field of Dreams, in our hometown of Adelaide, Australia, had to leave to host a crusade overseas. While he was away, I was to take on the governmental role within the church and conduct the meetings.

As I was driving to attend a meeting, I looked down and saw a ladybug (some might know it as a ladybird) on my left thigh. I hadn't seen one since I was a child, and I had definitely never seen one inside a car. It was walking up and down my thigh, and I thought it was quite strange. The Lord's Spirit spoke to me at that point: *"Adam, what do you see? This is a sign. I have sent an angel to strengthen you."*

In the natural, ladybugs protect fruit from aphids, which try to destroy a plant's fruitfulness. In other words, the ladybugs preserve the fruit. The left thigh is symbolic of your natural physical strength and your health. With the ladybug walking up and down my thigh, the Lord was showing me that He was strengthening me physically in the natural realm. He was equipping me to have a sound mind and protecting me from having my fruit destroyed. Spiritually, the scene conveyed that an angel had come against demonic powers that were trying to attack me and destroy the fruit in my life.

What Do You See?

The Lord speaks directly to us. Sometimes He will communicate through a thought, sometimes He will ask a question, and at other times He will use images and signs from the natural world to gain our attention or to deliver His message. For example, the Lord would often speak to the prophet Jeremiah by asking him what he saw in the physical or natural realm. As Jeremiah saw the sign or natural incident, he would then receive a revelation of what God was saying and he would then prophesy the word of the Lord. On one occasion, God instructed Jeremiah to visit the potter, and upon seeing the potter at work, he heard what God was saying to Israel:

> *Arise, and go down to the potter's house, and there I will cause you to hear My words. Then I went down to the potter's house, and, behold, he made a work on the wheels. And the vessel that he made of clay was marred in the hand of the potter: so he made it again another vessel, as seemed good to the potter to make it. Then the word of the Lord came to me, saying, O house of Israel, cannot I do with you as this potter? says the Lord. Behold, as the clay is in the potter's hand, so are you in My hand, O house of Israel* (Jeremiah 18:2-6 NKJV).

The Lord continued instructing Jeremiah and gave a word calling for repentance or else judgment would be passed over Israel. So I believe the Lord spoke to Jeremiah through a natural incident that was a prophetic sign. He released a prophetic word through that sign. This is how God can use us to release prophetic words and operate in the natural and spiritual realms today.

Prophetic Signs Are Our Birthright

In the New Testament, Acts 22:22-28, the apostle Paul was about to be flogged by Roman officials when he asked, *"Is it lawful for you to scourge a man who is a Roman, and uncondemned?"* (Acts 22:25 NKJV). Paul had a dual citizenship, and he used his Roman citizenship to save him from being flogged. The Romans backed off and released him. That was a prophetic sign; it was a sign that happened in the natural first, and there was a revelation behind it in the Spirit. Paul used his second citizenship (Roman) to save himself and to terrify the enemy.

We can use this prophetic sign in our own lives. We too have dual citizenships: we are citizens of our own country, and we are citizens of Heaven. Metaphorically, Rome back in that time was a superpower, and any superpower can be a metaphor for the Kingdom of God. We need to use our heavenly rights, knowing and exercising our heavenly citizenship. Once we start using our heavenly citizenship against the enemy, ask him, "Is it lawful for you to attack a son of God, a citizen of Heaven?" and then begin speaking in the name of Jesus, this brings alarm and terror to the enemy and he will withdraw and let you go.

Worship and Authority

The only way that we can access this prophetic authority and take up our position of being seated in heavenly places is through worship. Because we are blood-bought believers, worship grants us access to the Kingdom of Heaven, where we can enter the presence of the Father. This is where we will worship Him in Spirit and in truth. Jesus spoke about this to the woman at the well:

> But the hour comes, and now is, when the true worshipers shall worship the Father in spirit and in truth: for the Father seeks such to worship Him. God is Spirit: and they that worship Him must worship Him in Spirit and in truth (John 4:23-24).

When we come into this authority through worship, we will see clearly in the Spirit. It will be as if we are on a mountaintop, with an incredible panoramic view of everything around us. When I was in Switzerland, I was on top of the mountain in Zermatt and I could see the clouds beneath me, but I could also see so many other wonders. It gave me the ability to gain my bearings on the surroundings, and this built up my confidence. Many Christians are in a pit, looking up and begging God to help them. They are living in the natural and walking in the flesh. We do need to function in the natural, but we are called to walk in the Spirit. We are called to be mountaintop heavenly dwellers to see clearly.

In summary, as born-again believers, we are entitled to full access of God's Kingdom. Through worship we can have communion with our Father and be in a position to receive and hear from Him. There are various ways God can speak to us: through dreams, visions, an audible voice, a gentle whisper, and signs occurring in the natural. As our spiritual understanding develops, we are better able to interpret the prophetic signs that God leaves in our wake.

The Bible shares the various ways God spoke to His prophets. We learned about Pharaoh's dismantling through prophetic natural incidents. We witnessed how Hosea's own life in the natural became a prophetic symbol of God's love, grace, and mercy for His people, and we saw how God spoke through Jeremiah's observation of signs in the natural to call His beloved Israel to repentance.

As God spoke to His prophets of yesteryear through natural signs and wonders, so too can He speak to us, His modern-day prophets. All we have to do is pay attention to the events surrounding us and feel the gentle tug of His Spirit on our hearts as He intimately shares His thoughts, plans, and blessings for us.

Chapter Three

THE SPIRITUAL OVERLAY OF CREATION

EXTRACT FROM *THE LOST KINGDOM*

BY ADRIAN BEALE

The purpose of this chapter is to explore and confirm the connection between the physical realm and its spiritual counterpart. The scriptural base used to illustrate the importance of recognizing that a spiritual overlay exists is none other than the creation week itself.

The Creation Week

The very first verse of Scripture says that, *"In the beginning God created the heavens and the earth"* (Gen. 1:1 NKJV). The following verses then unfold that creation. What I find interesting is that with an initial reading of these verses it appears that physical creation takes precedence. We read of the progressive introduction of light, earth, seas, plant life, sun, moon, fish, birds, and land animals until finally man is presented as the climax of God's creation. However, the first verse seems to emphasize that the heavens, being mentioned before the earth, are foremost in God's plan. So is there a spiritual or heavenly truth we have not seen as we read rather cursorily through these verses? You be the judge as we unlock the spiritual truths hidden here. Please understand I am not calling into question anything of the awesomeness of the physical creation but rather simply looking at the majesty of our Creator on another level. What I would like you to do as we proceed through this spiritual overlay of creation is to note when Jesus dies and is resurrected in reference to the creation week (on what days are these events depicted?), because like the first verse, it reveals God's focus in the plan of redemption. First let us consider a basic outline of earthly creation:

- On day one God speaks light into existence and divides light from darkness.

- On the second day He separates the waters above from the waters below.

- On day three God gathers together the waters under the heavens and causes dry earth to appear. On the same day plant life comes forth from the earth.

- On day four God sets the sun into the heavens to have dominion over the day; then He sets the moon and stars into the night sky to likewise have rule over the night.

- On the fifth day He creates fish and birds to come forth from the seas.

- On day six He establishes land animals and then man, giving him dominion over all that has been created.

- Finally, on the seventh day God rests from all that He created.

Now, let's reread those events, looking at them through the lens of Scripture (see 1 Cor. 2:13b) so that we see them afresh.

Day One

On day one God revealed light to the world, which was shrouded in uncertainty, disorder, confusion, and emptiness.

And the earth was without form [formless, confusion], and void [emptiness]; and darkness [disorder, uncertainty] was upon the face of the deep... (Genesis 1:2 KJV).

By introducing light, He also separated and distinguished it from darkness.

And God saw the light, that it was good: and God divided the light from the darkness (Genesis 1:4 KJV).

Spiritually, this speaks of the manifestation of Jesus to a darkened and disordered world, a world shrouded in uncertainty. His introduction brought light to the world as it is He who is the light of the world, Just as He openly declared, *"I am the light of the world"* (John 8:12). Like the introduction of light into darkness, His presence similarly divided and polarized people.

And there was much murmuring among the people concerning Him; for some said, He is a good man: others said, No; but He deceives the people (John 7:12 KJV).

Day Two

Day two speaks of Jesus's death. How do we come to that conclusion? On every other day after He had created it is recorded that God saw that it was *"good."* However, on the second day God does not say it was good because the separation of the waters signifies the separation of Father (waters above) from Son (waters beneath).

And God said, Let there be a firmament in the midst of the waters, and let it divide the waters from the waters (Genesis 1:6 KJV).

Death is the separation of waters. Thus, when Moses led Israel through the Red Sea (see Exod. 14:16ff) and when Elijah led Elisha through the Jordan, each crossing symbolized passing through death.

And Elijah took his mantle, and wrapped it together, and struck the waters, and they were divided here [these waters] and there [those waters], so that they two went over on dry ground (2 Kings 2:8 KJV).

That the second day represents death is further reinforced as we come to day three.

Day Three

On the third day, God gathered the waters under the heavens into one place and then let dry land appear.

> *And God said, Let the waters under the heaven be gathered together unto one place, and let the dry land appear: and it was so. And God called the dry land Earth; and the gathering together of the waters called He seas: and God saw that it was good* (Genesis 1:9-10 KJV).

Then He imbued the earth with the ability to bring forth grass, herb, and trees that reproduce according to the very essence and core they bear within.

> *And God said, Let the earth bring forth grass, the herb yielding seed, and the fruit tree yielding fruit after its kind, whose seed is in itself, upon the earth: and it was so. And the earth brought forth grass, and herb yielding seed after his kind, and the tree yielding fruit, whose seed was in itself, after his kind: and God saw that it was good* (Genesis 1:11-12 KJV).

Unlike the second day—where there was no recognition of good—on the third day God saw that it was *"good"* twice. The first recognition of goodness is because the earth coming out of the waters symbolizes the resurrection. How is that so?

Well, in Scripture, man is presented as an earthen vessel. Paul makes direct reference to this when he says, *"But we have this treasure in earthen vessels"* (2 Cor. 4:7), a revelation that parallels Gideon having his men hide a flaming torch in an "earthen" vessel (see Judg. 7:16,20), which is linked to our origin in Adam as one drawn from the dust of the earth (see Gen. 2:7). Just as we baptize by full immersion, which depicts death, burial, and resurrection, the earth coming out of the water symbolizes man's resurrection in Christ.

Because men are as trees spiritually (see Ps. 1:3; Jer. 17:5-8; Mark 8:24), God's second mention of goodness is tied to the inherent ability He has placed in this new creation (redeemed man) to produce fruit in accordance with the seed carried within. Those seeds are the words that proceed from our mouths. While it is tempting to deepen the discussion by unpacking this truth more, the primary purpose of this chapter is to confirm the interplay between the physical and spiritual realms while observing that God has invested more in the cross than redemption.

Day Four

Day four sees the establishment of the heavenly luminaries to divide day from night, with the sun to rule the day and the moon and stars to have dominion over the night.

> *And God made two great lights; the greater light to rule the day, and the lesser light to rule the night: He made the stars also. And God set them in the firmament of the heaven to give light upon the earth, and to rule over the day and over the night, and to divide the light from the darkness: and God saw that it was good* (Genesis 1:16-18 KJV).

Following the resurrection on the third day, these events mirror the ascension of Christ, who is now enthroned and seated in Heaven (see John 6:62; 20:17; Eph. 4:8-10; Ps. 68:18; cf. Isa. 14:13). The apostle Paul confirms this for us when he says, "*...and set Him at His own right hand in the heavenly places*" (Eph. 1:20 KJV).

According to Malachi, only those with faith can see it:

> *But unto you that fear My name shall the Sun of righteousness arise with healing in His wings...* (Malachi 4:2 KJV).

Jesus the Son is also *"the Sun of righteousness,"* and His victory in the cross and His following ascension marks the establishment of a new Kingdom and His enthronement over it, where all authority has been given Him (see Matt. 28:18). The physical positioning of the sun above earth and sky depicts His jurisdiction above Heaven and earth. This speaks of His dominion over the roots of sickness in the spiritual realm and their earthly manifestations. The above verse also suggests that in His ascension, Jesus, as *"the Sun of righteousness"* is healing more today than during His earthly ministry. Now *that* is food for thought! If we position our hearts to be irradiated in His glorious presence, then this verse says He will overshadow us in healing.

As wonderful as that may be, it is not all that was set up on the fourth day. The moon and stars were also positioned to have dominion over the night. What is symbolized by this act is discovered when we look at this event in the light of other Scriptures. Firstly, as night is the absence of light, this speaks of a time when Jesus is physically absent from the earth, as in "now."

> *As long as I am in the world, I am the light of the world* (John 9:5).

Then consider that when Jacob interpreted his son Joseph's dream of the sun, moon, and eleven stars bowing down to Joseph (see Gen. 37:9-10), he understood the moon and stars as representing his wife and sons (Joseph's brothers).

...Shall I and your mother and your brothers indeed come to bow down ourselves to you to the earth? (Genesis 37:10).

Therefore, the moon is a picture of his wife as she radiates his glory (cf. 1 Cor. 11:7), just as we—the Church (the Bride of Christ)—are called to radiate Christ's glory into a darkened world. This is in accordance with the fact that we spiritually have also been described as "seated" (a place of authority) in heavenly places.

And has raised us up together, and made us sit together in heavenly places in Christ Jesus (Ephesians 2:6).

This prefigures us corporately as the Bride of Christ and individually as the promised stars of Abraham's offspring (cf. Gen. 15:5; Rom. 4:13-16; Gal. 3:29). All the heavenly luminaries of day four are also said to be for "signs" and "seasons." In Hebrew, these two words speak of "miracles" and "appointed times" respectively. As sons and heirs of the Kingdom, we have been brought forth for such a time as this to spread the knowledge of the glory of God in the face of Jesus Christ as He works miracles through us.

Day Five

On the fifth day, God spoke forth fish and sea creatures to populate the waters and birds to grace the physical heavens. Both fish and birds can be considered as having wings. A fish or sea creature's fins and flippers are to it as wings are to birds, enabling it to soar and glide through the environment of water like a bird flies through the air. The two just live in different environments. Spiritually, winged creatures may symbolize spirit beings (see Isa. 6:2; Heb. 1:7; Rev. 14:6), so these two arenas might be read as a depiction of the spirit realms above the earth and under the earth. How do I come to that conclusion, you ask? In the same way that baptism parallels an earthly death, burial, and resurrection. In the same way that Jonah's plunge beneath the waves reveals it to be a journey to *"the belly of sheol"* (Jonah 2:2) and *"to the foundations of the mountains"* (Jonah 2:6), where, he recounts, *"The earth with its bars closed upon"* him forever (Jonah 2:6 AKJV). Underwater is under the earth, and in the sky is above the earth (cf. Matt. 12:40). The New Covenant or Kingdom significance of this day's creation is revealed in day six when God, having made man in His image, also gives him dominion over every area of His creation, which spiritually includes these two spirit realms.

And God blessed them, and God said unto them, Be fruitful, and multiply, and replenish the earth, and subdue it: and have dominion over the fish of the sea, and over the fowl of the air, and over every living thing that moves upon the earth (Genesis 1:28).

Day Six

Before God made man on day six, He made every land-based creature on the earth. Their description is both general and broad; they are simply listed as being cattle, beasts, and creeping things (see Gen. 1:30). What is of interest to us is that although these words describe animals of various species, God also uses these names metaphorically at times to describe people, kingdoms, and spirit beings. So we read of men who are described as creeping things (see Hab. 1:14), kingdoms represented as lions (Jer. 4:7; 50:17; Ezek. 32:2), bears and leopard-like creatures (see Dan. 7:5-6), and Jesus on the cross being surrounded by His earthly foes, who are described as roaring bulls of Bashan who gape at Him like roaring lions (see Ps. 22:12-13). This latter scene can also be considered a picture of the spiritual forces using men as puppets arrayed against Him. Then, there is satan, who came to Eve as a serpent (see Gen. 3). Given everything that spiritually precedes this moment, it is apparent—having been made in God's image, and having been given dominion over His creation—that we, as sons of God, are to exercise a level of authority that we have generally ignored.

Day Seven

God blessed the seventh day and set it apart ("sanctified" it). It was not like all the other days. On all the preceding days, the Bible records, *"evening and morning were the... day"* (Gen. 1:5,8,13,19,23,31). On the seventh day, there is no record of evening and morning. Notice that evening is the forerunner to morning because evening speaks of the death of Christ (Sun going down) and morning speaks of His resurrection (Sun rising). This prophetic enactment took place six times (six days) until everything was complete and in place so that God could position man in total rest. The place of rest was not reached after three days, which signified Christ's resurrection. It was not complete even after the ascension depicted on the fourth day. No, God continued to add specific spheres of influence and authority so that the King's dominion (Kingdom) encompassed every area and dimension. Nothing is outside its jurisdiction. Just as Boaz placed six measures of grain into Ruth's cloak (see Ruth 3:15-18) to telegraph the message that he would not "rest" until her union and future was complete, so Christ has done the same here. Selah. The word *sanctified* (qadosh: qoof, dalet, shin), when used specifically to describe the Sabbath, spells out "what follows the threshing." Therefore, stopping at the cross effectively has us still on Boaz's threshing floor. Finally, the seventh day had no evening and morning because we now walk in the continuous light of an ever-growing knowledge of the glory of God in the face of Jesus Christ (see 2 Cor. 4:6; cf. Col. 1:12; 1 Thess. 5:5; 1 John 2:8; Prov. 4:18; 16:15). It is truly a new day. Oh, how He deserves our praise!

Summary

In unveiling the scene behind the physical creation, there is an even greater spiritual truth awaiting our discovery.

- Day One: Jesus came to earth.

- Day Two: He died for our sin.

- Day Three: He was resurrected.

- Day Four: In His enthronement, He has positioned us with Him in heavenly places.

- Day Five: He has given us dominion over the spirit realms above and under the earth.

- Day Six: He has created us in His image and included dominion over all that is upon the earth.

- Day Seven: We walk in the light of the glory of God in the face of Jesus Christ.

Of the six days of creation, the first three cover the manifestation, death, and resurrection of Christ, leaving four further days to describe the inheritance that His death has opened to us as sons. These last four days are a depiction of the everlasting Kingdom He has established. Where the Church has been focused on God's exit strategy (the cross as a source of salvation), the spiritual overlay of creation would suggest that God had a bigger plan. He has always sought sons who would step through the cross to access the Kingdom, a realm beyond these earthly constraints. The victory of the cross and the establishment of His Kingdom means:

- He has imbued man with creative abilities to be issued from his own mouth.

- He has privileged sons to receive healing in His presence by faith.

- He has seated sons in positions of authority.

- He has revealed His glory to sons that they may reflect it into a darkened world.

- He has called forth sons for such a time as this to see miracles.

- He has given sons dominion over the spirit realms above and under the earth.

- He has given sons rule over every physical and spiritual entity on earth.

While this chapter was originally written to illustrate and emphasize the weight God has placed upon the Kingdom into which Christ's death has brought us, it also serves to demonstrate powerfully the overlay of spiritual truth hidden beneath the physical creation. That said, if at the very beginning of time we are able to identify a correlation between the realms, why now would there be a disconnect? Surely, it is not unreasonable to expect that God's creation around us is still relating spiritual truth to those with eyes to see.

Chapter Four

SONGS, NAMES, AND NUMBERS

ADRIAN BEALE

As we have read in the previous chapters, God can speak to us in various ways. God can speak to us in general through His word; Second Timothy 3:16 states that all Scripture is "God breathed":

> *All scripture is given by inspiration of God, and is profitable for doctrine, for reproof, for correction, for instruction in righteousness* (2 Timothy 3:16).

We can hear God's voice as He speaks to us through His creation. *"For since the creation of the world His invisible attributes are clearly seen, being understood by the things that are made, even His eternal power and Godhead, so that they are without excuse"* (Rom. 1:20 NKJV). God spoke all that surrounds us into existence, and as we observe the glorious beauty of this world and take note of the natural signs He presents to us, we are better able to understand His goodness in wanting to guide us in our spiritual walk with Him.

In this chapter, we will learn that God can speak to us through music. One of the most common ways to feel God's presence and to hear His voice is through worship. How sweet are the words of the psalmist and our modern-day musicians who lift our spirits and bring clarity to our situations! But God can also speak to us through secular music, and He can gain our attention and convey His word even when no song is being audibly played. We will also explore how God can communicate with us through the names of people and places and through numbers.

Earworms

Have you ever woken up singing a song, or with a song replaying in your head? Technically, these are known as "earworms." A few years ago, I awoke with the words of the song "Hit the Road Jack" playing in my head. I can honestly say that song was never on my list of favorites, and I was therefore intrigued by its random re-emergence. Researching English sources, I found that the name Jack comes from the name John, which means "gift from God," or more accurately, "Yahweh is gracious." As such, when considering what God could be communicating through the song, I was inclined to conclude that it didn't make sense. Why would I be telling the grace of God to leave me? As I was contemplating its meaning and the puzzle it presented, the thought came to me to recall who it was that actually sang the song. A quick search on the Internet revealed that the song was written by Percy Mayfield and made famous by Ray Charles, both of whom were American. So, does the name Jack come from a different source in America? Sure enough, in the United States, the name Jack is derived from the name Jacob, which can describe the man of the flesh, when compared to Israel, the name he was later given by God. Through the song, God was able to get past my self-preservation defenses to address the re-emergence of a fleshly attitude at the time.

On another occasion, I awoke singing "The Times They Are A-Changin'," a song made famous by Bob Dylan. I was immediately reminded that there is a Scripture that says something like that, so I looked it up.

> *And He changes the times and the seasons; He removes kings, and sets up kings; He gives wisdom to the wise and knowledge to those who have under-standing* (Daniel 2:21 NKJV).

Through that song God was alerting me to an imminent change in leadership that would affect my life. That same day, it was announced that because of a vote within the political party that governed Australia, that nation now had a new prime minister. As the observable political arena is but a shadow of that which is above it, namely, the spirit realm, I could sense that concurrent with the leadership change there was a noticeable spiritual shift. Personally, I became aware of a new level of favor from that day on, as new relationships opened to me and with them new avenues of financial support (cf. Dan. 4:25).

Names

Because of their availability and the depth and range of information they can convey, God delights in using names as regular communication channels. Businesses and brands, auto models, street signs, and food and outlet chains are in abundance everywhere and are often used by God to guide you when you are thinking through decisions.

When our representative in the United States was importing our dream book into the country for the first time, she had to jump through hoops to meet government requirements, filling out forms and going from building to building in an area that was totally unfamiliar to her. While sitting at a stoplight, she asked God, "Should I be doing this if it is so hard?" Right then, just as the light changed to green, a semi-truck pulled up beside her (going in the same direction) with her grandmother's maiden name emblazoned on its side. Because the name had godly significance in her life, she took this as full confirmation that she was on the right path. She was immediately strengthened by the encounter to proceed, and sure enough, the details for importing the books fell into place.

Many years ago, while on holiday, my wife and I took the opportunity to ask God to speak to a married couple about a certain country town that needed a pastor. The next day, we went out sightseeing and decided to go to the tourist information center first. As we jumped out of the car, there in front of us a street sign bore the name of the very town we had prayed about the night before. In the information center, there was a rack that was supposed to display brochures relating to other tourist destinations, but the only one it contained was about the town for which we had prayed. Later that same day, we encountered that name again prominently displayed on a historic paddle steamer exhibition in a museum. Things were lining up to indicate that God was potentially speaking to us about taking on the pastoral role. At the time, my wife was reluctant to uproot our young family because the town didn't have the best reputation and it was in the country. To make a long story short, a week or so later, my wife was chatting to her mom on the phone. Her mom related how her sister, a regional nurse, had flown with the flying doctor service over the weekend. My wife asked to which hospital they had flown. You guessed it—they flew to the town in question. Needless to say, we moved, and we pastored in that country town for a number of years.

The Secret Place Revealed through a Name

Across the world, Harley Davidson is a renowned motorcycle brand. To some people and in some cultures, it may convey power, independence, or freedom; and yet, to others it may speak of rebellion. For me, the name itself is particularly powerful and carries what I believe is the bedrock for all these associations. *Davidson* is a compound of *David* and *son*. *David* means "beloved," so straight away here we have a "beloved son." *Harley* is a compound of *Har* and *ley*. As *ley* is also spelled *lee*, we have here the protected or sheltered side of a field, tree, rock, etc. The foundational meaning of the *Har* part is a reference to either hares or rocks. As we are not able to take shelter behind a rabbit, in context, Harley Davidson is a "beloved son in the cleft of a rock"! The root understanding for the motorcycle brand's name is the secret place of God's presence, which is the true foundation for all power, freedom, independence, and rebellion (from the world). Harley Davidson is really a call to the secret place.

Middle Names

I come from a working-class family. My mother was an orphan, and at the time of my birth, she and my father were wondering how they would cope financially with an extra unexpected child. One morning, with this issue on her heart, Mom was reading the personal columns of the newspaper. While browsing through them, she saw an advertisement directed specifically at her, put there by her two biological brothers who were searching for her. They were looking to pass on an inheritance to her from their birth mother. That discovery and its provision financially stabilized our family at the time. It was also the inspiration for me to receive two middle names—Leonard and Harold—the names of my mom's long-lost brothers. To be honest, while I was growing up, I thought of those two old-fashioned handles as a burden. If someone asked for my middle name, I would reluctantly offer up "Len." Today, I see God's hand of provision miraculously providing for a child He destined to come into the world. As your middle name sits midway between your first and last names, it may be indicative of your spiritual character or destiny. *Leonard* means "lion-like," and *Harold* describes a "strong fighter" or "army leader." Our names are more than just a label to identify us; they are an encoding of our calling and as such are dripping with layers of potential. For this reason, don't be afraid to dig deeper than the usual baby name books when exploring the meaning of your name(s).

There will be positive aspects to meditate on and endorse and possibly negative qualities to pray through.

Negative Names

When a name does carry with it a potentially negative connotation, it is important to look at it afresh with eyes of faith. For example, the name Cecilia means "blind," which, understandably, may not present a terribly exciting prospect for one's future. However, as believers we are called to *"walk by faith, not by sight"* (2 Cor. 5:7). Therefore, the name Cecilia is an encouraging reminder to live beyond the veil of this natural realm.

My own name, Adrian, means "dark," which by definition may be considered to mean "without light." Viewed merely as a label, the name may also be prone to be associated with evil, gloominess, shady dealings, or a sullen outlook. However, viewed through different eyes, darkness has some very positive associations. Darkness is used as a description of the domain of God: *"So the people stood afar off, but Moses drew near the thick darkness where God was,"* which perhaps suggests aspects of His secret, unknown, or mysterious nature (Exod. 20:21 NKJV). The maid in the Song of Songs describes herself as *"dark, but comely,"* a description that betrays her lowly yet attractive character (Song 1:5).

Similarly, if we were to look at the name Jordan from the natural perspective, we would not immediately be met with an inspiring meaning because Jordan literally means "death" or "descender." However, this river's place and role in Scripture clearly sets it apart as the threshold of the Promised Land and the site of believer's baptism, and as such it is the positive harbinger of new things.

Numbers

Very often God will communicate using numbers. These may come in the form of a riddle that may take one of many possible paths to decode. Frequently, the numbers are simply a Scripture you are to look up and apply; at other times their treasure may be found by adding them up, or by an association they trigger. Consecutive numbers, like 345, may speak of a timing issue, like "it is time to act" or "the clock is ticking." The sequence 123 may say "it's as easy as 123" or "things are falling into place." Repeated numbers like 333 may speak of Scriptures like Jeremiah 33:3, and the sequence 1111 may relate to John 11:11 or it may speak of alignment. See the table at the end of this chapter for a brief overview of numbers and their possible metaphoric meanings.

That God communicates spiritually with numbers is reinforced in the Gospels when Jesus first feeds five thousand men, plus women and children, using only five loaves and two fish and then subsequently does a similar miracle, but this time for four thousand men. The number five carries with it the meaning of "grace," and the number one thousand, according to Isaiah 60:22, can be considered as signifying a nation. Therefore, five thousand (five times one thousand) is representative of the nation of grace. That nation is Israel. After He fed the five thousand, there were twelve baskets of leftovers taken up. The twelve baskets, being concave vessels, are a picture of the twelve disciples' hearts, which were filled with His teachings as He poured Himself out to Israel. After He had presented the Gospel to Israel, His disciples would carry the Gospel to the rest of the world. The number four can be representative of rule and dominion, but in this context it carries with it the image of the four corners of the world. Thus, four thousand speaks of the nations of the world. Seven baskets of fragments were taken up after the feeding of the four thousand. The seven in this scenario means His desire is to see the hearts of the world come to rest (the meaning of the number seven). Hopefully you can see how there is much more communicated in the physical provision recorded in Scripture than we may have previously considered.

A young man in Sydney, Australia, who works in finance, was continually seeing the figure 121 everywhere. He would wake at night and see on the clock that it was 1:21 a.m., he would stop his car at the lights and be behind a model 121 Mazda, and he would visit clients and their street address would be 121. He asked me what it meant. Sometimes a series of numbers indicates a sequence over time or a series of heart dispositions. One is the number associated with God, as He is first and foremost, and the number two may, among other things, indicate division, unity, or witness. I asked him if there was a time when he walked away from God, and he admitted that that had been his experience. I said, "In that case, God is showing that you were with God (1), then away from God (2), and you are now again one with God (1)." Why would God communicate that? To reassure the young man that no matter what happened during his ebb, he was now totally accepted and one with Him again.

An older guy named Ken who lives in North Carolina, on waking from sleep, was given the five-digit number 77452. He googled it and found that it was the zip code of a town called Kenney in Texas. He did a bit more research and discovered that the town was named after the evangelist John Wesley Kenney. What does Ken do in the church? He heads up the street outreach team. God was confirming his ministry as an evangelist through this coded message.

I told this latter story to a congregation in Auckland, and a couple on the front row shouted out, "Well, what would the numbers 9637 mean?" I explained the meaning of the numbers individually and asked whether a sequence of their meanings made any sense to them. They replied that it did not. As I was speaking, a man at the back of the meeting punched the numbers into a search engine on his smart phone and then conferred with another gentleman. The two men approached me down the center aisle and asked whether they could say something. I gave them the OK to share what they had found. They announced that 9637 is the scientific identifier of a protein for nerve endings. The second of the two men was a medical doctor and verified what they had found. I asked the couple whether that connection had any meaning to them. They looked at each other shocked because the woman was suffering from a nervous condition. The two men prayed for the woman, and she was overcome in the Spirit and fell to the floor. A month later, I followed up on what had taken place by speaking to her husband in a private message on social media. He confirmed that previously, his wife's condition would cause her to drop things without warning, but now she was no longer experiencing that problem. God had healed her by encoding four numbers to her as she awoke!

A prophetic woman in the church I attend received a download of four numbers. She decided to look up the numbers in *Strong's Exhaustive Concordance*, and God spoke to her through the Hebrew entry.

A young man in Nigeria, who, like most Africans, loves soccer, had a dream in which a young nineteen-year-old man was offered a contract with Manchester United. What does it mean? In this situation, the form of the numerals is the telling factor. Nineteen (19), as a compound of two numbers, is a depiction of God (1) and a man in prayer (9), as seen in the bent form the nine makes. To become unified (Man. United) takes time in prayer with God. The dream indicates that the young man is experiencing a measure of double-mindedness and is being called to prayer to become one with God.

Signs and Natural Incidents with Numbers

ADAM F. THOMPSON

God often speaks to me using numbers as symbolic messages, and He can speak to you in the same way. Sometimes numbers can be used to highlight and reference Scripture verses, and at other times they can have other meanings. If a number pops up regularly over a couple of days and in the same format each time, God is most probably trying to get your attention. The occurrence of numbers are all about timing, and when the numbers jump out at you they will witness with your spirit. Don't go looking for the numbers; God will use them naturally, and they will be obvious to you. Below are some examples of how God can speak to you through the incidents of natural signs in numbers.

Let's say that a doctor has diagnosed you with a serious illness or even has pronounced that death could be imminent and you start to see the numbers 11/11 or 11:11 every time you look at a clock or pass a sign or read a book. God could be speaking to you by using the numbers 11:11 to say that you are not going to die—He is going to raise you out of this sickness or disease. The clock digits 11:11 can be a sign of resurrection power, and they are often used by God to encourage people when they are feeling fatigued, spiritually flat, or sick. Revelation 11 talks about the two witnesses who were martyred, and verse 11 says: *"But after the three and a half days the Spirit of life from God entered them, and they stood on their feet, and great fear struck those who saw them"* (Rev. 11:11). The resurrection power of God came upon the two witnesses, and they ascended into Heaven. A miracle had occurred, and it terrified those who were originally rejoicing in their deaths. This resurrection power was also witnessed in John 11:11 when Jesus said that He was going to wake up Lazarus: *"Our friend Lazarus sleeps; but I go, that I may awake him out of sleep."* Therefore, 11:11 may also mean a spiritual awakening.

I remember once I used to see the numbers 444 popping up. At the time, I was coming under a lot of persecution. I shared the occurrence of the numbers with Adrian, and he said it meant that a prophet is not honored in his own town; in this instance, the numbers referred to John 4:44: *"For Jesus Himself testified, that a prophet has no honor in his own country."* This confirmed the tumultuous time I was enduring.

The numbers 333 may mean that you are about to give birth to the promises of God. In the natural, they can also be an encouragement to women who have endured miscarriages or who have failed to conceive that God is going to bless them with a baby. Three times three equals nine, and nine is the number of a full-term pregnancy, when you are ready to give birth.

There was a time I was preaching at another church in Adelaide (not my home church, Field of Dreams). I was teaching on the prophetic, and I released a word about how God has a mandate for Australia and is raising up an army. God's mandate is for the Body of Christ to have a prophetic voice and to have influence over nations. This prophetic voice was going to move in the power of the spirit of Elijah. I saw the army, and I quoted Revelation 3:7: *"And to the angel of the church in Philadelphia write, 'These things said He who is holy, He who is true, 'He who has the key of David, He who opens, and no one shuts, and shuts and no one opens'"* (NKJV). The key of the house of David was mentioned in Isaiah 22:22: *"And the key of the house of David will I lay on his shoulder; so he shall open, and none shall shut; and he shall shut, and none shall open"* (AKJV). There is a door standing open in Heaven; Jesus is that door.

I also spoke on Ezekiel 37 and the army that God is raising up:

> *Again he said unto me, Prophesy upon these bones, and say unto them, O you dry bones, hear the word of the Lord. Thus says the Lord God unto these bones; Behold, I will cause breath to enter into you, and you shall live: And I will lay sinews upon you, and will bring up flesh upon you, and cover you with skin, and put breath in you, and you shall live; and you shall know that I am the Lord. So I prophesied as I was commanded: and as I prophesied, there was a noise, and behold a shaking, and the bones came together, bone to his bone. And when I beheld, the sinews and the flesh came up upon them, and the skin covered them above: but there was no breath in them. Then said He unto me, Prophesy unto the wind, prophesy, son of man, and say to the wind, Thus says the Lord God; Come from the four winds, O breath, and breathe upon these slain, that they may live. So I prophesied as He commanded me, and the breath came into them, and they lived, and stood up upon their feet, an exceeding great army. Then he said unto me, Son of man, these bones are the whole house of Israel: behold, they say, Our bones are dried, and our hope is lost: we are cut off for our parts. Therefore prophesy and say unto them, Thus says the Lord God; Behold, O My people, I will open your graves, and cause you to come up out of your graves, and bring you into the land of Israel.*

And you shall know that I am the Lord, when I have opened your graves, O My people, and brought you up out of your graves, And shall put My Spirit in you, and you shall live, and I shall place you in your own land: then shall you know that I the Lord have spoken it, and performed it, says the Lord (Ezekiel 37:4-14).

Ezekiel 37 talks about the dry bones and about the earthquake that marked the forming of skin and flesh back on the dry bones. This was about the re-establishment of the nation of Israel, but it has a symbolic layer relevant to our times. I continued to release the word of the Lord at this meeting: God has given us the keys, and He has opened the door that no one can shut. Later that night, there was an earthquake that shook South Australia. It measured 3.7 on the Richter scale. This was a prophetic incident and a sign that took place to confirm the Scripture verses of Revelation 3:7 and Ezekiel 37 that I had quoted. It also says in Amos 3:7: *"Surely the Lord God will do nothing, unless He reveals His secret unto His servants the prophets."* God had released His word to His prophet and confirmed that word through the sign of the earthquake.

Conclusion

The breadth with which God is able to communicate is endless. One time, while I was ministering in Canberra, Australia's capital city (a strongly multicultural city), a man stood up and pronounced a couple of words he had heard in the night. He had no idea what they meant. A woman in the congregation said, "Can you say that again?" He did, and she said, "That is Russian. It means 'wrong government.'" This was either a call to pray for our nation or for him to address wrong thinking, or both.

In conclusion, these brief examples of hearing God's voice outside the box we tend to put Him in highlight for me how well He knows the myriad of resources we have to interpret His message to us. We are not to be lazy, but to be "workmen that rightly divide the word of truth," no matter how it comes (see 2 Tim. 2:15).

If we consider that prophecy is the Word of God that goes before us, then it is evident from this discussion that there are many words of promise still waiting to be recognized, articulated, and stepped into. Wouldn't you agree?

INTERPRETING NUMBERS	
NUMBER	**POSSIBLE METAPHORIC MEANINGS***
1	God, foremost, first, beginning
2	division, union, witness, 2ic (second in charge), twins (alike), death
3	resurrection, fullness, Holy Spirit, Throne Room
4	dominion, rule, world-wide, the eternal realm, Harvest Eve
5	grace, favor, five-fold
6	man, flesh, physical, working toward rest
7	rest, Sabbath, perfection, complete
8	new beginnings, circumcision, octave, beyond time
9	gifts/fruit of the Spirit, judgment, man in prayer
10	completion
11	adding to what God made complete, taking from twelve
12	apostolic government
13	adding to twelve, rebellion
14	The meaning of seven doubled, Passover
15	resurrection
17	amplified seven (seventh prime number), final rest
20	expectancy, waiting
24	governmental perfection
30	right time to reign
40	gestation, testing, probation, time to reign
50	jubilee, freedom, debts cancelled, Pentecost
60	completion of the flesh
70	eldership, foundations, complete rest
100	full harvest, complete flock

INTERPRETING NUMBERS	
NUMBER	**POSSIBLE METAPHORIC MEANINGS***
120	period of waiting
200	insufficient
1000	nation, clan
1111	John 11:11, Hebrews 11:11, Revelation 11:11 alignment
2222	Isaiah 22:22
300	glory of God, glory of men
333	Jeremiah 33:3
444	Isaiah 44:4, John 4:44
555	Isaiah 55:5
666	antichrist, satan
888	Jesus
1234	sequence, time to act
234	Psalms 23:4, shepherd-teacher, discipline and nurture
121	associations, sequence, epochs of experience/heart
678	flesh > rest > new beginnings
777	Judges 7:7; Ps 77:7

For any number(s), first consider a corresponding chapter and verse.

Chapter Five

THE NEED FOR INTIMACY

ADAM F. THOMPSON

While this book focuses on developing the prophetic ability to hear from God through everyday phenomena, this chapter presents the need for a corresponding growth in our intimacy with God. It would be negligent of us to develop one without the other because the delivery of God's prophetic word has to come with the Father's heart of love.

The Call to Maturity

I believe that the Body of Christ has not embraced the prophetic voice like it should in this modern era, but this is the hour where there is a real need. The reason why it hasn't been embraced fully is because there is a lack of maturity with the prophets. Don't get me wrong, there are a lot of mature prophets ministering, and I have some good friends with amazing ministries; but there are also a lot of prophetic people operating in the Body of Christ who are not yet mature. Unfortunately, they can be the ones who operate in the day-to-day mechanics of the church and cause chaos within the church setting. They distract people from God's plan in this New Covenant era. This is not a new occurrence. It has been happening for years. However, I do believe that a change is coming.

The Prophetic Gift without Intimacy

I want to use an example from the life of King Saul; I'm not preaching out of the Old Covenant, but I'm using it as an example for the New Testament era. Regarding Saul, we read:

> *Then Samuel took a vial of oil, and poured it upon his head, and kissed him, and said, Is it not because the Lord has anointed you to be ruler over His inheritance? When you are departed from me today, then you shall find two men by Rachel's sepulcher in the border of Benjamin at Zelzah; and they will say unto you, The donkeys which you went to seek are found: and, lo, your father has left the concern of the donkeys, and sorrows for you, saying, What shall I do for my son? Then shall you go on forward from there, and you shall come to the oak of Tabor, and there shall meet you three men going up to God to Bethel, one carrying three kids, and another carrying three loaves of bread, and another carrying a skin of wine: And they will greet you, and give you two loaves of bread; which you shall receive of their hands. After that you shall come to the hill of God, where is the garrison of the Philistines: and it shall come to pass, when you are come to the city, that you shall meet a company of prophets coming down from the high place with a harp, and a tambourine, and a flute, and a lyre, before them; and they shall prophesy: And the Spirit of the Lord will come upon you, and you shall prophesy with them, and shall be turned into another man. And let it be, when these signs are come unto you, that you do as the occasion suits you; for God is with you. And you shall go down before me to Gilgal; and, behold, I will come down unto you, to offer burnt offerings, and to sacrifice sacrifices of peace offerings: seven days shall you tarry, till I come to you, and show you what you shall do* (1 Samuel 10:1-8).

Samuel prophesied correctly over Saul. Everything that he released over him happened. Furthermore, in First Samuel 19:23-24, Saul prophesied:

So he went on to Naioth in Ramah; and the Spirit of God came upon him also, and as he went on he prophesied until he came to Naioth in Ramah. He took off his royal robes and prophesied before Samuel and lay down stripped thus all that day and night. Therefore they say, Is Saul also among the prophets? (1 Samuel 19:23-24)

Saul was anointed as king, and he had a prophetic gift. The people even recognized he was also a prophet. However, though Saul knew about the spiritual realm and understood the supernatural, he lost the connection with his Heavenly Father; and, therefore, he lacked direction and became afraid.

And when Saul saw the host of the Philistines, he was afraid, and his heart greatly trembled. And when Saul inquired of the Lord, the Lord answered him not, neither by dreams, nor by Urim, nor by prophets. Then said Saul unto his servants, Seek me a woman that hath a familiar spirit, that I may go to her, and inquire of her. And his servants said to him, Behold, there is a woman that hath a familiar spirit at Endor (1 Samuel 28:5-7 KJV).

Saul consulted a medium for direction, and because he entered the spirit realm outside the counsel of God, when the familiar spirit that operated through her told him that he and all of his sons would surely die, he was out of his depth. If he had maintained his intimacy with His Heavenly Father he would have been able to draw from the wisdom of God to govern righteously. Fear gripped Saul, which activated the curse put upon him through the words spoken over him in this encounter. Saul and his sons subsequently fell in battle. This is a good example of someone receiving spiritual insight without the wisdom and authority to counter such a word.

Quenching a Grassroots Move of God

Similarly, some people can initially be anointed in releasing a prophetic word for the Body of Christ, but they may not have an intimate relationship with their Heavenly Father. Or they may have emotional problems or a dysfunctional character, and this may open a door for them to be tormented by demons. This can cause chaos in the Body of Christ. I have experienced this firsthand. In the early days, Todd Weatherly (a close friend and co-founder of our church, Field of Dreams) and I had meetings in my home. We had a move of God where His Spirit was being poured out in my home and in the homes where we gathered for prayer. We never told people about our gatherings. It is unethical to pursue people from another church and have them join an independent home group. If God moves and people come of their own accord, then that is fantastic, but don't pursue people who are already fellowshipping somewhere else to have them join your group or take sheep away from another church.

While we gathered for prayer in my home, the glory of God broke out. Within a month, we had twenty-four people in my living room. People were getting healed, and we even had pastors from other churches knocking on our door for prayer. Initially, we thought we were going to be questioned by the pastors, but they came only to receive healing. We were warned by a mentor—a spiritual mother—who said, "This is great, but be careful. There are people who are going to come who might be prophetic but can be tormented by demons. They come to cause chaos." The enemy wants to distract people from having their eyes on Jesus and the flood of the Spirit, and he wants your gatherings to turn into demon-focused meetings where he can get the glory. Sure enough, after God was moving for many weeks, some questionable people started to come, and they began to cause chaos and bring distraction. They were in emotional turmoil and tormented by demonic powers.

Bugs Are Attracted to the Light

Recounting this event reminds me of when I was sixteen or seventeen and was going to college in a suburb that wasn't as safe as my hometown. I used to catch a train each morning and evening to and from college, where I was studying graphic design. In the evenings, the train station was in complete darkness except for one streetlight. It was a very bright streetlight, and I used to be drawn to it because I could get my bearings and see clearly and I felt safe once I reached the light. But there was one thing I did not like about it—there were a lot of bugs. These bugs caused a lot of distraction because they would bite me. I would try to swat them away, but at the same time I had to try and keep my nostrils and mouth covered. One time I swallowed a bug, and it was traumatic for me.

This is an analogy of what can happen with a move of God. See, Jesus is the gate, and He is also the light. God is light. First John 1:5 says *"...that God is light, and in Him is no darkness at all."* When Jesus steps into a place, and the Holy Spirit is releasing the revelation of Jesus, and there are attributes of Jesus's signs, wonders, and miracles, it is awesome, but it also brings bugs that like to hang around the light.

The apostle Paul was an amazing man; he was a revivalist, and he moved in an apostolic calling. He was very intimate with the Lord, and the Father's glorious light was revealed through his ministry. In Acts 16:16, a woman was trying to imitate and piggy-back off the ministry of Paul.

> *And it came to pass, as we went to prayer, a certain damsel possessed with a spirit of divination met us, which brought her masters much gain by soothsaying: The same followed Paul and us, and cried, saying, These men are the servants of the most high God, which shew unto us the way of salvation. And this did she many days. But Paul, being grieved, turned and said to the spirit, I command thee in the name of Jesus Christ to come out of her. And he came out the same hour* (Acts 16:16-18 KJV).

She was like a bug buzzing around the light.

The enemy was quite cunning in sending this woman. It was a high level of deception at play. Wherever Paul ministered there would have been leaders and indecisive Jews, those that were sitting on the fence and had yet to make a decision to follow the Lord. Now, with this demon-possessed woman trying to endorse Paul's ministry, it would have caused these people to say, "Aha! See, I knew this was of the devil! She is a witch, and she is endorsing Paul's ministry!" Can you imagine the confusion that would have taken place? We need to be very wary of this happening in our churches.

Right Word, Wrong Spirit

Some people can operate in a gift in the church, but their mind is tormented and so they can operate outside the counsel of God. They acknowledge God, but their message is from the soulish realm. It is very important not to operate in the gift without a relationship with God. A prophetic word can be very accurate but come from a wrong spirit. If people are very accurate in their giftings but they're drawing people unto themselves, then they are false prophets. The modern-day prophet needs to equip people for the work of the ministry, to draw them to embrace the head, Jesus, the King of Glory, and to bring them into a relationship and intimacy with God.

Intimacy: The Key to Deeper Revelation

Intimacy with God and Jesus is crucial. John 13:23 says: *"Now there was leaning on Jesus' bosom one of His disciples, whom Jesus loved."* This disciple was John. Jesus was the cornerstone that the people rejected. He is also referred to as the "Rock." John the apostle reclined on the Rock and rested his head there. John was the disciple who was the most intimate with Jesus. Metaphorically, the *bosom* or *breast* means the "heart" of God. John was resting in the nurturing heart of God.

In the Old Testament, Jacob rested his head on a rock as well:

...and he took of the stones of that place, and put them for his pillows, and lay down in that place to sleep. And he dreamed, and behold a ladder set up on the earth, and the top of it reached to heaven: and behold the angels of God ascending and descending on it (Genesis 28:11-12 KJV).

In verse 17, he identifies Jesus as being the gate:

And he was afraid and said, "How awesome is this place! This is none other than the house of God, and this is the gate of heaven!" (Genesis 28:17 NKJV)

Jesus is the direct access or gate to the Father. Some translations use the word *door* instead of *gate*. John 10:7-9 says:

Then said Jesus to them again, Truly, truly, I say to you, I am the door of the sheep. All that ever came before Me are thieves and robbers: but the sheep did not hear them. I am the door: by Me if any man enter in, he shall be saved, and shall go in and out, and find pasture (AKJV).

A few verses earlier it says:

Truly, truly, I say to you, He that enters not by the door into the sheepfold, but climbs up some other way, the same is a thief and a robber. But he that enters in by the door is the shepherd of the sheep. To him the porter opens; and the sheep hear his voice: and he calls his own sheep by name, and leads them out. And when he puts forth his own sheep, he goes before them, and the sheep follow him: for they know his voice. And a stranger will they not follow, but will flee from him: for they know not the voice of strangers (John 10:1-5 AKJV).

Again, this is highlighting the importance of an intimate relationship with Jesus and that we need to be wary of false prophets.

Jesus had different levels of intimacy with His disciples. In First Corinthians 15:6, Jesus appeared to the five hundred followers (see 1 Cor. 15:6). In Luke 10, it mentions that Jesus had seventy disciples that He sent out (see Luke 10:1). Then He had the twelve disciples who were a part of His inner circle, so to speak. At a more intimate level, Jesus had three of the disciples—Peter, James, and John—with Him at the Mount of Transfiguration, where He revealed Himself as the true King of Glory. At the most intimate level was John the apostle.

In Revelation 4:1, John had an intimate encounter with the Godhead:

> *After this I looked, and, behold, a door was opened in heaven: and the first voice which I heard was as it were of a trumpet talking with me; which said, Come up here, and I will show you things which must be hereafter.*

John was the beloved disciple, and Jesus trusted him with the riches of the mysteries of the Kingdom. Through his intimacy with God, John was given the interpretation of these mysteries, and that brought revelation. John was intimate with Jesus *before* he did anything.

Right with a Wrong Spirit vs. Wrong with a Right Spirit

Many believers put the cart before the horse, so to speak. They uphold the gift and embrace it before they embrace a relationship with the Lord. It is not all about the gift; it's all about the relationship. For example, I have an amazing relationship with my daughter; I love her very much. When she was three years old, she drew a picture for me. Technically, the drawing was not 100 percent accurate. You know how kids can draw a person to look very skinny but then add really long arms or short legs and a big head? Well, it was similar to that. It looked like there was a tree, and the color blue was drawn across the sun, etc. My daughter gave this drawing to me as a gift, and I treasured it because of our relationship. If any other parent had handed me the drawing saying it was from their child, it would not have had the same impact on me.

Along these lines, I would like to highlight that we don't always use our gifts 100 percent correctly, but that is OK. If we have an intimate relationship with the Lord, He covers us. First Corinthians 13:9 says, *"For we know in part and we prophesy in part."* Sometimes we mess up or only prophesy in part, but God still loves us and still wants our relationship to go from strength to strength. Everything will flow into a divine order. As Romans 8:28 says, *"And we know that all things work together for good to them that love God, to them who are the called according to His purpose."*

To summarize, the prophetic and intimacy with God go hand in hand. When we step out of our intimate relationship with God, we can cause misunderstandings and even chaos. This not only causes us pain and confusion but affects those around us and can drive people away from our loving Father. Yes, we can operate out of our giftings, and at many times we have and still do. Remember that our gifts are without repentance, and as such God will not withdraw them from us (see Rom. 11:29). However, without an intimate relationship with God we will base our value on the manifested signs our gifts have left on others and we will begin to live only to perform the next sign or to deliver the next prophetic word. Soon we will find ourselves falling into sin and, worse yet, walking away from God and leaving a path of destruction behind us.

We are called to be the light of the world; wherever we go we are to manifest Jesus. But without a relationship with our Father we will only get to demonstrate our gifts and draw people unto ourselves instead of pointing others to an ever-loving God. The beauty of repentance is that with God's love, grace, and mercy, He quickly forgives our mistakes and invites us back into an intimate relationship with Him. Let's return to that secret place and fall in love with our Father again and allow Him to take us from glory to glory. Then let's step out and watch how God's love will be released through us to bring about significant change in the world.

Chapter Six

MAKING APPLICATION OF SPIRITUAL INSIGHT

ADRIAN BEALE

Recently, an unusual photograph on Twitter caught my attention. It showed eighty prized hunting falcons taking up the center cabin seats on an Emirates A330 flight. The birds, owned by a Saudi prince, were being transported by their master to Jeddah, a city in Saudi Arabia. These birds were being carried without a threat to other passengers by virtue of their leather hoods, which hide the birds from any visual stimulus from the world around them, thereby keeping them in a calm state. While I am told that this is not an unusual sight in the Middle East, it jumped out to me because it was something I personally had never seen before. And it is this kind of incident that is worth exploring from a godly perspective, especially when straight away you spot some key elements that carry with them strong spiritual overtones. For me, these were the following:

- Symbolically, birds can be representative of spirit beings because of their wings and ability to fly.
- The number eighty, as the product of eight times ten, is suggestive of "complete new beginnings."
- Like us, birds are at peace when they are closed to worldly stimulus.

After a photograph like this has gotten your attention, it is worth digging a little deeper by finding out characteristics of the scene's components. In this case, the peregrine falcon, also known as the duck hawk in the United States, is the fastest member of the animal kingdom—said to reach speeds of up to 240 miles per hour in its attacking dive. It is the most widespread bird-eating raptor. Rather interesting is the fact that the only other land-based bird species with a greater geographic coverage is the rock pigeon, which has proliferated as a result of human introduction. Pigeons, in turn, have supported the spread of falcons as a prey species.

The peregrine falcon's name means "wandering falcon" and derives from its migratory nature. Its diet consists mainly of medium-sized birds with the occasional small mammal, reptile, or insect. It attains sexual maturity after one year, mates for life, and nests in cliff edge "scrapes" or on tall man-made structures. Finally, it is respected for its hunting, its versatility, and its trainability.

"How does a photograph taken by someone else have application to us?" you may ask. The same way that God spoke to Gideon through a Midianite's dream, the same way that Joseph had his heart revealed and altered through the dreams of a butler and a baker, and the same way that Jesus's parables have application to those with ears to hear.

As you meditate on the information you may have uncovered in a situation like this, Holy Spirit will highlight relevant parallels.

INFORMATION	PARALLEL
Migratory bird	Our sojourning
Eighty	Complete new beginnings
Hood to hide it from the world	We walk by faith, not by sight (see 2 Cor. 5:7).
Feeds on pigeons	We destroy the poverty spirit.

INFORMATION	PARALLEL
Fastest member of the animal kingdom	Our authority is released at the speed of sound.
An attacking dive presupposes prior elevation	We have victory over issues/spirits revealed in prayer.
Medium-sized birds	Not afraid of man (spiritually another bird)
Mates for life	United with Christ
Lives in cliff scrapes	The secret place
Lives in towers	Our prophetic nature
Occasional diet of reptiles and insects	We have authority over demons and things that bug us.
Versatility and trainability	Our renewed mind

At this point, it is time to personalize elements from those listed above that speak to our hearts by recognizing, praying, confessing, decreeing, and/or applying the parallels that Holy Spirit quickens to us. For example, God may be addressing the tendency within us to dwell here and be consumed by all that is around us rather than recognizing that we are aliens here and that our home is Heaven. In which case, we would need to direct our attention to adjusting our hold on worldly pursuits and things. If finances are an issue in your life, such a revelation might be giving you a heads up on the fact that you are being robbed by a poverty spirit. If you are constantly battling financially and/or constantly confessing, "We can't afford this or that," God could be challenging you to recognize the depth of Heaven's resources and calling you to renew your mind and speak and decree from heavenly places in line with God's promises to you rather than your circumstances. Alternatively, the scene may be a call to shut the door to the world and spend time with Him in the secret place so that you receive revelation of His presence and are emboldened to speak to your peers. The potential personal applications are multiple. Now, in hindsight, seeing how potentially rich this attention-grabbing encounter has been, what a mistake it would have been to hastily pass over this opportunity and miss out on the spiritual fine-tuning it offered.

Roadside Harvest

During the latter part of 2016, Southeast Australia experienced storms that deposited tremendous amounts of rain. Not only were the winds associated with these storms so strong that many trees were uprooted and powerline towers twisted over like they were made of foil wrap, but the whole state of South Australia's power grid (which is totally reliant on wind turbines) was shut down repeatedly because of them. Three months later, during our summer vacation, my wife and I had the opportunity to drive through many different parts of the southeastern countryside. While we were not looking for the results of the earlier rains, they were unmistakably present, as we repeatedly encountered huge semi-trucks busily carrying grain to storage facilities and fields covered in hay bales from the bumper growth the rains had produced. What really caught my attention, though, wasn't the activity taking place in commercial farming, but rather the amount of unharvested grain on the sides of the road. It was everywhere. Seed had evidently blown or been washed from the fields after being sown and now, because it wasn't on farmland, stood as full heads of golden grain along the road. Because the scene was repeated in diverse places separated by hundreds of miles, we could not help but notice it and of course talk about it as we drove.

What would this mean if it were God speaking? From Scripture we understand that ripened grain speaks of souls ready for harvest, but how would you interpret the grain's position alongside miles of road throughout the country? I believe the scene has multiple applications. However, before jumping in and interpreting the harvest scene, the preceding storms and the rains they brought are also worth considering. So, the life-giving rains came accompanied with the inconvenience of power outages and a measure of destruction, as trees were uprooted and high voltage towers toppled. If an outpouring of rain is a parallel of the outflow of the Spirit of God and trees are viewed spiritually as men, it may be that some prominent people will struggle, resist, and be removed if their roots go no deeper than religion. The removal of high voltage towers also says that the next move is not going to come through the usual channels. Is this scenario biblical? Well, Scripture does record that pruning precedes harvest, as mentioned in John 15:2: *"Every branch in Me that does not bear fruit He takes away; and every branch that bears fruit He prunes, that it may bear more fruit"* (NKJV). Roads speak of transit, travel, and destiny, and the full heads of grain along the paths they scribe intimate a link between travel or travelers and harvest. This scene suggests that an outpouring in Australia will bring revival, with people going to and fro to be part of what God is doing.

If you personally have these types of experiences, recognize that there is often more than one level of interpretation. Your involvement may suggest that the revelation also applies to you personally and/or that you have a pivotal role in helping a scene material- ize. It may also be that an experience like this has been given to strengthen what God has been saying to others through other means.

As sons of God, we are called to be those who see Heaven come to earth. When we receive revelation from Heaven, it is often because God wants to use us as vehicles to usher in the very thing He has shown us. What He has revealed already exists in Heaven, and our role as sons is to be the portal through which it comes into substance here on earth. This means that the application of what we have been privileged to receive is vital. This will most definitely involve you thankfully praying and decreeing His purposes as discerned in what He has revealed, and it may or may not involve sharing what you are given. I personally do not share everything He shows me. Some things are just insights into the spiritual lay of the land, while others need additional people employed in prayer to usher them in.

At this point, it is important to repeat something that Adam and I teach at our confer- ences. When what is revealed appears negative in nature, we do not necessarily agree with or concede to it. This is because what is revealed may be the plans of the enemy. When this happens, the person receiving revelation should stand in their God-given authority as a son of God and pray, decree, and speak into being the opposite of what was revealed. For example, if sickness, death, financial loss, divorce, etc., were the discerned outcomes of what God may have shown, you would pray and release health, life, prosperity, or unity into the respective situation.

Blood Speaks

While I do not consider myself a Hebrew scholar, I do love to delve beneath the sur- face of the Scriptures to unearth truth only visible in the original language. One of the reasons for this interest is because Hebrew letters in their original form are pictograms or pictures. This means that a Hebrew word in its original form spells out its meaning in pictures. For example, the Hebrew word *esh* consists of two letters, *aleph* (ox head/horns: strong) and *shin* (teeth: devour). Together, they spell out "strong devourer." While the word *esh* is simply translated "fire" in our English Bibles, beneath it is the word picture of a "strong devourer." That may not mean much to you until we extend this root word and find in it the words *woman* and *blessing*. The Hebrew word *ishshah* (woman) is made up of the letters *aleph, shin,* and *hey,* which combine in sequence to say "what comes out of the fire" (meaning "pure"). Similarly, the word *blessed* or *happy,* which in Hebrew is the word *asher,* (*aleph, shin, resh* [head]) presents a word picture of "fire on the head" because fire on the head is symbolic of the presence of God.

HEBREW	WORD PICTURE	MEANING
Aleph shin	Strong devourer	Fire
Aleph shin hey	What comes from fire (pure)	Woman
Aleph shin resh	Fire on the head (God's presence)	Blessed, happy

As we have briefly seen here, the interesting thing about Hebrew root words is the amazing interconnectedness they present. Now, to take this discussion into an area relating to our topic of the relationship between the natural and spiritual realms, let's look at the Hebrew root word *dalet mem* (DM). This word, *dam* (DM), is translated "blood," and when spelled out, *dalet* (door) and *mem* (water) is literally prefigured as the "door of water." This is where it gets interesting because this Hebrew root word *dam* is found in the words *Adam, earth, tears, silence,* and *like.* Beneath the surface of these seemingly unrelated topics the root word *blood* links them all.

BLOOD:	דָּם	Dam: Door of water
ADAM:	אָדָם	Adam: First blood
GROUND:	אֲדָמָה	Adamah: Where Adam came from
TEARS:	דָּמַע	Dema: Blood of the eye
SILENCE:	דְּמָמָה	Dmama What comes from payment
LIKE:	דָּמָה	Dama: Of the blood
BLOOD:	דָּמִים	Dammim: (Plural) Money, payment, retribution

The Hebrew record of the origins of man (as listed in the first three rows above) confirms what indigenous people have been saying for years—that we are more connected to the land than most Western minds understand. This is because the root word *dam* in the Hebrew language links man to the earth, soil, and land (the word *adamah* is used for each of these). Therefore, it should come as no surprise that on occasion, the earth that we live on may want to communicate with us. Jesus called His disciples to brush the dust off their feet, and He said that the stones would cry out, not as a mere idiom or cliché (see Matt. 10:14; Luke 19:40). He said these things because the earth has been called as a witness and in one way or another speaks (see Deut. 4:26; 30:19; 31:28). The timing of the earthquakes at Jesus's crucifixion and Paul's deliverance from prison was not coincidental; each event was a declaration (see Matt. 27:51,54; Acts 16:26). Yes, there are tectonic plates that make up the earth's crust, and often they do move, causing earthquakes, but we also need to acknowledge that at times their movements are orchestrated to communicate. It is evident from their responses that the keeper of the prison and the centurion at the foot of the cross certainly heard what was being said.

At this point, it is important to know that the plural word for *blood* in Hebrew is *damim* and that this word also means "money," "payment," and "retribution." This is likely the real origin of the term "blood money." If we now revisit our list of words related through their Hebrew root *blood* (DM), we may consider that both blood and tears are shed. The shedding of blood is a cost to the body, and the shedding of tears is a cost to the soul. Recognizing also from Scripture that Jesus is referred to as the "last Adam," we sense that something is beginning to materialize through the mist of our understanding (see 1 Cor. 15:45). As the last Adam, Jesus in some way sealed and brought closure to that which was initiated in Adam. The giving of His all in body and soul as expressed through the falling to earth of His blood, sweat, and tears at His Passion brought full circle the call and failure of the first Adam (who was drawn from the earth). So that the earth, in witnessing His righteous sacrifice, declared the unlocking of the curses upon Adam and each successive generation and expressed the same through an earthquake. Jesus was silent before His accusers because His blood did the talking (see Heb. 12:24); and in His blood falling to the ground, He *"silence[d] the enemy and avenger"* (Ps. 8:2).

Adam's granted dominion over the earth has been redeemed by Christ and is now expressed, not through religion, but through God's sons. Understanding as sons (as blood relatives) that He has seated us in heavenly places with a commensurate authority means recognizing that we have been given jurisdiction on the earth (over natural and physical maladies), above the earth (over spiritual forces arrayed against us), and under the earth (over strongholds of the past and their spiritual roots).

It may be that you are reading this book because God has gained your attention through some supernatural or unusual event in your life. If you do not yet know God, then He is likely to be gaining your attention so that He can remove any curses operating in your life and move you into sonship with all its glorious provision. The Bible says, *"But as many as received Him, to them gave He power to become the sons of God, even to them that believe on His name"* (John 1:12). According to this verse, a person needs to invite Christ into their life based on what the Bible says He said and did. As we have already seen, His blood is the pivotal factor in redeeming mankind, and so it is in the application of that blood—which still speaks today—that we now appeal. If this is speaking to you, please feel free to pray this prayer:

> *Father, I recognize that You have been speaking to me through events in my life, and so I would now like to invite You into my life based on the shed blood of Your Son, Jesus. Jesus died for the sins of all mankind, which includes me. Therefore, I ask that You forgive me and my ancestors for all our sins and place them under the precious blood of Christ. I also invite Your Holy Spirit to come and fill me now to empower and teach me to live as a son of God, that I may arise to exercise the authority that You have given Your followers. Amen.*

Chapter Seven

WORKING TOGETHER WITH ANGELS

ADAM F. THOMPSON

Having discussed in previous chapters how to apply what we may have received through a natural revelatory experience, in this chapter I would like to go a step further by looking at our partnership with angels in releasing God's Word. As we know, God can speak to us through dreams and visions, and we can partner with angels to decree God's Word as given in those situations. When we see a natural event with a prophetic meaning, we can also call in God's angelic hosts to decree and release the word of the Lord for that event.

We Have Heaven Backing Us

Did you know that we are heirs to the Kingdom? We are part of God's royal family because we have been adopted as His sons and daughters, and as such we get to partake in the governing of the Kingdom on earth as it is in Heaven. We are also blessed to have the whole of Heaven backing us in our walk here on earth. God created angels to help us and minister to us. Angels are servants; they will never inherit what we will inherit once we join God's family. It is heresy to worship angels. Colossians 2:18-19 states:

> *Let no man beguile you of your reward in a voluntary humility and worshipping of angels, intruding into those things which he has not seen, vainly puffed up by his fleshly mind, and not holding the Head, from which all the body by joints and bands having nourishment ministered, and knit together, increases with the increase of God* (AKJV).

God is to be sought first and foremost, not angels.

The Eternal Family Business

I liken angels to being employees of the Kingdom, which is like an eternal family business. I even believe that there are servant quarters in the Kingdom of Heaven where the angels get to live. Picture a private organization: There is the owner or proprietor of the company, and working for the owner is the CEO. The CEO will never freely inherit the business, but he or she may have an opportunity to buy into it. Then, there is the owner's son. He comes in to learn and to be groomed for ownership of the organization. He will freely inherit and take over the company when the time is right. We, as the heirs of God, receive free access and all the perks from the business owner, as we will become the owner of the family business one day.

Now, this can intimidate the CEO because one day the son is going to be the new ruler or owner of the family business. I believe there is a parable behind this organizational structure that can be used to describe the fall of satan. Satan was delegated to a high level of control in the Kingdom of Heaven, but then the Son of God was to inherit the Kingdom, which meant that satan would never have full control of it. Proud and jealous, he was cast out without an inheritance.

Commanding Angels

We, as the new heirs to the Kingdom, have all the authority of the Kingdom and are seated higher than the angels, which means that we can command them, as mentioned in First Corinthians 6:3: *"Do you not know that we shall judge angels? How much more, things that pertain to this life?"* (NKJV). However, we cannot command angels or even demons with our own opinions. In the Book of Jude, chapter 1, verses 8 and 9, it says:

> *Likewise also these filthy dreamers defile the flesh, despise dominion, and speak evil of dignities. Yet Michael the archangel, when contending with the devil he disputed about the body of Moses, dared not bring against him a railing accusation, but said, The Lord rebuke you* (AKJV).

Not even Michael the archangel resorted to slanderous accusations or spoke out of his own opinion against the devil; he used the word of the Lord. We are to use the Word of God when we command angels into action, and we should never slander angels, nor use them for slanderous works against others.

This is true for rebuking fallen angels too. Although we call them "demons," they are in fact fallen angels, and as such we need to use the word of the Lord when we rebuke them. Psalms 103:20 states that angels do the bidding of the word:

> *Bless the Lord, you His angels, who excel in strength, who do His word, heeding the voice of His word* (NKJV).

Therefore, angels will only react to our commands when we start to decree out of a revelatory understanding of being a son or daughter, having the full domain of God inside us and recognizing the Kingdom we have inherited. We can decree healings, deliverance, and revival. We can call upon an army of angels to go forth as we release the revelatory Word of God over the people to whom we are ministering.

Ministering Spirits

Some people freak out when I start talking about angels; they think that by talking about them, I am worshiping them. I don't worship them. They work alongside all of us as ministering spirits.

> *Are they not all ministering spirits, sent forth to minister for them who shall be heirs of salvation?* (Hebrews 1:14)

When your pastor is speaking from the pulpit on a Sunday, he is ministering to you. Do you worship him? Surely not. You don't worship your pastor, but you are receiving from him. He is a ministering spirit who is releasing the Word of God. In the unseen world or spiritual realm, which supersedes this world, ministering spirits or angels exist. They release the word of the Lord, and you can receive from them like you receive from your pastor. They also work together with you when you speak and decree the revelatory word released to you.

Just as you are instructed to read your Bible and not just blindly follow what is being taught from the pulpit, you need to test the angels when they release words to you. Second Timothy 2:15 and First John 4:1, respectively, say:

> *Study to show yourself approved unto God, a workman that needs not to be ashamed, rightly dividing the word of truth* (2 Timothy 2:15 AKJV).

> *Beloved, believe not every spirit, but try the spirits whether they are of God: because many false prophets are gone out into the world* (1 John 4:1 KJV).

Various Angelic Roles

There are various types of angels who operate in different roles. There are revelatory angels, as mentioned in the Book of Revelation, who bring the revelation of Jesus Christ and the spirit of prophecy. Acts 7:38 and 53, Galatians 3:19, and Hebrews 2:2 all mention that angels are used by God to reveal His word. They also announce important messages, like the births of John the Baptist and Jesus in Luke 1:11 and 26 and Matthew 1:20, and, as mentioned in Revelation 14:6, they will be used to announce key events.

There are also healing angels as mentioned in John 5:4:

> *For an angel went down at a certain season into the pool, and troubled the water: whoever then first after the troubling of the water stepped in was made whole of whatever disease he had* (AKJV).

Angels can also impart physical strength to man as mentioned in the following Scriptures:

> *Suddenly, a hand touched me, which made me tremble on my knees and on the palms of my hands. And he said to me, "O Daniel, man greatly beloved, understand the words that I speak to you, and stand upright, for I have now*

been sent to you." While he was speaking this word to me, I stood trembling (Daniel 10:10-11 NKJV).

And suddenly, one having the likeness of the sons of men touched my lips; then I opened my mouth and spoke, saying to him who stood before me, "My lord, because of the vision my sorrows have overwhelmed me, and I have retained no strength. For how can this servant of my lord talk with you, my lord? As for me, no strength remains in me now, nor is any breath left in me." Then again, the one having the likeness of a man touched me and strengthened me. And he said, "O man greatly beloved, fear not! Peace be to you; be strong, yes, be strong!" So when he spoke to me I was strengthened, and said, "Let my lord speak, for you have strengthened me" (Daniel 10:16-19 NKJV).

And He was there in the wilderness forty days, tempted by Satan, and was with the wild beasts; and the angels ministered to Him (Mark 1:13).

Then an angel appeared to Him from heaven, strengthening Him (Luke 22:43).

There are delivering and protective angels:

For He shall give His angels charge over you, to keep you in all your ways (Psalms 91:11 NKJV).

The angel of the Lord encamps round about them that fear Him, and delivers them (Psalms 34:7).

In Acts 12, an angel set Peter free from prison and delivered him from the hands of Herod and the expectations of the Jewish people.

Now behold, an angel of the Lord stood by him, and a light shone in the prison; and he struck Peter on the side and raised him up, saying, "Arise quickly!" And his chains fell off his hands. Then the angel said to him, "Gird yourself and tie on your sandals"; and so he did. And he said to him, "Put on your garment and follow me." So he went out and followed him, and did not know that what was done by the angel was real, but thought he was seeing a vision. When they were past the first and the second guard posts, they came to the iron gate that leads to the city, which opened to them of its own accord; and they went out and went down one street, and immediately the angel departed from him (Acts 12:7-10 NKJV).

Below are more Scripture verses about delivering angels:

Now the two angels came to Sodom in the evening, and Lot was sitting in the gate of Sodom. When Lot saw them, he rose to meet them, and he bowed himself with his face toward the ground (Genesis 19:1 NKJV).

When the morning dawned, the angels urged Lot to hurry, saying, "Arise, take your wife and your two daughters who are here, lest you be consumed in the punishment of the city" (Genesis 19:15 NKJV).

For He shall give His angels charge over you, to keep you in all your ways. In their hands they shall bear you up, lest you dash your foot against a stone. You shall tread upon the lion and the cobra, the young lion and the serpent you shall trample underfoot (Psalms 91:11-13 NKJV).

My God sent His angel and shut the lions' mouths, so that they have not hurt me, because I was found innocent before Him; and also, O king, I have done no wrong before you (Daniel 6:22 NKJV).

Or do you think that I cannot now pray to My Father, and He will provide Me with more than twelve legions of angels? (Matthew 26:53 NKJV)

and laid their hands on the apostles and put them in the common prison. But at night an angel of the Lord opened the prison doors and brought them out, and said, "Go, stand in the temple and speak to the people all the words of this life" (Acts 5:18-20 NKJV).

There are even angels who provide or bring prosperity. Genesis 24:40 shares the story of Abraham's servant who was sent out to bring back a bride for Isaac:

...The Lord, before whom I walk, will send His angel with you and prosper your way; and you shall take a wife for my son from my family and from my father's house (NKJV).

The Lord sent an angel to prosper the way of the servant and provided him with Isaac's bride. First Kings 19:5-6 tells of the provision of bread and water for Elijah:

And as he lay and slept under a juniper tree, behold, then an angel touched him, and said unto him, Arise and eat. And he looked, and, behold, there was a cake baked on the coals, and a jar of water at his head. And he did eat and drink, and laid himself down again.

Matthew 4:11 shows that angels attended to Jesus after He was tempted by satan for forty days: *"Then the devil left Him, and, behold, angels came and ministered unto Him."*

There are destroying angels, or angels that bring judgment. Remember Sodom and Gomorrah? It took only two angels to wipe out sin and destroy a whole city. That is really intense, and I'm not sure if I would want those angels hanging out with me. Angels bringing judgment can be read about in the following Scriptures:

> *When the morning dawned, the angels urged Lot to hurry, saying, "Arise, take your wife and your two daughters who are here, lest you be consumed in the punishment of the city"* (Genesis 19:15 NKJV).

> *And when the angel stretched out His hand over Jerusalem to destroy it, the Lord relented from the destruction, and said to the angel who was destroying the people, "It is enough; now restrain your hand." And the angel of the Lord was by the threshing floor of Araunah the Jebusite. Then David spoke to the Lord when he saw the angel who was striking the people, and said, "Surely I have sinned, and I have done wickedly; but these sheep, what have they done? Let Your hand, I pray, be against me and against my father's house"* (2 Samuel 24:16-17 NKJV).

> *And it came to pass on a certain night that the angel of the Lord went out, and killed in the camp of the Assyrians one hundred and eighty-five thousand; and when people arose early in the morning, there were the corpses—all dead* (2 Kings 19:35; cf. Isaiah 37:36 NKJV).

> *And God sent an angel to Jerusalem to destroy it. As he was destroying, the Lord looked and relented of the disaster, and said to the angel who was destroying, "It is enough; now restrain your hand." And the angel of the Lord stood by the threshing floor of Ornan the Jebusite* (1 Chronicles 21:15 NKJV).

> *Then the Lord sent an angel who cut down every mighty man of valor, leader, and captain in the camp of the king of Assyria. So he returned shamefaced to his own land. And when he had gone into the temple of his god, some of his own offspring struck him down with the sword there* (2 Chronicles 32:21 NKJV).

> *Then immediately an angel of the Lord struck him, because he did not give glory to God. And he was eaten by worms and died* (Acts 12:23 NKJV).

More can be read in Ezekiel 9:2,5,7; Matthew 13:41-42;49-50; 24:30; and Revelation 7:1-2; 8:2-13; 9:15; 15:1; etc.

In Matthew 28:2-4, an angel brought resurrection power:

And, behold, there was a great earthquake: for the angel of the Lord descended from heaven, and came and rolled back the stone from the door, and sat upon it. His countenance was like lightning, and his clothing white as snow: And for fear of him the keepers did shake, and became as dead men.

This angel can also bring revival and the dunamis power of God. Even in Matthew 27, the dunamis power of God was witnessed:

And, behold, the veil of the temple was rent in twain from the top to the bottom; and the earth did quake, and the rocks rent; and the graves were opened; and many bodies of the saints which slept arose, and came out of the graves after His resurrection, and went into the holy city, and appeared unto many (Matthew 27:51-53 KJV).

What an intense revival that these people witnessed. We have yet to see such resurrection power in this modern age.

I believe that when I talk about and release the revelation of Jesus Christ and the word of the Lord, the angels activate it. As the following Scriptures suggest, angels are used to release words of encouragement:

And God heard the voice of the lad. Then the angel of God called to Hagar out of heaven, and said to her, "What ails you, Hagar? Fear not, for God has heard the voice of the lad where he is. Arise, lift up the lad and hold him with your hand, for I will make him a great nation" (Genesis 21:17-18 NKJV).

Then he said to me, "Do not fear, Daniel, for from the first day that you set your heart to understand, and to humble yourself before your God, your words were heard; and I have come because of your words" (Daniel 10:12 NKJV).

For there stood by me this night an angel of the God to whom I belong and whom I serve, saying, "Do not be afraid, Paul; you must be brought before Caesar; and indeed God has granted you all those who sail with you" (Acts 27:23-24 NKJV).

Angels also bring direction, as in the following Scriptures:

And the angel answered and said to him, "I am Gabriel, who stands in the presence of God, and was sent to speak to you and bring you these glad tidings" (Luke 1:19 NKJV).

Now in the sixth month the angel Gabriel was sent by God to a city of Galilee named Nazareth, to a virgin betrothed to a man whose name was Joseph, of the house of David. The virgin's name was Mary. And having come in, the angel said to her, "Rejoice, highly favored one, the Lord is with you; blessed are you among women!" (Luke 1:26-28 NKJV)

But while he thought about these things, behold, an angel of the Lord appeared to him in a dream, saying, "Joseph, son of David, do not be afraid to take to you Mary your wife, for that which is conceived in her is of the Holy Spirit" (Matthew 1:20; see also Matt. 2:13,19-20 NKJV).

Now an angel of the Lord spoke to Philip, saying, "Arise and go toward the south along the road which goes down from Jerusalem to Gaza." This is desert (Acts 8:26; see also Acts 10:3-6,22 NKJV).

The Chain of Command

Angels are all around us, and some of them must be bored out of their minds. They are waiting for us to activate them and awaken to the revelatory understanding of what it is to decree the word of the Lord and come into that place of authority where we can command angels. It's like in Matthew 8:5-9:

And when Jesus was entered into Capernaum, there came to Him a centurion, beseeching Him, and saying, Lord, my servant lies at home sick of the palsy, grievously tormented. And Jesus said to him, I will come and heal him. The centurion answered and said, Lord, I am not worthy that You should come under my roof: but speak the word only, and my servant shall be healed. For I am a man under authority, having soldiers under me: and I say to this man, Go, and he goes; and to another, Come, and he comes; and to my servant, Do this, and he does it (AKJV).

Jesus was blown away by the centurion's faith and his understanding of the chain of command. We need to understand God's chain of command. All we have to do is decree the word of the Lord, and the angels are activated. The Scripture verses throughout this chapter prove that angels are here to help us and minister to us. They are God's messengers, and they want us to call them forth and release the power of God. As the sons of God, we can enjoy decreeing the word of the Lord, and then we will surely see the Kingdom of God manifest as we work together with angels to bring transformation to this world.

Chapter Eight

HOW DO YOU INTERPRET SUPERNATURAL PHENOMENA?

ADRIAN BEALE & ADAM F. THOMPSON

How do you interpret everyday events that come as revelations? Start by asking Holy Spirit to help you understand what is being communicated in the event. Next, identify the elements that make up the scene, being sensitive to any related passages of Scripture that come to mind. After you have considered your own understanding of each of the elements comprising the scene, you might also like to use the metaphor dictionary included in this book to add depth to the spiritual landscape. If you are having difficulty getting a flow of thoughts, you might try starting the interpretation stage by using the metaphor dictionary as a catalyst for possibilities. Remember that it is more about your relationship with God than about following a specific formula. It is the Holy Spirit who will witness with your heart about the suitability and correctness of each element of the scene, and it is the Holy Spirit who will piece it all together.

The Scriptures are our standard for faith and practice. This means that our primary reference needs to be the Bible. If possible, look at the revelatory event through the lens of Scripture. By this we mean considering where in the Bible there is mention of certain elements that make up what you have experienced in the prophetic event, incident, or encounter. What meaning does God give those elements—for example, grasshoppers, lights, ships, grass, towers, fire, walls, etc.—in the Scriptures? However, we have often found that an event will include flora and fauna that hold specific characteristics and qualities that will require you to dig deeper using an Internet search engine or available textual resources. In researching the characteristics of elements like animals, insects, and plants, you will find new levels of potential understanding open up to unlock the meaning of the incident that gained your attention.

The day after one of our Prophetic Awakening conferences, a lady who had attended was driving down the highway after dropping her daughter off at work. As she drove home, a number of dandelion flowers started drifting across the road. Very quickly, their number increased, until hundreds of dandelions filled the air in front of her automobile. Having never experienced this before and noting that she could not see any dandelion plants on the ground in the area through which she was driving, the scene immediately caught her attention. As a consequence, she was interested in what, if anything, the event could mean prophetically.

The dandelion heads we see taking to the air are really the seed-bearers for the plants' on-going propagation. Being seed, they signify words. *"Now the parable is this: The seed is the word of God"* (Luke 8:11). Their ability to be carried by the breeze suggests, on a spiritual plane, that they are Spirit-carried words (see John 3:8). Being in front of her as she drove (she was moving into them) indicates that it is a future opportunity. The scene is one depicting the promises of God that could be passing her by. A little bit of research tells us that dandelion tea has healing properties, and this too could also be relevant.

To bring closure on the dandelion incident, I asked the lady who had the experience whether she had a situation for which she needed to make a demand on the promises of God. She acknowledged that there was an immediate family need weighing heavily upon her that required the healing of a relationship within the family. Through this incident, God was both bringing attention to His promises and empowering the family in question to harness them with focus for their need.

How do you know which interpretation for an element is the correct one? The answer is to consider, like we did above, the context of the whole incident and how it matches the life of the person who saw or experienced the event. In context, how does the interpretation for one element affect the interpretation of the other elements that make up the scene? There needs to be a cohesiveness in the interpretation of the elements so that the whole incident makes sense on a spiritual level.

To Whom Does the Prophetic Incident Apply?

After you have some elements pegged, start considering who it is that the event, encounter, or incident is for. In our experience, at least 90 percent of prophetic revelations are for the person experiencing them. Prophetic revelations often will address the concerns of your heart. They will also raise heart purification issues (sanctification). They will relate to questions for which you are looking for answers. They will focus on the big issues in your life—physical health issues, family and relationship issues, as well as ministry or working environment matters. Ask yourself what issues are weighing heavily on your heart. God's rhema word to you will center on you and the people over which you have influence and will also show people and organizations that have influence over you. This means that if you are in ministry, your prophetic, revelatory experiences will also address leadership, congregational, denominational, and other related concerns.

Receiving for Others

Our experience has been that the more prophetically sensitive a person is, the more likely they will receive revelation for others. It appears that for five-fold prophetic ministries (see Eph. 4:11), the greater the responsibility and the broader afield the prophet's revelations apply. This means that as well as receiving on a personal level, the prophet will get downloads on a congregational, city, national, and international level, depending on the nature of their calling. Be aware that there is a time period in the development of a prophet's credibility and accuracy of understanding before they are projected onto the world stage.

Before presuming the event is about others, also understand that people with traumatic childhood backgrounds are prone to interpret cataclysmic incidents on a world stage rather than recognizing how the revelations might relate to scars in their own hearts. In these situations, God uses what is happening in world events parabolically as a backdrop for the pain an individual may still be carrying in their heart.

Having said that, depending on your ministry role, God will give insights for counseling purposes to foster the spiritual well-being of others over whom you have responsibility or influence.

What Is the Purpose of What You Have Experienced?

Every prophetic experience sets forth a hope and a future produced by the interpretation, and it is moving by faith on that hope that bears fruit in people's lives. Without hope it is meaningless. God always speaks with purpose. As the interpretation comes to light, ask yourself what the purpose of the experience is. The purpose of a revelatory incident may take the form of a faith-building encouragement, a reassurance of His love, an answer to a question, a secret revealed, a warning, a major key for breakthrough, His guidance or direction, a correction, a prophetic promise, or an invitation to salvation.

Layers of Interpretation

We have all read a familiar passage of Scripture and seen layers—different perspectives—open to us. In the same way, whenever we are interpreting God's voice in prophetic events and incidents, understand that there will often be layers of interpretation possible in the same scene. It is true that taking your time and revisiting a certain scenario will usually allow the Spirit of God to open your heart to alternative meanings. Therefore, do not be in too much of a hurry to produce an early "fixed" interpretation. Also understand that more than one interpretation is possible from the same incident, and each may be valid and complementary.

Problems of Subjectivity

It is often difficult to see what is being said immediately after a revelatory experience because you are so close to it. It takes practice to be able to see objectively. You really have to see the initial imagery on another level. When you have difficulty doing this, write down a description of the experience and come away from it. Seek the Lord in prayer, and as you do, He will deposit fresh insights into your heart that will open up a new perspective from which to view the message. Getting someone else who is open to receive from God (and who also is growing in the gift of interpretation) to view the experience is also a good method of dealing with any problems of subjectivity. Your ability to hear the interpretation from God will improve with practice. Many times you will find yourself saying,

"What could that possibly be about?" As you acknowledge your own inability, suddenly Holy Spirit will drop a thought into your heart that will crack the code, and the whole thing will be revealed before your eyes.

Idols in Your Heart

Here is a word of warning: it is very dangerous to come before God seeking an interpretation while holding a preconceived agenda in your heart. If you do this, the Bible declares that God will give you what you want to hear. God warns Israel of this very thing through Ezekiel by stating:

> *...Everyone of the house of Israel who sets up his idols in his heart, and puts before him what causes him to stumble into iniquity, and then comes to the prophet, I the Lord will answer him who comes, according to the multitude of his idols (Ezekiel 14:4 NKJV).*

When coming before God for any form of guidance, we need to put our hearts into neutral before looking for an interpretation. That is not to say that we should blindly accept everything that someone puts forth as an interpretation of a prophetic revelation. What it does mean is that if we do hear the voice of God through an interpretation, then we need to be obedient to it. If we come prepared to hear only what we want to hear, then that is what we will hear, and that is dangerous.

Not a Forgone Conclusion!

Another vitally important point to remember is that when God gives a prophetic revelation, He does so with our best interests at heart. Prophetic downloads often show potential outcomes—either good or bad—but the outcome is not a fait accompli (a done deal). Without that understanding, we may become philosophical, fatalistic, or defeatist in our outlook, doing nothing to avoid a negative scenario. God may show a problem, risk, or hazard so that we may avert the danger. He may also be showing the plans of the enemy. We can take steps to put things right before they go awry.

When Nebuchadnezzar dreamed of a tree cut down and someone being treated as an animal, Daniel foresaw that God was warning Nebuchadnezzar to humble himself or be taken from the throne. It seems that Daniel did not believe it was an accomplished fact because he tried to prevent the dream's fulfillment by pleading with Nebuchadnezzar to change. He said:

Therefore, O king, let my advice be acceptable to you; break off your sins by being righteous, and your iniquities by showing mercy to the poor. Perhaps there may be a lengthening of your prosperity (Daniel 4:27 NKJV).

Daniel was giving Nebuchadnezzar the steps to avert the pending judgment of God. However, Nebuchadnezzar did not listen and was duly humbled in accordance with the dream (see Dan. 4:28-33). On the other hand, when the king of Nineveh heard of Jonah's prophetic words, he listened to God and had the city fast and repent, and the potential catastrophe was averted (see Jonah 3:6-10). Likewise, the prophet Isaiah was sent to Hezekiah to tell him to get his house in order because he was going to die. Hezekiah turned his heart toward the Lord, and the word of the Lord came again to Isaiah to tell the king his life had been extended fifteen years (see Isa. 38:1-5).

We also are not to use an interpretation as an excuse to do what we want to do contrary to the Word of God. For example, a revelation about sexual immorality or divorce is not justification for us to pursue these avenues of thought as our unalterable fate. No! These downloads are warnings about the state of our hearts so that we take steps to avoid these outcomes.

Judge All Interpretations

The importance of judging what is said in the interpretation of a revelatory experience cannot be overstated. In regard to prophetic ministry, Paul advised the Corinthian congregation to evaluate, or weigh, what was said. He said, *"Let two or three prophets speak, and let the others judge"* (1 Cor. 14:29 NKJV). When writing to the Thessalonian church, Paul also said, *"Do not despise prophecies. Test all things; hold fast what is good"* (1 Thess. 5:20-21 NKJV).

Paul is saying that when someone is operating in the prophetic, there is need for evaluation or judgment of what is said. This takes into account that we deliver God's treasure through earthen vessels and also acknowledges that none of us has arrived yet. We are all in the process of growing in the things of the Spirit. As interpretations of prophetic revelation equate to prophecy, they need to be judged and evaluated. When doing so, you might consider the following questions:

- Is it in line with Scripture?
- If what is being said is corrective, is it free of condemnation?
- Does the prophecy provide a future and a hope?

- Is there an inner witness or conviction that what is being said is truth?

- Does the prophecy meet a heart need?

- Does what is being said line up with what God has been saying through other avenues of guidance?

A negative response to one of these would put what is being said in question. At the very least, it should cause us to put the interpretation "on the shelf" until confirmation is received. A negative response to two or more of these questions would seriously put the prophecy in doubt. At such times, it is best to come away from interpreting until a later date. Often, future revelation will shed light on questionable interpretations.

The Metaphor Dictionary

The metaphor dictionary included in this book provides a comprehensive list of prophetic metaphors. However, due to the creativity of God, the individuality of our personal makeup, and cultural differences, there will be occasions when an entry does not provide an accurate interpretation for an element of a revelatory incident. On these occasions, you may know instinctively what is meant by an element, and if your inclination is correct, it will fit with the rest of the interpretation. If you are unsure of the interpretation, as mentioned earlier you may need to research a subject, animal, or person to discover what facet or characteristic of it God is communicating to you.

If God has given you a revelatory experience, don't be lazy. He knows what resources are available to you. Also, don't overlook a simple idiomatic interpretation. A bee may simply represent busyness, as in "busy as a bee." An ant may simply portray irritation, as in "ants in one's pants." Have fun decoding the messages God is giving you, and don't be afraid to think outside the box.

God bless,

ADRIAN and ADAM

Part II

RESOURCES FOR INTERPRETING VISIONS AND REVELATORY EXPERIENCES

THE METAPHOR DICTIONARY

Caution

It is important to read chapters 1-8 before attempting to use the dictionary. The dictionary contains possible interpretations for elements of individual prophetic incidents and natural events. It includes material that, up until the time of printing, we have found relevant to the interpretation of such events. The work is ever expanding, and as such, there will be interpretations for elements beyond those presented here. Therefore, the dictionary is set forth only as a catalyst of thought to be led and confirmed by the witness of Holy Spirit.

We strongly suggest that this material is not suitable for people who have or who are prone to suffer from neurosis. The authors take no responsibility for wrong interpretations and inappropriate actions taken based on this material.

BIBLE BOOK ABBREVIATIONS

Gen. = Genesis	Isa. = Isaiah	Rom. = Romans
Exod.= Exodus	Jer. = Jeremiah	1 Cor. = 1 Corinthians
Lev. = Leviticus	Lam. = Lamentations	2 Cor. = 2 Corinthians
Num. = Numbers	Ezek. = Ezekiel	Gal. = Galatians
Deut. = Deuteronomy	Dan. = Daniel	Eph. = Ephesians
Josh. = Joshua	Hos. = Hosea	Phil. = Philippians
Judg. = Judges	Joel	Col. = Colossians
Ruth	Amos	1 Thess. = 1 Thessalonians
1 Sam. = 1 Samuel	Obad. = Obadiah	2 Thess. = 2 Thessalonians
2 Sam. = 2 Samuel	Jon. = Jonah	1 Tim. = 1 Timothy
1 Kings	Mic. = Micah	2 Tim. = 2 Timothy
2 Kings	Nah. = Nahum	Tit. = Titus
1 Chron. = 1 Chronicles	Hab. = Habakkuk	Philem. = Philemon
2 Chron. = 2 Chronicles	Zeph. = Zephaniah	Heb. = Hebrews
Ezra	Hag. = Haggai	James
Neh. = Nehemiah	Zech. = Zechariah	1 Pet. = 1 Peter
Esther	Mal. = Malachi	2 Pet. = 2 Peter
Job	Matt. = Matthew	1 John
Ps. = Psalms	Mark	2 John
Prov. = Proverbs	Luke	3 John
Eccles. = Ecclesiastes	John	Jude
Song = Song of Solomon	Acts	Rev. = Revelation

A

Aardvark: (1) Ant-eater (destroyer of the diligent); (2) Nosey.
(1) Prov. 6:6-8; (2) As a physical attribute.

Abominable Snow Man: (1) Abuse (horrible cold-hearted person). Also see *Bigfoot.*
(1) Exod. 1:22; 7:14.

Aboriginal/s: See *Black Man, First Nations Peoples, Foreigner,* and *Native(s).*

Abortion: (1) Warning of an attempt to kill the promise (Herod spirit); (2) Actual abortion.
Also see *Birth* and *Child.*
(1) Exod. 1:16; Matt. 2:16; Rev. 12:4.

Above and Below: (1) Heaven and earth; (2) Spiritual and earthly (worldly); (3) Heaven and hell; (4) Head and feet; (5) Head and tail; (6) Heaven and the Deep; (7) Victorious and defeated.
Also see *Under* and *Underwater.*
(1-2) Exod. 20:4; Deut. 4:39; 5:8; 28:23; Josh. 2:11; John 8:23; Acts 2:19; (3) Job 11:8; Ps. 139:8; Amos 9:2; Matt. 11:23; (4) Eph. 1:22; (5) Deut. 28:13; (6) Gen. 49:25; (7) Deut. 28:13.

Accelerator Pedal: (1) Need to get in the Spirit (be quickened); (2) Need to speed up; (3) Go for it!
(1) John 6:63; Rom. 8:11; 1 Cor. 15:45; (2) 1 Sam. 20:38; 2 Sam. 15:14; (3) Rev. 3:8.

Accident: (1) Operating on the Flesh; (2) Needing spiritual revival; (3) Curse (continual accidents).
See *Automobile Accident.*
(1) 2 Kings 6:5; Acts 20:9; (1-2) Romans 6:19-25; (3) Prov. 26:2; 28:27; 30:10; 30:11; Eccl. 7:21-22; Jer. 11:3; 17:5; 48:10; Zech. 5:3; Mal. 3:9-10; 4:6; Gal. 3:13.

Acid: (1) Cutting or corrosive words; (2) Bitter; (3) Revenge (as in carrying an offense).
(1) Ps. 64:3; Prov. 25:18; (2-3) Acts 8:23; Heb. 12:15.

Acorn: See *Seed.*

Actions: See *Individual Movement* and *Directions.*

Adder: See *Snake.*

Adding: (1) Spiritual growth; (2) Salvations.
(1) 2 Pet. 1:5; (2) Gen. 50:20 (Joseph's name means "adding").

Adoption: (1) Inclusion into the family of God; (2) Spiritual sonship; (3) Freedom; (4) New creation; (5) Taking on something/someone; (6) Quick to take up new things (early adopters).
(1-3) Rom. 8:15; (4) Rom. 8:23; 2 Cor. 5:17; Gal. 6:15; (5) Matt. 10:14; Acts 4:4; 13:48; 17:11; (6) Acts 17:11.

Adorn: See *Wearing.*

Adrift: (1) Aimless; (2) Without direction; (3) Doubting; (4) Needing power; (5) Driven by circumstance/troubles.

Also see *Boat*, *Life Raft*, *Sea*, and *Ship*.

(1) Prov. 29:18; 2 Pet. 2:17; Jude 1:12-13; (2) Isa. 2:3; Mark 6:34; (3) James 1:6; (4) Acts 1:4, 8; (5) Acts 27:15.

Adultery: (1) Intimately sharing your heart with another who is not your spouse; (2) Worldliness; (3) Spiritual adultery (worship of other gods); (4) Lacking judgment; (5) Snare or trap; (6) Literal adultery; (7) Lust issue; (8) Heart stronghold; (9) Work of the flesh.

Also see *Fornication* and *Sex*.

(1) Prov. 6:32; Matt. 5:28; (2) James 4:4; (3) Jer. 3:8-9, 7:9; Ezek. 16:31-32; Hos. 4:13; Rev. 2:22; (4) Prov. 6:32; (5) Prov. 7:23; (6) Exod. 20:14; Jer. 29:23; (7) Matt. 5:28; (8) Matt. 15:19; 2 Pet. 2:14; (9) Gal. 5:19.

Adversary/ies: (1) The devil; (2) Human opposition; (3) Demon spirits; (4) Religious leaders; (5) Self (the flesh); (6) The world.

(1) 1 Pet. 5:8; (2) Matt. 5:25; Luke 12:58; 18:3; 21:15-16; Phil. 1:28; (3) 1 Cor. 16:9; (4) Luke 13:14-17; (5) Acts 18:6 (KJV); 2 Tim. 2:25-26 (KJV); (6) John 16:33; 2 Pet. 2:20; 1 John 5:4-5.

Adversity: (1) Test/trial; (2) Tribulation; (3) Trouble; (4) Suffering.

(1) Prov. 17:17; (2) 1 Sam. 10:19; 2 Chron. 15:6; Ps. 10:6; (3) Ps. 31:7; Prov. 24:10; (4) Heb. 13:3.

Advisor: (1) The Holy Spirit.

(1) John 14:26.

Aeroplane: (1) New heights; (2) Spiritual ministry or church; (3) High profile ministry (or high flyer); (4) Freedom in the Spirit; (5) Human-made imitation of the spiritual/spiritual things/church; (6) Travel; (7) Human-made structure.

(1) Isa. 40:31; (2) Isa. 60:8-9; Ezek. 3:14; 8:3; 11:1,24; Acts 8:39; (3) Gal. 2:9; (4) Ps. 51:12; Rom. 8:2; 1 Cor. 2:12; 2 Cor. 3:17; (5) Eph. 6:12b; Mark 8:33; (6) Acts 8:39-40; (7) Mark 14:58.

Aeroplane Landing: (1) Descending spiritually; (2) From Heaven; (3) Coming to town.

(1) 2 Sam. 1:4, 19; Rom. 11:12; (2) Isa. 14:12; (3) Luke 8:1; 10:38.

Aeroplane (Large Passenger Plane): (1) Church; (2) Big ministry.

(1-2) Ezek. 11:1; Acts 11:26.

Aeroplane (Fighter Plane): (1) Spiritual warfare; (2) Evangelist; (3) Evangelistic ministry; (4) Literal war plane.

(1) Isa. 31:5; (2-3) Acts 8:5-6,12,39; (4) Hab. 1:8.

Aeroplane (Freight Plane): See *Freight*.

Affair: (1) Person or church seduced by the world; (1) Sharing your spouse with work, church, or a hobby.

Also see *Adultery*.

(1) Hos. 2:5; (2) 1 Pet. 2:14-15.

African: See *Black Man* and *First Nations Peoples*.

After (Behind): (1) Past; (2) Following; (3) Later; (4) Seeking after.

Also see *Back, Backward*, and *Behind*.

(1) Phil. 3:13; (2) Matt. 10:38; 16:24; (3) John 13:36; (4) Rom. 9:31; 1 Cor. 14:1.

Afternoon: (1) Latter half of life (a day may parallel a lifetime); (2) Last days; (3) Late opportunity.

(1) Ps. 144:4; 2 Pet. 3:8; (2) John 9:4; (3) Matt. 20:9-14.

Age: (1) Literal years; (2) Generational association; (3) Age may also indicate a characteristic portrayed by the number of years (i.e., 15 may portray innocence; 18 may mean complete putting off of the old self; 92 may mean judgment and separation); (4) A woman's age could be the age of a person or church.

Also see *Baby, Grey, Individual Numbers, Old, Young*, and *Youth*.

(2) 1 John 2:12-14.

Ahead: See *Before*.

Air Conditioner: (1) Holy Spirit; (2) Full Gospel ministry.

(1) Acts 2:2,4a; (2) John 3:8.

Faulty Air Conditioner: (1) Hindering the Holy Spirit.

(1) John 3:8; Acts 7:51.

Air Force: (1) Ministering angel(s); (2) Spirit (good or evil); (3) Heaven.

(1-3) Rev. 8:13; 14:6; 19:17.

Air Force One: (1) Ministry with Christ onboard.

(1) Matt. 28:18-20.

Air Freshener: (1) The anointing of the Holy Spirit.

(1) Isa. 61:1-3.

Airmail: (1) Message from God; (2) Prophet to the nations (sending airmail).

(1) Gen. 8:11; (2) Jer. 1:9-10.

Airmail Parcel: (1) Gift from God; (2) Promise manifesting in the natural; (3) Fulfillment of the promise.

(1) Eph. 4:8; (2) 2 Cor. 1:20; (3) Luke 24:49; Acts 2:2.

Air Mattress (Airbed): (1) Holy Spirit.

(1) John 3:5, 8; Rom. 8:16; 1 John 5:6b.

Airplane: See *Aeroplane*.

Airport: (1) Waiting for destiny or ministry; (2) Transfer of ministries; (3) Spiritual grounding; (4) Spiritual refueling; (5) Waiting on the Holy Spirit; (6) Glory-gathering church; (7) Venturing out; (8) Church touching the nations.

Also see *Railway Station*.

(1) Isa. 40:31; Luke 2:25; (2) Acts 15:35-37,40; (3) Acts 2:42; 2 Tim. 3:16-17; (4) Acts 4:31; 6:3; 7:55; 11:24; 13:2-3,9; (5) Acts 2:1; (6) 1 Kings 10:2; (7-8) Acts 13:1-3.

Alarm: (1) Warning; (2) Warning of spiritual attack (smoke alarm); (3) Warning of judgment (fire alarm); (4) Conscience; (5) Prophetic decree; (6) Time to awaken spiritually.

Also see *Fire, Smoke,* and *Trumpet.*

(1) Amos 3:6; (2) Rev. 9:2-3; (3) Ezek. 16:41; 2 Pet. 3:7; (4) Rom. 2:15; 13:4-5; (5-6) Joel 2:1.

Alcohol: (1) False anointing; (2) Getting drunk on the spirit of the world; (3) Getting drunk with worldly power; (4) Glory (wine); (5) Baptism of the Spirit (wine); (6) Beguiling influence.

Also see *Alcoholic, Drunk,* and *Wine.*

(1) Eph. 5:18; (2) John 14:17; 1 Cor. 2:12; Eph. 2:2; 1 John 4:1; (3) Rev. 14:8; 18:3; (4) John 2:9-11; (5) Acts 2:15-17; (6) Gen. 19:32-35.

Alcoholic: (1) Rebellion; (2) Lawlessness; (3) Self-centeredness; (4) Recklessness; (5) Full of oneself; (6) Poison; (7) Prone to Excess; (8) Reckless words; (9) Taking it easy (following success).

Also see *Alcohol* and *Poison.*

(1) Isa. 24:20; (2) Eph. 5:18; 1 Pet. 4:3-5; Gal. 5:19-21; (6) Matt. 15:11; James 3:8; (7) Eph. 5:18; (8) James 3:8; (9) Gen. 9:21.

Aleph: (1) God; (2) Christ; (3) Strength; (4) One; (5) The door to eternity.

Also see *Horn(s).*

(1-2) Rev. 1:8; (3) Original in Hebrew: ox's head with horns; (4) Deut. 6:4; (5) Gen. 28:12 (the elements of the letter are thought to represent Jacob's ladder).

Aliens: (1) Unbelievers; (2) Fallen angels or familiar spirits; (3) Christians; (4) Angels or messengers from Heaven; (5) Outcast or scorned person; (6) Lying spirit (alien imitating a person); (7) Antichrist.

Also see *Foreigner* and *Stranger.*

(1) Eph. 2:12; 4:18; Heb. 11:34; (2) Gen. 6:2; Gal. 1:8; Heb. 11:34; (3) Heb. 11:13 (NIV); (4) Heb. 13:2; (5) Job 19:15; Ps. 69:8; (6) 1 Kings 22:22; (7) 1 John 4:1-3.

Alley: (1) Going through tough times; (2) Not on God's path or not yet on God's path; (3) Unprepared heart; (4) Sidelined; (5) Backslidden; (6) Low profile path; (7) Having something to hide; (8) Backstreet; (9) Demonic path.

Also see *Back Door.*

(1) 1 Sam. 22:1; (2) Ps. 119:105; (3) Isa. 40:3; (4) Acts 15:37-38; (5) Prov. 14:14; (6) Luke 14:23; (7-8) Judg. 5:6; (9) Ps. 23:4.

Alligator: See *Crocodile.*

Allowance: (1) Deposit of faith.

(1) Luke 12:42; Rom. 12:3b; Eph. 2:8.

Almond: (1) Resurrection; (2) Jesus Christ; (3) Watching; (4) God is watching over His Word to perform it; (5) Chosen.
(1) Num. 17:8; (2) John 11:25; (the almond is the first tree to blossom in Israel in spring); (3-4) Jer. 1:11-12 (Hebrew the word for almond means "watching"); (5) Num. 17:5.

Alms: (1) Good deeds; (2) Gifts God takes note of; (3) Gifts.
(1) Matt. 6:1; (2) Acts 10:4; (3) Acts 24:17.

Aloes: (1) Fragrance.
(1) Ps. 45:8; Song 4:14.

Aloe Vera: (1) Healing; (2) Holy Spirit anointing (healing balm).
(1-2) Jer. 8:22; 51:8.

Alpaca(s): (1) Mindful of things of the Spirit; (2) Believers with spiritual vision; (3) Sheep with authority; (4) Pride/fleshly man.
(1) Col. 3:1; Eph. 2:6; (1) 2 Kings 9:17; Hab. 2:1; (3) Dan. 4:17; (4) 1 Sam. 9:2; Isa. 3:16.

Alpha: (1) First; (2) Beginning; (3) Jesus Christ.
(1-3) Rev. 1:8, 11; 21:6; 22:13.

Altar: (1) Place of sacrifice and incense; (2) A place with God; (3) The human heart.
(1-2) Gen. 12:7; 2 Chron. 20:7b; (3) Jer. 17:1.

Altered: (1) Changed or exchanged; (2) Glorified.
Also see *Changed.*
(1) Lev. 27:10; Ezra 6:11; (2) Luke 9:29.

Alternative Therapist: (1) Faith ministry/church.
(1) Prov. 13:17b (NKJV); Matt. 9:22; Luke 17:19; Acts 14:9.

Aluminum: (1) Powerful Spirit-led ministry (quick and maneuverable); (2) Sensitive ministry/person.
(1) Rom. 8:14; (2) Acts 13:13.

Aluminum Foil: (1) Insulated.
Also see *Bake* and *Baker.*
(1) Prov. 1:30.

Ambassador: (1) A representative of God, satan, or a nation; (2) Peace-seeker; (3) Messenger; (4) Trouble or health; (5) Spy; (6) Deception.
(1) Ezek. 17:15; 2 Cor. 5:20; (2) Isa. 33:7; Luke 14:32; (3) Isa. 18:2; (4) Prov. 13:17; (5) 2 Chron. 32:31; (6) Josh. 9:4.

Amber: (1) Glory of God; (2) Caution; (3) Slow down or stop; (4) Fading glory.
Also see *Orange.*
(1) Ezek. 1:4; 8:2; (2-3) As with traffic lights; (4) 1 Sam. 4:21-22; Ezek. 10:4; (cf. Matt. 17:2).

Ambulance: (1) Warning of sickness; (2) Warning of serious accident; (3) Warning of death; (4) Someone who brings sinners to meet Christ; (5) Need of prayer help; (6) Emergency (ambulance with siren); (7) Urgency.

Also see *Paramedic*.

(1) Ezek. 33:5; Mark 6:55; (2) 1 Kings 22:34b; Ezek. 33:5; (3) 1 Kings 22:35; Ezek. 33:5; (4) Mark 2:4-5; (5) James 5:13-16; (6) Amos 3:6; (7) Exod. 12:33 (KJV).

Ambush: (1) Surprise demonic attack; (2) Going down wrong thought pathways can lead to the enemy ambushing your thought life.

Also see *Hijack*.

(1) Luke 10:30; John 10:10; (2) John 13:27; 2 Cor. 10:3-5.

Amen: (1) Truly; (2) So be it; (3) Yes; (4) Conclusion.

(1) John 1:51; 3:3,5,11; (2-3) 1 Cor. 14:16; 2 Cor. 1:20; (4) Matt. 28:28; Mark 16:20.

America: (1) In the Spirit (eagle); (2) Babylon.

(1) Isa. 40:31; (2) Rev. 17:5.

Amethyst: This stone, which is blue (heavenly) in color, relates to the tribe of Issachar (partnership). Therefore this stone means: (1) Heavenly partnership; (2) Python or divination spirit.

Also see *Python* and *Precious Stones*.

(1) Exod. 28:19; 39:12; Rev. 21:20; (2) As in the "amethyst python."

Amphetamines: (1) Hype (false excitement); (2) Speed.

Also see *Drugs*.

(1) Rom. 10:2; (2) 2 Kings 9:20.

Amphibious Vehicle: (1) Evangelistic ministry; (2) Ministry in the Spirit.

Also see *Hovercraft* and *Sea*.

(1) Matt. 4:19; (2) Rom. 8:14; Rev. 1:10.

Amplifier: (1) *The Divinity Code to Understanding Your Dreams and Visions* and *The Divinity Code to Hearing God's Voice through Prophetic Incidents and Natural Events* (make the message clearer); (2) Revelation (voice of God).

(1) Num. 12:6; Deut. 4:36; (2) Exod. 19:16; Rev. 10:3; 14:7.

Anaconda: See *Python*.

Anaemic: (1) Lacking spiritual strength (iron); (2) Lacking spiritual discernment (through no revelation).

Also see *Iron*.

(1-2) Heb. 5:13-14.

Anchor: (1) Jesus Christ; (2) Security; (3) Hope; (4) Brake; (5) Slow down.

(1-3) Heb. 6:19-20; (4) Acts 27:29; (5) As a "sea anchor" is used to slow a vessel.

Anchovy/ies: (1) School child/ren (small school fish); (2) Something that puts a bad taste in your mouth; (3) Someone who hasn't lost their saltiness.

(1) Matt. 4:19, 19:14; (2) 2 Kings 4:40-41; (3) Matt. 5:13.

Ancient: (1) Very old; (2) Lasting; (3) Forefather; (4) Long ago; (5) Wisdom. Also see *Antique* and *Old*.
(1-2) Deut. 33:15; Judg. 5:21; Ps. 119:100; (3) 1 Sam. 24:13; Ezra 3:12; (4) 2 Kings 19:25; Ps. 77:5; (5) Job 12:12.

Angel/s: (1) Messenger of God; (2) Guardian; (3) Minister; (4) God's Presence; (5) God's servants; (6) Spirits (good); (7) Reapers; (8) Assistant; (9) Spiritual warriors; (10) Worshipers; (11) Familiar spirit (morphing angel); (12) Jesus (Angel of the Lord); (13) Warring angels (angels with army boots).
Also see *Feather(s)* and *Wings*.
(1) Dan. 10:11,14; Luke 2:19-20; (2) Ps. 91:11; Matt. 18:10; (3) Matt. 4:11; Luke 22:43; (4) Luke 9:26; 15:10; (5) Matt. 13:41; (6) Ps. 104:4; Matt. 25:41; Heb. 1:7, 14; Rev. 12:9; (7) Matt. 13:39; (8) Heb. 1:14; (9) Dan. 10:13; (10) Heb. 1:6; (11) 1 Sam. 28:7; (12) Exod. 3:2-5, 14; (13) 2 Sam. 5:24.

Anger: (1) Literal anger; (2) Fear; (3) Frustration; (4) Insecurity; (5) Blocked goal; (6) Jealousy; (7) Grief; (8) Provocation.
(1) Matt. 5:22; (2) Ps. 20:2; (3) Luke 14:21; (4) 1 Sam. 18:8; (5) 1 Sam. 20:30; (6) Luke 15:28; Rom. 10:19; (7) Mark 3:5; (8) Col. 3:21.

Angle Grinder: (1) The living Word of God.
(1) Heb. 4:12; 1 Cor. 4:20.

Angler: See *Fisherman*.

Animals: As a very general rule, domestic animals may represent: (1) Christ; (2) Believers; (3) Israel.
Wild animals may represent: (4) Gentile nations; (5) Unbelievers; (6) People who return to the ways of the world; (7) Demon powers.
Also see entries under individual animal names.
(1) Lev. 4:3, 14, 23; (2) Isa. 53:6; (3-4) Jer. 50:17; (4-5) Dan. 7:3ff; 8:3,20; (6) 2 Pet. 2:12-15; Jude 10-11; (7) Scripturally unclean animals may represent demonic powers.

Ankle: (1) Walk; (2) Support; (3) Base/foundation; (4) New standing; (5) Preaching the Gospel with strength; (6) Strained relationship (sprained ankle); (7) Ineffective preaching (sprained ankle); (8) Unfaithful person (sprained ankle); (9) Relationship; (10) Broken relationship (broken ankle).
(1) Ezek. 47:3; (2-4) Acts 3:7; (5) Ps. 147:10; Rom. 10:15; 1 Cor. 4:20; (6) Eph. 4:16; (7) 1 Sam. 3:19; (8) Prov. 25:19; (9-10) Eph. 4:16.

Ankle-deep: (1) First steps; (2) Shallow; (3) Uncommitted.
(1) Ezek. 47:3.

Anniversary: (1) Revival; (2) Revival of memories; (3) Memorial or reminder.
(1) Ps. 85:6; (2-3) Exod. 12:14; Lev. 23:24; Num. 10:10.

Anointing: (1) The Holy Spirit; (2) Consecration; (3) Spiritual Coronation; (4) Divine equipping; (5) Leadership.

Also see *Perfume* and *Spray*.
(1) Acts 10:38; (2) Exod. 28:41; 29:29; 30:30; (3) 1 Sam. 15:1 & (1 Sam. 10:1; 11:15);
(1 Sam. 16:13; 2 Sam. 2); (4) Exod. 28:41; 2 Cor. 1:21; (5) 1 Sam. 10:1.

Anorexia: (1) Without spiritual revelation; (2) Depleted spiritually (no anointing/fat);
(3) Lying spirit; (4) Selfish heart; (5) Possible sign of abuse (verbal, emotional, sexual);
(6) Stress; (7) Actual anorexia.
(1-2) Prov. 28:25; Isa. 58:11; (3) 1 Kings 22:22; (4) Prov. 11:25; 28:25; (5-6) Dan. 6:18.

Answering Machine: (1) Religious mentality (one day God will answer my prayer); (2)
Automated response/empty words; (3) Put on hold; (4) Being treated impersonally.
(1) Job 30:20; Ps. 28:1; (2-4) Job 35:16; Eph. 5:6a; Matt. 12:36.

Ant(s): (1) Diligence; (2) Wise one; (3) Small; (4) Insignificant; (5) Irritation; (6)
Prophetic (ants sense rain coming).
Also see *Termites.*
(1) Prov. 6:6; (2-3) Prov. 30:24-25; (4) Prov. 30:25; (5) Judg. 2:3; (6) 1 Kings 18:41-45.

Antenna: (1) Spiritual sensitivity or senses; (2) Prophetic gifting.
(1) Matt. 11:15; (2) Jer. 29:19; Zech. 7:12.

Ant Hill: (1) Lowest mountain; (2) Works of the flesh.
(1) Isa. 40:4; (2) Gal. 5:19-21.

Anticlockwise: (1) Going back in time; (2) Turning back the clock; (3) Dealing with
past issues; (4) Living in the past; (5) Antichrist (against or instead of Christ).
(1-2) Isa. 38:8; (3) Exod. 20:5; Matt. 5:23-24; (4) Gal. 2:11-12; John 21:3; (5) Dan. 7:25;
cf. Gal. 4:4.

Antique: (1) Very old; (2) Valuable; (3) Collection; (4) Out of date; (5) Respect.
Also see *Ancient* and *Old.*
(1) Job 12:12; Ps. 77:5; (2) Matt. 13:52; (3) Luke 12:33; (4) 1 Sam. 2:22; 4:18; (5) Job
32:6.

Antlers: Mind of the Spirit (the piercing Word of God); (2) Mature spiritual leadership.
See also *Horns.*
(1) Heb. 4:12b; Rom. 12:2; (2) Acts 6:3-6; 1 Tim. 3:1-7.

Anus: (1) Seeing someone's anus may mean that you have been offended by them; (2)
Abomination.
(1) Gen. 20:9b; (2) Lev. 18:22; 1 Cor. 6:9; Rom. 1:27.

Ape: See *Monkey.*

Apostle: (1) Christ; (2) A "sent-out one"; (3) Church planter; (4) Miracle worker.
(1) Heb. 3:1; (2) From the Greek: *apostolos* means "sent forth, one sent"; (3) 1 Cor. 9:1;
(4) Acts 5:12; 2 Cor. 12:12.

Apple: (1) Love; (2) Temptation; (3) Fruit; (4) Health; (5) Precious (apple of the eye);
(6) Prized possession (apple of the eye); (7) New York; (8) Sexual sin (unripe apple); (9)
Looking for real love (picking apples and seeing if they are rotten inside).

(1) Ps. 17:8; Song. 2:5; Zech. 2:8; (2-3) Gen. 3:6 (loosely portrayed as an apple); (4) As in "an apple a day keeps the doctor away"; (5) Deut. 32:10; Ps. 17:8; Prov. 7:2; Lam. 2:18; (6) Zech 2:8; (7) Known as the "Big Apple"; (8-9) Song 2:5,7.

Apple Tree: (1) Young man; (2) Lover; (3) Christ; (4) One who bears good or bad fruit. (1-3) Song 2:3; (4) Matt. 7:17.

Apron: (1) Slave; (2) Serving; (3) Lay person. (1-2) John 13:4; (3) Acts 6:1-7.

Aqua: As *aqua* is Latin for "water," see *Water*.

Archer: (1) Hateful person who uses piercing words; (2) User of hurtful words; (3) Wounder; (4) Man or woman of the flesh/world. Also see *Arrows* and *Bow*. (1-2) Gen. 49:23; (2) Ps. 64:3; (3) 1 Sam. 31:3; 2 Chron. 35:23; Job 16:13; (4) Gen. 25:27; 27:3.

Architect: (1) God. Also see *Plan(s)*. (1) Ps. 127:1; 1 Cor. 3:9,16.

Archway: (1) Godly opportunity; (2) Open Heaven. Also see *Circle* and *Domed Roof*. (1-2) Gen. 9:13.

Arena: See *Spotlight* and *Stage*.

Ark: (1) Christ; (2) Presence of God; (3) Throne; (4) Vessel of salvation; (5) Mercy seat. (1) Exod. 25:10; Josh. 3:13, 16; Col. 2:9; (2) 2 Sam. 6:11-12; (3) Ps. 80:1; Rev. 11:19; (4) Gen. 6; (5) Heb. 9:4.

Arm(s): (1) Christ; (2) God; (3) Ministry assistant; (4) Church member; (5) Arms impaired indicates works affected; (6) Unable to assist (arms tied); (7) Strength or influence; (8) God's judgment (broken arm); (9) Without spiritual power (short arms). Also see *Left and Right*, *Limbs*, and *Legs*. (1) Isa. 40:10; 59:16; 63:5; (2) Jer. 32:17-18; (3) As in "my right-hand man"; Matt. 5:30; (4) 1 Cor. 12:14-15; (5) Isa. 44:12a; (6) Dan. 6:14-16; as in "my hands are tied"; (7-8) Ps. 18:34; Ezek. 30:21; Zech. 11:17; (9) Isa. 50:2; 59:1.

Armchair: (1) God (as a place of rest); (2) You as God's resting place; (3) The throne of God; (4) Lazy know-all (armchair expert). Also see *Chair* and *Sofa*. (1) Deut. 12:9; 2 Chron. 14:11; Isa. 30:15; Heb. 4:10; (2) 2 Chron. 6:41; Acts 7:49; (3) 1 Kings 10:19; (4) Prov. 26:16.

Armor: (1) Christ; (2) Divine protection; (3) Natural reasoning (non-faith); (4) Protection; (5) Insurance; (6) Rejecting individual talents (forcing conformity); (7) Human intervention; (8) Arguments; (9) Right standing with God.

(1) Rom. 13:12-14; (2) Rom. 13:12; Eph. 6:10-18; (3-6) 1 Sam. 17:38-39; (7) Isa. 22:8; (8) Luke 11:22; (9) 2 Cor. 6:7.

Army: (1) Spiritual force; (2) God's people; (3) Spiritual warfare; (4) Those spiritually in step (who keep rank, same heart).
(1) 2 Kings 6:16-17; (1-3) Eph. 6:12; (4) 1 Chron. 12:33, 38; Joel 2:7.

Arrest/ed: (1) Lawlessness; (2) Judgment; (3) Unforgiveness; (4) Unresolved sin; (5) Conscience; (6) Bringing thoughts into captivity (willful surrender); (7) Stronghold; (8) Betrayal (wrongful arrest); (9) Supposition (wrongful arrest); (10) Wrongfully accused; (11) Politics (wrongful arrest).
(1) Rom. 7:23; (2) Dan. 6:24; (3) Matt. 18:34; (4) Matt. 5:24-26; (5) John 8:9; Rom. 2:15; 13:5; (6) 2 Cor. 10:5; (7) 1 Cor. 5:5; (8) Matt. 26:48-50; (9) Acts 21:27-29; (10) Matt. 12:1-7,10; (11) Matt. 14:3-4.

Arriving: (1) Entering your destiny/Promised Land (arriving in vehicle).
(1) Josh. 1:11.

Arrow(s): (1) Piercing words; (2) False witness; (3) Evil words; (4) Children; (5) An individual as a ministry; (6) Conviction; (7) Judgment; (8) Adversity; (9) Deliverance; (10) Stay or depart; (11) Prophetic decree; (12) Slander (both kill at a distance); (13) Spiritual warfare; (14) Devouring words.
Also see *Archer*, *Broken Arrow*, and *Darts*.
(1) Ps. 38:2; 64:3; Prov. 25:18; (2) Prov. 25:18; Jer. 9:8; (3) Ps. 11:2; 91:5; (4) Ps. 127:4-5; (5) Isa. 49:2; (6) Job 6:4; (7) Deut. 32:23; Ps. 64:7; (8) Ezek. 5:16; Job 6:4; (9) 2 Kings 13:17; (10) 1 Sam. 20:20-22; (11) 2 Kings 13:19; (12) Ps. 11:2; 64:3-4; (13) 2 Kings 13:17; (14) Ps. 57:4.

Art: (1) Prophetic expression; (2) Expressing encounters; (3) Interpreting visions; (4) Visualisation; (5) Seeing in the Spirit.
(1-5) 1 Kings 6:29,32; Hab. 2:2; Rev. 1:19.

Art Class: (1) Prophetic school.
(1) 2 Kings 2:5; 6:1.

Art Gallery: (1) Prophetic conference; (2) Recognized prophetic ministry; (3) Recognized creative anointing; (4) Anointed to be creative.
(1) 2 Kings 2:3; (2) Gen. 37:3; 41:12; Dan. 5:11-12; (3) 1 Sam. 13:14; 16:13; (4) Exod. 31:2-4.

Arthritis: (1) Sin; (2) Inflamed within; (3) Incapacitated; (4) Stiff/rigid/religious; (5) Bitterness/unforgiveness; (6) Bondage; (7) Need for the Word of God (medicine).
(1) Lev. 21:17-19 (NIV); (2) Eccl. 7:26; Jer. 4:18; James 3:14; (3) Eph. 4:16 (contrasted with); Col. 2:19; (5) Acts 8:23; (6) Matt. 22:13; John 11:44; Acts 21:11; (7) Heb. 4:12.

Artifacts (Ancient): (1) Foundational Bible truths; (2) Things that tell of ancient ways of life; (3) Made by skilled artificers (inventors).

(1-3) 2 Chron. 34:11-14 (craftsmen = artificers), note that when they set about faithfully (v. 12) rebuilding the temple, God gave them the spiritual flooring, pillars, and roofing (v. 14) to truly rebuild: the Word of God!

(Also see 2 Kings 22:8-11; 1 Chron. 29:5; Neh. 3:6 [Old Gate]).

Artist: (1) Creatively anointed; (2) Seer prophet (expressing what is seen in a vision or painting pictures with words).
(1) Exod. 31:3; 35:31; (2) Dan. 7:1; 8:26; Matt. 17:9.

Ascend/ing: (1) Rising spiritually; (2) Turning to God; (3) New position/authority; (4) Progress; (5) Rising with self-effort/religion; (6) Spiritual gift.
See also *Steps*.
(1) Gen. 12:10–13:1; (2) Opposite of Jon. 1:3,5; (3) Eph. 2:6; (4) Ps. 24:3; (5) Gen. 11:4; Gal. 1:13-14; (6) Eph. 4:8.

Ash/es: (1) Worthlessness; (2) Judgment; (3) Shame; (4) Repentance and sorrow; (5) Contrasted with prosperity; (6) Tread down.
(1) Gen. 18:27; (2) Exod. 9:8-9; 2 Pet. 2:6; (3) 2 Sam. 13:19; (4) John 3:6-10; (5) Job 13:12; Isa. 61:3; (6) Mal. 4:3.

Ashtray: (1) Dealing with sorrow; (2) Disposing of oppression; (3) Odorous (bitter); (4) Spiritually devastated.
Also see *Smoking*.
(1) Esther 4:1; Isa. 61:3; Jer. 6:26; Ezek. 27:30; (2) Deut. 4:20; 26:7-8; (3) Gen. 27:34 (burned by his brother); Exod. 1:14; 15:23-24 (murmuring); Dan. 3:27b; (4) Neh. 4:2b.

Asian: See *Indigenous*.

Asleep: See *Sleeping*.

Asp: See *Snake*.

Ass: See *Donkey*.

Assassin: (1) Spirit of death; (2) False witness (character assassin); (3) Principality taking out leadership; (4) Character assassination (false witness).
Also see *Contract Killer*, *Kill/ing*, *Mafia*, *Murder*, and *Sniper*.
(1) Ps. 10:8, 94:6; John 10:10; (2) 1 Kings 21:10; Ps. 27:12; 35:11; (3-4) Matt. 26:31; Dan. 6:11-13.

Assistant: (1) Ministering angel; (2) One's partner; (3) The Holy Spirit.
(1) Heb. 1:14; (2) Gen. 2:18,20; (3) John 14:16-17.

Asthma: (1) Dying for want of the Spirit; (2) Dying spiritually; (3) Needing God.
(1) Job 33:4; Isa. 42:5; (3) Ps. 104:29; Isa. 42:5; (2) Job 15:30b.

Asteroid: (1) Message from Heaven; (2) Message of destruction/judgment; (3) Christ's return.
Also see *Meteor*.
(1) Rev. 8:10a, 9:1; (2-3) Matt. 24:29; Rev. 6:13.

Astray: (1) Sin; (2) Without God; (3) Lawless or unrighteousness; (4) Wrong teaching; (5) Off the path of life; (6) Lies; (7) Lost.
(1) Isa. 53:6; (2) Ps. 119:67; Jer. 50:6; Ezek. 14:11; (3) Ps. 119:176; Prov. 28:10; (4) Jer. 50:6; (5) Ps. 119:67; Prov. 5:21-23; (6) Ps. 58:3; (7) Ps. 119:176.

Astronaut: (1) Jesus; (2) Spiritual person raised up; (3) In the place of authority; (4) Abounding in spiritual blessings; (5) Enemy principalities or powers (foreign or threatening astronaut).
Also see *Space Suit*.
(1-4) Acts 1:11; Eph. 1:3, 20; 2:6; (5) Eph. 6:12b.

ATM: (1) Storehouse of the riches of Heaven; (2) Heart.
(1) Phil. 4:13; (2) Prov. 4:23; Col. 3:16.

Atonement: (1) Covering; (2) Make peace; (3) To make "at-one."
(1) Gen. 6:14 (the word *pitch* means "atonement"); (2) Lev. 4:26,31,35; (3) As in "At-one-ment."

Attic: (1) Head/mind; (2) Remembered (memories); (3) Heaven; (4) Place where old things are stored away.
(1) 2 Cor. 5:1; Gen. 40:17, 19; (2) Acts 10:4; 2 Cor. 10:5; (3) Gen. 28:12; Matt. 6:20; (4) Matt. 6:20.

Auction: (1) Exercising faith to take your inheritance; (2) Claiming your inheritance by faith; (3) Taking ownership of the true riches by faith.
(1) Heb. 11:1; (2) Ezek. 47:14; (3) Matt. 25:34.

Audit: (1) Test; (2) Financial test; (3) Being examined; (4) Being assessed; (5) Weighed in the balance; (6) Judgment; (7) Need to put your affairs in order.
(1-2) Acts 5:8; (3) Luke 13:9; 1 Pet. 5:8; (4) Heb. 4:13; (5) Dan. 5:27; (6) Dan. 5:28; (7) Luke 12:20.

Auger: (1) Portal of heavenly supply; (2) Multiple revelation; (3) Logos to rhema; (4) Intercession (words/seed going upward).
(1-3) Gen. 28:12; John 1:51; (4) 1 Kings 8:54; 2 Chron. 30:27; Acts 10:4.

Aunt: (1) Married Christian sister; (2) Actual aunt; (3) An aunt could speak about her character, name, or profession; (4) Church (related tribe); (5) Fellow Christian no longer close (distant relative).
(1) Lev. 18:14 (father's brother's wife); (4) Eph. 5:25; Jer. 3:10; Ezek. 23:4; (5) Ezek. 23:4.

Aura: See *Halo*.

Author: (1) Originator; (2) Jesus Christ; (3) Writer; (4) God.
(1-2) Heb. 12:2; (3) Job 19:23; Ps. 45:1b; (4) Gen. 1:1.

Automobile: (1) Ministry or ministry gift; (2) Person (an individual); (3) Church; (4) Business; (5) Powerful ministry (sports pack); (6) Authority issue (auto with no roof); (7) Family unit; (8) The "old self" (vintage car); (9) The ministry of God's Generals (1940-50s car); (10) Not conforming to the religious system (un-registered auto); (11) Ministry not yet recognized (unregistered vehicle); (12) Doing things without an anointing (driving unregistered car); (13) Revivalist (revamped vintage car); (14) Burned out ministry (breakdown); (15) Backslidden (breakdown); (16) Anger (overheating).
Also see *Auto Accident, Auto Stolen, Bus, Convertible, Driver, Parked Auto, Reversing Vehicle, Stalled Vehicle, Taxi,* and *Wrecking Yard.*
(1) Prov. 18:16; Eph. 4:8,11; Eph. 3:6-7; (2) Acts 20:24; Rom. 1:1 (Paul is a servant and bearer of the Gospel); (3) Heb. 11:7; (4) Jer. 18:3 (KJV); (6) Matt. 8:8-9; (7) Gen. 45:19; (8) Matt. 9:17; Rom. 6:6; (9) Isa. 61:4; Heb. 11:32-33; (10) Acts 4:13,19; (11) Acts 19:15-16; (12) Matt. 17:16; Acts 19:15-16; (13) 2 Kings 13:21; Matt. 17:10-12; (14) 1 Kings 19:10,14; Matt. 26:75; (15) 2 Tim. 1:15; (16) Exod. 32:19; Num. 20:10-11.

Auto Accident: (1) Warning; (2) Ministry threat, mistake, or catastrophe; (3) Potential clash of ministries; (4) Confrontation or conflict; (4) An attack on the destiny of a ministry.
Also see *Overtaking* and *Shipwreck.*
(1-2) Acts 20:23-24; 21:11; (3-4) Acts 15:36-40; (4) 1 Kings 19:2-3.

Auto Engine (Under the Hood): (1) Heart.
Also see *Engine.*
(1) Lam. 1:20 (KJV); Luke 1:17a.

Auto Interior: (1) Heart of the ministry; (2) The type of interior determines what type of ministry. (i.e., if the interior is worn out, it means the ministry is old, needing renewal).
(1) Acts 13:22; Eph. 3:16-17; 1 Pet 3:4 (KJV).

Auto Stolen: (1) Robbed by the devil; (2) Promise or destiny stolen; (3) Ministry stolen.
(1-3) Gen. 27:36; Matt. 16:22-23; John 10:10.

Auto Trunk: (1) Heart; (2) Baggage.
(1) Deut. 9:5; Prov. 14:14; 22:15; Heb. 13:9 (KJV); (2) Matt. 23:4; Luke 11:46; Acts 15:28.

Autumn: (1) End; (2) Fading; (3) Carried away; (4) Sin; (5) Moving toward winter.
(1) Jer. 8:20; (2-4) Isa. 64:6.

Avalanche: (1) Collapsing glorious landscape; (2) Escalating issue: (3) Danger of getting snowed under; (4) Warning of something getting out of control; (5) Past issues catching up to you (trying to out ski avalanche); (6) Judgment.
(1) 1 Kings 14:25-27; (2) Pr. 17:14; John 11:48; Acts 14:2; (3) Mk. 6:31; Lk. 10:41-42; (4) Acts 19:23-29; (5) 2 Sam. 12:1-7; (6) Rev. 6:16.

Aviary: (1) Stronghold of the enemy; (2) Restricted in the things of the Spirit.
(1) Ps. 91:3a; 124:7; (2) Isa. 40:31.

Awake: (1) Alert; (2) Watchful; (3) Resurrection; (4) Salvation; (5) Stirred spiritually.
(1) Isa. 52:1; 1 Cor. 15:34; Eph. 5:14; (2) Matt. 26:40; Rev. 16:15; (3) John 11:11; (4)
Eph. 5:8-14; (5) Hag. 1:14; Acts 17:16.

Awl: (1) Piercing; (2) Earmark; (3) Having loving (hearing) ears for.
Also see *Earrings.*
(1-3) Exod. 21:1-6.

AWOL: (1) Deserting God's army; (2) No longer fighting; (3) Giving up; (4) Cares of
the world choking the Word of God.
(1) 2 Sam. 23:9,11; John 6:66; 2 Tim. 1:15; (2) 2 Sam. 11:1-2; (3) 2 Tim. 4:10; (4) Matt.
13:22.

Axe: (1) Weighty/heavy/impacting word of warning; (2) Repentance; (3) Forgiveness;
(4) Judgment; (5) Instrument of judgment; (6) Chopper; (7) The Word of God.
(1) Dan. 4:14; Matt. 3:7-12; (2-5) Matt. 3:10-11; (5) Matt. 3:10-11; Acts 8:22; Luke
17:3-4; (there is a link between repentance and forgiveness); (6) 1 Chron. 20:3; Isa.
10:15; (7) Matt. 3:10-11.

Axis: (1) Turning point; (2) Going round the mountain.
(1) Exod. 17:11-13; Ps. 78:9; (2) Deut. 2:3.

B

Baboon: See *Monkey.*

Baby: (1) God's promise; (2) Holy Spirit (God's Promise); (3) New ministry; (4)
Immature; (5) New/young Christian; (6) Immature church; (7) New/young church;
(8) Birth or fulfillment of promise by faith (unexpected baby); (9) Future; (10) Blessing
(newborn baby); (11) The promise has arrived, but immature in the things of the Spirit
(premature baby); (12) Jumping ahead of God's timing (premature baby); (13) Forced
to move beyond what was anticipated (premature baby); (14) Thrown in the deep end
(premature baby); (15) Induced labor (trying to make it happen); (16) Induced labor.
Also see *Birthing, Boy, Girl, Pregnancy,* and *Twins.*
(1) Acts 1:4, 7:5,17; (2) Luke 24:49; (3) Rev. 12:2-4; (4) 1 John 2:12-14; Heb. 5:12-13;
(5-7) Matt. 1:25; 21:16; Luke 2:12; Acts 1:1; (8) 1 Sam. 1:17; Heb. 11:11; Gal. 4:23b;
(9) Isa. 7:14; Acts 7:19; (10) Deut. 7:13; (11) Gal. 4:4-6; (12) Exod. 2:14; 2 Sam.
18:19-31; Matt. 20:20-23; (13-14) Esther 4:11-5:3; Matt. 14:16; (15) Acts 1:6-7; Gen.
40:14-15; (16) Acts 11:25-26.

Babylon: (1) Place of captivity; (2) Place of fornication/harlotry; (3) Habitation of
devils and foul spirits; (4) Speaks of abundance, luxury, and riches; (5) Facing the wrath
of God; (6) Facing torment; (7) Symbolizes rebellion; (8) The world system and false
church; (9) Enticement; (10) Prostitution/ prostitute.

(1) Matt. 1:17; (2) Rev. 14:8; 17:5; (3) Rev. 18:2; (4) Rev. 18:3,12-14; (5) Rev. 16:19; 18:9; (6) Rev. 18:10; (7) Isa. 13:1-22; (8) Rev. 17:5; Isa. 13:11; (9) Josh. 7:21; (10) Rev. 17:5.

Babysitting: (1) Holding on to a promise; (2) Nurturing a new church/ministry; (3) Caretaking a young church.
(1) Heb. 10:23; (2) Exod. 2:2; 1 Sam. 1:23; (3) 1 Tim. 1:3; 6:20a.

Back: (1) Past; (2) Reverse; (3) Behind; (4) Secret exit; (5) Burden; (6) Return; (7) Trying to steer you (on your back); (8) Persistent (on your back); (9) Ignoring/ignorant to (back to someone/thing); (10) Moving away (back to you); (11) Not able/wanting to face you (back to you).
Also see *Backpack*, *Backwards*, *Before*, and *Behind*.
(1) Phil. 3:13; (2) Gen. 9:23; (3) Phil. 3:13; (4) Acts 27:30-32; (5) Matt. 23:4; Acts 15:28; (6) 1 Kings 13:16,19; (7) Matt. 16:22; (8) As in "on your back about something"; (9) 1 Sam. 15:11; 1 Kings 14:9; (10) Exod. 23:27; Josh. 7:8,12; (11) Exod. 33:23; Judg. 18:26.

Back Door: (1) Past; (2) Doubt/unbelief; (3) Undercover (hidden) entry/exit; (4) Not coming in the recognized way; (5) Backsliding; (6) Low profile entry/ exit; (7) Desertion; (8) Secret sin.
(1-2) Gen. 18:10,12-13; (3) Gen. 31:27; Jer. 39:4; (4) John 10:1; (5) Jer. 2:19; 5:6b; John 16:32; (6) Matt. 1:19; (7) John 10:12; (8) Luke 12:2.

Backhoe/Excavator: (1) Preparing spiritual foundations; (2) Unearthing hidden issues; (3) Dealing with hardened hearts; (4) Moving mountains.
See also *Excavate*.
(1) Luke 6:48; (2) 1 Sam. 18:6-11; Matt. 13:20-21; Matt. 19:20-22; (3) Ezek. 11:19; 36:26; (4) Mark 11:22-23.

Back Massage/Rub: (1) Nurturing; (2) Care; (3) Serving the needs of another; (4) Imparting the anointing and breaking yokes.
(1-3) Isa. 9:4; 10:27; Matt. 11:30; (4) Isa. 10:27.

Backpack: (1) Carrying baggage; (2) Burden; (3) Heart; (4) Burden on your heart; (5) Independent spirit with issues.
Also see *Bag*.
(1) Job 14:17a; (2) Matt. 11:29-30; (3) Matt. 16:9 (understanding is a heart issue); (4) Isa. 19:1 (the word *burden* in Hebrew has a double meaning: "a burden that is carried" and "the oracle of a prophet"); (5) 2 Kings 5:20; 2 Cor. 11:4-5; Jude 11.

Backpackers Hostel: (1) People coming and going with burdens or issues.
Also see *Youth Hostel*.
(1) Luke 11:46.

Backstage: (1) What is happening in the inner self (behind the scenes); (2) Giving Christ the glory.

Also see *Spotlight* and *Stage*.

(1) 1 Pet. 3:4; (2) Col. 3:3.

Backward: (1) Past; (2) Backslidden; (3) Turned away from God; (4) Not ready/preparation needed; (5) Retreat; (6) Need for introspection; (7) Not knowing where you are going.

(1) Gen. 9:23 (covering the past); Phil. 3:12; (2) Isa. 1:4; (3) Jer. 7:24; 15:6; Lam. 1:8; (4-5) Josh. 7:5,10-11.

Backyard (Garden): (1) That which is private; (2) Concerning you or your own family; (3) Past issues; (4) Hidden.

Also see *Front Yard* and *Garden*.

(1) Acts 5:2; (2) As in "take a look in your own backyard"; Mark 9:28; 13:3; (3) Phil. 3:13; (4) Gen. 3:8,10; Song 6:2.

Bacon: (1) Flesh; (2) Sin; (3) Religious teaching; (4) Partaking words that make you sluggish and unhealthy; (5) Doctrine of demons; (6) Bad influence; (7) Connecting with unbelievers.

Also see *Pig*.

(1) Isa. 65:4; (2-3) Deut. 14:8; (4) Phil. 3:19; James 5:5; (5) Matt. 8:29-32; (6) Eccles. 10:16; Luke 15:16; 1 Cor. 10:20; (7) Luke 7:34.

Badge: (Access Pass): (1) Honor; (2) Wisdom; (3) Evidence of the anointing; (4) Child/son of God (access to Kingdom); (5) Love slave; (6) Slave to the system.

(1-2) Prov. 1:9; Rom. 13:7; (3-4) Matt. 25:4; (5) Exod. 21:6; (6) Rev. 13:17; 14:9.

Bag: (1) Carrying baggage/burdens; (2) Heart; (3) Money; (4) Security; (5) Treasure; (6) Business; (7) Treasurer; (8) Thief; (9) Carrying; (10) Fashion accessory; (11) Putting yourself before God (bag with holes); (12) Carrying oppression or issues; (13) Carrying the anointing/mantle (a blue bag); (14) Heart full of faith (bag of money).

Also see *Backpack*.

(1) Job 14:17; Luke 11:46; Acts 8:18-20,22-23; (2) Matt. 6:21; (3) 2 Kings 5:23; 12:10; Prov. 7:20; Isa. 46:6; (4-5) Luke 12:33; (6) Deut. 25:13; Micah 6:11; (7) John 13:29; (8) John 12:6; 13:29; (9) 1 Sam. 17:40, 49; (10) Josh. 9:4-5; (11) Hag. 1:6; (12) Isa. 9:4 (NIV); (13) 1 Sam. 16:1; (14) 1 Sam. 2:35; Neh. 9:7-8; Rom. 10:8.

Bagel: (1) Spiritual food; (2) Manna; (3) Revelation.

(1) Being circular; (2-3) Deut. 8:3; Matt. 6:11.

Bait: (1) Temptation; (2) Trap/snare; (3) Potential offense; (4) Wrongly using the Word of God; (5) Word of God; (6) Signs and wonders; (7) Revelation; (8) The Gospel.

Also see *Fishing, Poison*, and *Worm(s)*.

(1) Luke 4:1b-2a,13; 1 Cor. 10:13; (2-3) Isa. 8:14; 29:21; Matt. 13:57; 18:6; (4) 2 Cor. 2:17; 1 Pet. 1:23; 2 Pet. 2:1; (5-6) Heb. 2:3-4; (7) Matt. 16:15-18; (8) Matt. 4:19b.

Bake: (1) Something of your own making; (2) Concocting or scheming something.

Also see *Baker* and *Cook*.

(1) Gen. 40:16-18; Jer. 17:9; Hos. 7:6a; (2) 2 Sam. 15:3-6; 1 Cor. 4:5; 2 Cor. 2:11.

Baked Beans: (1) Revelation (seed in sauce).
(1) Exod. 29:7; Luke 8:11.

Baker: (1) The devil; (2) Someone who causes things to rise by sowing sin; (3) Schemer; (4) Someone who appeals to the senses, but has something else in the heart (oven); (5) Craftsman of own heart; (6) One who has something to hide; (7) Angry person.
Also see *Bake, Bakery*, and *Oven*.
(1-2) Gen. 3:1; Hos. 7:4; (3) Gen. 40:22; (4) Gen. 40:1ff; (5) Hos. 7:6; (6) Gen. 40:16; (7) Hos. 7:6.

Bakery: (1) Your heart.
(1) Hos. 7:6.

Balaclava: (1) Spirit of fear; (2) Thief; (3) Unaware of the devil's schemes (unknown assailant).
Also see *Terrorist*.
(1) Rom. 8:15; (2) John 10:10; (3) 2 Cor. 2:11; Eph. 6:11.

Balances (Scales): (1) Judgment (weighed); (2) Justice; (3) Business; (4) Integrity; (5) Divide; (6) Deceit; (7) Falsehood; (8) Purchase; (9) Considered; (10) Vanity.
(1) Dan. 5:27; Rev. 6:5; (2) Lev. 19:36; Prov. 16:11; Ezek. 45:10; (3) Isa. 46:6; Hos. 12:7; (4) Job 31:6; (5) Ezek. 5:1; (6) Hos. 12:7; Amos 8:5; Micah 6:11; (7) Prov. 11:1; 20:23; Hos. 12:7; (8) Jer. 32:10; (9) Job 6:2; (10) Ps. 62:9.

Balcony: (1) Prophetic vision; (2) Position of a prophet.
(1) Num. 22:41; (2) Num. 22:41; 1 Sam. 9:19.

Baldness: Appears to have two predominant lines of thought, based on: (1) Humbling and humility; (+) (2) A sign of the cutting away of the flesh; (-) (4) Shame or humiliation; (5) Judgment; (6) Mourning; (7) Fully bald man, like a vulture, could be a demon if unfriendly.
It may be that naturally occurring baldness signifies the former (+), and shaved baldness the latter (-).
Also see *Hair, Hair Cut Off, Head, Razor, Shave, Skinhead*, and *Vulture*.
(1) Isa. 22:12; Mic. 1:16; (2) Lev. 13:40-41; 2 Kings 2:23; (4) Lev. 21:5; Ezek. 7:18; (5) Isa. 15:2; Jer. 47:5; (6) Amos 8:10; (7) Mic. 1:16.

Ball: (1) Words; (2) Prophetic words.
Also see *Football, Golf Course, Golfer*, and *Tennis*.
(1) See entries below; (2) John 6:63.

Ball (Catching Ball): (1) Listening; (2) Taking hold of someone's words; (3) Trying to catch you out in your words.
Also see *Catcher's Mitt*.
(1) Matt. 13:19; Mark 12:13; (2) Luke 20:20,26 (KJV); (3) Mark 12:13.

Ball (Deflated Ball): (1) Words without power; (2) Words without the Spirit; (3) Losing the Spirit.
(1-2) Job 33:4; 1 Cor. 2:4; 4:20; 1 Thess. 1:5; Heb. 1:3; (cf. Luke 4:32); (3) Judg. 16:20.

Ball (Hitting Ball): (1) Effective speaking; (2) Authoritative speaking.
(1) 1 Sam. 3:19; (2) Acts 5:40; 16:22.

Ball (Kicking Ball): (1) Passing on the message; (2) Going for goal; (3) Persecution; (4) Going against God; (5) Being proud and forgetting God.
(1) Judg. 11:17; 19; 2 Tim. 2:2; (3-4) Acts 9:5; 26:14; (5) Deut. 32:15,18; 1 Sam. 2:29.

Ball (Passing Ball): (1) Teaching (passing on knowledge).
(1) John 8:20; Acts 15:35.

Ball (Rolling Ball): (1) Writing words; (2) Written words.
(1-2) Ezra 6:1-2; Isa. 8:1; 34:4; Jer. 36:2ff; Ezek. 3:1-3; Zech. 5:1-2.

Ball (Scoring): (1) Winning souls.
(1) Acts 2:41.

Ball (Spinning Ball): (1) Lying; (2) Deceptive words; (3) Spinning yarns (storytelling).
(1) Prov. 6:19, 10:18, 12:19,22, 14:5,25, 19:5,9; 21:6; 26:28; 30:6.

Ball (Throwing Ball): (1) Speaking; (2) Passing on to others; (3) Casting away.
(1) Ps. 50:17; (2) 2 Tim. 2:2; (3) Isa. 22:18; Mark 12:13.

Ball (Transparent Ball): (1) Words without substance (no heart or spirit).
(1) 1 Sam. 3:19.

Ballet: (1) Full of grace (graceful); (2) Love.
(1) Gen. 6:8; John 1:14b; (2) 2 Cor. 8:7; 13:14.

Balloon/s: (1) Celebration; (2) Words; (3) Prophecy: as words that lift (helium balloons); (4) In the Spirit; (5) Filled with the Holy Spirit; (6) Childlike faith; (7) Relief, freedom.
Also see *Ball.*
(1) Luke 15:23-24; (2) Ps. 33:6 (words are carried on one's breath); Prov. 1:23; John 6:63; (3) 1 Cor. 14:3; (4) Rev. 17:3a; (5) Luke 4:1; (6) Matt. 18:3; (7) Matt. 11:30.

Bamboo: (1) Young Christian; (2) Hollow Christian (no heart); (3) China; (4) Discipline.
(1) Prov. 11:28; Isa. 60:21; (2) Isa. 29:13; Matt. 15:8; (3) As in "the Bamboo Curtain"; (4) Prov. 23:13 (the rod or cane).

Bananas: (1) Fruit; (2) Wages (fruit of the hands).
Also see *Fruit* and *Yellow.*
(1) Deut. 1:25; (2) Prov. 31:16, 31 (KJV).

Banana Skin: (1) Watch your step.
(1) Ps. 73:2.

Band-Aid: See *Plaster.*

Band (Rock): (1) Powerful worship; (2) False worship; (3) Rejoicing; (4) Revival.
Also see *Rock 'n' Roll*.
(1) 1 Chron. 6:31-32; 15:16; (2) Exod. 32:17-19; (3) 1 Sam. 18:6; (4) 2 Chron. 5:13-14.

Bank: (1) Your heart; (2) Heaven (God's treasury); (3) Jesus; (4) Reserve; (5) Sure thing;
(6) Wealth/money; (7) Storehouse; (8) Interest; (9) Your place of employment (where
you receive financially).
Also see *Riverbank*.
(1) Matt. 12:35; Luke 6:45; 12:34; 21:1-4; Rom. 2:5; 2 Cor. 4:7; (2) Matt. 6:19-20; Mark
10:21; Luke 12:33; 18:22; (3) Col. 2:2-3; Heb. 11:26; (4) Acts 5:3; (5) As in "You can
bank on that"; (6) Luke 19:23; (7) 2 Chron. 32:27; (8) Luke 19:23; (9) Matt. 20:2.

Banner: (1) Flag; (2) The protection of God; (3) Love; (4) Fearsome army; (5) A
warning; (6) Memorial; (7) Victory.
(1-2) Ps. 20:5; 60:4; (3) Song 2:4; (4) Song. 6:4,10; (5) Isa. 13:2; (6) Exod. 17:14-15; (7)
Ps. 20:5 (NIV).

Banqueting: (1) Intimate communion; (2) Sumptuous feast; (3) Joy; (4) To feed on; (5)
Fleshly indulgence (drinking parties).
Also see *Party*.
(1) Song 2:4; (2) Esther 5:4-6; (3) Esther 5:6; 7:2,7 (wine = joy); (4) Job 41:6; (5) 1 Pet.
4:3.

Baptise/d: (1) Burial of old life; (2) Death and resurrection; (3) Death to sin; (4) Burial
of a sinful aspect of one's life.
(1-4) Rom. 6:1-11; Col. 2:12-13.

Bar (Nightclub): (1) Church/altar (as the communal place where we drink of the Spirit);
(2) The world; (3) Haunt of the workers of the flesh; (4) Gathering place for lovers of
darkness.
Also see *Nightclub*.
(1) Eph. 5:18; (2) 1 John 2:16; (3) Gal. 5:19-21; (4) 1 Thess. 5:5-7.

Barbed Wire: (1) Prisoner; (2) Captive; (3) Bondage or stronghold; (4) Legalism; (5)
Prohibited area; (6) Boundary of the spiritual realm (should be entered through the
cross).
(1-2) 2 Tim. 2:25-26; (3) Luke 13:16; (4) Rom. 7:2; 1 Cor. 7:39; (5) John 10:1-2; (6)
Luke 16:26; John 10:1-2 (cf. Matt. 27:29).

Barbeque: (1) Heart; (2) Independent spirit (cooking something up outside); (3) Solid
Bible teaching (meatfest); (4) Outdoor preaching.
(1) Hos. 7:6a; as in "what's cooking?"; (2) Prov. 18:1 (cf. KJV); (3) Heb. 5:12; (4) Mark
6:12.

Barber: (1) Enemy; (2) Deceiver; (3) Seducer; (4) Groomer; (5) Cleaner.
(1) 2 Sam. 10:3; Isa. 7:20; (2-3) Judg. 16:19; (5) Lev. 14:8-9.

Barbershop: (1) Enemy's camp.

Also see *Hairdressers.*

(1) 2 Sam. 10:4; Ezek. 5:1.

Barefooted: See *Shoes.*

Barista: (1) Revelator (person distributing revelation); (2) Holy Spirit; (3) Revelatory angel.

See also *Coffee.*

(1) Exod. 3:8,17; 13:5; 20:24; Ps. 23:5; Matt. 13:36; 15:15; 16:19 (the keys are revelation); (2) John 14:26; 16:13-14; (3) Judg. 13:13; 2 Kings 1:3, 15; 1 Chron. 21:18; Zech. 1:9; 4:1ff; 6:4ff; Matt. 1:20-24; 2:13; Acts 7:53; 10:22; Heb. 1:14; 2:2; Rev. 1:1.

Barley: (1) Inferior grain; (2) Harvest.

(1) Judg. 7:13-14; (2) Ruth 1:22; 2:23; 2 Sam. 21:9.

Barn: (1) Church; (2) Storehouse of riches; (3) Increase; (4) Greed; (5) Call to trust God without a bank of resources behind you; (6) Judgment; (7) Harvest.

Also see *Building, House,* and *Stable.*

(1-2) Job 39:12; Mal. 3:10; Matt. 6:26; (3) 2 Chron. 32:28; Prov. 3:10; (4) Luke 12:18; (5) Matt. 6:25-33; Luke 12:22-24; (6) Joel 1:17 (broken down barns); (7) Matt. 13:30.

Barrel: (1) Heart (and therefore a person); (2) Storage place; (3) Vessel; (4) Fleshly vessel (individual).

Also see *Pans, Pots, Rifle,* and *Vessel.*

(1) A barrel holds water and wine; (2-3) 1 Kings 17:12,14,16; (4) As barrels are made of wood and wood is representative of the works of the flesh (see 1 Cor. 3:12-15).

Baseball: (1) Trying to get you out with words (pitching or catching); (2) Words with power (batting); (3) Spiritual warfare (batting and pitching); (4) Hitting hearts with your words (home runs); (5) The enemy getting at you or getting one past you (strike); (6) Lie (curve ball); (7) Making history (hitting the most home runs).

Also see *Ball, Bat, Cricket, Football Game, Sport, Umpire,* and *Winning.*

(1) Mark 12:13; (2) Eccles. 8:4; Luke 4:32; (3) Rom. 7:23 (internally: spirit vs. flesh); 2 Cor. 10:3; Eph. 6:12 (in the second heaven against evil spirits); 1 Tim. 1:18; (4) 1 Sam. 3:19; (5) Gen. 3:1; 1 Cor. 10:13; (6) Gen. 24:49; Ps. 33:4; Luke 20:21; (7) Esther 8:5,8 (it is recorded).

Baseball Bat: See *Bat.*

Basement: (1) Hell; (2) A person's heart; (3) Hiding place; (4) Depression; (5) A place of the flesh.

Also see *Upper Room.*

(1) Prov. 5:5; Matt. 11:23; Ps. 55:15; (2) Prov. 22:17; (3) John 1:5; (5) As in "opposite of the upper room."

Basket: (1) Heart; (2) First-fruits; (3) Blessed fruitfulness; (4) A day's work or provisions; (5) Overflow from faith; (6) Group of people (family, church, nation); (7) Cursed fruit; (8) Escape pod.

(1) Gen. 40:16-17; Deut. 28:5; (2) Deut. 26:2-9; (3) Deut. 28:4-5; Jer. 24:1; (4) Gen. 40:16-18; (5) Matt. 14:20; 15:37; 16:9-10; (6) Jer. 24:1-10; (7) Deut. 28:17; Amos 8:1-2; Jer. 24:1; (8) Acts 9:25; 2 Cor. 11:33.

Basketball Ring (Hoop): (1) Sinking heavenly goals; (2) Reaching forward to what lies ahead.
(1-2) Phil 3:13-14.

Bat(s) (Animal): (1) Evil spirits; (2) Unclean spirits; (3) Idolatry; (4) Children of darkness; (5) Blind spirit that develops and uses occultic/demonic senses to "see."
Also see *Vampire*.
(1-2) Lev. 11:13a, 19b; Deut. 14:18; (3) Isa. 2:20; (4) 1 Thess. 5:5; (5) 1 Sam. 28:8.

Bat (Baseball/Cricket): (1) The rhema word of God; (2) Your turn or innings; (3) Heart; (4) Discipline (rod of correction); (5) Verbal leverage (tongue).
Also see *Ball, Cricket, Sport,* and *Umpire*.
(1) Heb. 4:12; (2) Esther 4:14; Gal. 1:15-16; (3) Matt. 12:34-35; (4) Prov. 13:24; (5) Eccl. 8:4; Luke 4:32.

Bat without a Handle: (1) Position of no real leverage (influence); (2) Disempowered.
(1) 2 Kings 24:1, 17; (2) Gen. 49:6b.

Bath/ing: (1) Cleansing; (2) Purification; (3) Applying the Word; (4) Needing conversion (all of body washed); (5) Daily confession (washing parts of the body, i.e., feet/hands); (6) Baptism (immersion in a bath).
(1) Lev. 15:5; (2) Num. 19:9,17; (3) Eph. 5:26; (4-5) John 13:4-15; (6) Acts 8:38-39.

Bathroom: (1) Cleansing; (2) Heart (the mirror of God's Word reveals your heart); (3) Grooming; (4) Conviction/repentance; (5) Secret lust/sin; (6) Refreshing; (7) Old issue (old bathroom).
Also see *Faeces, Dung, Toilet,* and *Urination*.
(1) Eph. 5:26; (2) James 1:23-26; (3) Isa. 1:16; (4) Matt. 3:11; (5) Ps. 38:9; 51:6; Isa. 29:15; John. 7:4; (5) Acts 3:19; (6) Rom. 6:6; 2 Pet. 1:9.

Batsman: (1) Delivering the word; (2) Defending against the word (blocking/bunting); (3) Successful message/revelation (Home run).
See also *Baseball*.
(1) Mark 16:20; (2) Isa. 54:17; (3) Acts 2:14-41.

Battery: (1) Holy Spirit (power source); (2) Power; (3) Reserve power; (4) Life.
(1) Luke 1:35; Acts 1:8; Rom. 15:13; (2) Acts 10:38; (3) Matt. 25:3-4; (4) 2 Cor. 13:4.

Battery Charge: (1) Fresh infilling of the Spirit.
(1) Acts 1:8; 2:3-4; 4:8,31,33; 9:17; 13:9.

Battle: (1) Spiritual warfare; (2) Attack; (3) Conflict.
Also see entry under *Fight*.
(1) Judg. 3:10; Eph. 6:10-12; 1 Tim. 1:18; (2) Josh. 10:19; Ps. 27:2; (3) Ps 13:2; 80:6.

Battleship: (1) Powerful evangelistic ministry.

Also see *Ship*.

(1) Acts 27:31; 2 Cor. 2:4.

Beach: (1) Limit; (2) Boundary; (3) Boundary of the Kingdom of Heaven (where souls are won and lost); (4) Recreation; (5) Earth; (6) No foundation in the Word (standing on sand); (7) Safety; (8) Battleground.

Also see *Coastline* and *Sand*.

(1-2) Josh. 15:2; Prov. 8:29; (3) Exod. 23:31; Num. 34:12; Job 38:11; Ps. 93:4; (4) Exod. 32:6; 1 Cor. 10:7; (5) Matt. 13:2; (6) Matt. 7:26-27; (7) Acts 28:1-2; (8) As in "trying to get a beachhead."

Beach Ball: (1) Words said in jest/fun.

(1) Eccles. 2:1.

Beacon: (1) Sign; (2) Signal; (3) Warning; (4) Call for assistance; (5) Drawing your attention; (6) The Gospel; (7) Believer; (8) Christ.

Also see *Lighthouse* and *Torch*.

(1) Isa. 30:17; John 1:5; Acts 2:19; (2) Gen. 1:14; Judg. 20:38; Ps. 19:1; Jer. 6:1; (3) Prov. 6:23; Isa. 8:20b; John 1:7; (4) Luke 5:7; Acts 9:3, 6, 15; (5) Matt. 5:16; John 5:35; Acts 12:7; (6) 2 Cor. 4:4; (7) Phil. 2:15; (8) 2 Cor. 4:6; 1 John 2:8b; Rev. 21:23.

Beads: (1) Superficial adornment; (2) Worldly adornment.

(1-2) 1 Pet. 3:3; 1 Tim. 2:9.

Bean Bag: (1) Apathy; (2) Lethargy.

(1-2) Prov. 26:13-14; Heb. 6:12.

Bear: (1) Enemy; (2) Stealer of young Christians; (3) Powerful spiritual force; (4) Fierce anger; (5) Oppressive leader; (6) Russia; (7) Antichrist; (8) Religious spirit; (9) Iran; (10) Territorial spirit; (11) Lover of revelation (eats honey); (12) Anti-Christ spirit; (13) Devourer of the Word (+/-); (14) Financial swipe; financial downturn/poverty; spirit of poverty; (15) Enemy as in Giants in land; (16) Spirit of death; (17) Spirit that steals revelation (honey).

(1-2) 1 Sam. 17:34-37; (3) Rev. 13:2; (4) Prov. 17:12; (5) Prov. 28:15; (6) Ezek. 38:16,18; (7) Rev. 13:2; (8-9) Dan. 7:5 (cf. Dan. 2:39, 8:20-21, 10:20); (10) 1 Sam. 17:36; Num. 13:33; 1 Sam. 17:34-36; Lam. 3:10; (11-12,17) Hebrew for "bear": *devash* = eats honey; (14) Prov. 28:15; (15) Num. 13:33; (16) 2 Kings 2:23-24.

Beard: (1) Full manhood or spiritual maturity; (2) God's statutes and judgments; (3) Holy.

Also see *Hair*.

(1) 1 Chron. 19:5; (2) Ezek. 5:1-6; (3) Lev. 21:5-6.

Beard (Untrimmed Beard): (1) Law/Legalism; (2) A person who has made an oath.

(1) Lev. 19:27; 21:5; (2) 2 Sam. 19:24.

Beard (Shaved Beard): (1) Shame; (2) Grief/mourning; (3) Humbled; (4) Sign of coming destruction.

(1) 2 Sam. 10:4-5; Isa. 15:2; (2) Ezra 9:3-6; (3) Jer. 41:5; 49:37; (4) Ezek. 5:1.

Beard (Grabbed by the Beard): (1) Warning of danger/death.
(1) 1 Sam. 17:35; 2 Sam. 20:9.

Beard (Spittle [Saliva] in Beard): (1) Madness.
(1) 1 Sam. 21:13.

Beast: (1) Antichrist; (2) Godly or ungodly being; (3) King/doms (nations); (4) Principalities and powers.
Also see entries under individual animals.
(1) Rev. 13:11-18; 14:9-11; (2) Rev. 4:6-8; 11:7; 13:1-4; (3) Dan. 7:17, 23; (4) Eph. 6:12; Dan. 10:13,20.

Beastiality: (1) Reprobate mind; (2) Darkened heart; (3) Willful denial of God; (4) Diseased soul; (5) Abomination; (6) Demonic harassment; (7) Cursed.
(1-3) Rom. 1:21-31; (4) 1 Thess. 4:5; (5) Exod. 22:19; Lev. 18:23; 20:15-16; (7) Deut. 27:21.

Beaten Up: (1) Verbal abuse; (2) Verbal onslaught; (3) Warning of physical harm.
(1-2) Luke 22:64-65.

Beating Time: (1) Synchronization with God; (2) Slow down (slowing to get in synchronization; (3) Time is short (speeding up); (4) Lagging behind and need to push in (others beating faster than you).
(1) Gen. 5:22; (2) Eccles. 3:1; (3) 1 Cor. 7:29; (4) Mark 5:27.

Beautiful: (1) Warning of inner corruption; (2) Gospel preacher; (3) Well-favored; (4) Holy garments; (5) Holiness; (6) Seeing facets of God; (7) Salvation (upon the meek); (8) Desirable; (9) Reflects the heart; (10) Temptation; (11) Vanity; (12) Speaks of the timing of God; (13) At the right place at the right time; (14) Reflective of Christ's love relationship with you (or the Church); (15) Christ; (16) Temporary outward show; (17) In danger of pride.
Also see *Ugly*.
(1) Matt. 23:27; Prov. 6:25; (2) Isa. 52:7; Rom. 10:15; (3) Gen. 29:17; Ps. 90:17; (4) Exod. 28:2,40; (5) 1 Chron. 16:29; 2 Chron. 20:21; Ps. 29:2; 96:9; 110:3; (6) Ps. 27:4; 50:2; 90:17; (7) Ps. 149:4; (8) Deut. 21:11; Isa. 53:2b; (9) 1 Sam. 16:12; Acts 13:22; (10) 2 Sam. 11:2; (11) 2 Sam. 14:25; Ps. 39:11; Prov. 31:30; (12-13) Eccles. 3:11; (14) Song 6:4; 7:1; (15) Isa. 4:2; (16) Isa. 28:1,4; (17) Ezek. 28:17.

Beauty Shop: (1) Grooming; (2) Getting ready; (3) Call for inward beauty rather than outward; (4) Vanity.
(1-3) 1 Pet. 3:3-4; Rev. 21:2; (4) 2 Sam. 14:25.

Beaver: (1) Busy; (2) Diligent/hard working; (3) Banking up (saving) the Word/Spirit.
Also see *Dam*.
(1) As in "busy as a beaver"; Luke 10:40-42; (2) Prov. 4:23; 10:4; 12:24; 22:29; 27:23; (3) Matt. 7:2; Mark 4:24.

Bed: (1) God (as the place of our rest); (2) Heart (as the place of God's rest); (3) Agreement (sharing bed); (4) Alignment with (double bed); (5) Rest; (6) Sickness; (7) Intimacy; (8) Laziness; (9) Adultery; (10) Asleep; (11) Warmth; (12) Sexual issue; (13) Suffering; (14) Thoughts; (15) Meditation; (16) In the Spirit (water bed); (17) Heart; (18) Association (bunk bed); (19) Position; (20) Death; (21) Single person (single or bunk bed as opposed to a double bed).

Also see *Bedroom*, *Sex*, and *Sheets*.

(1) Jer. 50:6; Matt. 11:29; Heb. 4:9-11; (2) Isa. 66:1; Prov. 14:33a; Acts 7:49; (3) Isa. 57:8; Rev. 2:22; (4) 1 Kings 17:19,21; 2 Kings 4:34; (5) Isa. 57:2; (6) Gen. 47:31-48:1; Matt. 9:2; (7) Heb. 13:4; (8) Prov. 26:14; (9) Prov. 7:16-18; (10) Luke 11:7; (11) Eccles. 4:11; (12-13) Rev. 2:21-22; (14) Dan. 2:29; 4:5; As in "the place where you lay your head"; (15) Ps. 4:4; (16) Dan. 2:29; (17) Ps. 4:4; Eccles. 2:23; Hos. 7:14; (18) Eph. 4:16; (19) Jer. 35:4 (chambers are bedrooms); position as in "births/bunks" on a battleship; (20) Gen. 49:33 (death bed); (21) 1 Cor. 9:5.

Bed (Under Bed): (1) Hidden; (2) Secret; (3) Cover up; (4) Foundation.

(1-3) Mark 4:21-22; (4) 1 Cor. 3:11.

Bedhead: (1) Lazy authority; (2) Leadership spiritually asleep.

(1) Matt. 23:4; (2) Matt. 23:16.

Bedroom: (1) Private; (2) Intimacy or union; (3) Inner circle (confide in); (4) The place of heart communion.

Also see *Bed*.

(1) Matt. 6:6; (2) 2 Sam. 11:2-4; (3) Mark 9:2-9 (the mountain was Jesus' "secret place"); (4) Ps. 4:4; 63:6.

Bedside Table: (1) Storage of things close to you.

(1) 1 Sam. 26:7.

Bee/s: (1) Spiritual force/evil spirits; (2) Surrounded; (3) Busy; (4) People who sting; (5) People who make honey; (6) Laborers; (7) Angels; (8) Angels ascending/descending (bee flight path); (9) Stinging words (words of judgment); (10) Spiritual warfare.

Also see *Ants*, *Honey*, *Sting*, and *Wasp*.

(1) Deut. 1:44; Isa. 7:18; (2) Ps. 118:12; (3) "Busy as a bee"; (4) Deut. 1:44; Ps. 118:12; (5) Matt. 3:4; John 4:34; (7) Exod. 25:20 (mercy seat covered in gold like honey); Heb. 1:14; (8) Gen. 28:12; John 1:51; (9) 1 Cor. 15:56; (1) Eph. 6:12.

Beehive: (1) Busy (a hive of activity); (2) Heaven; (3) The Church; (4) Enemy stronghold.

(1-2) John 1:51; (3) Num. 13:16; Acts 13:4; (4) Deut. 1:44; Ps. 118:12.

Beetroot: (1) Heart/blood; (2) Communion (flesh and blood) leading to fruitfulness; (3) Idolatry (not liking beetroot).

(1) John 6:56; (2) John 6:56; 15:5; (3) Acts 15:20.

Before (In Front Of): (1) Future; (2) Next (in time).

Also see *Ahead, Back,* and *Behind.*
(1-2) Luke 10:1; Phil. 3:13.

Beggar: (1) Recognizing one's spiritual state without God; (2) This is a good sign as it is the first step in coming to know God; (3) Petition; (4) Desperate; (5) Prayer.
(1-2) Matt. 5:3; Luke 16:23; (3) Ps. 38; Jer. 42:2; Dan. 9:3; (4) Prov. 30:7; (5) Judg. 13:8 (NIV).

Beheaded: See *Decapitation.*

Behind: (1) Past; (1) After; (2) To follow; (3) Something that will happen in time; (4) Later; (5) Moving on from.
Also see *Ahead, Back,* and *Before.*
(1) Phil. 3:13; (1) Matt. 10:38; (2) Mark 8:34; (3-4) Joel 2:28; (5) Gen. 19:26 (Lot's wife failed to move on).

Belch: (1) Offense; (2) Moving on before you have digested what God has said (eating too fast); (3) Digesting words coming with a wrong spirit (sodas are full of CO_2); (4) Bringing up the past.
Also see *Breath* and *Vomit.*
(1) Ps. 73:15 (KJV); Prov. 18:19; (2) Josh. 1:8; (3) Prov. 14:15; 23:1-3; (4) Eccles. 3:15.

Bell: (1) Warning; (2) Proclamation of glory; (3) Attention gatherer.
Also see *Doorbell.*
(1) Matt. 24:3b; Mark 13:24-26; (2) Exod. 28:33-34; 39:25-26; Zech. 14:20; (3) Isa. 40:3; Matt. 3:1-5; John 1:8.

Belly: (1) Person's spirit (core of the person); (2) Heart; (3) Gut feeling; (4) Womb; (5) Meditating (spiritually digesting); (6) Intestinal system.
(1) Prov. 20:27; (2) Matt. 12:40; (3) Job 34:4; (4) Job 3:11; (5) Ps. 19:14; (6) Mark 7:19.

Belly Button Pierced: (1) Conviction or obedience of heart; (2) Penetrated by the Word of God.
(1) Acts 2:37; (2) Luke 2:35.

Below: See *Above and Below.*

Belt: (1) Truth; (2) The Word; (3) Prophecy; (4) Prophet; (5) Office (ministry/role).
(1) Eph. 6:14; (2) John 17:17; (3) Acts 21:11; (4) 2 Kings 1:8; (5) 2 Sam. 18:11.

Bench: (1) Not being used or not wanted (sitting on the bench); (2) Sidelined; (3) Rest; (4) Team.
Also see *Sit/ting.*
(1-2) 1 Sam. 4:13; (3) 2 Sam. 7:1; Zech. 1:11b; (4) Eph. 2:6.

Bench Top: (1) Heart; (2) Pulpit.
Also see *Chopping Board.*
(1) As an altar: Judg. 6:26; As a table: Exod. 34:28; 2 Cor. 3:3; (2) Ps. 104:15b; Matt. 4:4.

Bend (noun): (1) Change; (2) Transition; (3) Deviation from God's path; (4) Ungodliness (bent); (5) Perversion (bent).

Also see *Bend* (verb), *Corner*, and *Curve*.
(1) Exod. 13:17-18 (via an indirect route); Prov. 24:21; (2) Gen. 11:31 (at Haran, on way to Canaan); Exod. 13:17-18; (3) Deut. 5:32; Ps. 5:8; Isa. 40:3; (4) Acts 13:10; Jude 1:4; (5) Num. 22:32; Deut. 32:5; Acts 13:10.

Bend (verb): (1) Humbled/ing; (2) Readying an attack (of words); (3) Determined (bent on doing something); (4) Backsliding (no longer upright); (5) Being kept bound.
Also see *Arrow*, *Bend* (noun), *Bowing*, and *Knee*.
(1) Isa. 60:14; (2) Ps. 64:3; Jer. 9:3; (3-4) Hos. 11:7; (5) Luke 13:11-16.

Beneath: See *Above and Below* and *Under*.

Bent: See *Bend*, *Bowing*, *Curved*, and *Crooked*.

Berries: (1) Fruitfulness; (2) Resurrection.
Also see *Blueberries*, *Fruit*, and *Strawberries*.
(1-2) Isa. 17:6 (KJV); James 3:12 (KJV) (cf. Gen. 40:10,13).

Best Man: (1) Jesus; (2) John the Baptist (friend of groom); (3) Spirit of Elijah (friend of groom).
Also see *Bride*, *Groom*, and *Marriage*.
(1) Heb. 7:22, 12:24; (2-3) John 3:28-29; Song 5:1.

Bible: (1) Word of God; (2) Jesus Christ; (3) Christian walk; (4) What you believe to be truth; (5) Operating procedures.
(1) Josh. 1:8; (2) John 1:1; (3) Ps. 119:1,105; (4) John 17:17; (5) 2 Tim. 3:16.

Bible Character: (1) Mantle of the Bible character coming to or on the one having the experience; (2) Parallel incident happening in the life of the one witnessing the event or incident; (3) An incident in the life of the character that springs to mind.
(1-3) Ezek. 34:23-24; Matt. 11:14; 17:10-12.

Bicycle: (1) Individual on a humble/ing journey (no horsepower); (2) Self-propelled ministry (doing things in your own strength); (3) Inferior ministry; (4) Denying or without the power of the Holy Spirit; (5) Self-employed; (6) Spiritual framework linking God's Spirit with our spirit; (7) Wrong spirit (riding in wrong direction).
Also see *Handlebars*, *Inner Tube*, *Tandem Bicycle*, *Unicycle*, and *Wheel(s)*.
(1) Gen. 44:3; Dan. 5:21; Mark 11:2; (2) Zech. 4:6; (3-4) 1 Cor. 2:4; 4:20; 1 Thess. 1:5; (5) John 12:6; (6) Ezek. 1:20-21; (7) 1 Kings 16:31; Hos. 4:12; 2 Pet. 2:15; Jude 1:11; Num. 14:23-24.

Big/Bigger: See *Tall*, *Taller*, and *Smaller*.

Big Brother: (1) Government; (2) Leadership; (3) Jesus.
(1-2) 1 Sam. 9:2; (3) Heb. 2:11.

Bigfoot: (1) Spirit of antichrist (as in so-called "missing link") (2) Fear or torment of something that is not real (a hoax); (3) Threat (demon); (4) Authority putting its foot down (with threats).
Also see *Abominable Snow Man*.

(1) 1 John 2:22; 4:2-3, 5-6; (2) Num. 13:33; (3) 1 Sam. 17:44; Acts 13:8-10; (4) Acts 9:1; Dan. 3:13-15.

Biker/Bikie: (1) Rebels/rebellion; (2) Intimidation; (3) Strongman; (4) Evil spirit (hell's angel); (5) Gangster (underworld figures); (6) Beloved son in the cleft of the Rock.
(1) Mark 15:7; (2) Rom. 8:15; 2 Tim. 1:7; (3) Matt. 12:29; Luke 11:21-22; (4) Matt. 25:41; Jude 1:6; (5) Neh. 4:7-8; Phil 2:10b; (6) See earlier book content.

Bikini: (1) Revealing; (2) In the flesh; (3) Carnal; (4) Enticing temptation.
(1) Gen. 3:7; (2) Gen. 2:25; 3:7; 1 Pet. 4:2; Rom. 8:5; Gal. 6:8; (4) 2 Sam. 11:2-4.

Billiards: See entries under *Pool Hall*, *Pool Cue*, and *Pool Table*.

Bingo: (1) Casting lots; (2) Idol; (3) False gods of luck and chance.
(1) Matt. 27:35; Mark 15:24; Luke 23:34; (3) 1 Sam. 6:9b.

Binoculars: (1) Distant; (2) Spiritual vision; (3) Seeing Heaven or seeing from Heaven; (4) Fearful; (5) Distant in time; (6) Prophet; (7) Foreseeing; (8) Focusing; (9) Faith (not seen with the naked eye).
Also see *Horizon*.
(1) Gen. 37:18; Jer. 4:16; Matt. 26:58; (2) 2 Kings 4:25-27; Mark 5:6; Luke 16:23; (3) Mark 11:13; 13:34; (4) Mark 15:40; Exod. 20:18b; (5) Gen. 22:4; 37:18; Ezek. 12:27; Heb. 11:13; (6) 2 Kings 2:7; (7) Ezek. 12:27; (8) Matt. 7:5; (9) Heb. 11:1.

Bird/s: (1) Good or evil spirits (heavenly beings); (2) The Holy Spirit; (3) A church or the Church; (4) Angel; (5) Black birds = generally evil; (6) A curse (may be seen as a pale or yellow bird landing on someone/thing); (7) Spirit of death (black bird).
Also see individual bird names, *Dove*, *Raven*, and *Wings*.
(1) Gen. 40:17-19; Lev. 14:4-7 (Jesus and the Holy Spirit); Matt. 13:31-32; (2) Luke 3:22; (3) Acts 14:27 & Matt. 23:37; Ruth 2:12; (4) Rev. 8:13; 14:6; (5) Gen. 8:7-11 (the raven found no rest = no rest for the wicked); (6) Gen. 40:17-19; Prov. 26:2; (7) Jer. 9:21.

Birds (Swooping): (1) Demonic harassment; (2) Divine protection.
(1) Gen. 40:17; (2) Isa. 31:5.

Bird Bath: (1) Heart; (2) The Word of God.
(1) Ps. 73:13; Jer. 4:14; Heb. 10:22; (2) Exod. 30:18-19; Eph. 5:26.

Birth/ing: (1) Birthing a new ministry/church/venture; (2) Beginning of something new; (3) Bringing forward God's promises through prayer; (4) Travailing intercession; (5) Being born again; (6) Lost hope or promise (stillborn); (7) Judgment (stillborn); (8) Stopping God's promise (stillborn).
Also see *Baby*, *Caesarean Birth*, and *Pregnancy*.
(1) Rev. 12:2, 4-5; John 16:20-21; (2) Jer. 31:8; Mic. 4:10; (3) 1 Kings 18:1,41-45; (4) 1 Sam. 1:10-18; Rom. 8:25-29; (5) John 3:3; (6-7) Isa. 47:9; (8) Matt. 2:16.

Birthday: (1) Born again; (2) Start of something new; (3) Celebration; (4) Memorial; (5) Death (a woman goes through a death before birth).

(1) John 3:3; (2) Exod. 12:2; 2 Cor. 5:17; (3-4) Exod. 12:2-14; (5) John 12:24; 19:34; Rom. 6:4; 8:22; 1 Cor. 15:21-22.

Biscuit: See *Bread*.

Bishop: (1) Overseer (to watch over); (2) Covering; (3) Spiritual authority. Also see *Pastor* and *Priest*.
(1-3) 1 Tim. 3:1-2; 1 Pet. 5:2.

Bite/Bitten: (1) Infected (affected) by words; (2) Poisoned by words; (3) Destructive (devouring) words; (4) Falling to temptation; (5) Addicted (as in bitten by the gambling bug); (6) Test of faith; (7) Backbiting or slander (bite on back).
Also see *Eating*, *Snake*, and *Spider*.
(1) Matt. 27:20; (2) Gen. 3:1-6; Acts 13:8-10; (3) Ps. 52:4; (4) Gen. 3:1-6; (5) Prov. 23:2-3; (6) Mark 16:17-18; Acts 28:3-6; (7) Num. 21:5-6.

Bitter: See *Lemon*.

Bitumen: (1) Hard; (2) Traffic or commerce; (3) Busyness; (4) Sealant; (5) Preventing growth.
(1-3) Matt. 13: 4,19; (4) Gen. 6:14; (5) Deut. 29:23.

Black: (1) Without light or life; (2) Without the Spirit (operating in the soul); (3) Wicked; (4) Sin; (5) Deceitful; (6) Mourning; (7) Dead or unclean; (8) Burned; (9) Famine; (10) Hell; (11) Death; (11) Financially sound (in the "black"); (12) Financially viable/stable/profitable; (13) Power; (14) Hidden/secret.
Also see *Black Man*, *Black and White*, and *Woman* (black widow).
(1) Gen. 1:2-3; Lam. 4:8; (2) John 13:30b; James 2:26a; Matt. 25:8; (1 John 1:5b; Rom. 8:9); 1 Cor. 2:14; (3) Song 5:11; Gen 8:7; Isa. 48:22; (4) Lam. 4:8; (5) Prov. 7:9; (6) Jer. 8:21 (cf. NKJV & KJV); (7) Lam. 4:8; Matt. 23:27 (contrasted with white); (8) Jer. 14:2, 8; (9) Rev. 6:5-6; (10) 2 Pet. 2:17; (11) Job 3:5; (12) As in "in the black" financially; (13-14) Exod. 20:21; 1 Kings 8:12.

Black Eye: (1) Persecuted prophet; (2) Domestic violence; (3) Abuse (physical, emotional, or spiritual); (4) Darkness around the heart; (5) Wounded heart.
(1) 1 Kings 19; (2) 1 Sam. 22:19; Jer. 4:31; (3) Luke 22:63-64; (4) Rom. 1:21; Eph. 4:18; (5) Ps. 109:22; 147:3.

Black Man: [Note: The meaning of an African-American/ First Nations (Indigenous) person or Caucasian person in an incident or event may change dependent on the ethnicity (racial/cultural background) of the person experiencing it. An African-American/ First Nations person may see Caucasians as the fleshly man (due to their past inclination to be soulish, exploit and enslave). To a Caucasian a First Nations person may represent the fleshly man due to their color or order in the land (see 1 Cor. 15:46). A person of different race is generally interpreted as "Foreign." See *Foreign*.]

Black and White: (1) Judgment/al; (2) Double-minded; (3) Religious; (4) Lukewarm.
(1) John 8:5-6; Acts 23:3; (2) James 1:6-8; (3) Matt. 23:5-7; (4) Rev. 3:16.

Black Widow Spider (Red Back Spider): (1) Deadly entrapment; (2) Deception of sin holding someone to ransom; (3) Jezebel spirit.
(1) Prov. 5:3-5; 7:5-27; 9:13-18; (2) 1 Cor. 15:56; (3) 1 Kings 18:4; 19:2; 21:5ff.

Blanket: (1) Covering; (2) Authority; (3) Smothering (wet blanket).
(1) 1 Kings 19:13; (2) 2 Kings 2:14; (3) Ezek. 32:7.

Bleeding: (1) Losing spiritual life; (2) Hurting; (3) Suffering; (4) Wounded; (5) Dying; (6) Purification; (7) Atonement; (8) Martyr.
Also see *Blood*.
(1) Acts 22:20; Lev. 17:11; (2-3) Isa. 53:4-5,7; (4) 1 Kings 22:35; Ezek. 28:23; (6) Lev. 12:4; (7) Lev. 17:11; (8) Acts 2:20; Gen. 4:10.

Blimp: (1) High profiled Holy Spirit ministry; (2) Very discerning prophetic ministry.
Also see *Hot Air Balloon*.
(1) Ezek. 8:3; Acts 8:39; (2) Num. 22:41 (by virtue of the view).

Blind: (1) Spiritually blind; (2) In the dark spiritually or spiritually ignorant; (3) Unbeliever; (4) Received a bribe; (5) Hardened heart; (6) Lacking faith or love; (7) Hatred.
(1) Isa. 42:18; 56:10; Matt. 15:14; Luke 4:18; John 9:39; (2) 1 Cor. 12;1; Isa. 42:7, 16; Matt. 23:16-17; 23:26; Rev. 3:17; (3) Isa. 29:18; (4) 1 Sam. 12:3: Deut. 16:19; (5) John 12:40; 2 Cor. 3:14-15; 4:4; (6) 2 Pet. 1:9; (7) 1 John 2:11.

Blindfold: See *Blind* and *Veil*.

Blinds (Awning): See *Shutters*.

Blister: (1) Experiencing friction because of the Gospel; (2) Friction affecting your work (hand blister) or walk (foot blister); (3) Trouble adjusting to a new role (filling someone else's shoes).
Also see *Pimple*.
(1) Matt. 5:10; (Matt. 10:35; Eph. 6:15); (2) Matt. 13:20-21; (3) Mark 9:33-34.

Block of Units (Flats/Apartments): (1) Subculture or group; (2) Spiritually undeveloped individual (one unit/flat).
(1) Acts 16:3 (KJV); (2) 2 Cor. 5:1.

Blood: (1) Life (of the flesh); (2) Spirit (spirit parallels blood); (3) Family; (4) Atonement; (5) Redemption or redeemed; (6) Judgment; (7) Strife; (8) Guilt/ blame; (9) Money; (10) Sacrifice; (11) Murder; (12) Drunk; (13) Earnest search for repentance (tears of blood); (14) Anxiety (sweating blood); (15) Christ or His offspring (bloody husband); (16) Martyrdom (bloody bride); (17) Wounded; (18) War.
Also see *Bleeding*.
(1) Lev. 17:11; (2) Job 33:4; Ezek. 37:14; 1 Pet. 4:6; Rev. 11:11 (the Life of God is the Spirit); (3) Num. 35:21; Deut. 19:6; Josh. 20:5 (avenger of blood = kinsman); (4) Lev. 17:11; (5) 1 Pet. 1:18-19; (6) Gen. 4:10; Exod. 4:9; (7) Prov. 30:33; (8) Matt. 27:24; (9) Matt. 27:6 (blood-money); (10) Exod. 34:25; Ps. 106:38; Isa. 1:11; Ezek. 39:19;

(11) Gen. 4:10; (12) Jer. 46:10; (13) Heb. 12:17; (14) Luke 22:44; (15) Exod. 4:26; 1 Cor. 10:16; (16) Rev. 17:6; (17) 1 Kings 22:35; Ezek. 28:23; (18) 1 Kings 2:5.

Blood Bank: (1) Church.
(1) John 6:53-56; Lev. 17:11; as in "the place where spiritual life is renewed."

Blood Pressure: (1) Resistance to the Holy Spirit (high b.p.); (2) Lacking spiritual intimacy (low b.p.); (3) Lacking spiritual fortitude (low b.p.).
(1) Lev. 17:11 & (Job 33:4; Ezek. 37:14); Acts 6:10; (2) Isa. 40:30-31; (3) Heb. 12:3-4.

Bloody Nose: See *Nose Bleed*.

Blood Transfusion: (1) Salvation/conversion; (2) Spiritual life renewed. (1) Heb. 9:14; 1 Pet. 1:18-19; 1 John 1:7; (2) Lev. 17:11.

Blossom: (1) Potential fruitfulness; (2) Chosen by God; (3) Abundance; (4) Joy and rejoicing; (5) Beauty; (6) Pride; (7) Associated with spring (summer is harvest time).
(1) Gen. 40:10; Num. 17:8; (2) Num. 17:5; (3) Isa. 27:6, 35:2; (4) Isa. 35:2; Hab. 3:17-18; (5) Isa. 35:1; (6) Ezek. 7:10; (7) Song 2:11-12.

Blowing: (1) Opposition; (2) Testing; (3) Spirit; (4) Assisting a fire.
Also see *Hit*, *Trumpet*, and *Wind*.
(1-2) Matt. 7:25, 17; John 6:18; (3) Isa. 40:7; John 3:8; (4) Job 20:26; Isa. 54:16.

Blue: (1) Heaven/ly; (2) Spirit/ual; (3) Royalty (king); (4) Jesus; (5) Holy Spirit (dark blue); (6) Human spirit (light blue); (7) Healing (as a heavenly reality); (8) Complete; (9) Reminder of seeking the Kingdom first (if looking at blue).
(1-2) Exod. 28:31; 36:8,35; 39:1; Num. 4:7; 15:38; (3-4) Esther 8:15; (5) John 1:32; (6) Rev. 1:6; 5:10; (7-9) (cf. Exod. 39:24; Num. 15:38-39; Matt. 9:20-21).

Blueberries: (1) Fruit of the Spirit.
Also see *Berries*, *Blue*, and *Strawberries*.
(1) Gal. 5:22-23.

Blues Music: (1) Depression; (2) Cultural association with oppressed peoples.
(1-2) Ps. 137:1-3.

Blunt: (1) A blunt weapon means ineffective words; (2) Rude, outspoken, or tactless; (3) Dull; (4) Blunt words often require raised volume.
(1) Ps. 58:6; Isa. 54:17; (2) Eph. 5:4; (3) Isa. 59:1; (4) Eccles. 10:10.

Blushing: (1) Embarrassment; (2) Anger; (3) Shame; (4) Stress; (5) Guilty.
(1) Ezra 9:6; (2) Gen. 39:19 (NIV); (3) Ezra 9:6; Jer. 6:15; (4) Job 16:16 (5) Ezek. 16:63.

Board: (1) Secular leadership; (2) Religious council; (3) Elders.
(1) Acts 4:8; (2) Matt. 5:22; 10:17; 12:14; 26:59; (3) Acts 11:30; 14:23.

Boarding School: See *Private School*.

Board Meeting: (1) Communing over business matters; (2) Running a business; (3) Business plans and agenda; (4) Ambition; (5) Council; (6) Accountability.

(1) Acts 4:15; (2) Acts 4:16-21, 5:27,29; (3) Matt. 26:59; Luke 22:66-67; (4) 2 Sam. 15:12; John 11:47-48; (5) Matt. 5:22; 10:17, 12:14; 26:59; (6) Acts 15:6, 22.

Boardwalk: See *Jetty*.

Boat: (1) Ministry; (2) Life's journey; (3) Person; (4) Holy Spirit transport; (5) Church. Also see *Battleship, Canoe, Rowing, Ship, Shipwreck,* and *Speedboat*.
(1) Luke 5:3-10; (2) Mark 4:35; (3) John 3:8; Acts 18:21b; (4) 2 Sam. 19:18; (5) 1 Pet. 3:20; Matt. 14:22.

Boat Trailer: See *Trailer (Boat)*.

Body: (1) Death (dead body); (2) The Body of Christ; (3) The temple of God; (4) Sacrifice; (5) Spiritual body; (6) Organization; (7) The flesh.
(1) Ps. 79:2; 110:6; (2) Rom. 12:5; 1 Cor. 6:15; Eph. 5:30; (3) 1 Cor. 6:19 (individually); 2 Cor. 6:16 (corporately); (4) Rom. 12:1; (5) 1 Cor. 15:44; (6) 1 Cor. 12:25; (7) Rom. 8:13; 1 Cor. 6:16; Col. 1:22a.

Body Odor: (1) Offense/ive; (2) Works of the flesh. (1) Gen. 3:19; 4:2-5; (2) Ezek. 44:18.

Bogey/Boogie (Dried Nasal Mucus): (1) Person offended by the things of the Spirit; (2) If another person has the bogey, it may be that they have offended you; (3) Wrong spirit (resistance to the Spirit of God); (4) Evil spirit; (5) "Bogey man": under *Demon*.
(1) Matt. 13:57; John 6:61-63; (2) Matt. 16:23; (3) Acts 7:51; (4) Acts 13:8-10.

Boiling: (1) Anger; (2) Purification; (3) Enlivening.
Also see *Pressure Cooker*.
(1) Gen. 44:18; Num. 11:1; Isa. 42:25; (2) Num. 31:23; (3) Jer. 20:9.

Boils: (1) Test; (2) Anger; (3) Plague.
(1) Job 2:7; (2) Lev. 13:23 (burning boil); (3) Lev. 13:22 (spreading).

Bolts: (1) Assurance; (2) Sure words; (3) Immovable; (4) Build/ing; (5) Tie together or unite; (6) Foundation; (7) Lock.
Also see *Nails, Nuts* and *Bolts*.
(1) Ezra 9:8; Isa. 22:23; (2) Eccles. 12:11; (3) Isa. 41:7; Jer. 10:4; (4-6) Ezra 4:12; Neh. 4:6; Eph. 2:21; (7) 2 Sam. 13:17-18.

Bomb: (1) Words of sudden detrimental impact (dropped bomb); (2) Explosive or shocking words; (3) Sudden destructive event; (4) Shocking announcement (i.e., resignation); (5) Empowered by the Holy Spirit (loading a bombshell); (6) Words that burn (positive or negative); (7) Unresolved issue that will blow up in the future (time bomb); (8) Explosive outburst.
Also see *Arrow, Missile, Rocket,* and *Terrorism*.
(1) 1 Sam. 3:19; Prov. 18:21; (2) Matt. 26:21; Luke 22:21; (3) Jer. 51:8; 1 Thess. 5:3; (4) As in "she dropped a bombshell"; (5) Acts 1:8; (6) Jer. 20:8; Luke 24:32; (7) Gen. 4:2-3; (8) Prov. 18:21.

Bonds: See *Bound*.

Bones: (1) Dead; (2) Without spiritual life; (3) Broken-spirited; (4) Having sorrow of heart; (5) Hopelessness; (6) Feeling cut off from God; (7) Envy (rotten bones).
(1-2) Ezek. 37:4,11; (3) Prov. 17:22; (4) Prov. 15:13; (5-6) Ezek. 37:11; (7) Prov. 14:30.

Book: (1) Bible; (2) Judgment (Lamb's book of Life); (3) Literal book; (4) Words; (5) Law; (6) Go by the book; (7) Contract; (8) Meditate; (9) Life plan; (10) An individual (a heart).
Also see *Bookcase, Library,* and *Scroll.*
(1) Josh. 1:8; (2) Rev. 13:8; 21:27; (3) Luke 4:17; (4) Luke 3:4; (5) Josh. 1:8; (6-7) Exod. 24:7; (8) Josh. 1:8; (9) Ps. 40:7; Heb. 10:7; (10) Prov. 3:3; 2 Cor. 3:3.

Bookcase: (1) Mindset; (2) Ideals and beliefs; (3) Church full of head knowledge.
Also see *Book.*
(1-2) Josh. 1:8a; Col. 3:2; (3) 1 Cor. 8:1-2.

Bookmark: (1) Revelation; (2) Verse for meditation.
Also see *Highlighter* and *Tassels.*
(1-2) Josh. 1:8.

Bookshelf: (1) Intellectual; (2) Inactive church; (2) Stored knowledge (3) Study; (4) Someone or something on hold (books on the shelf). *If the bookshelf falls over it could mean:* (5) Warning of losing knowledge/memory; (6) Challenging your current understanding; (7) Mental shakeup.
See also *Book* and *Bookcase.*
(1) 1 Cor. 2:4; 4:20; (2) Rev. 3:14-22; (3) Prov. 10:14; (3) 2 Tim. 2:15; (4) Gen. 40:14-15; 23; 41:1; John 5:3; (5) Judg. 3:7; Dan. 4:33-34; (6) Acts 9:5; 26:14; 19:1-6; (7) Matt. 15:16; 16:6-12.

Boomerang: (1) What goes around comes around (positive or negative); (2) Something that the Spirit brings back to you; (3) Australia.
(1) Isa. 55:11; Gal. 6:7; (2) Gen. 41:9-14 (cf. Gen. 40:23); (3) By association.

Boom Gate: (1) Waiting on God.
(1) Ps. 62:5.

Boots: (1) External or outward walk (what you do out of the home); (2) Work; (3) Termination of a relationship; (4) Warfare; (5) Arduous path; (6) Readied to climb (hiking/climbing boots); (7) Muddying the waters.
Also see *Feet, Sandal,* and *Shoe.*
(3) As in "being given the boot"; Matt. 10:14; (4) Joel 2:7; (5) Gen. 35:16; Prov. 13:15; (6) 2 Sam. 22:34; Ps.18:33; Hab. 3:19; (7) Ps. 46:3; Isa. 57:20; Ez. 32:2,13.

Boss: (1) Jesus; (2) God; (3) Natural leadership; (4) Spiritual leadership; (5) Father.
(1) Matt. 10:24-25; John 13:13-14; (2) Ps. 123:2; Gen. 24:12; Isa. 40:22; (3) Gen. 39:2; 1 Sam. 24:6; (4) 2 Kings 2:3, 5; (5) Mal. 1:6.

Bottle(s): (1) Heart (as a vessel of the Spirit); (2) Old bottles may speak about the old self; new bottles the new self; new bottles (wine skins) are adjustable/ flexible/ stretchable; (3) Local church; (4) Wineskins need to be able to vent (that is, speak out or they will burst); (5) Old bottles may speak about deception; (6) Sharing a bottle speaks of friendship/communion/covenant meal; (7) Welcome; (8) Sucking the life out of people (emptying bottles and laying them down).
Also see *Vessels* and *Wine*.
(1-2) Jer. 13:12-13; Matt. 9:17; John 2:6-10; (3) Matt. 9:17; (4) Job 32:19; (5) Josh. 9:4, 13; (6) 1 Sam. 1:24; 10:3; 16:20; (7) 2 Sam. 16:1; (8) Jer. 48:12.

Bottle Cap/Top: (1) Stopping words coming out (+/-) (capping a bottle).
Also see *Bottle*.
(1) Matt. 9:17 (KJV); Prov. 30:32 (cf. Eccles. 10:12). As in "put a lid on it!"

Bought: See *Buy/ing*.

Bound: (1) Spiritually bound with words; (2) Under control; (3) Captive or confined; (4) Opposite of freedom; (5) To be dead spiritually.
A person can be bound: (6) By religion; (7) By the world; (8) By an unclean spirit; (9) By satan; (10) By iniquity; (11) In the Spirit; (12) By the state; (13) By people pleasing.
Also see *Cord*, *Loosing*, and *Rope*.
(1) Acts 23:12, 14, 21; Matt. 16:19; 18:18; (2) Mark 5:3-4; (3) Mark 6:17-20; John 18:12; (4) John 8:33; (5) John 11:44; (6) John 18:12; Acts 9:2,14,21; 21:11; (7) Acts 7:7; (8) Luke 8:29; (9) Luke 13:16; (10) Acts 8:23; (11) Acts 20:22-23; (12) Acts 22:29; (13) Acts 24:27.

Boundary: (1) Covering; (2) Kingdom of God; (3) Decision; (4) Heaven and hell; (5) Righteous and sinner; (6) Blessed and cursed; (7) Dividing God's Word or God's Word dividing.
(1) Gen. 19:8b; (2) Deut. 17:14; (3) Num. 13:30–14:1; (4-6) Matt. 25:33-34; Luke 16:26; (7) 2 Tim. 2:15; Heb. 4:12.

Bow (Bow and Arrow): (1) Heart (that which shoots words); (2) Words launched at a distance; (3) Deceitful heart (distorted bow); (4) Ready (bent bow).
Also see *Arrows* and *Left*.
(1) Ps. 64:3; Hab. 3:9; (2) 1 Sam. 20:20-22; (3) Ps. 78:57; Hos. 7:16; (4) Ps. 11:2.

Bowing: (1) Humbling oneself; (2) Greeting; (3) Worship; (4) Paying homage.
Also see *Bending*, *Duck*, and *Knee*.
(1) Isa. 2:11; (2) Eastern culturally accepted greeting; (3) Matt. 28:9; (4) Acts 10:25-26.

Bowl: (1) Heart; (2) Glorious being (golden bowl); (3) Man's glory (golden bowl); (4) The heart of God (golden bowl).
See also *Vessels*.
(1-3) Ps. 23:5; Eccles. 12:6; (4) Exod. 37:17; Heb. 8:5.

Bowling Alley: (1) Prophetic Training.

(1) 1 Sam. 3:9-10,19; 10:11; 17: 36; 2 Kings 2:1-14; 13:17-19; Ps. 64:3.

Bowling/Bowler (Ten Pin): (1) Prophet; (2) Preaching and hitting hearts (strike); (3) Spirit of death (strike); (4) Destroying angel.

(1) 2 Kings 1:10; (2) Acts 2:37; (3) 2 Kings 19:35; (4) Exod. 12:23.

Bowling/Bowler (Cricket): (1) Prophet; (2) Preaching; (3) Under spiritual attack (facing opposition bowler).

See also *Ball, Baseball,* and *Batsman.*

(1) Acts 15:32 (balls are words); Hos. 6:5; (2) Mark 16:20; (3) Ps. 64:3-4.

Box: (1) Heart; (2) Righteous/ness (white box); (3) Innocence (white box); (4) Insincere heart (plastic box); (5) Confined or restricted; (6) Spiritual gift or present; (7) Not unpacked or not in use (something boxed up).

(1) Matt. 26:7 (KJV); (2) 1 Kings 3:6; Rom. 10:10; (3) Ps. 106:38; (4) Isa. 29:13; (5) As in "put in a box"; (6) Mark 14:3 (as does the alabaster box, which was broken that the fragrance of the Holy Spirit may fill the house); (7) Luke 7:37 (KJV).

Boxing: (1) Spiritual Warfare; (2) Under attack; (3) Adversity; (4) Need for discipline.

(1-2) 2 Cor. 10:3-4; Eph. 6:12; (3) Isa. 30:20; Heb. 13:3; (4) 1 Cor. 9:26-27.

Boy: (1) The world; (2) Actual boy; (3) Legacy or heritage; (4) Inheritance; (5) Heir; (6) Future; (7) Young generation; (8) Promise.

Also see *Baby, Girl,* and *Son.*

(1) Luke 9:41; John 16:21; Gal. 4:3; (3-5) Matt. 21:38; Gal. 4:1,7,30; Heb. 1:2; Rev. 21:7; (6) Job 21:8; (7) Gen. 48:19b; Amos 2:11; (8) Gal. 4:28.

Bra: (1) Righteousness; (2) Integrity of heart; (3) Support; (4) Brazen (no bra); (5) Loose woman (no bra); (6) Feral (no bra); (7) Whore (no bra); (8) Nurture (bra as care and support).

Also see *Breast.*

(1) Eph. 6:14; (2) 1 Kings 9:4; (3) Rev. 1:13 (KJV); (4-6) Hos. 2:2; Prov. 5:19, 6:29; (7) Prov. 5:19-20; (8) Isa. 60:4.

Braces (Teeth): (1) Bound (restricted) by your words; (2) Ineffective bite/no power; (3) Speaking other than what God has directed you to say; (4) Legalism; (5) Hypocrisy; (6) Need for corrective speech.

Also see *Teeth.*

(1) Num. 21:5-6; Matt. 16:18; (2-3) Num. 22:38; (3) 1 Cor. 2:4; 1 Thess. 1:5; Heb. 4:12; (4) Matt. 23:4; (5) Matt. 23:2-3.

Brake(s): (1) Stop or slow down; (2) Stop speaking; (3) Stop hearing; (4) Slow down; (5) Feeling out of control (no brakes); (6) Feeling like you started something that you cannot stop (no brakes); (7) No limits (no brakes).

(1) Exod. 14:13; (2) Rom. 3:19; 2 Cor. 11:10; Titus 1:11; Heb. 11:33; (3) Acts 7:57; (4) Ps. 103:8; 145:8; Prov. 14:29; 15:18; 16:32; Joel 2:13; Acts 27:7; James 1:19; (5) Prov. 25:28; (6) James 3:5; (7) Matt. 9:17 (the new wineskin has no breaks!).

Branch: (1) Jesus; (2) Channel of the Holy Spirit (anointed one); (3) Believer/Christian; (4) Fruit bearer; (5) Honorable elder; (6) Influence (long branch = long reach); (7) Day; (8) Pride (endangered branches); (9) Union with God (flourishing branch); (10) The king (the highest branch).
(1) Isa. 4:2; 11:1; Jer. 23:5; 33:15; Zech. 3:8; 6:12; (2) Exod. 25:31-37; Zech. 4:12-14; (3) Matt. 13:31-32; John 15:5; (4) Num. 13:23; Isa. 4:2; 17:6; Ezek. 17:8; 19:10; John 15:2,4; (5) Isa. 9:14-15; 19:15; (6) Ezek. 31:5; Dan. 4:14; (7) Gen. 40:10-12; (8) Rom. 11:17-22; (9) Prov. 11:28; (10) Ezek. 17:22.

Brass: (1) Judgment; (2) Financial hardship; (3) Without love; (4) Third place. (1) Exod. 27:1-2; Rev. 1:15; (2) Matt. 10:9; (3) 1 Cor. 13:1; (4) Mark 12:42.

Breach: (1) Breakthrough/forth; (2) Fracture; (3) Break; (4) Spiritual gap; (5) Repair needed; (6) Wound; (7) Broken wall; (8) Hole.
(1) Gen. 38:29; 2 Sam. 5:20; 6:8; (2) Lev. 24:20; (3) Num. 14:34; (4) Judg. 21:15; 1 Kings 11:27; Ps. 106:23; Prov. 15:4; Isa. 22:9; (5) 2 Kings 12:5-7; 22:5; Isa. 58:12; (6) Job 16:14; Isa. 30:26; Jer. 14:17; Lam. 2:13; (7) Isa. 30:13; Ezek. 26:10; (8) Amos 6:11.

Bread: (1) Christ; (2) The Word of God; (3) Broken body (breaking bread); (4) Communion (breaking bread); (5) Death; (6) Words (our hearts feed on words); (7) Affliction (unleavened bread); (8) Life (bread sustains life).
Also see *Crumbs*, *Crusty Bread* (directly below), *Loaf*, *Toast*, and *Wine*.
(1) 1 Cor. 10:16; 11:27; (2) Deut. 8:3; Amos 8:11; Matt. 4:4; Luke 4:4; (3) Matt. 26:26; Luke 24:35; Acts 2:42; (4-5) Mark 14:1; 1 Cor. 11:26; (6) Amos 8:11; Matt. 4:4; (7) Deut. 16:3; (8) John 6:33,35,48,51,58.

Bread (Crusty Bread): (1) Old words; (2) Deception; (3) Thoughts and words from a fleshly heart (wood oven loaves).
(1-3) Josh. 9:4-6,12.

Bread (Moldy Bread): (1) Old manna/revelation; (2) Not exercising faith; (3) Need for daily bread.
(1-2) Exod. 16:20-21, 26; (3) Matt. 6:11.

Breakfast: (1) Breaking of a fast; (2) Feast after spiritual drought; (3) A new day; (4) New beginning.
(1) Judges 20:26; 2 Sam. 12:16-20; Esther 4:16-5:4; Dan. 6:18-23; Joel 2:12-14; Matt. 6:17-18; (2) Matt. 4:2-4; Matt. 4:11; Acts 10:30-44; (3-4) Isa. 58:6; Jon. 3:5-10; Matt. 4:11; Luke 2:36-38; Acts 10:30-44; 27:33.

Breaking: (1) Violating; (2) Stealing; (3) Destroying; (4) Brokenness; (5) Dying to self; (6) Repenting; (7) Desperate faith; (8) Cut short/nullified/without effect; (9) Physically broken; (10) Dispersing; (11) Pruning; (12) Giving the heart expression vocally (breaking forth).
(1) Matt. 5:19; John 5:18; 7:23; Rom. 2:23; (2) Matt. 6:19-20; 24:43; (3) Matt. 12:20; Mark 5:4; Luke 5:6; John 21:11; Acts 27:41; Eph. 2:14; Rev. 2:27; (4) Matt. 21:44;

Luke 20:18; Acts 2:42,46; 21:13; 1 Cor. 10:16; 11:24; (5) Matt. 14:19; 15:36-37; 26:26; Mark 14:3; Luke 24:35; (6) Judg. 21:15; Joel 2:13; (7) Mark 2:4-5; (8) John 10:35; (9) John 19:31-32, 36; (10) Acts 13:43; (11) Rom. 11:17,19; (12) Gal. 4:27.

Breast: (1) Nurtured; (2) Spiritual pioneer (e.g., Martin Luther); (3) Repentance (beating breast); (4) Embrace; (5) Sexually perverse spirit or spirit of lust (grabbing breast); (6) Close to the heart (love).
Also see *Bra, Harlot, Jezebel* (in Name and Place Dictionary), *Naked*, and *Woman*.
(1) Job 3:12; Song 8:1; Isa. 60:16; (2) Someone who distributes the milk of the Word that the Body may grow thereby; (3) Jer. 31:19; Luke 18:13; (4) Ruth 4:16; Prov. 5:20; (5) Matt. 5:28; (6) John 13:23; 21:20.

Breath: (1) Spirit; (2) Spiritual life; (3) Offensive (bad breath); (4) Unclean spirit (bad breath); (5) God's Spoken Word (rhema).
Also see *Belch*.
(1-2) Gen. 2:7; (3) Job 19:17; (4) Mark 1:26; (5) Ps. 33:6.

Breath Analysis/Testing: (1) Testing/measuring the Spirit. (1) 1 John 4:1.

Brewery: (1) Because it utilizes fermentation, it infers a process of corruption and evil; (2) Worldly church.
Also see *Yeast*.
(1) Exod. 34:25; Lev. 2:11 (leaven and honey were excluded from offerings because they symbolize people seeking their own glory, i.e., corrupt worship); (2) 1 Pet. 1:23-25; Rev. 2:15-18; 18:2.

Bricks: The Scriptural use of the word portrays: (1) people's attempt to reach Heaven; (2) People attempting to make a name for themselves; (3) Human-made empires; (4) Rebellion against God; (5) Bondage of the world (Egypt); (6) A works-based service of people; (7) Keeping people busy so that they do not have time to truly worship God; (8) Pride; (9) Human-made altars; (10) Human-made words (bricks instead of stone).
Also see *Stone(s)*.
(1-3) Gen. 11:3-4; (4) Gen. 9:1; 11:4; (5-6) Exod. 1:14; (7) Exod. 5:7-8ff; (8) Isa. 9:9-11; (9) Isa. 65:3; (10) Gen. 11:3-4.

Bride: (1) Church; (2) Heavenly Jerusalem; (3) Israel; (4) United with (union); (5) Relationship; (6) Spotless and ready for Christ's return (bride in white dress); (7) Martyrdom (bloody bride).
Also see *Best Man, Blood, Groom*, and *Marriage*.
(1) Eph. 5:25; (2) Rev. 21:9b-10; (3) Isa. 54:5; (4-5) Gen. 2:24; (6) Rev. 19:7; (7) Rev. 17:6.

Bridegroom: See *Groom*.

Bridesmaid: (1) Loss of first love (should be the bride); (2) Getting others ready to meet Christ; (3) Pastor/leader; (4) Holy Spirit; (5) Church next in line for a move of God/revival (catching bouquet); (6) Expectant church (catching bouquet); (7) Church missing out on the glory (failing to catch the bouquet); (8) Stepping on others (hurting others to catch the bouquet).
(1) Rom. 7:4; Rev. 2:4; (2) Matt. 25:10; Rev. 21:2; (3) Matt. 23:11; Eph. 5:26-27; (4) John 16:13; (5) Acts 10:44-45; (6) John 4:28-29; Acts 1:14; (7) Matt. 23:37; (8) Matt. 15:25-27.

Bridle: (1) Control the tongue.
(1) Job 30:11; Ps. 32:9; 39:1; James 1:26; 3:2.

Bridge: (1) The cross; (2) Jesus Christ; (3) The Church; (4) Filling the gap; (5) Means to an end; (6) Human-made destiny; (7) Human-made efforts; (8) Life's passage or journey; (9) A link; (10) Salvation ministry (working on bridge); (11) Relationship or communication; (12) Human-made structure.
(1) 2 Sam. 18:9 (see *Oak*); (2) John 1:51; 1 Pet. 3:18; (3) John 1:41-42; 2 Cor. 5:20; (4) Ezek. 22:30; (10) By virtue of the fact that the bridge is the cross of Christ; (11) Ps. 133:1; also, as in "building bridges"; (12) Gen. 11:4.

Briefcase: (1) Business; (2) Financial management; (3) Business transaction; (4) Teacher or teaching.
(1) John 12:6; Acts 1:18a; (2-3) Prov. 7:20; John 12:6; (4) Eph. 4:11.

Broad: (1) Destruction (road/gate); (2) All encompassing; (3) Easy (road/gate); (4) Made to impress; (5) Deep (river).
(1-3) Matt. 7:13-14; (4) Matt. 23:5 (adornments); (5) Eph. 3:18; Ezek. 47:3-5.

Broken: (1) Broken spirit; (2) Broken heart; (3) Ineffective work (broken hand); (4) Bad walk (broken foot); (5) Interrupted walk (broken feet).
(1) Job 17:1; (2) Prov. 15:13; (3) Job 22:9 (KJV); (4) Heb. 12:13; (5) 2 Sam. 4:4.

Broken Arrow (arrows = words): (1) Mute spirit; (2) Unbelief; (3) Lacking confidence; (4) Words of the flesh; (5) Disarmed the enemy; (6) Threat of unexpected catastrophe/conflict; (7) The cross.
(1-2) Luke 1:20; (3) Exod. 6:30; (4) cf. 1 Sam. 3:19; (5) Ps. 76:3-6; (6) Term for stolen nuclear warhead; (7) Ps. 76:2-3.

Broken Glass: (1) Disappointment; (2) Reproach; (3) Illegal entry into your spirit (breaking your spiritual window); (4) Cutting words.
Also see *Glass*, *Water* (water reflects like glass), and *Window*.
(1) Job 17:11; Ps. 38:8 (cf. Prov. 27:19; 20:5); also as in "shattered dreams"; (2) Ps. 69:20; (3) Matt. 6:19; (4) Ps. 22:13a.

Bronze: (1) Strength; (2) Righteousness; (3) Boldness; (4) Third place.
Also see *Brass*, *Gold*, *Pewter*, and *Silver*.
(1-3) Rev. 1:15; 2:18 (NIV); (4) Num. 31:22 (NIV); also as in Olympic medals.

Brook: (1) Resting place; (2) A defining moment; (3) A dividing place; (4) Hiding place; (5) A place of trees; (6) A place of harvest; (7) A place of blessing; (8) The Word of God; (9) A place of sustenance; (10) A place of judgment; (11) A place of passage; (12) Deceitful; (13) A place of stones; (14) A place of refreshing and honor; (15) The human spirit; (16) A place of mourning; (17) Defense; (18) Border; (19) The words from a person's mouth.

Also see *River* and *Stream*.

(1) 1 Kings 17:4-6; (2-3) Gen. 32:23; Num. 21:14-15; Deut. 2:13-14; 1 Sam. 30:9-10, 21; 2 Sam. 15:23; 17:20; 1 Kings 2:37; (4) 1 Kings 17:3; Job 40:22; (5) Lev. 23:40; (6) Num. 13:23-24; (7) Deut. 8:7; Job 20:17; (8) 1 Sam. 17:40; Ps. 42:1; (9) 1 Kings 18:5; (10) 1 Kings 18:40; 2 Kings 23:6; (11) Neh. 2:15; (12) Job 6:15; (13) Job 22:24; (14) Ps. 110:7; (15) Prov. 18:4; (16) Isa. 15:7;
(17) Isa. 19:6; (18) Jer. 31:40; (19) Prov. 18:4.

Broom: (1) Cleaning up; (2) Putting things in order; (2) Destruction.

Also see *Sweeping*.

(1-2) Luke 15:8; (3) Isa. 14:23.

Brothel: (1) Church whose members are selling themselves to the world or making money illegitimately; (2) House of sin; (3) Lust issue.

(1) Rev. 17:3-4; (2) Prov. 5:20-22; (3) Matt. 5:28.

Brother: (1) Fellow believer (male or female); (2) Jesus Christ; (3) Guardian; (4) Natural brother; (5) Brother in nationality.

(1) Rom. 14:13; 1 Cor. 5:11; 6:6; Matt. 22:30; 1 Pet. 3:1-4; (2) Matt. 28:10; John 20:17; Rom. 8:29; Heb. 2:11; (3) Eph. 6:21-22; Col. 4:7; (4) Gal. 1:19; (5) Rom. 9:3.

Brother-in-law: (1) Legalistic believer; (2) Someone who negates the Word through religious tradition; (3) Religious adversary; (4) Fellow believer wanting to impose their ways/culture opposing the flow of the Spirit; (5) New converts coming out of worldly ways.

Also see *Father-in-Law* and *Son-in-Law*.

(1) Gal. 2:16,21; 5:10; (2) Matt. 15:1-3; (3) Matt. 16:21; 26:57; (4) Gal. 2:12-13; 3:3; (5) Acts 11:3,18.

Brown: (1) Earthly or earthen (contrasted to heavenly); (2) Sin; (3) The imperfections of the flesh; (4) Marred, unwanted; (5) Dark-skinned.

(1) 2 Cor. 4:7; (2) Ps. 104:35; Eccles. 7:20; Matt. 9:6; (3) Gen. 6:12; 2 Cor. 4:7; (4) Gen. 30:32-40; (5) Song 1:5-6.

Bruise: (1) Strike and injure (or injured); (2) Have victory over; (3) To crush or bind a heart; (4) Wounded; (5) Been ill-spoken of.

(1) Gen. 3:15; (2) Gen. 3:15; Rom. 16:20; (3) Matt. 12:20; Luke 4:18; 9:39; (4) Isa. 1:6; 53:5; (5) Prov. 25:18.

Brush: See *Broom* and *Comb*.

Bubble: (1) Spirit being; (2) Life (the Spirit bubbling up); (3) Protection (surrounded by a bubble); (4) Thought or revelation (as in thought bubble); (5) Anger (as in boiling); (6) Speaks of an episode in one's life or time period; (7) Fragile; (8) Separation or difference. Also see *Balloon* and *Effervescence*.
(1) Ezek. 1:21; (2) John 4:14; (3) Job 1:10; Ps. 5:12; 32:7,10; (4) 2 Cor. 10:5; (5) Job 30:27 (KJV); (6) 1 Sam. 10:2-9; Heb. 1:1; (7) Ps. 80:12; 89:40; Isa. 5:5; (8) Eph. 2:14.

Bubble Gum: (1) Fear of public speaking/Tongue-tied (bubble gum inhibiting your ability to speak); (2) Meditation/revelation; (3) Not receiving an authoritative word (chewing gum under chair); (4) Communication breakdown (chewing gum under table); (5) Secret words; (6) Worthless information.
(1) Exod. 4:10; (2) Josh. 1:8; Ps. 1:2-3; (3) 1 Sam. 10:8; 13:13; (4) John 13:26,30; (5) Acts 5:2; (6) Eph. 5:6; 2 Thess. 3:11.

Bucket: (1) Unsaved person (wooden pail); (2) Insignificant; (3) Human vessel; (4) Preacher; (5) Superficial person (plastic bucket).
Also see *Plastic*, *Vessel*, and *Wood*.
(1) Exod. 7:19; (2) Isa. 40:15 (as in "drop in a bucket"); (3) Num. 24:7; (4) Num. 24:7; Luke 8:11; Eph. 5:26; (5) Matt. 15:8-9; Col. 2:18a.

Bud: (1) Resurrection life; (2) New life.
(1-2) Gen. 40:10; Num. 17:8; Job 14:7-9; Isa. 27:6; 55:10; Heb. 9:4.

Buddhist Monk: (1) Religious spirit; (2) Idolatry. (1) Mark 7:3,5,8a; (2) Exod. 20:4.

Buddy: (1) Jesus Christ; (2) The Holy Spirit; (3) Close associate.
(1) John 15:15; (2) John 14:16.

Budgie: See *Parrot*.

Bugs: (1) Annoyance; (2) Religious spirit (bug in the ear).
Also see *Insects*.
(1) Isa. 1:14; Luke 18:5; also, as in "stop bugging me!"; (2) John 7:12b (bad-mouthing those moving in the Spirit).

Building (noun): (1) The individual; (2) Strong individual; (3) The Church; (4) Prayer tower (watch tower); (5) A business; (6) The glorified person; (7) Greed (barns); (8) Heavenly mansion; (9) Establishment.
Also see *Barn* and *House*.
(1) 1 Cor. 3:9; 6:19; John 2:21; Matt. 7:24,26; (2) 1 Cor. 3:9; Gal. 2:9; (3) 2 Cor. 6:16 (corporate temple); Eph. 2:21-22; 1 Pet. 2:5; (4) Matt. 21:33; Mark 12:1; Luke 14:28; (5) Matt. 24:1; John 2:16; Mark 13:2; (6) Mark 14:58; 1 Cor. 5:1; (7) Luke 12:18; (8) John 14:2; (9) Ezra 3:10; Isa. 44:28.

Building (verb): (1) Preaching the Gospel; (2) Building the Church; (3) Building the individual; (4) Christian works; (5) Putting together; (6) Association.
(1) Rom. 15:20; (2) Matt. 16:18; (3) Jude 1:20; Prov. 24:3-4; (4) 1 Cor. 3:14; (5-6) Eph. 4:16.

Builder: (1) God; (2) Gospel preachers/believers; (3) False builders; (4) You; (5) Church builder; (6) Businessman (trying to make a name for oneself).
Also see *Workman*.
(1) Ps. 127:1; Heb. 3:4; 11:10; (2) 1 Cor. 3:10; (3) Matt. 21:42; (4) Jude 1:20; 1 Cor. 3:10b; (5) Matt. 16:18; Acts 8:5-6, 14-15; (6) Gen. 11:4-5.

Building Blocks (ABC): (1) A call for child-like faith; (2) A message spelled out; (3) If the blocks are moved and the message unread, it may mean lacking spiritual insight/ sensitivity; (4) Playing with building blocks with no message speaks of immaturity and entertainment-only value; (5) Early stage of building faith.
(1) Matt. 18:3-4; (2) Dan. 5:24-25; (3) Matt. 13:16-17; (4) 1 Cor. 13:11; (5) Jude 1:20.

Building Contractor: (1) Apostle; (2) Five-fold ministry; (3) Man-made kingdom.
See also *Building* and *Builder*.
(1) Eph. 2:20-21; (2) Eph. 4:12; (3) Gen. 11:4.

Building Frame: (1) The Holy Spirit; (2) Understanding; (3) Structure.
(1) Eph. 2:21-22; (2) Prov. 24:3; (3) Isa. 61:4.

Bull: (1) Idol; (2) Danger; (3) Strong evil spirit; (4) Bellower (loud speaker); (5) Offering; (6) Financial predator (red rag to a bull, being in the red); (7) Financial bull = stocks, prices rising; (8) Demon of anger/death; (9) Territorial spirit.
Also see *Ox* and *Calf.*
(1) Exod. 32:4ff; 1 Kings 12:28, 32; 2 Kings 10:29; (2) Exod. 21:29; (3) Ps. 22:12-13; (4) Jer. 50:11; (5) Lev. 9:2; (6) Isa. 34:7; Jer. 50:11; (7) Ps. 50:10; (8) Ps. 22:12-13; (9) Ps. 22:12-13.

Bulldog: (1) Determined; (2) Tenacious.
Also see *Dog.*
(1-2) Jer. 15:3.

Bulldozer: (1) Very powerful ministry (generally: constructive = good; destructive = evil); (2) Apostle, prophet, or evangelist; (3) Preparation ministry; (4) Heavy-handed leader; (5) Powerful trailblazing/groundbreaking ministry (pioneering).
Also see *Earthmover*, *Road Grader*, and *Truck*.
(1) Acts 8:5-6, 9-10; (2-3) Isa. 40:3-4; Matt. 3:3; Acts 8:5-6; (4) 1 Sam. 22:11-18; (5) Matt. 3:1-3.

Bullet/s: (1) Words against you; (2) Piercing words; (3) God's Word; (4) Wounds (used slugs); (5) Words lodged in your heart (used slugs).
(1) Ps. 64:3; Jer. 9:8; (2) Ps. 45:5; (3) Heb. 4:12; (4-5) Prov. 18:8; 26:22.

Bully: (1) Strongman; (2) Call of God (on bully's victim).
(1) Matt. 8:28; 12:29; Acts 13:10-11; (2) 1 Sam. 17.

Bulrushes: (1) Lying prophet.
(1) Isa. 9:14-15.

Bum (Buttocks): (1) Curse of disobedience (tail).

Also see *Homeless Person* and *Sitting.*
(1) Deut. 28:44.

Bundle: (1) Life; (2) Treasure; (3) A gathered group.
(1) 1 Sam. 25:29; (2) Gen. 42:35; Song 1:13; (3) Matt. 13:30; Acts 28:3.

Burden: See *Backpack.*

Buried Alive: (1) Hell.
See *Burying.*
(1) Exod. 16:30-33.

Burn/ing: (1) Judgment; (2) Holy; (3) Torment; (4) Not being able to hold back; (5) Being consumed by; (6) Dealing with potential gossip (back-burning); (7) Dealing with past issues (back-burning); (8) Lust.
Also see *Fire.*
(1) Ezek. 38:22; Mal. 4:1; (2) Isa. 10:17; (3) Rev. 14:10; (4-5) Jer. 20:9; (6) James 3:5; (8) Rom. 1:27.

Burning Bush: (1) The Menorah.
See also *Menorah.*
(1) Exod. 3:14.

Burnt: (1) Betrayed or let down by another; (2) Sacrificed; (3) Heart seared from abuse; (4) Needs to be healed by the love of God.
(1) Luke 21:16; (2) 1 Pet. 2:5; (3) Neh. 4:2; (4) Mark 12:33.

Burp: See *Belch.*

Burrow: (1) Resting place; (2) Hiding place.
(1-2) Ps. 104:18; Prov. 30:26.

Burst: (1) Trying to put things of the Spirit into the unsaved; (2) Not yet capable of containing the truth shared; (3) Unable to stop the flow of the Spirit.
(1) Mark 2:22; Luke 5:37; (2) John 16:12; (3) Jer. 20:9.

Burying: (1) Dying to self; (2) Baptism; (3) Being overcome by sin (being buried); (4) Hiding.
Also see *Underground.*
(1-2) Rom. 6:4; (3) Rom. 6:23; (4) Gen. 35:4; Josh. 7:19-21.

Bus: (1) Large ministry; (2) Church; (3) Commercial vehicle; (4) Vehicle to your destiny; (5) Prophetic teaching/ministry (double-decker bus).
Also see *Bus Queue, Bus Station, School Bus, Tourist Bus,* and *Missing the Bus.*
(1) Acts 9:15-16; (2) Acts 15:3; 3 John 1:6b-7; (3) John 2:16; (4) Acts 1:8; (5) 2 Kings 6:1.

Bus Queue: (1) Waiting for ministry.
Also see *Bus Station/Stop.*
(1) 2 Chron. 7:6; Rom. 12:7.

Bus Station/Stop: (1) Waiting for ministry; (2) Waiting for direction; (3) Awaiting the timing of God.

Also see *Bus Queue.*

(1-2) Acts 13:1-3; (3) Gal. 4:4; Luke 2:51a; 3:23.

Bush: (1) God's manifest Presence; (2) May speak of turning aside; (3) God wants to talk to you; (4) Hiding place; (5) Growing believer; (6) Unbelieving person of the flesh; (7) Humble person; (8) Person trusting in people; (9) Fleshly Christian (covered with leaves); (10) Hiding from sin; (11) Menorah (burning bush); (12) Seven spirits of God (burning bush).

Also see *Tree.*

(1) Exod. 3:2; Deut. 33:16; Acts 7:30,35; (2) Exod. 3:3; (3) Mark 12:26; (4) Gen. 3:8; (5) Ps. 1:1,3; (6) Jer. 17:5-6; (7) Exod. 3:2; (8) Jer. 17:5-6; (9-10) Gen. 3:8; (11) Ex. 3:2-3 & Ex. 25:31 & Rev. 4:5; (12) Isa. 11:2.

Bush Fire: See *Wildfire.*

Business: (1) God's work; (2) Secular work.

(1) 1 Cor. 15:58; Luke 2:49; Acts 6:3; Rom. 12:11; (2) 1 Thess. 4:11.

Business Card: (1) New venture; (2) New association; (3) Identity.

(1-2) Acts 13:2-3; (3) Rev. 2:17.

Blank Business Card: (1) New name; (2) New beginning; (3) Favor of God; (4) Losing identity; (5) God about to do something new with you.

(1-2) Isa. 62:2; Zeph. 3:20 (NLT); Rev. 2:17; (3) 1 Sam. 10:7; 2 Sam. 7:3; (4) Ps. 9:5; (5) Isa. 42:9; 43:19a.

Busy: (1) Other agendas; (2) Commerce; (3) Hardened hearts.

(1) Luke 10:31-32, 41; (2) John 2:14-16; (3) Matt. 13:4, 19 (the wayside is hardened by much traffic).

Butcher's Shop: (1) Place of solid Bible teaching; (2) Place of judgment.

(1) 1 Cor. 3:2; Heb. 5:12-14 (KJV); (2) James 5:5.

Butler: (1) Faithful servant; (2) Fruitful servant.

(1-2) Gen. 40:9-13.

Butter: (1) Prosperity; (2) Smooth talker; (3) Charming words; (4) Strife because of the Word; (5) Growth through the Word; (6) Provision; (7) Change (melted butter).

(1) Deut. 32:14; Job 29:6; (2-3) Ps. 55:21; (4) Prov. 30:33; (5) Isa. 7:15, 22; 1 Cor. 3:2 (moving beyond milk); (6) Judg. 5:25; 2 Sam. 17:29; (7) Ps. 97:5.

Butterfly: (1) New creation; (2) Believer; (3) Glorified body (heavenly); (4) In the Spirit; (5) Changed (no longer a caterpillar); (6) No longer earthbound; (7) Glorified through death; (8) A person who flits from church to church (spiritual butterfly); (9) Israel (from Jacob [worm] to Israel [butterfly]).

(1-2) 2 Cor. 5:17; Eph. 4:22-24; 1 Pet. 3:18; (3) 1 Cor. 15:40; (4) Rev. 1:10; (5) 2 Cor. 5:17; (6) Ezek. 3:14; 8:3b; 11:1; (7) 1 Cor. 15:53-55; (8) cf. 1 Cor. 12:18, 25; (9) Isa. 41:14a (cf. Gen. 32:28).

Button (Pushing): (1) Employing an emotional trigger; (2) Touching a sore spot; (3) Arousing interest; (4) Invoking a response; (5) Ready to explode (anger). Also see *Remote Control.*
(1) 1 Sam. 18:7-9; Ps. 106:32-33 (KJV); (2) Acts 23:6; (3) John 4:17-19; (4) John 6:60-61,66; (5) Acts 7:54.

Buy/ing: (1) Soul winning; (2) Caught up in money-making; (3) Anchoring oneself to the world (giving second-place to the salvation of souls); (4) Laying down your life (giving your all); (5) Commercial transaction; (6) Life as usual before judgment; (7) Seeing things from an earthly perspective; (8) Redeemed by God; (9) Commitment; (10) Believing; (11) Grabbing hold of (purchasing); (12) Taking something on board. Also see *Sale* and *Shop.*
(1) 1 Cor. 6:20; (2) Matt. 21:12-13; James 4:13; (3) Luke 14:18-19, 21-24; (4) Matt. 25:9-12; 13:44-46; Rev. 3:18; (5) Matt. 14:15; 27:7; John 4:8; Acts 7:16; Rev. 13:17; (6) Luke 17:28; (7) John 6:5-7; (8) 1 Cor. 6:20; 7:23; (9) As in "buying into"; (10) As in "I just don't buy it!"; (11) 1 Chron. 21:24; (12) Prov. 18:17.

C

Cab: (1) Driven by money; (2) Money-driven ministry or person (hireling); (3) The road you are traveling down is costing you (you as passenger); (4) Business opportunity to your destiny (you as driver).
(1) John 12:5-6; (2) John 10:12-13; (3) Matt. 16:26; (4) Matt. 26:15.

Cabin (Holiday): (1) Rest; (2) Relaxed; (3) Holiday or break; (4) Intimacy. Also see *Hut* and *Shack.*
(1-2) Ruth 1:9; 2 Sam. 7:1; 1 Chron. 28:2; Isa. 66:1; Ezek. 44:30b; Dan. 4:4; (3) Luke 9:10b; (4) Matt. 14:13.

Cabin (Ship's): (1) Heart. (1) Jon. 1:2-3,5b.

Cablecar: (1) Jacob's Ladder; (2) Rising prayer and descending revelation; (3) Heavenly encounter.
(1) Gen. 28:12; (2) Matt. 6:10-11; (3) 2 Cor. 12:2.

Caesar: (1) Allegiance to world system; (2) Conqueror; (3) Tyrant; (4) Deceitful temptation; (5) Worldly (money-focused) leader.
(1) Matt. 22:17-21; (2) Luke 2:1; 3:1; John 19:12,15; (3) Acts 12:1-2; (4-5) Matt. 22:17-21.

Caesarean Birth: (1) Releasing the inner child; (2) Breaking a generational curse; (3) Deliverance; (4) Supernatural, pain-free birth (birthing either spiritually a promise or normal child-bearing); (5) Man interfering with God's promise trying to make it happen in the natural.
Also see *Birth* and *Pregnancy*.
(1) Num. 15:25-26; 1 Kings 8:38-39; 1 John 2:12; (2) Exod. 34:7; Num. 14:18; (3) Luke 9:42; John 16:21; Rev. 12:2; (4) Luke 1:36; (5) Num. 14:39-45.

Cage: (1) Stronghold; (2) Being treated like an animal; (3) Bondage; (4) Being confined; (5) Restrictions; (6) Unclean spirits (bird cage); (7) Choking the Spirit.
Also see *Aviary*.
(1) 2 Cor. 10:4-5; (2) Jer. 37:15; (3-5) Gen. 40:5a; (6) Rev. 18:2; Jer. 5:27; (7) Acts 5:18-19.

Cake: (1) Something of your own making (flesh); (2) Divine provision or sustenance; (3) The Word; (4) Communion with God (particularly if there is also a drink involved).
Also see *Bread*.
(1) 1 Kings 17:12-13; (2) 1 Kings 19:5-8; (3-4) 2 Sam. 6:19 (KJV) (cf. NKJV).

Calcium: (1) Food for the spirit (strengthens bones); (2) Needed for a broken spirit.
(1-2) Ps. 34:18; Prov. 15:13; Prov. 17:22.

Calculation: (1) Trying to work it out; (2) Trying to work it out in your head (mental calculation).
Also see *Calculator*.
(1-2) Prov. 3:5-6.

Calculator: (1) Trying to work it out in the natural; (2) Financial focus.
Also see *Calculation* and *Slide Rule*.
(1) John 6:7; (2) Matt. 9:9.

Calendar: (1) Planning; (2) Appointment; (3) Date with destiny.
Also see *Day* and look up individual numbers.
(1-2) 1 Kings 20:22,25-26; (3) Dan. 9:25; Matt. 21:4-5.

Calf: (1) Increased wealth; (2) Sacrifice/offering; (3) Idol; (4) Celebration; (5) Fellowship.
(1) Ps. 50:10; (2) Heb. 9:12,19; (3) Acts 7:41; (4) Luke 15:23; (5) Gen. 18:7-8.

Calling (Your Name): (1) A calling to ministry; (2) Attention required; (3) A friend or family member calling your name could be God; (4) Hearing an unknown voice is possibly God calling you to deeper relationship; (5) A scary, threatening, or uncomfortable voice calling your name may represent demonic powers; (6) A voice may also be providing direction; (7) Temptation (a voice calling you to fulfill the flesh).
Also see *Knocking* and *Doorbell*.
(1) 1 Sam. 3:4-10; Exod. 3:4; (2) Gen. 22:11; (3-4) 1 Sam. 3:4-10; (5) Matt. 8:28-29; (6) Acts 16:9; (7) Matt. 4:3, 6-7,9.

Calm: (1) Peace; (2) Still; (3) Sign of the Presence of God; (4) Removal of threat.
(1-4) Ps. 23:2; Mark 4:39; Luke 8:24.

Calm Feelings: (1) Good Sign; (2) Means God's in control.
(1-2) Mark 4:39; Ps. 107:29.

Camel: (1) Servant; (2) Endurance; (3) Speaks of being well-resourced; (4) Beast of burden; (5) Bearer of treasures; (6) Caravan; (7) Journey; (8) Equipped in the wilderness; (9) Prophet (preparing the way); (10) Rich man; (11) Provision.
Also see *Camel's Hair* and *Caravan.*
(1) Gen. 24:10; Matt. 3:4; Mark 1:6; (2) Gen. 24; (3) Matt. 19:24; (4) Gen. 24:61; 2 Kings 8:9; Isa. 30:6; (5) Isa. 30:6; Matt. 2:11; (6-7) Gen. 24:10; (8) Gen. 24:10; (9) Matt. 3:4; (10-11) Matt. 19:23-24.

Camel's Hair: (1) Prophet's mantle or calling of a prophet (as burden-bearer).
Also see *Camel.*
(1) 2 Kings 8:9 (shows camels as burden-bearers); Matt. 3:4; 11:9.

Camera: (1) Focusing; (2) Publicity; (3) Memories; (4) Fame; (5) Revealed (made public); (6) Seeking recognition (posing in front of camera); (7) Mind (as the place of memories); (8) Heart (as the place of the promises of God); (9) Seeing in the Spirit.
Also see *Cameraman*, *Movie Camera*, and *Photograph.*
(1) Acts 3:4; Heb. 12:2; (2) Mark 1:45; 5:20; 7:36; (3) Matt. 26:13; Mark 14:9; (4) Matt. 9:26,31; 14:1; (5) Dan. 2:19; (6) Matt. 20:21; Mark 10:37; (7) Rom. 12:2; (8) 1 Cor. 2:9; (9) See *Window.*

Cameraman: (1) Seer; (2) Prophet; (3) Focused individual.
(1-2) Num. 24:4,16; (3) 2 Sam. 18:24.

Camouflage: (1) Hidden in the secret place; (2) Hidden agenda; (3) Hiding something.
See also *Chameleon.*
1 Sam. 19:2; (2) Jer. 23:24; (3) Jer. 49:10.

Camp: (1) Temporary location; (2) The army of God; (3) Army of angels; (4) Church (multiple tents); (5) Gathering of spiritual forces (good or evil); (6) Wilderness experience (refugee camp); (7) Church led by the Spirit.
(1) Exod. 19:2; Josh. 10:15; (2) Exod. 14:19-20; Josh. 6:18; Ps. 34:7; (3) Gen. 32:1-2. (4) Exod. 33:7; Num. 2:16-17 (KJV); 15:35-36; (5) Gen. 32:1-2; Joel 2:11; Judg. 7:11; (6) As a place of refuge from persecution in your own land, but not yet having moved into a new homeland (like Israel); (7) Exod. 13:21; John 3:8.

Canaan: (1) The Promised Land; (2) The land of God's promises; (3) The Kingdom of God within (the infilling of the Holy Spirit).
(1) Exod. 13:5, 11; (2) Luke 24:49; (3) Luke 17:21.

Canaanites: (1) Spiritual principalities/powers/spirits; (2) Bring low by traffic or trade (convenience, greed, materialism, and possessions); (3) They also remove spiritual uprightness (they "unwall" you).

(1) Exod. 3:8; (2) This is the meaning of the root of the name; Gen. 13:7; (3) Ps. 51:10; 2 Sam 12:1-7.

Cancer: (1) Sin; (2) Sin within the Church (Body of Christ); (3) Destructive self-consuming words; (4) Literal cancer/disease; (5) Doubt (eats away faith in one's heart); (6) Fear (eats away faith); (7) Bitterness; (8) Unforgiveness; (9) Stress.
Also see *Tumor*.
(1) Isa. 1:4; Hos. 9:9; (2-3) 2 Tim. 2:16-17; (5) Matt. 14:30-31; 21:21; (6) Matt. 8:26; Mark 4:40; (7) Job 21:25; (8) Num. 12:11-12; (9) Job 2:4-5.

Candle/stick: (1) Believer; (2) The Holy Spirit; (3) God's Word; (4) Church; (5) Wickedness (lamp put out); (6) Holy Spirit removed (candle snuffed out); (7) Losing first love (candle snuffed out).
Also see *Lampstand*, *Light*, and *Wax*.
(1) Matt. 5:14-15; (2) Rev. 4:5; (3) Ps. 119:105; (4) Rev. 1:20; (5) Prov. 24:20; (6-7) Rev. 2:4-5.

Candy (Sweets): (1) Words (often God's Words); (2) Treat; (3) Pleasurable to the flesh, but without spiritual nutrition; (4) Appealing to children or immature believers; (5) Temptation (tempting treats); (6) Without substance.
(1) Ps. 119:103; 141:6; Prov. 16:24; (2) Prov. 27:7b; (3) 1 Cor. 14:20; 2 Tim. 4:3-4; Rev. 10:9-10; (4) Rom. 16:18; (5) Eph. 4:14; (6) Heb. 5:14.

Cane Toad: (1) Plague/curse; (2) Plague of false religion; (3) Solution that becomes a bigger problem (in Australia).
Also see *Frog* and *Toad*.
(1-2) Exod. 8:2; (3) Gen. 16:1-2.

Cankerworm: (1) Subtle destruction; (2) Gangrene; (3) Rotting; (4) Corrosion.
Also see *Locust*.
(1) Joel 1:4; James 5:3.

Cannibals: (1) Something eating at you (issue not dealt with); (2) Church devouring one another; (3) Partaking/communing with Christ; (4) Communing with demons.
(1) Matt. 18:34; (2) Lev. 26:27-29; Gal. 5:15; (3) John 6:53; (4) Lev. 26:28; 1 Cor. 10:20-21.

Cannon: (1) Powerful voice; (2) Impacting words (unrelenting heart); (3) Very persuasive words; (4) Leader; (5) Anger; (6) Unbridled tongue/heart.
(1) Luke 4:32; Acts 7:22; Heb. 12:26; (2) 1 Kings 19:2-3; (3) Rom. 16:18; Col. 2:4; (4) Eccles. 8:4; (5) Dan. 2:12-13; (6) Ps. 32:9; James 3:5-6 (loose cannon).

Canoe: (1) Undeveloped (primitive) ministry or person; (2) The flesh (our "self"-propelled old vessel); (3) Ministry in own strength (paddling canoe); (4) Ministry without the Holy Spirit; (5) Holy Spirit-led individual (canoe/ kayak moving without paddle in running water).
Also see *Boat*, *Rowing*, and *Underwater*.

(1) Acts 19:2b; (2) Deut. 12:8; Judg. 21:25 (doing your own thing); (3-5) Zech. 4:6.

Canteen: See *Restaurant.*

Cap: (1) Casual or familiar authority; (2) Weak authority.
Also see *Hat.*
(1) 1 Cor. 11:10.

Cape: See *Mantle.*

Captain: (1) Jesus; (2) Authority gained through suffering; (3) Leader; (4) Pastor.
(1-2) Heb. 2:10; (3) Rev. 6:15; (4) Jer. 51:23; Acts 20:28; 1 Pet. 5:2.

Captive: (1) Fallen into sin; (2) Bound by iniquity; (3) Under demonic oppression; (4) Under the influence of a dominant personality.
Also see *Chains, Prisoners*, and *Yoke.*
(1) Lam. 1:5; Amos 1:6; (2) Acts 8:23; (3) Matt. 12:29; Mark. 3:22-27; (4) Matt. 20:25.

Car: See *Automobile.*

Caravan (Camel): (1) Gifts; (2) Enduring trip; (3) Gathering the Church (Bride).
Also see *Camel.*
(1-3) Gen. 24:10.

Caravan: See *Trailer.*

Carburetor: (1) Door to the heart; (2) Fueling the heart/ministry.
Also see *Automobile.*
(1) Prov. 4:23; Matt. 6:6; Rev. 3:20; (2) Gen. 4:7; 1 Kings 10:24; Ezra 7:27; Neh. 2:12.

Car Carrier/Transport: (1) Riding on someone else's ministry; (2) Big ministry about to release other ministries (new cars).
(1) 2 Kings 5:20; (2) Matt.28:19-20; Luke 9:1-2.

Carcass: (1) Unclean; (2) Dead to self.
(1) Lev. 5:2; (2) Matt. 24:28.

Cards (Playing): (1) Gambling; (2) Bluffing; (3) Partnership; (4) Entertainment; (5) Deception; (6) Chance; (7) Time filler; (8) Patience; (9) Playing games and not revealing what's in your heart (hand); (10) Not telling you everything (keeping things close to your chest).
(9) Matt. 19:3; 22:17-18; (10) As in "having not laid all your cards on the table"; Acts 5:8-9.

Cards (Pack of Cards): (1) Flimsy (as in "the whole thing fell over like a pack of cards").

Cards (Patience): (1) Time filler; (2) Boredom; (3) Needing patience.

Cards (Poker): (1) Gambling; (2) Bluffing; (3) Chance; (4) Deception.

Cards (Whist, etc.): (1) Entertainment.

Cards (Bridge, Canasta, etc.): (1) Partnership.

Cards (Birthday/Christmas): (1) Gift; (2) Celebration.
(1) Matt. 2:11b; (2) Matt. 2:10.

Cards (Tarot): (1) Familiar spirits; (2) Searching for hope (the wrong way); (3) Deception; (4) Shrouded in uncertainty; (5) Desire for destiny or answers; (6) Bypassing God for answers.
(1) 1 Sam. 28:8; Acts 16:16; (2) 1 Chron. 10:13-14a; (5) 1 Sam. 28:7; (6) Micah 5:12.

Care: (1) Concern for God, people, or the world; (2) Chokes the Word (worldly care); (3) Practical concern; (4) True heart for people.
(1) 1 Cor. 7:32-33; (2) Matt. 13:22; Mark 4:19; Luke 8:14; 10:40-41; 21:34; (3) Luke 10:34-35; (4) John 10:13; 12:6.

Caretaker: (1) God; (2) Pastor/leader.
Also see *Janitor.*
(1) Ps. 23:1; 1 Pet. 5:7; (2) Acts 20:28.

Cargo Plane: (1) Large spiritual ministry bearing and releasing international ministries.
(1) Acts 13:1-2.

Carnal: (1) In the Flesh; (2) Sinful; (3) Death.
(1) 1 Cor. 3:1,3; 2 Cor. 10:4; (2) Rom. 7:14; (3) Rom. 8:6.

Carnival: (1) Showy church; (2) Entertaining church; (3) The world; (4) Pleasure.
(1) Rev. 3:1; (2) 2 Tim. 4:3-4; 3:4b-5; (3) Heb. 11:25; James 5:5a; (4) 1 Cor. 10:7.

Car Park: (1) Ministry rest; (2) Church; (3) Going nowhere; (4) Stuck in the wilderness (no destiny); (5) Wilderness; (6) Transition.
(1) Car = ministry, park = rest; (2) Acts 14:28; (3) Exod. 14:15; Luke 4:42; (4) Num. 26:65; (5) Luke 1:80; (6) Mark 14:34.

Carpenter: (1) Jesus; (2) Creator; (3) Builder.
(1) Matt. 13:55; (2) Matt. 13:55a; (3) 2 Sam. 5:11; 2 Kings 12:11.

Carpet: (1) Foundation; (2) Purging (carpet cleaning); (3) Covering/hiding issues; (4) Moving into a new spiritual home (carpet rolled up); (5) Changing on the inside (new carpet).
Also see *Rug* and *Vacuum Cleaner.*
(1) Eph. 6:11-18 (we are to stand on foundational truth); (2) 1 Cor. 5:7a; (3) As in "sweeping under the carpet"; (4-5) Matt. 9:17; 2 Cor. 5:1.

Carport: (1) Exposed ministry going nowhere.
Also see *Car Park* and *Garage.*
(1) 1 Sam. 4:13.

Carrots: (1) Deposits to help someone see in the dark (sliced carrots); (2) Spiritual eyes opening.
Also see *Vegetables.*
(1) Ps. 112:4; Isa. 9:2; 42:16; (2) Dan. 1:12,17.

Carry/ing: (1) Burden (of the cross); (2) Heavy load; (3) Guilt; (4) Sickness; (5) Oppression; (6) Captive; (7) Extras; (8) Under the influence of the Spirit (being carried); (9) Dependent; (10) Dead.

Also see *Heavy* and *Weight*.
(1) Matt. 10:38; 16:24; (2) Matt. 23:4; (3) Lev. 5:17; Num. 5:31; (4) Matt. 6:55; (5) Acts 10:38; James 2:6; Ps. 106:42; (6) Matt. 1:11, 17; Mark 15:1; 1 Cor. 12:2; Gal. 2:13; Eph. 4:14; Heb. 13:9; Jude 1:12; (7) Luke 10:4; (8) John 21:18; Rev. 17:3; 21:10; (9) Acts 3:2; (10) Luke 7:12 (physically); Luke 16:22 (spirit-carried); Luke 24:51; Acts 5:6; 8:2; 1 Tim. 6:7.

Cart: (1) Traditional or human-designed ministry; (2) Old ministry; (3) Repeating history; (4) If cart is full, it means fruitfulness or abundance; (5) Heritage.
(1) 1 Sam. 6:7-8; 2 Sam. 6:3; (2) Gen. 45:27-28 (NKJV); (3) 1 Cor. 10:6-11; (4) Ps. 65:11; (5) Ps. 61:5; 111:6; 119:111; 127:3.

Cartoon Character: (1) Superficial person (not real); (2) Fable/myth; (3) Animated; (4) Relate the nature, personality, color of clothing, and the sayings of the character to ascertain the inferred meaning; (5) There may also be an automatic association between a known person and a cartoon character.
(1-2) 2 Tim. 4:7.

Carved: (1) Mark; (2) Ownership; (3) Deeply committed; (4) Costly; (5) Skilled workmanship; (6) Idolatry; (7) Permanent; (8) Identified.
(1) As in "he made his mark"; (2-3) Isa. 49:16; (4) Prov. 7:16; (5) Exod. 35:30-33; (6) Judg. 18:18; (7) Isa. 49:16; (8) Gen. 4:15; Exod. 28:11.

Cashew (Nuts): (1) Crooked words (bent nuts/seeds); (2) What does dreamer think of cashews? (could be positive if they are their favorite).
(1) Ps. 52:4; 2 Cor. 2:17; (2) Luke 8:11.

Cashier: See *Store Clerk* and *Salesman*.

Cassette Tape Player: (1) Old man.
(1) Rom. 6:6.

Castaway: (1) Lacking discipline; (2) Losing the battle with the flesh; (3) Backslider; (4) Reject.
(1-2) 1 Cor. 9:27; (3) Jer. 2:19; 3:8; (4) 1 Cor. 9:27.

Casting (Fishing): (1) Prophetic ministry; (2) Prophesying; (3) Stepping out in faith.
(1-2) Gen. 22:4-13; Casting, as in "lifting one's eyes"; (3) Eccles. 11:1.

Castle: (1) Beautiful Christian; (2) Eternal house in glory; (3) Human-made kingdom or church; (4) Stronghold; (5) Safe refuge; (6) Name of the Lord; (7) Heaven or heavenly home; (8) The kingdom of evil (haunted castle/s); (9) Demon possession (haunted castle).
(1) 2 Cor. 5:1; (2) John 14:2; (3) Gen. 25:16 (KJV); (4) Acts 21:37; 23:10; 1 Chron. 11:5,7; (5-6) Prov. 18:10; (7) John 14:2; Heb. 12:22; (8) Luke 11:21-22; Eph. 6:12; (9) Mark 1:23; 2 Cor. 5:1.

Cat (Domestic): (1) Vicious attack; (2) Witchcraft (black cat); (3) Independence; (4) Independent spirit; (5) Rebellious spirit; (6) Unteachable heart; (7) Rich person (fat cat); (8) Laziness (fat cat); (9) High ranking public servant (fat cat); (10) Curiosity; (11) Beginning, start, or young version of the above (kitten); (12) Innocence.

Also see *Dog*, *Mascot*, and *Pet*.

(1) Dan. 6:12,24 (This was a vicious attack that was judged with a vicious attack); (2-5) 1 Sam. 15:23; (6) 2 Tim. 3:7; (7-9) Rev. 3:17; (10) As in "curiosity killed the cat"; (11) Ezek. 19:3.

Catapult: See *Slingshot*.

Catcher's Mitt: (1) Sensitive or spiritual hearing; (2) Your spirit.

Also see *Ball*.

(1-2) 1 Kings 19:12; Matt. 11:7-15.

Catching: (1) Listening; (2) Trying to catch you out in your words.

Also see *Ball*, *Baseball*, *Catcher's Mitt*, and *Cricket*.

(1) Matt. 13:19; Mark 12:13; (2) Mark 12:13.

Caterpillar: (1) Unsaved individual (not yet a butterfly); (2) Progressive destruction; (3) Judgment or plague; (4) Restoration; (5) Something eating at you and stealing fruit (they eat leaves).

(1) 2 Cor. 5:17; (2) Joel 1:4; (3) 1 Kings 8:37; Ps. 78:46; 105:34; Isa. 33:4; (4) Joel 2:25; (5) Jer. 17:8; Jon. 4:7.

Cat Food: (1) Feeding independence; (2) Independent teaching; (3) Feeding witchcraft.

(1) Gal. 2:12; (2) Acts 18:26; (3) Acts 8:10-11.

Cathedral: (1) High-profile church.

(1) Acts 11:26.

Catheter: (1) Secretly offended; (2) Secretly uncomfortable about a situation/person.

See *Urination*.

(1) Matt. 15:12; (2) John 13:27-30.

Cattle: (1) Prosperity; (2) Wealth.

Also see *Calf* and *Cow*.

(1) Ps. 50:10; 107:38; (2) Gen. 13:2 (KJV), 30:43 (KJV).

Caucasian: [Note: The meaning of an African-American/ First Nations (Indigenous) person or Caucasian person in an incident or event may change dependent on the ethnicity (racial/cultural background) of the person experiencing it. An African-American/ First Nations person may see Caucasians as the fleshly man (due to their past inclination to be soulish, exploit, and enslave). To a Caucasian a First Nations person may represent the fleshly man due to their color or order in the land (see 1 Cor. 15:46). A person of different race is generally interpreted as "Foreign." See *Foreign*.]

Cauldron: (1) Witchcraft; (2) Mixing up trouble; (3) Spell casting; (4) Boiling; (5) Flesh; (6) City or location.

Also see *Cookbook* and *Pot.*
(1) Gal. 5:19-20; (4) Job 41:20; (5-6) Ezek.11:3,7.

Cauliflower: (1) Glory of God (in the shape of clouds).
(1) 2 Chron. 5:14.

Cave: (1) Hiding place; (2) Stronghold; (3) Refuge or shelter; (4) Grave (place of burial); (5) What is going on inside of you; (6) Recluse; (7) Secret place; (8) Temporary home; (9) Underground; (10) Hell.
Also see *Tunnel* and *Underground.*
(1) Gen. 1:30; 1 Kings 18:13; 19:9,13; (2) Judg. 6:2; 1 Chron. 11:15-16; (3) Ps. 142:5; 57:1; (4) Gen. 25:9; 49:29-32; 50:13; John 11:38; (5) 1 Pet. 3:4; (6) 1 Kings 19:9; Prov. 18:1; (7) Song 2:14; (8) 1 Kings 18:4; (9) Gen. 19:30; (10) 2 Pet. 2:4; Jude 1:6.

Cedar: (1) Royalty; (2) Mighty person; (3) Spiritual; (4) Evergreen.
(1) This tree is tall and upright and was used extensively for the royal residence and temple; 2 Sam. 5:11; 1 Kings 9:10-11; (cf. 2 Chron. 1:15, 9:27); (2) Zech. 11:2; (3) Jer. 17:8.

Ceiling: (1) In rule or dominating; (2) Limitation; (3) Covering; (4) Authority; (5) Heaven; (6) Spiritual heights.
Also see *Roof.*
(1) Deut. 28:13; Matt. 25:21; Rom. 6:14; Heb. 13:7; (2) 1 Kings 6:15; (3) Gen. 19:8; Matt. 8:8-9; 24:45; (4) Matt. 8:8-9; (5) Hebrew for Heaven is also a vaulted ceiling (see Ezek. 10:1); Acts 10:4; Rev. 4:1 (attic door in ceiling); (6) Isa. 57:15; Eph. 6:12; Rev. 21:10.

Cell Phone: See *Telephone.*

Cement: See Concrete.

Cemetery: (1) Death; (2) Without life (Spirit of God); (3) Superficiality; (4) No faith (open grave); (5) The end of something; (6) Putting something to rest or death.
Also see *Grave* and *Graveyard.*
(1) Matt. 8:22; Luke 9:60; Acts 2:29; (2) Ezek. 37:1-10; (3) Matt. 23:27-28; (4) Ps. 5:9; James 2:26; (5) John 19:30; (6) Gen. 35:2-4.

Censer: (1) Relates to prayer; (2) Judgment of the prayers of the saints.
(1-2) Rev. 8:3-5.

Censor: (1) Gag; (2) Edit; (3) Cut.
(1) Ps. 63:11.

Center: If something or someone is in the center it infers that they are: (1) In control; (2) Center of God's will; (3) Divine order; (4) Deeply involved; (5) In plain view; (6) The main culprit; (7) Heart; (8) Dividing; (9) Identifying with who or whatever they are with; (10) Being, seeking, or needing attention.
Also see *Corner, Heart, Middle, Left,* and *Right.*

(1) Mark 14:60; Acts 1:15; (2) Rom. 12:2b; (3) Prov. 11:1; (4) Luke 2:46; (5) John 8:3,9; Acts 17:22; (6) John 19:18; (7) Ps. 22:14; Prov. 14:33; Isa. 19:1; (8) Exod. 14:16, 22; (9) Luke 24:36; (10) As in "center of attention."

Cents: (1) Small amount of money; (2) May represent a large heart; (3) Don't look at the outward; (4) Unforgiveness issue.
(1-3) Mark 12:42; Luke 21:2-4; (4) Luke 12:58-59.

Chaff: (1) Waste; (2) Without heart (no substance); (3) Little weight (insignificant); (4) Easily blown away; (5) Momentary/quickly pass; (6) Separation of the unrighteous; (7) Judgment.
(1-4) Job 21:18; Ps. 1:4; Isa. 17:13; 33:11; 41:15; (5) Hos. 13:3; Zeph. 2:2; (6-7) Matt. 3:12; Luke 3:17; Isa. 5:24; Jer. 23:28b.

Chains: (1) Captivity or confinement test; (2) Pride; (3) Bound/bonds; (4) Spiritual warfare; (5) Oppression; (6) Joined in the Spirit (between people); (7) Negative soul-tie (between people); (8) Allurement (neck chain); (9) Sign of wealth or opulence (golden chain around neck).
Also see *Captive, Cord, Prison,* and *Prisoners.*
(1) Ps. 105:17-19; (2) Ps. 73:6; (3) Ps. 68:6; Jer. 39:7; Mark 5:4; Luke 8:29; (4) Ps. 149:6-9; (5) Isa. 58:6; (6) Acts 20:22; Eph. 4:3; (7) 1 Cor. 6:16; (8) Song. 4:9; (9) Prov. 1:9; Song 1:10; Ezek. 16:11.

Chair: See *Sit/ting.*

Chamber: (1) Place of torment; (2) Part of hell; (3) Old English term for bedroom.
(1-2) Prov. 7:27; (3) Jer. 35:4.

Chameleon: (1) Adaptable; (2) Deception; (3) Camouflage; (4) Person who is given to change.
See also *Camouflage.*
(1) 1 Cor. 9:22; (2) Gen. 27:12; Gen. 38:15; (4) Prov. 24:21.

Champagne: (1) Celebration; (2) Victory; (3) Breakthrough.
(1-3) Zech. 10:7.

Change/d: (1) Change of heart (clothes); (2) Liberated (clothes); (3) Change of ownership; (4) Conversion; (5) Role and authority (changed name); (6) Allegiance (changed name); (7) Glorification; (8) Moving to next stage of glory; (9) Glory to shame or vice versa; (10) Change of attitude (facial expression); (11) Unreliable (given to change); (12) Disobedience; (13) Change of destiny (times and laws); (14) Deception and greed (wages); (15) Just feigning; (16) To turn; (17) God is in control of all change.
Also see *Altered* and *No Change* (directly below).
(1) Gen. 35:2; 2 Sam. 12:20; Dan. 4:16; (2) Gen. 41:14 (no longer a prisoner); 2 Kings 25:2; Jer. 52:33; (3) Ruth 4:7; (4) 2 Cor. 5:17; (5) 2 Kings 24:17; (6) Num. 32:38; (7) Job 14:14; Ps. 106:20; 1 Cor. 15:51-52; (8) 2 Cor. 3:18; (9) Jer. 2:11; Hos. 4:7; Rom. 1:23;

(10) Dan. 3:19; 5:6-10; 7:28; (11) Prov. 24:21; (12) Ezek. 5:6; (13) Dan. 7:25; (14) Gen. 31:7, 41; (15) 1 Sam. 21:13; (16) Lev. 13:16; (17) Dan. 2:21.

No Change: (1) God does not change; (2) Lacking a fear of God; (3) Not having been emptied out; (4) Religious traditions (fight against change); (5) Stubbornness or hardened heart; (6) Not converted.
Also see *Change* (directly above).
(1) Mal. 3:6; (2) Ps. 55:19; (3) Jer. 48:11; (4) Acts 6:14; (5) Ps. 78:8; Heb. 3:8,15; (6) Matt. 18:3.

Charge: (1) Accusation; (2) Condemnation; (3) Enemy attack; (4) Govern; (5) Suing.
(1) Job 13:19; (2) Ps. 69:27; (3) Prov. 28:15; (4) Zech. 3:6; (5) Matt. 5:40.

Charging (Electrical): See *Battery Charging*.

Chariot: See *Automobile* and *Chariot of Fire*.

Chariot of Fire: (1) Angelic vehicle; (2) Rapture; (3) Passionate vehicle.
(1) Ps. 104:4; 2 Kings 6:15-17; (2) 2 Kings 2:11; (3) Ps. 39:3; Jer. 20:9.

Chasing: (1) Threatening (chasing someone); (2) Being threatened (being chased); (3) Call to prayer (being chased); (4) Obsessed with (whatever you are chasing).
Also see *Hiding* and *Running*.
(1) Lev. 26:7; (2-3) Deut. 1:44 (*Hormah* means "devotion"); (4) 2 Kings 5:20 (chasing the dollar).

Check/ing: (1) Testing; (2) Inspecting; (3) Confirming; (4) Ensuring.
Also see *Exam*.
(1-2) Gen. 22:1, 12; (3-4) Prov. 22:21; Luke 24:24.

Check ($): (1) Faith (the currency of the Kingdom); (2) Finances; (3) Prosperity (receiving a check); (4) Promise.
(1) Matt. 6:24; Luke 16:13; Acts 8:20; Rom 1:17; Heb. 11:4; (2) 2 Cor. 8:9; Phil. 4:12; (3) 1 Cor. 16:2; (4) Eph. 1:14.

Cheek: (1) Preparing for persecution; (2) Physical abuse; (3) Criticism/blame; (4) Responding to persecution with love; (5) Grief (tears on cheek); (6) Back chat.
Also see *Tears* and *Teeth*.
(1) Lam. 3:30; Matt. 5:39; (2) 1 Kings 22:24; (3) Job 16:10; (4) Isa. 50:6; (5) Lam. 1:2; (6) Job 15:6; Ps. 31:18; Lam. 3:62.

Cheekbone: (1) Making the enemies of God eat their words.
(1) Ps. 3:7.

Cheerleader: (1) Worshiper (including praise); (2) Believer; (3) Encourager.
(1-2) John 4:23-24; (3) 1 Sam. 18:7; Matt. 21:8-9.

Cheese: (1) Spiritual growth (maturing); (2) Words that sour or have soured (cheese is curdled milk); (3) Something has holes in it (Swiss); (4) Not real; (5) Gift of sustenance; (6) Neutral or non-committal words (Swiss cheese).

(1) 1 John 2:13-14; Rev. 12:11; (2) Job 10:10; (3) 2 Tim. 4:3-4; (4) Matt. 15:8; Mark 7:6; *cheesy* as in "cheesy grin"; (5) 1 Sam. 17:18; 2 Sam. 17:29; (6) Rev. 3:15.

Cheeseburger: (1) Palatable teaching (seeker friendly message); (2) Fable; (3) Childish, ill-prepared words.
Also see *Hamburger.*
(1-3) 2 Tim. 4:2-4.

Cheesecake: (1) Temptation.
(1) Gen. 3:6.

Cheezels (Cheese Balls): (1) Hollow/empty words.
(1) Esther 3:10; Prov. 23:1-3.

Chef: (1) Christ; (2) Pastor.
(1) 1 Pet. 5:2-4; (2) Acts 20:28.

Chemist Shop (Drug Store): (1) The Church as a dispenser of God's Word; (2) The Word of God; (3) Jesus Christ (healing dispensary); (4) A church without feeling (drugged up).
Also see *Shop.*
(1-2) Prov. 4:20-22 (the right script); (3) Matt. 4:23; (4) Rev. 3:1-2, 15-17.

Chest (Torso): (1) Heart; (2) Righteousness; (3) Faith and love.
(1) Exod. 28:29; (2) Isa. 59:17; Eph. 6:14; (3) 1 Thess. 5:8.

Cheque: See *Check ($).*

Chew/ing: (1) Meditating; (2) Thinking about.
(1) Josh. 1:8; (2) As in "chewing things over."

Chewing Gum: See *Bubble Gum.*

Chicken: (1) Church; (2) God; (3) Jesus Christ; (4) Gatherer; (5) Protector; (6) Scared; (7) Unclean spirit; (8) Revelation (chicken nuggets); (9) Criticism of the Church (fried chicken).
Also see *Hen.*
(1) Ps. 17:8; 50:5; 91:4; Isa. 49:5; Matt. 23:37; Acts 14:27; (2) Ps. 91:1,3-4; (3) Matt. 23:37; Luke 13:34; (4-5) Matt. 23:37; Luke 13:34; Ps. 17:8; (6) As in "He's nothing but a chicken"; (7) Lev. 20:25; (8) Matt. 23:37; John 6:51; (9) Acts 8:1; 3 John 1:10.

Chicks (Baby Chickens): (1) Children of God; (2) Your offspring.
(1-2) Matt. 23:37.

Chief: (1) Jesus Christ; (2) Best of or the strongest; (3) Main; (4) Leader.
(1) Eph. 2:20; 1 Pet. 5:4; (2) Prov. 16:28b; Dan. 10:13; (3) Ps. 137:6.

Child/ren: (1) Future of oneself or Church (children of God); (2) Innocence; (3) Inner child; (4) Immaturity; (5) Past childhood; (6) Humility; (7) Receiving, trusting, believing; (8) Young converts; (9) Followers of Christ or satan; (10) Undisciplined child (illegitimate children); (11) Children of the devil (illegitimate children); (12) Children of wrath (disobedient).

Also see *Younger* and *Youth*.
(1) Jer. 31:17; John 1:12; (2) Matt. 18:6; (3) Deut. 29:29; 2 Kings 17:9; 2 Chron. 28:11-12; (4) Luke 7:32; 1 Cor. 13:11; (5) 1 Sam. 12:2; (6) Matt. 18:4; Luke 9:46-48; (7) Matt. 18:3; (8) 1 John 2:12-14; (9) Acts 13:10; 1 John 3:10; (10) Heb. 12:8; (11) John 8:44; (12) Eph. 2:3; 5:6; Col. 3:6.

Children's Book(s): (1) Children's Bible (childlike faith); (2) Belief and trust; (3) Innocence; (4) Humble dependence.
(1-4) Matt. 18:3-6.

Chilies: (1) Hot; (2) India; (3) Mexico.
(1-3) 1 Kings 10:2,10,15.

Chimney: (1) Soul-tie or opening for the enemy.
(1) Eph. 4:27.

China/Chinese: (1) Foreign; (2) Diligent; (3) Literally Chinese; (4) Low cost; (5) Populous; (6) Demonic (dragon); (7) Honorable; (8) Atheistic (communism); (9) Antichrist (dragon); (10) Integrity; (11) "Take away"; (12) "Plastic"; (13) Huge, dominant commercial entity.
Also see *Foreign*.
(1) Isa. 49:12; (2-12) Other characteristic perceptions.

Chips (Potato): See *French Fries*.

Chiropractor: (1) Manipulation and adjustment; (2) Getting the body in alignment.
(1-2) Eph. 4:12.

Chocolate: (1) Money hungry; (2) Hungry for pleasure; (3) Self-indulgence; (4) Sweet, deceptive words; (5) Palatable; (6) God's Word; (7) Words spoken in love (chocolates); (8) Gratitude (thanksgiving).
Also see *Junk Food*.
(1) Matt. 6:24; Luke 16:8b-9,13; (2-3) 2 Tim. 3:4b; (4) Prov. 23:1-3, 6-8; (5-6) Ps. 119:103; 141:6; (7-8) Song 2:14; 4:11.

Choice: (1) Options; (2) Decision; (3) Prepared; (4) Best; (5) Refined.
(1) 1 Sam. 6:7-9; 1 Kings 18:21; (2) Josh. 24:15; (3) Matt. 20:16; 22:14; (4) Gen. 49:11; 1 Sam. 9:2; 2 Sam. 10:9; (5) Prov. 10:20.

Choir: (1) See *Worship*.
(1) 2 Chron. 29:28; Ps. 66:4.

Choke/ing: (1) Gagging communication (stopping words); (2) Stopping the life flow; (3) Demon oppression or possession; (4) Stifling the Spirit; (5) Attack; (6) Threat; (7) Incapable; (8) Care of the world and deceitfulness of riches; (9) Fear/anxiety; (10) Lust for things; (11) Pleasures of life; (12) Drowning; (13) Injustice; (14) Speaking lies; (15) Iniquity; (16) Dishonest gain; (17) Failing through nerves (choking under pressure).
Also see *Strangle/d*.

(1) 2 Kings 2:3; (2) John 5:24; 7:38; (3) Mark 9:17-18; (4) 1 Cor. 14:39b; (5) (cf. Matt. 17:15; 9:17-18); (6) Acts 4:18, 21; (7) Matt. 13:7,22; (8) Matt. 6:25; (9) Mark 4:7,19; (10) Luke 8:7,14; (11) Mark 5:13; Luke 8:33; (13) Job 5:16; (14) Ps. 63:11; (15) Ps. 107:42; Rom. 3:19; (16) Tit. 1:11; (17) Matt. 27:22-26.

Chopping Block/Board: (1) Judgment/al; (2) Harsh words; (3) Dealing with the flesh (cutting the fat); (4) Sermon preparation.
(1-2) Matt. 3:10; (3) Rom. 8:13; (4) Heb. 4:12.

Chopsticks: (1) Asia; (2) Imbibing words; (3) The need to get a grip on the word (rice and meat); (4) Precision in using the word (increased skill required); (5) Coordination and witness of two verses required (using two sticks); (6) Difficulty getting a grip on the word (if not Asian); (7) Nitpicking; (8) Discernment; (9) Study; (10) Foreign/different approach to the word (if not Asian); (11) Getting fed by a different source (if not Asian). See also *Foreign* and *Rice*.
(1) By association; (2) Luke 8:11; (3) Josh. 1:8; (4) 2 Tim. 2:15; (5) Matt. 18:16; 2 Cor. 13:1; (6) Heb. 5:11-14; (7) Matt. 23:24; (8) 1 Cor. 11:29; (9) 2 Tim. 2:15; (10-11) 2 Tim. 4:3.

Christmas: (1) Celebration; (2) Gifts; (3) Self-indulgence; (4) Revival (Christmas Day). Also see *Santa*.
(1) Luke 2:10-11, 13-14,20; (2) 1 Cor. 12:1, 9-11; (3) Luke 6:32-33; (4) Luke 2:9-11.

Christmas Tree: (1) Traditional person/church; (2) Glamorous ministry; (3) High-profile ministry (the Christmas tree takes center stage at Christmastime); (4) A person or ministry that looks outwardly attractive, but has no spiritual life; (5) Spiritual gifts; (6) Celebration; (7) Paganism/idolatry.
(1) Col. 2:8; (2-3) Matt. 13:32; (4) Matt. 23:27-28; (5) 1 Cor. 2:12; 12:1, 4, 7, 9-11; (6) Luke 2:10-11, 13-14, 20; (7) 2 Kings 16:4; 17:10-11.

Chrome: (1) Hard/ened; (2) Cold-hearted (hardened heart).
Also see *Biker/Bikie*.
(1) Zech. 7:12; (2) Matt. 24:12.

Church Building: (1) May refer to a particular or known congregation; (2) The reference may also be general; (3) May represent the individual (as a temple of worship); (4) A place of worship.
Rev. 2:1,8,12,18; (2) 1 Tim. 3:15; (3) 1 Cor. 3:16; 6:19; (4) Acts 24:11; 1 Sam. 1:3.

Church Service: (1) Worship; (2) Praise; (3) Fellowship.
Also see *Congregation* and *Temple*.
(1) 2 Chron. 29:28; (2) Heb. 2:12b; (3) Acts 2:42.

Cigar: (1) Big offense; (2) Celebration; (3) Lucrative business; (4) Thinking big (Mr. Big [positive (+) or negative (-)]).
(1) Job 19:17; (2) Prov. 13:9; (3) 1 Tim. 6:9; (4) Gen. 15:5 (+); Luke 12:18 (-).

Cigarette(s): (1) Offensive; (2) Odorous; (3) Taking up offensive words and language; (4) Temptation to return to an addictive lifestyle; (5) Stronghold; (6) Foul spirit.

Also see *Drugs* and *Smoking*.

(1) Job 19:17; (2) Joel 2:20; (3) Eph. 5:4; 4:29; Isa. 29:21; (4) Judg. 8:33; 1 Cor. 10:13; (5) Ps. 78:61; Ezek. 30:18b; (6) Mark 9:25 (stopping someone from hearing/speaking truth); Rev. 14:11; 18:2.

Cinema: See *Picture Theater*.

Cinnamon: (1) Love.

(1) Prov. 7:17-18; Song 4:14.

Circle: (1) God; (2) Eternally/eternity (as in a never-ending loop); (3) Covenant; (4) Earth; (5) Completion; (6) Repeating same mistake (going in circles); (7) Repeat relationship scenario (circle of friends).

Also see *Wheel*.

(1-2) Deut. 33:27; Jer. 10:10 (NIV); Eccles. 3:11; (3) Circumcision, which is the sign of covenant with God (Gen. 17:10-11), is a circle of flesh cut away; (4) Isa. 40:22; (5) As in "I saw the project through full circle"; (6) Ps. 78:41,57; (7) Deut. 2:3.

Circumcision: (1) Cutting away of the desires of the flesh; (2) Heart; (3) Believer; (4) Obedience.

(1) Jer. 4:4; Col. 2:11; (2) Rom. 2:29; Deut. 10:16; 30:6; Jer. 4:4; (3) Rom. 3:30; 4:9-12; Gal. 5:6; (4) Josh. 5:4-9.

Circus: (1) World; (2) Incompetent organization; (3) In the spotlight; (4) Circle of influence; (5) Entertainment; (6) Performance; (7) Itinerant flamboyant miracle evangelist (tent crusades).

Also see *Lion* and *Spotlight*.

(1) 1 John 2:16; (2) As in "The place is a circus!"; (3) Acts 9:3; (4) 1 Kings 12:8-13; Matt. 17:1; (5) Luke 7:32a; (6) Matt. 16:1; (7) Acts 13:2-3.

Cistern: (1) Heart (storage/supply); (2) Marital faithfulness; (3) Ease (reservoir); (4) Two evils; (5) Confinement or prison.

Also see *Deep, Reservoir, Swimming Pool, Water,* and *Well*.

(1) Prov. 5:15; Eccles. 12:6; (2) Prov. 5:15-20; (3) 2 Kings 18:31; Isa. 36:16; (4) Jer. 2:13; (5) Jer. 38:6.

City: (1) The world; (2) Populous; (3) Preaching place; (4) Pride; (5) Each city to be judged; (6) Place of persecution; (7) May speak of the spiritual authorities over the city; (8) Represents life; (9) Busy; (10) Note type or name of city; (11) International influence (if cities in different countries); (12) New Jerusalem (modern city); (13) Kingdom of Heaven; (14) Becoming well-known (going to a big city).

Also see *Bricks* and *Tower*.

(1) Gen. 11:4; Isa. 14:21b; Matt. 5:14; (2) Matt. 8:34; 21:10; Mark. 1:33; (3) Matt. 11:1; (4) Matt. 4:5-6; (5) Matt. 10:15 (cf. 10:11, 14); 11:20-24; (6) Matt. 10:23; 23:34b; Luke 4:29;

(7) Luke 19:17, 19; (9) Luke 17:28-29; (11) 1 Kings 10:24; (12) Isa. 62:1-4; Rev. 3:12; (13) Ps. 103:19; Dan. 2:44; Matt. 3:2; Rev. 12:10; (14) Gen. 13:12; 14:12; John 7:3-4.

Clap/ping: (1) Victory or triumph; (2) Approval; (3) Mocking; (4) Faith from revelation (heart and head in agreement); (5) Celebration.
Also see *Left* and *Right* (left hand [heart] and right hand [mouth]).
(1) Ps. 47:1; (2) 2 Kings 11:12; Isa. 55:12; (3) Job 27:23; Lam. 2:15; (4) Rom. 10:9-10; (5) 2 Kings 11:12.

Classroom: (1) Heart; (2) Teachable heart; (3) Place of training; (4) Equipping and preparation.
Also see *School.*
(1) Job 8:10; Ps. 90:12; Prov. 4:4; 16:23; Isa. 29:13; Col. 3:16; (2) Matt. 26:55; Mark 12:35a; 14:49; 20:1; 21:37; John 7:14, 28; (3) 1 John 2:13-14; (4) Mark 10:39, 42; 2 Tim. 3:16-17.

Claw: (1) Aggression; (2) If a claw is grabbing you or someone else, it could be a spirit of death; (3) In the grip of satan; (4) Torment (tearing claw); (5) Stronghold.
(1) Ps. 7:2; Jer. 5:6; Hos. 5:14; (2) Ps. 18:4 (AMP); Ps. 116:3; (3) 1 Sam. 17:34; Isa. 5:29; (Amos 3:4 & 1 Pet. 5:8); (4) Matt. 18:34 (KJV); 1 John 4:18; (5) 2 Cor. 10:4-5.

Clay: (1) Human/kind or humanity; (2) Being molded; (3) Weakness; (4) Fragile; (5) From the earth.
(1) Job 10:9; Isa. 64:8; Rom. 9:20-21; (2) Jer. 18:4-6; (3-4) 2 Cor. 4:7; Lev. 14:5; 15:12; (5) Job 4:19.

Clean: (1) Redemption; (2) Possibly speaks of an outward appearance versus inward reality; (3) Unused; (4) Readiness; (5) Under the blood.
Also see *Leprosy.*
(1) Tit. 2:14; Matt. 8:2-3; Mark 1:40-42; (2) Matt. 23:25-28; (3) Matt. 27:59; (4) Rev. 21:2; (5) 1 John 1:7.

Cleaning: (1) Confession and repentance; (2) Fasting.
(1) 1 John 1:9; Heb. 6:1; (2) Matt. 6:17.

Clean Slate: (1) Good record; (2) No debt; (3) Forgiveness of sins.
(1-3) Col. 2:13-14.

Clear water: (1) Holy Spirit; (2) Life; (3) Cleansing; (4) God's Word.
Also see *Water.*
(1) John 7:38; James 3:11; Rev. 21:6; (2) Rev. 22:1; (3) Ezek. 36:25; Heb. 10:22; (4) Eph. 5:26.

Cleave: (1) Join; (2) Split; (3) Embrace; (4) Cling.
All (KJV) References: (1) Gen. 2:24; Luke 10:11; Acts 11:23; (2) Ps. 78:15; 141:7; Eccles. 10:9.

Cliff: (1) On the edge; (2) On the edge of destruction; (3) Place where natural resources run out; (4) Place of decision; (5) Place of launching into the Spirit; (6) A leap of faith; (7) The place where earth meets Heaven; (8) Place of refuge (in God); (9) Prophetic insight (overlooking from a cliff).
Also see *Edge*.
(1-2) Luke 4:29; (3) 1 Kings 17:11-14; 2 Kings 4:1-7; John 6:5-7; (4) 1 Sam. 14:9-10; 1 Kings 18:21; (5) 1 Sam. 14:10, 13; Luke 4:29-30; 5:4-6; 8:22; Acts 27:4; (6) Matt. 14:29; 2 Cor. 5:7; (7) Matt. 27:33, 42; (8) Exod. 33:22; Ps. 104:18; (cf. Prov. 30:26); (9) Num. 22:41; 23:28.

Climbing: (1) Overcoming; (2) Overpowering; (3) Human effort; (4) Preparing for an encounter with Jesus; (5) Theft (climbing into); (6) Growing in the Spirit (climbing up); (7) Making spiritual progress (climbing up); (8) Growing up (children climbing up).
Also *Climbing Over, Down, Ladder,* and *Up*.
(1) 1 Sam. 14:13; (2) Joel 2:7,9; (3) Amos 9:2; (4) Luke 19:4; (5) John 10:1; (6-7) Isa. 40:31; (8) Hos. 9:12; Matt. 22:24.

Climbing Over: (1) Lack of sensitivity; (2) No longer an issue; (3) Self-aggrandizement; (4) Skipping a level; (5) Lacking humility; (6) Ambition; (7) Overcoming.
Also see *Overtaking*.
(1) Mark 9:33-37; (2) Matt. 9:10-13; as in "get over it!" (3) Isa. 14:13-14; Rom. 10:6; (4-5) Luke 14:8-11; (6) 1 Kings 1:5; (7) Rev. 12:11.

Cloak: See *Coat*.

Clock: (1) Time; (2) Waiting in (or on) God; (3) God appointed lifespan; (4) Hour is nearer; (5) End is near (five minutes to twelve); (6) Last hour; (7) Divine appointment; (8) Opportunity; (9) Timing is important; (10) Harvest; (11) Fullness of time; (12) Time to awaken; (13) Awaiting the timing of God to release a situation or ministry; (14) Note the time and look up individual meanings of the numbers.
Also see *Time* and *Watch*.
(2) 1 Sam. 13:8; (3) John 7:8; 8:20 (reference to His death); (4) Rom. 13:11; (5) Matt. 20:9; (6) 1 John 2:18; (7) Hab. 2:3; (8) Acts 16:25-26; (9) Eccles. 3:1; (10) Num. 13:20; (11) Luke 1:57; (12) Rom. 13:11; (13) Ps. 105:17-19; Dan. 4:16,33-34; Jer. 29:10.

Closet: (1) Private; (2) Secret; (3) Place of prayer; (4) Hidden sins from past.
Also see *Cupboard*.
(1) Joel 2:16; Matt. 6:6; (2-3) Matt. 6:6; Luke 12:3; (4) Ps. 32:5; 69:5.

Cloth: (1) Speaks of the need to be born again; (2) Speaks of a superficial patch-up job; (3) Death (wrapped in cloth); (4) Nakedness (clothes taken); (5) Cast away (unclean cloth); (6) Mourning (sackcloth).
(1-2) Matt. 9:16; Mark 2:21; (3) Matt. 27:59; (4) Mark 14:51-52; (5) Isa. 30:22; (6) Gen. 37:34.

Clothe: (1) God's glory; (2) Armor of God; (3) Armor of light; (4) Righteousness or salvation; (5) Speaks of growing up.
(1) Gen. 3:7; Rev. 16:15; (2) Eph. 6:11; (3) Rom. 13:12; (4) Isa. 61:10; Zech. 3:5; (5) 1 Sam. 2:19.

Clothes Dryer: (1) Losing the anointing; (2) Preparing a new anointing.
(1) Judg. 16:19-20; (2) Zech. 3:4.

Clothesline: (1) Being left out to dry; (2) Restored ministry.
Also see *Clothes Dryer.*
(1) Gen. 40:23; (2) Ps. 51:7.

Clothing: (1) God's glory; (2) Human-made cover up; (3) Adultery (burning clothes); (4) Guarantor issue (taken clothing); (5) A change of clothes is a change of role and authority; (6) Clothing depicts the state of our relationship with God (white = right); (7) Clothing may also be indicative of the state of one's heart; (8) Clean or new clothes may indicate conversion, separation, or preparation; (9) Something that doesn't fit (baggy clothes); (10) Warning of judgment/plague/death (wearing unbearably hot clothes); (11) Clothed with the zeal of God (non-tormenting fiery clothes).
Note also the color of the clothes and look up entries under individual colors. Also see *Bra, Clothe, Coat, Inside Out, Pants, Shirt, Skirt,* and *Suit.*
(1) Gen. 2:25; (2) Gen. 3:7; James 2:2; Matt. 7:15; (3) Prov. 6:26-27; (4) Prov. 20:16; 27:13; (5) Gen. 41:14; Luke 15:22; 2 Kings 2:12-15; (6) Job 29:14; Isa. 61:10; Mark 16:5; Lam. 4:7-8; (7) John 19:23 (Jesus wore a seamless tunic because of his faultless heart); 2 Kings 22:19 (torn clothes = humbled heart); (8) Exod. 19:14-15; Matt. 9:17; Luke 15:22; (9) 1 Sam. 17:38-39; (10) Zech. 3:2-3; (11) Isa. 59:17; Jer. 20:9.

Cloud: (1) Presence of God; (2) God's glory; (3) Holy Spirit; (4) Guidance; (5) God's favor; (6) Coming shower; (7) Promise (of blessing or judgment).
Also see *Dust Cloud, Shower,* and *Storm.*
(1) Exod. 16:10; 24:16; Num. 16:42; (2) 1 Kings 8:11; 2 Chron. 5:14; (3) Num. 11:25; (4) Exod. 13:21; Neh. 9:12; (5) Prov. 16:15; (6) Luke 12:54; (7) Gen. 9:14; 1 Kings 18:44-45.

Dark Cloud(s): (1) Tribulation; (2) Trouble; (3) Judgment; (4) Testing/trial; (5) Oppression; (6) Depression (no hope).
(1) Joel 2:10; Acts 2:20; (3) Ps. 18:11; Jer. 23:19; 25:32; (2) Rev. 9:2; (4) Matt. 24:29; (5) As in "under a cloud."; (6) Acts 27:20.

Cloudy: (1) Uncertainty; (2) Second Coming; (3) Coming blessing (shower); (4) Heavenly witnesses; (5) Empty hearts (no rain).
Also see *Dark Clouds, Shower, Storm,* and *Rain.*
(1) Luke 9:34; (2) Mark 13:26; 14:62; 1 Thess. 4:17; Rev. 1:7; (3) Luke 12:54; (4) Heb. 12:1; (5) Jude 1:12.

Cloven-Hoofed: (1) Clean; (2) Divided; (3) Sure-footed; (4) Word-guided.

(1-4) Deut. 14:6.

Clover: (1) Sports or fitness (three-leaf clover).
Also see *Grass* and *Mown Grass.*
(1) Ps. 147:10 (symbol of Adidas).

Clown: (1) Person always searching for laughs; (2) Entertainer; (3) Clumsy; (4) Attention grabber; (5) Fool or foolish; (6) Painted face; (7) Joker; (8) Playing with the things of God.
(1) Eccles. 2:2-3; (2) 2 Tim. 4:3-4; (3) 1 Sam. 25:25, 36; (4) Acts 8:9-11, 13, 18-24; 1 Pet. 3:3-4; (5) Eccles. 2:2-3; (6) 2 Kings 9:30; Jer. 4:30; Prov. 14:13; (7) Eph. 5:4; (8) John 6:66 (these were not serious or sincere in their search for truth).

Cluster: (1) Group of believers; (2) Fruit (good [sweet] or bad [bitter]); (3) Harvest; (4) Revival; (5) Blessing; (6) Breasts.
(1) See *Congregation*; (2) Gen. 40:10; Num. 13:23; Deut. 32:32; 1 Sam. 25:18; (3) Rev. 14:18; Gen. 40:10; Num. 13:23-24; (4) 1 Sam. 30:12; (5) Isa. 65:8; Mic. 7:1; (6) Song 7:7-8.

Coach (Sports): (1) Holy Spirit; (2) Jesus; (3) Five-fold ministry; (4) Mentor.
Also see *Pastor.*
(1) John 14:26; 1 John 2:27; (2) Luke 6:13-16; 9:10; (3) Eph. 4:11-12; (4) Exod. 18:19-22; 1 Tim. 1:18.

Coals: (1) Energy; (2) Cold (moving away); (3) Warm (moving closer); (4) Judgment or to condemn; (5) Angel (spirit); (6) Adultery (walking on coals); (7) Baptism of fire; (8) Cleansing; (9) Altar; (10) Fiery Stone; (11) Jealousy.
Also see *Fire.*
(1) (2-3) John 18:18; 21:9; (4) Ps. 140:10; Prov. 25:21-22; Rom. 12:20; (5) Ezek. 1:13; (6) Prov. 6:28-29; (7-10) Isa. 6:5-7; (11) Song 8:6.

Coastline: (1) Represents a boundary; (2) Represents the interchange between the spiritual and natural realms; (3) Dominion on sea and earth (Heaven and earth).
Also see *Beach, Boundary, Rocks, Sand,* and *Sea.*
(1-3) Gen. 1:9; Rev. 10:2, 5-6, 8; (2) John 21:4, 15-17; also consider that the sea speaks of humanity and fishing of evangelism; (3) Rev. 10:5-6.

Coat: (1) Righteousness; (2) Salvation; (3) Authority or position; (4) Spiritual anointing (mantle); (5) Commitment; (6) Spiritual growth (new coat); (7) People's character and role are displayed in what they wear. For example: In First Samuel 15:27-28, Saul's robe represented his kingdom; in Matthew 3:4, John wore a prophet's clothes; in Mark 10:50, Bartimaeus had a beggar's cloak; in John 19:23, Jesus wore a seamless coat; in John 21:7, Peter had a fisherman's coat.
Also see *Mantle, Rainbow* (coat of many colors), and *Robe.*
(1) Job 29:14; Isa. 61:10; (2) Isa. 61:10; (3) Gen. 37:3; John 19:2; (4) 1 Sam. 28:14; Lev. 21:10; Matt. 9:20; 14:36; (5) Mark 10:50; (6) 1 Sam. 2:19.

Cobblestones: (1) Ancient paths.

(1) Jer. 18:15.

Cobweb: See *Web*.

Cockroach(es): (1) Sin; (2) Unclean; (3) In the dark spiritually; (4) Creeping infestation; (5) Areas of the heart not yet brought to the light; (6) Lies; (7) Defiling thoughts (roaches in your hair).

(1-2) Lev. 5:2; 11:31,43; 20:25b; (3) 1 John 1:6-7; (4) 2 Tim. 3:6; Jude 1:4; (5) 1 Cor. 4:5; 2 Cor. 4:6; 2 Pet. 1:19; (6) 1 John 1:6-7; (7) Tit. 1:15.

Coconut: (1) Purity/holiness (white of coconut).

(1) See *White*.

Codes: (1) Deposits of revelation from God; (2) Dreams; (3) Mysteries (requires code-breaker: the Holy Spirit).

(1) Dan. 2:28a, 47; Prov. 25:2; Matt. 16:15-17; (2) Num. 12:6-8; (3) Job 11:7; Dan. 4:9; 1 Cor. 13:2; 14:2.

Coffee: (1) Stain (spilt); (2) Sin (spilt); (3) Stimulant; (4) Fellowship or communion (having coffee with someone); (5) Ground (to powder); (6) Revelation as a stimulant (coffee bean/plunger).

(1-2) Exod. 32:20-21; (3) 2 Tim. 1:6; 2 Pet. 3:1; (4) Rom. 14:17; 1 Cor. 10:21; (5) Exod. 32:20; Matt. 21:44; (6) Luke 8:11.

Coffin: (1) Death.

Also see *Grave* and *Graveyard*.

(1) Gen. 50:26.

Cogs: (1) Heart.

(1) As in "heart of the operations."

Coins: (1) Money; (2) Provision; (3) Relatively small or interim amount of money; (4) Money from many nations (various multi-colored coins).

Also see *Gold* and *Money*.

(1-2) Matt. 17:27; (3) Mark 12:42; (4) 2 Sam. 8:11; 1 Chron. 18:11.

Cold: (1) Hardened; (2) Without love; (3) Increase of wickedness; (4) Refreshing; (5) Resistant reception; (6) Alone; (7) Reluctance; (8) Away from God; (9) Dead/death; (10) Unforgiveness; (11) Evil presence.

Also see *Ice*.

(1) John 18:18; (2-3) Matt. 24:12; (4) Matt. 10:42; (5) Acts 28:2-6; (6) Eccles. 4:11; 2 Cor. 11:27; (7) As in "having cold feet"; (8) Matt. 24:12; (9) 2 Kings 4:34; (9) Matt. 24:9,12; (10) Matt. 24:10,12; (11) Job 4:15.

Cold Sore: (1) Sinning with the lips.

(1) Job 2:10b; Ps. 59:12; Prov. 10:19; Isa. 6:7.

Coles: See entries under Name and Place Dictionary.

Collision Center: See *Wrecking Yard*.

Colors: The color of clothing and vehicles is a very important indicator of the meanings they carry. Color may communicate: (1) Newness; (2) Personality and character; (3) Splendor; (4) Honor; (5) Heavenly glory; (6) Promise (rainbow); (7) Favor (multi-colored covering); (8) Innocence/purity (multi-colored covering); (9) Glory (multi-colored); (10) May relate to a recent association of someone/something or someplace using that color; (11) Prophetic anointing (multi-colored).
Also see *Multi-Colored*, *Rainbow*, and individual colors.
(1) Matt. 9:16; Rom. 6:4; 2 Cor. 5:17; (2) Rev. 6:2-5; (3-4) 2 Sam. 13:18; 2 Tim. 2:20; 1 Pet. 1:7; (5) Rev. 4:3; (6) Gen. 9:13; (7) Gen. 37:3; (8) 2 Sam. 13:18; (9) Gen. 37:3 (prefigures His glory); 1 Chron. 29:2; Ezek. 16:16; 17:3 (10) By association; (11) Gen. 37:3.

Coloring Book: See *Children's Book(s)*.

Colt: See *Horse* and *Donkey*.

Coma: (1) Spiritually dull; (2) Unreasonable; (3) Unresponsive; (4) Insensible; (5) Loss of God consciousness (or ineffective conscience).
Also see *Sleep/ing*.
(1) Matt. 15:16; (2-4) Gen. 19:33; Jer. 51:39b, 57; (5) 1 Tim. 4:2.

Comb: (1) Vanity; (2) Grooming oneself for self-glory; (3) Examining (combing).
(1-2) 2 Sam. 14:25-26; (3) Gen. 13:10-11.

Comet: See *Asteroid* and *Meteor*.

Commandments: (1) God is One, love God, love people (love, love, love); (2) Rules; (3) Instruction or guidance; (4) God's Word; (5) Law; (6) Tradition and ordinances of people (competing with).
(1) Mark 12:29-31; John 13:34; 14:21; 15:10, 12; 1 Tim. 1:5; (2) Matt. 15:9; (3) Matt. 8:18; John 10:18; 11:57; 12:49-50; 1 Thess. 4:2; Heb. 11:22; (4) Exod. 34:28; Num. 15:31; 1 John 2:7; (5) Rom. 7:9, 12; Eph. 2:15; 6:2; (6) Mark 7:8-9; Col. 2:21-22; Tit. 1:14.

Compass: (1) Bearings; (2) Direction; (3) God (God's habitation is known as the sides of the north).
Also see *North*, *South*, *East*, and *West*.
(1-2) Job 26:7; (3) Job 37:22; Ps. 48:1-2; Lev. 1:11.

Compass (Drawing): (1) Circle or circle of influence; (2) Growth rings (concentric circles).
(1-2) Acts 1:8.

Computer: (1) Heart (CPU); (2) Channel of communication; (3) Programmed.
Also see *Hard Drive*, *Hardware*, *Motherboard*, *Software*, and *Upgrade*.
(1) Prov. 4:23; (2) 2 Tim. 2:2; (3) Rom. 12:2.

Computer CD: (1) Impartation or teaching (loading a CD); (2) Programming (loading a CD); (3) Store of thoughts.
(1) 2 Tim. 2:2; (2) Prov. 22:6; (3) Rom. 12:2.

Computer Program: (1) A programmed way of thinking.
(1) Rom. 12:2.

Concealing: (1) Hiding; (2) Covering up; (3) Denying.
(1-2) Prov. 11:13; Judg. 3:16; (3) Matt. 26:70,72.

Concordance: (1) Seeking deeper understanding; (2) Seeking God.
(1) Prov. 15:14; (2) Prov. 28:5.

Concrete: (1) Hard-hearted; (2) Stronghold; (3) Human-made rock/stone; (4) Word foundation; (5) Solid as a rock; (6) City; (7) Foundation.
Also see *Brick*, *Rock*, *Stone*, and *Wall*.
(1) 1 Sam. 25:37; Job 41:24; Ezek. 11:19; 36:26; Zech. 7:12; 2 Cor. 3:3; (2-3) Nah. 3:14; (4-5) Luke 6:48; (6) As in "concrete jungle"; (7) Isa. 28:16.

Condom: (1) Ineffective Gospel witness; (2) Not sowing the seed (the Gospel or the Word of God); (3) Sexual promiscuity; (4) Fornication.
Also see *Genitals*.
(1) Mark 14:56; 1 Cor. 15:15; (2) Gen. 38:9; Luke 8:11; (3-4) Gal. 5:19.

Conference Room: (1) Prayer; (2) Spiritual dialogue; (3) Communion with God; (4) Fellowship; (5) Business decisions.
(1) Ps. 85:8; Mark 12:26; (2-4) Matt. 17:1; Luke 22:12; (5) 1 Kings 22:6; 2 Kings 6:11.

Coney: See *Guinea Pig*.

Conflict: (1) Warning; (2) Suffering for Christ; (3) Spiritual battle; (4) Inner battle.
Also see *Battle*, *Contend*, and *Fight*.
(2) Phil. 1:30; (3) Eph. 6:12; Col. 2:1; (4) Gal. 5:17.

Congregation: (1) Church (the Redeemed); (2) Gathering of good or evil; (3) Heavenly worshipers; (4) The Kingdom.
(1) Ps. 1:5, 26:12; 40:9-10; 74:2; 89:5; 149:1; (2) Acts 13:43; Ps. 22:22; 26:5; Prov. 21:16; (3) Ps. 22:25; (4) Isa. 14:13; Ps. 35:18.

Container: See *Sack* and *Vessel*.

Contend: (1) Argue; (2) Fight spiritually; (3) Compete against.
(1) Job 40:2; Prov. 29:9; Acts 11:2; (2) Deut. 2:9, 24; Isa. 41:12; 49:25; Jude 1:3,9; (3) Jer. 12:5.

Continuous: (1) Without end; (2) Ongoing; (3) Consistent; (4) Persistent faith; (5) Abiding; (6) Eternity (Heaven).
(1) Acts 20:7; Rom. 2:7; Heb. 7:3b, 23-24; 13:14; (2) Acts 1:14; 2:42, 46; Rom. 9:2; Heb. 13:15; 2 Pet. 3:4; (3) Acts 6:4; 18:11; (4) Luke 18:1-8; John 8:31; Acts 14:22; Col. 1:23; 1 Tim. 5:5b; James 1:25; (5) John 15:9-10; 1 John 2:24; (6) Isa. 57:15.

Contraceptive Pill: (1) Inability to reproduce spiritually; (2) Not sharing the Gospel (not reproducing your own kind); (3) Taking in a human-made contrivance that stops you from fruit-bearing; (4) Aborting the promise of God; (5) Pleasure without responsibility.

(1) Acts 4:17-18; (2) Rom. 10:14; 1 Cor. 1:21; (3) 2 Cor. 11:4; (4) Exod. 1:16; Matt. 2:16; (5) Judg. 16:1-3.

Contract Killer: (1) Angel of death; (2) The Law; (3) Legalism; (4) Judgment shown through grumbling; (5) The flesh; (6) Sin.

Also see *Assassin, Gunman, Rifle,* and *Sniper.*

(1) Exod. 12:23; 2 Sam. 24:16; (2-3) 2 Cor. 3:6-7a; (4) James 5:9; (5) Gal. 5:19-23; (6) Rom. 7:5-6, 8-11.

Cook: (1) Scheming (concocting something); (2) Work of the flesh; (3) Poison.

Also see *Bake, Baker, Cake,* and *Oven.*

(1-2) Gen. 25:29-34; (3) 2 Kings 4:39-40.

Cookbook: (1) Plan (recipe for disaster); (2) Witchcraft; (3) Ingredients; (4) Stirrer; (5) Formula; (6) Preparation; (7) Instructions; (8) *The Divinity Code to Understanding Your Dreams and Visions Dictionary* and *The Divinity Code to Hearing God's Voice through Prophetic Incidents and Natural Events.*

Also see *Baker* and *Cook.*

(1) Prov. 14:12; 16:25; (2-6) Acts 19:19; (7) 2 Tim. 3:16; (8) This interpretation suggests that you are not looking to the Holy Spirit enough and are looking more at dream interpretation as a formula.

Cooler/Cool Box: (1) Heart (preserving the Word); (2) Heart without love.

(1) Prov. 3:1; 4:4,21,23; Luke 8:15; Heb. 9:4; (2) Matt. 24:12.

Copper: See *Bronze.*

Cord: (1) Control; (2) Soul-tie; (3) Generational curse; (4) Emotional attachment; (5) Stronghold; (6) Bondage; (7) Life (the tie between spirit and body); (8) The blood of Jesus; (9) Protection or security; (10) Link; (11) Sin (or enslaved to sin); (12) Captivity; (13) Death; (14) Group of like-minded people.

Also see *Bound, Rope,* and *Umbilical Cord.*

(1) Ps. 2:3; (2) Gen. 44:30 (parent-child); 1 Sam. 18:1 (friends); 1 Cor. 6:16 (sexual partners); (3) Exod. 20:5; 34:7; Num. 14:18; Deut. 5:9; (4) Hos. 11:4; (5) Matt. 12:29; Mark 3:27; 2 Cor. 10:4; (6) Job 36:8; Ps. 118:27; Prov. 5:22; (7) Ps. 129:4; Eccles. 12:6; (8) Josh. 2:15, 18; (9) Eccles. 4:12; Ps. 129:4; Isa. 54:3; (10-11) Isa. 5:18; Prov. 5:22; (12) 1 Kings 20:31-32; (13) 2 Sam. 22:6; Ps. 116:3; (14) Ps. 119:61 (cf. KJV & NKJV); as in "band of brothers."

Corn: (1) Word of God; (2) Believer; (3) Spiritual fruit; (4) Blessing.

Also see *Seed.*

(1) 1 Cor. 9:9-11; 1 Tim. 5:17-18; (2) John 12:24-25; (3) Mark 4:28; (4) Deut. 7:13; Prov. 11:26.

Cornerstone: (1) Christ; (2) Chief; (3) Foundation.

(1-3) Ps. 118:22; Mark 12:10-11; Eph. 2:20.

Coroner: (1) Death confirmation; (2) The Lord declaring how a church has died; (3) Angel of the Lord investigating your death and possible judgment (get ready to meet the Lord); (4) Possible angel of death (if the subject is still alive, this is a warning of a predatory evil spirit).
(1-2) Rom. 6:11; (2) Rev. 3:1; (3-4) Job 4:15-17; Jude 1:9.

Correction Fluid (White Out): (1) Rewriting over a chapter in one's life; (2) Removing reproach.
(1-2) Gen. 30:22-23; Luke 1:24-25.

Corridor (Hallway): (1) Life journey; (2) Passage to and from the heart; (3) Past journey; (4) Future path; (5) Path to destiny; (6) Passing or passage of time; (7) Transition; (8) Pathway of the mind (soul-tie [godly or ungodly]).
Also see *Trench.*
(1, 3, 4) Exod. 14:22 (future), 29 (past); Num. 22:24; Also as in "pass-age"; Ps. 23:4; (2) Job 31:7; Isa. 65:2; (5) Jer. 29:11; (6) Gen. 4:3; 21:22; (7) Num. 22:24; (8) Ps. 119:59; Isa. 55:7.

Corrugated Iron: (1) Roofing material; (2) Leadership or covering (possible country church); (3) Strong faith; (4) Able to protect from and deflect storms, and at the same time, able to channel the flow of the Spirit; (5) No rust = strong character.
Also see *Fence, Iron,* and *Roof.*
(1) Gen. 19:8; Josh. 2:6; Matt. 8:8; 10:27; Mark 2:4-5.

Corrupt: (1) Unsaved; (2) Evil (bad fruit); (3) Bad company; (4) Mortal death; (5) Heart focused on earthly treasures; (6) The fleshly or old person; (7) Destructive or corrosive speech.
Also see *Corruption.*
(1) Eph. 4:22; 1 Tim. 6:5; 2 Tim. 3:8; (2) Matt. 7:17-18; 12:33; Luke 6:43-45; (3) 1 Cor. 15:33; (4) 1 Cor. 15:53-54; (5) Matt. 6:19-21; Luke 12:33-34; James 5:2; 1 Pet. 1:18; (6) Eph. 4:22; Jude 1:10; (7) Eph. 4:29.

Corruption: (1) Bad character; (2) Wickedness; (3) Deceitfulness; (4) Shortened life; (5) To be led astray; (6) Eternal death; (7) Weakness.
Also see *Corrupt, Decay,* and *Rust.*
(1) 1 Cor. 15:33; (2-4) Ps. 55:23; 2 Pet. 1:4; 2:19; (5) 2 Kings 23:13; Rev. 19:2; (6) Ps. 16:10; 49:9; Isa. 38:17; Jon. 2:6; Acts 2:27,31; Rom. 8:21; Gal. 6:8; (7) 1 Cor. 15:42-43.

Costume Hire: (1) Wanting to be someone else; (2) Feeling like you need to be someone else; (3) False Christian (façade).
Also see *Mask.*
(1) 1 Sam. 21:13; Rom. 7:18-19; (2) Eph. 1:6; (3) Gen. 27:15; Prov. 6:19; Gal. 2:4.

Cotton: (1) Glory of God; (2) Pure (+ heart) (white cotton).
Also see *Wool.*
(1) Rev. 1:14; (2) 2 Sam. 2:18.

Couch: (1) Heart (as the place of rest); (2) To lie down (lazy); (3) Reclining spiritually; (4) Sick; (5) Comfort/able; (6) Bed; (7) Somber place; (8) Seduction (woman lying on a couch).
Also see *Armchair* and *Sofa.*
(1) Prov. 14:33; Matt. 11:29; Acts 2:26; (2) Gen. 49:14; Job 7:13; 38:40; also as in "couch potato"; (3) Gen. 49:4; Luke 5:24; Acts 5:15; (4) Amos 6:4; Luke 5:19; Acts 5:15; (5) Amos 6:4; (6-7) Ps. 6:6.

Council: (1) Authority structure.
Also see *Government.*
(1) Matt. 5:22.

Counselor: (1) Holy Spirit; (2) Jesus Christ.
Also see *Teacher.*
(1) John 16:7; (2) Isa. 9:6.

Countenance: (1) Radiance; (2) Face; (3) Presence.
Also see *Face.*
(1) 2 Cor. 3:7; (2) Matt. 6:16; 28:3; Luke 9:29; Rev. 1:16; (3) Acts 2:28.

Counter (Shop): (1) Something on offer (something on the counter); (2) A deal; (3) Something deceitful (under the counter); (4) A bribe (under the counter); (5) The pulpit; (6) Hungry/searching for spiritual food (standing at a counter); (7) What you are having served up.
(1-2) Acts 24:26; (3) Ps. 26:10; Mark 12:13; (4) Prov. 21:14; (5) As the place where food is served up; (6) Ps. 78:19; Matt. 15:22-28; John 6:67-68; (7) John 12:2.

Country: (1) Offspring; (2) Consider what that country represents to you and the character of its people; (3) International (several countries); (4) Entering the Kingdom of God (entering another country).
Also see individual entries, e.g., *Chinese.*
(1) Gen. 10:20,31; 12:7a; (4) Josh. 1:11b; John 3:5.

Country Road: (1) Country ministry; (2) Alone; (3) Off track; (4) Wilderness training.
Also see *Dirt Road*, *Road*, and *Winding Road.*
(1) Acts 8:26; (2) 1 Kings 19:4; (3) Luke 15:4; (4) Deut. 8:2-3.

Countryside: (1) Pleasant; (2) Peaceful; (3) Restful/leisurely; (4) Fresh; (5) Creation.
Also see *Grass*, *Green*, and individual tree names.
(1) Gen. 2:9; (2) Ps.23:2; Isa. 55:12; (3) Gen. 49:15; Deut. 3:20; 12:10; Josh. 1:13; Ps. 23:2; (4) Song 7:13; (5) Gen. 1:12; 2:9.

Court (Law): (1) Tested; (2) Trial; (3) Judgment; (4) Salvation (judgment).
(1-3) John 18:28-38; 19:4-16; (3) Rom. 14:10; (3-4) John 3:17; James 4:12; Rom. 8:33-34; Rev. 20:12.

Courthouse: (1) Place of judgment; (2) Testing or trial; (3) Accusation; (4) Exposure of secrets of the heart; (5) Adjudication; (6) Brought before God/Christ.

(1) Rom. 14:10; 2 Cor. 5:10; (2) Matt. 22:35; Mark 10:25; (3) Acts 23:29; (4) Rom. 2:16; (5) John 19:10; (6) Acts 7:7; 10:42; Rom. 2:16; 2 Tim. 4:1; Heb. 12:23; 13:4.

Cousin: (1) Brother church (male cousin); (2) Sister from church (female cousin); (3) Brother or sister in the faith (spiritual relative).
(1) Ps. 68:6; Jer. 31:1; Eph. 3:15; (2-3) Luke 1:36,58; Rom. 16:1.

Cover: (1) Covering; (2) Hiding sin; (3) Protection; (4) Love.
(1) Ps. 32:1; 91:1; (2) Ps. 69:5; Prov. 28:13; Isa. 30:1; Luke 23:30; (3) Ps. 91:1; Matt. 23:37; (4) Song 2:4; 1 Pet. 4:8.

Coveralls: (1) Self-righteous works; (2) Armor of God; (3) Manual labor/er; (4) Covering; (5) Redemption (taking off coveralls).
(1) Isa. 64:6; (2) Eph. 6:11; (3) Gen. 3:19; (4-5) Zech. 3:3-4.

Covert: (1) Hidden; (2) Secret; (3) Shelter; (4) Shadow/shade.
(1-2) 1 Kings 18:13; (3) Isa. 4:6; 16:4; 32:2; Jer. 25:38; (4) 1 Sam. 25:20; Job 38:40; 40:21; Ps. 61:4.

Cow: (1) Wealth; (2) Cash; (3) Blessing; (4) Idol.
(1) Ps. 50:10; (2) As in "cash cow"; (3) Ps. 107:38; (4) Exod. 32:24; 1 Kings 12:28.

Cowboy: (1) Gung-ho believer; (2) Shady businessman; (3) Idolatry; (4) Jesus (as the Herdsman); (5) May describe a "driving" rather than a "leading" shepherd.
Also see *Cattle, Horse,* and *Whip.*
(1) Acts 19:14-16; (2) Gen. 31:7; (3) Exod. 32:24; (4) John 10:11; (5) Exod. 6:1; Num. 22:6; Luke 8:29.

Crab: (1) Believer with a tough exterior; (2) Believer with spiritual armor on; (3) Moody person; (4) Crabbing may represent evangelism amongst counter- culture groups; (5) Promise/s of God (as a living rock); (6) Believers in the armor of God; (7) Stronghold; (8) Partaking of an unclean thing (eating crab); (9) Spirit of cancer.
Also see *Fish, Lobster, Net,* and *Shrimp.*
(1) Matt. 4:19; as in "shellfish"; (2) Eph. 6:12ff; (3) As in "they were really crabby"; (5) 1 Pet. 2:4-5; (6) Eph. 6:11; 1 Pet. 2:4-5; (7) Job 21:6; Ps. 48:6; (8) Lev. 11:9-10.

Crack: (1) Old wineskin; (2) Flaw; (3) Lacking unity; (4) Barren ground (cracked ground).
(1) Josh. 9:4; Matt. 9:17; (2) Dan. 6:4; Hos. 10:2; (3) 1 Cor. 6:7; (4) 2 Kings 2:19.

Crackling: (1) Hot fire; (2) Fool's laughter.
(1-2) Eccles. 7:6.

Craftwork: (1) Witchcraft.
(1) 2 Kings 9:22; 2 Chron. 33:6; Mic. 5:12a; Gal. 5:19a-20a.

Crane (Bird): (1) Chatter; (2) Timely; (3) Honor and loyalty/fidelity (Japanese crane).
(1) Isa. 38:14; (2) Jer. 8:7; (3) Japanese tradition.

Crane (Machine): (1) Burden; (2) Burden lifting or lifted; (3) Made easy; (4) Powerful salvation ministry.

(1) Matt. 23:4; Luke 11:46; (2-3) Matt. 11:30; 27:32; (4) Isa. 49:22; 59:19b; Ps. 3:3; James 4:10.

Crash Dummy: (1) Test run; (2) Warning; (3) Observed impact; (4) Collision ahead.
(1-2) 1 Sam. 19:13-18; (3) Matt. 27:54; Mark 15:39; (4) Job 5:4; Isa. 8:9.

Crash Helmet: (1) Helmet of salvation; (2) Hardened heart (proud thoughts); (3) Fragmented/fragile mind.
(1) Eph. 6:17; (2) Dan. 5:20; Mark 6:52; 8:17; (3) James 1:8.

Crayfish: See *Lobster*.

Crazy: (1) Foolishness; (2) Anger/rage; (3) Fear; (4) Curse of disobedience; (5) Paranoia; (6) Obsession; (7) Demonic possession/oppression; (8) Person deep in the things of the Spirit (this looks like madness to the natural person).
(1) Hos. 9:7; (2) Luke 6:11; (3) 2 Tim. 1:7; (4) Deut. 28:28; (5) Matt. 2:16; (6) Prov. 19:13; 27:15; Luke 18:5; (7) Luke 8:35; (8) 1 Cor. 2:14.

Cream: (1) Best; (2) The Gospel.
Also see *Ice Cream*.
(1) Heb. 12:24; (2) Heb. 5:13 (the best part of the milk of the Word).

Cream (Color): (1) False holiness; (2) Self-righteousness.
Also see *White* and *Off-White*.
(1) Lev. 10:10; Ps. 51:7; (2) Isa. 64:6 (cf. Rev. 19:8).

Creativity: (1) In the Spirit; (2) Using the gifts of the Spirit.
(1) Gen. 1:2ff; (2) John 9:6-7.

Credit Card: (1) Accounted as having faith; (2) Financial issue; (3) Having no spiritual credibility (wrong use of credit card).
(1) Gen. 15:6; Gal. 3:6; (2) Luke 14:28; (3) Acts 19:15.

Creek: (1) Creeks and rivers often depict boundaries.
Also see *Brook*, *Stream*, and *River*.
(1) Gen. 32:22-23; Josh. 1:11.

Creep/ing: (1) Warning; (2) Suspicious; (3) Secretive; (4) Outward form of godliness without the Spirit; (5) Abomination.
(1) 2 Tim. 3:6; (2-4) 2 Tim. 3:6; (5) Ezek. 8:10.

Crib: (1) New beginning; (2) Blessing started; (3) Nurturing; (4) Baby; (5) Pregnancy; (6) Feed tray; (7) The hand that feeds you.
(1-5) Luke 2:7,12,16; (6) Prov. 14:4; (7) Isa. 1:3.

Cricket (Insect): (1) Annoying person; (2) Deserted or empty.
(1) 2 Sam. 16:5-9; (2) Matt. 23:27; Isa. 34:13.

Cricket (Sport): (1) Noble; (2) Partnership; (2 batsmen); (3) Trying to get you out with words (bowling); (4) Words with power (batting); (5) Spiritual warfare (batting and bowling taking place); (6) Making history (hitting a hundred runs).
Also see *Ball*, *Bat*, *Football Game*, *Sport*, *Umpire*, and *Winning*.

(1) Supposedly a gentleman's game; Also as in "that's just not cricket"; (2) Deut. 17:6; Matt. 18:19-20; (3) Mark 12:13; (4) Eccles. 8:4; Luke 4:32; (5) Rom. 7:23 (internally: spirit vs. flesh); 2 Cor. 10:3; Eph. 6:12 (in the second heaven: against evil spirits); 1 Tim. 1:18; (6) Esther 8:5,8 (it is recorded).

Cricket bat: (1) Innings (as in your turn/or your time to bat).
Also see *Bat.*
(1) Esther 4:14; Eph. 1:4.

Crimson: (1) Sin; (2) Blood; (3) Opulence.
Also see *Blood* and *Red.*
(1-2) Isa. 1:18; (3) Jer. 4:30.

Cripple: See *Polio.*

Crocodile: (1) Devourer; (2) Demon spirit; (3) The devil; (4) Death; (5) Religious hypocrite; (6) One with biting remarks; (7) Predator; (8) Financial predator; (9) Faking or pretending (crocodile tears); (10) Consumed by words.
(1) By virtue of its teeth; (2) Matt. 13:4; (3) Isa. 27:1; Mal. 3:11; 1 Pet. 5:8; Rev. 12:4; (4) Prov. 5:5; Ezek. 28:8 (KJV); (5) Matt. 23:14; Mark 12:40; Luke 20:47; (6) Gal. 5:15; (7) 1 Pet. 5:8; (8) Mal. 3:10-11; (9) Mal. 2:13; (10) Ps. 57:4; 124:3-7.

Crooked: (1) Faithless spiritual deviation; (2) Evil; (3) Ungodly; (4) Darkness; (5) Without peace.
Also see *Curved, Darkness, Straight,* and *Upright.*
(1) Prov. 3:4-5; Isa. 40:3-4; (2) Prov. 2:12-15; (3) Ps. 125:5; Isa. 40:4; Luke 3:5; (4) Isa. 42:16; Phil. 2:15; (5) Isa. 59:8.

Cross: (1) Jesus's cross; (2) Gospel of salvation; (3) Death; (4) Forgiveness (cancellation of debt); (5) Victory; (6) Healing; (7) Believer's cross; (8) Losing one's life for Christ.
Also see *Crucify.*
(1) John 19:17, 25; (2) 1 Cor. 1:17-18; Col. 1:20; (3) Phil. 2:8; (4) Col. 2:14; (5) Col. 2:15; Heb. 12:2; (6) Acts 4:10; (7-8) Matt. 10:38-39; 16:24; Mark 8:34; 10:21; Luke 9:23; 14:27.

Crossing (a bridge, lake, river, etc.): (1) Getting saved (entering Kingdom of Heaven); (2) Moving into the spiritual; (3) Journey of life; (4) Deliverance; (5) Exit from old; (6) Entry to new; (7) Double-mindedness (going backward and forward across); (8) The battle between the flesh and spirit (going backward and forward across).
Also see *Boom Gate* and *Railroad Tracks.*
(1) Exod. 14:16; 1 Pet. 3:20-21a; (2) 2 Kings 2:8-9, 14 (good); 2 Kings 21:6 (evil); (3) John 6:16-21; (4) Deut. 4:20; (5-6) Deut. 6:23; (7) James 1:6-8; (8) Gal. 5:17.

Crossroad: (1) Decision time; (2) Choice; (3) Vulnerable.
(1) Josh. 24:15; (2) Luke 22:42; (3) Matt. 25:36; 1 Cor. 4:11-13.

Crouching (1) Hiding; (2) Ready to attack.
Also see *Bending* and *Bowing.*

(1) Josh. 8:4; (2) Deut. 19:11.

Crow: See *Raven.*

Crowd: (1) Heavenly onlookers; (2) Busy; (3) Busyness; (4) Congregation; (5) Sheep without a shepherd; (6) Followers; (7) Public place; (8) Public opinion.
(1) Heb. 12:1; (2-3) Luke 9:10; (4) Matt. 5:1; (5) Matt. 9:36; (6) Mark 10:46; (7-8) Neh. 8:3; John 8:59.

Crown: (1) Victory; (2) Glory and honor; (3) Authority; (4) Life; (5) Righteousness; (6) Rejoicing; (7) Incorruptible; (8) Reward; (9) Pride.
Also see *Head.*
(1) 2 Tim. 2:5; Rev. 6:2; (2) Phil. 4:1; Heb. 2:7-9; 1 Pet. 5:4; Rev. 4:10; (3) Heb. 2:8; Rev. 4:10; (4) James 1:12; Rev. 2:10; (5) 2 Tim. 4:8; (6) 1 Thess. 2:19; (7) 1 Cor. 9:25; (8) Rev. 2:10; (9) Isa. 28:1,3.

Crucify: (1) Lay down one's life (death to self); (2) Human weakness; God's wisdom and power; (3) Nailing the flesh with its affections and lust to live in the Spirit; (4) Torturous death.
Also see *Cross.*
(1) Gal. 2:20; (2) 1 Cor. 2:2-5; 2 Cor. 13:4; (3) Gal. 5:24-25; Rom. 6:6; (4) Matt. 27:31ff; Mark 15:25ff.

Cruise Ship: (1) Life's path or journey; (2) Journey, voyage, passage; (3) Can also represent a life without God or running from God; (4) Spiritual apathy.
Also see *Holiday, Houseboat, Suitcase, Tourist,* and *Yacht.*
(1) Prov. 5:6; 6:23; 10:17; 30:19; (2-3) Jon. 1:3; (4) Luke 12:19; Rev. 3:17-18.

Crumbs: (1) Insufficiency (lacking spiritual nourishment); (2) Spiritual pauper; (3) Great faith.
Also see *Bread.*
(1-2) Luke 16:21; (3) Matt. 15:27-28.

Crying: (1) Sorrow; (2) Grief; (3) Pain; (4) Pouring out one's heart; (5) Rejected; (6) Seeking repentance; (7) Disgraced; (8) Anguish of heart; (9) Due for blessing; (10) Tears do not ensure sincerity.
Also see *Tears.*
(1-3) Rev. 21:4; (4) Lam. 2:18-19; Heb. 5:7; (5-6) Heb. 12:17; (7) Matt. 26:75; (8) John 11:35; (9) Ps. 126:5-6; 84:6; (10) Mal. 2:13.

Cry Out: (1) Torment; (2) Fear; (3) Attention; (4) Uproar; (5) Unclean spirit; (6) Wilderness; (7) Anger; (8) Authoritative instructions; (9) Heartfelt supplication; (10) Declaration; (11) Inner conflict.
(1) Matt. 8:29; Mark 9:24; 15:34, 39; Luke 8:28; (2) Exod. 14:11; Matt. 14:26; Mark 6:49; (3) Matt. 20:30; 25:6; Mark 10:47; Luke 9:38; Acts 14:14; 21:28; 23:6; (4) Matt. 27:23-24; Mark 15:13-14; Acts 19:34; (5) Mark 1:23, 26; Luke 4:33,41; 9:39; Acts 8:7; (6) Matt. 3:3; Mark 1:3; Luke 3:4; John 1:23; (7) Acts 7:57; 19:28; (8) Rev. 14:15,18; (9)

Exod. 8:12; Ps. 84:2; 3:4; 17:1; 18:6; Mark 9:24; (10) Matt. 21:15; Mark 11:9; (11) Mark 5:5-7.

Crystal/s: (1) Clear or pure; (2) Clarity; (3) Paganism; (4) New Age.
(1) Rev. 22:1; (2) Rev. 21:11; 22:1.

Crystal Ball: (1) Seeking direction; (2) Bypassing God (wrong entry into heavenlies); (3) Fortune telling; (4) Familiar spirit; (5) Occult practice; (6) Witchcraft.
Also see *Cards (Tarot)* and *Witchcraft.*
(1-2) Lev. 20:6; 1 Sam. 28:3-8; (3) Acts 16:16-18; (4) Deut. 18:11-12; (5-6) Deut. 18:10.

Cucumber: (1) Symbol of world; (2) Turning back to the world; (3) Besieged.
(1-2) Num. 11:5; (3) Isa. 1:8.

Cud: (1) Meditation (chewing cud); (2) Needs outworking.
(1) Lev. 11:3; (2) Lev. 11:4.

Cummin (Cumin): (1) Small matter; (2) Taking care of miniscule issues while neglecting more important ones.
(1) Matt. 23:23.

Cup: (1) A person as a human vessel (heart); (2) Blessing; (3) Covenant; (4) Resurrection/life; (5) God's fury/wrath/judgment (also known as the cup of trembling); (6) Salvation or redemption; (7) Death/baptism; (8) Consolation; (9) Responsibility or calling; (10) God's will (the Father's cup); (11) Portion.
Also see *Platter.*
(1) Matt. 23:25-27; (2) Ps. 23:5; 1 Cor. 10:16; (3) Luke 22:20; 1 Cor. 11:25; (4) Gen. 40:9-13,21; (5) Isa. 51:17,22; Lam. 4:21; Ezek. 23:32; (6) Gen. 44:2, 12 (Silver = redemption); Ps. 116:13; (7) Mark 10:38-39; (8) Jer. 16:7; (9) Matt. 26:39-42; (10) Luke 22:42; John 18:11; (11) Ps. 11:6; 16:5.

Cupboard: (1) Heart; (2) Storage; (3) Thoughts (mind); (4) Delay; (5) Reserve or preserve; (6) Abundance: (7) Accumulated; (8) Hidden.
Also see *Closet.*
(1) Prov. 13:12; Amos 3:10; (2) 2 Chron. 11:11; 1 Cor. 16:2; (3) 1 Chron. 29:18; Ps. 31:12; (4) Exod. 22:29; (5) Gen. 41:36; (6) 1 Kings 10:10; 2 Chron. 31:10-12; (7) 2 Kings 20:17; Ezek. 4:9 (NIV).

Curb: See *Kerb.*

Currency Exchange: (1) Conversion to faith (place where your values change); (2) Receiving financial blessing from Heaven.
(1) Matt. 6:24; Luke 16:11, 13; (2) Exod. 12:35-36; Prov. 13:22; Phil 4:19.

Cursing: See *Swearing.*

Curtain: (1) The fleshly veil; (2) The heart (beyond a curtain); (3) Heaven; (4) Cover; (5) Ending (closing curtain); (6) Death.
Also see *Veil.*
(1) Heb. 10:20; (2) 2 Cor. 3:15; (3) Ps. 104:2; Isa. 40:22; (6) As in "It's curtains!"

Curved: (1) Distorted or warped; (2) Leaning or having an inclination toward; (3) Deception; (4) Sin; (5) Bent on something; (6) Oppressed; (7) Bound; (8) Infirmity; (9) Mourning; (10) Not yet upright or straight; (11) Dismayed; (12) Flowing in the anointing; (13) Unrighteous.

Also see *Crooked*, *Straight*, and *Upright*.

(1) Ps. 62:3b; (2) Ezek. 17:7; (3) As in "He threw me a curve ball"; Ps. 78:57; (4) Ps. 51:10; (5) Hos. 11:7; (6-8) Luke 13:11, 16; (9) Ps. 35:14; 38:6; (10) Luke 3:5; (11) Isa. 21:3; (12) John 3:8; (13) Ps. 125:4-5; Prov. 13:6.

Cushion: (1) Comfort; (2) Easy life ("cushy" job); (3) Desensitize/d (spiritually asleep).
(1) 2 Cor. 1:4, 7:4; (2) Luke 16:19; (3) Matt. 13:13.

Cussing: See *Swearing*.

Cut: (1) Harsh words; (2) Using the Word of God; (3) Prune; (4) Edify; (5) Kill (cut off); (6) Cuts on the body can mean verbal abuse and/or wounded; (7) Cutting away the flesh.

(1) Luke 12:51; Acts 5:33; 7:54; (2) Eph. 6:17; Heb. 4:12; (3) John 15:2; (4) Heb. 12:11; (5) Dan. 9:26; Gen. 9:11; (6) Matt. 27:29-30; Mark 10:34; (7) Rom. 2:29.

Cutting Hair: (1) Breaking a vow; (2) Making a vow; (3) Shame; (4) Cutting away the flesh.

Also see *Hair*, *Razor*, and *Shave*.

(1) Num. 6:5; (2) Acts 18:18; (3) Jer. 7:29; Ezek. 5:1-2; (4) Lev. 14:8.

Cyclone: See *Storm*.

Cylinder: (1) 3-D object (spiritual); (2) Beyond the physical realm; (3) New dimensions.

Also see *Circle* and *Round*.

(1-3) Eph. 3:18 (multi-dimensional).

Cymbal: (1) All words no love; (2) Worship.
(1) 1 Cor. 13:1; (2) 1 Chron. 15:16,19,28.

D

Dad: See *Father*.

Dam: (1) Resisting or stopping the move of God; (2) Potential; (3) Controlled flow of the Spirit; (4) Holding back; (5) God's protection.

Also see *Deep*, *Lake*, *Pond*, *Reservoir*, and *Water*.

(1) Gen. 26:15; Deut. 2:30; Acts 2:17; 6:8-10; (2) Mal. 3:10; (3) 2 Chron. 32:3-5,30; (4) Gen. 26:18; (5) Josh. 3:13; Isa. 59:19b.

Dancing: (1) Worship/praise; (2) Joyful celebration; (3) Being led by the Spirit (as in ballroom dancing); (4) Sensuous/fleshly; (5) Partner hunting; (6) Sign of positive change/deliverance; (7) Youthful/immaturity; (8) Spiritually immature; (9) Change (turning); (10) Performance; (11) Also consider that the music to which you are dancing may be indicative of its meaning; (12) Union/love.

Also see *Turning*.

(1) 2 Sam. 6:14-16; Ps. 149:3; 150:4 (2) Judg. 11:34; 1 Sam. 18:6; Ps. 30:11; Luke 15:25; (3) John 21:18; Rom. 8:14; (4) Exod. 32:19; 1 Sam. 30:16; Job 21:17; Matt. 14:6; (5) Judg. 21:21-23; (6) Ps. 30:11; cf. Lam. 5:15 (reversed); (7) Jer. 31:13; Job 21:11; (8) Matt. 11:16-19; (9) Ps. 30:11; Jer. 31:13; Lam. 5:15; also as in "the dance of change" or "learning new steps"; (10) Matt. 14:6; Mark 6:22; (12) Amos 3:3.

Dandelion: (1) Seed led by the Spirit; (2) Undervalued, but embraced by children; (3) Healing properties.

(1) Ezra 37:1; John 3:8; Rev. 17:3; 21:10; (2) Matt. 18:3,4; (3) Dandelion tea is embraced for its healing properties.

Dandruff: (1) Renewing the mind (getting rid of the old wineskin); (2) Fragmented mind.

(1) Rom. 12:2; (2) Dan. 5:6; Luke 24:38; James 1:8.

Dark/ness: (1) Demonic presence; (2) Absence of Christ; (3) Separation from God; (4) Hell; (5) The kingdom of satan; (6) Spiritual blindness; (7) In sin; (8) Ungodliness; (9) Worldliness; (10) Lost; (11) Ignorant; (12) Judgment; (13) Secret/ly; (14) Lying; (15) Hatred; (16) Spiritually unaware or ignorant (in the dark); (17) Hidden Presence of God; (18) Death; (19) Subconscious; (20) Lost, not knowing the way (morally, ethically); (21) Rich (as in chocolate); (22) Hate brother (walking in darkness) (23) Foolishness; (24) Fear (of the unknown); (25) The mysterious, unknown, hidden, or secret; (26) The place of hearing.

Also see *Black*, *Night*, and *Shadow*.

(1) Ps. 22:12-13; Matt. 27:45; Mark 15:33; Luke 23:44; (2) John 13:30; 8:12; (3) Matt. 4:15-16; 1 John 1:5; (4) Matt. 8:12; 22:13; 25:30; 2 Pet. 2:4; Jude 1:13; (5) Luke 22:53; Acts 26:18; Eph. 6:12; Col. 1:13; (6) Matt. 6:23; John 1:5; Acts 13:11; (7) Eph. 5:11-12; (8) John 3:19; 8:12; 2 Cor. 6:14; 1 Thess. 5:5,7b; (9) Rom. 13:12; Eph. 6:12; (10) John 12:35,46; 1 John 2:11; (11) 1 Thess. 5:4; (12) Exod. 10:21; Acts 2:20; Jude 1:6; (13) Matt. 10:27; 1 Cor. 4:5; (14) 1 John 1:6; (15) 1 John 2:9,11; (16) Exod. 10:22-23; Deut. 28:29; 2 Sam. 22:29; (17) Exod. 20:21; Num. 12:8; Deut. 5:23; 1 Kings 8:12; (18) Job 10:21-22; 12:22; (19) 2 Cor. 4:6; (20) Isa. 50:10; (21) John 1:9; 3:19-20; 8:12; 9:5; 11:10; (22) 1 John 2:11; (23) Eccles. 2:13; (24) Gen. 15:12; (25) Exod. 20:21; (26) Matt. 10:27.

Darkroom (Photography): (1) Private exposure and developing vision.
(1) Matt. 10:26; 1 Cor. 4:5.

Darts: (1) Heart-piercing words; (2) Need for the shield of faith.

Also see *Arrows*.

(1) 2 Sam. 18:14; Prov. 7:23; (2) Eph. 6:16.

Daughter: (1) Your future; (2) Natural daughter; (3) Fellow believer—female—daughters of faith; (4) May refer to a work, church, ministry, or city planted by God or another; (5) Female descendant.

(1) Job 21:8; Ps. 103:5b; Joel 2:28; 2 Cor. 4:16; (2) Acts 21:9; (3) Matt. 9:21; Luke 13:16; 2 Cor. 6:18; 1 Pet. 3:6; (4) John 12:15; (5) Luke 1:5; 8:48.

Day: (1) Light; (2) Glory or honor; (3) Time to do the work of God; (4) Guidance; (5) In the Presence of Christ; (6) In Christ; (7) A day may equal a year.

Also see entries under individual numbers (one through seven) and individual days (Sunday through Saturday).

(1) Gen. 1:5; (2) Rev. 21:24-25; (3) John 9:4; (4) John 11:9; (5-6) John 8:12; 9:4; (7) Num. 14:34; Ezek. 4:6.

Dead: (1) Spiritually dead; (2) Unable to receive spiritual truth; (3) Literal, physical death; (4) An aspect of one's life laid down; (5) Death to self; (6) A dead person speaking to you may indicate soul-ties; (7) A dead person speaking to you may indicate demonic deception.

Also see *Death*.

(1) Matt. 8:22; (2) John 8:43,47; (3) John 11:14; (4-5) Matt. 10:38; 16:24; Mark 8:34; 10:21; Luke 9:23; 1 Cor. 15:30-31 (5) Gal. 2:20; (6) Gen. 42:38; (7) 2 Cor. 11:14; Gal. 1:8.

Dead End: (1) No hope; (2) Bad decision; (3) Turn back; (4) Wrong way; (5) Not giving out; (6) Disobedience.

(1) Eph. 2:12; Heb. 3:10-12; (2) Gen. 12:10; Gal. 1:6; Jude 1:11; (3) Gen. 13:1,3; James 5:20; (4) Gal. 2:18; (5) Mark 4:24; Luke 6:38; Matt. 10:8; (6) 1 Kings 13:9-22.

Deaf: (1) Lack of spiritual hearing; (2) Hardened heart; (3) Without spiritual understanding; (4) Unbeliever; (5) Deaf and dumb spirit.

Also see *Dumb*.

(1-3) Matt. 13:13-15; Mark 4:12; Luke 8:10; Matt. 13:15; Acts 28:27; Heb. 3:15; John 8:43; (4) Isa. 29:18; (5) Mark 9:25-26.

Dealer: (1) The authority figure; (2) The spiritually stronger one; (3) God; (4) Dominant one; (5) Rich with servants; (6) M.C. (Master of Ceremonies), host, or preacher.

(1) John 7:18-19; (2) John 4:9; (3) Luke 1:25; Rom. 12:3; Heb. 12:7; (4) 1 Sam. 17:4-10; (5) Prov. 22:7; (6) John 2:8-10.

Death: (1) Dying to self; (2) Literal death; (3) Spiritual death (result of sin); (4) Ending a relationship (with a known person); (5) Death of a ministry; (6) Separation; (7) Sin; (8) Martyrdom; (9) Condemned; (10) Judgment; (11) Conversion (salvation); (12) Crucifying the flesh; (11) If you know the name of the person, look up meaning (e.g., your friend Verity dies, means the death of truth).

Also see *Birth* and *Dead*.

(1) Matt. 10:38; 16:24; Mark 8:34; 10:21; Luke 9:23; 1 Cor. 15:30-31; (2) John 11:14; (3) Jer. 9:21; Rom. 6:23; (4) Rom. 16:17; 2 Cor. 6:14; Eph. 5:11; (6) Rom. 6:23 (spiritual death is separation from God); physical death is separation of the spirit from the body; (7) Rom. 6:23; (8) Matt. 10:21; Acts 7:60; (9) Matt. 20:18; (10) 2 Sam. 12:19-23; (11) Rom. 6:4-8; (12) Gal. 5:24.

Debt: (1) Unforgiveness; (2) Offense taken; (3) Sin.

Also see *Payment*.

(1) Matt. 18:21-35; (2-3) Luke 11:4.

Decapitation: (1) In trouble with the law (capital punishment); (2) Punishment; (3) Martyr; (4) Defeated; (5) Loss of authority or authority figure; (6) Losing one's head (insanity, paranoia, psychosis); (7) Silenced.

Also see *Head* and *Throat (Cut)*.

(1) 1 Sam. 5:4; Isa. 9:14; (2) 1 Sam. 17:51; 2 Sam. 16:9b; (3) Heb. 11:37a; (4) 1 Sam. 17:51; (5) 1 Cor. 11:3; Eph. 5:23; (6) John 10:20; Acts 12:15 (KJV), 26:24; (7) Mark 6:18-19,24.

Decay: (1) Eternal death; (2) Perish.

(1) Ps. 49:14; Acts 2:27; (2) Isa. 1:28; Rom. 2:12.

Deck (Timber): (1) Foundation; (2) Platform.

(1) 2 Tim. 2:19a; (2) Matt. 10:27.

Deed: (1) Contract; (2) Title (ownership); (3) Works of the flesh.

(1-2) Gen. 23:20; Jer. 32:44; (3) Rom. 3:20, 28.

Deep: (1) Heart; (2) Ocean/seas/waters; (3) Equivalent to death (deep sleep); (4) Well rooted/grounded; (5) Hell; (6) Profound; (7) Secrets; (8) The heart of God (Word of God).

(1) Gen. 1:2; 7:11; Lev. 13:3; Ps. 42:7; 64:6; Prov. 18:4; 20:5; Dan. 2:22; John 4:11; (2) Gen. 1:2; Neh. 9:11; Job 38:30; 41:31; Ps. 104:5-6; 107:24; Isa. 51:10; 63:13; Zech. 10:11; Luke 5:4; 2 Cor. 11:25; (3) Gen. 15:12; Gen. 2:21; John 19:34; Isa. 29:10; (4) Ps. 80:9; Luke 6:48; (5) Ps. 88:6; 140:10; Prov. 22:14; 23:27; Isa. 30:33; Jon. 2:3; Matt. 12:40; Luke 8:31; Rom. 10:7; (6-7) Ps. 92:5; Dan. 2:22; 1 Cor. 2:10; (8) Gen. 1:2; Dan. 2:22; John 4:11.

Deeper: (1) Greater commitment; (2) Further on in spiritual walk; (3) Revelation (deeper in the things of God); (4) Caught or entrapped (going to hell).

(1-2) Ezek. 47:3-5; (3) Prov. 3:20; (4) Ps. 18:4; Jon. 2:5-6.

Deep Water: (1) The heart of God; (2) Plans of a man's heart; (3) Out of your depth; (4) Thrown in the deep end.
(1) Ps. 42:7; (2) Prov. 20:5; (3) Ezek. 47:5; Matt. 14:16; (4) Jon. 1:15; Matt. 10:5ff.

Deer: (1) Someone who thirsts after God; (2) Strong spiritual walk and reaching new heights; (3) Sure footedness; (4) Spiritually sound.
(1) Ps. 42:1; (2) Ps. 18:33; (3) Song 2:17; 8:14; (4) Hab. 3:19.

Deer Hunting: See *Hunting*.

De Facto Relationship: (1) Person or church with one foot in world, one foot in Christ; (2) No commitment; (3) Lukewarm person or church.
(1-3) Prov. 7:7-8; Hos. 2:5; John 4:18.

Deliverance: (1) Dealing with a controlling issue; (2) Getting something out in the open; (3) Cleansing the inner temple of the human heart; (4) Casting out a literal demon; (5) The Rapture; (6) Released through the Presence of God.
(1) Exod. 34:24; Deut. 7:1-5; Jon. 2:4,10; (2) Lev. 18: 14-15,28; Job 39:3; Prov. 22:10; Jer. 16:12-13; Matt. 5:13; (3) Gen. 21:10; Deut. 9:4; 1 Kings 14:24; 21:26; Ps. 80:8; (4) Matt. 8:16; 9:33; 10:1,8; 12:28; (5) Isa. 26:19-21; (6) Ps. 44:2-3.

Demolition: See *House*.

Demon: (1) Fallen angel; (2) Evil spirit; (3) Unclean spirit; (4) Physical affliction; (5) Bondage; (6) Oppression; (7) Addiction; (8) Self-destruction; (9) Sickness; (10) Spirit of death; (11) Stronghold; (12) Issue (on which a demon might find ground to enter); (13) Spirit of infirmity; (14) Literal demon.
(1) Rev. 1:20; 12:4; (2) 1 Sam. 16:14; (3) Matt. 10:1; Mark 5:8; (4) Acts 10:38; (4-5) Luke 13:12,16; (6) 1 Sam. 16:14; (4-8) Matt. 17:15-18; (9) Matt. 8:16; Luke 8:2; (10) See *Reaper*; (11) Luke 8:29; (12) Matt. 18:34-35; Eph. 4:27; (13) Matt. 4:24; Luke 8:2.

Den: (1) Dark hiding place for greedy predators; (2) Hiding place.
(1) Job 38:39-40; Ps. 104:21-22; Dan. 6:16; Matt. 21:13; Mark 11:17; Luke 19:46; (2) Ps. 10:9; Judg. 6:2; Rev. 6:15.

Dental Nurse/Assistant: (1) Church.
Also see *Dentist*, *Nurse*, and *Teeth*.
(1) Song 4:2; Isa. 40:11.

Dentist: (1) Christ; (2) Pastor.
Also see *Teeth*.
(1-2) This is by virtue of the fact that teeth are as sheep (Song 4:2; 6:6), and the person who works on them would be their leader.

Deodorant: (1) Blessing (as a sweet fragrance); (2) Favor of God; (3) Covering up an offense; (4) Dealing with an offense.
Also see *Body Odor*.
(1-4) Song 4:10; Prov. 27:9; Matt. 11:6; Luke 7:23; Phil. 4:18.

Deposit: See *Credit Card*, *Currency Exchange*, and *Down Payment*.

Descend: (1) Dropping away spiritually; (2) Death; (3) Bringing from Heaven to earth; (4) To humble; (5) Give up.
Also see *Dropping* and *Down*.
(1) Gen. 12:10; 26:2; 46:4; Jon. 1:3,5; (2) Gen. 37:35; 44:29,31; Josh. 3:11,13,16, (*Jordan* means "descender/death"); Job 7:9; (3-4) Ps. 18:27; Phil 2:5-8; (5) Gen. 21:16.

Desert: (1) Testing place; (2) Place where heart is revealed; (3) Place of dependence on the Word; (4) Place of humbling; (5) Preparation for entry into Promised Land; (6) Without public profile; (7) Place of Spirit strengthening; (8) Barrenness; (9) Infertility; (10) Trials; (11) Place away from God.
(1-5) Deut. 8:2-3, 7-9; (6-7) Luke 1:80; (8) Job 39:6; (9) Gen. 29:31; Prov. 30:16; (10) Matt. 4:1; Acts 14:22; (11) Jer. 17:5-6.

Desk: (1) Speaks of a business or work situation/issue; (2) Schooling or learning; (3) Teaching.
(1) Matt. 9:9; (2-3) Deut. 6:7a; Matt. 26:55b.

Desktop Computer: See *Computer*, *Hardware*, *Laptop*, and *Software*.

Dessert: (1) Indulgence; (2) Inheritance/promise/blessing.
Also see *Ice Cream*.
(1) Prov. 25:16; (2) Lev. 20:24.

Destroy: (1) Ruin; (2) Kill; (3) Judgment; (4) Famine; (5) Devil.
(1) Jer. 4:7; (2) Esther 9:24; (3) Gen. 18:28; (4) Joel 1:10; (5) John 10:10.

Devil: (1) Chief of all evil; (2) Fallen angel; (3) Unclean spirit.
(1) Matt. 12:24; Mark 3:22; Luke 11:15; (2) Isa. 14:12-15; Ezek. 28:14-15; (3) Rev. 18:2.

Dew: (1) The favor of God; (2) A gift or blessing from God; (3) Eternal life; (4) Revelation from God; (5) That which comes from God because of prayer; (6) Replenishment/zest; (7) Judgment (no dew); (8) Guidance or confirmation.
(1) Prov. 19:12; (2) Ps. 133:3; Hos. 14:5; Mic. 5:7; (3) Ps. 133:3; (4) Exod. 16:13-15 (heavenly food); (5) Deut. 32:2; 1 Kings 17:1; (6) Ps. 110:3; (7) Hag. 1:10; (8) Judg. 6:38.

Diamond: (1) Jesus; (2) Precious work; (3) Permanent marker; (4) The word *diamond* comes from the Greek word *Adamas*, meaning "unconquerable"; (5) Resistance to abrasion; (6) Hardest natural substance known; (7) Excellent disperser of light; (8) Adamant/immovable/resolute; (9) Associated with the tribe of Gad.
Also see *Precious Stones*.
(1) 1 Pet. 2:4; (2) 1 Cor. 3:12; (3) Jer. 17:1; (4) Ezek. 3:8-9 (adamant); (9) Exod. 28:18.

Diaper: (1) Immaturity; (2) Spiritually unaware of offense.
(1-2) Eph. 4:14.

Diaper Soaking Solution: (1) Waiting on God (soaking) to remove stubborn fleshly characteristics.
(1) Ps. 69:2-3.

Diary (Personal): (1) Your heart (as the place where you record things of importance); (2) Agenda of your heart; (3) Date with destiny (Divine appointment); (4) Memory; (5) Record; (6) Memorable moment; (7) Anticipated event; (8) Personal secret.

(1) Deut. 11:18; (2) Num. 15:39; Prov. 19:21; Hab. 2:2; (3) Esther 4:14; Gal. 4:4; (4-6) 1 Sam. 30:6; Neh. 4:14; Ps. 78. (7) Tit. 2:13; (8) Matt. 13:35b.

Diary (Work): (1) Divine appointment; (2) Anticipated event; (3) Business event; (4) Schedule.

(1) Esther 4:14; John 15:16; 1 Pet. 2:9; (2) Dan. 9:24-27; Tit. 2:13; (3) John21:3; (4) Gal. 4:4.

Dice: (1) Chance; (2) Gambling; (3) Trying to find God's will.

For particular numbers on dice, see entries under individual numbers. For example, if you threw a five, you might be gambling with God's grace.

(1) 1 Sam. 6:9; (2) Mark 15:24; (3) Exod. 28:30; Num. 27:21; 1 Sam. 28:6.

Digging: (1) Uncovering truth; (2) Fertilizing; (3) Digging a well; (4) Preparing for a protracted battle; (5) Seeking.

Also see *Dirt, Shovel, Spade, Earthmovers*, and *Excavate*.

(1) Matt. 13:44; (2) Luke 13:8; (3) Gen. 26:18-19; (4) As in "digging in"; (5) Matt. 7:7; 13:45-46.

Dignity: See *Formal*.

Dim: (1) Lacking spiritual insight; (2) Calamity; (3) Sorrow or grief; (4) The Glory has departed; (5) Moving by faith; (6) Halfway between dark and light; (7) Compromise; (8) Lukewarm; (9) Lights are going out.

(1) Gen. 27:1; Deut. 34:7; 1 Sam. 3:2; 4:15; (2) Lam. 5:17; (3) Job 17:7; (4) Lam. 4:1; (5) Gen. 48:10, 13-20.

Dining Room: (1) Spiritual nourishment; (2) Intimacy; (3) Fellowship.

Also see *Bread, Restaurant*, and *Table*.

(1) Ps. 34:8; Heb. 5:12-14; (2-3) Ps. 23:5; Rev. 3:20.

Dinosaur: (1) Out of date (old); (2) Large predator; (3) Evil spirit/the devil; (4) Monster (wild); (5) Fierce (violent); (6) Untamable.

Also see *Monster*.

(1) Matt. 9:17; 2 Cor. 5:17; (2) Job 41:14; (3) Rev. 12:9; (4) Job 41:2-5; (5) Job 41:10; (6) Job 41:4.

Dirt: (1) Sin; (2) Finding someone's past sin; (3) Flesh; (4) Of humanity.

Also see *Dust* and *Earth*.

(1) Isa. 57:20; (2) As in "digging up dirt on someone"; (3-4) Gen. 2:7.

Dirt Road: (1) Doing your own thing (uncleanness); (2) Heading toward uncleanness; (3) Off of God's highway; (4) A path of unwholesome talk; (5) Scandal; (6) Accusation; (7) Country ministry; (8) Wilderness path; (9) Path to Promised Land; (10) Path of humbling dependence on the Word of God.

Also see *Country Road*, *Dirt*, *Road*, and *Winding Road*.
(1) Ezek. 36:17; (2) 1 Cor. 15:33; (3) Prov. 16:17; Isa. 35:8; 40:3; (4-6) Ps. 73:8; (7) Judg. 5:6; (8-9) Exod. 13:18; Deut. 1:19, 31; (10) Deut. 8:2-3.

Dirty Water: See *Water (Dirty Water)*.

Disability: (1) Unsaved (spiritually insensitive); (2) Not yet spiritually developed (spiritually dull); (3) Having a character flaw; (4) Curse (the result of sin); (5) Dependence on God (having been humbled).
Also see *Mentally Disabled Person(s)*.
(1) 1 Cor. 2:14; (2) 2 Kings 6:17; Matt. 14:29-30; (3) Matt. 26:35,69-75; (4) John 5:5-14; (5) Gen. 32:25,31.

Discount: (1) Disregard; (2) Favor.
(1) Mark 7:13; (2) Prov. 22:1; Matt. 18:27.

Disease: (1) Contagious sickness; (2) Common infirmity.
(1-2) Matt. 4:23-24; 9:20,35; 10:1.

Dish: (1) Heart; (2) Preparing or cleansing hearts (washing dishes).
Also see *Plate* and *Spoon*.
(1-2) Matt. 23:25.

Dishwasher: (1) The Holy Spirit; (2) Holy Spirit evangelist (cleaning hearts).
Also see *Dish*.
(1) Ps. 51:10-12; (2) Matt. 10:8; Luke 4:18-19.

Distance: (1) Time; (2) Old; (3) Physically separated; (4) Trust issue (someone standing at a distance).
Also see *Horizon*.
(1) Acts 2:39; (2) Josh. 9:13; (3) Gal. 2:12; Jude 1:19; (4) 1 Sam. 26:13-25.

Distant: (1) Shutting off from someone; (2) Feeling unworthy; (3) Fearful; (4) Unsociable.
Also see *Horizon*.
(1) Luke 17:12; 23:49; (2) Luke 18:13; (3) Rev. 18:10, 15; (4) Prov. 18:24a.

Distributor (Auto): (1) Heart.
(1) Matt. 15:18-19.

Ditch: (1) Enemy hindrance; (2) Trap; (3) Whore (deep ditch); (4) Hell; (5) Place of refuse; (6) Human-made watercourse; (7) Depression.
(1-2) Ps. 7:15; 57:6; Isa. 42:22; (3) Prov. 23:27; (4) Matt. 15:14; (5) Job 9:31; (6) 2 Kings 3:16-17; Isa. 22:11; (7) 1 Sam. 28:20-21.

Dividing: (1) Separating: (2) Separating between soul and spirit; (3) Between truth and lies; (4) Between believer and unbeliever; (5) Between husband and wife (divorce); (6) Between family members; (7) About to fall over.
(1-2) Heb. 4:12; (3) 2 Tim. 4:4; Tit. 1:14; (4) Matt. 25:32-33; 2 Cor. 6:14; (5) Matt. 5:32; (6) Matt. 10:34-35; (7) Matt. 12:25.

Diving: (1) Boldly stepping out in faith (confidence in the Spirit); (2) Lack of support; (3) Hiding; (4) Descending spiritually; (5) Launching into the deep things of God. Also see *Descending, Down*, and *Falling.*
(1) Acts 4:29-31 ("confidently diving in"); (2) Judg. 15:20b; (3) As in "diving for cover"; (4) Ps. 107:12; (5) Ezek. 47:5.

Diving Instructor (Scuba): (1) Teacher who takes people deeper in the Spirit.
(1) 2 Kings 2:8; John 14:26.

Divorce: (1) Separation; (2) Hard-heartedness; (3) Disagreement; (4) Severance at workplace; (5) Adultery; (6) Actual divorce.
(1) Matt. 19:5-6; (2) Matt. 19:8; (3) Deut. 24:1; Amos 3:3; (4) Exod. 9:28b; Luke 16:2; (5) Matt. 5:32; 19:9.

Dizzy: (1) Busy; (2) Confusion; (3) Under the anointing (drunk in the Spirit); (4) Warning of intoxication with drugs or alcohol.
(1) Matt. 6:28; (2) Job 12:25; Ps. 70:2; (3) 2 Chron. 5:14; Jer. 23:9; (4) Job 12:25; 1 Cor. 5:11.

Dock: See *Airport* and *Railway Station.*

Doctor: (1) Jesus; (2) Authority; (3) Holy Spirit balm; (4) Sick; (5) Possible sin; (6) Need to seek God for healing; (7) Need of medication.
(1) Mal. 4:2; Mark 5:26; (2) Acts 5:34; (3) Jer. 8:22; James 5:14-16; (4) Matt. 9:12; Luke 5:31; (5) Mark 2:17; (6) 2 Chron. 16:12; James 5:14-16; (7) Jer. 8:22.

Dog: (1) Unbeliever/fool; (2) An attitude that rejects God's authority; (3) Symbolizes the world; (4) The flesh; (5) Someone who turns on you; (6) Turning on you with their mouths; (7) Turning back to old ways (self-willed, walking in flesh, despising authority); (8) Deceitful doers (under the table); (9) Those who tear apart with their mouth; (10) Stronghold; (11) Comforting friend; (12) Despised or insignificant; (13) Watchman (good or bad); (14) Lazy; (15) Not dealing with an issue (sleeping dog); (16) Religious spirit (blue heeler); (17) Liar; (18) Vicious (junk yard dog); (19) Spirit of condemnation (big vicious dog that attacks another dog [the flesh]); (20) Demon (evil spirit); (21) Demon of lust; (22) Depression (big dog); (23) Fear of discovery (hound/terrier on your trail).
Also see *Bulldog, Mascot, Pet*, and *Puppy.*
(1) Deut. 23:18; Prov. 26:11 (cf. Ps. 14:1); Matt. 16:26-27; Rev. 22:15; (2) Ps. 22:16; (3) Matt. 7:6a; 15:26; (4) Isa. 56:11 (appetite is a mark of the flesh); Phil. 3:2 (AMP); (5) Prov. 26:17; Matt. 7:6; (6) Ps. 59:6-7; Phil. 3:2; (7) 2 Pet. 2:10, 22; (8) Mark 7:27-28; Luke 16:21; (9) Exod. 11:7; Jer. 15:3; Matt. 7:6; (10) Luke 16:21; (11) As in "A dog is man's best friend"; (12) 1 Sam. 17:43; 24:14; 2 Sam. 9:8; (13) Isa. 56:10-11; (14) "The quick brown fox... "; (15) Isa. 56:10; (16) Ps. 22:16; (Gen. 3:15; John 11:47-48,53); Phil 3:2; (17) Rev. 22:15; (18) Ps. 22:16; Jer. 15:3; (19) John 3:19; Rom. 5:16; 8:1; (20) Ps. 22:20; Phil. 3:2; (21) Isa. 56:11; (22) Isa. 56:10; (23) 1 Sam. 24:14.

Doggy Lodge (Kennels): (1) Live-in rehabilitation center.
(1) 2 Sam. 9:4-5,8.

Dog Poop: (1) Offense; (2) Taking on an offense (stepping in dog poop).
(1) Zeph. 1:17 (KJV); (2) Ps. 119:165 (KJV).

Dog Wash: (1) Rehabilitation ministry; (2) Ministry to the destitute or despised; (3) Secular rehabilitation.
(1) 2 Sam. 9:6-8; (2) 1 Sam. 17:43; 24:14; Luke 7:39; James 2:1-5; (3) Gen. 12:10.

Doll: (1) Woman's past childhood issues/memory; (2) Grooming for motherhood; (3) Childhood desire.
Also see *Mannequin* and *Toys*.
(1) 1 Cor. 13:11; Phil. 3:13; (2) Ruth 4:16; (3) Luke 2:49.

Dollar: See *Money*.

Dolphin: (1) Teacher; (2) Minor prophet; also see *Whale*.
(1) Job 12:7-8; 35:11; By virtue of the intelligence assigned to dolphins.

Domed Roof: (1) Religious stronghold (highly resistant mindset); (2) Church under law (mosque-type structure).
Also see *Archway* and *Circle*.
(1) Matt. 23:25, 27; (2) Matt. 23:23; Rom. 6:14-15; Gal. 3:23; 5:18.

Dominoes: (1) Spiritual momentum; (2) Others falling; (3) Sensitive balance; (4) Interconnectedness; (5) Repercussions; (6) Shock wave.
Also see *Cards* and *Falling*.
(1-6) 1 Sam. 14:15-16,20.

Donkey: (1) Humility; (2) Faithful burden-bearer; (3) Servant; (4) Judge (white donkey); (5) Hostile or stubborn person; (6) Determined individual or stubborn; (7) Unbeliever; (8) Needing guidance; (9) Without understanding; (10) Dishonorable person (burying a donkey).
(1) Zech. 9:9; Matt. 21:5; (2) Gen. 42:26; 49:14; Num. 22:30; Isa. 1:3; (3) Gen. 42:26; Exod. 23:5; (4) Judg. 5:10; (5) Gen. 16:12; (6) Prov. 26:3; Jer. 2:24; (7) Deut. 22:10; 2 Cor. 6:14; Job 1:14; (8) Prov. 26:3; (9) Ps. 32:9; (10) Jer. 22:19.

Donut(s): (1) Sweet words without heart (false promises); (2) Spiritual meal.
Also see *Circle* and *Wheel*.
(1) Prov. 23:1-3, 7-8; Isa. 29:13; Matt. 15:8; (2) Ezek. 1:16.

Door: (1) Christ; (2) Opportunity; (3) Mouth; (4) Entrance; (5) Faith; (6) Heart; (7) The unstoppable work of God; (8) Imposition (door pushed in); (9) Going through transition; (10) Temptation (door ajar or at the door); (11) Destruction (broad door); (12) Gateway into the spirit realm (arched doorway); (13) Decision (several doors to choose from); (14) Violence (bullet holes in door); (15) Witnessing (going door to door); (16) Needing the anointing (squeaky door); (17) Rape (door kicked in).
Also see *Back Door*, *Front Door*, *Key*, *Next Door*, and *Sliding Door*.

(1) Gen. 6:16; John 10:7; (2) Col. 4:3; (3) Ps. 141:3; Col. 4:3; (4) Col. 4:3; (5) Acts 14:27; (6) Rev. 3:20; (7) Rev. 3:7-8; (8) Ps. 109:22; (9) Judg. 11:16; Ps. 23:4; (10) Gen. 4:7; (11) Matt. 7:13; (12) See *Circle*; (13) Josh. 24:15; (14) Ezek. 8:7-9; (15) Rev. 3:20; (16) Prov. 26:14; Matt. 25:8-12; (17) Gen. 19:9.

Doorbell: (1) Call to prayer and communion with Christ; (2) Loss of first love; (3) Calling; (4) Opportunity (hearing a bell); (5) Arrival (you ringing a bell); (6) Looking for opportunities (you ringing a bell); (7) Anticipation or expectation.
Also see *Calling* and *Knocking*.
(1) Rev. 3:20; (2) Matt. 7:21-23; Rev. 3:20; (3) Matt. 20:16 (KJV); 22:14; (4) Luke 11:9-13; Acts 14:27; 1 Cor. 16:9; 2 Cor. 2:12; (5) Acts 12:13; (6) 1 Cor. 16:9; Col. 4:3; (7) Matt. 24:33.

Doorpost (Threshold): (1) The cross; (2) Love slave.
(1) Exod. 12:6-7; (2) Exod. 21:6.

Door within a door: (1) A mouth within a mouth (someone speaking for another); (2) An opportunity within an opportunity; (3) Subculture; (4) Voice in a voice.
(1) Prov. 27:2; Isa. 28:11; John 5:43; 14:26; 18:34; Acts 8:34; (2) Neh. 7:3; Esther 2:21; Prov. 8:3, 34; (3) Job 38:17; Acts 12:13,16 (door in a gate); (4) Matt. 10:20.

Dove: (1) Holy Spirit; (2) Innocent; (3) Poverty or poor; (4) See *Jonah* in Name and Place Dictionary.
Also see *Bird(s)*.
(1) Matt. 3:10; (2) Matt. 10:16; (3) Lev. 12:8.

Down: (1) Fallen; (2) Rest; (3) Hell; (4) Spiritual decline; (5) Humbled; (6) Worship or homage (bow down); (7) Sleep (lay down); (8) Without hope or depressed (downcast or looking down); (9) Disapproval or unsuccessful.
Also see *Descend, Dropping, Laying Down, Up*, and *Upright*.
(1) Ps. 20:8; (2) Ps. 23:2; (3) Ps. 55:15; Prov. 5:5; (4) Isa. 59:14; Jer. 8:4; Luke 8:13; 2 Thess. 2:3; (5) Job 22:29; Isa. 2:11; 10:33b; Jer. 13:18; Luke 18:14; (6) Gen 24:26,48; 43:28; Job 1:20; (7) Gen. 28:11; Ps. 3:5; 4:8; (8) Ps. 42:5,11; 43:5; (9) As in "thumbs down."

Download: (1) Revelation.
(1) Matt. 16:17; James 1:17.

Down Payment: (1) Being Spirit-filled; (2) Guarantee of what was promised.
(1-2) 2 Cor. 1:22; 5:5.

Drag/ging: (1) Evangelism (net); (2) Subjection and capture; (3) Failure and defeat; (4) Idolatry; (5) Holding back.
(1) John 21:8; (2) Gen. 37:28; (3) 2 Kings 19:28; Isa. 37:29; Ezek. 29:4; 38:4; Amos 4:2; (4) Hab. 1:15-16; (5) As in "Dragging your feet."

Dragon: (1) The devil; (2) China (foreign god); (3) Principalities (evil).

(1) Rev. 12:3-5, 7, 9, 13, 16-17; 13:2-4; 16:13; 20:2; (2) 1 Cor. 10:19-20; (3) Eph. 6:12; Rev. 12:7.

Dragonfly: (1) Principality; (2) Water spirit; (3) Helicopter gunship.
(1) Rev. 9:9-10; (2) Ezek. 32:2b; (3) Rev. 9:9-10.

Drag Queen: (1) Façade, human-run church; (2) Church trying to be attractive to people (detestable Bride of Christ).
(1) Rev. 2:14-15; (2) Jer. 7:18; Rev. 3:17.

Drain: (1) Lifeless soakage pit; (2) Detoxing; (3) Loss (down the drain); (4) Feeling low or negative (looking down the drain).
Also see *Gutter(s)*, *Overflow*, *Pipe*, and *Washbasin*.
(1) 2 Tim. 3:7; (2) Ps. 107:23; (3) Luke 15:8; Phil. 3:8; (4) Jon. 2:3-6.

Drawer: See *Cupboard*.

Dreadlocks: (1) Ungodliness (unclean); (2) Man or woman of the flesh; (3) Subcultural association; (4) Spiritually bound; (5) Unruly spirit (spiritually unkept).
(1) Dan. 4:33; (2) Gen. 25:25; (3) 1 Pet. 3:3; (4) Mark 5:2-5, 15; (5) Prov. 25:28.

Dregs: (1) The bottom of the cup of God's fury.
(1) Isa. 51:17,22.

Dress: See *Clothes*.

Dressing: (1) Putting on Christ; (2) Preparation; (3) New anointing.
(1) Rom. 13:14; Gal. 3:27; (2) Matt. 22:11-12; Eph. 6:11; (3) Lev. 16:32, 21:10; 2 Kings 2:13.

Dressing Gown: (1) Relaxed; (2) Just cleansed (showered); (3) Old.
Also see *Pajamas*.
(1) Jer. 43:12b; (2) Lev. 16:4, 24; (3) Cultural perception.

Dressing Room: (1) Heart; (2) Preparation for the King; (3) Preparation for self-glory.
(1) Rom. 13:14; Gal. 3:27; 1 Pet. 3:3-4; (2) Matt. 3:3; (3) 1 Pet. 3:3-4; 1 Tim. 2:9.

Dribbling/Drooling: (1) Desire for something; (2) Uncontrolled emotion; (3) Anticipation; (4) Madness.
(1) 2 Sam. 23:15; (2) 1 Sam. 1:10-13; (3) Consider Pavlov's dog; (4) 1 Sam. 21:13.

Dried Fruit: (1) Fruit that remains; (2) Promise not yet appropriated.
(1) John 15:16; (2) Num. 13:31-32ff.

Drinking: (1) Refreshing; (2) Drunkenness; (3) Partaking of the Spirit; (4) Uncovering the fleshly self (laying down the spiritual self); (5) Merriment; (6) Bitterness; (7) Revelry (excess); (8) Victory; (9) Revival; (10) Procrastination; (11) Satisfaction (often enjoying the fruit of one's labor); (12) Deception; (13) Adultery (drinking from another's cup); (14) Laying down one's life (living sacrifice); (15) A poured-out soul; (16) Prosperity; (17) Fellowship/alignment with another; (18) Disobedience; (19) Faith; (20) Arrogance; (21) Peace; (22) Desperation; (23) Pleasure; (24) The wrath of God; (25) Tears; (26) Brook; (27) Violence; (28) Partaking; (29) Wisdom; (30) Undeserved grace; (31) Receiving; (32) Heavy heart; (33) Perverted judgment; (34) Anesthetic; (35) Self-glory; (36) Non-satisfying; (37) Stupor/blindness/delusion; (38) Spiritual thirst; (39) Offerings; (40) Judgment; (41) Fouled water; (42) Defilement; (43) Hardened heart (lacking compassion); (44) Ease; (45) Redemption; (46) Celebration; (47) Provision; (48) Blood of New Testament; (49) Poison; (50) Old wine; (51) New wine; (52) Ease; (53) God's will; (54) Holy Spirit; (55) Spiritual Union; (56) Stumbling block; (57) Jesus Christ; (58) Fornication.

Also see *Brook*, *Cup*, and *Drinking Fountain*.

(1) Gen. 21:19; 25:34; Ruth 2:9; 2 Sam. 16:2; 1 Kings 19:6, 8; Matt. 10:42; (2) Gen. 9:21; 1 Kings 16:9; (3) John 4:14; (4) Gen. 9:21; 2 Sam. 12:3; Ps. 51:10; (5) Gen. 43:34; Judg. 19:21-22; 1 Kings 18:41-42; Eccles. 8:15; 9:7; (6) Exod. 15:23-24; Num. 5:24; Isa. 24:9; Jer. 8:14; 9:15; 23:15; Hos. 4:18; Matt. 27:34, 48; (7) Exod. 32:6; 1 Sam. 30:16; Isa. 5:11; Eph. 5:18; (8) Num. 23:24; Ezek. 25:4; (9) Judg. 15:19; 1 Sam. 11:13; Isa. 43:20; (10) Judg. 19:4,6; (11) Ruth 3:3; 1 Sam. 1:9; Eccles. 2:24; 3:13; 5:18; (12) 2 Sam. 11:13; Prov. 20:1; 23:7; Isa. 22:13 (self-deception); Hab. 2:15; (13) 2 Sam. 12:3; Prov. 5:15; Hos. 2:5; (14) 2 Sam. 23:15-17; Matt. 20:22-23; 26:42; Mark 10:38-39; (15) 1 Sam. 1:15; (16) 1 Kings 4:20-21; (17) 1 Kings 13:8; Job 1:4,13; Mark 2:16; Luke 5:30; 13:26; 1 Cor. 10:21; 11:25-29; (18) 1 Kings 13:19-22; (19) 1 Kings 17:10; (20) 1 Kings 20:12; Dan. 5:1-3; (21) 2 Kings 6:22-23; Isa. 36:16; (22) 2 Kings 18:27; (23) Esther 1:8; Joel 3:3; (24) Job 21:20; Ps. 75:8; Isa. 51:17,22; 63:6; Jer. 25:15; Rev. 14:8,10; 18:3; (25) Ps. 80:5; 102:9; (26) 1 Kings 17:4, 6; Ps. 110:7; (27) Prov. 4:17; (28) Prov. 5:15; Song 5:1; Jer. 2:18; 16:8; Ezek. 23:32-34; (29) Prov. 9:1-5; Matt. 11:18-19; (30) Prov. 25:21-22; Rom. 12:20; (31) Prov. 26:6; (32) Prov. 31:6; (33) Prov. 31:4-5; (34) Prov. 31:7; Mark 15:23; (35) Isa. 5:22; 37:25; Zech. 7:6; (36) Isa. 29:8; Amos 4:8; Hag. 1:6; (37) Isa. 29:9-10; 56:12; Jer. 51:57; Joel 1:5; (38) Isa. 32:6; John 7:37; (39) Jer. 7:18; 32:29; 44:17-19; (40) Jer. 25:17,26-29; 46:10, 49:12; Ezek. 4:10-11; 23:32-34; 31:14; (41) Ezek. 34:18-19; (42) Dan. 1:8; (43) Amos 4:1; 6:6; (44) Matt. 24:49; (45) Matt. 26:27; (46) Matt. 26:29; Mark 14:25; Luke 22:18; (47) Matt. 6:25; Mark 9:41; (48) Mark 14:23-24; (49) Mark 16:18; (50) Luke 5:39; (51) John 2:10; (52) Luke 12:19,45; 17:8,27-28; (53) Luke 22:42; John 18:11; (54) John 4:14; 1 Cor. 12:13; (55) John 6:53-56; (56) Rom. 14:21; (57) 1 Cor. 10:4; (58) Rev. 18:3.

Drinking Fountain: (1) Flow of the Holy Spirit; (2) Church or ministry; (3) Everlasting life; (4) A move of God; (5) Fulfillment in God.

Also see *Drinking.*

(1-2) John 7:37-39; (3) John 4:14; Rev. 21:6; 22:1, 17; (4) John 4:39-42 (cf. context); (5) John 4:32-34 (cf. context).

Dripping Tap: (1) Contentious wife; (2) Contentious church that is quenching the Spirit.

(1) Prov. 19:13; 27:15; (2) 1 Thess. 5:19.

Driver: (1) If you are driving, you are steering your own destiny; (2) If you are in the passenger seat and someone unknown is driving, it means God is driving; (3) If the driver is corrupt, it means you are probably being manipulated/controlled; (4) If someone you know is driving a bus, it means they will head up a ministry; (5) Going in the wrong direction means wrong spirit.

(1-2) John 21:18; (3) 2 Tim. 3:5-6; (4) 2 Sam. 5:2; (5) Ps. 51:10 (KJV).

Drive-Through: (1) Quick fix mentality.

(1) Matt. 14:15.

Driveway: (1) Entry; (2) Exit; (3) Awaiting ministry; (4) Parked ministry.

(1-2) Deut. 28:6; Ps. 121:8; (3-4) 1 Kings 3:7; Isa. 49:2b.

Drop/ping: (1) Heaven's provision; (2) Word of God (dew); (3) Teaching (rain); (4) Overflow; (5) Rain; (6) Enticement (lips); (7) Contentious wife/church; (8) Collapse; (9) A small and insignificant thing; (10) To fall away; (11) To let God's charge or promises go; (12) To let go of something.

Also see *Descend.*

(1) Judg. 5:4; Ps. 65:11; 68:8-9; Luke 22:44; (2) Ezek. 20:46; 21:2; Song. 5:2; (3) Deut. 32:2; (4) 1 Sam. 14:26; Song. 5:5; Joel 3:18; (5) 2 Sam. 21:10; Job 36:27-28; Ps. 65:11-12; 68:8-9; Prov. 3:20; (6) Prov. 5:3; (7) Prov. 19:13; 27:15; (8) Eccles. 10:18; (9) Isa. 40:15; (10) 1 Pet. 1:24-25; 2 Pet. 3:17; (11) Heb. 4:11; (12) Matt. 26:39; Acts 27:32.

Drought: (1) Tribulation and testing; (2) The grave; (3) Judgment; (4) Financial struggles; (5) Lacking the love of God; (6) Spiritual or natural famine; (7) Lack of the Spirit of God; (8) Lack of the Word of God.

Also see *Rain—No Rain.*

(1) Gen. 31:40; Deut. 8:15; Isa. 58:11; Jer. 2:6; 17:8; Hos. 13:5; (2) Job 24:19; (3) 1 Kings 17:1; Ps. 32:4; Jer. 50:38; Hag. 1:11; (4) 2 Cor. 8:9, 14; (5) Eph. 3:17-19; Rev. 2:4; (6) Amos 8:11; (7) Ezek. 37:5-6, 9-10; (8) Amos 8:11.

Drowning: (1) Judgment; (2) Overcome by the words of one's enemies; (3) Beyond one's depth; (4) Catastrophe; (5) In need of salvation.

Also see *Underwater.*

(1) Gen. 6:17; Jon. 2:3, 5; (2) Ps. 42:7, 10; (3) Matt. 14:30-31; (4) Isa. 43:2; (5) Isa. 59:19b.

Drug Dealer: (1) Tempter; (2) The devil; (3) The world (drug dealer's wife); (4) Profiteer; (5) Manipulation and control; (6) Witchcraft; (7) Dependence; (8) Familiar spirits.

Also see *Drug Use*.

(1-2) Matt. 4:1; John 10:10; (3) Luke 4:5-6; Rev. 12:9; (5) Acts 13:8-10; (8) 2 Kings 21:6.

Drug Store: See *Chemist Shop*.

Drug Use: (1) Rebellion; (2) Defiance of authority; (3) Unmanageable; (4) Offense; (5) Speaks of the flesh; (6) Looking for a quick fix; (7) Looking for instant pleasure/ gratification; (8) Deceived; (9) Addiction; (10) Counterfeit fulfillment; (11) Searching for an anesthetic; (12) Actual drug use; (13) Manipulation; (14) Witchcraft; (15) Stronghold; (16) Sickness; (17) Dependence; (18) Medication.

Also see *Amphetamines*, *Needle*, *Pills*, and *Speed (Drug)*.

(1-4) Consider that in Rev. 9:21 the word *sorceries,* elsewhere translated "witchcraft," is the Greek word *pharmakeia*, from which we get the word *pharmacy*, and put this into 1 Sam. 15:23; (5) Gal. 5:19-21; 2 Pet. 2:10; (6-7) 2 Tim. 3:1-4; (8) 2 Tim. 3:6-7; (10) Eph. 5:18.

Drum: (1) Spiritual warfare.

Also see *Beat*, *Drummer*, *Music*, and *Worship*.

(1) 2 Chron. 20:21-22; 2 Cor. 10:4.

Drummer: (1) God (as the One who is in charge of the timing); (2) Leader (pulse/ heartbeat of the ministry).

Also see *Beat*, *Drum*, *Music*, and *Worship*.

(1) Gal. 4:4; Eph. 1:10; (2) John 13:25.

Drunk: (1) Spirit-filled; (2) Issue with alcohol; (3) Under the influence of religion; (4) Power trip; (5) Using the tongue against brothers in the Lord; (6) Disgraced; (7) Guaranteed woe, sorrow, contentions, complaints; (8) Intoxicated with the world; (9) Love; (10) Overcome with something.

See *Alcohol* and *Alcoholic*.

(1) Eph. 5:18; Acts 2:4, 15; 1 Cor. 12:13; (2) Eph. 5:18; (3) Rev. 17:1-2; (4) As in "drunk with power"; (5) Jer. 46:10; (6) Gen. 9:31; Lam. 4:21; (7) Prov. 23:29-35; (8) Rev. 17:2; (9) Song 1:2; Hosea 3:1; (10) Deut. 32:42; Isa. 49:26; Rev. 17:2.

Dry: (1) Without the Spirit (dead); (2) Thirsting for God; (3) Barren place; (4) Wilderness; (5) Desert; (6) Valley.

(1) Ezek. 37:2, 9-10; (2) Ps. 42:1; (3) Job 15:34; (4) Isa. 50:2; Jer. 51:43; Ezek. 19:13; (5) Jer. 50:12; (6) Ezek. 37:1-2.

Duck (noun): (1) Unclean spirit; (2) Fleshly spirit being; (3) Migrating (in flight); (4) Unity (flying in formation); (5) Vulnerable (out of water); (6) Resisting the Spirit (water off a duck's back); (7) Easy target.

Also see *Birds* and *Mud*.

(1) Ps. 40:2; Isa. 57:20; ducks are muddy bottom-feeders with webbed feet; (2) 2 Kings 5:20,25-26; (3) Rev. 12:14; (4) Ps. 133:1; (5) As in "sitting duck"; (6) Acts 7:51; (7) As in "sitting duck."

Duck (verb): (1) Humble; (2) Hiding.

Also see *Bowing*.

(1) Isa. 2:11; (2) As in "ducking for cover."

Dugong: (1) Worldly idol (sea cow).

Also see *Walrus*.

(1) Exod. 32:24; 1 Kings 12:28.

Dumb: (1) Silence because of confidence in God; (2) No reproof; (3) Ignorance; (4) Idolatry; (5) Influence of evil spirit (deaf and dumb); (6) The product of doubting God's Word; (7) Unbelief.

Also see *Deaf* and *Mute*.

(1) Ps. 39:9 (NKJV); Isa. 53:7; (2) Ps. 38:13-14; (3) Isa. 56:10; (4) Hab. 2:18-19; 1 Cor. 12:2; (5) Matt. 9:32-33, 12:22; Mark 9:17-18, 25-26; (6) Luke 18:21; (7) As in "no confession of faith."

Dumb Waiter: (1) The Holy Spirit.

(1) John 16:13 (KJV).

Dune Buggy: (1) Powerful itinerant ministry.

(1) Luke 1:80.

Dung: (1) Works of the flesh that perish; (2) Offense; (3) Refuse, waste, garbage; (4) Fertilizer; (5) Dealing with, precedes the refreshing of the Holy Spirit.

Also see *Feces*, *Rubbish*, and *Urination*.

(1) Job 20:7; Ps. 83:10; 113:7; Jer. 8:2; Ezek. 4:12; Zeph. 1:17; Phil. 3:4-8; (2) Matt. 16:23; Luke 14:23; Rom. 5:17; (3) 1 Kings 14:10; 2 Kings 9:37; 18:27; Lam. 4:5; Phil. 3:8; (4) Jer. 16:4; 25:33; Matt. 13:8; (5) Neh. 3:14-15.

Dusk: (1) End times; (2) Running out of time.

(1) Luke 24:29; (2) Matt. 20:6; John 11:9.

Dust: (1) Human; (2) Humbled; (3) Numerous; (4) Under a cloud of controversy; (5) Under the feet; (6) Death; (7) Beginning and end of mortal humanity; (8) Dishonored; (9) Contempt or disapproval (throwing dust into air or dusting feet off).

Also see *Dust Storm* and *Earth*.

(1) Gen. 2:7; (2) Isa. 2:10-11; 47:1; (3) Gen. 13:16; 28:14; Num. 23:10; 2 Chron. 1:9; (4-5) Nah. 1:3; (6) Isa. 26:19; (7) Gen. 3:19; (8) Ps. 7:5; (9) 2 Sam. 16:13; Acts 22:23.

Dust Storm: (1) A declaration warning of pending judgment; (2) Earthly witness against a city or nation; (3) A call to come under the blood; (4) If no repentance, then the strength of the city or nation will be struck down; (5) A sign preceding deliverance and revival.

Also see *Dust* and *Whirlwind.*

(1) Nah. 1:3 (cf. Exod. 8:16; Matt. 10:14); (2) Exod. 8:16; Matt. 10:14 (cf. Deut. 4:26; 19:15); (3-4) Exod. 12:7,12-13 (cf. Gen. 49:3; Deut. 21:17; Ps. 78:51); (5) Exod. 12:31.

E

Eagle: (1) Spiritual self; (2) Prophet (seer); (3) God; (4) Strength; (5) Israel; (6) Swift; (7) Heavenly resting place (nest); (8) Lifted by the Spirit (not by effort); (9) Unsettled home/church (Time to move on); (10) Instrument of judgment; (11) Angel (white eagle); (12) Warring angel; (13) Person waiting on God; (14) Mystic.

(1) Isa. 40:31; Matt. 24:28; (2) Exod. 19:4; 1 Sam. 9:9; (3) Exod. 19:4; Deut. 32:11-12; the Book of John depicts Jesus as Divine (i.e., the Eagle); (4) Ps. 103:5; Isa. 40:31; (5) Rev. 12:14; (6) Deut. 28:49; 2 Sam. 1:23; Job 9:26; Jer. 4:13; Lam. 4:19; Hab. 1:8; (7) Job 39:27; Prov. 23:5; Jer. 49:16; Obad. 1:4; (8) Prov. 30:19; (9) Deut. 32:11-12; (10) Prov. 30:17; Ezek. 17:3-20; (11) Luke 17:37;
John 20:12; (12) Dan. 10:6,13; (13-14) Isa. 40:31.

Ear: (1) Heart; (2) Physical ear; (3) Turned to fables; (4) Hearing God's voice; (5) Eager to hear spiritually (cleaning ears).

Also see *Deaf, Hearing,* and *Itching.*

(1) Matt. 10:27; 11:15; 13:9,15,43; Luke 1:44; 9:44; Rev. 2:7,11,17,29; 3:6,13,22; (2) Luke 22:50-51; Acts 7:51, 57; 11:22; 28:27; (3) 2 Tim. 4:4; (4) John 10:3; (5) Isa. 50:4; Matt. 11:15.

Early: (1) Quickly; (2) Eager; (3) Measure of your desire for God; (4) Time of revelation; (5) Beginning; (6) Straight away or soon; (7) Diligently.

(1) Hos. 5:15b; (2-3) Ps. 63:1; Prov. 8:17; 24:22; Mark 16:2; Luke 21:38; John 8:2; (4) Prov. 8:17; Luke 24:1-6 (5) Matt. 20:1; Mark 16:9; (6) Ps. 46:5; 78:34; 90:14; 101:8; (7) Ps. 63:1 (the word *early* [Hebrew: *shackar*] also means "diligently").

Earring(s): (1) Hearing; (2) Having ears (obedience) for false gods; (3) Love slave (ears for God); (4) Spiritual sensitivity (feathered earring); (5) Hearing heavenly glory (flower earring); (6) Hearing the voice of God (gold earring); (7) Hearing the words of redemption (silver earring); (8) Hearing a false gospel (brass/bronze earring).

Also see *Adorn, Awl,* and *Hearing.*

(1) Deut. 5:1; Mark 4:9; (2) Gen. 35:2-4; (3) Exod. 21:1-6; (4) Matt. 11:15; (5) Rev. 19:1; (6) Exod. 21:5-6; Rev. 9:13; (7) Exod. 21:5-6; Matt. 26:15; (8) Exod. 21:5-6; 1 Kings 14:26-27.

Earth: (1) The non-faith realm; (2) Sight realm; (3) The natural non-spiritual realm; (4) Humanity; (5) God's footstool; (6) Land of our pilgrimage; (7) Physical domain.
Also see *Earthly, Four, Heaven, Sea,* and *Soil.*
(1) 1 Cor. 2:14; (2) Matt. 6:10; (3) 1 Cor. 15:46-47; (4) 2 Cor. 4:7; (5) Acts 7:49; (6) Heb. 11:13; (7) Matt. 6:10.

Earthly: (1) Human/flesh; (2) Worldly; (3) Without faith; (4) Secular; (5) Creation; (6) Worldly wisdom.
Also see *Earth, Orange,* and *Red.*
(1) Gen. 2:7; 1 Cor. 15:47; 2 Cor. 4:7; 5:1; (2) John 3:12, 31; Col. 3:2; (3) John 3:12; Phil. 3:19; Col. 3:2; (4) Phil. 3:19; (5) Matt. 13:35; Heb. 1:10; (6) James 3:15.

Earthmovers: (1) Leadership working in the flesh.
Also see *Digging.*
(1) 1 Cor. 15:47.

Earthquake: (1) Power of God; (2) Shaking; (3) Revival or eve of revival; (4) Voice of God; (5) Judgment; (6) Shock; (7) Opened heart(s); (8) Visitation by God.
(1) 1 Kings 19:11-12; (2-3) Acts 4:31; 16:26-34; 17:6; (4) Ps. 29:8; (5) Rev. 6:12; 8:5; 11:13,19; (6) 1 Kings 19:11-12; (7) Matt. 27:54; Acts 16:26; (8) Isa. 29:6; Zech. 14:3-5; Matt. 28:2; Luke 21:11; Rev. 16:18.

East: (1) Place of God's glory; (2) Sun (Son) rising; (3) Expectancy; (4) Waiting on God; (5) Praise and worship; (6) Looking to God; (7) Receiving a gift/message from someone noble from the east means it is God-given; (8) Receiving a gift from an unreliable source from the east may mean it is demonic (Eastern religion); (9) Consider aspects in your own environment relating to east.
Also see *West* and *Sun.*
(1-2) Ezek. 43:1-2; (3) The sun rises in the east; Mal. 4:1-2; (4) Jon. 4:5; (5) Num. 2:3 (*Judah* means "praise").

Eating: (1) Reading or studying the Word (assimilating the Word); (2) Communing; (3) Agreement with (covenant); (4) Friendship; (5) Given to fleshly appetites; (6) The best the world has to offer without God; (7) Receiving; (8) Revelation; (9) Devouring; (10) Taking; (11) Consuming.
Also see *Biting, Cannibals, Eating (Satisfied),* and *Eating (Not Satisfied).*
(1) Isa. 55:1,10-11; Jer. 15:16; Heb. 5:12-15; (2) Job 42:11; (3) Song 4:16; (4) Ps. 41:9; (5) Prov. 23:2; (6) Eccles. 2:24; 3:13; 8:15; (8) Matt. 16:15-17; (9) 1 Pet. 5:8; (10-11) Gen. 41:20,27-30.

Eating (Satisfied): All of these will be satisfied: (1) Tithers; (2) The meek; (3) The righteous; (4) The repentant.
(1) Deut. 14:28-29; (2) Ps. 22:26; (3) Prov. 13:25; (4) Joel 2:12,26.

Eating (Not Satisfied): Causes of not being satisfied: (1) Walking contrary to God; (2) Wicked; (3) Not listening to God; (4) Sin; (5) Neglecting God's house.

(1) Lev. 26:26; (2) Prov. 13:25; Isa. 9:18-20; (3) Isa. 55:2-3; (4) Mic. 6:14; (5) Hag. 1:4,6.

Echo: (1) Returning message; (2) Relayed message; (3) Bouncing words (hardened hearts); (4) Having your deeds/words return to you; (5) Not returning empty.
(1) Gen. 32:6; (2) Exod. 19:8; (3) Num. 13:26; (4) Ps. 7:16; (5) Isa. 55:11.

Ecstasy: (1) Speaking in tongues; (2) Bliss; (3) Revival; (4) Rapture; (5) Joy.
Also see *Drug Use.*
(1) 1 Sam. 10:4-6 (*prophesying* means literally "speaking in ecstasy"); (2) 2 Cor. 12:4; (3) Acts 2:4; (4) 1 Thess. 4:16-17; (5) John 16:24.

Edge: (1) Lip, border, shore; (2) Nervous (on edge).
(1) 1 Kings 7:23; Ezek. 43:13; Judg. 7:22; (2) Ps. 38:8; 42:5.

Effervescence: (1) New spiritual life.
Also see *Soda.*
(1) John 4:14; 7:38-39.

Egg(s): (1) Promise(s); (2) New beginnings; (3) Gift; (4) Schemes/plans; (5) Eggs without yolks speaks of promises without heart (i.e., empty promises); (6) Potential; (7) Fertility.
(1-3) Luke 11:12-13; 24:49; (4) Isa. 59:5.

Eggshells: (1) Sensitivity; (2) Fear of upset (walking on eggshells); (3) Proceed cautiously; (4) Vulnerable; (5) Empty promises.
Also see *Eggs*
(1-4) Job 39:14-15; (5) Prov. 23:7-8.

Egg Yolk/Yoke: (1) Promise; (2) The Holy Spirit; (3) Heart; (4) Life; (5) No egg yolk means no life or heart in a promise (empty promise).
(1-2) Luke 11:12-13; 24:49; (3-5) Job 6:6; Jer. 17:11 (KJV).

Egypt: (1) The world; (2) The unspiritual, materialistic system; (3) The place of slavery to Pharaoh (satan); (4) That kingdom ruled by philosophy and the physical senses; (5) Anti-God; (6) Superpower.
(1) Exod. 3:8; John 15:19; (Acts 7:34; Gal. 1:4); (2) Matt. 13:22; 16:26; 25:34; Mark 4:19; John 3:19; 8:23; Rom. 12:2; 2 Cor. 4:4; 2 Pet. 1:4; 1 John 2:16; (3) Gal. 4:3; (Exod. 6:5-6; Eph. 2:2-3); John 12:31; 14:30; 16:11,33; 17:15; 1 Cor. 2:12; 5:10; 1 John 4:4; (4) John 14:17, 19; Col. 2:8; (5) James 4:4; 1 John 2:15; (6) Ezek. 30:6.

Eiffel Tower: (1) The Cross; (2) Human achievement/pride; (3) France; (4) Jesus Christ; (5) Watchtower; (6) Prophetic company.
(1) As the world's most recognizable landmark. Likewise many of Israel's memorials point to the cross. Exod. 12:14 (Passover); Exod. 17:14 (victory over Amalek); Josh. 4:7 (crossing Jordan). (2) Gen. 11:4; (3) By association; (4) John 12:32; (5) Hab. 2:1; (6) "Eiffel": plateau of oaks.

Eight: (1) New beginnings; (2) Superabundant and satiating; (3) Abounding in strength; (4) To make fat or cover with fat or oil; (5) Worship; (6) Resurrection or regeneration; (7) Circumcision of the heart (cutting off the sins of the flesh); (8) Eternity (eight sideways is an eternal loop); (9) Metaphysical (on a plane above nature).
(1) Matt. 28:1; Eight marks the start of a new week; (2-4) These meanings come from the root of the Hebrew word for eight, *Shah'meyn*; (5) Ezek. 40:26, 31; (Seven steps led to the outer court [rest], eight steps led into the inner court [worship]); (6) Matt. 28:1,6 (first day of the week is the eighth day); 1 Pet. 3:20; 2 Pet. 2:5; (7) Gen. 17:12; Rom. 2:29; Col. 2:11; (8) Mark 10:30 (two worlds now and future); Matt. 28:1 (eighth day); Rev. 21:6 (alpha and omega); (9) Mark 16:2.

Eighteen: (1) 2 X 9 = 18; as such, 18 means: Judgment by the Word of God; or (2) Judgment by division (mutual destruction); or, (3) Fruitful association; alternatively 18 may mean: (4) 10 + 8 = 18; as such 18 means: Complete new beginning; or (5) Complete putting off of the old self.
(1) Judg. 3:12,14; 10:7-8; Luke 13:4-5; (2) Judg. 20:24-25, 42-44; (3) 2 Kings 22:3-10; (4-5) Luke 13:11-16 (v. 13, "made straight," i.e., upright in spirit cf. Ps. 51:10).

Electricity: (1) Power of God; (2) His Spirit witnessing with our spirits. Also see *Lightning*.
(1) Luke 8:46; (2) Rom. 8:16.

Elephant: (1) God Almighty; (2) Prominent person (Christ); (3) Powerful ministry; (4) High-profile ministry; (5) Large ministry; (6) Tough character; (7) Prophetic ministry; (8) Larger than life personality; (9) Insensitive (thick skinned); (10) Big issue; (11) A significant memory; (12) Great future (baby elephant); (13) Unwanted (white elephant); (14) Heavy-handed.
(1) Jer. 32:17; Rev. 11:17 (He is great and powerful as the largest land animal); (2) 1 Sam. 9:2b; (3) Acts 19:11; 1 John 4:4; (4) Luke 7:28; (5) John 6:10; (6) Exod. 11:3; Heb. 7:4; (7) Jer. 6:17; Ezek. 33:6; Amos 3:6-7; (elephants use their trunks as trumpets to sound alarm and have exceptional hearing and smell); (8) 1 Sam. 17:4; (11) Neh. 4:14.

Elephant Trunk: (1) Trumpet/voice; (2) Channel of the Spirit; (3) Arm of the Lord (strength).
(1) Rev. 4:1; (2) John 4:14; 7:38-39; (3) Isa. 51:9; 62:8.

Elevator: See *Lift*.

Eleven: (1) Disorder; (2) Disintegration; (3) Imperfection/incompleteness; (4) Open doors.
(1) Gen. 37:9; eleven stars: Joseph's dream marked disorder in Jacob's household; (2) Matt. 26:56; Acts 1:16-17,26; The eleven apostles speaks of disintegration of the twelve; (3) Deut. 1:2 (eleven-day journey from Horeb to Kadesh Barnea)—one more day would have carried them into divine government; the eleven sons of Jacob—"one is not" (Gen 42:32) speaks of incompleteness; (4) John 11:11,39.

Emaciated: (1) Something you are no longer feeding; (2) Losing its strength; (3) Anguish of soul; (4) Spiritually weak (lacking spiritual nourishment).
Also see *Skinny*.
(1) Job 19:20; (2) Ps. 102:5; (3) Lam. 4:7-8; (4) Lam. 4:9; Amos 8:11.

Embarrassment: (1) Shame/disgrace; (2) Nakedness (without God's glory); (3) People-conscious (fear of people); (4) Perceived failure.
(1) Gen. 9:22-23; 1 Sam. 20:34; 2 Sam. 19:5a; 2 Chron. 32:21; (2) Gen. 2:25; Exod. 32:25 (KJV); (3) Prov. 29:25; (4) Ps. 142:4

Embrace: (1) Taking to heart or opening one's heart; (2) Worship; (3) Love; (4) Showing affection; (5) False affection; (6) Taking teaching to heart; (7) Accept as your own.
(1) 1 Sam. 18:1; (2) Matt. 28:9; (3) 2 Kings 4:16; Song 2:6; 8:3; Acts 20:10; (4) Gen. 33:4; Prov. 5:20; Acts 20:1; (5) Gen. 29:13 (cf. Gen. 24:29-31); (6) Prov. 4:8; Heb. 11:13; (7) Gen. 48:10.

Emerald: (1) Mercy; (2) Praise.
Also see *Green*.
(1) Rev. 4:3; (2) Exod. 28:18 (KJV) (Some associate this stone with Reuben, others with Judah).

Employee: (1) Servant of God; (2) Worker in the harvest; (3) Bad employee causing division may mean demonic force or rebellious person; (4) Helper; (5) Actual employee.
(1) Rom. 1:1; 6:18,22; Phil. 1:1; 2 Tim. 2:24; (2) Col. 4:12; (3) Rom. 6:16; (5) Eph. 6:5-6; Col. 4:1; 1 Tim. 6:1; Tit. 2:9-10.

Empty: (1) Without the Spirit; (2) Without fruit.
(1) Matt. 12:44; Luke 1:53; (2) Mark 12:3; Luke 20:10-11.

Enemy: (1) satan; (2) Evil spirits in the heavenly realms; (3) Child of the devil; (4) The world; (5) The flesh.
(1) Matt. 13:39; 1 Pet. 5:8; (2) Eph. 6:12; (3) Acts 13:10; (4) 1 John 2:15-16; (5) Gal. 5:17.

Engaged: (1) Busy; (2) Unavailable; (3) Awaiting union; (4) Focused.
(1-3) Luke 10:40-42; (4) Mark 10:46-52.

Engine: (1) Heart; (2) Victorious new beginning (V8 engine); (3) Working in the flesh (V6 engine).
(1) Prov. 4:23; (2) 1 Cor. 15:54,57; 1 John 5:4; (3) Exod. 20:9.

Entering a Building via the Rear Entrance: (1) Not coming in via the system; (2) Secretly; (3) Keeping a low profile.
(1-3) John 7:10.

Entrapment: (1) Temptation; (2) Looking for legal ground to discredit; (3) Looking to catch in words.
(1) Matt. 4:3; (2) Matt. 19:3; (3) Matt. 22:15.

Envelope: (1) Communication; (2) Heart; (3) Person (vessel) carrying a message; (4) Consider color of envelope and stamp or title and address on envelope.
Also see *Colors*, *Letter*, *Mailbox*, *Name*, and *Postage Stamp*.
(1) 2 Cor. 3:1; 7:8; 10:9-10; (2) Prov. 3:3; Jer. 17:1; 2 Cor. 3:2-3; (3) 2 Sam. 18:20.

Eraser: (1) Starting again; (2) New beginning; (3) Cut off from God; (4) Redemption.
(1) Jon. 3:1; (2) John 21:15-17; (3) Deut. 9:14; (4) Isa. 43:25.

Escalator: See *Lift (Elevator)*.

Escape Pod: (1) Deliverance; (2) Salvation; (3) Rescue.
(1-3) Gen. 7:1; Acts 9:25; 2 Cor. 11:33.

Esky: See *Cooler/Cool Box*.

Evening: (1) Departure/absence of Christ; (2) Represents the time when Christ is in Heaven; (3) Close of the day (4) Time of reckoning.
(1) Matt. 27:57; Mark 14:17; (2) Matt. 14:15,23; Mark 1:32; 4:35; 6:47; 11:19; 13:35; 15:42-43; Luke 24:29; John 6:16; 20:19; (3) Matt. 20:8; Luke 24:29; (4) Matt. 20:8.

Evergreen: (1) Long life; (2) Feeding on the Word of God daily.
(1-2) Ps. 1:2-3.

Evidence: (1) Testimony (for or against); (2) Witness (for or against); (3) Substance of our faith.
(1-2) John 3:11; 1 Cor. 15:15; (3) Heb. 11:1.

Ewe: (1) Witness; (2) Wife; (3) Female believer; (4) Mother to young Christians.
(1) Gen. 21:28-30; (2) 2 Sam. 12:3; (3-4) Gen. 31:38; Ps. 78:71.

Exam: (1) Test; (2) Judgment; (3) A trial of life; (4) Temptation; (5) Searching the heart; (6) A look into the life and affairs of someone.
Also see *High School*.
(1) Matt. 4:1; (2) Rev. 20:12; (3) James 1:2-4; 1 Pet. 1:7; (4) Matt. 4:1ff; 26:41; Luke 4:13; (5) Ps. 26:2; 1 Cor. 11:28; 2 Cor. 13:5; (6) Acts 28:18; 1 Cor. 9:3.

Excavate: (1) Preparing foundations; (2) Opening your heart; (3) Searching your heart; (4) Uncovering the secrets of the heart; (5) Clearing your heart; (6) Enlarging your heart.
Also see *Digging*, *Dirt*, *Earthmovers*, *Shovel*, and *Spade*.
(1) Matt. 7:25; (2) Song 5:2; Acts 16:14; (3) 1 Chron. 28:9; Ps. 139:23; Jer. 17:10; Rom. 8:27; (4) Ps. 44:21; (5-6) Gen. 26:18; (cf. 2 Cor. 4:7).

Excavator: See *Backhoe/Excavator*.

Exercise Bike: (1) Not spiritually fit; (2) Armchair expert (over-opinionated and under-achieving); (3) Busy, but going nowhere (laboring in vain).
(1) John 16:12; (2) Matt. 23:3-4; (3) Luke 10:40-42; 1 Cor. 15:58.

Exercise Equipment: (1) Personal well-being; (2) Working for personal well-being; (3) Physical fitness; (4) Spiritual fitness; (5) Self-concern; (6) Image or health concerns; (7) Spiritual strengthening.

(1) 3 John 1:2; (2) 1 Cor. 3:12; (3-4) 1 Tim. 4:8; (5) Eph. 5:29; (6) Phil. 3:4; (7) Luke 1:80a; Jude 1:20.

Experiment: (1) Test; (2) Testing time.
(1) Gen. 22:1; (2) Job 2:5-5; 1 Cor. 10:13.

Explosion: (1) Sudden destruction; (2) Warning of impending judgment; (3) Incident involving tempers flaring.
(1) Isa. 29:6; 1 Thess. 5:3; (2) Jer. 4:19-21; (3) Matt. 22:7.

Eye of the Storm: (1) Heart of the issue (what's in the center is the reason for the storm); (2) Protected; (3) Peace with God.
(1) Prov. 4:23; John 6:70; 13:21; (2) Isa. 43:2; Mark 4:39; (3) Ps. 46:10; Isa. 43:2.

Eyes: (1) Heart/spirit; (2) Eyes of the Lord; (3) Second sight (eyes of the spirit); (4) Seer; (5) Prophetic gift (eyes wide open); (6) Spiritual perception (heart receptivity); (7) May refer to the outward person (as different from the inner person of the heart); (8) Pride (looking down); (9) Waiting on God (looking up); (10) Closed to the things of God (shut eyes or no eyes); (11) Cherubim; (12) Spiritual sight/imagination (right eye); (13) Fleshly leader (damaged or blind right eye).
Also see *Tears* and *Winking*.
(1) (Prov. 20:27; Matt. 6:22); Matt. 13:15; (2) Ps. 33:18; 34:15; 139:16; Prov. 5:21; 15:3; (3-5) Num. 24:4,16; 1 Sam. 9:9; Isa. 1:1; (6) Eph. 1:18; (7) Ps. 36:1; 73:7; 131:1; Prov. 4:21; 21:2; 23:26,33; Eccles. 2:10; 11:9; Isa. 44:18; Matt. 13:15; John 12:40; (8) Ps. 17:11; 131:1; Prov. 3:7; (9) Ps. 25:15; 121:1-2; 123:1-2; 141:8; 145:15; (10) Acts 28:27; (11) Ezek. 10:2; (12-13) Zech. 11:17.

Eyes (Seven or Many Eyes): (1) Spirit of prophecy (testimony of Jesus); (2) Perfect revelation; (3) Sign of prophetic anointing; (4) Spirit of God.
(1-3) Rev. 19:10; (4) Isa. 11:2; Rev. 5:6.

Eye Liner/Mascara : (1) Window dressing for appeal; (2) Vanity; (3) Beauty; (4) Applying mascara only to top eye lashes means to stop worrying about what the world thinks (people pleasing) and instead doing things to please God.
Also see *Above* and *Below*.
(1-4) 1 Cor. 7:33-34; 1 Pet. 3:3-4.

F

Fabric: (1) Life; (2) Life story; (3) The structure of a thing.
Also see *Cloth* and *Veil*, and see *Tucker* in Name and Place Dictionary.
(1) As in "the fabric of life"; Isa. 49:18; Luke 7:25; 2 Cor. 5:4; (2) Rev. 3:5; also as is depicted in some tapestries (e.g., Bayeux tapestry); consider that fabric is made up of individual strands of material woven together; (3) Definition of fabric from which we get the word *fabrication*.

Face: (1) Heart; (2) Life; (3) Someone's identity; (4) Revelation.
(1) Prov. 15:13; 27:19; (2) Prov. 16:15; (3) Exod. 34:10; Acts 20:25; (4) 2 Cor. 4:6.

Happy Face: (1) Cheerful heart.
(1) Prov. 15:13.

Hidden Face: (1) Afraid of God; (2) Fear of the Lord.
(1-2) Exod. 3:6.

Radiant Face: (1) God's Glory; (2) Wisdom.
(1) Exod. 34:30; 2 Cor. 3:7; (2) Eccles. 8:1.

Sad Face: (1) Sorrow; (2) Repentance (this can be a good thing).
(1) Eccles. 7:3; (2) 2 Cor. 7:10.

Facebook: (1) The state of the heart; (2) A person's journey; (3) Revealing the heart; (4) Communication platform; (5) Platform for voicing your passions/opinions; (6) Indirect communication; (7) Self-promotion; (8) Attempting to build a following.
(1) Prov. 27:19; (2) 2 Cor. 11:22-28; (3) Luke 2:35; (4) Jer. 33:30; Mal. 3:16a.; Eph. 5:19; Col. 3:16; (5) Matt. 10:27; (6) Dan. 8:13a; (7) 2 Sam. 16:6; Rom. 12:3; (8) 2 Sam. 15:6; Acts 5:36; 21:38.

Factory: (1) Productive church; (2) Business (good or evil); (3) Manufactured (made up = lies); (4) human-made; (5) Work of a repetitive nature; (6) Church operating as a business (manufacturing for their own interest); (7) Church based on works.
(1) Acts 2:41-42,47; (2) Ps. 127:1; 1 Tim. 3:3,8; Jude 1:11; (3) Eph. 4:25; Col. 3:9; 1 Tim. 4:2; (4) Gen. 11:3-5; (5) Prov. 15:27a; 1 Tim. 6:5; (7) Rev. 3:15-17.

Factory Shutdown: (1) Ministry/business closure; (2) Unexpected announcement; (3) Disillusionment; (4) Exodus /relocation; (5) Grief.
(1) 2 Chron. 36:19; Lam. 1:1; (2) Job 1:13-19; Matt. 16:21; John 13:21; (3) Luke 23:49; 24:11; John 13:22; (4) Exod. 12:31-33; Lam. 1:6; Luke 24:13-21; (5) Lam. 1:2; 2:11; Luke 19:41-44; 24:17.

Fade: (1) Die; (2) Death; (3) Temporary; (4) Losing touch with eternal life; (5) Aged or old.
(1) Isa. 1:30; 24:40; 64:6; Jer. 8:13; James 1:11; 1 Pet. 5:4; (2) 1 Pet. 1:4; (3) Isa. 28:1; (4) Ezek. 47:12 (KJV); (5) Josh. 9:13.

Fail: (1) Cease or stop; (2) Sin.
(1) Ps. 12:1; 1 Cor. 13:8; (2) 1 Sam. 12:23; Ps. 31:10.

Fair: See *Carnival*.

Fake: (1) Not the genuine article; (2) Not real; (3) Façade; (4) Superficial.
(1-3) Mark 7:6; Luke 6:42; (4) Matt. 8:19-22.

Falling: (1) Taking eyes off God; (2) Losing God's protection/support; (3) Ungodly; (4) Opposite to standing/walking/uprightness.
Falling also indicates: (5) Out of control; (6) Sinning; (7) Death; (8) Worship (down); (9) War/argument/disagreement (falling out); (10) Attack (upon someone);

(11) Embracing (upon someone); (12) Come under the influence of; (13) Talkative person who doesn't receive instruction; (14) Without counsel/support; (15) Person trusting in riches; (16) Pride/overconfidence; (17) Having a bad tongue/ways; (18) Gloating over someone else's misfortune; (19) Troubled spirit; (20) Someone trying to trap another; (21) Hardened heart.

Also see *Diving*, *Dropping*, and *Lift (Elevator)*.

(1-4) Ps. 20:8; 64:10; 91:7 (see all of psalm); 116:8-9; 118:13-14; Heb. 12:1-2; (5) Matt. 17:15; John 18:6; (6) Num. 11:4 (KJV); Acts 1:25; 1 Cor. 8:13. (AMP); (7) Gen. 14:10; Exod. 21:33-34; Acts 5:5, 10; (8) Gen. 17:3; John 11:32; (9) Gen. 45:24; Exod. 1:10; (10) Luke 10:30; (11) Gen. 33:4; (12) Lev. 19:29; (13) Prov. 10:8,10; (14) Prov. 11:14; Eccles. 4:10; (15) Prov. 11:28; (16) Prov. 16:18; (17) Prov. 17:20; 28:18; (18) Prov. 24:17; (19) Prov. 25:26; (20) Prov. 26:27; 28:10; Eccles. 10:8; (21) Prov. 28:14.

Falling (Endless Falling): (1) The abyss; (2) The bottomless pit.
(1-2) Rev. 9:2; 11:7; 17:8; 20:1-3.

Falling into Trouble: (1) Wicked messenger.
(1) Prov. 13:17.

Family: (1) Believers (those in the family of God); (2) The Church; (3) Those who speak the same language; (4) Spiritual fellowship; (5) Your own family.
(1) Eph. 3:15; (2) Ps. 107:41; (3) Gen. 10:5.

Famine: (1) Lack of the Word of God; (2) Poverty; (3) Actual famine.
(1) Amos 8:11; (2) Jer. 29:17.

Famous Person: (1) Jesus Christ; (2) Someone in your acquaintance who in some way relates as a parallel of a famous person; (3) The spirit of a famous person (if they are passed away and righteous); (4) Look up the meaning of the person's name (For example, imagine the prophetic incident involved Mel Gibson. *Mel* means "chief," therefore, this may symbolize Christ); (5) That actual person; (6) The world's glory (as in Hollywood personality); (7) The job, role, character, or passion of the famous person.
Also see *Superhero*.
(1) Mark 1:28; Luke 4:14,37; (2) Matt. 11:14; 17:12-13; (3) 1 Sam. 28:15; Matt. 17:3; 22:32; (6) Matt. 4:8; (7) Matt. 11:14.

Fan (verb): (1) Stirred by the Spirit; (2) Separate (winnow); (3) Judge; (4) Purge; (5) Increasing the heat; (6) Cooling.
(1) John 3:8; (2) Isa. 41:16; Jer. 4:11; (3) Jer. 15:7; 51:2; (4) Matt. 3:12; (5) Rev. 16:8-9; (6) Job 37:21b (KJV).

Fan (noun): (1) Spirit.
(1) John 3:8.

Fancy Dress: See *Costume Hire*.

Farm: (1) The harvest field; (2) Kingdom of Heaven; (3) God's Kingdom; (4) The world; (5) Israel; (6) The believer; (7) Evangelical ministry.

Also see entries under *Field* and *Harvest*.
(1) Matt. 9:36-37; 13:24-30; John 4:35; (2) Matt. 13:24-30; 20:1ff; (3) Matt. 21:28-32; John 10:9,16; (4) Matt. 13:38-39; 21:33-43; Rev. 14:15; (5) Isa. 5:1ff; Luke 13:6-9; (6) 1 Cor. 3:9.

Farmer: (1) Spiritual leaders (good and bad); (2) God the Father; (3) Christ (Sower); (4) Preacher; (5) Evangelist; (6) Minister; (7) The believer; (8) Laborer; (9) Worker.
(1) Matt. 21:33-45; Mark 12:1ff; Luke 20:9ff; 2 Tim. 2:6; (2) John 15:1; 1 Cor. 3:9; (3) Matt. 13:37; (4-9) 1 Cor. 3:6.

Fast: See *Fasting* and *Quick/ly*.

Fast Food: See *Junk Food*.

Fasting: (1) Dying to self; (2) Cleansing of the vessel or garment; (3) Humbling oneself before God; (4) Cutting off the flesh; (5) Empowering; (6) Hungering for Christ; (7) Denying the flesh to sensitize the spirit; (8) Not swallowing what is being served up; (9) Separation from the world; (10) Literal fast.
(1) Matt. 6:16; Luke 2:37; Acts 13:2; (2) Matt. 9:14-17; (3) Ps. 35:13; (4) 1 Cor. 9:27; (5) Matt. 17:21; Luke 4:2,14; (6) Mark 2:20; Luke 5:35; (7) Matt. 3:4; Luke 1:80; (8) Prov. 23:1-3, 6-8; (9) Dan. 1:8.

Fat & Fatness: The meaning of fatness breaks into two main categories: (+) Well-favored; or, (-) One who has forsaken God and become desensitized to the things of the Spirit because of opulence and pride.

Fat & Fatness (+) Well-favored: (1) Well-favored; (2) The best; (3) Flourishing; (4) Generous; (5) Plentiful; (6) Influential (for good); (7) Anointing of the Holy Spirit.
(1) Gen. 41:4; (2) Gen. 4:4; 45:18; 1 Sam. 2:29; 2 Sam. 1:22; Luke 15:23,30; (3) Num. 13:20; Ps. 92:14; (4) Prov. 11:25; (5) Isa. 30:23; (6) Ps. 92:14; Prov. 11:25; (7) Isa. 21:5; Acts 10:38 (anoint means "to smear with oil or fat").

Fat & Fatness (-) Proud/Desensitized: (1) Flesh; (2) Forsaken God; (3) Pride; (4) Desensitized; (5) Hired hands (in the ministry for money); (6) Living to fleshly appetites; (7) Influential (for bad); (8) Being spiritually lazy/resting in the flesh (fat backside); (9) This group are also being readied for judgment, as in "fattened for the slaughter"; (10) Self-indulgent.
Also see *Cat*.
(1) Deut. 32:15; Jer. 50:11; (1 Sam. 2:15-16; 4:18); (2) Deut. 31:20; 32:13-15; (3) Ps. 17:10; (4) Ps. 119:69-70 (fat heart = desensitized); Isa. 6:10; (5) John 10:13; (6) Ps. 78:29-31; (7) Ps. 78:31 (KJV); (8) Neh. 9:25-26; (9) James 5:5; (10) Judg. 3:17,21-22; James 5:5.

Father: (1) God (Heavenly Father); (2) Spiritual authority/covering; (3) Jesus Christ; (4) Spiritual leader or mentor (father in the faith); (5) Natural father; (6) Spiritual ancestors; (7) The past; (8) The devil (unbeliever, sinner, or liar's father).

(1) Matt. 6:9; 2 Cor. 1:2-3; 6:8; (2) 1 Chron. 24:19 (KJV); 25:3,6; (3) Isa. 9:6; (4) 1 Cor. 4:15; 1 Thess. 2:11; 1 Tim. 5:1; (5) Eph. 5:31; 6:2; (6) Heb. 1:1; (7) Job 21:8; (8) John 8:44; 1 John 3:8.

Father-in-Law: (1) Mentor; (2) Wise counsel; (3) Guide; (4) Mutual benefit; (5) Legalistic leader; (6) Actual father-in-law.
Also see *Brother-in-Law* and *Son-in-Law*.
(1-2) Exod. 18:18-24; (3-4) Num. 10:29, 31-32; (5) John 3:10.

Feathers: (1) Covering; (2) Protection; (3) Trust; (4) The Holy Spirit; (5) Glory; (6) Coward (white feather); (7) Evidence of angels; (8) Someone "feathering their own nest."
Also see *Angel(s)* and *Bird(s)*.
(1-3) Ps. 91:4; (4) Isa. 40:31; (5) Ezek. 17:3, 7; (6) Rev.21:8; (7) Exod. 25:20; Isa. 6:2; (8) 2 Sam. 15:6; 2 Kings 5:22-27.

Feces: (1) Dirty (defiled); (2) Sin; (3) Self-righteousness; (4) Clean up required.
Also see *Dung, Sewage, Toilet*, and *Urination*.
(1-4) Isa. 64:6; Phil. 3:8.

Fear of Man: (1) People-pleasing; (2) Telling people what they want to hear.
(1) Prov. 29:25; (2) 2 Tim. 4:3.

Feeding: (1) Speaking or teaching; (2) Fueling; (3) Doing the will of God.
(1) 1 Cor. 3:1-2; (2) Prov. 26:20; (3) John 4:34.

Feeling: (1) Spiritual sensitivity. How a person feels when they see or recognize an event as a prophetic incident may be a strong indicator of its meaning; (2) For example, a sense of peace while flying conveys we are comfortable in the Spirit. However, the same scene with a sense of impending danger is a warning about our spiritual state; (3) It should be noted that just as we have five physical senses, so we also have five spiritual senses: taste, touch, smell, sight, and hearing.
(1) Eph. 4:19; (3) Ps. 34:8; 1 Kings 18:44; 2 Kings 6:16-17.

Feet: (1) Messenger; (2) Bearer of good news; (3) Ministry; (4) Heart; (5) Walk; (6) Offense; (7) Stand; (8) Take authority over; (9) Trampled; (10) Assert authority; (11) Stomp (feet); (12) Disrespect (trample on); (13) Overpowered; (14) Close to you (at your feet); (15) Depression (feet hanging).
Also see *Broken* and *Shoes*.
(1) Rom. 10:15; (2 -3) Isa. 52:7; (4) Prov. 6:18; (5) Acts 14:8,10; (6) Prov. 6:18; Matt. 18:8; (7) Eph. 6:13; (8) Luke 10:19; (9) Luke 8:5; 12:1; (10-13) Luke 21:24; (14) Matt. 8:35; Luke 10:39; (15) Matt. 27:5.

Feet (Dirty Feet): (1) Sinful nature; (2) Offense (wiping dust off).
(1) John 13:10; (2) Luke 10:11.

Feet Cut Off: (1) Unreliable witness (fool); (2) Unable to preach the Gospel. (1) Prov. 26:6; (2) Rom. 10:15.

Feet On: (1) Defeat or oppression (someone's feet on you); (2) Victory (your feet on someone or something); (3) Being trampled on.

(1-2) Josh. 10:24; Matt. 5:13; Luke 10:19; (3) Matt. 5:13.

Feet (Stamping Feet): (1) Aggression; (2) Defiance; (3) Temper tantrum; (4) Crushing satan.

(1-3) Ezek. 25:6; (4) Gen. 3:15.

Feet (Webbed Feet): (1) Walking in the Spirit; (2) Seasoned in the things of the Spirit.

(1-2) Ezek. 47:5; Matt. 14:26; Gal. 5:16.

Female: See *Woman*.

Fence: (1) Barrier; (2) Boundary or demarcation; (3) Provides protection or rest; (4) Trust; (5) Garrison or army; (6) Fortified; (7) Blocked (fenced in); (8) Changing loyalties (jumping the fence); (9) Changing camps; (10) Control issue.

Also see *Hedge* and *Wall*.

(1-2) 2 Chron. 17:2; (3) Num. 32:17 (KJV); 2 Chron.14:6; Job 1:10; Isa. 5:2; (4) Deut. 28:52 (KJV); Jer. 5:17; (5) 2 Sam. 23:7; 2 Chron. 17:2; 32:5; (6) Deut. 9:1; Josh. 10:20; (7) Job 19:8; (8-9) 1 Sam. 29:4; (10) Num. 22:24, 26; 2 Kings 25:10; 2 Chron. 25:23; 2 Cor. 10:4-5.

Ferret(s): (1) Thief; (2) Seek and find; (3) Person who finds answers.

(1) From Latin *furunem* meaning "thief"; (2-3) As in "Ferret things out"; Matt. 7:7.

Ferris Wheel: (1) Eternity; (2) God's will (bringing Heaven to earth); (3) Life (ups and downs); (4) Unsettling change (fast ferris wheel and struggling to hold on).

(1) Gen. 9:11 (note the "never again"); Ezek. 1:18-20 (spirit is eternal); (2) Matt. 6:10; (3) Eccles. 3:6; (4) Matt. 6:28.

Fertilizer: (1) Word of God; (2) Words of encouragement; (3) Edification; (4) Praying in the Spirit; (5) Prophecy; (6) Love; (7) Five-fold ministry gift; (8) Trials (testing of the Word); (9) Preparing for fruit.

(1) 1 Pet. 2:2; (2-3) Rom. 14:19; Eph. 4:29; (4) Jude 1:20; (5) 1 Cor. 14:4; (6) 1 Cor. 8:1; Eph. 4:16; (7) Eph. 4:11-12; (8-9) Luke 13:8-9.

Fever: (1) Curse for disobedience; (2) Plague; (3) Suffering or torment.

Fever (Healing from Fever): (4) Healed in the Atonement; (5) Jesus rebuked fever; (6) Healed through faith in the Word.

(1-2) Deut. 28:15,22; (3) Luke 4:38-39; Acts 28:8; (4) Matt. 10:7-8 (the coming of the Kingdom); (5) Matt. 8:14-15; Mark 1:30-31; Luke 4:38-39; Acts 28:8; (6) John 4:47-52.

Field: (1) World; (2) The believer; (3) Harvest (someone in the field); (4) The Church or a church.

Also see *Farm* and *Harvest*.

(1) Matt. 13:38; (2) 1 Cor. 3:9; (3) Matt. 9:38; John 4:35; (4) Luke 15:25; 17:36.

Fifteen: (1) Acts of divine grace; (2) Resurrection.

(1) 3 (Spirit fullness) x 5 (grace); (2) 2 Kings 20:6; Esther 9:18,21; John 11:18 (KJV); Acts 27:28.

Fifty: (1) Jubilee; (2) Liberty/liberation; (3) Release/freedom; (4) Deliverance/rest; (5) Pentecost; (6) The perfect consummation of time; (7) Extreme grace.
(1-4) Lev. 25:10,40,54; Num. 8:25 (Levites freed from service at fifty years of age); (5) Lev. 23:16; Acts 2:1-4; (6) 7 x 7 +1 = 50; Acts 2:1; (7) 5 (grace) x 10 (complete).

Fig: (1) Represents political Israel; (2) False religion (fig leaves); (3) Prosperity; (4) Prayer (under the fig tree); (5) Judgment (falling fruit, no blossom); (6) Self-righteousness (fig leaves); (7) Dead religious system (bearing no fruit).
(1) Matt. 21:19; Hos. 9:10; (2) Gen. 3:7 (unable to cover sin); (3) 1 Kings 4:25; Song 2:13; (4) John 1:48-50; (5) Isa. 34:4; Nah. 3:12; Joel 1:7; Hab. 3:17; Matt. 21:19 (pending judgment); (6) Gen. 3:7 (own covering); (7) Matt. 21:19-20.

Fight: (1) Fight of faith; (2) Spiritual battle/warfare; (3) Outward afflictions; (4) Worldly lusts; (5) Angelic battle; (6) Fight using the Word of God.
Also see *Battle*.
(1) 1 Cor. 9:26; 1 Tim. 6:12; (2) John 18:36; Eph. 6:12; (3) Heb. 10:32; (4) James 4:1-2; (5) Rev. 12:7; Dan. 10:13,20; (6) Rev. 2:16.

Filing Cabinet: (1) Heart; (2) Memory.
(1) Prov. 3:1, 4:4b, 20-21; (2) 1 Chron. 28:9; Isa. 50:4.

Film: See *Movies*.

Filming: (1) Bringing focus to an issue or focusing on an issue; (2) Documenting (recording good/bad memories).
Also see *Camera* and *Movies*.
(1) 2 Sam. 12:1-7; Matt. 6:26; (2) Esther 1:19.

Filthiness: (1) Sinful; (2) Iniquity; (3) Self-righteousness; (4) The world's view of the Church; (5) Foul language; (6) Greed for gain.
(1) Job 15:16; Isa. 4:4; Ps. 14:3; 53:3; (2) Zech. 3:3-4; (3) Isa. 64:6; (4) 1 Cor. 4:13; (5) Col. 3:8; (6) 1 Tim. 3:3,8; Tit. 1:7,11; 1 Pet. 5:2.

Find: See *Lost* and *Found*.

Fine Print: (1) Details; (2) Instructions; (3) Contract; (4) Questionable content in a contract; (5) What is not said up front; (6) Revelation (mysteries revealed).
(1-3) Ezra 4:15,21-23; Esther 1:22; (4-5) Matt. 22:15; Mark 12:13; Luke 20:20,26; 1 Cor. 4:5; (6) Prov. 25:2; Rom. 16:25; Eph. 3:9.

Finger(s): (1) The Holy Spirit (The Finger of God); (2) Kingdom of God; (3) Ownership; (4) Recognition; (5) Speaks of looking for evidence through feelings; (6) Speaks of an amplification in intricacy and detail of what is being done (just as we use our fingers to amplify our touch); (7) Sensitivity; (8) God's government/rule (the finger of God).

(1-2) Matt.12:28; Luke 11:20; (3) Lev. 4:6,17,25,30,34; Isa. 2:8; (4) Exod. 8:19; (5) John 20:25,27; (6-7) Song 5:5 (fragrance); Isa. 59:3 (sin); Dan. 5:5 (judgment); Ps. 144:1 (warfare); (8) Luke 11:20 (cf. Exod. 31:18).

Finger(s) (Pointing Finger): (1) Accusation; (2) Blame-shifting; (3) Direction. (1-2) Prov. 6:13; Isa. 58:9.

Finger(s) (Tip of the Finger): (1) Amplifies the lesson; (2) Small amount; (3) Sensitivity.

(1-3) Luke 16:19-31 (note v. 24); Jesus teaches that even though the greatest faith (small amount of water [i.e., word]), be exercised after death, it is too late! (cf. Matt. 15:27-28). The small amount depicted in dipping the tip of the finger also amplifies the rich man's need/torment. Also note the great gulf between the believer and unbeliever. Therefore, Jesus amplifies here the need to outwork faith in love this side of eternity.

Fingernails: See *Nails (Finger)*.

Fingerprints: (1) Identity (source of the evidence); (2) Ownership; (3) Recognition; (4) DNA; (5) Wrong motive; (6) Being exposed (fingerprints found); (7) Signs and wonders (marks of the Holy Spirit); (8) God's handiwork.
Also see *Finger* and *Hand*.
(1) Exod. 8:19; (2) Prov. 7:3; (3) Job 37:7; John 20:25; (5-6) Prov. 6:12-13; (7) Matt. 12:28; Luke 11:20; (8) Exod. 31:18; Deut. 9:10; Luke 11:20.

Fire: (1) Presence of God; (2) Cleansing; (3) Judgment; (4) Strife; (5) Hell; (6) Affliction; (7) Tongue; (8) God's Word; (9) Gossip; (10) Passion; (11) Lust and adultery; (12) Anger or jealousy; (13) Glory of God; (14) Love.
Also see *Burn*, *Bush Fire*, *Flame*, *Forest Fire*, and *House Fire*.
(1) Deut. 4:24; (2) Num. 31:23; Luke 3:16-17; (3) Ps. 21:9; Ezek. 21:31; (4) Prov. 26:20-21; (5) Mark 9:43; (6) Deut. 4:20; Ps. 66:12; (7) Acts 2:3; James 3:6; (8) Jer. 5:14; 23:29; (9) Prov. 26:20; James 3:5-6; (10) 1 Cor. 7:9; (11) Prov. 6:25-28; (12) Ps. 79:5; 89:46; (13) Exod. 24:17; (14) Song 8:6-7.

Fire Engine: (1) Rescuer or deliverer; (2) Someone who tries to put out the fire of God; (3) Trouble (engine with siren); (4) Sign of fire out of control.
(1) Exod. 18:13-22; Zech. 3:2b; (2) Lev. 16:12; Ps. 39:3; Neh. 4:10, 12; 1 Tim. 5:12-13; James 1:6; (3) Prov. 12:13; 16:27; (4) James 3:5.

Fire Extinguisher: (1) Person who quenches the Spirit; (2) The Holy Spirit (right spirit/water); (3) Repentance.
Also see *Fire Engine*, *Fire Fighter*, and *Fire Warden*.
(1) Acts 2:3-4; 1 Thess. 5:19 (the fire of the Spirit); (2) John 7:38-39; Gal. 5:16,20 (The fire of anger, strife, contention is put out by love); Num. 16:1-33 (fighting fire with fire); (3) Matt. 5:22,25 (the fire of judgment).

Fire Fighter: (1) Revival police; (2) Opponents to the move of the Spirit; (3) Deliverer/Jesus/Angel of the Lord.

Also see *Fire Extinguisher*, *Fireman*, and *Fire Warden*.
(1-2) cf. Acts 2:3; 4:17; (3) Gen. 19:13-15; Zech. 3:2; Luke 4:18-19.

Fireman: (1) Jesus; (2) Deliverer.
Also see *Fire Extinguisher* and *Fire Fighter*.
(1) Dan. 3:25; (2) Zech. 3:2b.

Fireplace: (1) Heart; (2) Anger or jealousy.
(1) Jer. 23:29; (2) Ps. 79:5; James 3:5-6.

Fire Warden: (1) Religious spirit/controlling spirit; (2) Quencher of the Spirit; (3) Peacemaker.
Also see *Fireman*, *Fire Extinguisher*, and *Fire Fighter*.
(1) Acts 5:27-28a,32; (2) 1 Thess. 5:19; (3) Matt. 5:9.

Firewood: (1) Deeds done in vain; (2) Covenant sacrifice or meal; (3) Gossip; (4) Contentious person; (5) Ready for judgment/hell; (6) People burning through God's Word; (7) Words that stir up anger (fuel for the fire).
(1) 1 Cor. 3:12-14; (2) Gen. 22:6-7; Lev. 1:7; (3) Prov. 26:20; (4) Prov. 26:21; (5) Isa. 30:33; (6) Jer. 5:14; (7) Acts 6:11-12.

Fireworks: (1) Celebration; (2) Conflict or trouble; (3) Spiritual warfare (clash of spirits).
(1) Lev. 23:32,41; (2) Job 5:7; Acts 15:7; (3) Judg. 5:20; Rev. 12:7.

First Nations Peoples: (1) Innocence; (2) The old self (person of the flesh); (3) Ancestors; (4) Unsaved people.
Also see *Native(s)*, *Old Man*, and note under *Black Man* or *Caucasian*.
(1) Gen. 2:25; (2) Rom. 6:6; 2 Cor. 5:17; Eph. 4:22; Col. 3:9; (3) Amos 2:4b (NIV); (4) 1 Cor. 15:46.

Fir Tree: (1) Choice individual; (2) Used in temple building; (3) Thanksgiving; (4) Joy; (5) Blessing; (6) Glory.
(1) 2 Kings 19:23 (KJV); Isa. 37:24 (KJV), As trees are a symbol of people, the upright fir tree is a picture of a choice individual; (2) 1 Kings 5:10; 2 Chron. 3:5; (3) 1 Kings 6:33-34; Ps. 100:4; (4) Isa. 14:8; (5) Isa. 55:13; (6) Isa. 60:13.

Fish: (1) Believers; (2) Conversions (fish caught); (3) Humankind (potential believers); (4) Spiritual food (the Gospel); (5) Believers in the Spirit (flying fish); (6) Young believers (gold fish); (7) Financial blessing (money from fish's mouth); (8) Revival (fish jumping into boat); (9) Revelation of the truth (spiritual download); (10) A prospective spouse (a "catch").
(1-3) Eccles. 9:12; Hab. 1:14; Matt. 4:19; (4) John 6:11; 21:13; (5) Isa. 40:31; (6) 2 Cor. 3:18; (7) Matt. 17:27; (8) Luke 5:6-7; (9) John 21:10-19; (10) Prov. 18:22; Luke 5:7; 1 Cor. 7:28,36,38.

Fish and Chips: See *French Fries*.

Fish and Chip Shop: (1) Church feeding off battered fish (unhealthy believers); (2) Church/organization having a wrong spirit (dirty oil).
Also see *French Fries.*
(1) 1 Cor. 3:2-4; (2) 2 Cor. 11:4.

Fish Hooks: (1) Evangelistic ministries; (2) Taking the bait; (3) Messages from the Word of God; (4) Leading to Christ; (5) Dragged into or out of something against person's will.
Also see *Net.*
(1) Acts 8:5-7; (2) Gen. 3:6; (3) Matt. 17:27; 1 Cor. 9:14; (4) Acts 8:12; (5) Ezek. 38:4; Isa. 37:29.

Fishing: (1) Evangelism; (2) Soul winning; (3) Witnessing; (4) Investigating; (5) Looking for a partner; (6) Putting the Word out there (throwing a line); (7) Creative evangelism (fly tying).
(1-2) Matt. 4:19; (3) Acts 1:8,22; 2:32; 3:15; (4) Luke 20:20; as in "fishing around"; (5) Prov. 18:22; (6) Matt. 4:19; (7) 1 Cor. 9:22.

Fishing Line: (1) The means to catch fish; (2) The Gospel.
(1-2) Matt. 4:19; Rom. 1:16.

Fishing Pole: See *Fishing Rod.*

Fishing Rod: (1) Heart; (2) Tool of evangelism (person or thing used in evan- gelism); (3) Caught up in the world (black fishing rod).
(1) Jer. 9:8; Matt. 12:34b; (2) Matt. 4:19; John 21:6; (3) 1 John 2:16.

Fish Pond: (1) The world (sea of humanity); (2) Your fishing hole (evangelistic arena: workplace, school, town, etc.); (3) Church.
(1) Matt. 4:18-19; (2) Acts 8:5,26,29,39-40; (4) As in the place where fish are kept.

Fish Tank: (1) Church.
Also see *Fish Pond.*
(1) As the place where fish are kept.

Fist: (1) Threat of retribution; (2) Pending judgment; (3) Violence; (4) Grabbing; (5) Hitting/wickedness; (6) Aggression/contention.
Also see *Hand* and *Knuckles.*
(1-2) Isa. 10:32; (3) Exod. 21:18; (4) Prov. 30:4; (5-6) Isa. 58:4.

Five: (1) Grace; (2) Abundance; (3) Favor; (4) Redemption; (5) Multi-tasking (five-fold ministry).
(1) Gen. 45:11; (2) Gen. 1:20-23; (3) Gen. 43:34; Lev. 26:8; (4) Num. 18:16; (5) Eph. 4:11.

Fizzy Drink: See *Soda.*

Flag: (1) Surrender (white flag); (2) Nationality; (3) Spiritual warfare; (4) Praise; (5) Kingdom of God; (6) Love; (7) Covering/protection.
Also see *Banner.*

(1) Rom. 6:16 (KJV); (2-3) Ps. 20:5; Song 6:4,10; (4) Ps. 150:6; (5) Ps. 20:5; 60:4; (6-7) Song 2:4.

Flame(s): (1) The Holy Spirit; (2) God; (3) The human spirit; (4) Judgment; (5) Light; (6) Torment; (7) Apostolic ministry; (8) Baptism in the Spirit; (9) Anger; (10) Jealousy. Also see *Fire* and *Flamethrower.*
(1) Luke 3:16; Acts 2:3; 2 Cor. 4:6-7; Judg. 7:20; (2) Isa. 10:17; (3) Prov. 20:27; Ps. 18:28; (4) Isa. 29:6; (5) Ps. 18:28; (6) Luke 16:24; (7) Acts 20:24 (fiery passion); Rom. 1:15; (8) Acts 2:3-4; (9) Ps. 21:9; (10) Ps. 79:5.

Flame Thrower: (1) Outburst of anger; (2) Imparting the fire of God.
Also see *Fire* and *Flame(s).*
(1) Ps. 78:21; 147:18a; Isa. 30:27,30; (2) Acts 2:2-3.

Flashlight: See *Torch.*

Flat Tire/Tyre: (1) Spiritually flat (unable to go forward).
Also see *Tire* and *Wheel.*
(1) Job 27:3; 33:4; John 3:8.

Flea: (1) Parasite; (2) Itch; (3) Irritant; (4) Insignificant; (5) Hunted; (6) Secret, parasitic message that passes from person to person, stealing life.
Also see *Parasite.*
(1-3) See *Lice;* (4) 1 Sam. 24:14; (5) 1 Sam. 26:20; (6) John 7:12-13.

Flee: (1) Hide; (2) Fear; (3) Run away (move quickly); (4) Forsake; (5) Often associated with judgment; (6) Hired hands flee under threat.
(1) Matt. 2:13; 3:7; 24:16; (2) Matt. 8:33; (3) Matt. 10:23; 24:16; Mark 14:52; 16:8; (4) Matt. 26:56; (5) Luke 3:7; 21:21; (6) John 10:5.

Fleece: (1) Covering; (2) Stolen/stealing; (3) Looking for guidance (cut out rug entry); (4) Façade.
Also see *Cover* and *Rug.*
(1) Judg. 4:18; (2) John 12:6; (3) Judg. 6:37-40; (4) Matt. 7:15.

Flies: Beelzebub means "lord of the flies" and is a reference to the devil. Therefore flies represent: (1) Evil spirits; (2) satan; (3) Doctrine of demons (fly in drink).
Also see *Fly Spray*, *Frogs*, and *Odor (Bad).*
(1-2) Exod. 8:21-31; Matt. 12:24; (2) Matt. 12:24; 1 Cor. 10:21a.

Flood: (1) Verbal onslaught of the enemy; (2) Overflow of sin; (3) Harvest time; (4) Divine assistance; (5) Test of foundations; (6) Sudden; (7) Floods destroy the unrighteous; (8) Judgment.
Also see *Water—Dirty Water.*
(1) Isa. 59:19b; Rev. 12:15; (2-3) Josh. 3:15; (4) Isa. 59:19b; (5) Matt. 7:25-27; (6) Matt. 24:38-39; (7-8) Gen. 6:13, 17; 2 Pet. 2:5.

Floor: (1) Foundation; (2) Place of sorting/purging (threshing floor); (3) Storage area; (4) Ground; (5) Humbling.

(2) Ruth 3:3,6; Isa. 21:10; Matt. 3:12; Luke 3:17; (3) Deut. 15:14; Hos. 9:2; 13:3; Joel 2:24; Mic. 4:12; (4) Judg. 6:37; (5) Ruth 3:3.

Floorboards: (1) Foundation of the fleshly person (not of God).
(1) 1 Cor. 3:12.

Flour: (1) The cross (crushed Christ); (2) Humility; (3) The laying down of individual fame for the Body of Christ (one grain dying for the benefit of making a loaf); (4) Contrite heart (crushed seed); (5) Prosperity.
Also see *Bake, Barley, Bread, Mill/stone, Seed, Self-Raising Flour, Wheat*, and *Yeast*.
(1) 2 Kings 4:40-41 (cf. Isa. 53:5; John 12:24); (2) Exod. 11:5 (the lowest position); Lev. 5:11 (poor person's offering); cf. Num. 11:8; John 6:32-33; Phil. 2:7-8; (3) John 12:24; 1 Cor. 10:16-17; (4) Ps. 34:18; 51:17; (5) Ezek. 16:19; Rev. 18:13.

Flowers: (1) The righteous/upright; (2) Prosperity; (3) Brevity of life; (4) Offering praise (fragrance) to Christ; (5) Clothes; (6) Life; (7) Passing glory of people; (8) Glory.
(1) Prov. 14:11; (2) Ps. 103:15; Isa. 27:6; (3) James 1:10-11; (4) 1 Kings 6:29,32,35; (5) Matt. 6:28, 30; (6) Isa. 35:1; (7) 1 Pet. 1:24; (8) Matt. 6:28-29.

Fluorescence: See *Highlighter*.

Fly: See *Flies*.

Flying: (1) Rising up out of the flesh into the Spirit (breaking physical laws); (2) In the Spirit; (3) Worship; (4) Moving in the gifts.
(1) Ps. 55:6; Prov. 23:5b; Isa. 40:31; (2) Matt. 3:16b; 4:1; Luke 23:46b; Acts 8:39; (3) Ezra 8:6; Isa. 6:2; (4) 1 Cor. 12:7 (flying as a manifestation of the Spirit).

Flying a Kite: (1) Beginning to grow in the things of the Spirit.
(1) 2 Kings 6:17a.

Flying Saucer(s): (1) Demonic deception.
(1) Matt. 24:24.

Fly Screen: (1) Covering; (2) Protection from the demonic.
Also see *Flies*.
(1-2) Eccles. 10:1.

Fly Spray: (1) The anointing/the Holy Spirit (demonic powers fleeing in His Presence).
Also see *Flies*.
(1) Matt. 12:28; Luke 11:20 (See *Fly*).

Foam: (1) Easily blown away; (2) Without substance; (3) Demonic oppression (mouth).
(1) Hos. 10:7; (2) Jude 1:13; (3) Matt. 9:18; Mark 9:20; Luke 9:39.

Fog: (1) Sin; (2) Life snippet; (3) In darkness; (4) Hell; (5) Hidden; (6) Secret.
(1) Isa. 44:22; (2) James 4:14; (3) Acts 13:11; (4) 2 Pet. 2:17; (5-6) Ps. 18:11.

Folding: (1) Putting away; (2) Preparation for storage or travel; (3) Protecting or hiding; (4) Humbling; (5) Sorting; (6) Corruption (wrinkle and creased/crooked ways); (7) Giving up or quitting.
Also see *Spot* and *Wrinkles*.

(1) 1 Cor. 13:11 (childish things); Eph. 4:31 (evil speaking); Heb. 9:26 (sin); (2) Exod. 12:11 (KJV); (3) Josh. 7:11b-12a, 21; Acts 5:1-2; (4) Rom. 14:11; Phil 2:10-11; 2 Chron. 7:14; (5) Matt. 25:32-33; (6) Eph. 5:27; James 1:17; (7) Eph. 6:11,14 (standing is the opposite of folding).

Food: (1) Word of God; (2) Jesus; (3) Will of God; (4) What you're feeding on; (5) Doing God's business.
Also see *Meal, Meat*, and *Refrigerator*.
(1) Heb. 5:13-14; Matt. 4:4; (2) John 6:54; (3) John 4: 34; (4) John 4:34; (5) John 4:31-34.

Food Poisoning: (1) Tainted Gospel or ill-prepared preaching; (2) False promises; (3) Food of the world (newspapers, lies, gossip, false information, deceit); (4) Ungodly words that poison your spirit; (5) Curse.
(1) 2 Cor. 11:4; Gal. 1:6; 2 John 1:10; (2) Prov. 23:3, 6-8; (3) 1 John 2:15-17 (cf. John 4:34); (4) Ps. 58:3-4; 140:3; Rom. 3:13; (5) 2 Kings 40:4.

Fool: (1) Unbeliever; (2) Transgressor; (3) Despiser of wisdom and instruction.
(1) Ps. 14:1; 53:1; (2) Ps. 107:17; (3) Prov. 1:7b.

Foot: See *Feet*.

Football: (1) May represent the object of everyone's attention.
Also see *Ball, Goal*, and *Football Game*.
(1) 1 Sam. 9:20b.

Football Game: (1) Counterfeit worship/warfare; (2) False focus; (3) Idolatry; (4) May be representative of business (which for the most part is equally competitive and all about winning); (5) Life; (6) Spiritual warfare; (7) Ministry.
Also see *Goal, Sport*, and *Winning*.
(1-2) 1 Chron. 16:31-33; Ps. 74:4; 96:11-12; 98:7-9; (3) Exod. 20:3-4; (5) 2 Tim. 4:7; (6-7) See *Ball*.

Footpath: (1) Course of life (good or evil); (2) Hardened heart; (3) Busy heart; (4) Can be what lies ahead or in the past (behind you); (5) Child's path or journey; (6) Passage to hear the Gospel.
Also see *Pavement*.
(1) Ps. 17:5; 44:18; 119:101,105; Prov. 1:16; 4:14,26; (2-3) Matt. 13:4,19; Luke 10:31-32; (4) Ps. 199:105; Phil. 3:12-13; (5) Gen. 18:19; (6) Rom. 10:15.

Foot Pedal (Guitar): (1) Changing atmospheric dynamics; (2) Crushing satan's head through worship; (3) Rock stardom.
See *Feet* and *Guitar*.
(1) 1 Sam. 10:5-6; 1 Sam. 18:6-7; (2) Gen. 3:15; Luke 10:19; (3) Matt. 10:18a.

Footprints: (1) Steps of faith; (2) Jesus carrying you (as in the popular wall plaque); (3) Claiming your spiritual inheritance; (4) Evidence of angels (5) Evidence; (6) Evidence of strongholds.

(1) Ps. 119:105; 2 Cor. 5:7; (2) Matt. 11:29-30; (3) Gen. 32:1-2; Josh. 1:3; Ps. 91:11; (4) Ps. 34:7; (5) Heb. 11:1; (6) Num. 13:33.

Footsteps: (1) Following; (2) Someone's replacement (heir apparent); (3) Guidance; (4) Expectancy (getting louder); (5) Leaving (getting fainter).

Also see *Stepping* and *Walking.*

(1) Song 1:8; John 21:19,22; Rom. 4:12; Heb. 12:1-2; (2) 1 Kings 3:14; 8:25; as in "walking in the footsteps of his father"; (3) Ps. 25:9; (the word *guide* here means "to tread"); (4) 1 Kings 14:6; 2 Kings 6:32; 2 Sam. 5:24; Isa. 52:7; (5) Isa. 40:31b.

Footsteps inside Footsteps: (1) Same spirit; (2) Following someone's faith/ example.

(1) 2 Cor. 12:18; (2) Rom. 4:12; 1 Pet. 2:21.

Forehead: (1) The mind/thinking; (2) Mental strongholds.

(1-2) 1 Sam. 17:49 (our biggest giants are likewise defeated with a stone [word] to the mind!); 2 Cor. 10:4-5.

Foreign: (1) Non-believer; (2) Not operating in faith; (3) Christ (as not known by Him); (4) Made overseas; (5) Not familiar; (6) Not knowing a situation.

Also see *First Nations Peoples, Foreigner, Stranger, Unfamiliar,* and *Woman (Foreign Woman).*

(1) Exod. 12:45; Obad. 1:11; Eph. 2:19; (2) Rom. 4:11-12; (3) Luke 13:25,27; (4) 1 Kings 10:6-7; (5) 1 Sam. 17:39; Acts 17:23; (6) Heb. 11:9-10.

Foreigner: (1) Possible warning of potential ungodly threat; (2) If you are the foreigner, it may mean you are set apart from the world; (3) A father-figure who is a foreigner may refer to the fact that your relationship with God as Father is foreign to you; (4) Liar; (5) False hand of friendship; (6) Religious worker who professes to know Christ, but in reality does not; (7) Person not understanding the voice of the Spirit.

Also see *Aliens, First Nations Peoples, Foreign, Indigenous, Woman (Foreign Woman),* and *Stranger.*

(1) Eph. 2:12; 4:18; Col. 1:21; Heb. 11:34; (2) Deut. 14:2; 26:18; Heb. 11:9; 1 Pet. 2:9; (4) Ps. 144:11; (5) Ps. 144:11; (6) Matt. 7:22-23; (7) 1 Cor. 14:11.

Foreign Woman: See *Woman (Foreign Woman).*

Foreskin: See *Circumcision.*

Forest: (1) Lost/darkness; (2) Not out of the woods; (3) Harvest crop; (4) Church; (5) Multitude of people; (6) Army of mighty men; (7) Hiding place for predators; (8) Place of idolatry and works.

Also see *Beast, Cedar, Fir Tree, Forest Fire, Jungle, Park, Pine Tree, Rainforest,* and *Woods.*

(1) Ps. 104:20; (2) 1 Sam. 23:15; 2 Sam. 18:6-9; (3) Isa. 32:15-20; (4) 1 Chron. 16:33; Ps. 96:12; Song 2:3; Isa. 44:23; (5-6) Isa. 7:2, 10:18-19,34; 29:17-19; Jer. 46:23-24; Ezek. 20:47; Zech. 11:2; (7) 2 Kings 2:24; Ps. 50:10; 80:13; 104:20; Isa. 56:9; Jer. 5:6; 12:8; Amos 3:4; Mic. 5:8; (8) Isa. 44:13-15; Jer. 7:18, 10:3-5.

Forest Fire: (1) Judgment; (2) Gossip or rumor out of control.
Also see *Burn*, *Fire*, *Forest*, and *Wild Fire*.
(1) Ezek. 20:47-48; (2) James 3:6.

Fork: (1) Lying (forked-tongue); (2) Divided (paths/loyalties); (3) Choice (decision-making).
(1) Gen. 3:4 (serpent split-tongued); (2) Gen. 13:9-11; Mark 11:4 (KJV); (3) Mark 11:4 (KJV), (fork in the road).

Forklift: (1) Organizing (putting things in order); (2) Lying spirit (falsely raising hopes/ left on the shelf); (3) Burden lifter.
(1) Neh. 12:44a; (2) 1 Kings 22:22; Mic. 2:11 (as in lifting with a forked tongue); (3) Matt. 11:28.

Formal: (1) Religious; (2) Official/orderly (legitimate). (1) Isa. 10:1 (a prescribed form); (2) 1 Cor. 14:40.

Fornication: (1) Actual fornication; (2) Defiled by other lovers; (3) Idolatry; (4) Communing with or friend of the world.
Also see *Adultery* and *Sex*.
(2) Isa. 23:17; (3) 2 Chron. 21:11; (4) 1 Cor. 6:16; James 4:4.

Forty: (1) Test, try, prove; (2) No man's land (between two realms); (3) Wilderness before entering the Promised Land; (4) The distance to the Promised Land; (5) Probation before entry; (6) Humbling dependence on God; (7) Full term of reign; (Samson half term, David, Saul, Solomon); (8) Gestation (Pregnancy full term).
(1) Deut. 8:2 (Hebrew "prove"); (2-3) Acts 1:3; Matt. 4:2; 1 Sam. 17:16; (4) Exod. 16:45; Num. 14:34; Deut. 2:7; 8:2; (5) Acts 7:30,36; (6) Deut. 8:3; (7) Judges 16:31; 2 Sam. 5:4; Acts 13:21; 1 Kings 11:42; (8) Matt. 2:6.

Forty-Two: (1) Resurrection; (2) Blasphemy of Holy Spirit [Prefigures Christ's rejection by religious spirits (hair related to anointing) and length of His ministry]; (3) Witness of probation; (4) Probation.
See *Forty*.
(1) Matt. 1:17 (3 x 14, each representing a day); (2) 2 Kings 2:23-24; (3) 40 + 2; (4) James 5:17.

Forty-Five: (1) Undergoing testing and trials with the grace of God followed by revival.
(1) See *Forty* and *Five*.

Forty-One: (1) New beginning after testing/trial; (2) Love after trial.
Also see *Forty* and *One*.
(1) Luke 4:14-15; (2) Song 8:5.

Fossil: (1) Locked in the past.
(1) Gen. 19:26.

Found: See *Lost and Found*.

Foundation: (1) Christ; (2) Word of God; (3) Heart; (4) History; (5) Beginning; (6) Genesis; (7) Rock; (8) Love.
(1) 1 Cor. 3:11; (2) Matt. 5:18; 7:24-25; (3) Isa. 28:16; Matt. 13:23; Acts 13:22; Eph. 3:17; (4-5) Job 4:19; (7) Matt. 7:24-25; (8) Eph. 3:17.

Fountain: (1) Deep source; (2) Fountain of Life (Christ); (3) The Holy Spirit; (4) The human spirit/heart; (5) Abundant water supply; (6) Womb; (7) Cleansing; (8) Fear of the Lord; (9) Voice of the righteous; (10) Wisdom.
Also see *Waterfall.*
(1) Gen. 7:11; Lev. 20:18; Eccles. 12:6; (2) Ps. 36:7-9; Prov. 13:14; Jer. 2:13; Rev. 21:6; (3) John 7:38-39; (4) Matt. 12:34b; James 3:8-11; (5) Gen. 16:7; Num. 33:9; Ps. 114:8; Jer. 9:1; 17:13; (6) Lev. 20:18; Prov. 5:18; Song 4:12; (7) Lev. 11:36; Zech. 13:1; (8) Prov. 14:27; (9) Prov. 10:11; (10) Prov. 18:4.

Four: (1) Rule or dominion; (2) Earth or the physical; (3) Creation or creative works; (4) Material or earthly completeness; (5) Earthly dominion; (6) Earthly effort or flesh; (7) World (especially city); (8) Division; (9) Not enough; (10) Not known; (11) Not bearable; (12) May say someone is not changing (four corners and four sides to square); (13) The spirit realm (fourth dimension); (14) Time (as the fourth dimension); (15) Christ as fourth man in fiery furnace.
Also see *Earth* and *Earthly.*
(1) Gen 1:16; Prov. 30:31; (2) The fourth book of the Bible is Numbers; in Hebrew it is called *B'Midbar*, which means "the wilderness." This talks of the earth, which is a wilderness compared to Heaven; Prov. 30:24; Mark 13:27; (3-4) Fourth day saw material creation finished; Job 1:19 (Job's material completeness was taken that God may lead him into spiritual completeness); John 4:35; (5) John 11:17,39; 19:23; Acts 10:11,30; (6) Gen. 47:24; Acts 27:29; (7) Gen. 15:13; Acts 7:6 (Egypt is a picture of the world; [4 x 100; 100 = whole; 400 = complete earthly dominion or earthly dominion completed, beginning of spiritual dominion]); (8) Gen. 1:14-18; 2:10 (parted); (9) Prov. 30:15; (10) Prov. 30:18; (11) Prov. 30:22; (13) Eph. 3:18-19; (14) Exod. 3:14; Heb. 13:8; (15) Dan. 3:25.

Four Hundred and Forty: (1) Harmony with God (perfect pitch 440).
(1) 1 Cor. 6:17.

Fourteen: (1) Double measure of spiritual perfection; (2) Passover; (3) Deliverance and liberty.
(1) 2 x 7; (2) Exod. 12:6; Num. 9:5; (3) Gen. 31:41; Exod. 12:6, 31-33; Acts 27:27-44.

Four-Wheel Drive: (1) Powerful and independent ministry; (2) A ministry that does not have to stay on the road (traditional paths); (3) Full Gospel ministry; (4) Sign of opulence/wealth/prosperity (the "look" of success).
Also see *Jeep.*
(1) Luke 1:80; (2) Ps. 77:19; (3) Mark 16:15-18,20; (4) Matt. 23:5a.

Fox(es): (1) Little sins (apparently insignificant) that destroy fruitfulness; (2) Sly or cunning spirit/person; (3) Light-footedness (thief); (4) Vermin; (5) Cowardly (lacking spiritual fortitude); (6) Creature of the night; (7) Politician; (8) Stealer or attacker of sheep.
(1) Song 2:15; (2) Luke 13:32; (3) Neh. 4:3; (4) Ps. 63:10 (KJV); (5-6) Ezek. 13:4-5; (7) Luke 13:32; (8) Ezek. 34:12; Acts 20:29.

Foyer: (1) Exposure (common place); (2) Entry; (3) Exit; (4) Place of welcoming, greeting, or arrival; (5) First impressions.
(1) Gen. 19:1; Exod. 38:8; Num. 10:3; 1 Sam. 2:22; Jer. 1:15; Mark 1:33; (2-3) Deut. 28:6; (4) 1 Cor. 16:20; 2 Cor. 13:12; (5) Isa. 53:2; Matt. 23:27.

Fragile: (1) Handle with care; (2) Vulnerable; (3) Sensitive.
(1) Gal. 6:1; (2) Gen. 4:7; Judg. 16:19-20; (3) 1 Sam. 18:8.

Frame: (1) The believer; (2) The Church; (3) A support; (4) A devised plan; (5) Something made or about to be made; (6) Something spoken or about to be spoken; (7) Treasuring a memory; (8) Set up.
(1) Ps. 103:14; 139:15; (2) Eph. 2:21 (KJV); (3) Ps. 139:15; (4) Jer. 18:11 (KJV); Ps. 94:20 (KJV); (5) Isa. 29:16 (KJV); (6) Judg. 12:6 (KJV); Ps. 50:19; (7) Phil. 3:13; Eph. 2:11a (KJV); (8) Gen. 39:14; 1 Kings 21:10.

Freezer: (1) Heart; (2) Long-term issue in the heart (long-term storage); (3) Love gone cold; (4) Hardened heart.
Also see *Frozen* and *Ice.*
(1) Luke 6:45; (2) Gen. 42:9; (3) Matt. 24:12; (4) Job 38:30.

Freight: (1) Business.
(1) 1 Kings 10:15.

French Fries: (1) Flesh (that which clogs the arteries and stops the flow of life).
Also see *Fish and Chip Shop* and *Junk Food.*
(1) Gal. 6:8.

Friday: (1) Six; (2) Human; (3) Double income; (4) Eve of rest; (5) Eve or victory; (6) Day of the flesh.
Also see *Day* and *Five* (the secular world sees Friday as the fifth day of the week).
(1-2) Gen. 1:26-31; (3) Exod. 16:5,22,26,29; (4) Exod. 23:12; (5) Josh. 6:3; (6) As in, the world celebrates the end of the working week.

Fridge: See *Refrigerator.*

Friend: (1) Jesus; (2) Obedient disciple; (3) Literal friend; (4) Someone with whom you are familiar.
(1) Prov. 18:24; Matt. 11:19; Luke 12:4; John 15:13,15; (2) John 15:14; (4) Job 19:14; Ps. 41:9.

Frill-Necked Lizard: (1) Spirit of fear; (2) Demon.
Also see *Lizard.*
(1-2) 2 Tim. 1:7.

Frog: (1) Unclean spirit; (2) Demonic powers; (3) Demon; (4) Deception; (5) Lying spirit.
(1-4) Exod. 8:2-13 (each plague pointed to the ineptitude of Egypt's gods, which in turn were empowered by demons, cf. 1 Cor. 10:19-20); Ps. 78:45; 105:30; Rev. 16:13; (4-5) 1 Kings 22:22; Rev. 16:13.

Front: (1) Future (as in front of you); (2) First appearance; (3) Seeing on the surface; (4) Exposed; (5) Leadership.
Also see *Front Door*, *Front Yard*, and *Before*.
(1) Matt. 11:10; Luke 9:52; 10:1; Acts 7:45 (as in "what lies ahead or before me"); (3) As in "It was all a front for the mafia"; (4) As in "up front"; (5) Ps. 80:1; Isa. 40:11.

Front Door: (1) Entry to your heart; (2) Future (before you); (3) Face; (4) Mouth; (5) Meet; (6) Confront; (7) Seek, ask, knock; (8) Entrance; (9) Communication; (10) The door speaks for the household; (11) Spiritual sensitivity; (12) In secret (behind closed doors); (13) Not known (door shut); (14) Close/near/soon (at the door); (15) Jesus (the Door); (16) Salvation (open doors); (17) Hardened hearts; (18) Opportunity; (19) Opportunity to preach; (20) Door of Heaven; (21) Opening up to.
Also see *Door* and *Front*.
(1) Exod. 12:7; Ps. 24:7,9; Rev. 3:20; (2) Ps. 5:8; (3) Gen. 1:2; 4:6-7; (4) Judg. 11:31 (rash oath); Job 41:14; Ps. 141:3; Ezek. 33:30-31; (5) 2 Kings 14:8; (6) Gen. 19:6-7; 2 Kings 14:11; (7) 1 Chron. 16:11; Luke 11:7-13; (8) Gen. 6:16; Prov. 8:3; (9) Gen. 43:19; Exod. 33:9-11; (10) Exod. 12:22-23; Josh. 2:19; (11) Exod. 21:6; (12) Isa. 57:8; Matt. 6:6; (13) Matt. 25:12; Luke 13:25; (14) Matt. 24:33; Mark 1:33; 13:29; James 5:9; (15) John 10:7, 9; (16) Acts 16:26-28; (17) Acts 21:30 (doors shut); (18) 1 Cor. 16:9; 2 Cor. 2:12; Rev. 3:8; (19) Col. 4:3; (20) Ps. 78:23; Rev. 4:1.

Front Porch: See *Porch* and *Verandah*.

Front Yard (Garden): See *Yard (Front)*.

Frost: (1) Cold or hardship; (2) Judgment; (3) No love; (4) Wickedness. Frost settles overnight, therefore also see *Night*.
(1) Gen. 31:40; Jer. 36:30; (2) Ps. 78:47; (3-4) Matt. 24:12.

Frown: (1) Disapproval; (2) Pride (looking down on you); (3) Troubled or burdened spirit.
(1) Gen. 31:5; (2) Isa. 2:11; (3) Dan. 7:28.

Frozen: (1) Love gone cold (cold-hearted); (2) Spiritually inactive; (3) Sexual issue of fear.
Also see *Freezer*, *Frost*, and *Ice*.
(1) Matt. 24:12; (2) Rev. 3:16; (3) 2 Sam. 13:20.

Fruit: (1) Produce of the Spirit; (2) Attributes of the heart (good or bad); (3) New believers; (4) An outward display of the heart; (5) Children or descendants; (6) Earnings (fruit in hand); (7) Laziness or resting on your laurels (rotten fruit).

(1) Gal. 5:22-23; (2-3) Jer. 17:10; Matt. 7:16-20; (3) Col. 1:6; (4) Matt. 12:33; (5) Acts 2:30; (6) Prov. 31:16; (7) Luke 12:16,19.

Fruit Falling: (1) Untimely (too early/not ready/too late); (2) Ill-prepared; (3) Falling over in trials.
(1-3) Rev. 6:13.

Fruit Inspection: (1) Sampling for approval or quality; (2) Analyzing the heart.
(1) Matt. 3:8; 21:34-35; Luke 3:8; 13:6; John 15:5,16; (2) Hos. 10:1-2.

Fruit Tree: (1) Believer.
Also see *Orchard*, *Plantation*, and *Vineyard*.
(1) Ps. 1:3.

Frying Pan: (1) Heart (as the place where meals are prepared); (2) Passion/zeal. (1) Lev. 7:9; 1 Chron. 23:29; (2) Jer. 20:9.

Funeral: (1) Burying the past; (2) Death; (3) About to be resurrected; (4) Baptism.
Also see *Death* and *Mourning*.
(1-4) Rom. 6:4.

Furnace: (1) Hell; (2) Judgment; (3) Torment; (4) Affliction; (5) Purifying.
Also see *Dross*, *Gold*, and *Iron*.
(1) Matt. 5:22b; Rev. 9:2; (2) 2 Pet. 2:4; (3) Luke 16:23; (4) Isa. 48:10b; (5) Ps. 12:6.

Furniture: (1) Past makeup/issues (old); (2) Gifts, riches, and promises of God (new); (3) May represent what is going on within you (God's house), e.g., a table may speak about communion; a chair, authority; a couch, perhaps laziness, etc.
Also see *Chair*, *Couch*, *House*, *Sofa*, and *Table*.
(1-2) Prov. 24:3-4; 2 Cor. 5:17; (3) 2 Cor. 5:1.

Furniture Truck: See *Removal Van*.

G

Gambling: (1) Playing with your eternal destiny; (2) Flesh dominating the spirit (putting temporary fulfillment above eternity); (3) Addiction; (4) Stronghold; (5) Greed; (6) Deception; (7) Making decisions without God.
(1-2) Matt. 16:26; Luke 12:20; (3) Ps. 1:1 (*sinner* here is a habitual sinner); 1 Tim. 6:9; (4) Mark 10:21; (5) Prov. 1:19; 15:27; (6) Eccles. 5:10; 1 Tim. 6:10; (7) Gen. 16:2 (He didn't check with God); 2 Kings 1:3; 1 Chron. 10:14; Isa. 50:11.

Games: (1) Business (competitive sport); (2) Spiritually immature; (3) Toying with Christianity; (4) Missing the point (i.e., that it is about souls); (5) Life in the Kingdom of God.
Also see *Ball*, *Cards*, *Playground*, *Playing*, and *Toys*.
(1) Mark. 9:33-34; (2) 1 Cor. 13:11; (3) As in "They are just playing games"; (4) Matt. 11:16-19; (5) 2 Tim. 4:7.

Gang: (1) Fear; (2) Intimidation; (3) Spiritual warfare; (4) Anger and violence; (5) Unclean spirits; (6) Principality or power (gang leader); (6) Strongman (gang leader). Also see *Skinheads*.

(1-3) Josh. 1:4-9 (the word *Hittite* comes from a root word that means "affrighted with fear"); (4) Neh. 4:1-2; Ps. 22:16; (5) Mark 5:7-9, 13; (6) Matt. 12:27; Eph. 6:12.

Gap: (1) The connection between Heaven and earth; (2) Ministry of intercession; (3) Jesus Christ; (4) An opportunity or opening; (5) Hole needing filling; (6) Something missing; (7) Step, leap, or stand of faith.

(1-2) Ezek. 22:30; Heb. 7:25; Luke 16:26; (3) Heb. 7:25; John 1:51 (cf. Gen. 28:12,17); (4-6) Ezek. 22:30; (7) Matt. 14:28-29.

Garage: (1) Parked or retired ministry; (2) In storage; (3) Church; (4) Undergoing a spiritual tune-up; (5) Going nowhere; (6) Restoration of a fallen ministry (workshop); (7) Repair shop (workshop). Also see *Car Park* and *Parked Auto*.

(1) 1 Sam. 4:13-15; Luke 12:19; (2) Isa. 49:2; (4) Luke 1:80; (5) Gen. 42:16a; Luke 12:19; (3, 6-7) Rev. 3:2, 8; Gal. 6:1.

Garbage: (1) Sin; (2) Transgression; (3) The flesh; (4) Works of the flesh.

(1-2) Isa. 66:24 (garbage is taken to the dump!); Mark 9:43-45,47; (3) Phil. 3:8; (4) Gal. 5:19-21.

Garbage Truck: (1) Large deliverance ministry (removes rubbish/sin); (2) Removing sin; (3) Unclean ministry/church; (4) Corrupt business; (5) Unholy destiny. Also see *Flies* and *Rubbish*.

(1) Matt. 8:16; (2) Job 8:4; Isa. 31:7; Zeph. 1:17; (3) Isa. 64:6; John 2:14-16; Rev.17:4-6; 19:2-3; (4) Isa. 1:4; (5) Mark 9:43-44,46,48.

Garden: (1) The heart of the believer; (2) The human spirit; (3) The Church; (4) Growth; (5) Place of intimacy with God; (6) Workplace or that which is in your care; (7) Eternal life (evergreen garden); (8) Can be a place of death and burial; (9) Can represent sin (hiding in garden); (10) Can represent new life (fruitfulness); (11) Righteousness. Also see *Park*, *Yard (Back)*, and *Yard (Front)*.

(1) Song 4:16-5:1; Mark 4:7-8; (2) Song 4:15; Jer. 31:12; (3) Song 4:12; (4) Gen. 2:9; Luke 13:19; (5) Gen. 3:8; Song 4:12,15-16; 6:2,11; John 18:26; (6) Gen. 2:15 (7) Isa. 51:3; 58:11; (8) John 19:41; 2 Kings 21:18, 26; (9) Gen. 3:10 (also consider that it was the place of the first sin); (10) Num. 24:6; Jer. 31:12 (joy); (11) Isa. 61:11.

Gardener: (1) Heavenly Father; (2) Earthly or spiritual caretaker.

(1) Gen. 2:8; Song 5:1; 6:2; John 15:1; (2) Gen. 2:15; John 20:15; also as the one who maintains and cares for the fruit-bearing trees.

Gardening: (1) Father's business; (2) Ministry; (3) Preparing the heart; (4) Working in the harvest.

(1) John 15:1; (2) Luke 13:7-9; (3) Jer. 4:3-4; Hos. 10:12.

Garment: See *Clothes, Mantle, Robe,* and *Skirt.*

Gas: (1) Spirit (Holy or evil); (2) Your life.

Also see *Poison.*

(1) Job 15:13; 27:3; (2) James 4:14.

Gasoline: (1) Fuel; (2) The Holy Spirit; (3) Power; (4) Ignition; (5) Anger; (6) Refuel; (7) Worldly wine or dependence; (8) Money.

Also see *Automobile* and *Motor.*

(1) Zech. 4:12; Matt. 25:8-9; (2-3) Mic. 3:8a; Zech. 4:12-14; Matt. 25:3-4; (cf. Matt. 25:1-12); Acts 1:8; (4) Ps. 104:4; (5) Isa. 9:19; (6) Acts 2:4; 4:31; 9:17; 11:24; 13:9,52; 15:13; (7) Rev. 18:3; (8) Ezek. 27:17; Matt. 25:8-9.

Gas Station: (1) Church where you receive an infilling of the Holy Spirit; (2) An anointed ministry; (3) Place of refueling in the Spirit; (4) Place of restoration.

Also see *Gasoline, Mechanic,* and *Oil Rig.*

(1) Acts 2:4; (2) Luke 4:18; (3) Isa. 40:31; (4) Acts 9:17-19.

Gate: (1) Jesus Christ (The Gate of Heaven); (2) Heart; (3) Access; (4) Barrier (closed gate); (5) Opportunity (open gate); (6) Leadership (gatepost); (7) Not knowing Christ (shut gate); (8) Power; (9) Authority; (10) Narrow (life); (11) Broad (destruction); (12) Entry; (13) Separation; (14) Eldership; (15) Temple gate (beautiful); (16) The place of control; (17) The place of observation; (18) Exit; (19) Big entry; (20) Barred entry; (21) The place of sacrifice; (22) Protection; (23) The place of witness; (24) Locked up; (25) Death; (26) Thanksgiving; (27) The authority and strength of people (brass and iron); (28) Righteousness; (29) The place of wisdom; (30) The place of judgment; (31) The place of communication; (32) Worship (sheep gate); (33) Evangelism (fish gate); (34) Foundational teachings (old gate); (35) Death to self (valley gate); (36) Purging and refining (refuse gate); (37) Holy Spirit refreshing (fountain gate); (38) Word of God (water gate); (39) Intercession (horse gate); (40) Return of Christ (east gate); (41) Mustering or rapture (miphkad gate).

Also see *Door.*

(1) Gen. 28:12,17; John 1:51; Ps. 24:7,9; 118:20; 2 Sam. 23:15; (2) Ps. 24:7,9; (3) Ps. 100:4; (4) Neh. 7:3; 13:19; Rev. 21:25; (5) Prov. 1:21-22; 8:34; (6) Ruth 4:11; Prov. 31:23; Gal. 2:9; Rev. 3:12; (7) Luke 13:25; (8-9) Gen. 22:17; 24:60; Ps. 69:12; 127:5; Matt. 16:18; (10-11) Matt. 7:13-14; Luke 13:24; (12) Prov. 17:19; Luke 7:12; Acts 10:17; (13) Luke 16:20,26; (14) Gen. 19:1; 23:10; 34:20; Ruth 4:1-2,11; 1 Sam. 4:18; 9:18; Job 29:7; Prov. 31:23; (15) Acts 3:2,10; (16-17) Acts 9:24; (18) Acts 12:10; (19) 1 Sam. 21:13; Acts 12:13; Rev. 21:12; (20) Deut. 3:5; Acts 12:14; (21) Acts 14:13; Heb. 13:12; (22) Exod. 20:10; Deut. 3:5; (23) Ruth 4:10-11; (24) 1 Sam. 23:7; (25) Job 38:17; Ps. 9:13; 107:18; Matt. 16:18; (26) Ps. 100:4; (27) Ps. 107:16; (28) Ps. 118:19; (29) Prov. 1:20-21; 8:1,3,34; 24:7; (30) Ruth 4:1-2,10; Prov. 22:22; (31) Prov. 31:31; (32) Neh. 3:1; (33) Neh. 3:3; (34) Neh. 3:6; (35) Neh. 3:13; (36) Neh. 3:13; (37) Neh. 3:15; (38) Neh. 3:26; (39) Neh. 3:28; (40) Neh. 3:29; (41) Neh. 3:31.

Gather: (1) Harvest; (2) Revival; (3) Protect; (4) Church (a gathering).
(1) Luke 3:17; Rev. 14:15; (2) Mark 1:33; Luke 8:4; (3) Matt. 23:37; (4) Acts 14:27.

Gaunt: See *Emaciated* and *Skinny*.

Gear Lever: (1) Change or change agent; (2) Taking the ministry up or down a notch spiritually.
(1) Gen. 41:14; 2 Chron. 29:16; (2) 1 Kings 18:46; 19:3.

Gemstones: See *Precious Stones.*

General (Military): (1) Jesus Christ; (2) An archangel; (3) Apostolic ministry; (4) Authority; (5) Leader.
(1) Josh. 5:14-15; (2) Dan. 10:13; Jude 1:9; Rev. 12:7; (3) Acts 5:29; 6:2-7; 8:14-15; (4-5) 1 Chron. 11:6.

Generator: (1) Power of God; (2) The Holy Spirit; (3) Powerful Spirit-filled ministry.
(1) Ps. 62:11; 68:35; 71:18; (2) Mic. 3:8; Luke 4:14; (3) Luke 1:17.

Genitals: (1) Evangelism or evangelist; (2) Sex/uality; (3) Sexual perversion; (4) Exposed; (5) Vulnerable; (6) Revealed secrets (possible sexual secrets).
Also see *Naked, Sex,* and *Sexual Abuse.*
Note: if there is an accompanied sexual arousal or perversion associated with the prophetic incident or natural event then there may be a pornographic/sexual/lust/sex predator issue or evil spirit involved.
(1) Mark 4:14-20; as the reproductive organs of the Body of Christ (seed sowing); Lev. 15:16 (KJV); (2-3) Lev. 15:16-18 (KJV); (4) Gen. 3:7a; 9:22; (5-6) Deut. 25:11 (KJV).

Giant: (1) Big test; (2) Intimidation/fear; (3) Overwhelming; (4) Enemy resistance; (5) Large faith (if you are the giant); (6) Imposing obstacle; (7) Demons; (8) Need for the anointing (not conventional battle cf. Eph. 6:12); (9) We are to look to God, not ourselves; (10) Giants need dispossessing; (11) Angel.
(1) 1 Sam. 17:4,16; (2) Num. 13:32-33; 1 Sam. 17:11; (3) Job 16:14; (4) Deut. 3:1,11; 2 Sam. 21:16-22; (5) Matt. 8:10; (6) Matt. 15:22-28; (7) Gen. 6:4; (8) 1 Sam. 17:33-47; (9) Num. 13:33; (10) Deut. 2:20-21; 3:13; Josh. 13:12; 17:15; (11) Rev. 7:1; 10:5,8.

Gift: If your Father is giving you a gift, it can represent: (1) A spiritual gift; (2) The Holy Spirit; (3) The baptism in the Spirit (evidenced by speaking in tongues).
Alternatively, a gift could be: (4) A bribe.
(1) Heb. 2:4; (2) Eph. 1:17; Rom. 5:5; 2 Cor. 5:5; Gal. 3:5; (3) Luke 24:49; Acts 11:17; (4) Prov. 21:14.

Giraffe: (1) Pride; (2) Self-importance.
(1-2) Ps. 131:1; Isa. 2:11; 3:16.

Girl: (1) Young church; (2) Literal girl; (3) Young generation.
(1) Eph. 5:25; (3) Ruth 4:12b.

Glands: (1) Bitterness and unforgiveness [first sign of a spiritual infection] (swollen glands).

(1) Matt. 24:10 (note the progression: offense > betrayal > hatred).

Glass: (1) Heart; (2) Word of God; (3) Mirror; (4) Transparent and pure; (5) Seal; (6) Fragile (breakable); (7) Victory.

Also see *Broken Glass* and *Window.*

(1) Prov. 27:19; Matt. 5:8; John 2:25; (2-3) 1 Cor. 13:12; 2 Cor. 3:18 (KJV); James 1:23-25; (4) Rev. 21:18,21; (5) Job 37:18; (6) Ps. 2:9; 31:12; Matt. 9:17; (7) Rev. 15:2.

Glass (Drinking): (1) Heart; (2) Pure heart (crystal glass); (3) Church (as a vessel of the Holy Spirit); (4) Anointed ministry.

Also see *Glass* and *Glass of Water.*

(1) Prov. 20:5; 21:1; Lam. 2:19; Matt. 5:8; (3) Ezek. 39:29; Acts 2:17-18; (4) Acts 28:8.

Glass Door: Prophetic opportunity (walking through glass door).

(1) 1 Kings 19:19-20; Rev. 4:1.

Glasses (Spectacles): See *Reading.*

Glass Office: (1) Office of a prophet.

(1) 1 Sam. 9:9; Prov. 7:6.

Glass of Water: (1) Installment of revelation from God's Word; (2) Partaker of God's Spirit (if drinking); (3) Eternal Life; (4) Unselfish deed (giving glass of water); (5) Returning good for evil (giving to your enemy).

Also see *Glass (Drinking)* and *Water.*

(1) Prov. 18:4; Amos 8:11; Eph. 5:26; (2) John 4:11; (3) John 4:14; (4) Matt. 10:42; (5) Prov. 25:21.

Glass Table: See *Table (Glass Table).*

Glitter: (1) Glamor; (2) Self-glory; (3) Apparent appeal; (4) Looking good.

(1-4) 2 Cor. 11:14; 2 Tim. 3:5; 1 Pet. 3:3-4.

Gloves: (1) Warm and loving help; (2) Warmth; (3) Protection; (4) Deed in secret; (5) With or without sensitivity.

(1) James 2:15-16; (2) John 18:18; (3) Ps. 44:3 (KJV); (4) Matt. 6:4; (5) Heb. 4:15 (KJV).

Glue: (1) Stuck (or stick); (2) Joined; (3) Soul-tie; (4) Stronghold; (5) Love; (6) Word of power; (7) Having trouble moving on.

(1) 2 Sam. 18:9; Isa. 5:13; (2) Gen. 2:24; 1 Cor. 6:17; (3) 1 Sam. 18:1; (4) Matt. 12:29; (5) 2 Cor. 5:14; Col. 2:2; 3:14; Phil.2:2; (6) Heb. 1:3; (7) Gen. 19:26; Mark 6:48; Acts 27:41.

Goal: (1) Success; (2) Achievement; (3) Overcoming the world.

Also see *Hole in One.*

(1-2) 2 Tim. 4:7; Phil 3:12; (3) Rev. 3:21.

Goalkeeper: (1) Defense of the Gospel.

(1) Phil. 1:7,17.

Goat(s): (1) Unsaved; (2) Cursed; (3) One without compassion (heart); (4) Demon; (5) Hard-hearted.

Also see *Sheep*.

(1-4) Matt. 25:32, 41; (5) Matt. 9:34; 12:2,24; 23:13 (full of "buts").

Go Cart: (1) Immature Christian walk; (2) Incomplete Christian walk.

Also see *Racing Driver*.

(1) 1 Cor. 13:11.

Godson: (1) Promise; (2) Jesus.

(1) Rom. 9:9; Gal. 4:23; Heb. 11:17; (2) Matt. 27:54; Mk. 1:1.

Going Out: (1) Beginning a spiritual military campaign; (2) Leaving.

Also see *Coming In* and *Outside/Outdoors*.

(1) 1 Kings 3:7 (AMP); Josh. 14:11; 2 Sam. 3:25; (2) John 13:30.

Gold/en: (1) Refined/pure/holy; (2) Glory; (3) Wealthy, great, or powerful; (4) Anointing (gold honey); (5) First place; (6) Money; (7) Beautiful or valuable; (8) Deeds done in the Holy Spirit; (9) Honor/able; (10) Rich or blessed; (11) Religious glory.

Also see *Precious Stones* and *Yellow*.

(1) Job 23:10; Heb. 9:4; Rev. 21:15, 18-21; (2) Lam. 4:1; Isa. 60;9; 1 Pet. 1:7; (3) Ezek. 16:13; Dan. 2:38; (4) Zech 4:12; (5) 1 Kings 10:21; (6) 2 Kings 12:13; 2 Chron. 24:14; (7) Zech. 4:2-6; Rev. 5:8; (8) 1 Cor. 3:12; 2 Tim. 2:21; (9) 2 Tim. 2:20; (10) Rev. 3:18; (11) Rev.17:4.

Golden Gate Bridge: (1) Path to God's glory; (2) Path to riches.

(1-2) Rev. 21:21.

Golf Caddy: (1) Support role; (2) The Holy Spirit.

(1) 1 Sam. 14:6-7; (2) John 14:26.

Golf Course: (1) Progressing in faith (speaking the word and then following it).

Also see *Ball, Golfer, Golf Hole,* and *Hole in One*.

(1) Deut. 8:3; 30:14; Josh. 1:8; Ps. 119:105.

Golfer: (1) Someone walking by faith (following the Word).

Also see *Ball* and *Golf Course*.

(1) Ps. 119:133.

Golf Hole: (1) The goal or target God has for you; (2) The hole number may convey a message.

Also see *Golf Course* and *Golfer*.

(1) Phil. 3:14; (2) See individual number entries.

Golf Tee: (1) Preaching platform.

Also see *Ball, Trees,* and *Water*.

(1) As the launching place for words (the ball).

Google: (1) God (as all-knowing); (2) Searching for answers.

(1) John 16:30; Col. 2:2-3; 1 John 3:20; (2) Gen. 2:3; Matt. 7:7.

Gorilla: See *King Kong.*

Government: (1) Kingdom of God; (2) Church (government installation/dept.); (3) Authority.
(1-2) Eph. 1:20-23; (3) Rom. 13:1.

Governor: (1) Christ; (2) Ruler; (3) Authority and power; (4) Organizer and coordinator; (5) Judge; (6) Decision maker; (7) Justice of the peace; (8) The Law; (9) Helmsman (the person steering the ship).
(1) Matt. 2:6; (2) Matt. 2:6; (3) Luke 20:20; Rom. 13:1; (4) John 2:8-9; (5) Acts 24:10; (6) Matt. 27:2,11,14,21; (7) 2 Cor. 11:32; (8) Gal. 4:2; (9) James 3:4 (KJV).

Grader (Road): See *Road Grader.*

Grades: (1) Hot for God (A-grading); (2) Cold in my zeal for the things of God (F-grading); (3) Lukewarm (C-grading).
(1-3) Rev. 3:15-16.

Graffiti: (1) Spraying someone with words; (2) Self-promotion (graffiti initials); (3) Warning (The writing's on the wall).
(1) 2 Chron. 32:17; Mark 15:29; Luke 23:39; 1 Cor. 5:11; (2) 2 Sam. 15:4; (3) Dan. 5:25.

Grandchild: (1) The future or distant future; (2) The recipient—good and bad—of parental and grandparental influence; (3) Offspring; (4) Consider the meaning of their name.
(1) Exod. 2:9; Deut. 6:6-8; Ps. 34:11; 132:12; Prov. 13:22; (2) Exod. 34:7; Prov. 13:22; 2 Kings 17:41 (idolatry); Ps. 78:5-6 (Word of God); Ps. 103:17 (righteousness); Ezek. 37:25 (land).

Grandfather Clock: (1) Unsaved people with time running out; (2) The past/history (time of old); (3) Living in the past.
(1) Ps. 89:47; Rev. 12:12; (2) Josh. 24:15.

Grandparent: (1) The past; (2) Heritage or generation; (3) Inheritance (good or bad); (4) Tradition (especially if depicted as a nationality rich in tradition); (5) Church history (grandmother); (6) May represent those that give up the call (retire); (7) God; (8) Patron.
(1) Heb. 1:1; (2) Gen. 50:24; (3) cf. Exod. 34:7; Prov. 13:22; (4) Gal. 1:14; 1 Pet. 1:18; (5) 2 Tim. 1:5; (6) Deut. 4:25; (7) Dan. 7:9; (8) Prov. 17:6.

Grapes: (1) Good fruit; (2) Blood; (3) Sacrifice (crushed).
(1) John 15:16; (2) Gen. 49:11; (3) Gen. 40:11 (sacrificing the grape for its juice).

Grapes (Big Grapes): (1) Blessing; (2) The time to act (harvest); (3) Possible resistance to move on in God due to insecurity and low self-worth.
(1) Num. 13:27; (2-3) Num. 13:23,33.

Grass: (1) Humanity or flesh; (2) Peace (tender grass); (3) The righteous; (4) Little faith; (5) A place to feed; (6) A dying rich person; (7) Judgment; (8) People of small power; (9) Numerous; (10) Spiritual food/provision; (11) Evildoers; (12) Flourishing; (13) A troubled heart (withered grass); (14) Speaks of the frailty and brevity of life; (15) Favor (dew on grass); (16) A time to be diligent; (17) Speaks of humbling; (18) Blessing.
(1) Isa. 40:6; James 1:10; 1 Pet. 1:24; (2) Ps. 23:2 (*green pastures* means literally "pastures of tender grass"); (3) Prov. 11:28; (4) Matt. 6:30; (5) Matt. 14:19; Mark 6:39 (green grass); John 6:10 (much grass); (6) James 1:10-11; (7) Isa. 15:6; 40:6-8; Jer. 14:5-6; Rev. 8:7; (8) 2 Kings 19:26; Isa. 37:27; (9) Job 5:25; (10) Job 6:5; Jer. 50:11; Zech. 10:1; (11) Ps. 37:1-2; 92:7; 129:6; (12) Ps. 72:16; (13) Ps. 102:4,11; (14) Ps. 103:15; Isa. 51:12; (15) Prov. 19:12; (16) Prov. 27:23-27; (17) Dan. 4:15,23,25,32-33; 5:21; (18) Deut. 11:13-15.

Grass (Mown Grass): (1) Humanity's mortality; (2) Sinful people; (3) Humbled person (cutting away the flesh); (4) Harvesting (mowing grass); (5) Death or destruction.
(1-2) Ps. 37:1-2; (3) Ps. 72:6 (KJV); (4) Ruth 1:22; John 4:35; (5) Ps. 37:1-2.

Grasshopper: (1) Little, small, or insignificant.
Also see entries under *Locust*.
(1) Num. 13:33.

Grave (Stone): (1) Death; (2) Darkness; (3) Grief; (4) A sure thing; (5) Resurrection for the righteous (an upright gravestone can represent resurrection); (6) Levels pride; (7) Hypocrite (whitewashed tomb); (8) Victory.
Also see *Cemetery, Coffin, Death,* and *Graveyard*.
(1) Exod. 14:11; Job 33:22-30; 38:17; (2) Ps. 88:6; (3) Gen. 50:10; 2 Sam. 3:32; John 11:31; (4) Ps. 89:48; Prov. 30:15b-16a; (5) Gen. 35:20; 28:18; Ps. 49:15; Ezek. 37:12-14; Matt. 27:52-53; John 12:17; (6) Isa. 14:11; (7) Matt. 23:27; Luke 11:44; (8) 1 Cor. 15:55-57.

Gravel: (1) Deceit; (2) Shame; (3) Stony issues in the heart.
Also see *Dirt, Dust, Gravel Road,* and *Rocks*.
(1) Prov. 20:17; (2) Lam. 3:16; (3) Matt. 13:20-21.

Gravel Road: (1) Ungodly path.
Also see *Dirt Road, Gravel,* and *Sandy Path/Trail*.
(1) Ps. 17:5.

Graveyard: (1) Valley of death; (2) Valley of dry bones; (3) Spiritually dead; (4) Religious or hypocritical.
Also see *Cemetery, Coffin, Grave,* and *Death*.
(1) Job 10:21-22; (2) Ezek. 37:1-14; (3) Ps. 107:10-11, 14; (4) Matt. 23:27-28.

Gravy: (1) The Anointing.
(1) Joel 2:28; Acts 2:17; Heb. 6:4.

Gray: See *Grey* and *Grey Hair*.

Green: (1) Righteousness; (2) Envy; (3) Peace; (4) Hypocritical; (5) Prosperous; (6) Productive; (7) Life; (8) Growth; (9) Zealous; (10) Youth; (11) Joy; (12) Fruitful; (13) Fruitless; (14) Work of the flesh/self; (15) Flesh; (16) Wickedness; (17) Idolatry; (18) Earth; (19) Mercy; (20) Anointing or anointed one (olive green); (21) Resurrection. (1) Ps. 92:12; Prov. 11:30; (2) Prov. 14:30; Ezek. 31:9; Acts 7:9; 13:45; (3) Ps. 23:2; (4) Matt. 23:28-29; (5) Luke 23:31; (6) Song 2:13; Isa. 15:6-7; (7) Exod. 10:15-17; (8-10) Isa. 53:2; (12) Jer. 11:16; 17:8; Hos. 14:8; (13) Mark 11:13; (14) Ps. 37:35; (15) Isa. 40:6-8; 1 Pet. 1:24; (16) Ps. 37:5; (17) Deut. 12:2; 1 Kings 14:23b; 2 Kings 16:4; 17:10; (18) Gen. 1:30; Exod. 10:15; Rev. 8:7; 9:4; (19) Gen. 9:12 (central color of rainbow); (20) Zech. 4:12-14; (21) Gen. 8:11.

Grey: (1) Depression; (2) Uncertainty or ill-defined; (grey area); (3) Double-minded (mixture of black and white); (4) Lukewarm; (5) Death; (6) Old or mature; (7) Loss of strength; (8) Honor.
Also see *Grey Hair.*
(1) Job 3:5; 16:16; (2) Matt. 4:16; Luke 1:79; (3) James 1:8; Rev. 3:15-16; (4) Rev. 3:15-16; (5) Rev. 6:8 (pale horse); (6) Gen. 42:38; 44:29,31; Deut. 32:25; (7) Hos. 7:9; (8) Lev. 19:32.

Grey Hair: (1) Old or mature; (2) Wisdom; (3) God; (4) Close to death; (5) Deserving honor and respect; (6) The devil (accusing, arrogant, proud, lying, or deceptive individual).
Also see *Hair.*
(1) Gen. 42:38; (2) Job 12:12; Prov. 16:31; 20:29; (3) Dan. 7:9,17,22; (4) Gen. 42:38; 44:29, 31; Deut. 32:25; Hos. 7:9; (5) Lev. 19:32; (6) Rev. 12:9; 20:2.

Grief: See *Mourning.*

Griffin: (1) Commanding angel; (2) Powerful prophetic angel from God.
Also see *Lion* and *Eagle.*
(1) 2 Sam. 1:23b; Dan. 7:4; (2) Rev. 22:6.

Grim Reaper: See *Death* and *Destroy.*

Grind: (1) Proud person judged; (2) Judgment coming; (3) Sexual relations; (4) Harsh treatment; (5) Confinement and slavery.
(1) Matt. 21:42,44; (2) Matt. 24:41; (3) Job 31:10; (4) Isa. 3:15; (5) Lam. 5:13; Judg. 16:21.

Groaning: (1) Symbolizes heartache and a desire for release or birth of the spirit; (2) Bondage or affliction; (3) Oppression; (4) Complaint; (5) Wounded or vexed soul; (6) Grief (heartache); (7) Bruised heart; (8) Pain; (9) Death; (10) Awaiting release.
(1) Rom. 8:26; 2 Cor. 5:2,4; (2) Exod. 2:23-24; 6:5; Ps. 102:20; Acts 7:34; (3) Judg. 2:18b; (4) Job 23:2; (5) Job 24:12; Ps. 6:3, 6; 38:8-9; Jer. 51:52b; (6) Ps. 6:6-7; John 11:33,38; (7) Ps. 102:4-5; (8) Rom. 8:22; (9) Ezek. 30:24b; Ps. 102:20; (10) Rom. 8:23.

Grocery Store: See *Supermarket.*

Groom: (1) Jesus; (2) You in union with someone or something; (3) Christ or His offspring (bloody groom).
Also see *Best Man*.
(1) Mark 2:19-20; John 3:29; (3) Exod. 4:26; 1 Cor. 10:16.

Grotto: (1) Heart; (2) Earthly treasure; (3) Religious shrine.
Also see *Cave*, *Shrine*, and *Treasure*.
(1-3) Matt. 6:19-20.

Guarantee: (1) The Spirit; (2) Promise; (3) Assurance in Christ; (4) Faith.
(1) 2 Cor. 5:5; (2) Luke 24:49; (3) Acts 2:36; 17:31; (4) Heb. 11:1 (AMP).

Guide: (1) The Holy Spirit; (2) Jesus; (3) Mentor/leader; (4) An angel; (5) The Bible; (6) The rhema word (a word spoken in season).
Also see *Map* and *Pointing*.
(1) John 16:13; Rom. 8:14; (2) John 10:27; 21:19,21; Heb. 12:2; (3) 1 Kings 19:21b; Acts 8:30-31; (4) Gen. 19:15-16; (5) Ps. 119:105; (6) Prov. 15:23b; Isa. 50:4; Acts 8:30-31.

Guinea Pig: (1) Feeble; (2) Fearful; (3) Wise; (4) Timid; (5) Pawn; (6) Experiment; (7) Sin that you want to keep (as a pet).
Also see *Pet*.
(1-4) Prov. 30:24-26 (conies KJV); (5) As in "being used"; (6) As in "They are just using me as a guinea pig"; (6) Heb. 12:1.

Guitar: (1) Person; (2) Musician; (3) Worshiper; (4) Prophetic worship.
See *Music*, *Musical Instrument*, and *Rock 'n' Roll*.
(1) It has a body, neck, head and vocal chords; (1-4) 1 Sam. 10:5; 1 Chron. 25:1.

Gums: (1) Issue of the heart (bleeding gums).
(1) Matt. 15:18; Luke 6:45.

Gun: (1) Words; (2) Weapon; (3) Accusation; (4) Threatening words (loaded gun).
Also see *Bow* and *Bullets*.
(1-2) Isa. 54:17; (3-4) Ps. 22:13.

Gunman: (1) The accuser of the brethren; (2) Condemnation.
Also see *Assassin*, *Contract Killer*, *Gun*, *Sniper*¹ and *Rifle*.
(1) Rev. 12:10; (2) Matt. 12:37; John 5:24 (KJV); Rom. 8:1; 1 Tim. 3:6; James 3:1-9; 5:12.

Gutter(s): (1) Channel of the Spirit; (2) Lowest point (rock bottom); (3) Water catchment; (4) Humble soul recognition of being spiritually poor.
Also see *Drain*, *Curb/Kerb*, *Plumber*, and *Trench*.
(1) Judg. 15:19; Isa. 44:3; John 7:38-39; (2) Mic. 7:10; (3-4) Matt. 5:3.

Dirty Roof Gutters (1) Not dealing with issues in your life/church/ministry (the run-off of wrong authority structures).
(1) Matt. 23:26.

H

Haemorrhoids: See *Hemorrhoids.*

Hail: (1) Judgment; (2) Wrath.
(1) Ps. 78:47; Isa. 30:30; Ezek. 13:13.

Hair: (1) Anointing; (2) Vanity or self-glory; (3) Sin; (4) Separation unto God; (5) Speaks of covering (woman); (6) Glory; (7) Strength; (8) Fine line (accurate); (9) Protection or care; (10) Prophet or recluse; (11) Innumerable; (12) Humbling love and devotion; (13) Speaks of shame (long hair on male); (14) Self-glory (long hair on male); (15) Set apart for God (long-haired boy); (16) Person in the world (ponytail); (17) Glory (curly hair like a lion's mane); (18) Stronghold of thoughts (caught in the hair); (19) Self-glory/pride (caught by the hair); (20) Renewal of the mind (+/-) (washing hair).
Also see *Baldness, Grey Hair,* and *Hairy.*
(1) Judg. 16:19-20; (2) 2 Sam. 14:26; 1 Tim. 2:9; 1 Pet. 3:3; (3) Lev. 13:3-4,10ff; (4) Num. 6:5-8,18-19; (5) 1 Cor. 11:15; (6) Prov. 16:31; Dan. 7:9; 1 Cor. 11:15; Rev. 1:14; (7) Judg. 16:22,28-30; (8) Judg. 20:16; (9) 1 Sam. 14:45; 2 Sam. 14:11; 1 Kings 1:52; Matt. 10:30; Acts 27:34; (10) 2 Kings 1:8; (11) Ps. 69:4; (12) Luke 7:38,44; John 11:2; 12:3; (13) 1 Cor. 11:14; (14) Judg. 16:17; 2 Sam. 14:26; (15) Judg. 13:5; (16) Isa. 31:1; (17) Song 4:1; Dan. 7:9; Rev. 1:14; (18) Gen. 40:17; (19) 2 Sam. 18:9; (cf. 2 Sam. 14:26); (20) Tit. 3:5; Rom. 12:2.

Haircut: (1) Cleansing from sin; (2) Rejection; (3) Loss of/or removing the anointing.
(1) Lev. 14:8; (2) Jer. 7:29; (3) Judg. 16:19-20.

Hair Cut Off: (1) Shame; (2) Subjection; (3) Judgment; (4) Humbling; (5) Breaking of a vow.
Also see *Baldness.*
(1-3) Isa. 3:24; 7:20; 15:2; Jer. 7:29; Ezek. 5:1; (4-5) Judg. 16:19-21.

Hairdressers: (1) Vanity; (2) Grooming (self-glory); (3) Church (as the place where hair [the flesh] is trimmed).
Also see *Barber Shop.*
(1-2) 2 Sam. 14:26; 1 Tim. 2:9; 1 Pet. 3:3; (3) Num. 6:19.

Hair Extensions: (1) Authority/covering; (2) Not happy with your covering (pulling out extensions).
(1-2) 1 Cor. 11:15.

Hair (Not Singed): (1) God's protection.
(1) Dan. 3:27.

Hair Pulled Out: (1) Abuse; (2) Ashamed; (3) Being taken advantage of (some/part of hair pulled out); (4) Frustration.
(1) Isa. 50:6; (2) Ezra 9:3; Neh. 13:25; (3) Isa. 50:6; (4) As in "I'm pulling my hair out because nothing is being done about it!"

Hair (Wanting It White or Black): (1) Warning to watch what is coming from your mouth; (2) Promises you can't keep.
(1-2) Matt. 5:36-37.

Hairy: (1) Fleshly person (hairy arms, legs, back).
Also see *Legs—Hairy Legs.*
(1) Gen. 25:25; Rom. 9:13.

Half: (1) Division; (2) Part unknown; (3) Something beyond human knowledge; (4) Half-truth; (5) Incomplete; (6) Equal share with another.
(1) Gen. 1:6; (2-3) 1 Kings 10:7; Eph. 3:18-19; (4) Acts 5:1-2; Rev. 3:16; (5) Gen. 2:18; Ps. 55:23; (6) Esther 5:3,6; 7:2.

Hallway: See *Corridor.*

Halo: (1) Glory of God; (2) An angel.
(1) Matt. 17:2; Rev. 1:16; 10:1.

Hamburger: (1) Fast food; (2) Sermon; (3) Words or teaching quickly or ill-prepared; (4) Not balanced nutrition; (5) Words spoken without consideration of impact or consequences.
(1) Heb. 5:14; (2) Heb. 5:12-14; (3) 1 Tim. 3:15-16; 2 Tim. 4:3; (4) Mark 4:19; an example of this might be where someone says that fasting is no longer applicable based on Isaiah 58, though Jesus plainly says that we are expected to fast in Matthew 6:16; (5) Eccles. 5:2.

Hammer: (1) God's Word; (2) Using the Word of God to bring thoughts captive and killing wrong (human-made) thoughts; (3) Speaks of human-made building; (4) Unholy efforts of people; (5) Idolatry; (6) Babylon (or warlike nation); (7) Communism.
Also see *Mark* in Name and Place Dictionary.
(1) Jer. 23:29; (2) Judg. 4:21; 5:26; (*Sisera* means "binding in chains" and may speak of strongholds [attitudes of mind]) cf. 2 Cor. 10:3-5; (3) 1 Kings 6:7; (4-5) Ps. 74:6; Isa. 44:12; Jer. 10:2-5; (6) Jer. 50:23; (7) As in "hammer and sickle" on flag.

Hammerhead Shark: (1) Predator that uses the word; (2) Copping a flogging from a demon.
(1) Jer. 23:29; Matt. 4:6; (2) Acts 19:14-16.

Hand(s): (1) Heart; (2) Flesh; (3) Work of the flesh; (4) Works; (5) Crippled heart (withered or malformed hand); (6) The Church (God's hands); (7) God's provision or doing; (8) Taking; (9) Responsibility; (10) Dominion, control, or authority; (11) Oath or pledge; (12) Opposition; (13) Help; (14) Leading out; (15) Carrying; (16) Grabbing or grasping; (17) Gift or giving; (18) Payment; (19) Harm, hurt, or hit; (20) Readily available (at hand); (21) Within reach; (22) Custody or capture; (23) Reaching out; (24) Power or strength; (25) Invitation; (26) Direction; (27) Laziness (poor)/diligence (rich); (28) United; (29) Diligence (rule)/slothful (are ruled); (30) Doing (own); (31) Purchase; (32) Hidden (slothfulness); (33) Silence; (34) My side of the agreement (a hand); (35) Despondency and disappointment (hands hanging down).

Also see *Broken, Fingers, Fist, Handle, Hands Folded, Hands Laid On, Knuckles, Palm, Left and Right,* and *Shaking Hands.*

(1) Ps. 24:4; 58:2; Prov. 21:1; Eccles. 7:26; Song 5:4; James 4:8; (2) Luke 24:39; Eph. 2:11b; (3) Exod. 32:3-4; Dan. 2:34; (4) Gen. 4:11; 5:29; 31:42; Deut. 3:24; Prov. 12:14; Eccles. 2:11; (5) Luke 6:6-11; (6) 1 Cor. 12:12; (7) Eccles. 2:24; 9:1; (8) Gen. 3:22; (9) Gen. 9:2; (10) Gen. 14:20; 16:6,9; 24:10; 41:35; (11) Gen. 14:22; 21:30; 24:2; 38:20; 47:29; (12) Gen. 16:22; (13) Gen. 19:10; (14) Gen. 19:16; (15) Gen. 22:6; (16) Gen. 22:10; 25:26; Prov. 30:28; (17) Gen. 24:18; 33:10; Prov. 31:20; (18) Gen. 31:39; (19) Gen. 32:11; 37:21-22; Prov. 6:17; (20) Gen. 32:13; (21) Gen. 33:19; (22) Gen. 38:18; Prov. 6:5; (23) Gen. 38:28; (24) Gen. 49:24; Exod. 13:16; Prov. 3:27; (25) Prov. 1:24; (26) Prov. 4:27; (27) Prov. 10:4; (28) Prov. 11:21; 16:5; (29) Prov. 12:24; (30) Prov. 14:1; Eccles. 9:10; (31) Prov. 17:16; (32) Prov. 19:24; 26:15; (33) Prov. 30:32 (hand to mouth); (35) Heb. 12:12.

Handbag: See *Bag.*

Hand Grenade: (1) Anger needing/wanting release; (2) Carrying tension; (3) Wanting to throw cell phone (not being able to free oneself from people wanting you); (4) Fear of something erupting; (5) Wanting to get rid of— distance yourself from—a potential hazard (throwing hand grenade).

(1) Num. 24:10; Lam. 2:3; (2) Jer. 17:22; (3) Mark 3:7, 20; 7:33a; (4) Job 22:10b; (5) 2 Sam. 11:15.

Handkerchief: (1) Speaks of great faith and anointing; (2) Speaks of indirect acts of faith and healing; (3) Miracle; (4) Releasing the anointing for healing or deliverance (giving handkerchief); (5) Receiving the anointing for healing or deliverance (receiving handkerchief).

(1-5) Acts 19:12.

Handle: (1) To understand and gain control over something/someone; (2) Spiritual stranglehold; (3) No longer held captive (handle falling off); (4) No longer out of control; (5) Uncontrollable (too hot to handle); (6) Deceit and deception (secretive or wrong handling); (7) Truth (handling something openly).

(1) As in "I've got a handle on my new position now"; (2-3) John 14:30 (NIV); (4-5) As in "He's not able to handle it." (6-7) 2 Cor. 4:2.

Handlebars: (1) Leadership (steering the ministry); (2) Person getting in your way (someone on the handlebars); (3) Freeloader/burden to the ministry (someone on the handlebars); (4) Someone uncomfortable with the way things are going/or the way you are going about things (carrying someone on the handlebars).
(1) Ps. 23:2-4; (2) Gen. 13:1,14; (blocking your vision); (3) Acts 15:36-39; (4) John 6:60,66.

Hand Rail: (1) Barrier; (2) Support.
(1) Deut. 3:5 (KJV); Job 38:10-11; Ps. 107:16; (2) Job 40:18.

Hands Folded: (1) Laziness; (2) Famine; (3) Self-destruct.
(1) Prov. 6:10; 24:33; (2) Eccles. 4:5.

Hand Shaking: See *Shaking Hands.*

Hands Laid On: (1) Impartation; (2) Blessing; (3) Hurting; (4) Identifying with; (5) Death (hands on the eyes); (6) Healing; (7) Persecution.
(1-2) Gen. 48:13-20; (3) Gen. 22:12; (4) Gen 48:16; (5) Gen. 46:4; (6) Mark 6:5; 16:18b; (7) Luke 21:12; 22:53 (KJV).

Handwriting on a Wall: (1) The future is determined; (2) Judgment; (3) Weighed and found wanting; (4) Rumor.
(1-3) Dan. 5:5,27; (4) As in hearsay.

Hanging: (1) Cursed; (2) The Cross; (3) Conversion; (4) Christ; (5) Despondency (hands hanging down); (6) Feeling regret and guilt; (7) In the second heaven (positive experience).
(1) Mark 9:42; Gal. 3:13; (2) Luke 23:39; (3) Gal. 2:20; (4) Acts 5:30; 10:39; (5) Heb. 12:12; (6) Matt. 27:4-5; (7) Ezek. 3:14; 8:3.

Hang Glider: (1) Ministry in the Spirit; (2) Waiting on God.
(1-2) Isa. 40:31; John 3:8.

Harbor: See *Port.*

Hard/Hardened Heart: (1) Pride; (2) Stubbornness; (3) Resistant to the will of God.
(1-2) Neh. 9:16; Dan. 5:20; (3) Exod. 7:14.

Hard Drive: (1) Intellect (mind of the flesh); (2) Mind of the Spirit (supernatural quick thinking without boundaries).
Also see *Hardware* and *USB.*
(1) Rom. 8:5; Col. 2:18; (2) 1 Cor. 2:16.

Hardware (Computer): (1) The body of flesh/temple.
Also see *Computer, Hard Drive, Laptop, Desktop,* and *Software.*
(1) 1 Cor. 6:19; Col. 1:22.

Hardware Store: (1) Heaven; (2) Faith's storehouse (Faith is the substance...).
(1) Phil. 4:19; (2) Heb. 11:1.

Harlot: (1) Seducing spirit (sexual immorality); (2) An idolatrous or adulterous church; (3) A Christian dabbling with other gods; (4) A Christian dabbling in immoral sex; (4) Prostitute; (5) Church relying on enterprise; (6) Babylon; (7) Escort to hell (seducing harlot).

Also see *Woman*.

(1) Judg. 16:5; Prov. 7:10; (2) Jer. 3:1,6; Ezek. 16:15-17,32; Rev. 17:5; (3) Jer. 2:20; (4) 1 Cor. 6:15-18; (4) Prov. 29:3; (5-6) Rev. 16:19; 17:4-5; 18:2-3; (7) Prov. 5:3-5; 7:10-27; 23:27.

Harvest: (1) Soul winning; (2) The end of the world/final ingathering of souls.

Also see *Farm* and *Field*.

(1) John 4:35-42; (2) Matt. 13:39.

Hash Brown: See *French Fries*.

Hat: (1) Identity; (2) Role or responsibility; (3) Covering; (4) Authority; (5) Honor; (6) Dishonor.

Also note the type of hat. For example: If you are wearing a captain's hat, it means you will steer a ministry. If you had a Captain Cook's hat, it may mean you are going to take a nation for Christ. A helmet means either salvation or spiritual warfare and the need to guard your thoughts (see Eph. 6:17).

Also see *Cap* and *Helmet*.

(1) Deut. 1:15; Judg. 11:11; 1 Sam. 10:1; (2) As in "I'm wearing so many hats"; (3-6) 1 Cor. 11:3-16.

Hatred: (1) Murderer.

(1) 1 John 3:15.

Hawk: (1) Sharp-eyed; (2) Under surveillance; (3) Soaring on spiritual thermals; (4) Spiritual predator.

(1-2) As in "Hawk-eye"; (3) Job 39:26; (4) Hawks prey on other birds as well as small mammals.

Hay: (1) Carnal motives; (2) Carnal works.

(1-2) 1 Cor. 3:12-13.

Hay Fever: (1) Being spiritually shut down by the works of the flesh; (2) Having been overcome and caught up in the world.

(1) 1 Cor. 3:12,15; (2) 1 John 2:16.

Head: (1) Jesus Christ; (2) Authority; (3) Leadership; (4) Father; (5) Blessed; (6) Foundation (Dan. 2:31-33, note that this image starts at the head not the feet); (7) Disapproval or disgust (shaking of the head).

Also see *Decapitation* and *Platter*.

(1) 1 Cor. 11:3; Eph. 4:15; 5:23; (2) Exod. 18:25; (3-4) Exod. 6:14; Num. 1:4; 1 Chron. 29:11; Ps. 133:2; (5) Deut. 28:13; (6) Ps. 133:1-3; Dan. 2:37-39; (7) Ps. 44:14; 109:25.

Head (Hitting Head): (1) Mocking Christ or leadership; (2) Mocking; (3) Scorned; (4) Sarcasm; (5) Disrespect; (6) Abuse; (7) Deadly blow; (8) Serious injury.
(1-6) Matt. 27:31; Mark 15:19; (7-8) Gen. 3:15.

Head (Over the Head): (1) Accusation (if sign over head); (2) Overwhelmed; (3) Subjection (if feet over head); (4) Transferring (if hands over head); (5) Deliverance; (6) Blinded or veiled; (7) Point missed.
(1) Matt. 27:37; (2) Ezra 9:6; Ps. 38:4; (3) Ps. 66:12; (4) Lev. 16:21; (5) Jon. 4:6; (6) As in "That went over his head."

Headphones: (1) Hearing from God; (2) What someone is listening to (positive or negative).
(1) Mark 4:9; (2) Rom. 12:2; 2 Cor. 10:5.

Heal/ed/ing: (1) Heart conversion; (2) Through the cross; (3) Literal healing; (4) Confirms that God's Kingdom is within and has now come; (5) A call to act by faith on receiving a word [which can be a prophetic incident]); (6) A call to walk in the Spirit; (7) Demonic deliverance; (8) Counterfeit healing (e.g., through cultic or occultic religion).
(1) Matt. 13:15; Luke 4:18; John 12:40; (2) Isa. 53:5; (3) (4) Matt. 4:23; 9:35; Luke 9:2,6,11; 10:9; (5) Matt. 8:8; (cf. Mark 6:4-5; Luke 4:16, 22-23); (6) Mark 6:13; Luke 4:18; Acts 10:38; (7) Luke 8:2,36; 9:42; (8) 2 Thess. 2:9.

Heap: (1) To amass or gather; (2) Witness; (3) Ruin; (4) Lots (heaps); (5) Do good to an enemy (heaping coals on his head).
(1) Gen. 31:46; Job 16:4; 27:16; Rom. 12:20; 2 Tim. 4:3; James 5:3; (2) Gen. 31:48,51-52; (3) Isa. 17:1b; 25:2; Deut. 13:16; Josh. 8:28; 2 Kings 19:25; (4) Judg. 15:16 (KJV); (5) Prov. 25:21-22.

Hearing: (1) Receiving in your heart; (2) Obedience; (3) Understanding.
(1) Ezek. 3:10; Mark 4:9; 8:18b; (2) Ps. 49:1; the Hebrew word for hearing, *shama*, also carries with it the thought of obedience; (3) 1 Kings 3:9.

Hearse: (1) Death; (2) Burial/burial of an issue.
(1) 2 Kings 23:20; Luke 7:12; (2) Gen. 23:4; 49:29; Rom. 6:4; Col. 2:12-13.

Heart: (1) The real person; (2) The inner part of person; (3) The spirit; (4) God's measure of a person; (5) Innermost thoughts; (6) The mind; (7) The emotions; (8) The will; (9) The core or middle; (10) The place where wisdom is deposited; (11) The deep; (12) The real altar of God.
Also see *Hard/Hardened Heart*.
(1-2) Ps. 19:14; 24:4; 28:3; 55:21; (3) Rom. 2:29; 8:27; 2 Cor. 1:22; (4) 1 Sam. 15:7b; (5) Gen. 6:5; 27:42; (6) Gen. 24:45; Exod. 4:21; (7) Gen. 42:28; Exod. 4:14; Lev. 26:16; (8) Exod. 7:23; 25:2; 35:5, 21-22; (9) Exod. 15:8; (10) Exod. 35:25-26,35 (KJV), 36:1-2; (11) Ps. 64:6; (12) Jer. 17:1.

Heat: (1) Adversity; (2) Pressure; (3) Anger; (4) Fire; (5) Wilting under pressure; (6) Judgment; (7) Noon (heat of the day); (8) Sun.

Also see *Fire*.

(1-2) Jer. 17:8; Luke 12:55; Rev. 16:9; (3) Deut. 29:24; Ezek. 3:14; (4) Acts 28:3; (5) James 1:11; (6) 2 Pet. 3:10,12; Rev. 16:9; (7) 2 Sam. 4:5; 1 Sam. 11:11; Matt. 20:12; (8) Ps. 19:6.

Heater: (1) Turning up the heat (pressure, adversity).
Also see *Fire, Fireplace, Kitchen*, and *Oven*.
(1) Dan. 3:19.

Heaven: (1) The spiritual realm (second heaven); (2) The home of God (The Father); (3) Eternity; (4) The spiritual Kingdom; (5) The place of reward; (6) Permanent treasury; (7) The home of believers; (8) The angelic realm; (9) The throne of God (third heaven); (10) Sky (first heaven); (11) God-given (from Heaven); (12) The place of unlimited blessings; (13) The place from which the Church is to exercise its dominion.
(1) Matt. 3:16; 6:10; Luke 10:18; Acts 10:11; (2) Matt. 3:17; 5:16,34,45,48; 6:1,9; (3) 2 Cor. 5:1; (4) Matt. 4:17; John 3:12; (5) Matt. 5:12; (6) Matt. 6:20; 19:21; (7) Matt. 8:11; Luke 10:20; 2 Cor. 5:1; (8) Matt. 18:10; 22:30; 24:36; 28:2; Luke 22:43; Gal. 1:8; (9) Matt. 23:22; Acts 7:49; 2 Cor. 12:2; (10) Matt. 24:30; Luke 4:25; James 5:18; (11) Luke 20:4; John 3:27; 6:51; (12) Eph. 1:3; (13) Eph. 3:10; 2:6.

Heavy: (1) Depression; (2) Grief; (3) Sorrow; (4) The glory of God; (5) Burden; (6) Responsibility; (7) Serious; (8) The big guns; (9) Physical thugs or spiritual giants; (10) Wealth/prosperity; (11) Honor/esteem; (12) Sin/guilt.
Also see *Carrying, Fat*, and *Weight*.
(1-3) Ps. 119:28; (4) 1 Kings 8:11; 2 Cor. 4:17; (5-6) Exod. 18:18; (7) As in "Things were getting heavy"; (8-9) As in "He sent in the heavies"; (10) Gen. 31:1 (cf. KJV & NKJV); (11) Mal. 1:6 (*Honor* is the Hebrew *kabod*, which carries the sense of weightiness); (12) Ps. 38:4; Heb. 12:1.

Hebrew: (1) God's language; (2) Eternity (*aleph–tav*: first and last letters of Hebrew alphabet convey beginning and end or eternity); (3) Encoded language; (4) A call to decode Scripture or verse; (5) A call to go deeper; (6) Number association (each letter also conveys a number); (7) Pictorial meaning (each letter has an associated pictorial meaning). See *Aleph* and *Jews*.
(1-2) Gen. 1:1 (the letters *aleph–tav* appear in the Hebrew text and yet not in English translations); (3) Prov. 25:11; (4-5) Prov. 25:2; (6-7) John 7:15 (KJV).

Hedge: (1) Protection; (2) Restricted or channeled; (3) Painful restriction; (4) A call to stand in the gap; (5) Wall.
Also see *Fence* and *Wall*.
(1) Job 1:10; Ps. 80:12; Matt. 21:33; Mark 12:1; (2) Job 3:23; (3) Prov. 15:19; (4) Ezek. 13:5; 22:30; (5) Hos. 2:6.

Heel: (1) Betrayal; (2) Strike from behind; (3) Past life; (4) Past revealed; (5) Trap/snare; (6) Hold back.
Also see *Wall*.

(1) Gen. 3:15; Ps. 41:9; John 13:18; (2) Gen. 49:17; (3) Ps. 49:5; (4) Jer. 13:22 (KJV); (5) Jer.18:9; (6) Gen. 25:26.

Height: (1) Measure of something; (2) Spiritual dimension; (3) The measure of a person (in human terms); (4) Heaven; (5) Spiritual high ground; (6) Pride; (7) Strength; (8) God's home; (9) Greatness and dominion.

Also see *High, Smaller, Tall,* and *Taller.*

(1) Rom. 8:39 (love); (2) Eph. 3:18; (3) 1 Sam. 17:4; Dan. 3:1; (cf. 1 Sam. 16:7b); (4) Job 22:12; Ps. 102:19; 148:1; Prov. 25:3; (5) Jer. 31:12; Ezek. 20:40; (6) Jer. 49:16; Ezek. 31:10; (7) Jer. 51:53; Amos 2:9; (8) Ezek. 20:40; (9) Dan. 4:20-22.

Helicopter: (1) Christ or a ministry of salvation (rescue); (2) Spiritual ministry; (3) Vertical lift; (4) Quick ascension; (5) In danger of pride (quick ascension); (6) Evil spirit (spying helicopter).

Also see *Helicopter Rotor Blades.*

(1-3) Ps. 91:12; Matt. 17:27; Luke 1:69; John 6:39; (4-5) 1 Tim. 3:1, 6; 1 Sam. 15:17; (6) 1 Pet. 5:8.

Helicopter Rotor Blades: (1) Leader's words that keep you ducking for cover; (2) Uplifting words.

Also see *Helicopter* and *Propeller.*

(1) Esther 7:6-7; Matt. 14:3-4, 8; (2) 1 Cor. 14:3.

Helmet: (1) Salvation; (2) Hope; (3) Protect your mind; (4) Keep your head down (watch pride); (5) Spiritual warfare.

Also see *Cap, Hat,* and *Motorcycle Helmet.*

(1) Isa. 59:17; Eph. 6:17; (2) 1 Thess. 5:8; (3) 2 Cor. 10:5; 1 Pet. 1:13; (4) Rom. 12:16; (5) 2 Cor. 10:3-5; Eph. 6:11.

Hem: (1) The place of overflow.

(1) Ps. 133:2; Matt. 9:20; 14:36.

Hemorrhoids: (1) Stress; (2) Straining to get rid of a burden/sin.

(1-2) 1 Sam. 6:11 (KJV).

Hen: (1) Christ; (2) Comfort, nurture, and protect; (3) Church.

Also see *Chicken.*

(1-2) Matt. 23:37; Luke 13:34; (3) Matt. 23:37; Acts 14:27.

Herbs: (1) Bitterness.

Also see *Spices.*

(1) Exod. 12:8; Num. 9:11.

Hidden: (1) Dead to self; (2) Safe.

(1-2) Col. 3:3.

Hiding: (1) Guilt (awareness of sin); (2) Fear; (3) Shame; (4) Protection; (5) Ignoring an issue.

Also see *Chasing, Concealing,* and *Running.*

(1) Lev. 5:2-4 (*unaware* means "hidden from Him"); Prov. 28:1 (The Hebrew word for "wicked" here is *rasha*—amongst its meanings is the thought of "guilty"); (2) Matt. 24:24-25; (3) Gen. 3:8,10; (cf. Gen. 2:25); (4) Exod. 2:2-3; Job 5:21; Ps. 17:8; (5) Lev. 20:4; Deut. 22:1,3.

High: (1) God; (2) Exalted; (3) Heaven; (4) Spiritual ground; (5) Secure (tower)/Security; (6) Spiritually lifted; (7) Proud; (8) Praise; (9) Wisdom; (10) Abomination to God (that which is highly esteemed among men).
Also see *Height, Hills,* and *Mountains.*
(1) Gen. 14:18-20; Ps. 18:13; 78:35; 83:18; (2) Exod. 14:8; Num. 33:3; 2 Sam. 23:1; Job 5:11; Luke 14:8,10; (3) Exod. 25:20; Job 11:8; 16:19; 22:12; Ps. 68:18; 103:11; Isa. 6:1; (4) 1 Sam. 9:12, 14; 10:5; 1 Kings 3:4; (5) 2 Sam. 22:3 (KJV); Ps. 18:2 (KJV); Ps. 61:2-3; 91:14; 144:2; (6) 2 Sam. 22:49; 23:1; (7) Job 21:22; Ps. 18:27; Ps. 62:9; 75:5; 101:5; Prov. 21:4 (KJV); (8) Ps. 149:6;
(9) Prov. 8:1-2; 9:1,3; 24:7; (10) Luke 16:15; 20:46.

High Heels: (1) Woman in authority; (2) Businesswoman; (3) Woman wanting more authority (to appear taller); (4) Gospel outreach to homosexuals (man in high heels); (5) Worldly woman.
(1) Judg. 4:4,9; (2) Acts 16:14; (3) 1 Kings 21:7; (4) 1 Cor. 9:22; (5) Prov. 7:10.

Highlighter: (1) Illumination/revelation; (2) Outstanding; (3) Glory of God.
(1) Dan. 5:24-25; Rev. 19:16; (2) 1 Sam. 9:2; (3) Ps. 18:12; Isa. 60:19; Ezek. 1:28.

High-Rise Apartment: (1) Sudden elevation; (2) Prophetic office; (3) Preoccupation with non-practical matters (ivory tower).
Also see *Tower.*
(1) Gen. 41:14; (2) Num. 22:41; (3) 2 Sam. 11:1-2.

High School: (1) Spirit training; (2) Place of higher learning; (4) Passing into eternity (exams/graduation); (5) Moving into spiritual adulthood (exams/graduation).
(1) Isa. 50:4; Luke 1:80; (2) Matt. 5:1-2; (4) Rev. 20:12; (5) Matt. 5:9 ("sons" are mature sons who have become like their Father).

Highway: (1) God's path (the "high" way); (2) Commercial path; (3) Broad, easy, or quick road (way of the world); (4) Highway to hell; (5) Unsafe; (6) The main route; (7) The path of life (faith); (8) Spiritual decline (empty highways); (9) A heart prepared for God; (10) The highway to Heaven; (11) Prayer (the "high" way).
Also see *Path, Road,* and *Street.*
(1) John 14:6; (2) Matt. 22:9-10; Mark 10:46; (3-4) Matt. 7:13; (5) Judg. 5:6; (6) Judg. 20:31-32; 21:19; Num. 20:19; (7) Prov. 16:17; Isa. 35:8; Jer. 31:21; (8) Isa. 33:8; (9) Isa. 40:3; (10) Isa. 62:10; John 1:51; (11) 2 Chron. 7:14; cf. John 14:6; 14:13-14.

Highway Patrol: (1) Being assessed for ministry (road worthiness); (2) Angels. Also see *Automobile.*
(1) 1 Tim. 3:1-7; (2) Heb. 1:14.

Hijacking: (1) Warning of potential derailed destiny; (2) Warning of diverted destiny; (3) Warning of a destroyed destiny; (4) Someone trying to influence you with a hidden agenda; (5) Interference in the second heaven.

Also see *Ambush.*

(1-2) Luke 10:30-34; (3) Num. 13:32-14:2; (4) Matt. 16:22-23; (5) Dan. 10:13.

Hill: (1) Strength; (2) Place of prosperity; (3) Exposed; (4) Proud person; (5) Pride; (6) Place of revelation; (7) Hiding place; (8) Spiritual high ground; (9) Home of God; (10) Place of idolatry; (11) Lasting; (12) Place to cut off the flesh; (13) Reference point; (14) Military high ground; (15) Rural land.

Also see *Mountain* and *Strength.*

(1) Ps. 95:4; (2) Ps. 50:10; (3) Isa. 30:17; Matt. 5:14; (4) Isa. 40:4; Luke 3:5; (5) Isa. 2:12-14; Jer. 49:16; Luke 4:25-29; (6) Num. 23:9; 2 Kings 1:9; 4:27; Luke 9:37; (7) 1 Sam. 23:19; 26:1; Ps. 104:18; Jer. 16:16; (8) Exod. 17:9-10; 1 Sam. 10:10; Ps. 2:6; 3:4; 15:1; 24:3; 43:3; (9) Ps. 68:15-16 (KJV); 99:9; 121:1; (10) Deut. 12:2; 1 Kings 11:7; 14:23; 16:4; 17:10; Jer. 2:20; Ezek. 6:3-4; Hos. 4:13; (11) Deut. 33:15; (12) Josh. 5:3; (13) Josh. 15:9; 18:13-14; 24:30; (14) 1 Sam. 9:11; 10:5; (15) Ps. 50:10; 65:12; Isa. 5:1.

Hippopotamus: (1) Horse.

Also see *Horse.*

(1) *Hippo* is a Greek name meaning "horse."

Hips: (1) Strength of the flesh; (2) Call to change from being self-reliant to rely more on the Spirit (hip replacement).

(1-2) Gen. 32:25,28,32.

Hire Car: (1) Living beyond your means (flash vehicle); (2) Non-sustainable destiny/ expectations; (3) Faith that yields under pressure; (4) Superficial ministry; (5) Ministry that will not be there under pressure; (6) Ministry that doesn't care about the people.

See *Limousine, Cab/Taxi,* and *Uber.*

(1) Dan. 5:1-30; Matt. 23:27; (2) Num. 22:21-31; 2 Kings 5:22-27; (3) Jn. 10:12; (4) 2 Cor. 11:5; (5) Jn. 10:12; (6) Jn. 10:13.

Hit: (1) Judgment; (2) Death.

(1-2) Exod. 12:7,22; Deut. 21:4-5; 2 Sam. 12:15; Isa. 53:4,8.

Hole: (1) Hiding place; (2) Home, den, lair, or nest (resting place); (3) Snare; (4) Clay pit; (5) Spiritual portal; (6) Cave; (7) Flawed (in garment); (8) Empty; (9) Outlet; (10) Worn-out (in garment); (11) Not changed (garment); (12) Missing something (not complete); (13) Time to replace (in garment); (14) Your heart (hole in ground); (15) Covenant (a ring created by the rim).

(1) 1 Sam. 14:11; Isa. 2:19; 7:19; Jer. 13:4; 16:16; Mic. 7:17; (2) Isa. 11:8; Jer. 48:28; Matt. 8:20; Luke 9:58; (3) Isa. 42:22; (4) Isa. 51:1; (5) Ezek. 8:7-12; (6) Nah. 2:12; (7-9) Hag. 1:6; (10-11) Matt. 9:16; (13) Luke 5:36-38; (14) 2 Cor. 4:7; (15) Gen. 9:12-13.

Hole in One: (1) Accurate word that penetrates the heart; (2) Saying the right thing at the right time.
(1) Luke 2:35; Heb. 4:12; (2) Isa. 50:4.

Holiday: (1) Rest; (2) Celebration; (3) Caught up in religion/working your way to Heaven (holy day); (4) Letting down your guard.
Also see *Tourist*.
(1) Exod. 20:11; 31:17; (2) Exod. 12:14; (3) Gal. 4:9-10 (this is particularly true if the scene also pictures works); (4) 1 Pet. 5:8.

Hollow: (1) Empty (without substance); (2) Not solid; (3) Spirit.
(1-2) 1 Tim. 1:10; 4:3; 6:3-5; (3) Judg. 15:19.

Hollywood: (1) Fame (worldly glory); (2) Superficiality.
(1) Acts 8:9-10; 12:22-23; (2) Matt. 23:27; John 5:44.

Home: (1) Heaven; (2) On our way to Heaven (on our way home); (3) Home; (4) Comfort/rest.
Also see *House*.
(1-2) John 14:2-4; Heb. 11:10; (3) Literal home; (4) Ruth 1:9; Isa. 66:1; Dan. 4:4.

Homeless Person: (1) Christ; (2) True disciple; (3) Without a spiritual house; (4) Poverty; (5) Cursed.
Also see *Bum*.
(1) Matt. 8:20; (2) Mark 10:29; (3) Luke 13:35; (4-5) Gen. 4:12.

Homework: (1) Getting our hearts in order; (2) Understanding and studying the Word.
Also see *House*.
(1) 2 Kings 20:1; Isa. 38:1; (2) 2 Tim. 2:15.

Honey: (1) God's Word; (2) Pleasant words; (3) Grace or mercy; (4) Flourishing fruitfulness; (5) Manna from Heaven; (6) Blessing and abundance; (7) Own glory; (8) The provision of God; (9) Sweet words; (10) Spiritually enlightening; (11) Money; (12) Unadulterated Word of God (wild honey); (13) Revelation; (14) Partaking of the Promised Land.
Also see *Bees*.
(1) Judg. 14:8; Ps. 19:9-10; 119:103; Prov. 24:13-14; Isa. 7:15; Ezek. 3:3; (2) Prov. 5:3; 16:24; Song 4:11; (3) Matt. 3:4 (where locust speaks of judgment, and honey speaks of grace); (4) Exod. 3:8,17; 33:3; Lev. 20:24; (5) Exod. 16:31; (6) Num. 13:27; 14:8; Deut. 8:8; (7) Lev. 2:11; Prov. 25:27; (8) Deut. 32:13; 2 Sam. 17:29; Ps. 81:16; (9) Prov. 5:3-4; 25:16; Rev. 10:9-10; (10) 1 Sam. 14:27,29; (11) As in "land of milk and honey"; (12) Matt. 3:4; Mark 1:6; (13) Exod. 16:31; Deut. 8:2-3; (14) Exod. 13:5b.

Honeycomb: (1) Speaks of solid spiritual food; (2) Those who loathe it are full of other things.
(1) Song 5:1; (2) Prov. 27:7.

Hooded: (1) Blinded mind/veiled heart; (2) Covering or hiding something; (3) Covered; (4) Dishonor or shame; (5) Needing Christ; (6) Fear; (7) Mischievous lips; (8) Mourning.
(1) 2 Cor. 3:13-15; (2) Gen. 38:15; (cf. Gen. 3:8); (3-4) Jer. 14:4; Ezek. 7:18; 1 Cor. 11:4; (5) 2 Cor. 3:16; Jer. 14:4; (6) Exod. 34:30; (7) Ps. 140:9; Prov. 10:6; (8) 2 Sam. 15:30; Esther 6:12.

Hook: (1) Promise; (2) The Gospel; (3) The Word with power; (4) Politically dragged by force into something (trap); (5) Snare of temptation.
(1) Acts 2:38-39; 7:17; Eph. 3:6; (2) Matt. 4:19; (3) 1 Cor. 2:4. (4) Ezek. 19:4; 38:4; (5) Gen. 4:7.

Horizon: (1) The foreseeable future; (2) Expectancy.
Also see *Binoculars*, *Distance*, and *Distant*.
(1) Matt. 24:33-34; (2) Luke 15:20.

Hornet: See *Wasp*.

Horn(s): (1) Strength; (2) Power; (3) Influence; (3) Voice; (4) Crown (king) or leader; (5) God's power (The Spirit); (6) Pride; (7) Strength of heart; (8) Christ (horn of salvation); (9) Appeal to God; (10) Human-made strength; (11) Dominion; (12) Alarm or warning (blowing "shofar" ram's horn); (13) Celebration; (14) Omnipotence, or full of power (seven horns); (15) Nations.
Also see *Anointing* (cf. 1 Sam. 16:1,13) and *Shofar*.
(1-2) Gen. 22:13 (This is a prefigure of Christ laying down His strength); Ps. 89:17; 92:10; Lam. 2:17; Dan. 8:7-8; Amos 6:13 (KJV); Hab. 3:4 (KJV); (3) Josh. 6:4-8 (spiritual voice); Ezek. 29:21; Dan. 7:11,24; (4) Ps. 75:10; Dan. 7:24; 8:20-21; Rev. 17:12; (5) 1 Sam. 16:13; (6) Ps. 75:4-5 (horn lifted up); (7) Jer. 17:1 (horns of the altar); (8) Ps. 18:2; 132:17; Luke 1:69; (9) 1 Kings 1:50-51; 2:28 (grabbing the horns of the altar); Ps. 118:27; Amos 3:14; (10) 1 Kings 22:11; 2 Chron. 18:10 (iron horns); (11) Zech. 1:21; (12) Num. 10:4, 9; (13) Lev. 23:24; (14) Rev. 5:6; (15) Zech. 1:21.

Horse: (1) Looking to the world; (2) The flesh; (3) Hiring the world; (4) Not looking to God; (5) Swiftness; (6) Strength; (7) Power; (8) Authority; (9) Famine (black horse); (10) Death (pale horse); (11) Warfare (red horse); (12) Worldly spirit (sea horse); (13) Divine (white horse); (14) Competitive spirit (race horse).
(1) Deut. 17:16; 1 Kings 10:28; 2 Chron. 9:28; Isa. 31:1; (2) Isa. 31:3; Rev. 19:18; (3) 2 Kings 7:6; (4) Deut. 17:16; Isa. 31:1; (5) Jer. 4:13; Hab. 1:8; (6) Isa. 31:1; Jer. 47:3; (7) Rev. 9:19; (8) Rev. 6:2; (9) Rev. 6:5; (10) Rev. 6:8; (11) Rev. 6:4; (12) Jer. 6:23; 50:42; (13) Rev. 6:2; (14) 2 Sam. 18:22; Ps. 147:10.

Horse (White Horse's Rider): (1) Jesus Christ; (2) Warrior; (3) Faithful & true; (4) Justice; (5) Judge.
(1-5) Rev. 19:11-13.

Hose (Garden): (1) The flow of the Spirit; (2) Outpouring of the Spirit.

Also see *Sponge.*

(1-2) Acts 2:17.

Hospital: (1) Church; (2) Healing & rebuilding ministry; (3) Sick church; (4) Heaven; (5) Needs healing (going to hospital).

(1) 1 Cor. 12:28; Eph. 4:12,16; (2) Gal. 6:1-2; (3) 1 Cor. 1:10; Rev. 3:17; (4) Rev. 21:4; (5) Mark. 2:3-4.

Hostage: (1) Being held to ransom; (2) An area in your life not redeemed; (3) Stronghold; (4) Extortion.

(1) Job 33:24; Hos. 13:14; (2) Isa. 51:10-11 (KJV); Jer. 31:11; Matt. 20:28; 1 Tim. 2:6; (3) Jer. 38:6; (4) Prov. 6:1-3; Isa. 16:4.

Hot: (1) Anger; (2) Trouble; (3) On fire for God; (4) Passionate; (5) Confronting; (6) Fierce; (7) Purifying; (8) Judgment; (9) Devouring; (10) The latest.
Also see *Cold* and *Fire.*

(1) Exod. 32:19,22; 22:24; Deut. 9:19; (2) As in "They landed in hot water"; (3) Rev. 3:15-16; (4) Ps. 39:3; Jer. 20:9; (5) Mal. 4:1; (6) 2 Sam. 11:15; (7) Ezek. 24:11; (8) Dan. 3:22; (9) Hos. 7:7; (10) As in "hot off the press."

Hot Air Balloon: (1) Ministry in the Spirit.
Also see *Blimp.*

(1) Ezek. 3:14; 8:3; 11:1.

Hot Chocolate: (1) Anointing.

(1) Ps. 23:5.

Hotel: (1) Temporary place; (2) Passing through; (3) A place to pause on the way; (4) In Scripture, staying overnight at an inn can be a place of revelation; (5) Church (as the place where we drink); (6) A church at rest; (7) Denomination (hotel chain); (8) Place of rest.

(1-3) Gen. 42:27; 43:21; Exod. 4:24; Luke 2:7; 10:35; (4) Luke 24:28-31; Gen. 28:11-15; (5) Eph. 5:18; (8) Heb. 4:1,5,9-11.

Hotel Reception: (1) New temporary ministry or venture (checking in); (2) Leaving temporary ministry or phase in one's life (checking out).

(1) Gen. 24:23b; (2) Gen. 24:56.

Hot Dogs: (1) Feeding you what you want to hear (convenient food); (2) Being spiritually lazy (wanting fast food).

(1) Isa. 30:10; Jer. 5:31; (2) Matt. 25:8-9.

Hot Rod: (1) Someone moving with anger; (2) Moving too quick; (3) Showing ministry without perseverance.

(1) Exod. 32:19; (2) 2 Sam. 18:19ff; (3) Heb. 10:38.

Hot Water: See *Water (Hot).*

House: (1) An individual; (2) Church; (3) Someone's home or household; (4) Yourself; (5) Covering; (6) Ministry; (7) Business; (8) Israel; (9) Glorious individual, church, or ministry (western red cedar house); (10) Death (demolition); (11) Spiritual renewal (interior renovation/decoration); (12) Superficial change (exterior renovation); (13) Delivered from a demon (clean house); (14) Demon-oppressed or -possessed (unclean home).

Also see *Building, Home, Interior of a House, Mansion, New House, Old House, Palace, Real Estate, Run-Down House,* and *Temple.*

(1) 2 Cor. 5:1; Heb. 3:6; (2) 1 Tim. 3:15; 2 Tim. 2:20; Heb. 3:6; 1 Pet. 2:5; (3) 1 Tim. 3:4; 5:13; (5) Gen. 19:8; Matt. 8:8; also as in "under the head of the house"; (7) John 2:16; (8) Heb. 8:10; (9) 1 Kings 6:9; (10) John 2:19-21; (11) 2 Chron. 24:4; (12) Joel 2:13; Matt. 13:20-21; 1 Pet. 3:3; (13-14) Luke 11:24-25.

Houseboat: (1) Family; (2) Flowing in the anointing; (3) Taking things easy (cruising).
Also see *Cruise Ship* and *Yacht.*
(1) Gen. 7:1; (2) Ezek. 47:9; (3) See *Holiday.*

House Fire: (1) Judgment; (2) Words against your ministry; (3) Power of God, revival, or Pentecost (non-destructive fire); (4) Fire of God; (5) Angry individual.
Also see *Fire* and *House.*
(1) Rev. 18:8; (2) James 3:5-6; (3) Exod. 3:2-3; Acts 2:3; (4) Obad. 1:18; (5) Gen. 44:18.

House for Sale: (1) Soul in the balance; (2) Not yet purchased by Christ; (3) Selling out; (4) Vulnerable to exploitation.
(1) Joel 3:14; (2) 1 Cor. 6:19-20; (3) 2 Tim. 4:10a; (4) Matt. 26:14-16.

Hovercraft: (1) Spiritual vehicle or spirit; (2) (+) Angel; (3) (-) Demonic spirit (doing negative things or if the hovercraft is dark in color).
Also see *Amphibious Vehicle.*
(1) Job 4:15; Ezek. 10:17; (2) Mark 6:49; (3) Matt. 12:43.

Hundred: (1) Complete count (10 x 10 = complete completeness); (2) Whole; (3) Complete blessing; (4) Maximum blessing; (5) Financial wholeness ($100); (6) The debt of unforgiveness; (7) The glory of God (300); (8) The shame of people (300); (9) Full harvest.
(1-2) Luke 15:4-6 (the whole flock); (2) The tithe is one-tenth and means, as we have given the first tenth of our income, we acknowledge His right to the rest. It also means "as is the first round" (1-10), so the rest is likewise God-given; (3-4) Matt. 13:8; Mark 4:8; (6) Matt. 18:28; (7) Gen. 5:22; 45:22; Judg. 7:2,6-7; 1 Kings 10:17; (8) Mark 14:4-5 (Mary was shamed); 2 Chron. 12:9-10; (9) Matt. 13:23.

Hunger: (1) Humbling; (2) Spiritual desire for God and His Word; (3) Judgment; (4) Desire for righteousness; (5) In need; (6) Denying the flesh; (7) Vulnerable to false doctrines.
Also see *Fasting* and *Thirsty.*

(1-2) Deut. 8:3; (3) Deut. 28:48; 32:24; Job 5:5; (4) Matt. 5:6; (5) Job 22:7; (6) Ps. 107:5; (7) Prov. 27:7; Matt. 4:6; Luke 4:10-11.

Hunter/Hunting: Everything about hunting in Scripture carries a negative or anti-Christian tone. Examples of meanings are: (1) The enemy; (2) The fleshly person; (3) A hunter of people or godly people; (4) Evil (hunts the violent person); (5) Surety for another; (6) Laziness (not roasting that which is caught); (7) Adultery (hunt for lives); (8) Being hunted may be a sign of iniquity/sin; (9) False prophets hunt for souls; (10) Corruption, disloyalty, or unfaithfulness.
(1) Prov. 6:5; 1 Pet. 5:8; (2) Gen. 25:27; 27:5; (3) Gen. 10:9; 1 Sam. 24:11; 26:20; (4) Ps. 140:11; (5) Prov. 6:1-5; (6) Prov. 12:27; (7) Prov. 6:26; (8) Jer. 16:16-18; (9) Ezek. 13:18-21; (10) Mic. 7:2.

Hurricane: See *Storm.*

Hurry (In a Hurry): (1) Get prepared (sense of urgency); (2) Quick departure; (3) Journey ahead; (4) Birth of a ministry; (5) Time running out (urgency); (6) Driven by the world; (7) God is not in a hurry; (8) Turning away from God; (9) Act quickly; (10) Escape; (11) Decisiveness required; (12) Eager to sin; (13) Not blessed; (14) Urgent repentance required.
Also see *Running* and *Urgency.*
(1-3) Gen. 19:15; Exod. 12:11; (4) Gen. 41:14; (5) Luke 14:21; 2 Pet. 3:12 (Christ is coming back); (6) Exod. 5:13; (7) Josh. 10:13; Isa. 28:16b; (8) Judg. 2:17; Ps. 16:4; (9) 1 Sam. 20:38; Acts 12:7; Rev. 2:5; (10) 1 Sam. 23:26; 2 Sam. 4:4; 17:16; Ps. 55:8; Acts 22:18; (11) 1 Sam. 25:17-18,34; (12) Prov. 1:16; 7:23; 19:2; (13) Prov. 20:21; 28:20; 29:20; (14) Rev. 2:16.

Husband: (1) Jesus; (2) God; (3) Natural husband.
Also see *Groom.*
(1) Matt. 9:15; 25:1,13; John 3:29a; (2) Isa. 54:5; (3) John 4:16.

Hut: (1) Spiritually impoverished individual.
Also see *Cabin* and *Shack.*
(1) 2 Sam. 9:4; (cf. 1 Cor. 6:19).

Hyena: (1) Warning of an attack upon a spiritual sleeper; (2) Call to stay awake spiritually.
(1-2) Isa. 52:1a; Luke 22:45-46.

Hysterectomy: (1) No longer able to win souls (unfertile church/person); (3) Barren church/person; (4) Robbed of the promises of God.
Also see *Birth.*
(1-2) Rev. 3:1; (4) Gen. 20:18.

I

Ice: (1) Cold; (2) Cold person; (3) No love (increase of wickedness); (4) Stopping the flow of the Spirit; (5) Deceitful heart; (6) Hardened hearts who melt under pressure. Also see *Black* and *Cold*.
(1-2) Ps. 147:17 (KJV); (3) Matt. 24:12; (4) Job 38:30; Ps. 147:17-18; (5-6) Job 6:15-17.

Ice Cream: (1) Not sharing the Gospel; (2) Preaching the Gospel without love; (3) Promises of God; (4) Deceptive food (a sweetener).
Also see *Cream* and *Dessert*.
(1) Heb. 5:13 (cream is the best part of the milk); (2) Matt. 24:12; Phil. 1:17; (3) Exod. 3:8 (milk and honey); Lev. 20:24; (4) Prov. 20:17; Prov. 23:1-3.

Ice Skating: (1) Gracious in a cold and hard environment; (2) In jeopardy (on thin ice); (3) At risk (thin ice); (4) Walking by faith in a cold-hearted environment (walking on water).
Also see *Slide* and *Slip*.
(1) Lam. 3:30a; Matt. 5:39; (2-3) 2 Sam. 23:17; Lam. 5:9; Rom. 16:4; 1 Cor. 15:30; Phil. 2:30; (4) Matt. 14:28-29.

Icing (Cake): (1) Sugar-coating the message.
(1) 2 Tim. 4:3-4.

Idol: (1) Devils; (2) False god; (3) Snare; (4) Silver and gold.
(1) 1 Cor. 10:19-20; (2) Ps. 96:5; (3) Ps. 106:36; (4) Ps. 115:4; 135:15.

Immigration: (1) Coming into the Kingdom; (2) Entering into the Promise.
(1) Matt. 12:28; Luke 17:21; John 3:5; (2) Deut. 27:3b.

Incense: (1) Prayers; (2) Worship; (3) Idol worship.
Also see *Perfume*.
(1) Ps. 141:2; Rev. 8:3-4; (2) Exod. 25:6; 30:7; 2 Chron. 32:12b; (3) Jer. 1:16; 44:19.

Indian (American): Explore associations held by the person experiencing or recognizing the event as prophetic.
Also see *First Nations Peoples*, *Old Man*, and *Native(s)*.

Indian (Asian): (1) Explore associations held by the person experiencing or recognizing the event as prophetic; (2) See *Foreign* and *Foreigner*.
Also see *Black Man*, *Caucasian*, and *First Nations Peoples*.

Indigenous: See *First Nations People* and *Native(s)*.

Industry/ial: (1) Big business; (2) Commercialization; (3) Mechanical.
Also see *Business*, *Busy*, and *Machines*.
(1-2) 1 Kings 10:14-15; 2 Chron. 1:17; (3) 2 Chron. 26:15a.

Information Desk: (1) Approaching God for guidance.
(1) Prov. 4:11; Jer. 29:11-14a.

In Front Of: See *Before*.

Ingrown Toenail: (1) Hurt leader that affects the Body's walk (big toe); (2) Self-inflicted problem that becomes painful and affects your walk; (3) Problems with your children/ spiritual children (smallest members of your body); (4) Small issue that causes a lot of pain; (5) A nation's suffering which affects other nations around it.

Also see *Toes*.

(1) 1 Cor. 12:12; (2) 1 Sam. 2:29-30; Prov. 29:15; (3) 1 Cor. 12:12; Gal. 6:10; cf. Matt. 10:35-36; (4) 1 Sam. 2:29-30; (5) Dan. 2:41-42.

Injection: See *Needle*.

Ink: (1) Writing; (2) Book (as in becoming an author); (3) The Spirit written on people's hearts; (4) May speak of coming face to face rather than writing; (5) An ink spot in a pocket speaks of writing that may offend.

(1-2) Jer. 36:18; (3) 2 Cor. 3:3; (4) 2 John 1:12; 3 John 1:13.

Inner Tube: (1) The Spirit; (2) The spiritual person.

Also see *Balloon*, *Bicycle*, and *Wheel*.

(1) Ezek. 1:20; John 3:8; (2) Eph. 3:16.

Insect: (1) Pest; (2) Plague; (3) Small.

Also see *Bugs*.

(1-2) Exod. 5:3; 8:21; (3) Matt. 23:24.

Inside Out. Like back to front: (1) A person who has things reversed (e.g., money before Kingdom); (2) Revealing or perceiving the secrets of the heart.

(1-2) Matt. 6:33; 23:25-28.

Insincere: (1) Heart not in something.

(1) Prov. 23:7b; 1 Cor. 5:8; Phil. 1:16-17.

Institution: (1) Church.

(1) Acts 11:26; 15:5.

Insurance: (1) Covering; (2) The Holy Spirit; (3) Salvation (house insurance); (4) Mercy (goodness of God); (5) The grace of God.

(1) Exod. 12:7,13; (2) 2 Cor. 1:22; 5:5; Eph. 1:13-14; (3) 1 Cor. 3:9; 2 Cor. 5:1; (4) Ps. 27:13; 103:4-5; Jon. 2:6-8; (5) Jer. 31:2; Acts 11:23; 15:11.

Intel (CPU): See *Computer (CPU)*.

Interior Decoration: See *House*.

Interior of a House: (1) Within the believer; (2) A new interior suggests renewal; (3) A run-down interior suggests the old self in operation.

Also see *House*.

(1) 2 Cor. 5:1.

International Flight: (1) Multinational ministry; (2) From earth to Heaven (entering Heaven); (3) Traveling from the earthly realm to the heavenly one.

Also see *Overseas*.

(1) Acts 19:26; (2) John 1:51; Rev. 4:1; (3) 2 Kings 2:11; Acts 1:9.

Intersection: See *Crossroads*, *Road*, and *T-Junction*.

Intestines: (1) Eating disorder (pulling intestines out of mouth); (2) Trials (pulling intestines out of mouth); (3) Wickedness (intestines spilling out); (4) Condemned to judgment (intestines spilling out).
Also see *Belly*.
(1) Matt. 15:17; (2) Prov. 18:14 (can't stomach or tolerate it anymore); (3) Acts 1:18; (4) 2 Sam. 20:10; Acts 1:18.

Investing: (1) Sowing into God's Kingdom/harvest.
(1) Prov. 31:16.

Iron: (1) Man; (2) Strong/Strength; (3) Dominion; (4) Strength of people; (5) Judgment; (6) Hard; (7) Hardened/Obstinate/Stubborn; (8) Bound; (9) Barrier; (10) Permanent; (11) Strong leadership; (12) Oppression (furnace of iron); (13) Works; (14) Earthly (from the earth).
(1) Prov. 27:17; (2) Josh. 17:16-18 (iron chariots symbolize the strength of people); Judg. 1:19; 1 Kings 22:11; Jer. 1:18; Dan. 2:40; (3) Deut. 33:25; Josh. 17:16-18; Judg. 4:3; 2 Sam. 12:31 (subjection); (4) 2 Sam. 23:7; Job 41:7 (KJV), 27; 1 Kings 22:11; 2 Chron. 18:10; Prov. 27:17; (5) Deut. 28:23; Ezek. 22:20-22; Amos 1:3; (6) Job 19:24; Jer. 17:1; (7) Lev. 26:19; Isa. 48:4; Jer. 6:28; (8) Ps. 105:18; 149:8; Jer. 28:13-14; (9) Lev. 26:19; Ps. 107:16; Acts 12:10; (10) Jer. 1:18; (11) Ps. 2:9; Rev. 2:27; 12:5; 18:12; 19:15; (12) Deut. 4:20; 1 Kings 8:51; (13) Deut. 27:5; Josh. 8:31; Job 41:27; (14) Job 28:2a.

Iron Furnace: (1) The world (Egypt).
(1) Deut. 4:20; 1 Kings 8:51.

Ironing: (1) Seared conscience; (2) Liar; (3) Hypocrisy; (4) Dealing with sin; (5) Spotless ready for Christ (ironing shirt or dress); (6) Starchiness (proud); (7) Rebellion.
(1-3) 1 Tim. 4:2; (4) Eph. 5:26-27; (5) Eph. 5:27; (6) Ps. 75:5; (7) Deut. 31:27.

IRS: (1) Giving grudgingly (feels like you are being taxed); (2) Money-hungry church; (3) Literal tax issue; (3) Sowing into the heavenly treasury; (4) Respecting/fearing God's financial right.
(1) 2 Cor. 9:7; (2) Rev. 3:17; (3) Mal. 3:10; 2 Cor. 9:6; (4) Deut. 8:18; Acts 5:3-4.

Islam: (1) "Submission to Allah"; (2) Legalistic church; (3) Militant church; (4) Counterfeit Christianity; (5) Antichrist spirit.
(1) Literal translation; (2) Gal. 3:7-11; (3) Matt. 26:52; (4) 2 Cor. 11:4; (5) 1 John 2:22.

Island: (1) Offshore; (2) Independent; (3) Remote; (4) Peaceful and serene; (5) An individual; (6) Independent culture.
(1) Rev. 1:9; (2) Gen. 10:5; (3) Ps. 72:10; Jon. 1:3; (4) Rev. 1:9; (5) Job 22:30 (KJV); as in "no man is an island"; (6) Gen. 10:5 (KJV).

Israel: (1) In the place of God's promises; (Promised Land); (2) The Kingdom; (3) Spiritual place/heavenlies; (4) Literal Israel; (5) Spiritual man (versus Jacob: man of the flesh); (6) Real believers; (7) Landing pad for Christ.

See also *Hebrew* and *Jews*.
(1) Exod. 12:25; Deut. 6:3; (2) John 12:13; (3) Gal. 4:26; (4) Matt. 2:20-21; (5) Gen. 32:28; 35:10; (6) John 1:47; Rom. 11:26; (7) Zech. 14:4.

Itching: (1) Judgment; (2) Hearing what you want to hear (itching ears).
(1) Deut. 28:27; (2) 2 Tim. 4:3.

Ivory: (1) Strong revelation (powerful word); (2) Righteousness; (3) Beauty and strength.
Also see *Elephant*, *High-Rise Apartment*, and *Rhino*.
(1) Song 5:14 (the heart of God); (2) 1 Kings 10:18 (cf. Ps. 96:10, Jer. 23:5); (3) Song 7:4.

J

Jacket: (1) Mantle; (2) Authority; (3) Position or role; (4) Limited authority (short-sleeved jacket).
Also see *Coat*, *Mantle*, and *Robe*.
(1-3) 2 Kings 2:13-15; (4) 1 Sam. 15:27-28.

Janitor: (1) Minister content with the status quo; (2) Minister just doing a job; (3) Minister working to keep everybody happy.
Also see *Caretaker*.
(1) Ps. 55:19; Jer. 48:11 (maintenance person); (2) John 10:12-13; (3) Matt. 27:15-17,22,24; Acts 12:1-3.

Japanese: (1) Technology; (2) Technology-driven entertainment; (3) Strong traditional culture.
Also see *Foreign*.
(1) 2 Chron. 26:15; (2) Rev. 3:17-18; (3) Gal. 1:14; 1 Pet. 1:18.

Jaw/Jaws: (1) Mouth; (2) Words; (3) Greed (jaws); (4) Vicious attack of words (jaws).
Also see *Shark*.
(1) Judg. 15:16-19 (this passage prefigures Christ's victory and the outpouring of the Spirit); (3) Job 29:16; (4) Prov. 30:14.

Jazz: (1) Improvised or spontaneous worship; (2) Ad libbing.
Also see *Jazz* in Name and Place Dictionary.
(1-2) Josh. 5:14; 2 Sam. 6:16.

Jealousy: (1) Spiritually unfaithful; (2) Anger; (3) Displacement (if a prophetic event stirs up jealousy consider if you have in some way been replaced by those persons that the event/incident relates to. This will need to be repented of and soul-ties cut in the spirit).
(1) 2 Cor. 11:2,4; 1 Cor. 10:21-22; (2) Rom. 10:19; Zech. 8:2; (3) 1 Sam. 18:7-8.

Jeep: (1) Spiritual warfare.
Also see *Four-Wheel Drive*.

(1) Eph. 6:10-11.

Jello /Jelly: (1) Spiritual food without substance.

(1) 1 Cor. 3:2.

Jerusalem: (1) Actual Jerusalem; (2) Your spirit; (3) City of God; (4) New Jerusalem (spiritual/heavenly home); (5) Mother/church: (6) Bride of Christ; (7) Epicenter of the world; (8) Date with destiny.

(1) Matt. 23:37; (2) Acts 1:8; (3-4) Matt. 5:35; Heb. 12:22; Rev. 3:12; (5) Gal. 4:26; (6) Rev. 21:2; (7) Acts 1:8; (8) Matt. 16:21; 21:18.

Jesus: (1) Literally Jesus (God); (2) A husband; (3) Your pastor.

Also see *Husband*, *Pastor*, and *Shepherd*.

(1) Exod. 3:13-14; John 8:58; 2 Cor. 4:4; (2) Eph. 5:22-23; (3) John 10:11.

Jet Ski: (1) Thrill-seeker.

(1) Acts 8:18-19.

Jetty: (1) Church (as an outreach to the world [sea]); (2) Preaching platform.

Also see *Sea*.

(1) Acts 11:22; 13:1-3; (2) Matt. 4:19; Rom. 10:14-15.

Jewelry: (1) Gifts of the Holy Spirit; (2) Worldly favor; (3) Willing heart; (4) Spoils of war; (5) Godly favor; (6) Discretion; (7) Lips of knowledge; (8) Over-emphasis on the outward; (9) Salvation, righteousness, and joy; (10) Worldly allurements; (11) Those who bring glory to God; (12) The adornment of the harlot church.

(1) Gen. 24:53; (2) Exod. 3:22; 11:2-3; 12:36; Job 28:12-18 (cannot be compared to wisdom); (3) Exod. 35:22; (4) Num. 31:51,53-54; 2 Chron. 20:25; (5) 2 Chron. 32:27-29; Ezek. 16:12; (6) Prov. 11:22; (7) Prov. 20:15; (8) Isa. 3:21; (9) Isa. 61:10; (10) Ezek. 23:26-27; Hos. 2:13-14; (11) Mal. 3:17; 1 Cor. 3:12; 1 Pet. 2:5; (12) Rev. 17:4-5; 18:12.

Jews: (1) Chosen people; (2) Spiritual family; (3) Persecuted group; (4) Religious hierarchy (associated with Jerusalem's religious elite in Gospels).

See also *Israel* and *Hebrew*.

(1) Deut. 7:6; 14:2; 1 Pet. 2:9; (2) John 4:22; (3) Acts 7:34; (4) John 5:16; Gal. 1:13-14.

Jezebel: See *Jezebel* in Name and Place Dictionary.

Job Interview: (1) Date with destiny; (2) Test before service; (3) New job. (1) Acts 9:6,15; Gal. 1:15-16; (2) Luke 4:13-14.

Jogging: (1) Lukewarm (half-hearted).

See also *Running*.

(1) Rev. 3:16.

Join: See *Cleave*.

Joking: (1) Not taking a situation seriously.

Also see *Laughter*.

(1) Eccles. 2:1-2, 7:4b; Isa. 24:11.

Judge: (1) God; (2) Jesus Christ.
(1) Acts 7:7; Heb. 12:23; 13:4; Rev. 20:12; (2) Acts 10:42; Rom. 2:16; 2 Tim. 4:1.

Jugular Vein: (1) Poisoned thoughts (snake or spider bite on neck); (2) Spiritual life drained (blood sucked from neck).
Also see *Neck* and *Throat*.
(1) Ps. 58:4; Gal. 3:1; (2) Lev. 17:11.

Jumping: (1) Joining (jumping on something); (2) To assail someone (jumping on someone); (3) Overcoming; (4) Without patience or taking the shortcut; (5) Sudden discipline (being jumped on); (6) Sudden response to a command.
Also see *Leaping.*
(1) As in "jumping on the band wagon"; (2) Luke 10:30; (3) Ps. 18:29; John 16:33; (4) As in "jumping the queue"; (5) As in "they jumped on her straight away"; (6) Matt. 8:9.

Junction (T or Y): See *T-Junction.*

Jungle: (1) World; (2) Trials; (3) Complicated journey; (4) Lush growth.
Also see *Forest* and *Rainforest.*
(1) John 13:31; 1 Pet. 5:8; 16:11; (2) Jer. 6:21; (3) Isa. 57:14; (4) Prov. 11:28.

Junk Food: (1) Wrong doctrine; (2) Not doctrinally sound; (3) Convenient food.
(1) 1 Tim.1:3-4; 4:1,6-7; 2 Tim. 4:3-4; (3) 2 Tim. 4:3.

K

Kaleidoscope: (1) Turmoil in relationship and emotions (possible nightmare as a child); (2) Receiving the glory of God as a child; (3) Confusion.
(1) Matt. 19:14; (2) Matt. 18:10; Rom. 8:17; (3) 1 Cor. 14:33; James 3:16.

Kangaroo: (1) Jump; (2) Bounce; (3) Boxing; (4) Australia; (5) Pouch; (6) Someone who has energy (bounce); (7) In the wilderness; (8) Someone who doesn't respect boundaries (fence jumper); (9) Australian church(es).
(3) 1 Cor. 9:26; (6) 1 Kings 18:44b-46; (7) Luke 1:80; (8) Exod. 20:17; Luke 12:39; John 10:1; (9) By association.

Kayak: See *Canoe.*

Kebab: (1) Mixed diet [God's Word and world's word intermixed] (e.g., meat, onions, capsicum, meat, etc.).
(1) Job 12:11; Heb. 5:14; 13:9.

Kerb (Curb): (1) Boundary on God's path; (2) The Love of God; (3) The Fear of God.
Also see *Gutter(s).*
(1) Num. 22:24; (2) 2 Cor. 5:14a (The love of God keeps us from legalism); (3) Ps. 36:1 (The fear of God keeps us from lasciviousness [fleshly lifestyle]).

Key(s): (1) Authority; (2) Opportunity; (3) Access; (4) The rhema word (off your tongue); (5) Control; (6) Way out; (7) Heart; (8) God's will; (9) Prayer; (10) Faith; (11) Unity; (12) Praise; (13) Revelation; (14) Prophecy; (15) Knowledge; (16) Pivotal or indispensable person (i.e., "key player"); (17) Love; (18) The gifts of the Spirit; (19) Signs and wonders; (20) *The Divinity Code to Under- standing Your Dreams and Visions* and *The Divinity Code to Hearing God's Voice through Prophetic Incidents and Natural Events.* Also see *Door.*

(1) Isa. 22:22; Matt. 16:19; (2) Luke 11:52; (3) Judg. 3:25; Rev. 9:1; 20:1; (4) Matt. 16:18-19 (tongue: small instrument that opens your destiny); (5) Matt. 16:19; Rev. 9:1; (6) Rev. 9:1-3; (7) Song 5:2-6; Acts 13:22; 16:14; Rev. 3:7; (8) Isa. 22:22; 45:1; Luke 22:42; Col. 4:3; (9) Matt. 16:16-19; (cf. 1 Kings 18:1,41-45); (10) Rom. 5:2a; 2 Cor. 5:7; Gal. 3:5; 5:6; Eph. 2:8; Heb. 11:5,8,29,30; (11) Ps. 133:1-3; 1 Pet. 3:7; (12) Ps. 100:4; (13-14) Matt. 16:16-19; (15) Luke 11:52; (16) Mark 12:28, 30; Rom. 2:4b; (17) John 3:16; (18) Matt. 16:19 (give = gift); (19) Deut. 6:22-23; (20) Prov. 25:2.

Kicking: (1) Resisting; (2) Aggression; (3) Using strength, power, or force. Also see *Ball.*

(1) Acts 9:5; (2) Num. 22:23-25; Ps. 36:11; (3) Ps. 147:10.

Kidnap/ped: (1) Take/n away; (2) The devil holding someone for ransom.

(1) Gen. 30:15; (2) Tim. 2:25-26.

Kill/ed/ing: (1) Crucifying the flesh; (2) Stopping something; (3) Getting rid of; (4) Slandering or speaking against. Also see *Assassin*, *Mafia*, *Murder*, and *Strangle/d.*

(1) Gal. 2:20; (2) John 19:30; (3) 2 Sam. 12:9; (4) Matt. 5:21-22.

Killer Whale: (1) Prophetic warrior; (2) Familiar spirit (appears friendly, but is dangerous); (3) Church leader who is a predator; (4) Spiritual predator. Also see *Dolphin*, *Walrus*, and *Whale.*

(1) 1 Sam. 15:32-33; 1 Kings 18:40; (2) Matt. 7:15; (3) John 12:6; (4) Acts 8:18-19.

King: (1) Jesus Christ; (2) Authority; (3) Dominion.

(1-3) Rev. 1:5.

King Cobra: (1) The devil. Also see *Snake.*

(1) Eph. 6:12; Rev. 12:9.

King Kong: (1) Defiant stronghold; (2) Strong man; (3) Stronghold of affluence; (4) Strength.

Though a fictitious character, he may be encountered as a child's toy, a movie premiere, statue, or amusement park ride, etc. See also *Monkey.*

1 Sam. 17:4,23-25; (2) Matt. 12:29; (3) 1 Kings 10:22: 2 Chron. 9:21.

Kiss: (1) Empty promises; (2) Affection or embrace; (3) Seduction; (4) Betrayal; (5) Departure/farewell; (6) Welcome/greeting; (7) Deception; (8) Enticement; (9) Worship; (10) Union (joined); (11) Confession of faith in; (12) Encountering God through worship.

(1) Ps. 12:2b; 55:21; (2) Gen. 29:11; 48:10; 1 Sam. 10:1; 1 Kings 19:18; Ps. 2:12; 85:10; Prov. 24:26; Hos. 13:2; Song 1:2; 8:1; 1 Pet. 5:14; (3) 2 Sam. 15:5; Prov. 7:13; (4) 2 Sam. 15:5-6; Matt. 26:48-49; Mark 14:44-45; (5) Gen. 31:28,55; 50:1; Ruth 1:9,14; (6) Exod. 4:27; 18:7; 2 Sam. 14:33; 1 Kings 19:20; Luke 7:45; 15:20; Acts 20:37-38; Rom. 16:16; 1 Cor. 16:20; (7) Gen. 27:26-27; 2 Sam. 20:9; Prov. 27:6; (8) Job 31:27; (9) Luke 7:38; (10) Ps. 85:10; (11) 1 Kings 19:18; (12) Song 1:2.

Kitchen: (1) Heart; (2) The human spirit; (3) The place of preparation; (4) The Church (especially a commercial kitchen); (5) The place of storage; (5) Mind (upstairs kitchen); (7) Under pressure (turning up the heat).

Also see *House.*

(1) Hos. 7:6; Neh. 13:5; the kitchen is the heart of the house and the house is a temple; (3) Gen. 18:6; 27:17; Exod. 12:39; Judg. 6:19; 2 Kings 6:23; Neh. 5:18; Ps. 23:5; Matt. 22:4; 26:17-19; Luke 14:17; Acts 10:10; (4) Acts 6:1 (as a distribution center); (Matt. 16:18; John 21:17b); (5) Neh. 13:5; (6) As the place where we "cook up" ideas; (7) Dan. 3:19; Luke 10:40.

Kite Flying: See *Flying Kite.*

Kitten: See *Cat (Domestic).*

Kiwi Fruit: (1) Fruit of new zeal in God (New Zeal-land); (2) Undergoing a spiritual clean-up.

(1) Ps. 69:9; 119:139; Isa. 9:7; 59:17; (2) John 2:14-17.

K-Mart: See *Shop* and *K-Mart* in Name and Place Dictionary.

Knee(s): (1) Relate to the heart; (2) Birthing; (3) Prayer/supplication; (4) Humbling submission/subjection; (5) Submission to Christ; (6) Devotion to God or false gods; (7) Fear (particularly knocking knees); (8) Weakness; (9) Being comforted (sitting on the knees); (10) To be blessed (kneeling).

(1) Rom. 10:9-10; Phil. 2:10-11; Rom. 11:4; (2) Gen. 30:3; 1 Kings 18:42; Job 3:12; (3) 1 Kings 8:54; 2 Chron. 6:13; Ezra 9:5-6; Dan. 6:10-11; Eph. 3:14; (4) Gen. 41:43; 2 Kings 1:13; (5) Phil. 2:10; Rom. 14:11; (6) 1 Kings 19:18; Ezek. 47:4; Rom. 11:4; (7) Isa. 35:3-4; Ezek. 7:17; 21:7 (on the receipt of bad news); Dan. 5:6; Nah. 2:10; (fear indicates a melted heart); (8) Ps. 109:24; Heb. 12:12; (9) 2 Kings 4:20; Isa. 66:12-13; (10) Gen. 48:9, 12 (the Hebrew *barakh* means "to bend the knee and to bless").

Knife: (1) Words; (2) Person who causes division (good or bad); (3) Cut away the flesh (pocket knife); (4) Hold your tongue (knife to throat); (5) Threat; (6) Fear and intimidation; (7) Protection; (8) Dividing [judging] truth (butter knife); (9) Words of people.
(1) Prov. 30:14; Heb. 4:12; (2) Judg. 19:29; Luke 12:51-53; Heb. 4:12-13; (3) Josh. 5:2-3; (4) Prov. 23:2; (5-6) Isa. 54:17; (7) 2 Kings 11:8; (8) 2 Tim. 2:15; (9) Prov. 30:14.

Knit: (1) Joined; (2) United; (3) Woven; (4) Love; (5) Holding together.
(1) Acts 10:11; (2) Judg. 20:11; Col. 2:2; (3) Col. 2:19; (4) 1 Sam. 18:1; 1 Chron. 12:17; (5) Col. 1:17.

Knives: See *Knife*.

Knock/ing: (1) Desire; (2) Opportunity (if you are knocking, it may mean you are seeking opportunities; if you hear knocking, it may mean an opportunity opening to you); (3) Jesus's desire for intimacy; (4) Desire for answers/seeking God; (5) Heart asleep; (6) Need for readiness; (7) Seeking fellowship; (8) Not known by Christ (too late in entering into intimacy); (9) Call to wait on God; (10) God trying to get your attention (a sign).
Also see *Door*, *Doorbell*, and *Calling*.
(1) Matt. 7:7-8; (2-3) Rev. 3:20; (opportunity knocks) (3) Matt. 7:7-8; Luke 11:9-10; (4) Song 5:2; (5) Luke 12:36; (6) Acts 12:13-16; (7) Luke 13:25; (9) Luke 12:36; (10) Rev. 3:20.

Knot: (1) Stronghold; (2) Secured; (3) Enigma or parable; (4) Tied up; (5) Having trouble finding release.
(1-2) Matt. 12:29; Mark 3:27; (3-4) Dan. 5:16 (*enigma* is literally "knot" [tied up]); (5) John 19:12.

Knuckles: (1) Fight or violence; (2) Disciplined; (3) Get serious and put in hard work.
(1) Exod. 21:18; Isa. 58:4; (2) As in "wrapped over the knuckles"; (3) As in "knuckle down."L

Kombi Van: (1) Alternative or unconventional ministry.
(1) Matt. 9:33; Mark 2:12.

Kookaburra: (1) Mocking spirit.
(1) Prov. 1:26; Isa. 28:22.

L

Labor Pains: See Birth/ing.

Ladder: (1) The cross; (2) Christ; (3) Entry into the spirit realm; (4) Salvation ministry; (5) Portal in Heaven; (6) Angelic activity; (7) Hierarchical system; (8) A son.
Also see *Steps* and *Lift*.

(1) John 3:14; 8:28; 12:32-33; that which stands between Heaven and earth; (2-3) Gen. 28:12; John 1:51; (4) John 12:32-33; (5) Rev. 4:1; (6) John 1:51; (7) Rev. 2:15; (8) John 1:51.

Lady: See *Woman*.

Ladybug/Ladybird: (1) Angel that strengthens and preserves fruit; (2) Obsessed with a woman god.
(1) 1 Kings 19:7; Luke 22:43; (ladybugs kill aphids); (2) Jer. 7:18; 44:17.

Lake: (1) Harvest field; (2) Place of testing; (3) May symbolize your life journey (crossing lake); (4) Place of final judgment (lake of fire); (5) Church (as a corporate reservoir of the Spirit); (6) The peace of God; (7) Restricting the move of the Spirit.
Also see *Dam, Pond*, and *Water*.
(1) Luke 5:2,4; (2) Luke 8:23-26; (3) John 6:15-21; (4) Rev. 19:20; (5) John 7:38-39; 2 Cor. 6:16 (corporate temple); (6) Ps. 23:2; (7) Acts 6:10; 7:51.

Lamb(s): (1) Young Christians; (2) Christ; (3) Sacrifice/offering; (4) Innocence; (5) Covenant witness; (6) Redemption price; (7) Poor man's wife.
(1) John 21:15; 1 Sam. 17:34; Isa. 40:11; (2) Isa. 53:7; John 1:29, 36; Acts 8:32; 1 Pet. 1:19; Rev. 5:6-13; (3) Gen. 22:7-8; Exod. 12:3; 29:38ff; Lev. 4:32; 12:6; 1 Sam. 7:9; (4) Luke 10:3; (5) Gen. 21:28-32; (6) Exod. 12:3-17; 13:13; (7) 2 Sam. 12:3-9.

Lamington: See *Cake*.

Lamp: (1) God's Word; (2) The believer's heart; (3) A church; (4) The Spirit of God (seven lamps).
Also see *Candle, Lampstand, Light, Flame*, and *Torch*.
(1) Ps. 119:105; (2) Prov. 20:27; Matt. 5:14; (3) Rev. 1:20; (4) Rev. 4:5.

Lampstand: (1) Church; (2) Revelation (enlightenment).
Also see *Lamp*.
(1-2) Rev. 1:20.

Land: (1) The promises of God; (2) The believer filled with the Holy Spirit; (3) The Kingdom of God; (4) This is our inheritance.
(1) Exod. 12:25; Deut. 6:3; 9:28; (2-3) Luke 11:20; 17:21; (cf. Luke 24:49; Acts 2:1-4; This parallels Israel physically entering Canaan. Also note that Jesus explains a two-fold fulfillment to the question of Acts 1:6-8. He says there is a future physical fulfillment and a present one through the indwelling of the Holy Spirit. Also note that it is the person who waits that inherits the land [see Ps. 37:9] and also is anointed [see Isa. 40:31]); (4) Gen. 12:7; Deut. 19:8.

Landlord: (1) The devil; (2) Lord Jesus
(1) John 14:30b; (2) Luke 12:45.

Landmark: (1) The cross; (2) Point of reference for guidance or direction; (3) Memorial to faith; (4) Memorial to God's provision; (5) Point of remembrance.
Also see *Lighthouse* and *Monument*.

(1) Col. 2:14-15; Gal. 6:14; (2-4) Josh. 4:3-7; Matt. 26:13; (5) Exod. 17:14-15.

Laneway: (1) The narrow way; (2) Side-tracked to another Christ/Gospel; (3) The way of Balaam.

Also see *Alley.*

(1) Matt. 7:13-14; (2) John 14:6; 2 Cor. 11:4; (3) Num. 22:26; 2 Pet. 2:15; Jude 1:11; Rev. 2:14.

Lap (noun): (1) Comfort; (2) Heart.

(1) 2 Kings 4:20; (2) 2 Kings 4:39; Neh. 5:13 (KJV); Prov. 6:27 (NIV); Eccles. 7:9 (NIV).

Laptop Computer: (1) Heart; (2) Mind; (3) May represent whatever you use it for (work, writing, games, presentations, etc.); (4) Itinerant ministry.

Also see *Computer, Desktop, Hard Drive, Hardware, Motherboard,* and *Software.*

(1) Ps. 139:23 (KJV); Esther 1:20-22; (2) Eph. 4:23; (3) 1 Cor. 4:12a; (4) Neh. 2:7.

Laser: (1) Revelatory word (precise word); (2) Prophecy; (3) Judgment; (4) Word of judgment; (5) Alarm or warning; (6) Made a target in the spirit (laser dot on a person/item); (7) Study focus (laser pointer); (8) Measuring/analyzing levels (being measured up).

(1) Ps. 119:105,130; Heb. 4:12; (2) 2 Pet. 1:19; (3) Hos. 6:5; (4) Isa. 51:4; Zeph. 3:5; (5) Joel 2:1; (6) 1 Kings 22:34; Job 2:5-6; (7) Isa. 50:4; (8) Amos 7:7.

Late: (1) ill prepared or feeling ill prepared; (2) Behind the times; (3) Feeling out of synch with the rest; (4) Feeling like you have missed the boat; (5) Change of heart; (6) Lacking respect (continuously late for appointments); (7) Over committed (hence too busy).

(1) Matt. 25:1-13; (2) 1 Cor. 15:8; (3) Pr. 20:4; Jn. 20:24; (4) Gen. 18:12; Matt. 25:1-13; (5) Matt. 21:29; (6) Pr. 29:7; Isa. 5:12; Lam. 4:16b; Matt. 22:3-10; (7) Lk. 10:38-42.

Laundry: (1) Cleansing.

(1) Mal. 3:2b.

Laughter: (1) Rejoicing; (2) Ridicule and scorn; (3) Faith's receipt; (4) Can cover a heavy heart; (5) Fool (quickly spent); (6) Unbelief.

Also see *Joking.*

(1) Job 8:21; James 4:9; (2) 2 Kings 19:21; Ps. 2:4; 22:7 (KJV); Matt. 9:24 (KJV); Mark 5:40 (KJV); Luke 8:53 (KJV); (3) Gen. 21:6-7; Ps. 126:1-2; (4) Prov. 14:13; Eccles. 7:3; (5) Eccles. 7:6; (6) Gen. 17:17-18; 18:12-15.

Lava: (1) Wrath of God; (2) Sudden destruction; (3) Judgment; (4) Presence or glory of God.

Also see *Fire* and *Volcano.*

(1) Mic. 1:3a-5a; (2) 2 Pet. 3:10, 12; Num. 26:10; (3) Ezek. 22:20; (4) Ps. 46:6; 97:5; Nah. 1:5.

Law: (1) The Word of God; (2) Legalism; (3) Love; (4) The law of faith; (5) The law of the mind (that written on our hearts); (6) The law of the Spirit of Life; (7) Liberty; (8) The writings of Moses; (9) All the Old Testament; (10) The law of sin and death; (11) The civil legal system; (12) Brings sin to light.
(1) James 1:25; 2:12-13; (2) Matt. 12:2, 10; 22:17; 27:6; (3) Mark 12:29-31; Rom. 13:8,10; Gal. 5:14; James 2:8; (4) Rom. 3:27-28; 4:13,16; Gal. 3:23-24; (5) Rom. 7:23, 25; Heb. 8:10; (6) Rom. 8:2,4; (7) James 1:25; (8) Luke 2:22; John 1:17,45; 7:19,23; 8:5; Acts 13:39; 15:5; 28:23; Rom. 2:12-13; 1 Cor. 9:9; (9) Ps. 82:6; John 10:34; Micah 4:7; John 12:34; John 15:25; Ps. 35:19; Ps. 69:4; 109:3-5; Isa. 28:11-12; 1 Cor. 14:21; (10) Rom. 7:7-9,23; 8:2; 1 Cor. 15:56; (11) Matt. 5:40; Acts 22:25; 1 Cor. 6:1,6-7; (12) Rom. 3:20.

Lawn: See *Grass*.

Lawnmower: (1) Ministry in the flesh; (2) Ministry keeping everybody under control (tall poppy syndrome); (3) Harvest ministry.
(1) Ps. 37:1-2; (2) Rev. 2:15 (hierarchy); (3) Joel 3:13a; John 4:35; Rev. 14:15.

Lawyer: (1) Someone giving counsel; (2) Holy Spirit as Counselor or Advocate; (3) Christ as Advocate; (4) Someone who is legalistic; (5) One who attempts to trap you with your words; (6) Tester; (7) Hypocritical believer who knows the Word, but not the Spirit; (8) Intercession.
(1) Rev. 3:18; (2) John 15:26; (3) 1 John 2:1; (4) Gal. 3:10; Tit. 3:9; (5-6) Matt. 22:35-36; Luke 10:25; (7) Luke 11:45-48,52; Luke 14:3-5; (8) Rom. 8:26.

Lay-By (Shopping): (1) Promise of God held in Heaven.
(1) Matt. 6:20; Eph. 1:3; Phil. 4:19; Col. 1:5.

Laying Down: (1) Not standing in faith; (2) Spiritually dead; (3) Not upright; (4) Resting; (5) Evil; (6) Overcome by the glory of God; (7) Bound; (8) Not true to the Gospel; (9) Sinful.
Also see *Death, Down, Sleeping, Standing,* and *Upright.*
(1) Rom. 5:2; 11:20; 1 Cor. 2:5; 16:13; 2 Cor. 1:24b; (2-3) Ps. 51:10-11 (KJV); (4) Jon. 1:5; (5) Prov. 16:17; (6) 1 Kings 8:11; Dan. 8:18; (7) Lev. 26:13 (opposite to upright); (8) Gal. 2:14; (9) 2 Sam. 22:24; Ps. 37:37-38 (opposite to upright).

Lead (Metal): (1) Heavy; (2) Shield.
Also see *Metal.*
(1) Zech. 5:7-8; (2) Lead is so dense that it is impenetrable by X-rays.

Leaf: (1) A life: (a) Righteous life; (b) New life; (c) Driven to and fro; (d) Evergreen life; (e) The temporary nature of; (f) Abundant life/prosperity; (g) Fearful life; (2) Words: (a) As in "leaves of a book"; (b) Pages; (c) All words, no fruit (the fig tree is a picture of Israel); (d) Dead words/without fruit (dead leaves); (3) Covering up or hiding; (4) Healing.

(1a) Prov. 11:28; (1b) Gen. 8:11; (1c) Job 13:25; (1d) Ps. 1:3; Jer. 17:8; Ezek. 47:12; (1e) Isa. 64:6b; Jer. 8:13; (1f) Dan. 4:12,21; (1g) Lev. 26:36; (2b) Jer. 36:23 (KJV); (2c) Matt. 21:19; (2d) Mark 11:13; (3) Gen. 3:7; Matt. 24:32; (4) Rev. 22:2b.

Leaning On: (1) Have faith in (trust); (2) Show affection (love); (3) Without physical strength; (4) Sign of old age; (5) Being supported; (6) Look to for support.
(1) 2 Kings 18:21; Isa. 36:6; Heb. 11:21; cf. Prov. 3:5; (2) Song 8:5; John 13:23; 21:20; (3) Judg. 16:26; Heb. 11:21; (4) 2 Sam. 3:29; (5) 2 Kings 5:18; (6) 2 Kings 7:2, 17; 2 Kings 18:21.

Leap/ing: (1) Joy; (2) Worship; (3) In the Spirit; (4) Overcoming an obstacle; (5) Revival; (6) Healing; (7) Being attacked (being leapt on).
Also see *Jumping*.
(1) Luke 1:44; 6:23; (2) 2 Sam. 6:16; 1 Kings 18:26; Acts 3:8; (3-4) 2 Sam. 22:30; Song 2:8; (5) Isa. 35:6; Luke 1:41; (6) Acts 14:10; (7) Acts 19:16.

Lease: (1) Union or association; (2) Bond (tied to); (3) Contract.
(1-2) Matt. 26:14-16; (3) Gen. 23:15-20.

Leash: (1) Having control of; (2) Being controlled by.
(1-2) Isa. 10:27; (1) Lev. 26:13; Deut. 28:48; (2) Acts 15:10; 2 Cor. 6:14; Gal. 5:1; Isa. 9:4.

Leather Jacket: See *Jacket*.

Leaven: See *Yeast*.

Leaves: See *Leaf*.

Lectern: See *Pulpit*.

Leech: (1) Someone sucking the life out of you; (2) Soaking up your resources and strength; (3) Sponge; (4) Someone with an insatiable appetite to steal the life of others.
Also see *Mosquito* and *Parasite*.
(1-4) Prov. 30:15.

Left: (1) Weakness; (2) Flesh (natural), unbelief, cursed, death, goat, judgment; (3) Heart; (4) Below, after; (5) Riches and honor (left side of wisdom); (6) Foolishness; (7) Carefree and casual; (8) Intellect, soul, teaching; (9) God (facing Jesus on His left side).
Also see *Bow* and *Right*.
(1) Ps. 62:8; 80:17; Luke 22:69; (2) Matt. 25:41,33-46; Luke 23:33-43; (3) Judg. 7:20 (see note in entry 3 under *Right*); Ezek. 39:3; (4) Gen. 48:13-22; (5) Prov. 3:16; (6) Eccles. 10:2; (7) Exod. 15:26; Prov. 15:19; (8) John 21:5-6 (right = faith); (9) Acts 2:33; 5:31; 7:55.

Left (Turning Left and Right): (1) Searching elsewhere; (2) Distraction; (3) Taking eyes off God; (4) Without a goal/vision.
(1) Gen. 24:49; (2) 2 Sam.11:1-4; (3) Heb. 12:1-2; (4) Prov. 29:18.

Left (Not Turning Left or Right): (1) Obedience/blessing; (2) Long life; (3) Straight/narrow path; (4) Determined.

(1) Deut. 28:14; Josh. 1:7; (2) Deut. 5:33; 17:20; (3) Josh. 23:6; Matt. 7:13-14; (4) 2 Sam. 2:19-22.

Legs: (1) Strength/power; (2) Strength of humans; (3) Speaks of the walk; (4) Support; (5) Uncovered legs may speak of shame or uncovering of one's strength; (6) Hand under the leg (thigh) speaks of an oath; (7) Spiritual walk affected (legs impaired); (8) Long-term influence (long legs).
Also see *Broken Legs* (below), *Hairy Legs* (below), *Knees*, *Limbs*, *Shin*, *Thigh*, and *Tracksuit Pants*.
(1) Gen. 32:25; Ps. 147:10; Song 5:15; (2) Ps. 147:10; Dan. 2:33-34; (3) Lev. 1:9,13 (speaks of a cleansed walk); 2 Cor. 5:7; (4) Gen. 32:25; John 19:31-33; (5) Isa. 47:1-3; (6) Gen. 24:2-3,9; 47:29; (7) 2 Sam. 4:4; 2 Cor. 5:7; (8) Gen. 6:4; (cf. Num. 13:33; 1 Sam. 17:4).

Legs (Broken Legs): (1) Broken strength; (2) Unable to stand and fight; (3) Laziness; (4) Death; (5) Wisdom spoken by a fool.
Also see *Knees* and *Legs*.
(1) Ps. 147:10; (2) Eph. 6:11, 13-14; (3) Prov. 22:13; 26:13; As in "What's the matter with you?" "Are your legs broken or something?!" (4) John 19:31-33; (5) Prov. 26:7.

Legs (Hairy Legs): (1) Not walking in the Spirit (unattractive); (2) Walking in the flesh; (3) Person walking in own strength.
Also see *Hairy*.
(1-2) Gal. 5:16; (3) Gen. 25:25 (person of the flesh).

Leg Wax: (1) Freeing oneself from the flesh to walk in the Spirit; (2) Beautiful walk.
(1-2) Rom. 8:1,4; Gal. 5:16.

Lemon: (1) Sour or bitter; (2) Sour (disagreeable/unpleasant) fruit; (3) Issue over which one has become bitter; (4) Complaint; (5) Fruit.
Also see *Fruit*.
(1-2) Ezek. 18:2; (3) Acts 8:23; (4) Job 7:11b; (5) Gal. 5:22.

Length: (1) Measurement of time; (2) Age.
Also see *Measure* and *Tall*.
(1-2) Deut. 25:15; 30:20; 1 Kings 3:14b; Job 12:12; Ps. 21:4; Prov. 3:2,16.

Leopard: (1) Fast or swift; (2) Unchangeable; (3) Ambusher (lies in wait); (4) Predator that preys on the young/weak in faith; (5) Predator suddenly on the scene; (6) Evil principality in place over a city.
(1) Dan. 7:6; Hab. 1:8; (2) Jer. 13:23; (3) Jer. 5:6; Hos. 13:7; (4) Isa. 11:6; (5) Dan. 7:6; (6) Jer. 5:6; Eph. 6:12.

Leper: (1) Sinner.
(1) Sin is spiritual leprosy (see Lev. 13:14-17). Lepers were not healed but cleansed (see Matt. 10:8); Note how they were declared clean in Leviticus 14:2-8. Two birds were taken (heavenly beings = Jesus and the Holy Spirit). One is sacrificed in an earthen vessel

(cf. 2 Cor. 4:7) over living water, while the other is dipped in his blood and released! The leper is to shave (cut off the flesh) and wash (apply the Word).

Also see Num. 5:2; 2 Kings 5:1ff, 7:8; 2 Chron. 26:16-21; Luke 17:12-19.

Lesbian: (1) Church with its eyes on another church instead of Christ (infatuated with the "successful" mega church); (2) Literal lesbian.

(1) Rev. 2:18,20.

Letter: (1) Word; (2) Written instruction; (3) Written communication; (4) Reference to Bible epistle; (5) Orders; (6) Authoritative word; (7) Important (large letter); (8) Invitation.

Also see *Envelope, Mailbox,* and *Postage Stamp.*

(1) Esther 9:26,30; Jer. 29:1; 2 Cor. 10:11; Heb. 13:22; (2) Acts 15:23; (3) Acts 28:21; (4) 2 Cor. 7:8; (5-6) Acts 9:2; (7) Gal. 6:11; (8) Esther 5:8; Acts 7:14.

Letterbox: See *Mailbox.*

Levitating: (1) In the Spirit.

(1) Ezek. 3:12,14; 8:3.

Liar: (1) The Devil; (2) Deception.

(1) John 8:44b; (2) Ps. 5:6; 101:7; 109:2.

Liberty Bell: (1) Proclamation of salvation; (2) The Gospel; (3) Eve or proclamation of revival (outbreak of the Spirit).

(1-2) Luke 4:18-19; (3) 2 Cor. 3:17.

Librarian: (1) The Holy Spirit (female librarian) (as caretaker of the Word).

(1-2) Gen. 1:2; Eph. 5:26; John 14:26.

Library: (1) Seeking of knowledge; (2) Seeking knowledge of God; (3) Heavenly wisdom or riches (upstairs library); (4) Books; (5) Study; (5) Reference or research; (6) History; (7) Be still and know.

Also see *School.*

(1) Rom. 15:4; (2) Prov. 2:3-5; 2 Tim. 3:16; (3) Rom. 11:33; James 3:17a; (4) Eccles. 12:12; (5-6) Ezra 4:15; Esther 6:1; (7) Ps. 46:10.

Lice: (1) If you have lice, it may mean you have been taken advantage of; (2) That someone has become a parasite; (3) It may also mean that someone is "in your hair"; Scriptural meanings include: (4) Plaque; (5) Curse; (6) Parasite; (7) Judgment; (8) Anger and frustration/annoyance (as in,"I'll get out of your hair").

Also see *Fleas* and *Parasite(s).*

(4-6) Exod. 8:16-17; Ps. 105:31; (7) Exod. 8:16-17; (8) Luke 18:5.

License: (1) Authority to minister; (2) Marriage covenant; (3) Permit.

Also see *Automobile.*

(1) Matt. 28:18-20; (2-3) 1 Cor. 7:39.

License Plate: (1) Identity.

(1) Rev. 13:18.

Licking: (1) Getting a taste for something; (2) Succumbing to the flesh; (3) Precursor to eating/partaking; (4) Flattering words; (5) Sweet lies; (6) Self-righteous independent spirit (cat licking).

See also *Tongue*.

(1) Ps. 34:8; (2-3) Prov. 5:3-4; (4) Ps. 12:2-3; (5) Pr. 26:28; (6) 1 Kings 1:5ff; Gal. 2:12.

Lifeguard: (1) The Holy Spirit; (2) Jesus Christ; (3) Pastor (shepherd).

(1) Job 33:4; Isa. 59:19b; John 6:63; Tit. 3:5; (2) Gen. 45:5,7 (Joseph is a type of Christ); Matt. 8:25-26; Luke 23:39; Acts 4:12; (3) Acts 20:28; 1 Pet. 5:2-4.

Life Raft: (1) Needing salvation; (2) Lost; (3) In danger of losing salvation; (4) Ark (Christ).

Also see *Adrift*, *Boat*, and *Sea*.

(1-2) Matt. 18:11; (2) Luke 15:3-32; (3) Luke 9:25; Acts 27:30-31; (4) Gen. 6:13-16; Matt. 24:37-39; (cf. Luke 17:26ff.); Heb. 11:7.

Lift (Elevator): (1) Entering the spiritual realm; (2) Moving in the Spirit; (3) Rapture; (4) Looking for spiritual growth; (5) Looking to get to God; (6) Praise; (7) Gateway to Heaven; (8) Heaven's Kingdom coming to earth (particularly like an escalator with people coming and going); (9) Suicide (falling lift); (10) On way to hell (lift to basement); (11) Church (as the vehicle to bring Heaven to earth); (12) For different floor levels see entries under individual numbers.

Also see *Angels*, *Ascending*, and *Steps*.

(1) 2 Cor. 12:2; (2) Isa. 40:31; John 3:8; Heb. 2:4; (3) 1 Thess. 4:17; (5) Isa. 14:13; (6) Ps. 68:4 (AMP); (7) Gen. 28:12; (8) John 1:51; (9) Isa. 38:18; (10) Ps. 55:15; Prov. 7:27; (11) Matt. 16:18-19; Eph. 3:10; Heb. 12:22-24.

Lifting: (1) Bringing into the Spirit (lifting up); (2) Bringing into heavenly places; (3) Redeeming (lifting out); (4) Receiving spiritual vision (lifting eyes); (5) Bringing into the Kingdom (lifting up); (6) Releasing captives (lifting up); (7) Looking unto the Father (lifting eyes); (8) Believing (lifting eyes); (9) Dying to self (lifted by cross); (10) Bruise (lifting heel); (11) Preaching (raising voice); (12) Resurrecting (lifting up); (13) Pride (lifting up).

Also see *Lifting Hands*, *Loosing*, and *Pit*.

(1) James 4:10; (2) Eph. 1:3; 2:6; (3) Matt. 12:11; (4) Matt. 17:8; Luke 16:23; John 4:35; 6:5; 8:7 (KJV), 10; (5) Mark 1:31; Acts 3:7-8; (6) Mark 9:27; (7) Luke 18:13; 21:28; John 11:41; 17:1; (8) John 3:14-15; (9) John 8:28; 12:32; (10) John 13:18; (11) Acts 2:14 (KJV); (12) Acts 9:41; (13) 1 Tim. 3:6 (KJV).

Lift/ed hands: (1) Worship or sacrifice; (2) Making an oath; (3) Surrender; (4) Exercising spiritual authority (moving in judgment); (5) Pronouncing a blessing; (6) Opposition or rebellion; (7) A claim to not have the means to help; (8) Prayer; (9) Healing or deliverance (lifting into the Kingdom); (10) Resurrection; (11) Encouragement; (12) Helping with a burden.

Also see *Lifting*.

(1) Neh. 8:6; Ps. 134:2; 141:2; (cf. Gen 22:5,10 this is the first place worship is recorded in the Bible); (2) Gen. 14:22; Deut. 32:40; Ps. 106:26; Isa. 49:22; Ezek. 20:4-6, 15; 44:12; Rev. 10:5-6; (3) Universal signal of surrender; (4) Exod. 14:16; Num. 20:11; Isa. 26:11; Mic. 5:9; (5) Lev. 9:22; Ps. 63:4; Luke 24:50; (6) 2 Sam. 18:28; 20:21; 1 Kings 11:26 (KJV); (7) Job 31:21; (8) Ps. 28:2; Lam. 2:19; 3:41; 1 Tim. 2:8; (9) Mark 1:31; 9:27 (lifting someone else's hands); Acts 3:7; (10) Acts 9:41; (11) Heb. 12:12; (12) Matt. 23:4b.

Light: (1) Christ or God; (2) Revelation or illumination; (3) A righteous heart; (4) Life; (5) A guide to the right way; (6) The word as a guide; (7) God's glory; (8) Manifest/ exposed; (9) Fellowship (walking in light); (10) Not walking in the Spirit (no lights on); (11) Without Christ (no lights on); (12) Lost (no lights on).
Also see *Black, Candle, Lamp, Spotlight,* and *Torch.*
(1) John 8:12; Acts 9:3-5; 1 John 1:5; (2) Dan. 2:22-23; Acts 26:18; (3) Ps. 97:11; 112:4-7; Prov. 13:9; (4) Isa. 8:20; John 1:4; 8:12; (5) Exod. 13:21; Luke 1:79; (6) Ps. 119:105, 130; 2 Pet. 1:19; (7) Acts 22:11; 2 Cor. 4:6; Rev. 18:1b; 21:11a; (8) John 3:21; 1 Cor. 4:5; Eph. 5:13; (9) 1 John 1:7; (10) John 8:12; (11) John 11:9-10; (12) John 12:35.

Light Fitting: (1) Heart.
(1) 2 Cor. 4:6; 2 Pet. 1:19.

Lighthouse: (1) Jesus Christ; (2) Church; (3) Powerful believer; (4) Landmark.
(1) Matt. 4:16; Luke 2:32; John 1:9; 8:12; 9:5; (2-3) Matt. 5:14, 16; Luke 16:8; John 12:36; (4) Matt. 5:14-16.

Lightning: (1) Powerful Word from God; (2) Power of God; (3) The glory of God; (4) Instantly/quickly; (5) Judgment; (6) Destruction; (7) Fallen; (8) Angel; (9) Angels going back and forth to Heaven.
(1) Exod. 19:16; 20:18; 2 Sam. 22:14-15; Job 37:2-4; Ps. 29:7 (NIV); Ps. 77:17-18 (see *Arrows*); (2-3) Ps. 97:4-6; Dan. 10:6; Matt. 28:3; Rev. 4:5; (4) Nah. 2:4; Matt. 24:27; Luke 10:18; (5) Ps. 144:6; Luke 10:18; (6) Rev. 8:5; 16:18; (7) Luke 10:18; (8) Ezek. 1:13-14; (9) Ezek. 1:14.

Light Pole: (1) Jesus; (2) Believer.
(1) John 8:12; (2) Matt. 5:14-15.

Lily: (1) Jesus Christ; (2) Love; (3) Grows in the secret/hidden place (valley); (4) Lips (speaking sweet fragrant words); (5) Speaks of being clothed in spiritual glory.
Also see *Lips* and *Valley.*
(1) Song 2:1; (2) Song 2:1-2; [cf. 2:16; 6:3; 7:10 the progression of love]; (3) Song 2:16; 6:3; Hos. 14:5; (4) Song 5:13; 6:2; (5) Matt. 6:28-29; Luke 12:27.

Limbs: (1) Members; (2) Instruments of sin (flesh) or righteousness (Spirit); (3) The Body of Christ (the Church); (4) Loss of spiritual strength (limbs cut off); (5) Crucifying the flesh (you cutting your limb off).

Also see *Arms* and *Legs*.
(1) Matt. 5:30; (2) Rom. 6:13,19; 7:5,23; (3) Rom. 12:4-5; 1 Cor. 6:15; 12:12,14,26-27; (4) 1 Sam. 2:31; Jer. 48:25; (5) Matt. 5:29-30.

Limousine: (1) Glamour; (2) Opulence: (3) High profile.
(1-3) Song 3:9-10.

Linen: (1) Symbolizes the robe of righteousness (white linen); (2) the garment of salvation; (3) Well-valued and expensive garments.
(1) Lev. 6:10; Rev. 15:6; 19:8,14; (2) Isa. 61:10; (3) Luke 16:19; Rev. 18:12,16.

Lion: (1) Symbolizes authority (king); (1) Jesus Christ; (2) The devil; (3) Powerful spiritual forces (good or evil); (4) Angels/servants/instruments of judgment; (5) Strong-mouthed individuals; (6) Strong or strength; (7) Brave/courageous/valiant; (8) Enemy; (9) Fierce; (10) Lying in wait (ambush); (11) Bold believer (you as a lion); (12) Young believer or immature leader (lion without a mane); (13) Nation; (14) Anointing (lion's mane); (15) Territorial spirit.
(1) 1 Kings 10:18-20; consider also the Gospel of Matthew shows Jesus as the Lion/King; (1) Rev. 5:5; (2) 1 Pet. 5:8; (3) Rev. 4:7-8; 13:2; (4) 1 Kings 13:24-26; 20:36; 2 Kings 17:25-26; Rev. 9:8, 13-21; (5) Ps. 22:13; 57:4; 58:6-7; Heb. 11:33; (6) Num. 23:24; Judg. 14:14-18; 2 Sam. 1:23; (7) 2 Sam. 17:10; 23:20; (8) Judg. 14:5-6; 1 Sam. 17:34-37 (stealer of young Christians); (9) Job 10:16; 28:8; (10) Ps. 10:9; 17:12; (11-12) Prov. 28:1; (13) Num. 23:24; (14) Judg. 16:20 (Samson shaking himself is a picture of a lion shaking his mane); (15) (Jud. 14:5-6; Matt. 4:3-11); 2 Sam. 1:23.

Lips: (1) Voice/Words; (2) Flattery; (3) Praise; (4) Deceit; (5) Lying lips; (6) Seduction; (7) Wisdom; (8) Snare; (9) Destruction; (10) Call to depart (from lips of folly); (11) Digging up dirt on someone (burning lips); (12) Contention (fool's lips); (13) Perverse (fool's lips); (4) Precious jewel (lips of knowledge); (15) Hatred (disguised lips); (16) Fool (lips swallowing self); (17) Unrighteous (poisoned lips); (18) Saying something you regret (fat lip); (19) Double confession (split lip); (20) Doubt (split lip).
Also see *Kiss*, *Mouth*, and *Tongue*.
(1) Ps. 17:1; (2) Ps. 12:2; Prov. 20:19; (3-4) Ps. 17:1; (5) Ps. 31:18; Prov. 10:18; 12:22; 17:4; (6) Prov. 5:3; 7:21; (7) Prov. 10:13, 19 (can be restrained lips); 16:23; 17:28; (8) Prov. 12:13; 18:7; (9) Prov. 13:3 (wide lips); (10) Prov. 14:7; (11) Prov. 16:27; (12) Prov. 18:6; (13) Prov. 19:1; (14) Prov. 20:15; (15) Prov. 26:24; (16) Eccles. 10:12; (17) Rom. 3:13; (18) Prov. 18:6; Eccles. 10:12; (19-20) Ps. 12:2.

Lipstick: (1) Drawing attention to your words; (2) Being outspoken; (3) Sinful words (red lipstick); (4) Words of death (black lipstick); (5) Alluring; (6) Feminine/womanhood; (7) Love.
(1) Ps. 19:14; Prov. 12:6; (2) Num. 12:1; (3) Ps. 59:12; Prov. 10:19; Isa. 6:5; (4) Prov. 10:21; 16:30; 18:21; (5) Prov. 5:3; (6) 1 Sam. 25:3; (7) Song 4:3.

Liquid Nails: (1) Stronghold; (2) Bondage. (3) Soul-tie.

(1-2) Matt. 12:29; Luke 13:16; (3) 1 Sam. 18:1.

Listening to: (1) Receptive heart; (2) Spiritual understanding; (3) Building faith.
(1-2) Matt. 13:18-23; (3) Rom. 10:17.

Little: (1) Child; (2) Beginning; (3) Seed; (4) Weak; (5) Insignificant; (6) Humble.
Also see *Short, Tall*, and *Smaller.*
(1) Exod. 10:24; Num. 14:31; (2) Job 8:7; Zech. 4:10; (3) 1 Kings 17:11:14; (4-5) Num.
13:33; (6) 1 Sam. 15:17 (cf. Acts 13:9).

Liver: (1) Heart.
(1) Prov. 7:23; Lam. 2:11.

Living Room: (1) Expose; (2) Public place; (3) Truth; (4) Revealed; (5) Flourishing; (6)
Can be a place to relax; (7) Vulnerable (where all can see).
(1-4) 2 Kings 9:2-3, 20:4-5; 2 Chron. 29:16; Esther 2:11; Jer. 26:2; (5) Ps. 92:13; (6) Isa.
32:18; (7) Matt 26:55; Mark 14:49.

Lizard: (1) The devil; (2) Unclean spirit; (3) Tenacity (clinging on).
Also see *Frill-Necked Lizard* and *Snake.*
(1) Isa. 27:1; (2) Lev. 11:30; (3) Prov. 30:28 (see marginal note).

Loaf: (1) Christ; (2) The Church; (3) Speaks about receiving and distributing that which
is given; (4) Speaks about brokenness to create unity.
Also see *Bread* and *Table.*
(1) Matt.14:19-22 (speaks about Christ's death inexhaustibly providing for humanity);
Matt. 26:26; 1 Cor. 10:16; 11:23-24; (2) 1 Cor. 10:17; (3) Matt. 14:19; (4) 1 Cor.
10:16-17.

Lobster: (1) Partaking in opulence.
Also see *Crab* and *Shrimp.*
(1) Dan. 1:8.

Locker: (1) Heart.
(1) Prov. 4:23.

Locust: (1) Judgment/plague/pestilence; (2) Speaks of curse of the Law; (3) Demons;
(4) Possibly battle helicopters; (5) Devourer; (6) Death; (7) Call for humble prayer;
(8) Individually weak; (9) Army (en masse); (10) Recovery possible; (11) Numerous
(swarms); (12) Fickle (here today, gone tomorrow); (13) Prophet (as an instrument of
judgment); (14) Famine.
Also see *Grasshopper* and *Honey.*
(1) Exod. 10:3-4; Deut. 28:38, 42; 1 Kings 8:37; Ps. 78:46; 105:34; Joel 1:4; (2) Deut.
28:15,38; Matt. 3:4; (3) Rev. 9:2-3,7; (4) Rev. 9:7-10; (5) 2 Chron. 7:13; (6) Exod.
10:17-19; (7) 2 Chron. 7:13-14; (8) Ps. 109:22-23; (9) Prov. 30:27; (10) Joel 2:25; (11)
Nah. 3:15; (12) Nah. 3:17; (13) Matt. 3:4 (cf. Matt. 5:17; 7:12; 11:13; 22:40); (14) 1
Kings 8:37.

Lodge: (1) Boy's club; (2) Religious and traditional church; (3) Occult (Masonic).

Also see *Holiday*, *Homosexual*, and *Ski Lodge*.
(1) Mark 10:35-37; cf. Mark 10:9; Eph. 5:31-32; (2) Matt. 15:6b; Gal. 1:14; 1 Pet. 1:18; (3) Matt. 4:10; Luke 4:8.

Log(s): (1) Imperfection(s) (faults, mistakes, or sin); (2) Flesh; (3) Unrighteous person (logs laying down).
(1) Matt. 7:3-4; (2) 1 Cor. 3:12-15; (3) Ps. 1:3; 51:10 (steadfast = upright).

Lollies: See *Candy*.

Long: See *Length*.

Long-Legged: (1) Influential; (2) Tenacious; (3) Haughtiness or pride.
(1-2) Prov. 30:28 (As in Jezebel); (3) Luke 20:46.

Looking: See *Lookout*.

Looking Back: (1) Not fully committed; (2) Disobedience/rejection of God; (3) Held by the world; (4) Desirous for past pleasure; (5) Looking at the past; (6) Not appreciating the grace of God.
(1) Luke 9:62; (2) Acts 7:39; (3) Heb. 10:38; (4) Gen. 19:26; (5-6) Num. 11:5-6.

Looking through Window: (1) Prophet (godly person); (2) Perversion (ungodly person); (3) Demon/evil spirit (ungodly character).
Also see *Window*.
(1) 1 Sam. 9:9; Dan. 6:10; (2) Gen. 26:8; Jer. 9:21; Dan. 6:10-11; Joel 2:9; (3) Jer. 9:21.

Lookout: (1) Seeing prophetically; (2) Prophetic office.
Also see *Seeing* and *Window*.
(1-2) 1 Sam. 9:9b.

Loosing: (1) Operating with spiritual authority; (2) Healing (releasing those satan has bound); (3) Forgiving (releasing a debt); (4) Deliverance from demons; (5) Breaking a soul-tie; (6) Untying, releasing, opening, freeing, and bringing liberty; (7) Abiding in the Word of God.
Also see *Bound* and *Rope*.
(1) Matt. 16:19; 18:18; Rev. 5:2; (2) Mark 7:35; Luke 13:12-16; (cf. Rom. 7:2, 8:2) (3) Matt. 18:27 (KJV); (4) Luke 8:29; (5) Gen. 35:18-21 (after Rachel's death, Jacob becomes Israel); (6) Acts 13:25; 16:26; 22:30 (KJV); (7) John 8:31-33.

Losing Footing: See *Falling*.

Lost and Found (Lost): (1) Unsaved or sinner; (2) Spiritually dead (out of the Father's house); (3) Anxiety; (4) Through ignorance; (5) Through negligence; (6) Through greed, pleasure, or independence; (7) Through legalism or religion; (8) Losing one's destiny and calling; (9) Distracted (disoriented).

Lost and Found (Found): (1) Repentance or salvation; (2) Spiritually alive; (3) Revelation; (4-6) Joy and/or celebration (could symbolize Holy Spirit infilling); (7) Grace or Spirit.

(1) Luke 15:4-7; (2) Luke 15:32; (3) 1 Sam. 9:20; (4) Luke 15:4-7; (5) Luke 15:8-10; (6) Luke 15:11-24; (7) Luke 15:25-32; (8) Ps. 1:1; Prov. 10:17; (9) Prov. 9:15-18; Isa. 42:24; 1 John 2:11.

Lost and Found (Saying Something Is Lost When Found): (1) Deceitful gain; (2) Extortion; (3) Avoiding responsibility.
(1-2) Lev. 6:2-4; (3) Deut. 22:3-4.

Lottery: (1) Gambling; (2) Quick-fix mentality; (3) Looking for a financial breakthrough.
(1) See *Gambling*; (2) Isa. 28:16b; (3) Matt. 17:27.

Lounge Room: See *Living Room*.

Lowering Hands: (1) Lacking courage; (2) Despondency.
(1-2) Jer. 47:3 (cf. KJV & NKJV); Heb. 12:12.

Lunar Eclipse: (1) Religion (the flesh getting in the way of seeing the glory of God on the Church); (2) No witness; (3) Tribulation.
Also see *Moon*.
(1) Deut. 4:19; Job 25:5-6; 1 Cor. 15:41; (2) Ps. 89:37; (3) Matt. 24:29; Mark 13:24.

Machete: (1) Harsh/cutting words; (2) Trailblazing.
(1) Acts 5:33 (KJV); 7:54; (2) Matt. 3:2-3 (cf. Isa. 40:3; Mal. 3:1); Heb. 6:20.

Machines: (1) Human-made mechanisms; (2) Method or system; (3) Potential source of pride; (4) Sign of affluence; (5) Possible devices of warfare; (6) Reliance on people; (7) Representative of the strength of humanity; (8) human- made assistance; (9) Looking to the world; (10) Employing a method of greater efficiency and less effort.
(1-5) 2 Chron. 26:15-16; (6-10) 1 Kings 10:29; 2 Kings 18:24; Isa. 31:1.

Machine Gun: (1) Speaking in tongues; (2) Praying in the Holy Spirit; (3) Powerful preaching ministry.
(1-2) Acts 2:3-4; 10:46; 19:6; 1 Cor. 14:2,4-5; Jude 1:20; (3) 1 Sam. 3:19.

Mafia: (1) Thug; (2) Racketeer; (3) Underground or subversive activity; (4) Mocker (hit man).
(1-3) John 12:5-6; (4) John 18:2-3.

Magazine: (1) Gossip; (2) Lies; (3) Renewing the mind (home magazines); (4) Sex issue; (5) Worldly influence; (6) Publication/publicity; (7) Glamor.
Note: a lot will depend on the type of magazine depicted in the incident/event.
(1) Prov. 6:19; 11:13; 20:19; (2) Prov. 6:19; 12:22; 14:5; (3) Rom. 12:2; (4) cf. Prov. 6:32; Matt. 5:28; (5) 1 John 2:16; (6) 1 Sam. 31:9 (KJV); Ps. 68:11 (KJV); Isa. 52:7 (KJV); (7) 1 Pet. 3:3.

Maggot: (1) Disobedience; (2) Decay; (3) Judgment; (4) Death; (5) Corruption; (6) Despised person; (7) Eternal death; (8) Feeds on the flesh; (9) Someone who feeds off the Body (Church) grows wings and flies away (not really part of the Body).
Also see *Flies* and *Worm*.

(1-2) Exod. 16:20, 24; (3) Deut. 28:39; Isa. 66:24; Acts 12:23; (4) Jon. 4:7; Acts 12:23;
(5) Job 17:14; (6) Job 25:6; Ps. 22:6; Isa. 41:14; Mic. 7:17 (KJV); (7) Mark 9:44,46,48;
(8) Job 19:26 (KJV); 24:20; (9) Gen. 13:5-11; John 6:70; 12:6.

Magnifying Glass: (1) Faith; (2) Undergoing scrutiny; (3) In the spotlight.
(1) Heb. 11:1; 2 Cor. 4:18; (2) Acts 5:7-11; (3) 1 Sam. 18:7.

Mailbox: (1) Heart; (2) Invitation; (3) A letter may mean a dream or message is coming;
(4) Wanting to hear from God (going to mailbox); (5) Written communication.
Also see *Envelope* and *Letter.*
(1) Ezek. 3:10; Matt. 13:19; (2) Mark 1:37; John 11:3; (3) 2 Sam. 18:20; (4) Exod.
33:13b; 1 Sam. 27:15b; (5) 2 Kings 5:7.

Main Road: See *Highway.*

Maintenance Man: See *Janitor.*

Makeup: (1) Trying to impress people; (2) Pretentious (false prophet); (3) Superficial or
spiritually shallow person; (4) Marks those tainted with hypocrisy and sin (white-washed
face).
(1-3) 2 Kings 9:30; Jer. 4:30; Acts 4:19; (4) Matt. 23:27-28.

Man: The colors worn by men in an incident/event is a good indicator of who or what
they represent: (1) Often the old man is represented [man of the flesh] as is often wearing
red or black; (2) Also prominent is Christ; (3) Your spirit self (often dressed in light
blue); (4) The Holy Spirit (often dressed in white or dark blue); if colors are not evident,
then the old self often appears as Jim, James, Jacob, or Jackie; (5) Another character seen
is your will, identified by the name Bill or William. William comes from the German
name Wilhelm, which stands for "will, desire and protection, helmet"; (6) If a man is
unknown and kind, it may represent God, Jesus, or an angel; (7) An angel (messenger);
(8) If unfriendly or tempting, it may represent the devil or a demon; (9) Spiritual or
fleshly man; (10) Strongman (big and muscular man); (11) The flesh (strong-man); (12)
Spiritual principality or power (may appear as an intimidating figure); (13) Deceiving
spirits keeping people from the truth/true Gospel (men in black/M.I.B./blues brothers);
(14) The flesh/carnal ways; (15) Antichrist; (16) Sin; (17) Denomination of people; (18)
Governing authority.
Also see *Name* and *Woman.*
(6) Gen. 1:26; Judg. 13:6; (7) Zech. 4:1; Heb. 13:2b; (8) Matt. 4:5-6; 8:28; 13:38-39; (9)
Gen. 32:28; Gal. 5:17; (10) Matt. 12:29; (11) Matt. 12:25,29; Mark 3:24-27; (12) Dan.
10:13,20; Rom. 8:38; Eph. 1:21; 3:10; 6:12; Col. 1:16; 2:10,15; (13) 1 John 4:6; 2 Tim.
3:5; (14) Matt. 16:23; (15) 2 Thess. 2:3; (16) Gen. 4:7 (KJV); Rom. 5:12; 6:6; 7:1; (17) 1
Cor. 1:12; 3:3; (18) Matt.
22:16-17.

Manhole (in Ceiling): (1) Trying to get into Heaven or God's presence in the flesh; (2)
Self-righteously trying to get to Heaven.

(1) Luke 16:15; 18:10-14.

Manhole (in Ground): (1) Heart; (2) Gateway to hell (to the chambers of death).
(1) 2 Cor. 4:7; (2) Prov. 7:27.

Mannequin (Dummy): (1) No life or dead; (2) Superficial person; (3) New clothing; (4) Being fitted for new position; (5) Growing in God; (6) Special occasion; (7) A Christian who is into fashion, but not secure with God;
(1) Rom. 8:11b; (2) Luke 20:46; (3-5) 1 Sam. 2:19; (6) Matt. 22:11-12; (7) James 4:4.

Mansion: (1) Mature Christian; (2) Heavenly home; (3) Your current spiritual dwelling; (4) Church; (5) The household of faith/Christ/God; (6) Nation.
Also see *House* and *Palace*.
(1) 2 Cor. 5:1; (2) John 14:2; 2 Cor. 5:1-2; (3) 2 Cor. 5:1-2; (4) 1 Tim. 3:15; 2 Tim. 2:20; (5) Heb. 3:3, 6; 10:21; (6) Ezek. 27:14; 38:6; Heb. 8:10.

Mantle: (1) Spiritual authority; (2) Covering; (3) Spiritual position or office; (4) Anointing; (5) Mourning or humbling oneself before God (tearing one's mantle); (6) Reverting to the natural self (taking off the mantle); (7) Under the influence of evil (Dracula-like cape).
Also see *Coat* and *Robe*.
(1) 2 Kings 2:14; (2) 1 Sam. 28:14; Ps. 109:29; (3) 1 Sam. 15:27-28 (KJV); 1 Kings 19:19; 2 Kings 2:8, 13-14; (4) Exod. 29:21,29; 40:13; Lev. 8:30; (5) Ezra 9:3 (KJV); Job 1:20 (KJV); 2:12 (KJV); (6) John 21:7; (7) John 8:44.

Manufacturer's Manual: (1) Bible; (2) Instructions; (3) Basics; (4) Step-by-step guide.
(1) Josh. 1:8; Ps. 40:7-8; 139:16; (2) Prov. 4:4b-6; 7:2-3; 22:17-21; (3-4) Isa. 28:10.

Map: (1) Seeking directions; (2) Guidance; (3) Life map; (4) Plan for your life; (5) Holy Spirit; (6) The Bible; (7) Wanting to know where we are at in the plan of God.
Also see *Guide*.
(1) Jer. 6:16; (2) Judg. 18:5; Song 1:8; (3-4) Jer. 29:11; Luke 19:32; John 14:4-6; (5) John 16:13; Exod. 33:14; (6) Ps. 119:105; (7) Exod. 33:13a.

Marble: (1) Sign of opulence and wealth; (2) Solid and strong; (3) Spiritually dead (cold).
(1) Esther 1:6; Rev. 18:12; (2) Song 5:15; (3) Luke 22:55-57; Rev. 3:15-16.

Marijuana: (1) Offense; (2) Spirit of deception; (3) Counterfeit spirit; (4) Entering into the things of the Spirit (getting high).
(1) Job 19:17; (2) 1 Kings 22:22; (3) Acts 8:9-10; (4) Acts 7:48 (no high like the Most High!) (cf. Eph. 5:18); 1 John 1:4.

Mark: (1) Identification; (2) Ownership; (3) Note well; (4) Target; (5) Watch (gain understanding); (6) Measure; (7) Easily seen; (8) Open the heart to understand; (9) Noted; (10) Goal; (11) Impression.
Also see *Mark* in Name and Place Dictionary and *Scar* in the Metaphor Dictionary.

(1) Gen. 4:15; Gal. 6:17; Rev. 13:16; (2) Exod. 21:6; (cf. Isa. 49:16; Acts 20:28b); (3) Ruth 3:4 (KJV); 2 Sam. 13:28 (KJV); 1 Kings 20:7 (KJV); Ps. 37:37; Ezek. 44:5; Rom. 16:17 (KJV); (4) 1 Sam. 20:20 (KJV); Job 7:20 (KJV); 10:14; 16:12 (KJV); Ps. 56:6; Lam. 3:12 (KJV); (5) 1 Kings 20:22 (KJV); Job 18:2 (KJV); 33:11 (KJV); (6) Isa. 44:13; (7) Jer. 2:22; (8) Jer. 23:18; (9) Luke 14:7 (KJV); (10) Phil. 3:14; (11) Isa. 49:16.

Marketplace: (1) Corporate or commercial world; (2) Commercial church (profiteering); (3) The World (outside of Christ); (4) Babylon; (5) Trading place; (6) Gathering place; (7) Public place; (8) Those in position to buy or sell (entering the marketplace); (9) God's provision (bountiful market).
(1) Luke 12:18; 17:28; James 4:13; (2) Matt. 21:12; John 2:16; (3) 1 John 2:16; (4) Rev. 18:2-3; (5) Ezek. 27:17; (6) Matt. 11:16; (7) Matt. 23:7; (8) Prov. 31:24; (9) Phil. 4:19.

Marquee: (1) Celebration/party; (2) Temporary home.
Also see *Tent*.
(1) 1 Kings 8:66; 2 Chron. 7:10; (2) 1 Chron. 21:29a; Acts 7:44.

Marriage: (1) Conversion (union with Christ); (2) Union or joined; (3) Partnership; (3) Soul-tie; (4) Two being made one; (5) Christ and His Church; (6) Faith; (7) Christ's return; (8) Cares of the world; (9) Communion (reception); (10) Literal marriage.
Also see *Best Man*, *Bride*, and *Groom*.
(1) 1 Cor. 6:17; (2) Gen. 2:24; Matt. 19:4-6; (3) Gen. 26:26-28; 1 Sam. 18:3; (3) 1 Sam. 18:1 (friends); 1 Cor. 6:16 (sexual partners); (4-5) Eph. 5:31-32; (6) 1 Tim. 5:11-12; (7) Rev. 19:7; (8) 1 Cor. 7:33; (9) Rev. 19:9.

Mars: (1) War/ hostility.
Also see *Planets*.
(1) Mars is the Roman god of war.

Marshmallow: (1) Without substance (not solid); (2) Sweet and pleasurable; (3) People-pleasing messages.
Also see *Rock* and *Sand*.
(1) Heb. 5:14; (2) 2 Tim. 4:3; (3) Gal. 1:10.

Mascot: (1) Represents the team, organization, or company associated with it.
(1) Num. 2:2-3.

Mashed Potatoes: (1) Baby food.
(1) Rom. 14:2; Heb. 5:14.

Mask: (1) Hypocrisy; (2) Falsehood/deception; (3) Hiding; (4) Two-faced.
Also see *Costume Hire*.
(1) Matt. 23:27; (2) Gen. 38:14-16; Prov.14:13; (3) Ps. 10:11; (4) Gal. 2:11-12.

Mast: (1) Upright; (2) Mighty person; (3) Sail; (4) Strength; (5) Drunk; (6) Speaks of being led by the Spirit (in contrast to chimney stacks); (7) Prophet (lookout or watchman).
Also see *Rowing*, *Sail*, and *Ship*.

(1-2) Ezek. 27:5 (See *Cedar*); (3-4) Isa. 33:23; (5) Prov. 23:34; (6) John 3:8; (7) 2 Kings 2:15; Ps. 74:9; Isa. 30:10.

Master's Degree: (1) Trained by God; (2) Refined by God.
(1) Matt. 3:1-4; (2) Zech. 13:9; Mal. 3:3.

Mathematics: (1) Finances; (2) Income.
(1-2) 1 Kings 10:14; Luke 16:4-8.

Material: See *Fabric*.

Matryoshka Dolls: (1) The inner person; (2) Levels hidden in a person; (3) Painted faces.
(1) Eph. 3:16; (2) 1 Cor. 4:5; 1 Pet. 3:4; (3) Matt. 23:27.

Maze: (1) Trying to find the heart of God (maze in a house); (2) Trying to find one's way through a situation that is not straightforward (has many turns); (3) Feeling lost because the path ahead looks complicated; (4) Need for a consistent series of godly decisions; (5) Need to walk closer with God to make it through.
Also see *Lost*.
(1) 1 Sam. 13:14; Acts 13:22; (2) Exod. 18:20; 33:13a; (3) Matt. 10:39; 16:25; (4) Josh. 24:15; Luke 3:4-5; (5) Isa. 40:22 (He can see your way forward); Exod. 33:14-15; Ps. 37:5; Prov. 20:24; Jer. 10:23.

Meal: (1) Assimilating the Word; (2) Feeding on Christ; (3) Fellowship; (4) Intimate sharing; (5) Trust; (6) Provision; (7) Favor; (8) Healing; (9) Covenant.
Also see *Cup*, *Meat*, *Milk*, and *Table*.
(1) Heb. 5:12-14; 1 Cor. 3:1-3; (2) John 6:53-58; (3-5) Gen. 18:6-17; John 13:1b-2a; (6) Dan. 1:5a; (7) Ruth 2:14; (8) 2 Kings 4:41; 1 Cor. 11:24-25 (cf. Num. 21:8-9; 1 Pet. 2:24); (9) Luke 22:20; 1 Cor. 11:24-25.

Measure/ing: (1) Faith; (2) Growing in God; (3) Duration or time (e.g., days or years); (4) Decision; (6) Precision; (7) Judgment; (8) Reciprocity (as you use or do, so God measures to you); (9) Gauge of heart receptivity (hearing).
Also see *Length*, *Tape Measure*, *Time*, and *Weighing*.
(1) Rom. 12:3; (2) Eph. 4:13; (3) Ps. 39:4; (4) Deut. 21:2; (5) Josh. 3:4; (6) Job 28:25; Isa. 40:12; (7) Isa. 65:7; Dan. 5:27; Matt. 7:1-2; (8) Luke 6:38; (9) Mark 4:24.

Measure/ing (Different Measures): (1) Moral dishonesty.
(1) Prov. 20:10.

Measure/ing (Precise Measurement): (1) Rightly dividing the Word (diligent study); (2) A precise set of measures may be a confirmation of a future event.
(1) 2 Tim. 2:15; (2) Ezek. 40:2ff; Zech. 2:1-5.

Measure/ing (Same Measurement): (1) Balance; (2) Harmony; (3) Dividing.
(1) 1 Kings 6:25; (2) 1 Kings 7:37; (3) Heb. 4:12.

Measuring Self Against Others: (1) Comparing; (2) Foolishness.
(1-2) 2 Cor. 10:12.

Meat: (1) The Word of God; (2) Solid Bible teaching; (3) Doing the will of God.
(1) Job 12:11 (KJV); 34:3 (KJV); 1 Cor. 3:2; Heb. 5:12; (2) Heb. 5:14; (3) John 3:34 (KJV).

Meat Cleaver: (1) Word of God.
(1) Heb. 4:12.

Mechanic: (1) The Holy Spirit; (2) An angel; (3) Jesus Christ; (4) God; (5) Spiritual tune-up; (6) Helper correcting or helping your ministry; (7) Healer (evangelist); (8) One who maintains and repairs.
Also see *Automobile, Engine, Motor,* and *Oil.*
(1) John 14:16,26; (2) Dan. 10:11; Heb. 1:13a-14; (3) John 1:33 (the Holy Spirit also being symbolized by oil); (4) Ps. 51:10; (5) Acts 18:25-26; (6) Exod. 18:14; (7) Luke 4:18; (8) Isa. 58:12.

Mechanical: (1) Human-driven; (2) Works; (3) Strength of humanity.
(1-3) 2 Chron. 26:15-16.

Medal: (1) Honor; (2) Glory; (3) Rewards.
(1-2) Exod. 15:1; Ps. 8:5; 2 Cor. 2:14; Heb. 2:7; (3) Rev. 22:12.

Medicine: (1) Healing; (2) Prayer; (3) The Blood of Jesus; (4) The Word of God; (5) Holy Spirit joy; (6) Anointing oil; (7) Leaves (from Christ, the Tree of Life).
Also see *Doctor, Healed, Hospital,* and *Nurse.*
(1-2) James 5:14-15; (3) Isa. 53:5; John 6:53; (4) Prov. 4:20-22; (5) Prov. 17:22; (6) Jer. 46:11; James 5:14-15; (7) Ezek. 47:12b; Rev. 22:2.

Megaphone: (1) Make widely known; (2) Loud/ly.
(1) Matt. 10:27.

Memento: (1) Reminder; (2) Trophy (self-glory).
(1-2) 1 Sam. 17:54; (2) 1 Sam. 15:9,12.

Men: See *Man.*

Menorah: (1) Christ as the anointed, beaten, and resurrected Light Bearer; (2) Those crucified with Christ through whom He shines; (3) Seven spirits of God.
(1) Exod. 37:17-24; (2) Gal. 2:20; Matt. 5:16; (3) Isa. 11:2; Rev. 4:5.

Mentor: (1) The Holy Spirit; (2) In need of a mentor.
(1) John 16:7,13; 1 John 2:27; (2) 1 Kings 19:21.

Mentally Disabled Person(s): (1) Innocent child of God; (2) Evil spirit (aggressive and intimidating).
Also see *Disability.*
(1) 1 Cor. 1:27; (2) Mark 5:5, 15; Acts 19:16.

Message: (1) Word from God; (2) Letter; (3) Dream.
(1) 1 John 1:5; 3:11; (2) 2 Sam. 11:14; (3) Num. 12:6; Jer. 23:28; Matt. 2:13.

Messy: (1) Speaks of the works of people; (2) Not of God; (3) Busyness.
(1-2) 1 Cor. 14:33; (3) Mark 2:2,4; Acts 6:1.

Metal: (1) Represents the strength of the natural human (human-made); (2) Strong; (3) Earthly treasure; (4) Prone to rust; (5) Valued by the world; (6) Trade or commerce; (7) Money.
Also see *Lead*.
(1) Josh. 17:16,18; (2) Dan. 2:40; (3-4) Matt. 6:19; (5-7) Ezek. 27:12; Matt. 22:19-21; 25:16.

Meteor: (1) Message from Heaven; (2) Revival (meteor shower); (3) Judgment.
Also see *Asteroid*.
(1) Deut. 4:36; Isa. 55:10-11; also consider that Christ (The Word of God) is our Rock from Heaven; (2) Ps. 72:6-7; (3) Isa. 30:30; Ezek. 38:22.

Meter: (1) Power supply; (2) Assessing the anointing; (3) Heart (like a parking meter); (4) Opportune time.
(1-2) Mark 5:30; Luke 6:19; 8:46; (3) Neh. 7:5; (4) Esther 4:14; Dan. 2:21.

Meter Man: (1) Measuring the strength of the Spirit/power of God.
(1) Acts 8:18-19; 1 Cor. 2:4.

Microphone: (1) Opportunity to speak or sing; (2) Speaking platform; (3) Amplifying the message.
(1-3) Matt. 10:27; Luke 12:3.

Microscope: (1) Nit-picking; (2) Under examination (detailed inspection); (3) Detail; (4) Science; (5) Biological, bacterial, or viral situation.
(1) Matt. 7:2-6; 23:24; (2) Ps. 26:2; Luke 23:14; Acts 22:24; 1 Cor. 11:28; 2 Cor. 13:5; (3) Heb. 4:15; 9:5; James 2:10; (4) The microscope is an accepted symbol for science; (5) Matt. 24:7; Luke 21:11.

Microwave Oven: (1) Heart; (2) Cooking on the inside; (3) Quick work; (4) Convenience; (5) Penetrating; (6) Sudden boil-over.
(1) Hos. 7:6; (2) Ps. 39:3; Jer. 20:9b; (3) Isa. 43:19; (4) Gen. 25:29-34 (consider the cost of convenience); (5) Luke 2:35; (6) 1 Sam. 18:8.

Middle: See *Center*.

Midnight: (1) The darkest hour; (2) Death; (3) Deliverance; (4) A turning of the situation; (5) End of the second watch; (6) Time to ask, seek, and knock; (7) Decision time; (8) The end of time.
(1) Ps. 119:62 (giving thanks at the darkest hour); Acts 16:25; (2) Exod. 11:4-5; 12:29; (3) Judg. 16:3; Acts 16:25-26; (4) Ruth 3:8; Matt. 25:6; (5) Mark 13:35; (6) Luke 11:5,8-10; (7) Acts 16:25-26; 27:27; (8) Exod. 12:29 (judgment); Matt. 25:6-12.

Midwife: (1) The Holy Spirit; (2) An angel; (3) Intercessor; (4) Assistant or guide to help birth the promises of God.
(1) Rom. 8:22,26; (2) Ps. 34:7; (3) Rom. 8:22,26; (4) Gen. 35:17-18 (Here it is interesting to note the birth of Benjamin, meaning "son of my right hand," who is a type of Christ); Exod. 1:15-21; (cf. Gen. 50:24; Acts 7:19-25).

Milk: (1) God's Word for young believers; (2) Foundational Bible teaching; (3) Immature Christian.

(1) 1 Pet. 2:2; (2-3) 1 Cor. 3:1-2; Heb. 5:12-14.

Millipede: (1) Annoyance; (2) Pest.

Also see *Worm.*

(1-2) Mark 10:41.

Mill/stone: (1) Judgment; (2) Place of humbling.

Also see *Flour.*

(1) Matt. 18:6; Mark 9:42; Luke 17:2; Rev. 18:21; (2) Acts 8:33 (cf. Isa. 53:5; Phil. 2:8).

Mine: See *Cave* and *Tunnel.*

Mirror: (1) The Word of God; (2) The human heart; (3) Vanity; (4) Focus on self; (5) Deception (as in "smoke and mirrors"); (6) On reflection; (7) Past (looking behind you).

Also see *Broken Mirror.*

(1) 1 Cor. 13:12; James 1:23-24; (2) Prov. 27:19; (3-4) 2 Sam. 14:25-26; (5) Prov. 12:17,20; 14:8,25; 26:26; (6) Luke 15:17; John 14:9 (Jesus is in one sense a "reflection" of the Father); (7) Gen. 19:26 (looking back can paralyze you); Josh. 8:20 (looking back may disempower you); Phil. 3:13.

Mirror: (Broken Mirror): (1) Broken heart; (2) Broken focus/vision; (3) Letting go of the promises of God; (4) Double (mirror image); (5) Heaven; (6) Looking to self and not Jesus; (7) Vanity; (obscured mirror).

Also see *Mirror.*

(1) Prov. 27:19; 20:5 (the heart is a body of water that reflects); (2) Prov. 29:18; Lam. 2:9; Hab. 2:2; (3) Hab. 2:2; Matt. 14:29-30; (4) Ps. 12:2; (5) 1 Cor. 13:12; 2 Cor. 3:18; Rev. 4:6; (6) 2 Tim. 3:2b; (7) Job 7:3.

Miscarriage: (1) Lost promise; (2) Aborting the promise of God; (3) Promise robbed; (4) Death of a new ministry; (5) Judgment; (6) Curse; (7) Injustice; (8) Lacking spiritual strength.

(1-4) Matt. 2:16-18; Acts 7:19 (KJV); (5) Hos. 9:14; (6) Gen. 31:38; Exod. 23:26; (*birth* means "blessed," therefore, *miscarriage* means "cursed"); (7) As in "a miscarriage of justice"; (8) Isa. 37:3.

Missile: (1) Powerful words; (2) Words of destruction; (3) Word of God (guided missile); (4) Sermon; (5) Attack; (6) Judgment; (7) Infliction.

Also see *Arrow, Bomb, Nuclear Warhead, Rocket,* and *Spear.*

(1) Isa. 54:17; Luke 4:32,36; 1 Cor. 2:4; (2) 1 Sam. 18:11; 19:9-10; 20:33; (3) Heb. 4:12; Isa. 55:11; (4) Matt. 3:1-2, 4:17; (launched or pointed words); (5) Ps. 109:3; Jer. 18:18; (6) Job 20:23-25; Ps. 64:7; Ezek. 39:3; (7) Job 34:6 (see alternative rendering).

Missing the Bus: (1) Missing opportunity; (2) Missing big ministry; (3) Doing things independently; (4) Waiting (not your time in God to go and minister).

(1-2) Luke 10:38-42; (3) Luke 9:49-50; (4) 1 Cor. 16:12.

Mobile Phone: See *Telephone*.

Mom: See *Mother*.

Monday: (1) Two; (2) Death; (3) New beginnings.
Also see *Day* and *One*.
(1-2) Gen. 1:6-8 (Note there is no mention that "it was good"). This is the death that precedes resurrection; (3) The secular world sees Monday as the first day of the week.

Money: The use of money seems to break into three groups. Positive: (1) Faith; (2) Income; (3) Blessing of putting God first in your life; (4) Representative of gifts or talents; (5) Purchase rights; (6) Redemption (to buy back); (7) Deposits of the glory of God (gold coins); (8) Making a sacrifice or offering; (9) Thanksgiving (currency); (10) The Word of God; (11) Seed. How you use it: (12) Decision between God or money; (13) Need to invest spiritually; (14) It is not the amount, but the heart that is important. Negative: (15) Root of evil (i.e., it has the power of manipulation and control); (16) Trading in church; (17) Greed (takes away the spiritual life); (18) Deceitfulness; (19) Possible betrayal; (20) Worldly power; (21) Bribe.
Also see *Currency Exchange*, *Riches*, *Seed*, and *Treasure*.
(1) cf. Prov. 23:23; John 17:17; Rom. 10:17 (as the currency of the Kingdom); 1 Pet. 1:7; (2) 2 Kings 12:11a; Prov. 10:4; (3) 2 Chron. 1:11-12; Matt. 6:33; Prov. 10:22; (4) Matt. 25:15; (5) Acts 7:16; (6) Lev. 25:51; Num. 3:49; Isa. 52:3; (7) Isa. 60:9; (8) Mark 12:41; (9) Ps. 100:4; (10) Gen. 44:2 (cf. Luke 8:11); (11) Mal. 3:10; (12) Mark 6:8; Luke 16:13; Acts 4:36-37; 8:18-20; (13) Matt. 25:27; Luke 19:23; (14) Mark 12:42-44; (15) 1 Tim. 6:10; (16) John 2:14-16; (17) Prov. 1:19; 15:27; Isa. 56:10-11; Acts 24:25-26; (18) Matt. 13:22; 28:12-13,15; Acts 24:25-26; Rev. 3:17; (19) Mark 14:11; (20) Eccles. 10:19 (universal language); Matt. 22:17-21; (21) 1 Sam. 8:3; Ps. 26:10; Amos 5:12.

Mongoose: Defeats the cobra: (1) Rhema word; (2) Jesus Christ; (3) God's general.
(1) Heb. 4:12; (2) 1 Cor. 15:56-57; (3) Acts 28:3-5.

Monkey: (1) Making you look like a fool; (2) Not serious; (3) Affluence; (4) Mischievous spirit; (5) Mood swings (depression [up one minute down the next]).
Also see *King Kong*.
(1) Someone "trying to make a monkey out of me"; (2) As in "monkeying around"; (3) 1 Kings 10:22-23; (4) Ps. 38:12 (KJV); Prov. 24:8 (KJV); (5) James 1:8.

Monster: (1) Demon; (2) Evil spirit; (3) Fear.
Also see *Dinosaur*.
(1-2) Luke 4:33; Rev. 12:9; (3) 1 Sam. 17:11.

Month: January through December, see Name and Place Dictionary.

Monument: (1) The cross; (2) Remembrance. In the cross we see the fulfillment of the memorials in the Old Testament; (3) "I Am" (the name of God); (4) The sacrifice of the Passover lamb; (5) The escape from Egypt (the world); (6) Victory under "The Lord our Banner"; (7) Judgment upon the High Priest for the children of Israel; (8) The Feast of Trumpets; (9) The Bread of Life; (10) Death defeated (Jordan cut off).
(1-2) 1 Cor. 11:24-25; 2 Tim. 2:8; (3) Exod. 3:15; John 8:24; (4) Exod. 12:6-7, 13-14; (5) Exod. 13:3,8; (6) Exod. 17:14-15; (7) Exod. 28:29-30; (8) Lev. 23:24; (9) Lev. 24:7; (10) Josh. 4:7.

Moon: (1) Wife or mother or woman or sister; (2) The Church; (3) Faithful witness; (4) The moon rules and has dominion in the night, and is a reflection of the sun (cf. Mal. 4:2); (5) God's glory reflected; (6) Celebration; (7) Resurrection; (8) satan.
Also see *Lunar Eclipse*.
(1) Gen. 37:9-10; 1 Cor. 11:7; (2) Song 6:10; (3) Ps. 89:37; (4) Gen. 1:16; Ps. 136:9; (5) 1 Cor. 15:41; Rev. 21:23; (6-7) 1 Sam. 20:5 (the new moon); (8) Matt. 17:15, where the word *epileptic* is literally "moonstruck" or "lunatic"; here the moon symbolizes satan as the ruler of the darkness.

Mortgage: (1) Debt or curse; (2) Financial pledge; (3) The blood of Christ (frees us from the mortgage).
Also see *House*.
(1) Deut. 28:12; Rom. 13:8; (2) Gen. 28:20-22; (3) 1 Cor. 6:19-20; 1 Pet. 1:18-19.

Mosquito: (1) Little irritation that steals spiritual life; (2) Spiritual parasite; (3) Unseen attack that saps the life out of you (or poisons you); (4) Evil spirit; (5) Spirit stealing financially from you.
(1) Lev. 17:11; (2) John 12:6; (3) Deut. 25:18; (4) John 10:10; (5) Mic. 7:2-3; Matt. 27:6 (blood-money) (cf. Exod. 21:30; Lev. 17:11).

Motel: (1) Stopover; (2) Place of refreshment and rest; (3) Speaks of a journey (or life path); (4) Place of encounter; (5) Place of discovery.
Also see *Bed*.
(1-3) Gen. 42:27; 43:21; Luke 10:34-35; (4) Exod. 4:24; (5) Luke 24:28-31.

Moth: (1) Corruption; (2) Decay; (3) Rotten; (4) Destruction; (5) Vulnerability; (6) Fleeting and brief existence (transient life); (7) Temporary shelter (cocoon); (8) Judgment; (9) Building earthly treasures.
(1-3) Job 13:28; Isa. 50:9; 51:8; Hos. 5:12; Luke 12:33; (3-4) Job 4:19; (5) Isa. 50:9; (6) Ps. 39:11; (7) Job 27:18; (8) Hos. 5:12; (9) Matt. 6:19-20; James 5:2.

Mother: (1) The Church; (2) The Holy Spirit; (3) Natural mother; (4) Spiritual mother; (5) Heavenly Jerusalem; (6) Israel; (7) The past; (8) Nurturer; (9) The law/legalism.
(1) Eph. 5:25,31-32; (2) Gal. 4:29b; (3) 2 Tim. 1:5; (4) Gal. 4:19; (5) Rev. 21:2; (6) Rev. 12:1-2; (7) Job 21:8; (8) Song 8:1; Isa. 49:23; (9) Prov. 1:8; 6:20.

Motherboard: (1) Mind; (2) Mother soul-tie; (3) Counsel of God.

Also see *Computer*, *Hard Drive*, *Laptop Computer*, and *Desktop*.

(1) Rom. 12:2; 1 Cor. 2:16; (2) Gen. 25:28; 27:6; (3) Col. 2:9-10.

Mother-in-Law: (1) Legalistic church; (2) Meddler; (3) Illegitimate church; (4) Counselor; (5) Church history (religious mother-in-law); (6) Actual mother-in-law.

(1) Gal. 3:23-25; (2) 1 Tim. 5:13; (3) Acts 19:2-5; (4) Ruth 3:1, 3-4; (5) Rev. 1:19-20.

Motor: (1) Power; (2) Holy Spirit; (3) Human-made power; (4) The human spirit; (5) Heart.

Also see *Ass*, *Automobile*, *Gasoline*, and *Ox*.

(1-2) Mic. 3:8a; Luke 1:17; 4:14; Rom. 15:19; (3) Zech. 4:6; Eph. 2:2; (4) Ps. 39:3; 104:4; Prov. 20:27; (5) As in "The heart is the engine room."

Motorcycle: (1) Powerful and responsive individual ministry; (2) Independent ministry.

Also see *Trail Bike*.

(1) Acts 8:4-7, 26-39; (2) 1 Cor. 3:4-5; 12:15-16,21.

Motorcycle Helmet: (1) Helmet of salvation; (2) Call to know and stand on what Christ achieved at Calvary; (3) Call to choose godly thoughts; (4) Guarding your mind from the enemy.

Also see *Helmet*.

(1-2) Eph. 6:17; (3) 1 Cor. 2:16; (4) Eph. 6:17.

Motor Scooter: (1) Individual ministry; (2) Young ministry.

(1-2) Acts 21:9.

Mountain: (1) Spiritual high place; (2) Heaven; (3) Impossibility; (4) Obstacle; (5) Refuge/hideaway; (6) Meeting place with God (God's presence); (7) Triumph; (8) Place of prayer; (9) Place of worship; (10) Place of transformation; (11) Separation; (12) Ancient; (13) Apostolic calling (walking up mountain with Jesus); (14) Seeing God's glory (top of mountain); (15) God; (16) Doubt and unbelief; (17) Pride.

(1) Luke 4:5; (2) Ezek. 28:16; Heb. 12:22; Rev. 21:10; (3-4) Song 2:8; Mark 11:23; 1 Cor. 13:2; Luke 3:5; (5) Luke 21:21; Rev. 6:15; (6) John 6:3; 2 Pet 1:18; (7) 1 Kings 18:20-40; (8) Luke 6:12; 9:28; 22:39-40; (9) John 4:20-21; (10) Mark 9:2; (11) Song 2:17 (*Bether* = separation); (12) Deut. 33:15; (13-14) Matt. 17:1ff; (15) Ps. 48:1; (cf. Deut. 33:15; Ps. 90:2); (16) Deut. 1:20-26; Matt. 17:20; (17) Isa. 2:12-17; 40:4.

Mountain Bike: (1) Self exaltation.

Also see *Bike* and *Mountain*.

(1) Matt. 23:12; John 10:1.

Mourning: (1) Suffering loss.

Also see *Death*.

(1) 1 Sam. 25:1; Matt. 2:18.

Mouse/Mice: (1) Hidden unclean spirit; (2) Indicator of a lack of spiritual maintenance; (3) Unbeliever (unclean); (4) Small; (5) Plague; (6) Judgment; (7) Insignificant.

Also see *Rat*.

(1) Matt. 10:1; (cf. Rev. 16:13); (2) Luke 11:24-25; (3-4) Lev. 11:29; (5-6) (cf. 1 Sam. 5:12; 6:5 [KJV]); (7) Judg. 6:15.

Moustache: See *Mustache.*

Mouth: (1) Heart; (2) Word of faith; (3) Confession; (4) Silenced or mute (no mouth). Also see *Dumb, Lips, Mute,* and *Teeth.*
(1) Matt. 12:34; 15:18; Luke 6:45; (2) Rom. 10:8; (3) Rom. 10:9-10; (4) Luke 14:5-6; 20:26.

Mouth (Hurt Mouth): (1) Pain in the heart; (2) Inability to open up (unable to speak freely); (3) Speaking out of hurt.
Also see *Gums.*
(1) 1 Sam. 1:12-14; (2) Matt. 12:34b; 15:18; (3) Gen. 4:23; 31:29; Ps. 38:12.

Movie: (1) Your life as a story (Book of Life); (2) The title or plot of a movie may reflect a past, present, or future episode in your life; (3) Entertainment.
Also see *Picture Theater.*
(1-2) Rev. 3:5; 20:12; 1 Tim. 6:12; (3) 1 Cor. 10:7.

Movie Camera: (1) Capturing the action; (2) Get ready for action; (3) Making history; (4) Documenting the past; (5) Becoming a person of renown.
Also see *Camera.*
(1-3) Acts 2:40-41; 3:6-10; 4:33; (4) Esther 6:2; (5) Num. 16:2b; Ezek. 23:23.

Moving House: (1) Salvation (moving from old to new house); (2) A call to get saved (get into God's house); (3) Changing allegiances (possibly a person easily moved by circumstance); (4) Changing churches; (5) Transition of God (growing or shrinking in God); (6) Not happy with or within yourself.
Also see *Removal Van.*
(1-2) Heb. 11:7; (3) Isa. 7:2; (4) 1 Cor. 16:19; (5) Matt. 9:17; Heb. 10:38; (6) Rom. 7:24.

Moving Offices: (1) Changing ministry roles.
(1) Eph. 4:11.

Moving Van: See *Removal Van.*

Mucky: (1) A slanderous accusation; (2) Muckraking.
(1) Jude 1:9-10,13a; (2) Ezra 4:6; 2 Pet. 2:11.

Mud: (1) Stuck; (2) Backsliding (going back to the world); (3) Speaks of humanity; (4) Humbled; (5) Without solid footing (no foundation in God); (6) Sinking; (7) Bad name (someone covered in mud); (8) Accusation (throwing mud at someone); (9) Trodden down; (10) Creating (wet clay); (11) Dungeon; (12) Working through issues (making your way through mud); (13) Not able to let go of the past; (14) Flesh; (15) Sin; (16) Defiled words.
Also see *Clay, Dirt, Earth, Mud Cake, Mudslide, Mud Slinging, Water,* and *Dirty Water.*
(1) As in "stuck in the mud"; (2) Ezek. 47:11; 2 Pet. 2:22b; (3) Job 33:6; Dan. 2:43; John 9:6; (4) Job 30:19; (5) Ps. 40:2; (6) Ps. 69:2,14; Jer. 38:6b,22; (9) Isa. 10:6b; 41:25b;

Mic. 7:10; Zech. 10:5; (10) John 9:6-7; (11) Jer. 38:6 (no water, but mud); (12) Luke 15:15-17; (13) 2 Pet. 2:22; (14) Ps. 40:2; (15-16) Isa. 57:20.

Mud Cake: (1) Indulgence in fleshly words.
Also see *Mud*.
(1) 1 Cor. 2:4.

Muddy Water: See *Water (Dirty Water)*.

Mudslide: (1) Path into the world; (2) Falling back into the flesh.
Also see *Mud*.
(1-2) 2 Pet. 2:22.

Mud Slinging: (1) Slanderous words.
Also see entries under *Mud*.
(1) Ps. 69:14; Eccles. 7:21; Isa. 57:19-20.

Mule: (1) No longer in the world, but not yet humble (half way between a horse and a donkey); (2) Lukewarm; (3) Stubborn (no wisdom).
Also see *Donkey* and *Horse*.
(1) Deut. 8:2 (still in the wilderness); (2) Rev. 3:16; (3) Ps. 32:9.

Multi-Colored: (1) Glorious or clothed in glory; (2) Multi-faceted; (3) Having chameleon-like tendencies; (4) Covenanted.
Also see *Parrot(s)* and *Rainbow*.
(1) Gen. 37:3; 2 Sam. 13:18-19; the coat of many colors prefigures the glorified Joseph and the glorious Bride of Christ; (2) The glory of God is made of a multitude of pure qualities, just as white light is a composite of the colors within; (3) 1 Cor. 9:22b; 10:33a; (4) Gen. 9:11-12.

Mum: See *Mother*.

Murder: (1) Hatred; (2) Self-hatred; (3) Anger; (4) Battle between fleshly (old) self and spirit (new) self; (5) Root of offense.
Also see *Assassin*, *Kill/Killing*, *Mafia*, and *Strangle/d*.
(1-2) 1 John 3:15; (3) Matt. 2:16; 5:21-22; (4) Gal. 5:17; Eph. 6:12; (5) Matt. 24:10; 1 John 3:15.

Muscle Building: (1) Praying in the Holy Spirit; (2) Literal muscle building; (3) Muscling in; (4) Flexing muscle.
(1) Jude 1:20; (3) Gen. 27:36; (4) 1 Sam. 17:5-10.

Museum: (1) Old; (2) History; (3) Dead church; (4) A church that is honoring tradition and worshiping its history.
Also see *War Heroes/Museum*.
(1-3) Deut. 32:7; Ps. 44:1; (4) Matt. 23:29-30.

Mushroom: (1) Ignorant; (2) Willfully ignorant of God; (3) Deception; (4) Ignorant decisions (picking mushrooms); (5) Overnight sensation without foundation.

(1) Prov. 30:2; (2) Isa. 45:19; (3) As in "kept in the dark and fed lies"; 2 Cor. 4:2a; (4) Gen. 16:2 (Abram made this decision without consultation with God, i.e., in the dark); (5) Matt. 7:26b; 13:5-6; 15:13.

Music: (1) Worship; (2) Praise; (3) Celebration; (4) Victory; (5) Joy; (6) Language of love.
Also see *Guitar* and *Musical Instrument*.
(1) Dan. 3:5,7,10; (2) 2 Chron. 5:13; 7:6; 23:13; (3) Luke 15:25; (4) Exod. 15:20-21; 1 Sam. 18:6; (5) 1 Chron. 15:16; Lam. 5:14-15; (6) Ps. 45 intro; Ezek. 33:32; Zeph. 3:17.

Musical Instrument: (1) Ministry (particularly if you are a musician); (2) Ministry of worship; (3) Prophecy; (4) Entering the spirit realm/moving in the gifts (playing instrument); (5) Heart.
(1-2) 1 Chron. 6:32; 16:4; 2 Chron. 7:6; (3) 1 Chron. 25:1; (4) 2 Kings 3:15; (5) Ps. 9:1; Job 29:13; Ps. 108:1-3; 138:1.

Mustache: (1) Shady character; (2) Flesh in what is being said (hair on lip); (3) Authority (uniformed as motorbike cop, Indian military (consider size and style of moustache); (4) Hiding truth (hair covering lip); (5) Woman in man's role; (6) Inferiority/self-concept issue (woman with moustache); (7) Prophesying in the flesh.
(1) Gen. 31:36; (2) Gen. 25:25,27; 27:11; (3) Matt. 8:9; (4) Ps. 140:9; Prov. 26:24; (5) Jude 4:4; (6) Gen. 29:32; (7) Jer. 28:15.

Mute: (1) Unable to speak; (2) Trauma; (3) Broken spirit; (4) Silenced; (5) Fear.
Also see *Dumb*.
(1) Luke 1:20; (2) Gen. 45:3; (3) Prov. 15:13; 17:22; (4) Ps. 32:3; 50:21; Eccles. 3:7; Amos 5:13; Luke 14:5-6; 20:26; (5) 2 Sam. 3:11.

N

Nail Clippers: (1) Taking precautions not to hurt others.
(1) Eph. 6:12; 2 Cor. 10:3-4.

Nail Gun: (1) Penetrating words; (2) Harsh words.
(1-2) Eccles. 12:11.

Nails (Builder's): (1) God's Word; (2) Riveting words (words that engrave the heart and mind) that are God-given; (3) Permanent and secure fastening; (4) Memory peg (not forgotten); (5) Debt paid in full; (6) Preparation; (7) Resistance (buckled nail); (8) Jesus.
Also see *Screw*.
(1) Isa. 22:23 (KJV); Col. 2:14; (2) Judg. 4:21-22; 5:26; Eccles. 12:11; Col. 2:14; (3) Ezra 9:8 (KJV); Isa. 22:23 (KJV); 41:7 (KJV); Jer. 10:4; Col 2:14; (4) Isa. 49:15-16; John 20:25; (5) Col. 2:14; (6) 1 Chron. 22:3; (7) 2 Tim. 4:15; (8) Isa. 22:23.

Nails (Finger): (1) Female conflict; (2) Womanhood (painting fingernails); (3) Preparing to make an advance (flirting); (4) Disarming conflict (cutting nails).

Also see *Thumbnail.*

(1) Ps. 144:1b; Gal. 5:15; (2-3) Ezek. 23:40; (4) Ps. 46:9.

Naked: (1) Seeing the person as they really are; (2) Shame or ashamed; (3) Clothed in glory; (4) Demonic influence; (5) Death; (6) Unashamed Gospel preaching; (7) Not spiritually clothed (heart revealed); (8) Not ready or ill-prepared; (9) Without the anointing; (10) Call to wait upon God; (11) Feeling vulnerable.

Also see *Dressing* and *Clothes.*

(1) Heb. 4:13; (2-3) Gen. 2:25; Rev. 3:18; (4) Luke 8:27; (5) Job 26:6 (AMP); (6) Rom. 1:16 (cf. Gen. 2:25); (7) Mark 14:52; (8) Mark 14:51-52; (9) Lev. 16:32; 21:10; (10) Ps. 69:6; Isa. 49:23b; (Isa. 25:9; 61:10); (11) Rev. 3:17; 16:15.

Name: (1) A named person in an incident/event may refer to: (a) Literally that person; (b) The meaning of the name, which displays its truth. Look up meaning in the name section of this book. If not listed, search in a comprehensive name book or on the Internet; (c) Someone with that same character/position (ask yourself how you see that person); (d) An organization, business, church, or denomination that the person represents relating to their position (ask yourself what that person represents); (e) The marking of a period of time when you were in association with a person or place with that name. The incident/event may show you what has happened between now and then or what lies ahead should you continue on this course; (f) Incidents between you and that person that are now being paralleled spiritually.

Name (Calling Someone by a Different Name): (1) Attack on a person's character or mistaken character; (2) Mistaken identity; (3) Offended person (Sometimes when we call someone by a different name, we may offend them); (4) Call to put on the spiritual self and change character; (5) Trying to force someone to be something they are not.

(1) 2 Sam. 16:7; (2) Gen. 27:24; (3) Gen. 20:2,5,9-10; (4) Gen. 32:28; (5) Dan. 1:7-8.

Nappy: See *Diaper.*

Narrow: (1) The path of life (often difficult); (2) Pressured situation; (3) Distress; (4) Restriction; (5) Too small; (6) Trap; (7) A call to live not by sight, but by faith (narrow windows); (8) God often leads those He wants to use into pressured situations to build a determination and resolve within them that breaks through to new spiritual levels. He achieves this through affliction, confinement, and relational pressure; (9) Inability to grab hold of new mental models (narrow-minded); or (10) Inability to absorb new information because of personal bias.

(1-2) Matt. 7:13-14; (3) 1 Sam. 13:6; 14:4; (4) Num. 22:26; Job 13:27 (KJV); (5) Josh. 17:15 (KJV); Isa. 49:19 (cf. NKJV & KJV); (6) Prov. 23:27; (7) Gen. 6:16; Ezek. 40:16 (KJV); 41:16 (KJV), 26 (KJV); (8) 1 Sam. 1:6,10,11,17; 1 Sam. 17:28; Matt. 11:12; (9-10) John 8:43,47.

Nation: To determine the meaning of a country appearing in an incident or natural event, search out the meaning of the name and its etymology. Also consider the nation and its people's characteristics and think through any relationship the person experiencing the event has with that nation. (1) A country or countryman may be involved in an incident/event as a pointer for direction.
(1) Acts 16:8.

Nationality: See *Indigenous* and *Nation*.

Native(s): (1) People who are born and raised in a certain environment; (2) Spiritually aware (e.g., environmentally aware).
Also see *Alien*, *First Nations People*, *Foreign*, and *Foreigner.*
(1) Gen. 13:7b; (2) 2 Kings 6:16-17.

Navel: See *Belly.*

Neck: (1) Decision-making/maker; (2) Subjection (foot on neck); (3) Victory (foot on neck); (4) Dominion (yoke on neck); (5) Pride (stretched neck); (6) Death (broken neck); (7) Glory; (8) Strength/support; (9) Pride (stiff neck); (10) Stubborn (stiff neck).
Also see *Jugular Vein* and *Throat.*
(1) Ps. 73:6; Prov. 3:3-4; (2-3) Josh. 10:24; (4) Gen. 27:40; (5) Isa. 3:16; (6) 1 Sam. 4:18; (7) Song 4:4; 7:4; (8) Job 41:22; Ps. 133:1-2; Song 4:4; (9) 2 Chron. 36:13; Ps. 75:5; (10) Ps. 32:9; Jer. 17:23.

Necklace: (1) What's on the heart; (2) Condition of the heart; (3) Decision-maker/making; (4) Pride; (5) Yoke; (6) Subjection/service.
(1-2) Exod. 28:30; Isa. 59:17; Eph. 6:14; 1 Thess. 5:8; 1 Pet. 3:3-4; (3) Exod. 28:15,22; (4) Ps. 73:6; (5) Deut. 28:48; (6) Jer. 28:14.

Necrophilia: (1) Soul-tie to dead relationships; (2) Contact with the dead (divination); (3) In relationship with an unbeliever; (4) Obsession.
(1) Rom. 7:24; (2) 1 Sam. 28:8; (3) Matt. 8:22; (4) Judg. 19:24-29.

Needle: (1) Looking for life; (2) Injection of life; (3) Accompanied with horror or fear may be a sign that the enemy is trying to corrupt you (as in poisoning your blood); (4) Taking on an offense (poisoning your heart); (5) Impartation (injecting).
Also see *Drug Use* and *Syringe.*
(1-2) Lev. 17:11; (3-4) 1 Sam. 15:23; Rev. 9:21; (5) Rom. 1:11; 1 Thess. 2:8.

Neighbor: (1) Someone not in Christ (i.e., not in the household of faith); (2) Someone in close proximity, not a relative (a companion); (3) Someone needing compassion; (4) The person of the flesh in you (particularly if that person is at enmity with you); (5) Enemy; (6) Someone with whom you have experienced separation or division (i.e., a fence has been erected between you).
Also see *Next Door.*
(1) Luke 10:29-37; 1 John 3:1 (if sons, then in the household); (2) Mark 12:31; (3) Luke 10:36-37; (4) Rom. 8:1-5; Gal. 4:29 (cf. Rom. 7:14); (5) Matt. 5:43-44; (6) Gen. 13:11.

Nest: (1) Bed; (2) Home/house; (3) Forced growth (breaking up nest); (4) Security; (5) A place of security for the young; (6) Vulnerable (cast out of the nest); (7) Pride (high nest); (8) Sojourners (no nest).
(1) Matt. 8:20; (2) Num. 24:21; Ps. 84:3; 104:17; (3) Deut. 32:11-12; (4) Job 39:27; Jer. 22:23; 48:28; 49:16; (5) Ps. 84:3; (6) Prov. 27:8; Isa. 16:2; (7) Obad. 1:4; (8) Luke 9:58.

Net: (1) Evangelism for either Kingdom of God or the kingdom of darkness; (2) Kingdom of Heaven; (3) Ministry; (4) Trap; (5) Poetic justice (falling into your own net); (6) Seductive heart; (7) Death; (8) Trapped in the Internet.
Also see *Fishing*, *Hook*, and *Web*.
(1) Matt. 4:19; 23:15 (KJV); (2) Matt. 13:47; (3) Matt. 4:19; (4) Ps. 57:6; 140:5; Prov. 29:5; (5) Ps. 141:10; (6) Eccles. 7:26; (7) Eccles. 9:12.

New: (1) Regenerated or born again (new vessel); (2) New level of glory of God.
(1) Matt. 9:16; 2 Cor. 5:17; Tit. 3:5; as in "new wineskin"; (2) 2 Cor. 3:18; 1 Sam. 2:19.

New House: (1) The new nature (the born-again believer in Christ).
Also see *House* and *Old House*.
(1) 2 Cor. 5:1,17.

News: (1) The Gospel; (2) What God is doing; (3) A news report you need to see; (4) Reference to recent or up and coming events; (5) Something about to make headlines; (6) Mass exposure; (7) Sudden exposure (breaking news); (8) Sudden (newsflash).
Also see *Newspaper*.
(1) Isa. 61:1 (NASB); Luke 2:10 (NASB); Rom. 10:15; (2) Luke 1:19b; 2:8-10; Acts 11:20-22; (3) Luke 19:2-5; (4) Amos 1:1; (5) John 13:19; 14:29; (6) Isa. 52:7; Matt. 24:30; 26:64; (7) Gen. 45:13; 1 Sam. 4:14b; (8) Acts 22:17-18.

Newspaper: (1) God's Word; (2) Headlines; (3) Public Exposure; (4) Gossip; (5) Listening to the world.
Also see *News* and *Delivering Newspapers*.
(1) Ps. 68:11; Isa. 52:7; (2-3) Acts 26:23, 26; (4) Eccles. 10:20; (5) Matt. 16:13.

Newspaper (Delivering Newspapers): (1) Gospel preaching; (2) Making something public; (3) Publishing; (4) Distributing Bibles.
(1) Isa. 61:1 (NASB); Matt. 3:1-2; 24:14; (2) Mark 1:45; Luke 5:15; (3) Ps. 68:11 (KJV); Isa. 52:7; (4) Ps. 68:11 (KJV); Acts 10:37-38 (KJV); 13:49 (KJV).

Next Door: (1) Signifies a parallel from your life of what is happening in the Spirit; (e.g., earthly to spiritual; business to spiritual); (2) Close in time or place; (3) Next opportunity; (4) Neighbor; (5) Associate or friend (someone close to you); (6) At hand.
Also see *Door* and *Neighbor*.
(1) 1 Sam. 15:27-28; Hos. 3:1; Jer. 18:6; (2) John 4:46b-47, 49-53 (the miracle was performed at the same time, which means that there is no distance in prayer!); (3) 1 Cor. 16:9; (4) Luke 10:29; (5) Mark 12:31; (6) As in "nearby" in time or space (cf. Matt. 3:2).

Night: (1) Darkness; (2) Evil; (3) Betrayal; (4) Absence of Christ; (5) Stumbling (walking at night); (6) Secret or hidden (under cover of dark); (7) Walking at night is indicative of the old self (the unbelieving you); (8) Judgment; (9) Ignorance; (10) The realm of unbelief.

Also see *Darkness* and *Day*.

(1) Gen. 1:2,5; 1 Thess. 5:5; (2-3) John 13:30; 1 Cor. 11:23; (4) John 8:12; 9:4; 11:10; (5) John 11:10; (6) John 3:2; 7:50; 19:39; (7) John 3:2; (Matt. 27:4; John 13:30. Judas failed to see who Jesus was!); (8) Jude 1:6; (9) John 3:2,4; as in "they are in the dark about..."; (10) John 3:2; 13:30.

Nightclub: (1) The world (place where those in the dark congregate); (2) Church without Christ.

Also see *Bar* and *Hotel*.

(1) Gen. 1:5; 1 John 1:5-6; (2) John 8:12; 11:10; 13:30.

Nine: (1) Finality and judgment; (2) End or conclusion; (3) Fruitfulness; (4) Number of the Holy Spirit (The Fruitful One); (5) Not giving glory to God.

(1-2) The last digit nine marks the end and conclusion of a matter; (3) Gen. 17:1-2; Abraham was promised *exceeding fruitfulness* at 99 years of age; Matt. 7:16; John 15:8; Fruit is the final evidence of Christian growth and discipleship; (4) Gal. 5:22-23 (nine fruit); (5) Luke 17:17-18.

Nine O'Clock: (1) Time to be filled with the Spirit (holy happy hour).

(1) Acts 2:15.

Nineteen: As combinations of 9 + 10 = 19: (1) Complete judgment; (2) Certain finality; (3) Complete fruitfulness; (4) Fullness of the Spirit.

For Scriptures, see *Nine* and *Ten*.

Nineteen Seventy (1970): (1) A generation full of the Spirit.

For Scriptures, see *Nineteen* and *Seventy*.

Ninety: (1) Complete judgment; (2) Finality.

For Scriptures, see *Nine* and *Ten*.

Ninja: (1) Spiritual special agent (mighty people of valor); (2) Evil spirit/demon; (3) Spirit of death.

(1) 2 Sam. 23:8-12; (2-3) Jer. 9:21; Joel 2:9.

Nit: (1) Nit-picking; (2) Fault-finding; (3) Judgment (if someone is going through your hair).

Also see *Lice*.

(1) Matt. 7:2-6; 23:24; (2) Mark 3:2; (3) Matt. 22:15-17.

Noise: (1) Distraction; (2) Interference; (3) Busyness; (4) Annoying interference; (5) God's voice (loud trumpet noise); (6) A multitude.

(1) Matt. 13:22; Mark 10:21; Luke 9:59-62; Rev. 2:4; (2) Matt. 23:13; (3) Luke 10:40-42; (4) 1 John 2:15-17; (5) Exod. 19:19; (6) Isa. 13:4; 17:12.

Non-Deciduous: See *Evergreen*.

North: (1) Place of God's throne; (2) Place of judgment; (3) Location of the enemy; (4) Moving into your spiritual inheritance (turning northward); (5) Literally going somewhere north of your current location (turning northward); (6) Consider aspects in your own environment relating to north.

Also see *South*.

(1) Lev. 1:11; Ps. 75:6-7; Isa. 14:13-14; (2) Jer. 1:13-14; (3) Ezek. 38:6; (4-5) Deut. 2:3.

Nose: (1) Spiritual senses; (2) Spirit; (3) Led; (4) Insensitive; (5) Pride; (6) Offense (smoke in nostrils); (7) Offended; (8) Broken spirit (broken nose); (9) Unrelenting (hard-nosed); (10) Proud and insensitive to the Spirit (hard-nosed); (11) Unapproachable (hard-nosed); (12) Spiritually insensitive (no nose).

Also see *Nosebleed*.

(1) Ezek. 23:25; Ps. 45:7-8; (2) Job 27:3 (KJV); (3) 2 Kings 19:28; Isa. 37:29; (4) Ps. 115:6; (5-6) Isa. 65:5; (7) As in "Who put their nose out of joint?"; (8) Ps. 51:17; (cf. Gen. 2:7; Isa. 42:5); (9-10) Job 41:2; (11) Job 41:2; Ps. 115:6; (12) Ezek. 23:25.

Nosebleed: (1) Strife; (2) Possible family anger issue; (3) Damaged sensitivity.

Also see *Blood* and *Nose*.

(1-2) Prov. 30:33.

Nuclear Warhead: (1) Power of the Spirit; (2) Impact in a nation; (3) Potential massive outburst with multiple casualties; (4) Sudden destruction; (5) Serious destructive threat to a city, community, or church; (6) The Day of the Lord/Judgment Day.

See *Bomb* and *Broken Arrow*.

(1) Luke 3:16-17; Acts 4:31; (2) Isa. 34:2; John 11:50; Acts 1:8; (3) Prov. 29:22; Dan. 2:12-13; (4) Zech. 14:12; Jer. 4:20; 1 Thess. 5:3; (5) Gen. 19:13,24-25; Jonah 3:4; Acts 9:1-2; (6) Joel 2:30-31; Rev. 16:8.

Nudity: See *Naked*.

Numbers: See individual entries.

Number Plate: See *License Plate*.

Nun: (1) Purity.

(1) 2 Tim. 5:2.

Nurse: (1) Christ; (2) Holy Spirit; (3) Caring church; (4) Gentle nurturer of young Christians; (5) Ministers who affectionately impart the Word; (6) Feeder and provider of the young; (7) Carer; (8) Male or female servants; (9) Angels; (10) Healing angel (messenger of God ushering in the healing power of God).

Also see *Doctor* and *Hospital*.

(1) Isa. 40:11; (2) John 14:26; 15:26 (KJV); (3) Acts 4:35; (4) Exod. 2:7,9; 1 Thess. 2:7; (5) 1 Thess. 2:7-8; (4) Num. 11:12; (5) Ruth 4:16; (6) Isa. 49:23; (7) Matt. 18:10; Heb. 1:14; (10) John 5:4.

Nuts (Fruit): (1) God's Word; (2) Words of promise; (3) Someone distorting God's Word (sugar-coated nuts).
Also see *Seed*.
(1-2) Matt. 13:19-23; Luke 8:11; 1 Pet. 1:23; (3) Matt. 4:6.

Nuts and Bolts: (1) Underpinning truths.
Also see *Bolts*.
(1) Heb. 6:1-2.

O

Oak: (1) Longevity; (2) Stable (deeply rooted); (3) Kingdom pillar (landmark); (4) The cross; (5) Place to shelter; (6) Place to bury the past; (7) Idolatry; (8) Represents a proud enemy; (9) Durable (used for oars); (10) Strong.
(1) Zech. 11:2 (KJV); (2) Amos 2:9; (3) Josh. 24:26; (4) 2 Sam. 18:9-10,14 (KJV);
(5) 1 Kings 13:14; (6) Gen. 35:4,8 (KJV); 1 Chron. 10:12 (KJV); (7) Isa. 1:29 (KJV);
44:14-15; Ezek. 6:13; Hos. 4:13; (8) Isa. 2:12-13; (9) Ezek. 27:6; (10) Amos 2:9.

Oath: (1) Promise; (2) Pledge; (3) Allegiance; (4) Covenant.
(1-4) Gen. 21:22-31; 24:2-3,8; Eccles. 8:2.

Ocean: See *Sea*.

Octopus: (1) Fleshly control or influence (tentacles); (2) Controlling spirit; (3) Soul-tie stronghold (octopus on head).
Also see *Eight* and *Squid*.
(1) Exod. 2:14; Prov. 6:5; Gal. 2:4; (2) 1 Kings 21:7-10; (3) 2 Cor. 10:4-5.

Odor (Bad): (1) Foolishness; (2) Monstrous deeds; (3) Demons; (4) Deception; (5) Wrong spirit; (6) Offensive.
Also see *Incense* and *Perfume*.
(1) Eccles. 10:1; (2) Joel 2:20; (3) Eccles. 10:1 (see *Flies*); (4) Mark 9:25; Eph. 4:14; also as in "something is off" or "I smell a rat"; (5) Ps. 32:2; Mark 1:23-24; (6) Matt. 13:21; 16:23.

Office: (1) Business; (2) Kingdom office or position; (3) Pastor, teacher, evangelist, prophet, and apostle; (4) The heart (as the place where we do business with God); (5) Heaven (place where God sits running everything).
(1) 1 Sam. 21:2; (2-3) Eph. 4:11-12; (4) Ps. 91:1; (5) Gen. 28:12; Heb. 12:22-23.

Offspring: (1) Future; (2) Fruits of faith.
(1) Job 21:8; (2) Rom. 4:13.

Oil (Dirty): (1) Unclean spirit; (2) Foolishness.
(1) Eccles. 10:1; (2) Eccles. 10:1.

Oil (Olive): (1) Anointing; (2) Crowned by God; (3) The Holy Spirit; (4) Light; (5) Spiritual strength; (6) The Glory of God.

Also see *Olive*.

(1) Exod. 29:7,21; 30:24-31; Lev. 8:12; Ps. 23:5; 133:2; (2) Lev. 21:12 (KJV); 1 Sam. 10:1; 16:13; 1 Kings 1:39; 2 Kings 9:3; Ps. 45:7; 89:20; (3) 1 Sam. 16:13; Isa. 61:3; Eph. 1:13; 4:30; (4) Exod. 25:6; 35:8,28; (5) Ps. 92:10; (6) Zech. 4:12.

Oil Rig: (1) Church in the Spirit; (2) Anointed ministry.

Also see *Gasoline* and *Gas Station*.

(1-2) Matt. 25:9; 1 Sam. 16:13; John 7:38-39.

Oil Slick: (1) Wrong spirit (slick on a road/path); (2) Someone causing others to backslide; (3) Slippery character; (4) Out of control (positive or negative).

Also see *Oil Spill*.

(1) Ps. 32:2; Isa. 19:14; (2) Prov. 14:14; Jer. 2:19; 3:6; 8:5; (3) Ps. 55:21; (4) John 21:18.

Oil Spill: (1) Stopping the flow of the Spirit; (2) Tragic environmental changes (ecological disaster); (3) Anointing; (4) Outbreak of the Spirit, which is an offense to the world.

Also see *Oil Slick*.

(1) 1 Thess. 5:19; (2) Matt. 27:51, 54; (3) 1 Sam. 16:13; (4) Matt. 12:24, 28 (offended by the Spirit of God); Acts 2:15.

Old: (1) Past; (2) Unregenerate (not renewed by the Spirit); (3) Former life; (4) Memories.

(1-2) 2 Cor. 5:17; (3) Isa. 43:18-19a; (4) Isa. 65:17.

Old House: (1) The old self (prior to Christ); (2) The past; (3) Grandfather/mother; (4) Heritage.

(1-2) 2 Cor. 5:1 (KJV); 1 Cor. 3:9b; Heb. 3:6; (cf. 2 Cor. 5:17); (3) 2 Sam. 8:3,6; (4) Luke 1:27,69; 2:4; (cf. Gen. 15:4 (spiritual lineage); Luke 19:9).

Old Man: (1) Person of the flesh; (2) Unbeliever; (3) Past or history; (4) Grandfather; (5) Patriarch; (6) Wisdom; (7) God; (8) Stronghold; (9) The enemy (devil).

Also see *First Nations Peoples* and *Native(s)*.

(1) Rom. 6:6; Eph. 4:22; Col. 3:9; 2 Cor. 5:17; Jude 1:4; Matt. 9:17; (2) Luke 1:18; John 3:4; (3) 2 Pet. 1:21 (KJV); (4) Prov. 17:6; 1 Sam. 2:31; 4:18-19; (5) Gen. 25:8; 43:27; (6) Job 12:12; (7) Dan. 7:9,13,22; (8) Gen. 25:23; Lam. 1:7; Hos. 7:9; (9) Rev. 12:9.

Old Woman: (1) Person of the flesh; (2) Church history; (3) Grandmother; (4) Matriarch; (5) Wisdom; (6) Holy Spirit; (7) Past or history.

(1) Rom. 6:6; (2) Eph. 5:25,27,31-32; (3) 2 Tim. 1:5; (4) Gen. 18:11; 1 Pet. 3:5-6; (5) Prov. 8:1-2, 22-23; (6) Gen. 2:24 (cf. Eph. 5:31-32; Phil. 2:7); (7) 2 Tim. 1:5.

Olive: (1) Fruit of the Spirit; (2) Depositing or birthing the anointing; (3) Spiritual offspring.

Also see *Oil (Olive)* and *Olive Tree*.

(1) Isa. 61:3; Gal. 5:22-23; (2) 1 Sam. 16:13; (3) Deut. 28:40-41.

Olive Tree: (1) Anointed person.

(1) Zech. 4:11-14; Rev. 11:3-4.

One: (1) God; (2) Literally one; (3) Beginning; (4) Source; (5) Commencement; (6) First in order, time, rank, or importance; (7) Compound unity; (8) Only; (9) Indivisible; (10) Love; (11) First heaven (the physical realm).
(1) Gen. 1:1; (2) Literally one; (3) Gen. 1:1; 8:13; (4) God is the source of all that follows; (5) Genesis is the commencement of all that follows; (6) Isa. 44:6; 48:12-13; Rev. 1:11, 17; 2:8; 22:13; (7) Gen. 2:24; Num. 15:16; Mark 12:29; Acts 28:25; Gal. 3:28; (8-9) Isa. 43:10-11; (10) John 17:23; 2 Cor. 13:11; Phil. 2:2; (11) 2 Cor. 12:2.

One Hundred: See *Hundred*.

One Hundred and Eighty (180): (1) Repentance.
(1) Luke 17:4; Acts 26:20.

One Hundred and Twenty (120): (1) The end of the flesh (life in the Spirit); (2) A period of waiting; (3) One accord/Spirit utterance; (4) The Glory of God.
(1-2) Gen. 6:3,13; (Deut. 34:7; Matt. 17:3); (Luke 24:49; Acts 1:15); (3) Acts 2:1-13; (4) Exod. 34:29-33 (Moses revealed the Glory of God); Deut. 34:7; Luke 9:30-31; Jude 1:9; (after 3 x 40 year periods Moses entered into glory); Luke 2:22; [cf. Lev. 12:2,4]; Matt. 4:2; Acts 1:3; John 17:5 (After 3 x 40 day periods Jesus ascended to the Father and was glorified).

Onion: (1) Represents the World (Egypt); (2) Dwelling in the past and getting upset over nothing (tears from peeling onions); (3) Focusing on the past, having murky vision; (4) Layers or levels; (5) New York; (6) Chicago; (7) Dealing with heartfelt issues (chopping onions); (8) Dealing with issues of the heart (removing layers of the onion).
(1-3) Num. 11:5; (4) As in the rings of an onion; (5-6) These cities also known as the "Big Onion"; (7) Matt. 3:10; (8) Deut. 10:16; 30:6.

Open: (1) Opportunity (door); (2) Release; (3) Reveal/ed; (4) Manifest (tangibly seen); (5) Spiritual (in)sight; (6) In the Spirit; (7) Receive; (8) Freely; (9) Having a receptive heart; (10) Alive; (11) Released to speak; (12) Explain; (13) Bring to salvation; (14) Hear (open ears); (15) Opposite to secretly; (16) Opposite to shut.
Also see *Window (Open Window)*.
(1) 1 Cor. 16:9; 2 Cor. 2:12; Col. 4:3; (2) Mark 7:34-35 (to speak); Acts 5:19; 12:10; 16:26; Rev. 5:5; 6:1; (3) Matt. 5:2; 9:30; 13:35; Luke 24:27,32; Rom. 3:13; Eph. 6:19; Heb. 4:13; (4) Matt. 6:4,6,18; 27:52-53; Luke 4:17-21; John 7:4; Col. 2:15 (cf. NKJV & KJV); (5) Matt. 7:7-8; (6) Matt. 9:30; Luke 24:31-32; (7) Matt. 25:1-12; Luke 12:35-36; (8) Mark 1:45; 8:32; John 7:13; 11:54; 18:20; (9) Matt. 13:19; Luke 24:45; Acts 16:14; 2 Cor. 3:17-18 (KJV); Rev. 3:20; (10) Acts 9:40; (11) Acts 10:34; (12) Acts 17:3 (cf. NKJV & KJV); Luke 24:31-32; (13) Acts 26:18 (bring to the light); (14) 1 Pet. 3:12; (15) John 7:10; (16) Rev. 3:7.

Open Heaven: (1) Revelation or vision; (2) Blessing; (3) Gift from God; (4) Abundance; (5) Righteousness comes down, and with open hearts, salvation is the response; (6) Easy to witness.

Also see *Windows of Heaven*.

(1) Ps. 78:23-24; Ezek. 1:1b; John 1:51; Acts 7:56; 10:11; Rev. 4:1; (2) Deut. 28:12; Mal. 3:10; Matt. 3:16; (3) Ps. 78:23-24; (4) Gen. 7:11; (5-6) Isa. 45:8.

Op Shop: (1) Looking for an opportunity; (2) Middle-aged person looking for a second-hand spouse; (3) Church full of old wineskins.

Also see *Secondhand Store*.

(1) Gal. 6:10; (2) Ruth 3:7-9 (wanting to be covered by another's clothes); (3) Matt. 9:17; Acts 21:30.

Optician: (1) God; (2) Jesus Christ; (3) The Holy Spirit; (4) Developing spiritual vision/faith (eye testing); (5) Prophet (as someone who helps you see).

Also see *Eyes*, *Window*, and *Windows of Heaven*.

(1) Gen. 21:19; 2 Kings 6:17; (2) John 9:6-7; (3) Ezek. 11:24; Joel 2:28; John 14:17; Acts 2:17; (4) Heb. 11:1,3,7,27; (5) 1 Sam. 9:9; Eph. 4:11-12.

Orange (Color): (1) Glory; (2) Wisdom.

See *Amber*.

(1) Ezek. 1:4,27; (2) Prov. 3:35; Rom. 16:27; 1 Cor. 2:7.

Orange (Fruit): (1) Fruit; (2) Fruit of the Spirit; (3) Words of wisdom.

(1) Gen. 1:11; (2) Gal. 5:22-23; (3) Dan. 9:22; 10:3.

Orange Juice: (1) Strengthening physical immunity; (1) Words of warning; (2) Cautionary words.

(1) 3 John 2; (2-3) Ps. 16:5; Esther 4:6.

Orb: (1) Spirit; (2) Life.

Also see *Ball*, *Circle*, and *Wheel*.

(1-2) Ezek. 1:16,19-21.

Orbit: (1) Life's path; (2) Being led by the Spirit.

Also see *Flying*, *Planet*, and *Satellite*.

(1) Ps. 16:11; 19:4; (2) Rom. 8:14.

Orchard: (1) Fruitfulness.

Also see *Fruit Tree*, *Plantation*, and *Vineyard*.

(1) Eccles. 2:5; Song 4:13.

Ornament: (1) Something left on the shelf and forgotten about.

Also see *Trophy*.

(1) Gen. 40:23.

Ostrich: (1) Without wisdom and understanding.

(1) Job 39:13-17.

Other Side: (1) Opposite or opposed; (2) Enemy; (3) Separate; (4) Destiny or destination; (5) Heaven (spirit realm); (6) Avoidance or denial; (7) The believing or unbelieving side.

Also see *Passing Over Something* and *River.*

(1) John 8:44; 1 Sam. 17:3; (2) 1 Sam. 17:3; (3) Matt. 8:18; (4) Matt. 14:22; (5) 1 Sam. 28:11; 2 Cor. 12:2-4; (6) Luke 10:32; (7) Matt. 25:33; John 19:18 (cf. Luke 23:39-43).

Otter: (1) Joy (fun/playful).

(1) Gal. 5:22-23.

Outboard Motor: (1) Power of the Spirit; (2) Evangelism.

(1) Mic. 3:8; Luke 4:14; 1 Cor. 4:20; (2) Mark 1:17.

Out-of-Body Experience: (1) In the Spirit; (2) Death.

(1) Ezek. 3:12,14; 8:3; 1 Cor. 15:44b; (2) John 19:30.

Outside/Outdoors: (1) Open or exposed; (2) Desire to make known; (3) Not intimate or not in fellowship (in contrast to inside); (4) Outside of Christ; (5) Independent or separate; (6) In the Spirit (heavenly places/eternity); (7) Interacting with the world; (8) Cut off from God.

Also see *Going Out.*

(1) 2 Sam. 11:11; (2) John 7:4; (3) John 13:30; (4) Eph. 2:12; (5) Acts 13:2; (6) 2 Cor. 12:2; Rev. 3:20; (7) Luke 15:12-13; John 13:30; (8) Matt. 25:10-12; Rev. 22:15.

Oven: (1) Heart; (2) Adulterer; (3) Place where sin develops (yeast rises); (4) Hot (devouring); (5) Place of judgment; (6) Black.

Also see *Black* and *Yeast.*

(1) Lev. 2:4; Hos. 7:6; (2-3) Hos. 7:4; (4) Hos. 7:7; (5) Ps. 21:8-9; Mal. 4:1; Matt. 6:30; (6) Lam. 5:10.

Overalls: See *Coveralls.*

Overflow/ing: (1) Fullness of the Spirit/power; (2) Building oneself up by speaking in tongues; (3) Overcoming; (4) Holy Spirit ministry; (5) Abundance.

Also see *Flood.*

(1) Ps. 23:5; Mark 5:30; Acts 2:4; 13:9; (2) John 7:38-39; 2 Tim. 1:6-7; Jude 1:20; (3) Gen. 49:22; (4) Ps. 133:2-3; (5) Ps. 115:13-14; Matt. 13:12; 24:12.

Overseas: (1) Different kingdom (kingdom of self or Kingdom of God); (2) Prior to conversion; (3) Journey to Heaven (crossing sea); (4) Life's journey (crossing sea); (5) Going on a mission; (6) Ministering outside your domain.

Also see *International Flight.*

(1) Matt. 24:7; (2) Josh. 2:10; (3-4) Mark 6:45; (5-6) Acts 13:4-5; 28:1,8.

Overtaking (Vehicle): (1) Decision necessary to go forward; (2) Decision necessary to get past perceived obstacle; (3) Ambition; (4) Jostling for position; (5) Spiritually blind decision (blind corner); (6) Impatience (not waiting); (7) Misuse of power (immaturity); (8) Presumption (without faith); (9) Moving to the expectation of others; (10) Call for humble obedience (being overtaken); (11) Call to beware of jealousy; (12) Disaster and judgment; (13) Won't wait; (14) Wanting leadership.

Also see *Automobile, Auto Accident*, and *Waiting*.

(1-2) 1 Kings 12:1-6; (3) 2 Sam. 15:4-6; (4) Matt. 20:21; Mark 9:34; (5) Prov. 3:5-6; (6) Gen. 16:1-4; 1 Sam. 13:5-13; (7) 1 Kings 12:8-10; (8) Gen. 16:1-2; (9) 1 Sam. 15:24; Prov. 29:25; (10) 1 Sam. 18:7; (11) Luke 15:28-30; (12) Gen. 19:19; (13) 2 Kings 18:19-23; (14) Mark 9:34.

Owe: See *Debt*.

Owl: (1) Seer prophet (possesses spiritual wisdom); (2) Loner; (3) Inhabits the desolate waste; (4) Astute unbeliever (creature of the night); (5) Wisdom; (6) Demon.

(1) Matt. 23:34; Luke 11:49; (2) Job 30:29 (KJV); Ps. 102:6-7; (3) Isa. 13:21; 34:10-15; Jer. 50:39 (KJV); (4) Lev. 11:13,17; Deut. 14:12,15; (cf. Isa. 34:14) (5) As in "wise old owl"; (6) Isa. 34:14 (night creatures).

Owl (White Owl):.

Ox: (1) Strength; (2) Believer; (3) Time to plow; (4) Unknowingly following someone to your death; (5) Servant.

Also see *Ass* and *Plowing*.

(1) Prov. 14:4; (2) Deut. 22:10; Job 1:14; (these verses contrast the ox and ass as believer and unbeliever); (cf. Deut. 25:4; 1 Cor. 9:9-10); (3) Deut. 22:10; 1 Kings 19:19; Job 1:14; (4) Prov. 7:22; (5) 1 Kings 19:19; Luke 17:7.

Oyster: (1) You can achieve whatever you want (nothing is impossible).

(1) As in "The world is your oyster"; Gen. 11:6; Matt. 17:20; Luke 1:37.

P

Pad (Paper): (1) Heart.

Also see *Paper* and *Scroll*.

(1) Rom. 2:15; Heb. 8:10.

Paddock: See *Field*.

Padlock: (1) Security or secured; (2) Hard nut to crack; (3) Fear; (4) Shame; (5) Unforgiveness; (6) Yoke (or union); (7) Stronghold.

(1) Acts 5:23a; 16:23; (2) Josh. 6:1; (3-4) Prov. 29:25; (5) Matt. 18:30, 34; (6) 2 Cor. 6:14; (7) Ps. 89:40.

Paedophile: See *Pedophile*.

Pail: See *Bucket*.

Pain: (1) Spiritual childbirth; (2) A call to birth something in the Spirit; (3) Discipline; (4) Judgment against sin; (5) A heart pained; (6) Struggling to understand the prosperity of the wicked; (7) Pain of death; (8) Bad news.
(1) 1 Sam. 4:19; Ps. 48:6; Isa. 13:8; 66:7-8; Jer. 22:23; Mic. 4:10; Rom. 8:22 (KJV); Acts 2:24; Rev. 12:2; (2) 1 Sam. 1:12-17; 1 Kings 18:42-44; Rom. 8:26-27; (3) Job 33:19; Isa. 21:3; 26:16-18 (Note that God's chastening leads to birth); (4) Ps. 25:18; Jer. 15:18-19; 30:23 (KJV); 51:8-9; (5) Ps. 55:3-4 (by hateful words); Jer. 4:19; 6:24; (6) Ps. 73:16; (7) Ps. 116:3; Acts 2:24; (8) Isa. 23:5 (KJV).

Paintball Skirmish: (1) Playing church (not real warfare).
(1) Rev. 3:1.

Painting (noun): (1) Representation; (2) Image; (3) Illustration; (4) The likeness of something or someone; (5) Idol; (6) A conception; (7) View or vision; (8) Lacking the spiritual dimension (depth).
Also see *Painting (verb)* and *Photographs.*
(1-3) Matt. 13:3 (a word picture); (4) Gen. 5:3; (5) Num. 33:52 (KJV); (6-7) Hab. 2:2; (8) 1 Cor. 2:10.

Painting (verb): (1) Interior painting speaks of inner renewal or refurbishment; (2) Refreshing of the Spirit; (3) Exterior painting may refer to an outward show or hypocrisy; (4) Cover up; (5) Mere outward adornment; (6) Moving in faith (ad libbing); (7) Prophesying (inspired painting); (8) Preparation.
Also see *Artist* and *Painting (noun).*
(1-2) 2 Kings 12:14; 2 Kings 22:5; 2 Chron. 24:4,12; 29:3; 34:8-10; (3-4) Matt. 23:25-27; Luke 11:39; (5) 2 Kings 9:30; (6) Rom. 4:17; (7) 1 Sam. 9:9; Rom. 12:6; (8) Matt. 3:3; Luke 7:28.

Pajamas: (1) Unprepared; (2) Spiritually unaware; (3) Sleeping on the job.
Also see *Dressing Gown* and *Sleeping.*
(1-3) Matt. 26:40-41; Luke 12:35-38.

Palace: (1) Spiritually rich Christian; (2) The place of the Presence of the King (God); (3) The place of the throne (authority); (4) The place of feasting; (5) The place of audience before the king; (6) The place of decrees; (7) The place of glories; (8) The place of rejoicing; (9) The place of prosperity; (10) The place to flourish; (11) The place of pride and judgment.
(1) 2 Cor. 5:1; (2) Ps. 45:8-9; 48:3; (3) Esther 1:2; (4) Esther 1:5; (5) Esther 2:3 (KJV); (6) Esther 3:15 (KJV); 8:14 (KJV); (7) Ps. 45:13-14; (8) Ps. 45:15; (9) Ps. 122:7; (10) Dan. 4:4; (11) Amos 6:8.

Palm (Hand): (1) Be buffeted; (2) Struck by words; (3) Heart (left palm); (4) Powerless (no hands); (5) Remembered (inscribed palms).
Also see *Hand.*

(1) Matt. 26:67; Mark 14:65 (struck by palm); (2) 2 Chron. 18:23; John 18:22; (3) Lev. 14:15-16, 26-27 (left palm represents the heart while the right finger its application, cf. Rom. 10:9-10); (4) 1 Sam. 5:4; (5) Isa. 49:16.

Palm (Tree): (1) Victory; (2) Salvation; (3) Believer; (4) Flourish; (5) Righteous (upright believer); (6) Leader (palm branch).
(1-2) Deut. 34:3; Judg. 4:5ff; John 12:13; Rev.7:9-10; (3-4) 1 Kings 6:29, 32; Ps. 92:12; (5) Song 7:7 (upright); (cf. Jer. 10:5a); (6) Isa. 9:14-15.

Palsy: (1) Bedridden; (2) Spiritually lying down due to sin.
Also see *Bed*.
(1) Matt. 8:6 (KJV); 9:2 (KJV); (2) Ps. 51:9-10 (KJV); Mark 2:3-5 (KJV).

Pant: (1) Long for; (2) Birthing.
Also see *Birthing* and *Thirsty*.
(1) Ps. 42:1; (2) Ps. 48:6.

Pants (Underwear): (1) Self-righteous.
Also see *Genitals*, *Legs*, *Trousers*, and *Underwear*.
(1) Gen. 3:7.

Pantry: (1) Heart full of resources (The Word of God).
(1) 1 Kings 17:16; Matt. 14:14-21.

Paper(s): (1) Documents; (2) Record; (3) Certificate; (4) Deeds; (5) Account or debt; (6) Plans.
Also see *Pad (Paper)*.
(1-2) Ezra 4:15; Esther 2:23; 6:1; 10:2; (3) Jer. 3:8; (4) Gen. 23:17-18; (5) Matt. 18:23-24; (6) 1 Chron. 28:11-12.

Paper(s) (Scrunched-Up Paper): (1) Debt or contract cancellation; (2) Failed plans.
(1-2) Col. 2:14-15.

Paper(s) (Torn Paper): (1) Division; (2) Divorce; (3) Loss.
(1) Matt. 5:32; (3) 1 Sam. 15:27-28.

Paper Bag: (1) Temporary issue; (2) Hiding/cover up something.
(1) Matt. 5:25a; (2) Matt. 5:15.

Paper Cut: (1) Document, certificate, or deed that afflicts you.
(1) Ezra 4:18-19,21.

Paper Plane: (1) Rhema word (words carried by the Spirit); (2) Words carried by a spirit (-); (3) Prayer requests (thrown into the air); (4) Someone trying to get your attention by sending you a message (someone throwing a paper plane at you).
Also see *Aeroplane* and *Paper*.
(1) 1 Sam. 3:19; 1 Cor. 2:4; (2) Eph. 6:16 (-); (3) Jon. 2:7; (4) 1 Kings 19:2; Luke 7:22.

Parachute: (1) Bringing Heaven to earth by the Spirit; (2) Leap of faith (no parachute); (3) Escape plan; (4) Way out; (5) Safety net; (6) Survival mentality; (7) Self-preservation; (8) Love.

(1) Matt. 6:10; John 5:36; (2) Matt. 14:29; (3) Josh. 2:15,18; (4) Acts 9:25; (5) Acts 5:1-2; (6) Num. 13:31; Mark 14:50; (7) Luke 22:54-60; (8) Song 2:4; 6:4; Rom. 8:38-39; 2 Cor. 5:14a (KJV).

Paramedic: (1) Evangelist (someone who brings people to meet the Physician/Healer [Christ]); (2) Ministering angels.
(1) Mark 2:3-11; John 1:40-42; (2) 1 Kings 19:5-6; Dan. 10:10-11; John 5:4.

Parasite(s): (1) Someone who lives by stealing the spiritual life of another; (2) Someone who is just along for the ride—for what they can get out of it.
Also see *Flea, Leech,* and *Maggot.*
(1) Lev. 17:11; Prov. 30:15; 2 Tim. 3:4-7; (2) John 12:6.

Parents: (1) Past; (2) Guardians; (3) Careers or guides; (4) Forebears; (5) Leadership or management; (6) Spiritual parents; (7) Jesus and the Church; (8) The Father and Holy Spirit; (9) Literal parents.
Also see *Father* and *Mother.*
(1) Luke 18:29-30; John 9:2; (cf. Exod. 20:5; 34:7); 2 Cor. 12:14b; (2) Luke 2:27; John 9:23; Heb. 11:23; (3) Rom. 1:30; (4) John 9:2; (5) Col. 3:20; (6) 1 Cor. 4:15; (7) 1 Cor. 4:15b; Eph. 5:25; (8) Ps. 68:5; Heb. 12:9; (Gen. 2:24; Phil. 2:7).

Park (Noun): (1) Resting place; (2) Pleasure and recreation; (3) Informal; (4) Lush; (5) Appeals to the eyes; (6) Egypt (human-made park); (7) The Promised Land (natural park); (8) The Church; (9) The believer.
Also see *Garden.*
(1) Ps. 23:2; (2) Eccles. 2:5-6; (3) Esther 7:8; (4-5) Gen. 13:10; (6-7) Deut. 11:10-11; (8) Song 4:12; 8:13; (9) Song 4:12,15.

Parked Auto: (1) Awaiting ministry; (2) Rest; (3) Being worked on (place of preparation); (4) Retirement.
Also see *Garage.*
(1) Luke 1:80; 2:51-52; (2) Ps. 23:2; Mark 6:31; (3) (cf. Deut. 6:23; 8:2-3) Ps. 105:19; (4) Luke 16:2; 2 Tim. 4:7-8.

Park Ranger: (1) Informal Authority.
Also see *Gardener.*
(1) Matt. 11:29.

Parrot(s): (1) Repeater or gossip; (2) Angel(s).
Also see *Multi-Colored.*
(1) Prov. 17:9; Eccles. 10:20; (2) Luke 2:9; 9:26; Rev. 18:1.

Party: (1) Revival; (2) Celebration; (3) The world.
Also see *Banqueting* and *Birthday.*
(1-2) Luke 15:23-24; (3) Gal. 5:21; 1 Pet. 4:3.

Passenger: Being a passenger is generally a good sign as it says: (1) I'm giving or handing my destiny/my ministry over to God; (2) God's in the driver's seat.

(1-2) Ps. 23:3; Prov. 3:5-6; 8:20 (KJV); John 21:18; Rom. 8:14.

Passing Over Something: (1) Deliverance; (2) Moving into possession of a promise; (3) Ownership (taking possession); (4) Victory; (5) Glory.

(1) Gen. 8:1; Exod. 12:27; Isa. 31:5 (and preservation); (2) Deut. 2:29 (KJV); 3:18; 27:3; Ps. 23:5; (3) Deut. 3:18; 9:1; 11:31; Josh. 1:11; (4) Deut. 2:24; 9:1-4; Josh. 5:1; Judg. 11:32 (KJV); 1 Sam. 14:6-14; 2 Sam. 10:17-19; (5) Prov. 19:11; Mark 4:35-41; Luke 8:22-25.

Passing Under Something: (1) Owned and counted; (2) Tested; (3) Judged; (4) Death; (5) In subjection.

(1-3) Lev. 27:32; Jer. 33:13; (4) 1 Cor. 10:1-2; (5) Neh. 2:14; Isa. 28:15; Jer. 27:8; Ezek. 20:37.

Past Friend/Acquaintance/Employer, etc.: (1) This may speak of someone similar in character; (2) Doing the same deeds in a spiritual setting; (3) God may be showing you they need prayer; (4) Them literally.

Also see *Aunt*, *Brother*, *Sister*, and *Uncle*.

(1) Matt. 11:14; (2) John 3:14; (3) Luke 22:31-32.

Pastor: (1) Jesus (as the head); (2) A shepherd; (3) Actual pastor; (4) Meaning of his/her name.

Also see *Priest*.

(1-2) John 10:11; Heb. 13:20.

Path: (1) What lies ahead; (2) The way of the righteous or the way of darkness; (3) Guidelines; (4) Pathways of your mind (wherever the path leads to is the way you are thinking); (5) The journey of life; (6) The way of pride; (7) Ancient paths.

Also see *Cobblestones* and *Road*.

(1-2) Prov. 2:13; Isa. 42:16; Jer. 18:15 (ancient paths = righteous paths); (3) Ps. 17:4; 119:105; (4) Prov. 23:7a; James 1:8; 2 Pet. 3:1-2; (5) Ps. 119:105; (6) Dan. 4:37; Prov. 8:13; (7) Jer. 18:15; see the book *The Mystic Awakening*.

Pattern: (1) Example; (2) Spiritual blueprint; (3) Repeating issue.

(1) 1 Tim. 1:16; Tit. 2:7; Heb. 8:5; (2) Exod. 25:9,40; Josh. 22:28 (KJV); 1 Chron. 28:11-12; Heb. 8:5; 9:23; (3) Num. 14:22.

Pavement: (1) Commercial pathway; (2) Busy pathway; (3) Judgment.

Also see *Footpath*.

(1-2) Matt. 13:4; (3) John 19:13.

Payment (Incoming): (1) Reaping a harvest (blessing); (2) Issuing forgiveness.

(1) Mark 10:29-30; Gal. 6:7; (2) Luke 11:4.

Payment (Outgoing): (1) Jesus's sacrifice for sin; (2) Cost; (3) Forsaking all to follow Christ; (4) Laying down one's life; (5) Debt cancellation; (6) Receiving forgiveness.

Also see *Debt*.

(1) 1 Cor. 6:20; Col. 2:14; (2) Luke 14:28; (3) Luke 14:33; (4) Matt. 16:24-25; (5-6) Matt. 18:30.

Peacock: (1) Vainglory (bringing attention to self); (2) Pride; (3) Clothed in glory of God.

(1) Prov. 25:27 (self-promotion); John 5:44; 7:18; 12:43; (2) 2 Tim. 3:2; (3) Gen. 37:3.

Peanut: (1) Word of God; (2) Fool (simpleton).

Also see *Seed.*

(1) Luke 8:11; (2) Ps. 14:1,4.

Peanut Butter/Paste: (1) The Word simplified (smooth peanut paste); (2) Solid food (crunchy peanut paste); (3) Heart (a jar of peanut butter); (4) Deception (professing to be smooth, but actually crunchy).

(1-2) Heb. 5:12-14; (3) Prov. 14:14 (heart as a vessel); John 16:6; (4) Ps. 55:21.

Pearl(s): (1) Jesus Christ; (2) Revelations of God's Word (spiritual treasure); (3) The Kingdom; (4) Arrogance and pride; (5) Gate of the heavenly Jerusalem; (6) Faith; (7) Religious glory.

Also see *Precious Stones.*

(1) Matt. 13:46; (2) Matt. 7:6; (3) Matt. 13:45-46; (4) 1 Tim. 2:9; Rev. 17:4; 18:12, 16; (5) Rev. 21:21; (6) Rev. 21:21 (only entered by faith); (7) Rev. 17:4.

Pedestrian: (1) Sidelined ministry; (2) Spectator; (3) Not part of the race of faith.

Also see *Sidewalk.*

(1) Matt. 11:2-3; (2) Luke 6:7; (3) Acts 13:13; 15:38; Heb. 12:1.

Pedicure: (1) Preparation to preach the good news.

(1) Isa. 52:7.

Pedophile: (1) An authority figure abusing young Christians; (2) Warning of sex predator (evil spirit); (3) Cult leader that spiritually/psychologically overpowers the vulnerable; (4) Warning of an actual pedophile.

(1) 1 Sam. 2:22; (2) Gen. 19:5; (3) Acts 13:10; (4) Lev. 18:10.

Peel: (1) Cover; (2) Flesh; (3) Heart laid bare; (4) Judgment; (5) Labored (shoulders rubbed raw); (6) Affliction; (7) Aftermath of being burned (peeling skin).

(1) 2 Cor. 5:4; 2 Pet. 1:13-14; (2) Col. 1:22; (3) Luke 2:35; (4) Joel 1:7; (5) Ezek. 29:18; (6) Job 30:30; (7) Exod. 29:14.

Pelican: (1) Jesus Christ; (2) Prophetic evangelist (by virtue of the fact that this bird is white, soars, and fishes); (3) A person in the wrong environment (pelican in the wilderness); (4) Loner or alone; (5) Non-believer (unclean bird).

(1) Luke 5:4-5; (2) 1 Kings 18:21-22; Acts 2:40-41; (3-4) Ps. 102:6-7; (5) Lev. 11:13,18 (KJV); Deut. 14:17 (KJV).

Pellet Gun: See *Spud Gun.*

Pen/Pencil: (1) Words; (2) Writing; (3) Written record; (4) Tongue; (5) Something written in pencil may indicate that it is temporary or not confirmed.

(1) Ps. 45:1b; (2-3) Job 19:23-24; (4) Ps. 45:1b; (5) James 4:14.

Penguin: (1) Legalistic church (black and white); (2) Religious spirit (flightless bird, feeds on fish).

(1) Rev. 2:2-4; (2) Matt. 23:15, 25.

Penis: See *Genitals*.

Pepper: Contrasted against salt, salt is white and pepper black. Pepper, therefore, may represent: (1) Decay; (2) Sin; (3) Death; (4) Bad; (5) Lacking character; (6) No peace (without God); (7) Speech without grace; (8) Anger (hot and spicy); (9) Flavoring things to your own liking.

Also see *Salt*.

(1-4) Matt. 5:13; Mark 9:50; (5) Mark 9:49; (6) Mark 9:50; (7) Col. 4:6 (8) Exod. 32:19; Judg. 2:14; (9) Deut. 4:2; Prov. 30:6; Rev. 22:18.

Pepperoni: See *Sausage*.

Perfume: (1) Anointing; (2) Presence of Christ; (3) Joyful heart; (4) Love/Intimacy; (5) Seduction; (6) Infidelity; (7) Love offering; (8) Womanhood (femininity).

Also see *Incense*.

(1) Exod. 30:25; 37:29; Ps. 45:8; (2) Ps. 45:6-8; (3) Prov. 27:9; (4) Exod. 30:35-38; Song 3:6; (5) Prov. 7:17; (6) Isa. 57:8-9; (7) Matt. 26:7; (8) Esther 2:12.

Pergola: See *Verandah*.

Period: (1) No unity with partner; (2) Yearning for unity; (3) Loss of promise; (4) Grief; (5) Self-righteousness; (6) Embarrassment/shame (period exposed).

(1-4) Lev. 15:19,25; Matt. 9:20-22; (5-6) Isa. 64:6.

Pet: (1) Something you are feeding (fueling); (2) Habit; (3) Companion or friend.

Also see *Cat*, *Guinea Pig*, *Mascot*, *Dog*, and *Veterinarian*.

(1) Rom. 13:14; 2 Cor. 10:5; Gal. 4:8-9; 5:16-21; (2) 2 Pet. 2:14b; (3) As in "A dog is man's best friend."

Petrol: See *Gasoline*.

Petrol Station: See *Gas Station*.

Pewter: (1) Wickedness (dross); (2) Spiritually poor.

Also see *Tin* and *Tin Man*.

(1) Isa. 1:25; Ezek. 22:18 (pewter has approximately 90 percent tin content); Ps. 119:119; Prov. 26:23; (2) Num. 31:22 (low on the scale of metals).

Pharmacy: See *Chemist Shop*.

Photocop/ier/ying: (1) Reproducing; (2) Spreading the Word; (3) Publishing; (4) Exaggerating (multiplying) the past.

(1) 1 Cor. 11:1; (2-3) Ps. 68:11 (KJV); Acts 10:37 (KJV); 13:49 (KJV); (4) 2 Sam. 1:8-10; (cf. 1 Sam. 31:4).

Photographer: See *Cameraman*.

Photographs: (1) Memories; (2) Identity; (3) A call to remember; (4) Nostalgic longing for the past.

Also see *Camera, Cameraman*, and *Painting (noun)*.

(1) Exod. 17:14; (2) 1 Cor. 6:20; 7:23 (who you are is found in whose you are); Gal. 3:27; (3) Neh. 4:14; Ps. 78; (4) Num. 11:5; Ps. 137:1.

Piano: See *Music*.

Pickpocket: (1) Stealing your or other's hearts; (2) Stealer; (3) Being robbed unawares; (4) Loss of things close to you (husband, wife, or children taken unawares).

Also see *Pocket, Steal*, and *Thief*.

(1) 2 Sam. 15:6; Song 4:9; Prov. 4:23; (2-3) John 10:10; (4) 1 Sam. 30:2.

Picnic: (1) Desiring casual and relaxed fellowship; (2) Pleasurable and personal communion; (3) Desire for your pleasure versus God's pleasure.

(1) 2 Sam. 11:1; (2) Luke 8:14; (3) Luke 12:29-34; 1 Tim. 5:6; 2 Tim.3:4.

Picture: See *Camera, Painting*, and *Photographs*.

Picture Theater: (1) Your life passing before you (before God on Judgment Day).

Also see *Movie*.

(1) Rev. 20:12.

Pie: (1) Works (something of your own making); (2) Something you desire; (3) Something from the heart; (4) Meddling or busy-body; (5) A heart (good or evil).

Also see *Bake, Baker*, and *Oven*.

(1) Gen. 40:16-17; (2) As in "wanting a piece of the action"; (3) Hos. 7:6; (4) As in "finger in the pie"; (5) 2 Cor. 4:7 (as contents enclosed).

Pier: See *Jetty*.

Pierce: (1) Sorrow and grief.

(1) Luke 2:35; 1 Tim. 6:10.

Pierced Ear: (1) Pledging love; (2) Pledging slavery; (3) Sensitivity to Master's (God's) voice.

(1-3) Exod. 21:5-6.

Pig: (1) Unbeliever; (2) Sin; (3) Unclean spirit; (4) Devil/demon; (5) Woman without discretion.

(1-2) Matt. 7:6; Luke 15:13-18; (3-4) Matt. 8:30-32; Mark 5:16; (5) Prov. 11:22.

Pigeon: (1) Christ; (2) Spirit of poverty (poor person's sacrifice/offering).

Also see *Bird(s), Dove, Park*, and *Spirit of Poverty*.

(1) Lev. 1:14-17; 14:5-7; (2) Luke 2:24; (cf. Lev. 12:8).

Pillar: (1) Reliable and strong load-bearing (responsible) leadership; (2) Christ; (3) The Church; (4) The Holy Spirit; (5) Resurrection; (6) Stability and firmness; (7) Covenant witness; (8) Gravestone; (9) Corrosive person (salt); (10) Wisdom's seven pillars; (11) Warning of Christ's return (pillars of smoke).

(1) Gal. 2:9; Rev. 3:12; (2) Gen. 35:14-15; (3) Gen. 35:14-15; 1 Tim. 3:15; (4) Exod. 13:21-22 (fire and cloud); (5) Gen. 28:18 (a pillar erected); (6) Song 5:15; (7) Gen. 31:51-52; (8) Gen. 35:20; (9) Gen. 19:26; (10) Prov. 9:1; (11) Joel 2:30.

Pillow: (1) Christ (He on whom we rest, and dream); (2) Resting in faith, regardless of circumstance; (3) Heart; (4) Covering that guards your heart (pillowcase); (5) Thoughts (as that which we think about); (6) Meditation; (7) Rest; (8) Dream.

(1) Gen. 28:11-18 (in setting the stone upright and anointing it Jacob prefigures the resurrection); (2) Mark 4:38, 40; (3) Matt. 11:29; (4) Prov. 4:23; (5) Isa. 26:3; (6) Ps. 1:2; Dan. 2:29; (7) Exod. 33:14; (8) 1 Kings 3:5.

Pills: See *Drug Use.*

Pilot: (1) The Holy Spirit; (2) One who is steering; (3) Spiritual guidance.

(1) Ps. 43:3 (The light is fueled by oil); Luke 4:1; (2-3) Acts 13:2,4.

Pimples: (1) Fleshly imperfections; (2) Adjust spiritual diet by being obedient; (3) Spiritual detoxification and heart revealed (facial pimples); (4) Spiritual immaturity; (5) Pimples on the body may indicate physical health issues relating to that part of the body. Also see *Face* and *Spot.*

(1) 2 Cor. 7:1; (cf. Gal. 5:19-21); (2) John 4:34; (3) 2 Tim. 2:21; (4) 1 Cor. 13:11.

Pin: (1) Word; (2) Tie/fastener; (3) Jesus Christ; (4) End of relationship/project (as in "pulling the pin").

Also see *Nail* and *Pierce.*

(1) Eccles. 12:11; Col. 2:14; (2) Judg. 16:14; Isa. 22:23; (3) Isa. 22:23; (4) John 13:30.

Pinch: (1) Invitation of the flesh; (2) Fleshly seduction; (3) Offense.

(1-3) Gen. 4:7.

Pine (Tree): (1) Upright person.

(1) Isa. 60:13 (cf. Ps. 92:12).

Pink: (1) Flesh; (2) Sensual; (3) Immoral; (4) Sex; (5) Childhood innocence; (6) Feminine; (7) Young and delicate; (8) Calm.

(1) Rom. 2:28; (2-4) Deut. 22:15-17; (5) 1 Sam. 17:42; (6) As in "pink for girls and blue for boys"; (7) 1 Sam. 17:42; (8) As in "pink room."

Pipe (Smoking): See *Smoking.*

Pipe (Water): (1) Vessel (person or church) of the Word and Spirit; (2) Being led by the Spirit and Word of God.

(1) 2 Kings 20:20 (cf. 1 Kings 18:1,6-7a); (2) 2 Sam. 5:8.

Pirate: (1) Immoral get-rich-quick lifestyle; (2) Gold-digger.

Also see *Thief.*

(1-2) John 12:4-6.

Pistol: (1) Close range attack of words/thoughts; (2) Someone close speaking against you; (3) Spirit of lust (9mm).

Also see *Bullets, Gun, Rifle,* and *Smoking.*

(1) Gen. 44:18; Mal. 3:5; (2) Matt. 26:14-16; (3) 2 Sam. 13:14-15.

Pit: (1) Hell; (2) Trap; (3) Prison; (4) Heart.

(1) Gen. 37:20; Prov. 1:12; Isa. 14:15; Ezek. 26:20; Rev. 9:1-2,11; 11:7; (2) Prov. 22:14; 23:27; 26:27; 28:10; Jer. 18:22; (3) Jer. 38:10-13; (4) 2 Cor. 4:7.

Pitchfork: (1) Lies; (2) Devil.

Also see *Fork*.

(1-2) John 8:44; (2) By association.

Pizza: (1) Quick and easy fix for the flesh; (2) Temptation to doubt genuine revelation as a "pizza dream"; (3) Word of God (as bread); (4) Communion (pizza + drink).

(1) Luke 4:3; (2) Acts 26:24; (3) Deut. 8:3; Matt. 26:17; (4) Matt. 26:26-27.

Plague: (1) Curse; (2) Judgment; (3) Sin.

(1-3) Ps. 106:29.

Plain: The plain is contrasted against the mountain; therefore, plain represents: (1) Spiritual low place; (2) Place of the efforts of people; (3) Appealing to the natural eyes; (4) Lacking spiritual sight; (5) Place of vulnerability; (6) Place of preparation; (7) Straight or righteous (opposite of crooked).

Also see *Crooked* and *Mountain*.

(1) Gen. 19:17; (2) Gen. 11:2-4; (3) Gen. 13:10-12; (4) Deut. 34:1; (5) Gen. 19:17; (6) Num. 22:1-26:3,63; 31:12; (7) Isa. 40:4 (KJV).

Plan(s): (1) God's destiny for you; (2) Blueprints of Heaven.

(1) Jer. 1:5; 29:11 (NIV); (2) Exod. 25:40; Luke 1:31-32.

Planet(s): (1) May represent people.

Also see *Mars*, *Orbit*, *Pluto*, and *Satellite*.

(1) Gen. 37:9-10; 1 Cor. 15:47.

Plank: (1) Fleshly issue of the heart.

(1) Matt. 7:3.

Plant (noun): (1) Individual or significant plants represent people, churches, or nations. (2) Small plants may represent children.

(1) Isa. 5:7 (Judah); Isa. 53:2 (Christ); Matt. 15:13 (individuals); Matt. 21:33ff; (2) Ps. 144:12, Isa. 53:2.

Plant (verb): (1) Established by God; (2) Burying the flesh; (3) Spreading the Gospel; (4) Be born again; (5) Flourish; (6) Leading to harvest; (7) Planting weeds.

Also see *Sowing*.

(1) Gen. 2:8; Matt. 15:13; Luke 20:9; (2) Rom. 6:5; (cf. John 12:24); (3) 1 Cor. 3:6; (4) Eccles. 3:2; Isa. 61:3; (5) Ps. 92:13; (6) Ps. 107:37; (7) Matt. 13:25; 15:13.

Plantation: (1) Church; (2) Kingdom of God.

Also see *Fruit Tree*, *Orchard*, and *Vineyard*.

(1) As a gathering of fruit trees (cf. Ps. 1:3); (2) Matt. 21:28-31.

Plant Regeneration: (1) Resurrection; (2) New beginnings; (3) Confirmation of selection.
(1) Matt. 28:7; (2-3) Exod. 17:3-8.

Plaque: (1) Public declaration.
(1) Esther 8:13.

Plaster (Medical Strip): (1) Covering up the real issue; (2) Superficial patch-up job; (3) Placebo.
(1) Matt. 15:8; (2) Matt. 9:16; 2 Kings 12:2-3; 15:3-4, 34-35.

Plastic: (1) Superficial; (2) Not real; (3) Saying it, but not living it; (4) Cheap; (5) Not yet open to view (sealed plastic bag); (6) Not real; (7) Non-Christian hearts (plastic bags and bottles).
(1) Col. 2:18a; (2-3) Matt. 15:8-9; (4) Matt. 8:19-20; Luke 9:61-62 (looking for "easy believism"); (5) Isa. 29:11; Dan. 12:4,9; (6) Rev. 3:1-2; (7) Matt. 5:29-30; 9:17 (these will perish!).

Plate: (1) Heart. (2) What is seen on a plate may be showing a heart's desire; (3) Someone's agenda; (4) Portion and serving; (5) Ration; (6) Resources and supply; (7) Workload and responsibility; (8) Food; (9) Provisions; (10) What someone deserves.
Also see *Platter*, *Pots and Pans*, and *Vessel*.
(1) Ps. 78:18; Prov. 3:3 (KJV); 23:7-8; (2) Ps. 73:25-26 (a *portion* is what you get on a plate); Eccles. 2:10 (KJV); Dan. 1:8; (3) Prov. 23:6-7; (4) Luke 12:42; (5) 1 Kings 17:12; (6) 2 Sam. 9:11 (what's on the plate speaks of the extent of resources available); (7) As in "I have a lot on my plate at the moment"; (8-9) Prov. 23:1-3; (10) Luke 12:46.

Platform: (1) Pulpit.
Also see *Pulpit*.
(1) Gen. 23:3; Matt. 10:27.

Platter: (1) Represents the heart; (2) Too good to be true (silver platter); (3) Blessing; (4) Spoilt; (5) Martyr (head on a platter); (6) Influence of a Jezebel spirit (head on a platter).
Also see *Cup* and *Plate*.
(1) Matt. 23:25-28 (KJV); Luke 11:39 (KJV); (2) As in "handed to him on a silver platter"; (3-4) As in "handed to him on a platter"; (5-6) Matt. 14:8.

Platypus: (1) Adaptive person; (5) Five-fold ministry.
(1) 1 Kings 19:19-21; (2) Has (1) fur, (2) beak, (3) spurs, (4) on land and (5) under water.

Playing: (1) Childlikeness; (2) Spiritual immaturity; (3) Spiritually deaf; (4) Looking for outward response; (5) Sexual defilement; (6) Spiritual idolatry; (7) Worship; (8) Foolishness; (9) Entering into the Spirit; (10) Innocence; (11) Sign of peace; (12) Not serious.
Also see *Toys*.

(1-4) Matt. 11:15-19; Luke 7:32; (5) Lev. 21:9; Judg. 19:2; Hos. 2:5; (6) Exod. 32:6; Jer. 2:20; 3:6; 1 Cor. 10:7; (7) 1 Sam. 16:16-18,23; 2 Sam. 6:5; 1 Chron. 15:29; (8) 1 Sam. 26:21; (9) 2 Kings 3:15; (10) Isa. 11:8; (11) Zech. 8:5; (12) As in "He's just playing around."

Playground: (1) Spiritually immature and idolatrous church.
(1) Exod. 32:6,8.

Pliers: (1) Grabbing words (looking for leverage); (2) Gripping and tearing words (grabbing and pulling with pliers); (3) Can be looking for release from something (pulling out a nail).
(1) Mark 12:13; (2) Job 16:9; (3) Eccles. 12:11 (words); Isa. 22:23-25; Jer. 10:4 (idols).

Plowing: (1) Believer; (2) Preparation for harvest; (3) Call to seek God; (4) Hope; (5) Preparing or opening hearts; (6) Breaking up hardened hearts; (7) Working the heart with words (good or evil); (8) Questioning; (9) Whipping; (10) Wanting the past (looking back); (11) Looking forward; (12) Intercourse (seed sowing); (13) Worship.
Also see *Farmer* and *Plowman.*
(1) Luke 17:7,10; (2) Job 4:8; Prov. 20:4; 21:4; Isa. 28:24-25; Hos. 10:11; 1 Cor. 9:10; (3) Hos. 10:11-12; (4) 1 Cor. 9:10; (5) (Isa. 28:24-25; Matt. 13:18-19 cf. Luke 3:4-5); (6) Hos. 10:12; (7) Job 4:8; Prov. 21:4; Hos. 10:13; (8) Judg. 14:18; (9) Ps. 129:3; (10-11) Luke 9:62 (plowing requires that the plowman look forward, having two targets (the immediate and distant future) to
keep his lines straight); (12) Deut. 22:10 (cf. 2 Cor. 6:14); Judg. 14:18 (social intercourse); (13) Hos. 10:11.

Plowman: (1) One who prepares the hearts; (2) God; (3) Pioneer; (4) Servant; (5) Believer.
See also *Farmer* and *Sower.*
(1) Isa. 28:24-25; Matt. 3:3; (2) Hos. 2:23; 1 Cor. 3:9; (3) 1 Cor. 3:6; (4) Luke 17:7; (5) Luke 9:62.

Plumber: (1) The Holy Spirit; (2) Anointed ministry connecting others to the life-giving Spirit; (3) God/Jesus Christ.
(1) Isa. 44:3; John 7:38-39; (2) Judg. 15:19; John 7:38-39; (3) John 1:33; 4:14; Acts 2:17-18.

Pluto: (1) Hell; (2) The devil; (3) Distant person.
(1-2) Pluto is an alternative name of hades; (3) Matt. 2:1.

Pocket: (1) Heart; (2) Profiting; (3) Stealing; (4) Hiding place; (5) Holding place; (6) Money.
Also see *Pick-Pocket.*
(1) 1 Cor. 4:5; 1 Pet. 3:4; (2-3) John 12:6; (4) Job 10:13; (5) 1 Sam. 25:29b; (6) John 12:6; as in "hip-pocket."

Pocketbook: *Wallet/Billfold.*

Pointing: (1) The Finger of God (pointing to God's handiwork); (2) Accusation; (3) Giving direction (pointing the way).
Also see *Finger(s)*, *Guide*, and *Poking*.
(1) Exod. 8:19; 31:18; Luke 11:20; (2) Isa. 58:9; (3) Exod. 14:16.

Poison: (1) Lies (something a person is being asked or forced to swallow); (2) Death; (3) Words against someone; (4) Sin; (5) Excessive alcohol.
Also see *Bait*.
(1) Ps. 140:3; Rom. 3:13; 1 Kings 13:18; (2) 2 Kings 4:40; (3) Ps. 56:5; 140:1-3; (4) Rom. 6:23; (5) Prov. 23:30-32; Eph. 5:18.

Pokemon: (1) Evil spirits; (2) Angels; (3) Spiritual warfare.
(1-2) Dan. 10:13.

Poker Machine (One-Armed Bandit): (1) Get-rich-quick scheme.
Also see *Gambling*.
(1) Prov. 28:20,22.

Poking: (1) Accusation; (2) Offense; (3) Authority; (4) Correction; (5) Being stirred to action.
Also see *Pointing*.
(1-2) John 19:3; (3) Acts 9:5; (4) Eccles. 12:11; (5) Acts 12:7.

Polar Bear: (1) Religious spirit.
(1) Matt. 23:27; Mark 7:13.

Pole: (1) Cross; (2) Word of God.
Also see *Rod* and *Staff*.
(1) Num. 21:8-9; (cf. John 3:14); (2) Exod. 14:16 (the Word divides).

Police: (1) Authority; (2) Spiritual authority; (3) You exercising spiritual authority (you as policeman); (4) Angel(s); (5) God; (6) Protection; (7) Punishment of evil doers; (8) Point to legal implications; (9) Law; (10) Legalism/critical spirit.
Also see *Plainclothes Police* (below).
(1) Rom. 13:1; (2) 1 Cor. 6:1; 2 Tim. 4:1-2; (3) Luke 10:19; (4) Exod. 23:20; Ps. 91:11; Isa. 63:9; Luke 4:10; Acts 7:53; (5) Job 5:17; Heb. 12:23; Rev. 20:12; (6) Rom. 13:4; (7) 1 Pet. 2:13-14; (8-9) Acts 7:53; (10) Matt. 22:35-36; Acts 4:1-3a; 5:17-18.

Plainclothes Police: (1) Pastor; (2) Father or husband (unrecognized authority); (3) Angel in disguise; (4) God; (5) Unaware inspection; (6) Undercover; (7) Taxation (IRS); (8) Accountant.
Also see *Police*.
(1) 1 Cor. 6:1; 2 Tim. 4:1-2; (2) Eph. 5:23-24; (3) Gen. 19:1, 5; Heb. 13:2b; (4) Gen. 18:1-3, 20-21; (5) Prov. 24:12; (6) Josh. 2:1; (7) Matt. 17:24; (8) John 12:5-6.

Polio: (1) Spiritually impaired.
Also see *Legs* and *Wheelchair*.
(1) Matt. 14:29-31 (failing to walk by faith); John 5:6-7.

Polish: (1) To glorify; (2) Make shine; (3) Fine tune; (4) Make reflective.
(1) Lam. 4:7 (KJV); Dan. 10:6 (KJV); (2) Ps. 144:12 (KJV); (3) Isa. 49:2; (4) 1 Cor. 11:1.

Politics: (1) Denominationalism; (2) Buying votes; (3) Jobs for the boys; (4) Telling people what they want to hear; (5) Not being totally upfront with people; (6) Using people for personal gain.
(1) 1 Cor. 1:12; 3:3; (2) 2 Sam. 15:4; (3) 1 Sam. 22:7. (4) 2 Tim. 4:3; (5-6) 2 Sam. 15:4.

Pollution: (1) Defiling words; (2) Defiled heart; (3) Sin; (4) Oppression in the atmosphere (bad morale).
Also see *Mud, Sewage, Smoke,* and *Water—Dirty Water.*
(1) Job 16:4; Ps. 109:3; Matt. 12:32; (2) Exod. 15:23-25 (purified by the cross); (3) Isa. 1:4; Hos. 9:9; (4) 2 Cor. 10:3-5; Eph. 6:12.

Pomegranate: (1) Heart; (2) Joyful and fruitful (Fruit is round and full of seeds).
(1) Song 8:2; (2) Exod. 28:33-35; Song 4:3 (beautiful mind and fruitful thoughts).

Pond: (1) Church; (2) Local community; (3) Looking to or worshiping a past move of God; (4) Dam (old water not moving); (5) Place for fish.
Also see *Fish.*
(1-2) Isa. 19:10b; Matt. 4:19; (3) John 8:33; (4) 1 Sam. 3:1; 4:15.

Pool: See *Lake, Pond,* and *Swimming Pool.*

Pool Cue: (1) Powerfully impacting word (authoritative word); (2) Preparing to speak with authority (chalking cue).
(1) Exod. 14:16; Luke 4:36; (2) Isa. 49:2.

Pool Hall: (1) Group that is Christian by name only (no pool); (2) Cult group (haunt of underworld figures, plenty of words [balls], lots of gathering [tables], but no real Spirit [no pool]).
Also see *Swimming Pool.*
(1) Rev. 3:1. (2) 1 John 4:1-2.

Pool Table: (1) Communion; (2) Religious hearts (tables of stone); (3) Load of words around a table.
Also see *Sport* and *Winning.*
(1) 1 Cor. 10:21; (2) 2 Cor. 3:3 (KJV); (3) 1 Kings 13:20; Ps. 78:19; Dan. 11:27; John 13:28.

Popcorn: (1) Revelation; (2) Revelation of your life story.
(1) Prov. 29:18; (cf. Luke 8:11); (2) Rev. 20:12.

Porch (Front Verandah): (1) Out in the open; (2) Exposed; (3) Waiting or expectancy; (4) Could represent an extension of covering, as in missionaries.
(1) Mark 14: 68; Acts 3:11-12; (2) Matt. 26:71 (KJV); (3) Judg. 11:34; (4) Luke 9:1-2.

Port: (1) Jesus Christ; (2) Place of departure (leaving); (3) Place of arrival; (4) Looking for a rest in a storm; (5) Haven.

Also see *Airport*.

(1) Ps. 107:28-30 (cf. John 6:18-21); (2) Acts 27:6-7; (3) Acts 28:12; (4-5) Acts 27:12.

Portal: (1) Open Heaven (portal in sky).

(1) Gen. 28:17; Ps. 78:23; Rev. 4:1.

Postage Stamp: (1) Coming communication; (2) Registered or authorized message; (3) Message bearer; (4) Small.

Also see *Envelope* and *Letter*.

(1-3) Esther 8:8,10,12b; 1 Kings 21:8.

Postman: (1) Angel (messenger); (2) Bearer of good news; (3) Courier; (4) Carrier of the Word; (5) Preacher.

(1) Gen. 22:11; Dan. 10:5,11; (2) Rom. 10:15; (3) Esther 3:15; (4) Matt. 11:10-11; (5) Rom. 10:15.

Post Office: (1) Heavenly distribution centre; (2) Heart.

(1) Gen. 28:12; (2) Prov. 4:23; Matt. 12:34b.

Potatoes: (1) Works of the flesh (unwashed potatoes); (2) Heart full of earthly treasures (bag of potatoes).

(1) Gen. 3:17; Jer. 17:5; (2) Matt. 6:19.

Potted Plant: (1) Believer's heart; (2) Young believer (with limited root structure); (3) The Church.

(1) Ps. 1:3; Song 4:12; Isa. 61:3; Matt. 13:8; (2) Jer. 17:7-8; (3) Song 4:12.

Potholes: (1) Faulty foundations; (2) Uncomfortable journey ahead; (3) Experiencing a shake-up; (4) Hardship; (5) Slowing down the ministry; (6) Downtrodden or issues in the heart; (7) Crooked ways.

Also see *Dirt Road*.

(1) Matt. 7:26-27; 1 Cor. 3:11-15; (2-3) Num. 22:32b; Prov. 28:10; Isa. 24:18; Luke 6:47-48; (4) Prov. 13:15; Jer. 2:6; (5) Judg. 16:4; Prov. 23:27; (6) Prov. 22:14; Matt. 12:11; (7) Luke 3:5.

Pots and Pans: (1) Heart (a person as a vessel for the Holy Spirit to fill).

Also see *Barrel*, *Dish*, *Plate*, and *Vessel*.

(1) 2 Kings 4:3-7; 2 Cor. 4:7.

Potter: (1) God.

(1) Jer. 18:6.

Pottery: See *Vessels*.

Powder: (1) Judgment; (2) Ground.

Also see *Dust*.

(1-2) Exod. 32:20; Deut. 28:24; 2 Kings 23:6; Matt. 21:44; Luke 20:18.

Power: (1) Holy Spirit anointing; (2) Authority; (3) Miracle ability.

Also see *Strength*.

(1) Acts 1:8; (2) Luke 4:36; 9:1; Rev. 13:2; (3) Acts 10:38.

Power Lines: (1) Power of God's Word; (2) Flow of the Holy Spirit; (3) Principles of the Kingdom.
(1) Luke 4:32; Heb. 1:3; (2) Luke 4:14; Acts 10:38; (3) Mark 9:1; 1 Cor. 4:20.

Pram: (1) Someone carrying the promise of God; (2) Faith (that which carries the promise through to manifestation); (3) Beginning of a new ministry; (4) Empty promise (empty pram); (5) Expecting something to be birthed (promise/church/ministry); (6) Someone in whom the promise of God has died (black pram).
(1-2) Rom. 4:20-21; Heb. 6:15; (3) Acts 13:9 (beginning of Paul's ministry); (4) Isa. 29:13; Matt. 15:8; (5) 1 Sam. 1:18; (16) Gen. 16:1-3; Prov. 13:12.

Prawn: See *Shrimp*.

Praying Mantis: (1) Prophet; (2) Spiritual predator; (3) Cancer (predator that eats its victims while they are alive).
(1) 2 Kings 2:11-13 (mantis = mantle); (2) 1 Kings 19:2; Judg. 16:10; Prov. 7:21-27; (3) 2 Tim. 2:17 (KJV).

Preacher: (1) Bearer of the Good News; (2) Anointed speaker; (3) Prophet; (4) Jesus; (5) Your spiritual oversight; (6) False teacher; (7) Your conduct (particularly under pressure).
(1) Rom. 10:14-15; (2) Isa. 61:1a; Mark 3:14-15; 16:15; 2 Tim. 1:11; (3) Jon. 3:2; Matt. 3:1; (4) Matt. 4:17; (5) Acts 20:28; 1 Pet. 5:2; (6) Gal. 1:8-9; (7) 1 Pet. 3:1.

Precious Stone(s): (1) Christ; (2) Believer(s); (3) Gift(s); (4) Spiritual gift(s); (5) Spiritual work(s); (6) Foundation(s); (7) Adornment of the harlot church; (8) The glory of God; (9) Something or someone of value or dear to you; (10) Wisdom.
Also see *Amethyst, Rubies, Stones,* and *Treasure.*
(1-2) 1 Pet. 2:4-7; (cf. Luke 21:5); (3) Prov. 17:8; (4) Prov. 2:3-4; 8:10-11; 20:15; 24:4; (cf. 1 Cor. 12:8); Rev. 2:17; (5) 1 Cor. 3:12-13; (6) Rev. 21:19; (7) Rev. 17:4; (8) Rev. 21:10-11; (9) Matt. 13:46; (10) Job 28:5-6, 12-18.

Pregnancy: (1) Expectancy; (2) Awaiting birth of a ministry; (3) Promise; (4) Warning of fornication (adolescent pregnant); (5) On the eve of revival (new life); (6) May show something ungodly/demonic is about to be unleashed (context and feeling will determine whether it is good or bad).
Also see *Baby.*
(1) Matt. 1:23; Luke 2:5; (2) Luke 1:13-17,76,80; (3) Judg. 13:3; (4) Matt. 1:18-19 (Joseph suspected fornication, v. 20); (5) Gen. 21:1-6; Prov. 13:12; Luke 1:57-58, 67-79; (6) Gen. 10:8-10 (Some suggest Nimrod was a hunter of people).

Premature Baby: See *Baby.*

Prescription: (1) The Word of God; (2) Something you are asked to swallow; (3) Solution to the problem; (4) Positive words.
(1) Prov. 4:20-22; (2) 1 Sam. 18:7-8; 2 Sam. 12:5-7; (3) Gen. 41:34-36; (4) Prov. 16:24.

President: (1) Jesus Christ; (2) Company boss; (3) Literally the president.

Also see *Air Force One* and *Prime Minister.*

(1) John 20:28; (2) Rom. 13:1.

Pressure Cooker: (1) Pending explosion (arguments, destruction, conflict).

Also see *Boiling* and *Bomb.*

(1) 1 Sam. 20:30-33.

Priest: (1) Religious or legalistic leader; (2) Believer; (3) Jesus Christ; (4) Holy man; (5) Religious spirit; (6) A father (priest of the home).

Also see *Pastor.*

(1) Heb. 8:4; 10:11; (2) 1 Pet. 2:9,5; Rev. 1:6; 5:10; 20:6; (3) Heb. 7:17,26; 8:1; 9:11; 10:19-21; (4) Exod. 31:10; (5) Num. 5:30b; (6) Judg. 18:19.

Prime Minister: (1) Jesus Christ; (2) Senior minister; (3) Literally the prime minister.

Also see *President.*

(1) Heb. 3:1; 1 Pet. 5:4; (2) Acts 20:28; 1 Tim. 1:12; 1 Pet. 5:1-2.

Prince: (1) Jesus Christ; (2) satan; (3) Principality (ungodly); (4) Seated in heavenly places.

(1) Isa. 9:6b; (2) Matt. 12:24; Eph. 2:2; (3) Eph. 3:10; 6:12; (4) Eph. 2:6; Col. 3:1.

Printed Circuit Board: (1) The mind; (2) Power of the Spirit.

See also *Wire/Wiring.*

(1) Rom. 12:1; (2) Rom. 8:11; Acts 1:8.

Printer (Computer): (1) Mouth; (2) Words.

(1) Job 15:13; Ps. 26:7; 68:11; (2) Ps. 19:14.

Prison: (1) The world; (2) Captivity and bondage; (3) Stronghold; (4) Place of confinement; (5) Place of heart refinement; (6) Place to develop truth; (7) satan's kingdom; (8) Place of judgment/punishment; (9) Hell; (10) Taken captive; (11) Prisoner of Christ; (12) Constrained by the love of God; (13) Bound by your own thoughts/words.

(1) Col. 1:12-13; 2 Tim. 2:25-26; (2) Isa. 20:4; 61:1; (3) Zech. 9:12; (4-6) Gen. 42:16 (KJV); (cf. Ps. 105:17-19); (7) 2 Tim. 2:26; (8) 2 Pet. 2:4; (9) 2 Pet. 2:4 (NIV); Jude 1:6; (10) 2 Tim. 3:6; (11) Eph. 3:1; Philem. 1:1, 9; (12) 2 Cor. 5:14; (13) Prov. 23:7.

Prisoners: (1) Unbelievers; (2) Captives of satan; (3) Captive sinners; (4) Captives of false religion; (5) Oppression; (6) Addiction.

(1-2) Luke 4:18; 2 Tim. 2:26; (3) Rom. 7:23; (4) 2 Tim. 3:6; (5-6) Prov. 23:29-32.

Private School: (1) Holy Spirit schooling; (2) Mentoring (outside system); (3) Restricted or exclusive training; (4) Cult or religious church (boarding school).

(1) Luke 1:80; 1 John 2:27; (2) 1 Kings 19:19-21; Matt. 5:1-2; (3) Acts 4:13; (4) Matt. 5:20 (full of rules and you don't get to go home [Heaven])

Propeller: (1) Spirit-driven (good or evil).

Also see *Helicopter.*

(1) Mark 1:12 (KJV); Luke 8:29.

Prophetic Incident or Natural Event: (1) Message; (2) Word; (3) Direction; (4) Instruction; (5) Warning; (6) Prophecy.
(1) Gen. 37:8; Dan. 2:9; Matt. 2:13; (2) Ps. 105:17-19; (cf. Gen. 37:5-10); Matt. 2:13,19-20.

Prosthetic Limbs: (1) Not real; (2) Human-made; (3) False walk (legs); (4) False strength (legs or arm).
(1) 2 Sam. 20:9-10; Zech. 13:6a; (2) Ps. 147:10; (3) Num. 22:32b; Jer. 7:9; (4) Ps. 84:5a.

Prostitute: See *Harlot*.

Prostitution: (1) Exploited for money; (2) Selling yourself; (3) Sexual favors; (4) Unlawful trading; (5) Clandestine trading.
(1-5) Gen. 38:15-18.

Prune: (1) Discipline; (2) Judgment.
Also see *Purge* and *Trimming*.
(1) John 15:2; (2) Dan. 4:14; Matt. 3:10.

Psychiatrist: (1) Someone inside your head.
(1) Prov. 23:7a; Lam. 3:60-61 (cf. Ps. 119:95).

Public Toilet: (1) Slander; (2) Gossip; (3) Church that repeats a matter; (4) Church, ministry, business, or household whose sin is exposed publicly (possibly about to be exposed by media).
(1-2) Prov. 6:16-19; (3) Prov. 17:9; (4) Rev. 3:1.

Puddle: (1) Deposit of the Spirit.
(1) Acts 2:17-18.

Puffer Fish: (1) Proud Christian; (2) Wanting to appear more important/spiritual than they really are; (3) Christian filled with head knowledge; (4) Christian lacking love; (5) Religious spirit.
(1-2) 1 Cor. 4:18-19; 5:2; (3) 1 Cor. 8:1; (4) 1 Cor. 13:4; (5) Col. 2:18.

Pulley: (1) The Holy Spirit; (2) Encourager.
Also see *Crane*.
(1) Ezek. 3:14; 8:3; 11:1; (2) Prov. 12:25.

Pulling: (1) Saving (pulling into/out); (2) Redeeming (pulling in again); (3) Rescuing (pulling out); (4) Sheltering (pulling to you); (5) Destroying (pulling down); (6) Humbling (pulling down); (7) Selecting (pulling out); (8) Demolishing (pulling down); (9) Dismembering (pulling in pieces); (10) Uprooting (pulling up); (11) Stripping (pulling off); (12) Rebelling (pulling away); (13) Cleansing (pulling out); (14) Discouragement (pulling down).
Also see *Pushing* and *Towing*.
(1) Gen. 19:10; Jude 1:23; (2) 1 Kings 13:4; (3) Ps. 31:4; Luke 14:5; (4) Gen. 8:9; (5) Ezra 6:11; (6) Isa. 22:19; Jer. 1:10; 18:7; (7) Jer. 12:3; (8) Jer. 24:6; 42:10; Luke 12:18; 2

Cor. 10:4; (9) Lam. 3:11 (KJV); Acts 23:10; (10) Ezek. 17:9; Amos 9:15; (11) Mic. 2:8; (12) Zech. 7:11 (KJV); (13) Matt. 7:4 (KJV); Luke 6:42 (KJV); (14) Deut. 1:28.

Pulpit: (1) Preaching ministry; (2) Church's teaching; (3) Pastor; (4) Sermon; (5) Invitation to speak.
(1-2) Matt. 4:23; 9:35; Luke 20:1; Acts 5:42; 15:35; (3) Eph. 4:11; Tit. 1:7a, 9; (4) 2 Tim. 4:2; (5) Acts 10:22.

Pulse: (1) Life.
(1) Lev. 17:11.

Pump: (1) Building up in the Holy Spirit; (2) Pressure; (3) Receiving spiritual life (pumping).
(1) John 7:38-39; Jude 1:20; (2) As in "under the pump"; (3) Lev. 17:11; John 6:63.

Pumpkin: (1) Witchcraft; (2) Disappointment (something turns into a pumpkin); (3) Fruit of the world (pumpkin is the world's largest fruit).
Also see *Witchcraft*.
(1) 2 Chron. 33:6b-7a; (3) Num. 11:5.

Punch: (1) Spiritual warfare; (2) Exercising faith; (3) Impacting word; (4) Getting knocked around a bit.
Also see *Fist*.
(1) 1 Cor. 9:26; (2) 1 Tim. 6:12; 2 Tim. 4:7; (2) 1 Sam. 3:19; (4) Prov. 25:18.

Puppet: (1) Manipulative or controlling spirit; (2) Someone else is calling the moves; (3) Under someone's control; (4) Mouthing words without heart; (5) Not real.
Also see *Parrot* and *Remote Control*.
(1-3) 1 Kings 21:7-8; (4) Isa. 29:13; Matt. 15:8; (5) John 12:5-6.

Puppy: (1) Immature unbeliever; (2) Someone needing attention and support; (3) Uncommitted follower; (4) Someone who is going to grow into a dog.
Also see *Dog*.
(1) Rev. 22:15; (2) John 6:26 (someone following because they want their flesh satisfied); also consider puppies are in need of constant care; (3) Matt. 8:19-22; 10:38; (cf. John 6:2,66); (4) Matt. 13:32 (just as seeds grow into trees).

Purchase: See *Buying*.

Purge: (1) Purify; (2) Cleansed; (3) Sort/separate; (4) Pruning.
(1) Heb. 1:3 (KJV); (2) Mark 7:19 (KJV); Heb. 9:14,22 (KJV); 10:2 (KJV); 2 Pet. 1:9; (3) Matt. 3:12 (KJV); Luke 3:17 (KJV); 1 Cor. 5:7; 2 Tim. 2:21 (KJV); (4) John 15:2 (KJV).

Purple: (1) Royalty; (2) Kingship; (3) Luxurious and/or indulgent; (4) Righteousness.
(1-2) Judg. 8:26; Dan. 5:7; John 19:2; (3) Acts 16:14; Rev. 18:12; (4) Exod. 28:15; Eph. 6:14.

Purse: See *Wallet*.

Pushing: (1) Doing things in own strength; (2) Without the Spirit; (3) Fleshly or immature leadership; (4) Struggling; (5) Forcing someone into something they don't want to do; (6) Working their/your agenda; (7) Forcing back; (8) To undermine; (9) Exerting dominance; (10) Expanding dominion and influence; (11) Exerting pressure upon; (12) Overflow (good measure pushed down).
Also see *Button Pushing* and *Pulling*.
(1-2) Rom. 8:14 (being led instead of pushing); (3) Ps. 80:1; Isa. 40:11; (4) As in "I feel like I'm pushing uphill"; (5) As in "She was pushed into it"; (6) As in "pushing your own barrow"; (7) 1 Kings 22:11 (KJV); (8) Job 30:12; (9-10) Dan. 8:4; (11) Dan. 11:40 (KJV); (12) Luke 6:38.

Puzzle: (1) Confusion; (2) Test; (3) Riddle/parable; (4) Searching out mysteries. (1) 2 Chron. 20:12; John 13:7; (2) Gen. 22:1; (3) Num. 12:8; (4) 1 Cor. 14:2.

Pyjamas: See *Pajamas*.

Python: (1) Divination; (2) Fortune-telling spirit (familiar spirit); (3) Forecasting spirit catering to the will of people; (4) Spirit that seeks to squeeze out the spiritual life by applying pressure.
Also see *Snake*.
(1-2) Acts 16:16; 1 Sam. 15:23 (*rebellion* means "divination" in Hebrew); (3) Matt. 16:21-23; (4) 1 Thess. 5:19.

Q

Quarry: (1) Faith (moving mountains); (2) Removing major sin.
Also see *Rock(s)*.
(1) Matt. 21:21; Mark 11:22-23; (2) Ezek. 11:19; 36:26; Zech. 7:12.

Queen: (1) The harlot of the false church; (2) Manipulation and control (Jezebel); (3) Queen of heaven (false god); (4) Brought forward for a time such as this (you as the queen); (5) Judgment.
(1) Rev. 17:1–18:7; 17:4; 18:7; (2) 1 Kings 19:1-2; 21:5-16; Rev. 2:20; (3) Jer. 7:18; 44:17-19; (4) Esther 4:14b; (5) Matt. 12:42; Luke 11:31.

Quench: (1) Smother; (2) Put out (fire or light); (3) Stop or restrict; (4) Satisfy their thirst.
(1) Matt. 12:20; (2) Num. 11:2; 2 Sam. 21:17; Mark 9:43-45; Eph. 6:16; Heb. 11:34; (3) 1 Thess. 5:19; 2 Kings 22:17; (4) Ps. 104:11.

Queue: (1) Waiting.
Also see *Ticket* and *Waiting*.
(1) Luke 8:40.

Quick/ly: (1) Holy Spirit upon; (2) Given spiritual life; (3) Importance; (4) Window of opportunity; (5) Time running out; (6) Salvation; (7) Suddenly; (8) Soon; (9) Can be a sign of unbelief.
(1) Rom. 8:11 (KJV); 1 Kings 18:46; 1 Cor. 15:45 (KJV); 1 Pet. 3:18 (KJV); (2) John 5:21 (KJV); 6:63 (KJV); Rom. 4:17 (KJV); Heb. 4:12; (3) Matt. 28:7-8; Luke 14:21; John 11:29; (4) Acts 12:7; Rev. 2:5,16; (5) Matt. 5:25; John 13:27; Rev. 3:11; (6) Eph. 2:1,5 (KJV); Col. 2:13 (KJV); (7) Rev. 11:14; (8) Rev. 22:7,12,20; (9) Isa. 28:16; John 13:27.

Quiet: When people are quiet, it may indicate: (1) They are uncommitted; (2) They are showing prudence (cautiousness); (3) They have received correction; (4) They respect your wisdom; (5) They are fearful of reprisal; (6) They are meditating (thinking through the word); (7) They are waiting on God.
(1) 1 Kings 18:21; (2) Amos 5:13; (3) Job 6:24; (4) Job 29:10; (5) Esther 4:13-14; (6) Josh. 1:8; (7) Ps. 46:10.

Quilt: (1) Protected by God; (2) Covering (bed quilt); (3) Grand/mother's influence (ornate quilt); (4) Warmth.
Also see *Blanket*.
(1) Ps. 91:4-5; (2) Judg. 4:18; 1 Sam. 19:13; Prov. 7:16; (3) Gen. 24:67; (4) Job 31:20.

Quiver (noun): (1) Home; (2) Ready and waiting; (3) Spiritual warfare; (4) Threat of death; (5) Brace yourself with faith.
Also see *Arrows*.
(1) Ps. 127:4-5; (2) Isa. 49:2; (3) Gen. 27:3; Isa. 22:6; (4) Jer. 5:16; (5) Eph. 6:16.

R

Rabbit: (1) Unbeliever; (2) Sin; (3) Unclean spirit; (4) Multiplication; (5) Spirit of lust; (6) Pestilence (pestilent to farmers).
(1-2) Lev. 11:6; Deut. 14:7 (unclean and not dividing God's Word); (5) 2 Sam. 13:14. (as measured by the rabbit's prolific ability to reproduce); (6) Matt. 13:19.

Raccoon: (1) Ungodly, adaptive, and opportunistic thief.
(1) John 12:5-6.

Race: (1) The race of faith; (2) Christ's life; (3) The course of life.
(1) Gal. 2:2; 2 Tim. 4:7; Heb. 12:1-2; (2-3) Ps. 19:1-6.

Race Course: (1) Race of faith; (2) Church with a competitive spirit.
Also see *Race Horse*.
(1) Heb. 12:1; (2) Matt. 26:33; Mark 9:33-34.

Race Horse: (1) Competitive spirit (pride).
Also see *Horse*.
(1) Matt. 26:33; Mark 9:33-34.

Racing Driver: (1) Competitive spirit; (2) Fast life; (3) Ambition.
(1) Prov. 14:29b (KJV); 1 Tim. 6:5; (2) Prov. 19:2b (KJV); Isa. 28:16b; Acts 27:17; (3) Prov. 20:21; 28:20; Matt. 20:21.

Radio: (1) Prophet (receiver of the prophetic word); (2) Tuning in to God.
Also see *Stereo* and *Television*.
(1) Jer. 1:4, 9; (2) 2 Kings 3:15; Rev. 1:10.

Radio Station: (1) Spirit of the world; (2) Prophetic/evangelistic voice; (3) Declaring in the heavens/intercession (battling principalities in the heavenlies).
(1) Eph. 2:2; (2) Luke 8:39 (KJV); Acts 13:49; (3) Eph. 6:12.

Radio Tower: (1) Christ (The Word of God).
(1) John 1:1.

Rags: (1) Lethargy or drowsiness; (2) Self-righteousness; (3) Sin.
(1) Prov. 23:21b; (2-3) Isa. 64:6.

Railroad Crossing: See *Boom Gate*.

Railroad Platform: (1) Waiting place.
(1) Acts 1:4; Rom. 12:7 (KJV).

Railroad Track: (1) Particular job or ministry path; (2) Means of passage for powerful ministry; (3) The plans and purposes of God; (4) Holy Spirit ministry; (if the train is moving without tracks); (5) Guaranteed destiny (tracks can mean "no deviation").
Also see *Hand Rail*.
(1) Exod. 18:20b; Ps. 25:4; Isa. 2:3b; (2) Ps. 143:10 (KJV); Matt. 4:1; (3) Isa. 2:3; Mic. 4:2; (4) Rom. 8:14; John 3:8; (5) Num. 14:8; 1 Kings 11:38 (KJV).

Railway Station: (1) Awaiting release into ministry; (2) Coming and going; (3) Place of interchange; (4) Busy, outreaching church; (5) Base or foundation.
Also see *Airport* and *Train*.
(1) Isa. 49:2; Acts 12:25-13:1,2-3; (2-4) Acts 11:26,30; 12:25; 14:26-28; 15:2,30,35-36; 18:22; (5) Acts 1:8.

Rain: (1) Revival or resurrection; (2) Favor of God; (3) Judgment from on high; (4) Fruitfulness; (5) The Word of God; (6) Spiritual life; (7) Abundance; (8) Teaching; (9) Winter.
Also see *Shower*.
(1) James 5:18; 1 Kings 18:1; (2) Deut. 11:10-12; Prov. 16:15; (3) Gen. 7:4 (heavy); Exod. 9:18 (hail); Ps. 11:6 (coals); (4) Lev. 26:3-4; (5) Isa. 55:10-11; (6) Deut. 11:14; (7) Deut. 28:12; Job 36:27-28; Ps. 72:6-7; (8) Deut. 32:2; (9) Song 2:11.

Rain (No Rain): (1) Sin; (2) Judgment.
Also see *Drought*.
(1) 1 Kings 8:35-36; 2 Chron. 6:26-27; (2) 2 Chron. 7:13-14; Isa. 5:6; Jer. 3:2b-3.

Rainbow: (1) Covenant promise; (3) Remembrance; (3) God's glory; (4) Heavenly vision; (5) Angel or heavenly being; (6) Seven spirits of God.

Also see *Multi-colored* and individual colors.

(1-2) Gen. 9:12-15; (3) Ezek. 1:28; (4) Rev. 4:2-3; (5) Rev. 10:1; (6) Isa. 11:2; Rev. 4:3,5.

Rainforest: (1) Fruitfulness of the Spirit; (2) Revival.

Also see *Forest*, *Jungle*, and *Rain*.

(1) Ps. 147:8; (2) Isa. 35:1.

Rainwater Tank: See *Cistern*.

Raise: See *Ascend* and *Lift*.

Rake (Garden): (1) Gathering/gatherer.

Also see *Fork*.

(1) 1 Chron. 13:2.

Ram: (1) Christ; (2) Offering; (3) Compared to obedience; (4) Symbol of a strong person, city, or nation state; (5) Hard-headed individual; (6) Powerful individual; (7) Leadership.

(1) Gen. 22:13; (cf. Exod. 12:5; 1 Cor. 5:7); (2) Lev. 5:15-18; 8:18-22; 9:2-4; (3) 1 Sam. 15:22; (4) Dan. 8:20; (5) Gen. 22; (6-7) Dan. 8:3-6.

Ransom: (1) Christ's life; (2) Redemption price; (3) Freed from hell; (4) Freed from slavery; (5) Wealth cannot redeem a soul; (6) Life for a life; (7) Adultery (unredeemable by ransom); (8) Price paid for an individual's atonement.

(1) Prov. 21:18; Matt. 20:28; Mark 10:45; 1 Tim. 2:5-6; (2) Exod. 21:30 (KJV); (3) Job 33:23,24-28; Jer. 31:11; (4) Isa. 35:10; 51:10-11; Jer. 31:11; (5) Ps. 49:6-10; (6) Isa. 43:3-4; (7) Prov. 6:32-35 (KJV); (8) Exod. 30:12-15.

Rape: (1) Overpowered and stolen from; (2) Forced theft; (3) Purity stolen; (4) Lust; (5) Spirit of lust; (6) Humbled; (7) Murder; (8) Morally violated; (9) Humiliation; (10) Taking on lies (unwelcome seeds sown).

(1-4) 2 Sam. 13:1-2, 11-14; (cf. Prov. 6:26-32; 2 Sam. 12:4, 7-9); (5) Gen. 19:5-9; Judg. 19:22-27; (6) Deut. 22:28-29; (7) Deut. 22:25-26; (8) Gen. 34:2,5; (9) 2 Sam. 13:19; (10) Isa. 59:4,13.

Rash (Bodily): (1) Sin; (2) Uncleanliness (away from God).

Also see *Leper*.

(1-2) Lev. 13:2-3 (NIV); Lev. 14:56-57 (NIV); as in "cleanliness is next to godliness."

Rat: (1) Unbeliever (unclean animal); (2) Evil spirit; (3) Plague; (4) Someone who spreads disease by words; (5) Undermining (ratting on you).

Also see *Mouse/Mice* and *Teeth*.

(1) Lev. 11:29; (2) 1 Sam. 6:4 (idolatry); 1 Cor. 10:20 (demons); (3) 1 Sam. 5:12; 6:5a; (4) Ps. 22:13; (5) Acts 13:8.

Rattlesnake: (1) Noisy and poisonous person; (2) Deadly threat.

(1) Acts 13:8; (2) 1 Kings 19:2.

Raven: There are two main lines of interpretation: (1) Unbeliever; (2) Cared for by God; (3) Support from the world; (4) Evil spirit/demon; (5) Taker of spiritual sight.

Also see *Bird(s)*.

(1) Gen. 8:7; Isa. 57:21; Lev. 11:13,15 (unclean bird); (2) Job 38:41; Ps. 147:9; Luke 12:24; (3) 1 Kings 17:4,6; (4) Birds are heavenly beings, ravens are black and, therefore, carry the emphasis of being without light/life. (5) Prov. 30:17; (cf. Matt. 13:4).

Rave Party: (1) Counterfeit revival.

(1) 1 Cor. 4:20 (words without power); 2 Thess. 2:9; 2 Tim. 3:5.

Razor: (1) Deceitful tongue; (2) Instrument of judgment.

Also see *Hair* and *Shave*.

(1) Ps. 52:2-4; (2) Isa. 7:20; Ezek. 5:1ff.

Reading: (1) Washing (in what is being read); (2) Hearing; (3) Learning/teaching; (4) Understanding; (5) Spiritual conviction; (6) Receiving revelation; (7) Meditating (rereading).

Also see *Unable to Read* (Directly Below).

(1) Eph. 5:26; (2) Deut. 21:11; (3) Deut. 17:19; Josh. 8:35; (4) Neh. 8:8; (5) 2 Kings 22:10-11; Neh. 13:1-3; (6) Rom. 10:17; (7) Ps. 1:2.

Reading (Unable to Read): (1) Unsaved and therefore unable to understand sealed truth; (2) Being superficial (mouth and heart different) before God; (3) Unworthy (not under the blood); (4) Hardened heart (without understanding); (5) Spiritual blindness; (6) Unbelieving.

Also see *Reading*.

(1) Hos. 4:6; Matt. 13:11; (2) Isa. 29:9-16; (3) Rev. 5:2,9; (4) Matt. 13:4, 19; (5-6) Matt. 17:17-21.

Real Estate: (1) The Kingdom of God; (2) Soul winning; (3) Building wealth (positive or negative); (4) Promise of investment.

Also see *House*.

(1-2) 2 Cor. 5:1; (3) Deut. 8:12-13; Luke 12:18; (4) Jer. 32:44.

Reaper: (1) Spirit of death; (2) Harvest; (3) Angel; (4) Preacher or evangelist; (5) Sower; (6) Person with perseverance.

Also see *Farmer*, *Sower*, and *Seed*.

(1) Joel 3:13; Rev. 6:8; Rev. 14:19; (2) Lev. 19:9a; 23:22; Matt.13:30; Rev. 14:15; (3) Matt. 13:39; (4) John 4:35-38; Acts 2:40-41; (5) 2 Cor. 9:6; Gal. 6:7-8 (reaping what you sow); (6) Gal. 6:9.

Rear: (1) Past; (2) Unseen; (3) Not in authority; (4) Humbly or in subservience; (5) Less.

Also see *Back*, *Back Door*, and *Backyard*.

(1) Phil. 3:12-13,14; Luke 9:62; (2) Matt. 9:20; (3) Deut. 28:13, 44; Matt. 16:23; (4) Luke 7:38; (5) 2 Cor. 12:11.

Rearview Mirror: (1) Past; (2) Looking back; (3) Back up; (4) Reverse.

Also see *Mirror*.

(1-2) Gen. 19:26; Luke 9:62; (3) Gen. 9:23; (4) 2 Kings 20:10-11.

Receipt: (1) Faith; (2) The Holy Spirit; (3) Guarantee; (4) Proof of purchase or service.
(1) Heb. 11:1 (AMP); (2) Eph. 1:13-14; (3) 2 Cor. 1:22, 5:5; (4) Ruth 4:7.

Receptionist: (1) Someone who receives (the Word); (2) Prophet; (3) Preacher; (4) Writer; (5) Believer; (6) The Holy Spirit; (7) Evangelist (that which leads us to Christ).
(1-4) Prov. 2:1; Jer. 9:20; Ezek. 3:10; (5) Matt. 10:14; 13:23; John 12:48; James 1:21; (6) John 16:13; (7) Acts 8:5-6.

Recognition: (1) Fruit; (2) Evidence; (3) Tell-tale signs; (4) Familiar person or surrounding; (5) Known; (6) Friend of the world (not recognized).
(1-3) Matt. 7:16-20; (4-5) Matt. 7:23; John 15:15; 18:2; (6) James 4:4.

Record (Vinyl): (1) Stuck in a rut (repeating record); (2) Old-fashioned worship; (3) Nostalgia.
(1) Deut. 2:3 (NIV); Ps. 78:41,57; (2) Ps. 144:9; (3) Gen. 19:26.

Record Player: (1) Heart; (2) Replaying the same old song; (3) Going around the mountain.
See *Record (Vinyl)*.
(1) Eph. 5:19; (2) cf. Rom. 12:2; (3) Deut. 2:3.

Recycling: (1) Trying to repair the old nature (recycling in church); (2) Trying to reinvent the flesh (old nature); (3) Coming up with nothing new; (4) Working on superficial change; (5) Outward change, but no heart change; (6) Trying to bring change without God; (7) Equivalent to trying to change a caterpillar into a butterfly; (8) Something you have used/done before.
(1-7) Ps. 127:1a; Matt. 9:17; 1 Cor. 15:50; 2 Cor. 5:17; 10:3; (8) John 21:3.

Red: (1) Sin; (2) Person of the flesh (red garments); (3) Blood shed for sin; (4) Wrath of God; (5) War; (6) Anger or provocation; (7) Redemption; (8) Rebellion; (9) Power; (10) Whore (false church); (11) Glorious individual, church, or ministry (western red cedar house); (12) Passion; (13) Babylon; (14) Holy Spirit fire; (15) In debt; (16) Fear of the Lord; (17) Feeling like a target; (18) Embarassed.
(1) Lev. 13:19-20; Prov. 23:31-32; Isa. 1:18; (2) Gen. 25:25, 30; (3) Exod. 25:5; 36:19; Heb. 10:20; Num. 19:3-22; (4) Ps. 75:8; Isa. 63:2-3; (5) Rev. 6:4; 12:3-7; (6) Ps. 75:8; 106:7 (KJV); (7) Ps. 106:9 (8) Ps. 106:7 (NKJV); (9) Rev. 6:4 (KJV); (10) Rev. 17:1-4; (11) 1 Kings 6:9; (13) Rev. 17:4-5; (14) Acts 2:3; (15) As in "in the red"; (16) Rev. 20:15; (17) 2 Kings 1:13; (18) Acts 16:38.

Redback Spider: See *Black Widow Spider*.

Redhead: (1) Evil spirit operating through a person; (2) A spiritually immature and lustful individual; (3) A powerful and influential fleshly church or individual (girl/woman); (4) Witch (girl/woman); (5) Fiery or passionate woman; (6) A fox; (7) Earthly man (man of the flesh); (8) Man or woman on fire for God/living sacrifice.
Also see *Fox*.

(1) Gen. 25:25,34; Gen. 28:6-9; (2) Gen. 25:25-34; (3-5) See combinations of *Red* and *Woman;* (6) Ezek. 13:3-4; (7) Gen. 25:25,27; Matt. 13:38; (8) Acts 2:3.

Reed: (1) Someone easily shaken (double-minded person); (2) Symbol of Egypt/the world; (3) A false support or trust; (4) Someone moved by circumstance; (5) Damaged people (bruised reed); (6) Mock scepter.
(1) 1 Kings 14:15a; Matt. 11:7; (2-3) 2 Kings 18:21; Isa. 36:6; Ezek. 29:6; (4) Matt. 11:7; (5) Isa. 42:3; Matt. 12:20; (6) Matt. 27:29-30.

Referee: See *Umpire.*

Refining: (1) Purifying; (2) Purging; (3) Trial of faith; (4) Passing through the fire of affliction to bring dross (scum, rubbish) to the surface; (5) Often the world is used to purify us; (6) God is with you through the fire; (7) God is refining you as gold.
(1) 1 Chron. 28:18; 29:4; (2) Mal. 3:3; (3) 1 Pet. 1:7 (KJV); Zech. 13:9; (4) Isa. 48:10; Mal. 3:2; (5) Deut. 4:20; (6) Isa. 43:2; (cf. Dan. 3:25); (7) Rev. 3:18.

Refrigerator: (1) Heart; (2) Cold person, church, or situation; (3) Feeding the flesh; (4) Sin; (5) No fire; (6) Without the Spirit; (7) Without love.
(1-2) Rev. 3:15; Matt. 24:12; (3) Phil. 3:19; 1 Cor. 6:13; (4) Matt. 24:12; (5) Lev. 6:13; (6) Matt. 25:8; (7) Matt. 24:12.

Refuge: (1) God; (2) Strong shelter from trouble/harm; (3) Place of security; (4) A fortress; (5) A place of trust; (6) A hiding place; (7) The fear of the Lord.
(1-2) Ps. 9:9; 14:6; 46:1; 59:16; 62:7-8; 71:7; 91:9-10; (3) Ps. 57:1; (4) Ps. 91:2; (5) Ps. 91:2; (6) Ps. 104:18; (7) Prov. 14:26.

Relay Race: (1) Successive generations; (2) Passing on father to son.
(1) Gen. 5:1-32; (2) 2 Kings 2:9-13; Rom. 1:11.

Remote Control: (1) Laziness; (2) "Easy believism" without real works of service; (3) Someone else is calling the shots (puppet); (4) Non-committal/at a distance.
Also see *Button Pushing* and *Remote Control Car.*
(1) Judg. 18:9; Prov. 18:9; 21:25; (2) James 2:13; (3) 2 Kings 24:17; (4) Mark 14:54.

Remote Control Car: (1) Spirit-led ministry (God steering you); (2) Someone else steering you (controlling or manipulative person).
Also see *Jezebel* in Name and Place Dictionary and *Remote Control* (directly above).
(1) John 3:8; Rom. 8:14; (2) John 19:10-11.

Removal Van (Moving Van): (1) Moving out of the fleshly home into the spiritual one; (2) Ready to be born again (changing homes); (3) God wanting you to grow spiritually (come into victory); (4) Possible preparation for death (going to a heavenly home); (5) Actual physical move of home or church.
(1) Eph. 4:22; Col. 2:11; 3:8-10 (cf. 2 Cor. 5:1); (2) Deut. 21:13; John 6:56; 14:15-17; (3) Ps. 30:11; (4) John 14:2-3; 2 Pet. 1:14; (5) Gen. 45:27.

Repeated Words: (1) Important need of attention—particularly if your name is repeated; this is a call to turn aside and listen to God.

(1) Gen. 22:11; Exod. 3:4; Acts 9:4.

Reporter: (1) History.
(1) Esther 2:23; 6:1.

Rerun: (1) Repeating or covering old ground; (2) Dealing with past issues
(un- forgiveness); (3) Not growing in God.
(1) Mark 11:15-18; John 2:13-22 (2) Matt. 18:24, 28; (3) Heb. 5:12-14.

Reserved: (1) Set aside for a particular task; (2) A set aside blessing; (3) Set aside for
judgment; (4) Protected; (5) Hold or keep back.
(1) Isa. 49:2; Acts 9:15; 2 Tim. 2:20-21; (2) Gen. 27:36; 1 Pet. 1:4; (3) 2 Pet. 2:4,9,17;
3:7; Jude 1:6; (4) Rom. 11:4; (5) 2 Sam. 8:4 (KJV); Jer. 3:5 (KJV).

Reservoir: (1) God; (2) Holy Spirit ministry; (3) Holy Spirit not flowing.
Also see *Cistern, Dam,* and *Pond.*
(1) Jer. 10:13; (2) John 7:37-39; (3) 1 Thess. 5:19.

Rest: (1) Faith in the finished work of Christ; (2) Entry into the Kingdom; (3) Eternal
security in the Presence of God; (4) Release of burdens; (5) Peace; (6) Sleep; (7)
Refreshment; (8) Finding a home (good and evil); (9) Heart of person; (10) Trust; (11)
No longer laboring; (12) The true spiritual union of God and people.
Also see *Bed, Seven,* and *Sitting.*
(1) Heb. 4:1-11; (2) Exod. 33:14; Heb. 3:11,18; (3) Acts 2:26-28; (4) Matt. 11:28; 2
Thess. 1:7; (5) Matt. 11:29; Acts 9:31 (cf. KJV & NKJV); 2 Cor. 2:13; 7:5; (6) John
11:13; (7) Mark 6:31; (8) Matt. 12:43; Luke 11:24; 2 Cor. 12:9; 1 Pet. 4:14; (9) Acts
7:49; (10) Rom. 2:17; (11) Rev. 14:13; (12) Acts 7:48-49.

Restaurant: (1) Heart (as the place of communion and fellowship with God); (2)
Church; (3) Communion and fellowship; (4) In the confidence of someone; (5) Heaven.
See *Meal, Sitting,* and *Table.*
(1) Rev. 3:20; (2) 1 Cor. 11:20,33-34; (3) Gen. 18:4-8; (4) Gen. 18:16-17; (5) Rev. 19:9.

Reunion: (1) Return to a former position; (2) Renewing an old association.
(1) John 6:66; Acts 7:39; Heb. 10:38; (2) Luke 15:20; Eph. 4:22.

Reverend: See *Pastor* and *Priest.*

Reversing Vehicle: (1) Backsliding; (2) Going over the past; (3) Wanting to go back to
how things used to be.
(1) Prov. 14:14; Jer. 2:19; Hos. 11:7; (2) Isa. 43:18; 65:17; (3) Prov. 26:11; 2 Pet. 2:22;
Heb. 6:4-6.

Revolver: See *Pistol.*

Rewiring: See *Wiring.*

Rhino: (1) God (white rhino); (2) Africa; (3) Bulldozer in the Spirit; (4) Prophet.
Also see *Elephant, Horn,* and *Ivory.*
(1) Ps. 18:2; (2) By association; (3) Judg. 15:14-15; (4) Judg. 7:18.

Rib: (1) Heart; (2) Spiritual birth; (3) Bloodshed; (4) Wife.

(1) As the place of spiritual birth and due to the rib's proximity to the heart; (2) Gen. 2:21-23; John 19:34; (3) 2 Sam. 2:23 (KJV); 3:27 (KJV); 4:6 (KJV); 20:10 (KJV); Dan. 7:5; (4) Gen. 2:21-23.

Ribbon: (1) Gift; (2) Finish line.
Also see *Bookmark*, *Silver Cord (Silver Ribbon)*, and *Tassel*.
(1) Eph. 4:8; (2) 2 Tim. 4:7.

Rice: (1) The Word of God.
Also see *Seed*.
(1) Luke 8:11.

Rich(es): When you see riches in an incident/event, it is important to understand: (1) There are two types of riches: heavenly and worldly. (2) The key is the state of the heart. Heavenly Riches include: (3) Fellowship with God; (4) God's Glory; (5) Faith; (6) The inestimable and inexhaustible riches of Christ; (7) Goodness, forbearance, and longsuffering; (8) Wisdom and knowledge; (9) The gifts of the Spirit; (10) Understanding; (11) Forgiveness; (12) Mercy/love; (13) Grace. Worldly Riches: (14) May focus the heart on materialism; (15) Create a crowded heart which chokes faith; (16) Tend to self-reliance (trusting riches) instead of faith in God (making it difficult to enter the Kingdom); (17) Blind the heart to the spiritual dimension and the needs of others; (18) Lead hearts to look for the rewards here and now; (19) Earthly riches decay; (20) Deceive us into thinking we are rich when we are actually spiritually poor.
Also see *Poor* and *Treasure*.
(1) Luke 16:11; (2) Mark 12:41-44; Luke 19:2-10; (3) Heb. 11:26; (4) Rom. 9:23; Eph. 1:18; 3:16; Phil. 4:19; Col. 1:27; Rev. 3:17-18; (5) James 2:5; (6) Eph. 3:8; (7) Rom. 2:4; (8) Rom. 11:33; (9) Rom. 11:33; 1 Cor. 12:8; (10) Col. 2:2; Rev. 3:17-18; (11) Eph. 1:7; (12) Eph. 2:4; (13) Eph. 2:7. (14) Luke 1:53; 6:24; 18:23-25; (15) Matt. 13:22; Mark 4:19; Luke 8:14; 1 Tim. 6:9; (16) Matt. 19:16, 23-24; Mark 10:23-25; 1 Tim. 6:17; (17) Luke 12:16-21; 16:19-31; James 2:6; Rev. 6:15-18; (18) Luke 6:24; 14:12-14; 1 Tim. 6:18-19; James 1:10-11; (19) James 5:1-3; (20) Rev. 3:17 (cf. Rev. 2:9).

Rifle: See *Bow*, *Shooting*, and *Sniper*.

Right: (1) Strength; (2) Faith; (3) Spirit, blessed, or righteous direction; (4) Mouth; (5) Preferred, preeminence, above, before, double portion; (6) Authority; (7) Longevity; (8) Contentious woman; (9) Wisdom; (10) Future destiny; (11) Spiritual realm.
Also see *Left* and *Turning Left and Right* (under *Left*).
(1) Ps. 20:6; Isa. 41:10; 62:8; (2) John 21:6; Heb. 12:2; (3) Matt. 25:33,34-46; Luke 23:33-43; (4) Judg. 7:20 (right hand depicts the mouth while the left hand the heart); (5) Gen 48:12-22; (6) 1 Pet. 3:22; (7) Prov. 3:16; (8) Prov. 27:15-16 (oily right hand); (9) Eccles. 10:2; (10) Matt. 25:34; (11) Col. 3:1.

Right Eye: (1) Imagination; (2) Spiritual vision.
(1) Matt. 5:29; (2) John 21:6; Col. 3:1.

Ring: (1) Identity and seal; (2) Authority and position; (3) Covenant; (4) Marriage or family; (5) Hands; (6) Wealth; (7) Pride; (8) Promise; (9) Independent spirit (worn on middle finger).
(1) Gen. 38:18; Esther 3:12; 8:8; Dan. 6:17; (2) Gen. 41:42-43; Esther 3:10; 8:2; Luke 15:22; (3) Gen. 9:13 (A rainbow is a ring from the sky); Gen. 17:11-14; (4) 1 Cor. 7:39; (5) Song 5:14 (KJV); (6) James 2:2; (7) Isa. 3:1621; (8) Gen. 9:10-13; (9) Esther 3:10-11.

Ripe: (1) Harvest time; (2) Ready; (3) Best; (4) Perfect or mature; (5) Good and edible.
(1) Joel 3:13-14; John 4:35; Rev. 14:15,18; (2) Gen. 40:10; (3) Exod. 22:29; Num. 18:12-13; Isa. 18:5; (4) Isa. 18:5; (5) Jer. 24:2.

River: (1) Holy Spirit; (2) Move of the Spirit; (3) Word of God; (4) Life (River of Life); (5) Love; (6) Boundary or border; (7) Death to self (river crossing or dirty river); (8) Moving into Promised Land (river crossing); (9) Peace; (10) Eternity; (11) Prosperity; (12) A spirit (good or evil).
Also see *Brook, Creek, Riverbank, River Bed (Dry),* and *Stream.*
(1-2) Ezek. 47:1-12; John 7:38-39; Acts 11:16; (3) Prov.18:4; Amos 8:11; Eph. 5:26; (4) Ezek. 47:9; Rev. 22:1; (5) Eph. 3:18-19 (consider that this describes something that has length, width, and depth; its height depicts where it comes from!); (6) Josh. 1:11; (7-8) Deut. 27:3; Josh. 3; 2 Kings 5:12; (9) Isa. 48:18; (10) Dan. 12:7; (11) Ps. 1:3; (12) James 3:11.

Riverbank: (1) Out of the Spirit; (2) Not entering in; (3) About to enter in; (4) Decision time (place of decision); (5) Place of prayer; (6) Fruitfulness and prosperity.
Also see *River.*
(1) Ezek. 47:6; John 7:37-38; (2-4) 2 Kings 5:10-14; (5) Acts 16:13; (6) Ps. 1:3.

River Bed (Dry): (1) Without the Spirit of God; (2) Making a path; (3) Judgment; (4) Grieving the Spirit; (5) Quenching the Spirit.
(1) Isa. 44:3; Luke 11:24-26; John 7:37-38; (2) Josh. 5:1; Rev. 16:12; (3) Isa. 19:4-6; 42:15; 44:27; 50:2b; Ezek. 30:12; (4) Eph. 4:30: (5) 1 Thess. 5:19.

Roach: See *Cockroach.*

Road (path): (1) Jesus Christ (Christianity); (2) The path of life (faith); (3) What lies ahead for you; (4) The path of the righteous; (5) Peace; (6) Decision (middle of road or intersection); (7) Following their path (someone you know driving you down the road); (8) Destruction (broad road); (9) Changing sides (crossing the road).
Also see *Country Road, Highway, Path, Roadblock, Roadside, Roadwork, Rocky Road, Street, T-Junction,* and *Winding Road.*
(1) John 14:6 (The Way); (2) Ps. 16:11; Prov. 2:19; (3) Exod. 23:20; Prov. 5:21; 22:6; Luke 10:3; (4) Ps. 23:3; Prov. 2:13,20; 4:11; (5) Isa. 59:8; (6) Josh. 24:15; (7) Ps. 1:1,6; 18:21; 95:10; 119:3; 139:24; (8) Matt. 7:13; (9) Acts 9:11-15.

Road (Road Lighting Conditions): (1) Light = just; Darkness = wicked.

(1) Prov. 4:18-19.

Road (Turning off the Road): (1) Evil; (2) Greed; (3) Adultery.
(1) Prov. 4:26-27; Rom. 3:12; (2) Jude 1:11; (3) Prov. 7:25.

Roadblock: (1) Delay (awaiting the timing of God); (2) Sin stopping destiny; (3) Inspection (being checked/tested); (4) Ambush; (5) Warning; (6) Alternative route required; (7) Go back from where you came; (8) A personal agenda that needs to be changed; (9) Potential physical heart or artery issue.
(1) Acts 16:6-7; (cf. Acts 19:10; 1 Pet. 1:1); Ps. 105:19; John 11:6; (Luke 19:38; John 6:15); (2) Num. 14:22-24; (3) Gen. 42:16; Judg. 12:5-6; Ps. 105:19; Matt. 4:1; (4) Prov. 7:6-23; (5) Num. 22:22-35; (6) Acts 16:6-10; (7) Hos. 2:6-7; (8) Num. 22:22-35 (cf. Rev. 2:14); (9) Deut. 2:30.

Road Grader: (1) Restoration ministry; (2) Prophetic ministry.
Also see *Bulldozer* and *Earthmover*.
(1) Gal. 6:1; (2) Isa. 40:3-4.

Roadside: (1) Love (right side); (2) Legalism (left side); (3) Going nowhere (standing on roadside); (4) Spectating (standing on roadside); (5) Walking in the flesh.
(1-2) Mercy and truth; Prov. 3:3-4; (3) Rev. 3:16; (4) Luke 19:3-4; (5) Luke 10:31.

Road Traffic Authority: See *Highway Patrol*.

Road Work: (1) Preparing one's destiny; (2) Improving one's destiny; (3) Building a path for others; (4) Preparing hearts for God; (5) Warning to slow down; (6) Detour; (7) Removing a barrier in your path; (8) Problems ahead; (9) Changed destiny; (10) Delay; (11) Diversion (detour).
(1) Exod. 23:20; Isa. 40:3-4; (2) 2 Chron. 27:6; Isa. 57:14; (3) Isa. 62:10; (4) Mal. 3:1; Matt. 3:3; 11:10; (5) Num. 22:22-35; (6) Exod. 3:2-4; John 4:3-4 (divine appointment); Matt. 2:13-15 (protection); Mark 6:31 (rest); Luke 4:1-2,14 (testing); (7) Isa. 40:3-4; (8) Num. 22:22-33; (9) Acts 8:26-39; 9:3-6; (10) Gen. 11:31; (11) Deut. 5:32.

Roar: [A] Fearless authority making a declaration: (1) God's voice; (2) Loud voice; (3) A leader's anger; (4) Fearless (as a lion); (5) Territorial warfare (lion's roar). [B] The spiritual enemies of God trying to paralyze their prey: (6) Voice of the spiritual enemies; (7) The adversary; (8) A wicked leader. [C] The cry of a heart in anguish: (9) Heart cry; (10) The Second Coming; (11) The world (sea).
Also see *Lion* and *Sea*.
(1) Job 37:4-5; Isa. 42:13 (KJV); Jer. 25:30; Joel 3:16; Amos 1:2; (2) Job 3:24 (KJV); Rev. 10:3; (3) Prov. 19:12; 20:2; (4-5) Isa. 5:29; 31:4; (6) Judg. 14:5; Ps. 22:13; 74:4; 104:21; Jer. 2:15; 6:23; 50:42; Ezek. 22:25; Zech. 11:3; (7) 1 Pet. 5:8; (8) Prov. 28:15; (9) Ps. 22:1(KJV); 32:3 (KJV); 38:8 (KJV); (10) Luke 21:25; (11) Ps. 46:3; 96:11; 98:7; Isa. 5:30; 51:15; Luke 21:25.

Roast: (1) Purified (in fire); (2) Covenant memorial of deliverance; (3) Diligence; (4) Intimate fellowship.

Also see *Cooking.*
(1) Exod. 12:8-9; (2) Deut. 16:6-7; 2 Chron. 35:13; (3) Prov. 12:27; (4) 1 Cor. 10:21; (cf. Luke 22:8; John 15:15).

Roast Chicken: (1) Church criticism.
See Fried Chicken
(1) 1 Cor. 15:9; Gal. 1:13; Phil. 3:6.

Roast Lamb: (1) Jesus.
(1) Exod. 12: 3-14.

Robe: (1) Righteousness; (2) Authority; (3) Spiritual equipping; (4) Covenant; (5) Pride; (6) Humbling oneself (taking off robe).
The length, fabric, and color of a robe may be indicators of its meaning.
Also see *Clothing, Coat,* and *Mantle.*
(1) Job 29:14; Isa. 61:10; Rev. 7:9 (see *White*); (2) 1 Kings 22:10; Luke 15:22; (3) Lev. 8:6-7; (4) 1 Sam. 18:3-4; (5) Jon. 3:6; Luke 20:46; (6) Jon. 3:6.

Robbery: (1) Devil; (2) The result of disobedience/sin; (3) Inviting demonic interference; (4) Failure to tithe; (5) Cursed; (6) Not having the right to something; (7) Denial of God; (8) Pending destruction; (9) Fornication; (10) Election rather than recognized godly appointment of leadership; (11) Robber's chance for redemption.
Also see *Steal* and *Thief.*
(1) John 10:10; (2) Lev. 26:21-22; Isa. 42:24; (3) Amos 3:10-11; Matt. 12:29; Mark 3:27; (4) Mal. 3:8-9; (5) Mal. 3:9; (6) Phil. 2:6; (7) Ps. 62:10, 12b; Prov. 28:24; (8) Prov. 21:7 (KJV); Isa. 17:14; (9) Hos. 6:9; (10) John 10:1-2; Rom. 13:1; (11) Ezek. 33:15-16; (cf. Luke 19:8-9).

Robot: (1) Programmed person; (2) Religious (mechanical) person; (3) Without heart (heartless); (4) Person with technological skills.
(1) Matt. 16:22-23; Rom. 12:2; (2) Mark 7:3-9; (3) Matt. 15:8; Mark 12:28-33; (4) 1 Chron. 22:15b; Song. 7:1b.

Robotics: (1) Technology; (2) Computing/internet; (3) Electronic gadgetry; (4) Human-made.
(1-4) 1 Chron. 22:15b; Song 7:1b.

Rock(s): (1) Christ; (2) God; (3) God's Word or revelation (rhema); (4) Human hearts as the natural place of worship (the true altar); (5) Hardened hearts; (6) Word-doer; (7) Christ as an offense or stumbling stone; (8) Hiding place, refuge, or fortress; (9) Foundation of the Church; (10) Salvation; (11) Hope; (12) Strong/strength; (13) A solid and secure foundation; (14) False gods; (15) Barren (as in the top of a rock); (16) Place of destruction for the children of Babylon; (17) Permanence.
(1) Exod.17:6; Num. 20:8,10-11; (also see *Seven*); 1 Cor. 10:4; (2) Deut. 32:4,18,30; 1 Sam. 2:2b; 2 Sam. 22:2-3,32; Job 29:6; 39:27-30; Ps. 18:2, 31; 28:1; 42:9; 61:2; 78:35; 92:15; Song 2:14; Isa. 51:1; (3) Matt. 7:24; 16:18; (4) Job 28:5-11; John 4:24; (1 Sam.

14:4; Bozez and Seneh possibly represent David and Saul; *Bozez* means "shining" and *Seneh* means "thorn"); (cf. Judg. 6:20-21,26; 13:19); (5) Luke 8:6, 13; Jer. 5:3 (see *Face*); Jer. 23:29; (6) Matt. 7:24; (7) Isa. 8:14; Rom. 9:33; 1 Pet. 2:8; (8) Exod. 33:21-22; Num. 24:21; 1 Sam. 13:6; 1 Sam. 23:25; 24:2; Ps. 27:5; 31:3; 71:3; 94:22; Jer. 49:16; (9) Matt. 16:18; (10) Deut. 32:15; Ps. 18:46; 62:2a, 6; 89:26; 95:1; (11) Job 14:18-19; (12) Ps. 19:14b (see marginal note), 31:2 (KJV); 62:7; Isa. 17:10 (KJV); (13) Ps. 40:2; Matt. 7:24; (14) Deut. 32:31, 37; (15) Ezek. 26:14; (16) Ps. 137:8-9; (cf. Ps. 91:12); (17) Ps. 71:3; 78:35.

Rocket: (1) Powerful ministry; (2) Quickly established; (3) Growing quickly. Also see *Bomb* and *Missile*.
(1-2) Gen. 41:14; (3) As in "taking off like a rocket."

Rocking Chair: (1) Spiritual retirement.
(1) Gen. 27:1-4, 21 (cf. Gen. 35:28-29; 48:10-21).

Rock 'n' Roll: (1) Rebellion; (2) Witchcraft; (3) Sexual fornication; (4) Anger; (5) Spiritual warfare (worship).
(1-2) 1 Sam. 15:23; (The foundation of rock 'n' roll is rebellion. See the DVD *Hell's Bells 2* by Eric Holmberg if you want to explore rock's roots); (3) Prov. 30:19b; (5) Ps. 144:1; 2 Cor. 10:4.

Rocky Road: (1) Double-mindedness (unstable path); (2) On shaky ground (or going through shaking); (3) Going through a rough patch; (4) Journey with a hardened heart. Also see *Road*.
(1) James 1:8; (2) Ps. 18:7; (3) Prov. 13:15; Isa. 63:17; (4) Hos. 10:12.

Rod: (1) Discipline; (2) Judgment; (3) Dominion or rule; (4) Word of God (as a divider); (5) Jesus Christ; (6) Protection.
Also see *Staff* and *Stick*.
(1) Ps. 23:4; Prov. 13:24 (NKJV); Rev. 2:27; (2) Exod. 7:19; 8:5,16; 9:23; 10:13; Ps. 2:9; (3) Exod. 17:9-11; Rev. 12:5; 19:15; (4) Exod. 4:17; 7:10; 14:16; 17:6; (5) Exod. 7:10,12; John 3:14; (6) Ps. 23:4.

Roll (verb): (1) To have the heart moved; (2) To move or be moved; (3) Removing the heart's hardness; (4) Mourning (rolling on the ground); (5) Moving on in God (changing).
Also see *Circle, Round, Square,* and *Wheel*.
(1) Matt. 28:2 (an earthquake); Mark 16:3-8; Luke 24:2; (2) Rev. 6:14 (KJV); (3) Gen. 29:3; (cf. Deut. 10:16; Josh. 5:8-9; Jer. 4:4); (4) Mic. 1:10-11; (5) Josh. 5:8-9.

Roller Coaster: (1) Life out of control—up and down—carried by circumstance; (2) Unstable; (3) Emotionally driven; (4) Trials; (5) A call for preparation of heart (repentance); (6) Lifting despair and humbling pride.
(1-3) Ps. 109:23 (KJV); (4) James 1:2, 6; (5) Isa. 40:3-4; Mark 1:4; (cf. Acts 13:24); (6) Luke 3:4-6.

Roller Blades/Skates: (1) Free-spirited or in the Spirit; (2) Young Christian; (3) On a roll (when preaching); (4) Out of control.
Also see *Scooter* and *Wheels*.
(1-2) Ezek. 1:20; John 21:18; (3) Rom. 10:15; (4) James 1:8.

Roof: (1) Spiritual leadership; (2) Covering and protection (authority structure); (3) Preaching platform; (4) Reference to a household (those under one roof); (5) High profile; (6) Determined faith; (7) Peak of your ministry; (8) Refuge; (9) Attitude (e.g., self-destructive attitude—roof on fire); (10) Thoughts/thinking; (11) Authority.
Also see *Ceiling*.
(1) Acts 20:28; 1 Pet. 5:2; (2) Gen. 19:8; (3) Matt. 8:8-9; Matt. 10:27; (4) Matt. 8:8; (5) Exod. 17:9; 1 Sam. 26:13; Prov. 8:2a (KJV); Ezek. 31:3; (6) Mark 2:4-5; (7) 2 Sam. 11:2a; (8) Prov. 21:9; 25:24; Isa. 22:1; (9) Phil. 2:5; 3:19; (10) Rom. 12:3; 2 Cor. 5:1; (11) Matt. 20:25; Mark 10:42.

Roof (Leaking Roof): (1) Indicates wrong authority structures; (2) Wrong covering; (3) Absence of confidentiality in leadership.
(1-2) Luke 5:17-19; (3) Judg. 14:15-16.

Roof on Fire: (1) Pentecost; (2) Lust; (3) Anger; (4) Judgment.
(1) Acts 2:3-4; (2) Eph. 2:3; Rom. 1:27; (3) Prov. 25:24; (4) Gen. 19:24.

Rooms: (1) Chambers of the heart; (2) Mental strongholds; (3) Position or place; (4) Storage areas (memory); (5) History or generations (compartments of time); (6) Periods of time (e.g., years); (7) Departments.
Also see *House*, *Mansion*, and *Upper Room*.
(1) 1 Kings 6:5; Neh. 10:37-39; 13:4-5, 7-9; (cf. 1 Cor. 6:19); (2) 2 Cor. 10:4-5; (3) 1 Kings 2:35 (KJV); Prov. 18:16; Matt. 23:6 (KJV); Luke 14:7-10 (KJV); (4) Luke 12:17; (5) 1 Kings 8:20; 19:16 (KJV); Walking backward through rooms is going back through generations or time; (6) Acts 24:27 (KJV); (7) 1 Kings 20:24 (KJV).

Rooms (Large Room): (1) Blessing or fruitfulness.
(1) Gen. 26:22; Ps. 31:8 (KJV); Mal. 3:10.

Rooms (No Room): (1) Difficulty or discomfort; (2) Poor; (3) Prosperity or abundance.
(1) Mark 2:2; (2) Luke 2:7; (3) Mal. 3:10.

Rooms (Spinning Room): (1) Turmoil; (2) Sickness; (3) Drunkenness.
(1) 2 Cor. 6:5 (tumult); (2) Luke 13:11; (3) Ps. 107:27.

Rooster: (1) Leadership (profile figure with a loud voice); (2) A new day; (3) Loud individual who wants to run the place; (4) Witness of denial.
(1) Isa. 40:3; (2) Mark 13:35; (3) Gen. 37:26; (4) Matt. 26:34,74; Mark 14:72; John 18:27.

Root: (1) Heart; (2) Foundation; (3) Jesus Christ; (4) Past ancestry/heritage; (5) Stronghold; (6) Evil heart; (7) Bitter heart; (8) The remnant; (9) Love; (10) That which is the foundation of fruit; (11) That which taps into God's Word; (12) The righteous; (13) Soul-tie.
Also see *Uprooted.*
(1-2) Job 29:19; Matt. 13:6; 15:8,13; Eph. 3:17; (3) Isa. 53:2; Rev. 5:5; 22:16; (4) Isa. 11:1; (5) Heb. 12:15; (6) 1 Tim. 6:10 (love of money); (7) Deut. 29:18; Heb. 12:15; (8) 2 Kings 19:30; Isa. 27:6; (9) Eph. 3:17; (10) Prov. 12:12; Matt. 3:10; (11) Job 29:19; Jer. 17:8; Ezek. 31:7; (12) Prov. 12:3; (13) Exod. 20:5.

Rope: (1) Bound; (2) Influenced by (being pulled); (3) Influencing (pulling); (4) Noose; (5) Strength in unity (three-fold cord); (6) Being held back; (7) Being tied down; (8) Having a few "loose ends" (trailing rope); (9) Sin; (10) If you are tied to something or someone, it can refer to a soul-tie (positive or negative); (11) Renewing the mind (cutting a rope [soul-tie]); (12) Dependency.
Also see *Bound, Cord, Leash, Loosing,* and *Thread.*
(1) Judg. 16:11-12; (2-3) Isa. 5:18; Acts 27:30-32; (4) (5) Matt. 27:5; (6) Eccles. 4:12b; (7) Acts 24:27; Gen. 49:11; (9) Isa. 5:18b; (10) Gen. 44:30 (parent-child); 1 Sam. 18:1 (friends); 1 Cor. 6:16 (sexual partners); (11) Rom. 12:2; (12) Acts 27:32.

Rose(s⊠ (1) Jesus; (2) The Church; (3) Love; (4) Beauty; (5) Death (black roses).
(1-3) Song 2:1; (5) Isa. 9:2.

Rotten: (1) Curse/d; (2) Wickedness; (3) Consume; (4) Diseased; (5) Cancer; (6) Hell.
(1) Num. 5:21-22,27; Joel 1:17 (KJV); (2) Prov. 10:7; (3) Job 13:28 (KJV); (4-5) 1 Sam. 5:6 (NKJV); Job 13:28 (KJV); (6) As in "Go rot in hell!"

Rough: (1) Unprepared or untilled heart; (2) Harsh; (3) Attire of a prophet.
(1) Luke 3:5 (cf. 3:9); Deut. 21:4; Isa. 40:4; (2) Gen. 42:7; 1 Sam. 20:10; 1 Kings 12:13; (3) Zech. 13:4 (KJV); Matt. 3:4; Mark 1:6; Rev. 11:3.

Round: (1) God; (2) Of God; (3) Speaks of cutting away the flesh; (4) Changed or changing.
Also see *Circle, Roll, Square,* and *Wheel.*
(1) Rev. 4:2-3; (2) Gen. 9:13; (3) Josh. 5:8-9; (4) Josh. 5:9.

Roundabout: (1) Experience a turnaround of the situation; (2) Turn from fleshly into spiritual or vice versa; (3) Repentance; (4) Change of direction; (5) Going around the mountain.
(1-2) Matt. 9:22; 16:23; (3) Luke 17:4; Acts 26:20; (4) Deut. 2:3; (5) Deut. 1:6.

Rowboat: (1) Ministry or life of self-effort; (2) Need for the Holy Spirit; (3) Going backward; (4) Old or limited thinking; (5) Not changing or adapting.
See *Rowing.*

Rowing: (1) Self-effort or doing things in your own strength; (2) Opposing the Holy Spirit (going against the wind).

Also see *Boat* and *Canoe.*

(1) Mark 6:48; (2) John 3:8.

Rubber Band: (1) Stretching the truth (exaggeration); (2) Not really letting go; (3) Bouncing back; (4) Falsely bound.

(1) Gen. 20:10-12; (2) Gen. 19:26; 30:25-27; (3) Luke 22:32; (4) Rom. 8:1-2.

Rubber Boots: (1) Protection from sin.

(1) Ps. 18:36.

Rubbish: (1) Religious achievement (dead works); (2) Product of the world; (3) Fleshly build-up; (4) That which needs discarding; (5) That which putrefies if not emptied out; (6) That which gets in the way; (7) That which accompanies someone who has been burned.

Also see *Dung, Garbage*, and *Urination.*

(1-5) Phil. 3:4-8; (6) Neh. 4:10; (7) Neh. 4:2.

Rubbish Bag/Bin: (1) Heart filled with worldly/religious philosophies; (2) Sinful heart; (3) Removing sin (taking out the rubbish bag).

(1) Phil. 3:8; (2) Matt. 12:34; 15:18; (3) Phil. 3:8; 2 Pet. 1:9.

Rubbish Truck: See *Garbage Truck.*

Ruby: (1) Jesus Christ; (2) Heart; (3) Wisdom; (4) Virtuous wife; (5) Priceless; (6) Precious; (7) Incomparable; (8) Red; (9) Righteousness.

Also see *Precious Stones, Red*, and *Treasure.*

(1) Prov. 31:10 (the price paid for the Church); (2) Prov. 31:10-11; (3) Job 28:18; Prov. 3:13,15; 8:11; (4) Prov. 31:10; (5) Job 28:18; (6) Prov. 3:15; (7) Prov. 8:11; (8) Lam. 4:7; (9) Matt. 23:25.

Ruddy (facial skin): (1) Spiritually strong; (2) Healthy; (3) Young.

(1-2) Lam 4:7; Song 5:10; (3) 1 Sam. 16:12; 17:42.

Rug: (1) Looking for guidance (a fleece); (2) Foundation; (3) Undermined; (4) Purging (rug cleaning).

(1) Judg. 6:37; (2) Eph. 6:11-14 (we are to stand on foundational truth); (3) As in "having the rug pulled out from under you"; (4) Matt. 3:12a; Luke 3:17a.

Ruin: (1) Pride; (2) A flattering mouth; (3) Need to be born again; (4) Disobedient heart (not doing the Word); (5) Iniquity; (6) Judgment.

Also see *Run-Down House.*

(1) Prov. 16:18; Ezek. 31:9-13; Jer. 50:32a; Hos. 5:5 (KJV); 1 Tim. 3:6; (2) Prov. 26:28; (3) Acts 15:16; Amos 9:11; Gen. 12:8; 13:3 (consider that *Ai* means "heap of ruins" and *Bethel* means "house of God"); (4) Luke 6:44-49; (5) Ezek. 18:30; (6) Isa. 23:13, 25:2.

Ruler (Measuring): (1) Someone or something used to bring order; (2) Judgment.

Also see *Tape Measure.*

(1) 1 Cor. 11:34; 14:40; (2) Isa. 11:4.

Run-Down House (Collapsing): (1) Laziness; (2) Lazy Christian; (3) Sin; (4) Not looking after yourself; (5) No self-control.

(1-2) Eccles. 10:18; (3) Amos 9:10-11; (4) 1 Cor. 6:19-20; (5) Prov. 25:28.

Running: (1) The race of faith; (2) Hurry; (3) Fearful (running away); (4) Meet (run toward); (5) Engage (run toward); (6) Being self-willed/self-driven; (7) Courage; (8) Showing eagerness/commitment; (9) Greed (running after); (10) Searching (running to and fro); (11) Attack; (12) Natural or spiritual strength; (13) Abundance/overflow (running over); (14) Sure-footedness; (15) To seek after; (16) Contend (a "run in with"); (17) Be unstoppable; (18) To gather (running together); (19) Disciplined; (20) Your mission; (21) Have an alliance with (to run with); (22) Outrun your enemies.

Also see *Chasing, Hiding, Hurry,* and *Runner.*

(1) Gal. 5:6-7; Heb. 12:1-2; (2) Gen. 18:7; Judg. 13:10a; (3) Judg. 7:21 (defeat); 9:21; (4) Gen. 18:2; 24:17; 2 Kings 4:26; (5) 1 Sam. 17:48; (6) 2 Sam. 18:23-24; Rom. 9:16; (7) 2 Sam. 22:30; Ps. 18:29; (8) 1 Kings 19:20; Luke 19:4; John 20:4; (9) 2 Kings 5:20-21; Jude 1:11; (10) 2 Chron. 16:9; (11) Job 16:14; Acts 7:57; (12) Ps. 19:5; Isa. 40:31; (13) Ps. 23:5; 78:15; 119:136; 133:2; Luke 6:38; (14) Prov. 4:12; (15) Song 1:4; Isa. 55:5; (16) Job 15:26; Jer. 12:5; (17) Joel 2:7; (18) Acts 3:11; (19) 1 Cor. 9:24-27; (20) Gal 2:2; Isa. 40:31; Phil. 2:16; (21) 1 Pet. 4:4; (22) 1 Kings 18:46.

Running Water: (1) Living Water (The Holy Spirit).

Lev. 14:5-6, 50-52 (two birds = two heavenly beings = Jesus and the Holy Spirit); Song 4:12, 15; Isa. 44:3; Jer. 2:13; 17:13; John 4:10-11; 7:38-39; Rev. 7:17.

Runner: (1) Entrant in the race of faith; (2) Discipliner of the flesh; (3) Waiter on God (stamina); (4) Greed; (5) Sinner; (6) Messenger; (7) Herald.

Also see *Running.*

(1) Gal. 2:2; Heb. 12:1-2; (2) 1 Cor. 9:24-27; (3) Isa. 40:31; (4) Jude 1:11; (5) Prov. 1:16; 6:18; (6) 1 Sam. 4:12; 17:17; 2 Sam. 18:19-23; Jer. 51:31; (7) 1 Sam. 8:11.

Russia/n: (1) Busyness/Rushing.

See *Bear.*

(1) Luke 10:41.

Rust: (1) Decay; (2) Corruption; (3) Earthly treasures; (4) Need for heavenly treasure; (5) Without discipline (needing maintenance); (6) Lacking character; (7) Cancer; (8) Greed; (9) Old issue (rusty).

(1-4) Matt. 6:19-20; James 5:3 (KJV); (5) Eccles. 10:18; (7) James 5:3; (8) Matt. 6:19; James 5:3; (9) Matt. 6:19-20; Heb. 8:13 (KJV).

Rustling Sound: (1) Something being stirred up; (2) Fear of something coming.
(1) 2 Sam. 5:24; (2) Dan. 4:14.

RV: (1) Family unit (vehicle); (2) Recreation; (3) Holiday; (4) Relaxed.

Also see *Automobile, Trailer*, and *Truck*.
(1-4) Mark 3:31-32; 6:31; Luke 9:10.

S

Sack: (1) Human body; (2) The flesh; (3) Human vessel; (4) Working container; (5) Burden (carrying sack); (6) Baggage (carrying sack).
(1-2) (cf. Gen. 43:23; 2 Cor. 4:7); (3-4) Lev. 11:32; (5-6) Gen. 49:14; Josh. 9:4; Isa. 30:6.

Sacrifice: (1) Life; (2) Praise; (3) Jesus; (4) You as a living sacrifice (His will, not yours); (5) A gift; (6) Doing good and sharing; (7) Idolatry; (8) Evil spirits; (9) Sin; (10) The Law.
(1) Heb. 11:4; (2) Heb. 13:15; (3) Eph. 5:2; Heb. 7:27; 9:26; (4) Luke 22:42-44; Rom. 12:1; Heb. 10:7; (5) Phil. 4:18; Heb. 8:3; 9:9; (6) Heb. 13:16; (7) Acts 7:41; 14:13, 18; Rev. 2:14, 20; (8) 1 Cor. 10:20; (9) Heb. 5:1; 10:3; (10) Luke 2:23-24.

Sadness: See *Sorrow*.

Safe (Bank): (1) Heart; (2) Stronghold; (3) Secure.
(1) Ps. 57:7; 112:7-8a; Prov. 31:11a; (2) 2 Cor. 10:4; (3) Ps. 91:1.

Sail: (1) Led by the Spirit; (2) Waiting on the Holy Spirit (unfurled or empty sail); (3) Journey; (4) Test of faith; (5) Broken spirit (torn sail or broken mast).
Also see *Mast* and *Ship*.
(1-2) John 3:8; Acts 13:4; (3) Acts 13:4; (4) Luke 8:23-25; (5) Prov. 15:13.

Salami: See *Sausage*.

Sale: (1) Investment in one's destiny (good or evil); (2) Soul winning; (3) Moving in faith; (4) Redemption (purchase of used items); (5) Faithful service; (6) Preparation for ministry.
Also see *Buying*.
(1) Acts 1:18a; (2) Acts 20:28; 1 Cor. 6:20; 7:23; Eph. 1:14; (3) cf. Acts 8:20; 20:28; (4) Eph. 1:14; (5) 1 Tim. 3:13 (KJV); (6) Matt. 25:9-10; Rev. 3:18.

Salesman: (1) The Devil; (2) Profiteer; (3) Preacher.
Also see entries under *Buying, Sale*, and *Store Clerk*.
(1) Gen. 3:1-6; (2) John 2:14-16; Rev. 18:3; (3) Acts 8:12; Rom. 10:14 (Consider that "buying" can be the equivalent to "believing," as in "I"m just not buying it!').

Salmon: (1) Real believer (dying to reproduce); (2) Swimming against the flow of the world.
(1) Matt. 4:19; John 12:24; 15:13; (2) Matt. 7:13-14; 1 John 2:15-17.

Salt: (1) Purity or purification; (2) Loyalty of covenant; (3) Barrenness (overdosing with salt); (4) Fertilizer (of spiritual growth); (5) Fruitfulness; (6) Believers; (7) Tasting or seeing the goodness of God; (8) Seasoning; (9) Healing; (10) Offering or sacrifice; (11) Bitter words; (12) Mariner; (13) Flavoring things to your own liking; (14) Salary;

(15) Dead spiritually; (16) Spiritual warfare; (17) Faithful person.

Also see *Pepper*, *White*, and *Yeast* (salt's opposite).

(1) 2 Kings 2:19-22; Mark 9:49-50; (2) Lev. 2:13; Num. 18:19; 2 Chron. 13:5; (a covenant of salt refers to lifelong loyalty); (3) Deut. 29:23; Judg. 9:45 (In this context, sowing with salt was a symbolic action of cursing the land with barrenness); (4-5) Matt. 5:13; Col. 4:6; (Rock salt was used as a fertilizer in Jesus's day); (6) Matt. 5:13; (7) Job 6:6; Ps. 34:8; Mark 9:50; Col. 4:6; (8) Lev. 2:13; Mark 9:50; Col. 4:6; (9) 2 Kings 2:20-22; (10) Mark 9:49 (Salt was added to offerings as an anti-leavening agent); (11) James 3:10-12; (12) Ezek. 27:8-9; Jon. 1:5; as in "He is an old salt"; (13) Rev. 22:18; (14) The word *salary* comes from the Roman practice of paying its army a *salarium* or allowance of salt; (15) Gen. 19:26; Ezek. 47:11; (16) 2 Kings 2:19-22; (17) Matt. 5:13.

Sand: (1) Believers; (2) Multiplication; (3) Innumerable; (4) Many or multitude; (5) Spiritual boundary (beach); (6) Faulty foundations; (7) Disobedience (hearing and not doing the Word of God); (8) God's thoughts toward you; (9) Getting bogged or weighed down; (10) Deceptive foundation or false security in God (compacted sand); (11) Long-standing issue (compacted sand); (12) TV (words without weight/foundation); (13) Offspring; (14) Seed.

Also see *Beach*, *Coastline*, and *Quicksand*.

(1-2) Gen. 22:17; 32:12; (3) Gen. 41:49; Job 29:18; Jer. 33:22; (4) Josh. 11:4; Judg. 7:12; 1 Sam. 13:5; (5) Jer. 5:22; Rev. 13:1; (6-7) Matt. 7:26-27; (8) Ps. 139:17-18; (9) Exod. 14:25 (KJV); Job 6:3; Prov. 27:3; (12) Eph. 5:6; (13-14) Gen. 22:17.

Sand (Wet): (1) Heavy-hearted; (2) A fool's wrath.

(1) Job 6:2-4; (2) Prov. 27:3.

Sandal: (1) The Gospel of peace; (2) Preparation; (3) Sending out; (4) Humility; (5) Holy ground (taken off); (6) Deception (old); (7) Dominion; (8) Legal title (walking over land); (9) Transfer of title (sandal in hand); (10) Renunciation of title (removal of sandal); (11) Dishonor.

Also see *Shoes*.

(1) Rom. 10:15; Eph. 6:15; (2) Exod. 12:11; Eph. 6:15; (3) Mark 6:7-9; Acts 12:8; (4) John 1:27; (5) Exod. 3:5; Josh. 5:15; Acts 7:33; (6) Josh. 9:5; (7) Ps. 108:9; (8) Deut. 11:24; Josh. 1:3; (9) Ruth 4:7; (10-11) Deut. 25:7-10.

Sand Castle: (1) Unstable person (without foundations); (2) Individual who is hearing, but not doing the Word; (3) Church hearing only and not applying the Word (a people easily moved by the tide of public opinion/persecution).

(1-3) Matt. 7:26-27 (cf. 2 Cor. 5:1).

Sandpaper: (1) Preparation; (2) Affliction; (3) Judgment; (4) Abrasive person; (5) Having your rough edges knocked off.

(1) Isa. 49:2b; (2) Deut. 16:3; Job 2:8; Ps. 119:67; (3) Ezek. 26:4 (KJV) (4) Acts 8:3; (5) Isa. 49:2b.

Sandwich: (1) Spiritual meal; (2) Sermon; (3) Chicken sandwich is a church sermon. (1-3) 1 Cor. 3:1-2; Heb. 5:12-14.

Sandy Path/Trail: (1) Paths taken without divine revelation; (2) Taking steps in your own strength.
Also see *Gravel Road*.
(1-2) Exod. 2:12; Matt. 7:26.

Santa: (1) Alternative to Christ; (2) Giver; (3) An imbalanced Christian leader preaching lifestyle (giving false hope without suffering or persecution).
Also see *Christmas*.
(1) 1 John 2:18,22; 4:3; 2 John 1:7 (An antichrist can be either opposed to Christ or instead of Christ); (2) Acts 4:37; (3) Matt. 5:11; 1 Pet. 4:1.

Santa Hat: (1) Giving; (2) Traditional believer.
(1) Eph. 4:8; (2) Zech. 6:11.

Sap: (1) Life; (2) Anointing; (3) Human spirit (as the core of the tree).
Also see *Tree*.
(1-3) Ps. 104:16 (KJV); John 15:4-5.

Sapphire: (1) Foundation; (2) Throne of God; (3) Christ; (4) Some associate this stone with the tribe of Simeon (and others with the tribe of Reuben).
Also see *Blue*.
(1) Exod. 24:10; Isa. 54:11b; Rev. 21:19; (2) Ezek. 10:1; (3) Ezek. 1:26; (4) Exod. 28:18.

Satellite: (1) Worldwide prophetic evangelism; (2) Individual set apart; (3) Independent organization or church (led by the Spirit);
(1) Mark 16:15; (2) Gen. 49:26; (3) Acts 24:5.

Satellite Dish: (1) Communication with God.
Also see *Television*.
(1) Matt. 6:9.

Satin: See *Silk*.

Saturday: (1) Seven; (2) Rest.
Also see *Day* and *Six* (The secular world sees Saturday as the sixth day of the week).
(1-2) Gen. 2:2.

Saturn: (1) Godly person; (sixth planet with rings: person with halo).
Also see *Halo*, *Rainbow*, *Ring*, and *Six*.

Sauce: (1) The anointing; (2) Righteousness (through the blood); (3) Redemption.
(1) Exod. 29:7; Prov. 1:23; (2) Job 29:14; Isa.10:22; Amos 5:24; Rom. 3:21-26; Eph. 4:24; (3) Luke 22:20 (NIV); 1 Cor. 11:25.

Sauna: (1) Hot house (Anger in the home); (2) Sweating it out.
(1) Exod. 11:8; 32:19,22; Ps. 6:1; Prov. 19:13b; (2) Josh. 2:1-7; Ps. 130:5; Luke 22:44.

Sausage: (1) Processed message; (2) Packaged message; (3) Old message (salami); (4) Fiery message (pepperoni).

See *Meat*.

(1-2) John 16:25,29; 1 Cor. 3:2; (3) Acts 15:21; 2 Cor. 3:6; (4) Ps. 39:3; Jer. 20:9; Matt. 23:13-36.

Scaffold: (1) Superficial/temporary structure; (2) Preparatory structure; (3) Support. Also see *Trellis*.

(1-2) Exod. 26:15 (NIV); 35:11 (NIV); Acts 7:47-48; 1 Cor. 15:46; (3) Acts 20:35; 1 Thess. 5:14.

Scales (Over Eyes): See *Veil*.

Scales (Lizard/Fish): (1) Protection (armor); (2) Pride; (3) Hardened heart.

(1-3) Job 41:15,24.

Scales (Weight): (1) Heart (as the means of judgment); (2) Measuring the heart; (3) Judgment; (4) Weighed in the balance; (5) Balance (6) Deceit/deception (false balance); (7) Worth.

Also see *Weighing*, *Weight*, and *Weight Loss*.

(1) 1 Kings 3:9; Ps. 58:2; (2) Prov. 16:2; 25:20; 31:6; (3-4) Dan. 5:27; (5-6) Prov. 11:1; 20:23; Amos 8:5; (7) Zech. 11:12.

Scalp: See *Bald*, *Hair*, *Head*, and *Razor*.

Scalpel: (1) The Word of God.

(1) Heb. 4:12.

Scar: (1) Been hurt (scarred face = damaged heart); (2) Reminder (unable to forget); (3) Identity affected; (4) Walk affected.

(1) Ps. 35:12; (2) Isa. 49:16; (3-4) 2 Sam. 4:4; 9:4.

Scarf: (1) Growing cold (hardened heart); (2) Cold atmosphere; (3) Getting warmer (taking scarf off); (4) Insensitive (taking scarf off someone); (4) Enduring hardship for Christ; (5) Glory; (6) Hiding glory; (7) Covering; (8) The scarlet thread (red scarf).

(1-3) Matt. 24:12; (4) Prov. 25:20; (4) 2 Cor. 11:27; (5-6) Song 4:4; 7:4; (7) Exod. 34:33 (see *Veil*); (8) Josh. 2:18.

Scarlet: See *Red*.

School: (1) Place of teaching or learning; (2) Church; (3) Bible college; (4) Discipleship. Also see *Classroom*, *Library*, *Old School*, *Private School*, *Schoolmaster*, and *Teacher*.

(1) Matt. 5:1-2; Acts 20:20; (2) Matt. 4:23; 9:35; 13:54; Mark 1:21; 6:2; Luke 4:15; 6:6; (3) John 18:20 (church and temple); Acts 5:42; (4) Isa. 50:4.

School (Old School): (1) Old teaching; (2) Traditional church; (3) Pharisees.

(1) Matt. 16:6,12.

School Bus: (1) Teaching ministry; (2) Itinerant preacher.

Also see *Bus* and *School*.

(1-2) Acts 13:1-4; 21:28a; 1 Cor. 4:17b.

Schoolmaster: (1) Authoritative teaching ministry; (2) Christ; (3) The Law; (4) The Holy Spirit; (5) Natural teacher.

(1-2) Matt. 7:29; John 3:2; 6:45; (2) Gal. 3:24-25; (3) John 14:26; 1 John 2:27.

Scientist: (1) Trying to work it out in your head; (2) Reasoning away the supernatural; (3) Trying to get to God through human wisdom (intellect); (4) Anti-christ evolutionists; (5) Christian Scientists (wisdom of God).
(1) Matt. 16:7-10; (2) Isa. 10:12-13; John 20:25; Acts 2:15; (3) 1 Cor. 1:25; 2:5; 2 Tim. 3:5; (4) Rom. 1:25; 2 Pet. 3:4-7; (5) 1 Kings 4:29; Matt. 2:1.

Scissors: (1) Word of God.
See *Hairdressers*.
(1) Heb. 4:12.

Scorpion: (1) Demonic power; (2) Stinging words; (3) Torment; (4) Betrayal; (5) Harsh discipline; (6) Deception (temptation); (7) Politics (attack when threatened); (8) Sin; (9) Legalistic person/church (grabs and paralyzes its prey); (10) Spirit of fear (as in paralyzed by fear); (11) Demon spirits (flying scorpions).
(1) Luke 10:19; 11:12; Rev. 9:5; (2) Ezek. 2:6; (3) Rev. 9:5; (4) Luke 11:11-12; (5) 1 Kings 12:11; (6) Deut. 8:15; (cf. Luke 4:1-13); (7) Rev. 9:3, 5; (8-9) 1 Cor. 15:56; (10) 2 Tim. 1:7; (11) Rev. 9:9-10.

Scooter: (1) Young Christian; (2) Undeveloped ministry or person; (3) May represent the youngest in the family.
Also see *Motor Scooter*, *Roller Blades*, and *Wheels*.
(1) Ezek. 1:20-21; (2-3) 1 Cor. 13:11.

Scratch: (1) Reciprocal favors (scratching someone's back); (2) Irritation; (3) Imperfection; (4) Wounded heart (scratched face).
(1) 1 Pet. 4:10; (2) Prov. 17:25; (3) Luke 23:4; John 18:38; (4) Ps. 109:22; 147:3.

Screw: (1) Secured in place; (2) Stronghold (screw in head); (3) The placement of the screw may indicate the area over which the stronghold operates (i.e. a screw in the jaw may indicate a problem of speech); (4) Intellectually challenged or crazy (loose screw).
Also see *Nail*.
(1) Isa. 22:23a; Col. 2:14; (2-3) 2 Cor. 10:4-5 (entrenched in wrong thought pattern); (4) As in, having "a screw loose."

Script: (1) Saying what you want to hear; (2) Someone speaking one thing with another thing in their heart; (3) Rehearsed lines.
(1) Matt. 21:30; Luke 22:71; (cf. Luke 18:23); (2) Prov. 23:7b; Jer. 23:16; (3) John 11:21,32; it appears that Martha and Mary had said these words to each other while they waited in vain (as they thought) for Jesus.

Scroll: (1) The Word of God; (2) Ancient book; (3) Heaven; (4) Words typed on a computer; (5) Personal calling/destiny; (6) Unfolding revelation.
Also see *Book* and *Library*.
(1) Jer. 36:2,4,6; Ezek. 2:9-3:3; (2) Ezra 6:1-2; (3) Isa. 34:4; Rev. 6:14; (4) Computer screens scroll; (5) Ps. 40:7; 139:16; (6) 1 Sam. 10:2-6; Ps. 119:105; Luke 4:17-18.

Scuba Diving: (1) Exploring the world; (2) Exploring the things of the Spirit.
See *Deep* and *Deep Water.*
(1) Num. 13:1; Ps. 71:20; (2) Ps. 42:7; 1 Cor. 2:10.

Scum: (1) Rubbish that comes to the surface when heated (sin revealed); (2) That which is to be purged (filth).
Also see *Dross.*
(1-2) Ezek. 24:6,11-13.

Sea: (1) The world (sea of humanity); (2) The unbelieving world; (3) Baptism; (4) Raised voices (rough sea).
Also see *Beach, Coastline, Sand,* and *Wave.*
(1) 1 Kings 18:44 (the cloud represented the prayers of Elijah!); Ps. 98:7; Isa. 17:12; Jer. 50:42; Hab. 1:14a; Rev. 17:15; (2) Isa. 60:4-5; (cf. Ps. 2:1; 89:9-10); (3) 1 Cor. 10:1-2; (4) Jer. 6:23a.

Seafood: (1) Lust (What the world feeds on).
(1) 2 Pet. 1:4; 1 John 2:16-17.

Séance: (1) Inviting unclean spirits (familiar spirits).
(1) 1 Sam. 28:7,11.

Seat: See *Sitting.*

Seatbelt: (1) Exercising restraint; (2) Buckling up because of turbulence ahead; (3) Truth (protection against attack); (4) Protection from hindrance; (5) Secure in ministry or destiny.
Also see *Automobile* and *Auto Accident.*
(1) Exod. 19:12; (2) 1 Pet. 5:8; (3-4) Prov. 6:20-22a; Eph. 6:14; (5) Luke 10:42; Acts 21:11-13.

Second: (1) Spiritual; (2) Horizontal love; (3) Denial; (4) Servant (ox); (5) Made known; (6) Not first place or choice; (7) Not the best.
Also see *Two.*
(1) John 3:3-4; 1 Cor. 15:46-47; Heb. 8:7-8; 9:3,7; 10:9; Rev. 2:11; 21:8; (2) Matt. 22:39; Mark 12:31; (3) Mark 14:72; (4) Rev. 4:7; Also second book (Mark) of New Testament shows Christ as the tireless servant; (5) Luke 13:34-35; Acts 7:13; (6) Matt. 22:25-26,39; (7) As in "second rate."

Secondhand: (1) Something revisited.
(1) 2 Pet. 2:21.

Secondhand Shop: (1) Church of Old wineskins (men of the flesh).
(1) Eph. 4:24; Col. 3:10.

Second Place/Seat/Row: (1) Second best; (2) Inferiority; (3) Possibly feeling not worthy to take God's appointed position for you.
(1-3) Judg. 6:15; 1 Sam. 10:22; Matt. 22:25-26.

Secret: (1) Heart; (2) Private plans or counsel; (3) Revelation from God; (4) In the dark (darkness); (5) Brought to light; (6) Not open; (7) Private/ly; (8) Hidden; (9) God's Presence; (10) Personal issue; (11) Unknown; (12) Mystery.
(1) 2 Kings 4:27; Ps. 44:21; 139:15; Prov. 20:27; Matt. 6:6,18; 1 Cor. 14:25; 1 Pet. 3:4; (2) Gen. 49:6 (KJV); Ps. 64:2, 4-5; Prov. 11:13; 20:19; (3) Deut. 29:29; Ps. 25:14; Prov. 3:32; Dan. 2:47; Amos 3:7; Matt. 13:35; (4-5) Ps. 18:11; Isa. 45:3; Dan. 2:22; Mark 4:22; Luke 8:17; Eph. 5:12-13; (6) John 7:10; 19:38; (7) Deut. 13:6; Jer. 38:16; John 11:28; (8) Ps. 10:9; 27:5; 31:20; Prov. 9:17-18; 27:5 (KJV); (9) Ps. 81:7; 91:1; (10) Prov. 25:9-10; (11) Dan. 2:18-19; (12) Rom. 16:25.

Secret Passage: (1) Entering in to spiritual mysteries; (2) Spiritual truth that leads to your destiny; (3) Walking in the Spirit.
(1) Isa. 45:3; Dan. 2:22; (2) John 8:31-32; (3) 1 Cor. 14:2.

Seed: (1) God's Word; (2) Words; (3) Potential; (4) Faith; (5) Christ; (6) Believer; (7) Children/offspring; (8) Money to sow (investment); (9) Multitudes; (10) Multiplication; (11) Death.
Also see *Nuts*.
(1) Matt. 13:19-23; Luke 8:11; 1 Pet. 1:23; (2) Luke 19:22; (cf. 2 Cor. 9:6); (3) Matt. 13:32; (4) Matt. 17:20; Luke 17:6; (5) Gen. 3:15; Gal. 3:16; John 7:42; (6) Matt. 13:38; John 12:24; (7) Matt. 22:24 (KJV); Mark 12:19-22 (KJV); John 8:37 (KJV); Heb. 11:11; (8) Matt. 6:19-20; 2 Cor. 9:5-6; (9) Rom. 4:18 (KJV); (10-11) John 12:24.

Seed Sower: (1) Christ; (2) The devil; (3) Pastoral leadership; (4) Believers; (5) Any or every person; (6) Worker in the harvest.
(1) Matt. 13:37; (2) Matt. 13:25,28; (3) 1 Cor. 9:11; (4) 2 Cor. 9:6,10; James 3:18; (5) Gal. 6:7-8 (good and evil); (6) 1 Cor. 3:6.

Seeing: (1) Being born again; (2) Prophetic insight.
Also see *Lookout* and *Window*.
(1) John 3:3; (2) 1 Sam. 9:9.

Self-Rising Flour: (1) Wrong teaching; (2) Treading on others to elevate yourself; (3) Religious works; (4) Self-righteous works.
Also see *Yeast*.
(1) Matt. 16:11-12; (2) Luke 11:53-12:1; (3-4) Matt. 12:2; Mark 2:16; 7:2-13; Luke 11:38.

Semi-Trailer: See *Truck*.

Sequins: See *Glitter*.

Seven: (1) Divine perfection; (2) Rest; (3) Spiritual completion; (4) Blessed; (5) Full/satisfied/have enough of; (6) To swear an oath; (7) Seven items may = seven days or years; (8) Complete range/scale/cycle—colors of rainbow; musical scale, days of week); (9) Complete; (10) Revelation and Wisdom (11) Humility (Namaan); it takes humility to rest; (12) Sufficiency; (13) Promise (seven colors rainbow).

(1) Gen. 2:2 (God rested because creation was full, complete, good, and perfect); Ps. 12:6; (2) Gen. 2:2; Ruth 3:15-18; (3) Rev. 1:4; 3:1; (4) Gen. 2:3; (5) The Hebrew for seven is *shevah*, from the root *savah*, which means "full/satisfied/have enough of "; (6) Gen. 21:29-31; (7) Gen. 41:26; Dan. 4:16; Josh 6:4; (8) Deut. 28:7; (9) Gen. 2:1-2; (10) Isa. 11:2-3; (11) 2 Kings 5:10-14; (12) From word meaning Matt. 18:22; (13) Gen. 9:12-17.

Seventeen: (1) The perfection of spiritual order; (2) Walk with God; (3) Complete rest. Also see *Seven.*

(1) Seventeen is the seventh prime number (1, 3, 5, 7, 11, 13, 17); it therefore intensifies the meaning of number seven. Seventeen is the sum of 10 (complete order) + 7 (spiritual perfection); Gen. 8:4: The ark rested on the seventeenth day of the seventh month, likewise Christ's resurrection was on the seventeenth of Abib (Passover + 3 days) (cf. Exod. 12:6); Rom. 8:35-39, seventeen things as being impossible to separate us from the love of God; (2) Two who *"walked with God"*—Enoch (7th from Adam) and Noah (10th); (3) Gen. 8:4; (also as the sum of 10 + 7).

Seventy: (1) Perfect spiritual order; (2) Fullness of accomplishment; (3) Release from Babylon; (4) Set for increase; (5) A generation (years); (6) Complete rest; (7) Elder.

(1) As the product of 7 (perfect) x 10 (order); (2) Gen. 46:27; 50:3, 70 days mourning for Jacob; Exod. 1:5, 70 souls went into Egypt; Ps. 90:10, 70 years (life-span); Dan. 9:24, 70 weeks of Daniel; (3) Jer. 29:10; (4) Exod. 1:5; 15:27; Num. 11:25; Luke 10:1; (5) Ps. 90:10; (6) As the product of 10 x 7; (7) Num. 11:24.

Sewage: (1) Flesh; (2) Shame and offense; (3) Cleansing or detoxing; (4) Manure; (5) Religious recognition or religious leverage; (6) Perishing; (7) Needy; (8) Despised; (9) Defiled/polluted.

Also see *Feces* and *Urination.*

(1) Zeph. 1:17 (KJV); (2) Mal. 2:3 (KJV); (3) Neh. 3:13-14; The refuse gate was the gate through which refuse was taken; (4) 2 Kings 9:37 (KJV); Ps. 83:10 (KJV); Jer. 8:2 (KJV); 9:22 (KJV); Luke 13:8; (5) Phil. 3:7-8 (KJV); (6) Job 20:7 (KJV); Ps. 83:10 (KJV); (7) Ps. 113:7 (KJV); (8) Jer. 16:4 (KJV); (9) Ezek. 4:12-15.

Sewing: (1) Joining; (2) Uniting; (3) Sealing; (4) Mending; (5) Trying to put spiritual truth into the fleshly person;

(1-2) Gen. 3:7; (3) Job 14:17 (KJV); (4) Eccles. 3:7; (5) Mark 2:21.

Sewing Machine: (1) Joining or binding; (2) Manufacturing/fabricating; (3) Producing righteousness; (4) Repair or mend.

(1) Col. 3:14; (2) Judg. 16:13; (3) Isa. 61:10; John 19:23b; (4) Matt. 9:16.

Sex: (1) Union or agreement with someone (good or evil); (2) Lust; (3) Spirit of lust; (4) Adulterous heart; (5) Fleshly self; (6) Uncrucified Christian; (7) Feeding the flesh (you hunger for what you feed on!); (8) Stronghold of lust; (9) In love with the world; (10) Lover of pleasure; (11) Denial of the power of God; (12) Conceiving sin; (13) Contaminating or polluting the godly with the world.

Also see *Adultery*, *Fornication*, *Genitals*, and *Sexual Abuse*.

Note: if the person recognizing the prophetic incident or natural event experiences an awareness of perversion in the experience then it is likely that there is a pornographic/sexual/lust/sex predator issue or evil spirit involved.

(1) 1 Cor. 6:16; (2-3) Gen. 19:5; Judg. 19:22,25; Ps. 81:12; Prov. 6:25; Rom. 1:24-27; (4) Matt. 5:28; James 4:2-4; (5) Gal. 5:16-17,19; Eph. 4:22; (6) Gal. 5:24 (KJV); (7) Gal. 5:17; 2 Tim. 2:22; (8) 2 Tim. 2:22; (9) 1 John 2:16-17; (10-11) 2 Tim. 3:4b-6; (12) James 1:14-15; (13) 2 Pet. 2:10.

Sexual Abuse: (1) Perverted doctrine; (2) Literal abuse.

(1) Luke 20:47.

Shack: (1) Poor person; (2) Poor in spirit; (3) Actual spiritual state (while thinking you are rich).

Also see *Cabin* and *Hut*.

(1-2) 2 Sam. 9:5-6,8; Matt. 5:3; (3) Rev. 3:17; (cf. 2 Cor. 5:1).

Shade: See *Shadow* and *Under*.

Shadow: (1) Darkness; (2) Sin; (3) Hiding or away from God; (4) Sickness; (5) Death; (6) Hiding place; (7) Under the influence of (positive or negative); (8) Preview; (9) Without real substance; (10) Under; (11) Protection (refuge); (12) Sign; (13) Brevity (of life); (14) Covered; (15) Trust; (16) Bound.

Also see *Darkness* and *Under*.

(1) Ps. 107:11,14; Song 2:17; 4:6; Isa. 9:2; (2-3) Gen. 3:8; Job 34:22; John 3:19-21; James 1:17; (4) (5) Job 3:5; 10:21-22; 16:16; Ps. 23:4; 44:19; Matt. 4:16; Luke 1:79; (6) Ps. 17:8; Isa. 49:2; Mark 4:32; (7) Judg. 9:15; Acts 5:15; (8-9) Col. 2:17; Heb. 8:5; 10:1; (10) Song 2:3; Heb. 9:5; (11) Gen. 19:8; Ps. 91:1; 63:7; Isa. 4:6; 25:4; 30:2; Dan. 4:12; (12) 2 Kings 20:9-11; (13) 1 Chron. 29:15; Job 8:9; 14:1-2; Ps. 102:11; 109:23; 144:4; Eccles. 6:12; (14) Job 40:22; Ps. 80:10; (15) Ps. 36:7; 57:1; (16) Ps. 107:10,14.

Shake: (1) Fear; (2) Facing adversity; (3) Presence of God; (4) Easily moved by circumstances; (5) Sift or purge; (6) Taking responsibility for their own judgment (shaking shoes or clothes in front of someone); (7) Change; (8) Poor foundation; (9) Empowered by the Holy Spirit.

(1) Dan. 5:6; Matt. 28:4; (2) Ps. 10:6; (3) Isa. 19:1; (4) Matt. 11:7; (5) Luke 22:31; (6) Mark 6:11; Acts 18:6; (7) Luke 21:26; as in, "There was a shake-up of staff"; (8) Luke 6:48; (9) Acts 4:31.

Shaking Hands: (1) Pledge; (2) Agreement or unity; (3) Contract or covenant; (4) Surety (guarantor).

Also see *Fingers*, *Fist*, and *Hand*.

(1) Job 17:3; (2-4) Prov. 6:1; 17:18; 22:26.

Shark: (1) Worldly predator; (2) Sex predator; (3) Person greedy for gain (financial predator); (4) Devil; (5) Evil spirit.

Also see *Jaws* and *Wolf.*
(1) Ps. 17:9-14; 124:2-7; (2) Judg. 16:4-5; Prov. 23:27-28a; (3) Ezek. 22:27; (4) 1 Pet. 5:8; (5) Mark 9:20 (KJV).

Shave/d (Beard): (1) Separation; (2) Cutting off the flesh; (3) Spiritual cleansing; (4) Near miss; (5) Expression of grief; (6) Shame; (7) Vow of consecration (keep- ing or breaking a vow); (8) Losing the anointing; (9) Mourning; (10) Humbling; (11) Humiliation; (12) Repentance (when pulled on or shaved by oneself).
Also see *Cutting Hair, Hair,* and *Razor.*
(1) Num. 6:18-19; (2) Gen. 41:14; (3) Lev. 14:8-9; Num. 6:9; 8:7; Deut. 21:12; Acts 21:24; (4) As in "That was a close shave"; (5) Lev. 21:1-5; Job 1:20; Jer. 41:5; (6) 2 Sam. 10:4-5; 1 Chron. 19:4; 1 Cor. 11:5-6; (7) Num. 6:18-19; (8) Judg. 16:17-20; (9) Mic. 1:16; (10-11) 2 Sam. 10:4,5; Isa. 7:20; (12) Ezra 9:3; Jer. 41:5; 48:37; (Gen. 41:14; Ps. 105:19).

Shed: (1) Fleshly or immature Christian; (2) Person or organization built on greed (rusty shed); (2) Workshop business.
(1) 2 Cor. 5:1; (2) James 5:3; (3) 1 Sam. 13:19; Isa. 54:16.

Sheep: (1) Believers; (2) Christ; (3) Sinners (lost or astray); (4) Shepherdless (scattered sheep); (5) Church (flock of sheep).
Also see *Goat(s)* and *Shepherd.*
(1) Matt. 10:16; 25:32; Luke 15:4-7; John 10:3-4,7,14; John 21:16-17; 1 Pet. 5:2-3; (2) Acts 8:32; (3) Isa. 53:6; (4) Matt. 9:36; (5) Acts 20:28; 1 Pet. 5:2.

Sheet: (1) Covering; (2) Garment; (3) Veil over the mind/mind-set; (4) Thoughts; (5) Wrong thoughts (dirty sheets).
Also see *Bed.*
(1-2) Judg. 14:12-13 (KJV); (3-5) Acts 10:11-15; 1 Pet. 1:13.

Shells: (1) Protection; (2) Home or roof; (3) Currency; (4) Explosive projectile; (5) Cover; (6) Going into hiding; (7) Withdrawing; (8) Spiritual gifts.
(1) Job 41:7,13,15,24,26; (2) Gen. 19:8; (3) Matt. 13:45-46; (4) Acts 4:31; (5) Matt. 10:26; Luke 8:16; (6) 1 Kings 19:9; (7) As in "going into his shell"; (8) Gen. 24:53; Prov. 17:8.

Shepherd: (1) Christ; (2) God; (3) Pastor; (4) Hireling; (5) Greedy pastors; (6) False shepherds.
Also see *Sheep.*
(1) Matt. 25:31-32; 26:31; John 10:2,11,14; Heb. 13:20; 1 Pet. 2:25; (2) Gen. 49:24; Ps. 23:1; 80:1; Isa. 40:10-11; (3) Gen. 46:34b; Acts 20:28; 1 Pet. 5:2; (4) John 10:12-13; (5) Isa. 56:11; Ezek. 34:2-5; (6) Jer. 50:6.

Shield: (1) Faith; (2) Word of God (truth); (3) Protector; (4) God; (5) Spiritual warfare/battle; (6) Spiritual warriors; (7) Righteous; (8) Ruler; (9) Grace; (10) Mighty person; (11) Salvation; (12) House.

(1) Ps. 28:7; 115:9-11; Prov. 30:5; Eph. 6:16; (2) Ps. 91:4; 119:114; (3) Gen. 15:1; Ps. 33:20; (4) 2 Sam. 22:3; Ps. 3:3; 84:9 (KJV); 115:9-11; (5) 1 Chron. 12:8; Ps. 76:3; (6) 1 Chron. 12:24; (7) Ps. 5:12; (8) Ps. 47:9; (9) Ps. 84:11; (10) Song 4:4; Nah. 2:3; (11) 2 Sam. 22:36; Ps. 18:35; (12) As in a coat of arms or heraldic shield.

Shin: (1) Sensitivity affecting your walk or ability to stand; (2) Protection over a sensitive area (shin guard).

(1) Deut. 11:25; Josh. 10:8; 2 Chron. 20:17; Dan. 10:8; Hos. 4:14b; (2) Eph. 6:11.

Ship: (1) Big Ministry; (2) Big church (fellowship); (3) Christ; (4) Believer; (5) The C/church (the entire Body of Christ or individual congregations); (6) Trade; (7) Business; (8) Wealth; (9) Strength; (10) Cargo; (11) Journey, voyage, or passage.

Also see *Battleship*, *Boat*, *Freight*, and *Shipwreck*.

(1) Gen. 6:14-15; (2) Matt. 14:22-33; Mark 6:45-54; Luke 5:3b,10b; John 6:15-21; (Each incident describes Jesus's departure and the Church's subsequent opposition in the sea of humanity until His return); (3) Gen. 6:13-14 (Christ is God's vehicle of salvation today); Acts 27:31b; (4) James 3:4-5; (5) Gen. 6:13-16; Matt. 24:37; (6) 2 Chron. 9:21; Prov. 31:14; Rev. 18:17; (7) 1 Kings 10:15; Ps. 107:23; (8) 1 Kings 9:26-28; Rev. 18:19; (9) Isa. 23:14; (10) Acts 21:3; (11) Matt. 9:1; Mark 5:21.

Shipwreck: (1) Not moving in faith; (2) Blasphemy; (3) Disobedience; (4) Listening to people; (5) Moved by wrong motives; (6) Seeking personal fulfillment and pleasure above work of the Kingdom (capsized boat); (7) This may also be a person or ministry that began OK, but has been lured into seeking fulfillment through finances; (8) Spiritual forces arrayed against the ministry.

Also see *Auto Accident*, *Storm*, and *Waves*.

(1-2) 1 Tim. 1:19-20; Matt. 8:25-26; Heb. 11:29; (3) 1 Sam. 15:26-28; (4-5) Acts 27:10-11,41; (6) Jude 1:11,13 (cf. Matt. 6:33); (7) 1 Tim. 6:9-10; (8) Acts 27:14-18; Matt. 8:25-26.

Shirt: (1) Servanthood (taking shirt off); (2) Undue worry; (3) Little faith (over-emphasis on); (4) Fleshly self (old shirt); (5) Color is a very important indicator of the meaning behind clothing, so check entries under individual colors.

Also see *Clothing* and *Robe*.

(1) John 13:4; (2-3) Matt. 6:28-30; (4) Matt. 9:16.

Shoe: (1) Gospel; (2) Word; (3) Walk; (4) Preparation; (5) Authority; (6) Ministry.
(1, 4) Eph. 6:15; (2) Ruth 4:7; (3) Deut. 25:4-10; (5) Luke 15:22 (Sons wore shoes; slaves did not); (6) Rom. 10:15.

Also see *Ballet Shoe*, *Sandal*, *Slippers*, and *Walking*.

Shoes Off: (1) Holy ground/God's Presence; (2) Not prepared; (3) Communion; (4) Affecting your work for God; (5) Walking in the flesh; (6) Disgraced; (7) Testimony; (8) Enslaved.

(1, 3) Exod. 3:5; Josh. 5:15; (2) Eph. 6:15; (4) Deut. 25:4-10; (5) Rom. 8:1,4; 2 Cor. 10:2; 2 Pet. 2:10; (6) Deut. 25:9; (7) Ruth 4:7-8; (8) Isa. 20:2-4.

Shoes (Pair): (1) Witness (as in two words); (2) Balance; (3) Covenant.
(1) See *Two* and *Shoe*; (2) 2 Sam. 23:12; Prov. 3:3-4; (3) Amos 3:3; Ps. 86:11; Ruth 4:7-10.

Shoes (Two Pairs): (1) Two different aspects of the same walk (e.g., different person at home compared to outside).
(1) Ruth 1:15-16.

Shofar: (1) Prophet; (2) Prophetic voice.
Also see *Horn* and *Trumpet*.
(1) As one who has had the flesh cut out that the breath of God may flow through them; (2) Josh. 6:8.

Shooting: (1) Damaging words; (2) Rifle shooting means words spoken against you from afar; (3) Rifle can also mean words spoken against you distant in time (e.g., from your childhood); (4) Confronting or penetrating words to your face.
Also see *Arrows*, *Bullets*, *Gun*, and *Sniper*.
(1-3) Ps. 22:7-8; 64:3-4, 7-8; Isa. 54:17; (4) Ps. 22:7-8.

Shooting Star: (1) Revelation coming; (2) Word from God; (3) Angelic activity; (4) Timely movement in the Spirit; (5) Fallen believer.
(1) Matt. 2:2,9; Acts 9:3; (Also as 'a light globe moment'; (2) Gen. 1:15, 17; Acts 26:13-14; 2 Pet. 1:19; (3) Gen. 28:12;(4) Esther 4:14 (Esther means 'Star'); cf. Gen. 1:14; (5) Gen. 15:5; 22:17; 26:4; Matt. 24:29.

Shop: (1) Ministry; (2) Church; (3) Spiritual (food) supplier; (4) Materialistic church; (5) Commercial church; (6) Business.
Also see *Butcher's Shop*, *Hardware Store*, and *Shopping Center*.
(1-2) Jer. 3:15; Matt. 13:45; (3) Mal. 3:10; 1 Pet. 5:2; (4) John 2:16; (5) 1 Pet. 5:2; Rev. 18:3,11; (6) Gen. 43:4.

Shoplifter: See *Thief*.

Shopping Cart: (1) Agenda (something you are trying to fulfill); (2) Provision; (3) Poverty/famine (empty cart); (4) Searching (shopping around).
(1) John 1:13 (will of people); (2) Deut. 26:2; 1 Kings 4:22ff; (3) Jer. 42:14; (4) Matt. 7:7.

Shopping Center: (1) Multi-faceted commercial church.
(1) Matt. 21:12-13.

Shopping Trolley: See *Shopping Cart*.

Short: (1) Little time; (2) Brief or briefly; (3) Soon (Lord's return); (4) Humble; (5) Sin; (6) Missing God's best; (7) Restless; (8) Insufficient; (9) Powerless (short arm or hand); (10) Soon angry (short-tempered).
Also see *Little* and *Tall*.

(1) Rev. 12:12b; (2) Ps. 89:47; (3) 1 Cor. 7:29; (4) 1 Sam. 15:17 (cf. Acts 13:9); (5-6) Rom. 3:23; (7) Heb. 4:1; (8) Isa. 28:20; (9) Num. 11:23; Isa. 50:2; 59:1; (10) Tit. 1:7; James 1:19.

Shoulder: (1) Burden; (2) Authority; (3) Responsibility; (4) Bearing or carrying (5) Rank (height); (6) Reminder (memorial); (7) Departure (worldly goods on shoulder); (8) Rebellion (turning or shrugging the shoulder); (9) Putting your back into it (commitment); (10) Hurt the fatherless (arm falls off); (11) Redeemed (laid on shoulder); (12) Ignoring someone (cold shoulder).
(1) Gen. 12:6 (*Shechem* means "burden"); 2 Chron. 35:3; Isa. 10:27; Matt. 23:4; (2) Isa. 9:6; (3) Gen. 9:23; 21:14; Num. 7:9; Isa. 9:6; (4) Gen. 24:15; Judg. 16:3; 1 Chron. 15:15; Isa. 46:7; (5) 1 Sam. 9:2; 10:23; (6) Exod. 28:12; Josh. 4:5-7; (7) Exod. 12:34; (8) Neh. 9:29 (KJV); Zech. 7:11; (9) Job 31:36; Luke 9:62; (10) Job 31:21-22; (11) Luke 15:5.

Shout: (1) Joy or rejoicing; (2) Triumph; (3) Battle (can be the shout of victory or defeat in battle); (4) Praise; (5) Associated with the presence of God or at the entrance of a king (praise or triumph).
(1) Ezra 3:11-13; Ps. 5:11; 35:27; (2) Josh. 6:5,16,20; Ps. 47:1; (3) Exod. 32:17-18; Job 39:25; Amos 1:14; (4) Ezra 3:11; Isa. 44:23; (5) Num. 23:21; 2 Sam. 6:15; Ps. 47:5; Isa. 12:6; 1 Thess. 4:16.

Shovel: (1) Need to empty; (2) Labor or works; (3) Speaks of winnowing or separation; (4) Digging deeper in God (shoveling); (5) Faith.
Also see *Digging* and *Spade*.
(1) Exod. 38:3; (2-3) Isa. 30:24; (4) Gen. 26:15,18; (5) Matt. 17:20; 21:21; 1 Cor. 13:2.

Shower (Bathroom): (1) Cleansing; (2) Seeking cleansing in words (e.g., confession); (3) The Holy Spirit; (4) Human-constructed and controlled spiritual flow.
(1) John 13:10; (2) John 15:3; 17:17; 1 John 1:9; (3) Isa. 44:3; Joel 2:28; Acts 2:17; (4) Matt. 23:4, 15.

Shower (Rain): (1) Blessing; (2) God's favor; (3) God's strength; (4) Teaching; (5) Poor and needy (a wet person); (6) Softened hearts (soil); (7) God coming down; (8) Judgment for wickedness (withheld showers); (9) The remnant of Jacob; (10) Latter rain; (11) God's Word.
Also see *Cloud* and *Rain*.
(1) Ezek. 34:26; (2) Prov. 16:15; (3) Job 37:5-6; (4) Deut. 32:2; (5) Job 24:4,8; (6) Ps. 65:10; (7) Ps. 72:6; (8) Jer. 3:1-3; (9) Mic. 5:7; (10) Zech. 10:1; (11) Isa. 55:10-11.

Showing Off: See Entry 3 under *Tricks*.

Shrek: (1) Anger problem (ogre/tyrant); (2) Demon.
(1) 1 Sam. 20:30; (2) Mark 5:2ff.

Shrimp: See *Crab* and *Lobster*.

Shrine: (1) Place of idolatrous pilgrimage; (2) Place of false worship.
(1) 2 Kings 10:29; Ps. 97:7; (2) Deut. 8:19; Rom. 1:25.

Shrinking: See *Smaller*.

Shrub: See *Bush*.

Shutters: (1) Shutting out the glory; (2) Not prepared/able to receive the glory; (3) Spiritual blindness.
(1-2) Exod. 34:30,33-35; 2 Cor. 3:15; (3) Rom. 1:21; 2 Cor. 3:14; Eph. 4:18.

Sick: (1) Sin; (2) Parts of the anatomy may refer to structures within a family, church, business, group, or nation (e.g., a head wound may indicate a sick leader, hands may relate to workers, etc.); (3) Lacking spiritual well-being; (4) Actual physical ailment; (5) In need of healing; (6) Hope deferred; (7) Lovesick; (8) Lacking self-examination.
(1) Mark 2:17; Luke 5:20, 23-24, 31-32; John 5:14; James 5:14-15; (2-3) Isa. 1:5-6; (3) Matt. 10:7-8; (5) Matt. 4:24; 8:16; (6) Prov. 13:12; (7) Song 2:5; 5:8; (8) 1 Cor. 11:28-30.

Sideburns: (1) Heading toward maturity (not yet a beard).
(1) 1 Sam. 17:33; 1 John 2:13.

Sidewalk: See *Footpath* and *Pavement*.

Sieve: (1) Judgment; (2) Shake; (3) Test of the heart.
(1) Isa. 30:27-28; Amos 9:9-10; (2-3) Luke 22:31-32.

Signature: See *Signed*.

Signs: (1) Miracles; (2) Word/message/voice; (3) Confirmation/witness/evidence; (4) Divider; (5) Indicator; (6) Signal; (7) Directional pointer; (8) Warning; (9) Declaration; (10) Memorial/reminder; (11) End times/indication of His return.
(1) Deut. 7:19; 13:1-2; Matt. 12:38-39; Mark 8:11-12; Acts 2:43; 4:30; (2) Exod. 4:8-9,17; Ezek. 12:6,11; 24:24; Luke 11:30; John 20:30; (3) Exod. 4:28,30; 13:9; 31:13-14; Num. 14:11; 1 Sam. 10:2-9; 1 Kings 13:3; 2 Kings 20:8-9; Isa. 7:11,14; 19:20; Mark 16:17,20; John 2:18; 6:30; Acts 2:22; (4) Gen. 1:14; Exod. 8:23; 31:17; (5) Exod. 10:1-2; Judg. 6:17; 1 Sam. 14:10;
Matt. 16:1-4; 24:3; Mark 13:4; Luke 2:12; 21:7; (6) Judg. 20:38; Matt. 26:48; (7) Exod. 13:9; Deut. 6:8; 11:18; (8) Num. 26:10; Matt. 24:3; (9) Ezek. 24:24; John 19:19-22; (10) Josh. 4:6-7; Isa. 55:13; Ezek. 20:12,20; (11) Matt. 16:3; 24:30; Mark 13:4.

Signed: (1) Sealed agreement; (2) Confirmed authority; (3) Ownership; (4) Miracle (signature of the Spirit); (5) Token (seal of authenticity); (6) Confirmation of God's Word.
(1-2) Dan. 6:8-12,17; (3) 1 Cor. 16:21; Gal. 6:11; (4) Rom. 15:19; Heb. 2:4; (5) 2 Thess. 3:17; (6) Mark 16:20.
Also see *Shaking Hands*.

Silhouette: (1) Profile; (2) Exposure; (3) Eclipse; (4) Outline; (5) Icon.
(1) 1 Sam. 9:2; Matt. 23:5; (2) Job 20:27; (3) Ezek. 32:7; (4) Matt. 23:5b; (5) Matt. 22:20-21.

Silk: (1) Honor; (2) Glory; (3) Opulence; (4) Seduction; (5) China.

Also see *Fabric*.

(1-2) Gen. 41:42; (3) Luke 16:19; (4) Prov. 7:16-18; (5) By association (silk road/routes).

Silver: (1) Redemption; (2) Redemption money; (3) Second; (4) Secondary class.

(1-2) Exod. 30:11-16; 36:24 (Silver [redemption] is the foundation of the Christian); there is no record of silver in Heaven, we do not need redeeming in Heaven; Matt. 27:3-9; (3-4) 1 Kings 10:21.

Silver Cord: (1) Life and death; (2) Spinal column.

(1-2) Eccles. 12:6-7.

Sim Card: (1) Heart.

(1) Matt. 12:34.

Singing: See *Music*.

Sink (Bathroom/Kitchen): See *Washbasin*.

Sinkhole: (1) Judgment; (2) Poor foundation; (3) Unstable community.

(1) Exod. 16:30-33; (2-3) Jer. 2:13; Matt. 7:24-27.

Sinking: (1) Death of a ministry/relationship/chapter in one's life; (2) Death; (3) Judgment; (4) Struggling in faith (fearful); (5) Overwhelmed (positive or negative); (6) Sometimes this can be a positive sign as it may mark the end of a facet of the old self.

(1-3) Gen. 7:20-22; Exod. 15:5,10; 1 Sam. 17:49; 2 Kings 9:24; Ps. 9:15; (4) Matt. 8:24-26; 14:30-31; (5) Luke 5:7; (6) Rom. 6:3.

Sister: (1) The Church; (2) Kindred spirit (person, city, province, nation); (3) Fellow believer; (4) One's natural sister; (5) Wisdom; (6) Judah and Israel (sisters).

(1) Song 4:9-10,12; 5:1-2; (2) Jer. 3:8; Ezek. 16:45ff; 23:1-4; (3) Matt. 12:50; Rom. 16:1; 1 Cor. 7:15; 1 Tim. 5:2; James 2:15; (4) Mark 6:3; (5) Prov. 7:4; (6) Jer. 3:7-8,10.

Sister-in-Law: (1) Legalistic or religious church; (2) Religious female; (3) One's natural sister-in-law.

See *Sister*.

Sit/ting: (1) Authority; (2) Finished work; (3) Rest; (4) Judgment; (5) Position; (6) Honor; (7) Doing business.

Also see *Bench*.

(1) Eph. 2:6; Rev. 2:13 (KJV); Rev. 13:2 (KJV); (2) Ps. 110:1; Heb. 10:11-14; (3) Ruth 3:18; 2 Sam. 7:1 (KJV); Zech. 1:11 (KJV); (4) Matt. 19:28; Rev. 4:2-3; (5) Eph. 2:6; (6) Matt. 23:6; (7) John 2:14 (cf. NKJV & KJV).

Six: (1) Human; (2) Humanity in independence and opposition to God (flesh or sin); (3) Human labor contrasted with God's rest; (4) Not of God; (5) Rest (six full days bring us to seven: rest); (6) Works.

(1) Gen. 1:26,27,31 (humanity created on sixth day); John 2:6; (2) John 19:14-15; (3) Exod. 20:9; 21:2; 23:10-12; 31:15; 34:21; 1 Kings 10:19; (4) Luke 23:44-45; (5) Ruth 3:15-18; (6) Luke 13:14.

Sixteen: This number is derived three ways: (1) 4 x 4 = 16, as such it means a double emphasis of the rule of humanity (abomination); (2) 2 x 8 = 16, as such it means renewal of relationship with God because of the Word of redemption, or association of resurrection; (3) 10 + 6 = 16, as such it means the complete order of humanity.
(1) 2 Kings 13:10-11; 16:2-3; (2) Exod. 26:25; 36:30; 2 Kings 14:21; 15:2-4, 33-34; 2 Chron. 26:1, 4; (3) Josh. 15:41; 19:22.

Sixty: (1) Completion of the flesh.
Also see *Six* and *Ten*.
(1) As the product of 6 and 10.

Skateboard: (1) Youth ministry; (2) Use of gifts (tricks); (3) Spirit (wheels); (4) Immature path.
(1) Isa. 40:30-31; (2) Ps. 71:17; (3) Ezek. 1:20; (4) 1 Cor. 13:11.

Skateboard Deck: (1) Standing in the Spirit; (2) Walking by faith.
(1) Phil. 1:27; (2) 2 Cor. 5:7.

Skeleton: (1) Without the Spirit of God; (2) Dead/death; (3) Fear; (4) Framework; (5) Famine (black skeleton).
Also see *Skin* and *Skull*.
(1-2) Ezek. 37:7-9; (3) Ps. 64:1; 1 Cor. 15:26; (cf. Deut. 20:3; Josh 10:25); (4) Ps. 139:15; (5) Lam. 4:8-10; 5:10 (KJV).

Skiing: (1) In the Spirit (water skiing); (2) Moving by faith (water skiing); (3) Carried by the Glory of God (snow skiing).
Also see *Snowshoes*.
(1) John 6:19; 21:18b; (2) Matt. 14:29; (3) See Entry 3 under *Snow*.

Ski Lodge: (1) Church in the Glory; (2) Heaven.
Also see *Snow*.
(1-2) Dan. 7:9; (Mark 9:3; 2 Pet. 1:17); Rev. 1:14.

Skin: (1) Covering; (2) The flesh; (3) A life; (4) Clothing; (5) Narrowest margin (skin of the teeth); (6) Troubled heart (emaciated); (7) Indicative of the heart; (7) Wrath of God (old skin); (8) Famine (black skin).
Also see *Emaciated*.
(1) Gen. 3:21; Exod. 26:14; Ezek. 37:6,8; (2) Lev. 13:2ff; (3) Job 2:4; 18:13; 19:26; (4) Job 10:11; (5) Job 19:20; (6) Job 19:20; Ps. 102:4-5; Lam. 4:8; (7) Jer. 13:23; (7) Lam. 3:4; (8) Lam. 5:10 (KJV).

Skinhead: (1) Rebellion; (2) Aggression; (3) Anarchy; (4) Anti-authority.
Also see *Baldness*, *Gang*, *Teenager*, and *Youth*.
(1-4) Num. 12:1-2; Prov. 30:11; Amos 3:10; Gal. 5:19-21.

Skinny: (1) Lacking the Word of God; (2) Spiritual poverty; (3) Poverty; (4) Famine; (5) Cursed (gaunt).
Also see *Emaciated*, *Fat*, and *Thin*.
(1-2) Amos 8:11; (3-4) Gen. 41:19; (5) Deut. 28:17-18.

Skip Bin: (1) Waste; (2) Clean up; (3) Demolition; (4) Refurbishment.
Also see *Garbage Truck*, *Rubbish*, and *Rubbish Bag*.
(1-4) Neh. 4:2.

Skip/ping: (1) Youthfulness; (2) Overcoming (impossibility); (3) Joy.
(1) Ps. 29:6; 114:4; (2) Song 2:8; (3) Jer. 48:27 (KJV).

Skipping Rope: (1) Repetitive childhood issue(s); (2) Childlike joy.
(1) Gen. 42:24; (2) Ps. 29:6; 114:4,6.

Skirt: (1) Area of influence (kingdom/domain); (2) Protection; (3) Impurity (dirty skirt); (4) Anointed servant (anointed skirt); (5) Shame or disgrace (lifted skirt); (6) Sin (dirty skirt); (7) Covered.
(1) 1 Sam. 15:27-28; 24:5-6; (2) Ruth 3:9 (KJV); (3) Lam. 1:9; (4) Ps. 133:2 (KJV); Matt. 9:20; 14:36; (5) Jer. 13:22,26; Nah. 3:5; (6) Lam. 1:8-9; (7) Ezek. 16:8.

Skull: (1) Thoughts and plans; (2) The cross; (3) Death or warning of death; (4) Warning of poison; (5) Curse/d; (6) Piracy.
Also see *Skeleton*.
(1) Judg. 9:52-53 (his thoughts and plans were dashed); (2-3) John 19:17-18; (5) 2 Kings 9:34-35; (6) Associated with skull and crossbones.

Sky: (1) Heaven; (2) Mirror; (3) Blessing; (4) Drought (clear sky); (5) Christ's return (blood-red moonlit sky); (6) Blessing (red sky at night); (7) Tribulation (red sky in morning).
Also see *Cloudy*, *Open Heaven*, and *Storm*.
(1) Deut. 33:26; 2 Sam. 22:12-14; Ps. 77:17; Isa. 45:8; Jer. 51:9; Matt. 16:1-3; Heb. 11:12; (2) Job 37:18; (3) Mal. 3:10; (4) 1 Kings 18:43-44; (5) Acts 2:20; (6-7) Matt. 16:1-3. It is possible that the red night sky symbolizes Christ's death and birth of the day of salvation and alternatively that the red morning sky symbolizes His return and pending tribulation.

Skyscraper: See *Building* and *Tower*.

Slate: (1) Heart; (2) Writing; (3) Record of a debt; (4) Give credit; (5) A list of candidates; (6) To criticize.
(1-2) 2 Cor. 3:3; (3-5) From dictionary meanings; (6) As in "to slate someone."

Sleep/ing: (1) Prayerlessness (spiritual death); (2) Death; (3) Rest and refreshment; (4) In the flesh (spiritually dead); (5) Spiritually naked; (6) Spirit willing, weak flesh; (7) Exhaustion; (8) Danger; (9) Warning of temptation; (10) Captive; (11) God-induced sleep; (12) Dormant or inactive; (13) Place of revelation; (14) Unaware; (15) Insensitive to the things of the Spirit.
Also see *Coma*, *Pajamas*, and *Television* (asleep in front of the television).
(1) Matt. 26:40-41; (2) John 11:11,14; Acts 7:60; 1 Cor. 15:6; Eph. 5:14; (3) Matt. 8:24; 26:45; Mark 4:36-40; John 11:13; Ps. 127:2; Song 5:2; (4) Rom. 13:11-13; Eph. 5:14; (5) Rev. 16:15; (6) Matt. 26:40-41; (7) Mark 4:38; (8) Acts 20:9; (9) Matt. 26:40-41;

(10) Isa. 52:1-2; (11) 1 Sam. 26:7,23; (12) 1 Kings 18:26-27; (13) Dan. 7:1; 10:9; (14) 1 Sam. 26:12; (15) Judg. 16:20.

Sleeping Bag: (1) A heart that is spiritually unaware/insensitive; (2) Non-Christian; (3) Individual itinerant ministry.
(1) Judg. 16:20; Luke 21:34 (KJV); (2) John 3:3-5; (3) Luke 9:4; 2 Cor. 11:26-27.

Slide: (1) No integrity; (2) Not trusting God; (3) Word not in heart; (4) Deceit; (5) No repentance; (6) Spiritual adultery; (7) Backslide; (8) Judgment.
(1-2) Ps. 26:1; (3) Ps. 37:31; (4-5) Jer. 8:5; (6) Hos. 4:16 (KJV); (7) Jer. 8:5; Hos. 4:16 (KJV); (8) Deut. 32:35 (KJV).

Slide Rule: (1) Trying to work it out by yourself; (2) Precision; (3) Calculating.
Also see *Calculator.*
(1) Matt. 19:26; Eph. 2:9; (2) Matt. 10:30; (3) Luke 14:28.

Sliding Door: (1) Convenient way out; (2) Unannounced entrance; (3) Opportunity to backslide.
Also see *Door.*
(1) 1 Sam. 19:10; (2) John 10:1-2; 20:26; (3) Acts 7:39; Isa. 31:1.

Sling/Slingshot: (1) Faith (carries the stone to its target); (2) The heart (the pouch of the sling); (3) The Word of God (the stone that is slung).
(1) 1 Sam. 17:34-37; Heb. 11:32; (2) 1 Sam. 25:29 (*pocket* in Hebrew is *kaph*, which describes a concave vessel); (3) 1 Pet. 2:8 (KJV).

Slip: (1) Sin (Unrepentant); (2) At ease despising guidance; (3) Envious; (4) In danger of losing your salvation.
Also see *Slippery.*
(1) Ps. 38:16-18; (2) Job 12:5; (3) Ps. 73:2; (4) Heb. 2:1 (KJV).

Slippers: (1) Domestic walk (what you do at home).
(1) Matt. 11:8.

Slippery: (1) Without God; (2) Without the Word; (3) Plotting against the godly; (4) Ungodliness and wickedness; (5) Hard to handle; (6) Hard to grasp.
Also see *Slip.*
(1) 2 Sam. 22:37; (2) Ps. 17:4-5; 35:6 (in the dark); (3) Ps. 35:6; (4) Ps. 73:3,18; Jer. 23:11-12; (5) Luke 20:26 (KJV); (6) 2 Pet. 3:16.

Slow Motion: (1) God appears to be taking His time; (2) Slow down; (3) Long-lasting.
(1) Gen. 15:2; Ps. 42:9; Prov. 20:21; Isa. 28:16b; Luke 18:6-7; 1 Pet. 3:8-9; (2) John 11:6; (3) 1 Tim. 1:16; 6:19.

Slug (Snail): (1) Lawlessness; (2) Unclean issue; (3) Abomination; (4) Eating away righteous truth.
(1) Hab. 1:14; (2-3) Lev. 11:41-45; 20:25; 22:5-6; (4) 2 Tim. 2:17.

Slug Gun: See *Spud Gun.*

Small: See *Little* and *Smaller.*

Smaller: If something is smaller than it was originally, it may mean that: (1) Its influence is diminishing; (2) You are getting stronger in relation to it; (3) People are leaving. (1) Num. 33:54 (KJV); Ezek. 29:15b; (2) Exod. 1:9; (3) 1 Sam. 13:11.

Smell: (1) The Presence of Jesus (fragrant); (2) Love and adoration (fragrant perfume); (3) An acceptable sacrifice (sweet); (4) Fragrance of renewal (floral); (5) Deception/corruption; (6) Pride; (7) Battle; (8) Demons (bad or sulphur smell); (9) Offence/disfavor (bad smell); (10) Good or bad memory (reminder of an issue); (11) Discerning of spirits (smelling); (12) Spirit of death (bad smell); (13) Wrong spirit (bad smell); (14) Resurrection (scent of water); (15) Good counsel (sweet smell); (16) Royalty (smell of cedar); (17) Idolatry (inability to smell); (18) Love (smell of apples).
Also see *Nose*, *Odor*, and *Smelling Smoke*.
(1) Ps. 45:7-8; Song 1:13; 3:6-7; (2) Song 1:12; 4:10-11; 5:5,13; (3) Gen. 8:20-21; Phil. 4:18; (4) Hos. 14:6; (5) Gen. 27:27; Isa. 34:3; As in "I smell a rat"; (6) Isa. 3:16-24; (7) Job 39:25; (8) Eccles. 10:1; Rev. 9:2-4; (9) Gen. 34:30 (KJV); Exod. 7:21; 8:14; 16:20; 2 Sam. 10:6 (KJV); Eccles. 10:1; Isa. 3:24; (10) Num. 11:5; (11) 1 Cor. 12:17; (12) John 11:39; (13) Exod. 7:18; 8:14;
(14) Job 14:9; (15) Prov. 27:9; (16) Song 4:11; Hos. 14:6; (17) Deut. 4:28; Ps. 115:4-6; (18) Song 7:8.

Smelling Smoke: (1) Serious warning of danger or emergency; (2) Judgment.
Also see *Smell* and *Smoke*.
(1) Judg. 20:40-41; Acts 2:19-21; (2) Dan. 3:27.

Smile: (1) Anointing and joy of the Holy Spirit upon someone; (2) Grace or favor upon someone; (3) A blessing imparted; (4) Pleased; (5) Glory of God upon someone; (6) Wisdom of God imparted (revelation); (7) Love.
(1) Ps. 104:15; (2-3) Ps. 67:1; 119:135; (4) Ps. 80:3-4,7,19; Luke 3:22; (5) Isa. 60:1; Matt. 17:2; (6) Eccles. 8:1; (7) Ps. 31:16.

Smoke: (1) Judgment and torment (wrath of God); (2) Presence of God or Glory of God; (3) Anger; (4) Signal (sign of trouble); (5) Vanish (like smoke); (6) Painful annoyance; (7) Consumed; (8) Prayers of the saints; (9) Evil spirits; (10) Wickedness.
Also see *Smoking* and *Toxic Vapors*.
(1) Gen. 19:28; 2 Sam. 22:9; Ps. 18:8; 74:1; Joel 2:30-31; Rev. 9:17; 14:11; 18:8-10; (2) Gen. 15:17; Exod. 19:18; Isa. 4:5; 6:1,4; (3) Ps. 74:1; (4) Josh. 8:20; (5) Ps. 68:2; Isa. 51:6; Hos. 13:3; (6) Prov. 10:26; Isa. 65:5; (7) Ps. 102:3; (8) Rev. 8:4; (9) Rev. 9:2-3; (10) Isa. 9:18.

Smoking: (1) Offence (offended and/or offending); (2) Jealousy; (3) Consumed (in anger); (4) Worthless pursuit; (5) Bound by the world; (6) Evidence; (7) Shared or joint offense (passing pipe or bong).
Also see *Cigarettes* and *Smoke*.
(1) Job. 19:17a (NKJV); Isa. 65:5; (2) Deut. 29:20 (KJV); (3) Ps. 37:20 (KJV); Isa. 34:10; (4) Prov. 10:26; Matt. 16:23b (smoking may well be filling our lungs with the

devil's substitute for the Holy Spirit!); Ps. 102:3; Isa. 34:10; (5) Deut. 4:20; 1 Kings 8:51; Jer. 11:4; (6) As in "We found no smoking gun"; (7) Matt. 13:57; 15:12.

Smooth: (1) Spiritual; (2) Spiritually effective (of God); (3) Deceitful words; (4) Preparation.
(1) Gen. 27:11 (Esau [hairy] speaks of the flesh, therefore, by comparison, here Jacob's skin speaks of the Spirit); (2) 1 Sam. 17:40 (These have had the edges knocked off in God's Word [the brook]); (3) Ps. 55:21 (sounded fantastic, but his heart was saying other things); Prov. 5:3; Isa. 30:10b; (4) Luke 3:5.

Smuggling: See *Thief*.

Snail: See *Slug*.

Snake: (1) Sin; (2) A person who speaks poisonous words; (3) satan; (4) An evil spirit; (5) Curse; (6) A tempter; (7) A lying spirit; (8) Deception; (9) False teacher; (10) Jesus; (11) Hypocrisy; (12) Curse of poverty (skinny snake); (13) Deceptive person pretending to be righteous/false prophet (white snake); (14) False prophet (snake in a sock); (15) Seduction; (16) Fear; (17) A low-life full of deception (snake in the grass); (18) Strife in marriage (snake in bed); (19) White lies (white snake); (20) God/Jesus (white python); (21) Curse (yellow snake); (22) Revisiting an issue or spirit (double-headed snake); (23) Double-mindedness (double-headed snake); (24) Witchcraft; (25) Healing (snake on stick/pole); (26) Spirit of division (snake with two tails); (27) Doctor's pronouncement (snake on wrist: as in "medic alert" bracelet); (28) Wisdom; (29) Tongue.
Also see *Python, Spider, Snake—Bitten by a Snake*, and *Snakeskin*.
(1) John 3:14; 2 Cor. 5:21; (cf. Num. 21:7-9); (2) Ps. 58:3-4a; James 3:8; Rom. 3:13b-14; (3) Rev. 20:2; (4) Luke 10:19; (5) Gen. 3:14; Gal. 3:13; John 3:14; (6) Gen 3:1-15; (Ps. 91:9-13; cf. Matt 4:6-7); Rev. 12:9; (7) Gen. 3:4; John 8:44b; (8-9) 2 Cor. 11:3-4; Jude 1:4; (10) Exod. 7:12; Num. 21:8-9; John 3:14; (11) Matt. 3:7; 12:34; (12) See *Fat*; (13) Matt. 26:48-49; (14) Matt. 7:15; Acts 16:16; (15) Gen. 3:1-5,13; 2 Cor. 11:3; (16) Gen. 3:15; 2 Cor. 11:3; (17) Gen. 3:1; Esther 3:6; Luke 22:47-48; (18) Gen. 3:1,12 (unclean spirit causing division); (19) Gen. 12:13,18; (20) Exod. 7:12; John 3:14 (cf. Num. 21:8-9); (21) See *Yellow*; (22) Gen. 12:13; 20:2; (23) James 1:8; (24) Exod. 7:11-12; (25) Num. 21:8-9; (26) Ezek. 21:21; (Num. 22:7; Jude 1:11) (27) Exod. 15:9; Prov. 17:9b; (28) Matt. 10:16; (29) James 3:7-8.

Snake (Bitten by a Snake): (1) Disobedience; (2) Sin; (3) Breaking of protection; (4) Attack of the enemy; (5) Venomous words spoken against you; (6) Conflict; (7) Judgment.
(1-3) Num. 21:5-9; Eccles. 10:8; (4) Acts 28:3; (5) Num. 21:5-6; (6) Acts 28:3; Rev. 9:19; (7) Num. 21:7-9.

Snakeskin: (1) satan now present in a different guise; (2) Deliverance and transformation; (3) Signs/evidence of demonic activity.
(1) Gen. 3:1; 2 Cor. 11:14; (2) Acts 9:17-18; (3) Ezek. 28:17; Matt. 17:15; Luke 4:13.

Snakeskin Boots: (1) Walking in deception; (2) Walking in a curse/law; (3) Walking in wisdom.

(1) Ps. 38:12; 39:6; Jer. 2:5; 18:15; 2 Cor. 4:2; Eph. 4:17; (2) Deut. 29:19; Neh. 10:29; (3) Prov. 2:7; 13:20; 28:26; Matt. 10:16.

Snare: (1) Trap; (2) Offense; (3) Unforgiveness; (4) Lust; (5) Suddenly/unawares; (6) Legalistic restriction; (7) Manipulative control; (8) Thought strongholds; (9) Idolatry; (10) Work of the proud, wicked, and devil; (11) God is the deliverer from snares; (12) Secretly conspired against; (13) Surety for others (particularly unbelievers); (14) Unwise and unbelieving words; (15) Death; (16) Anger; (17) Fear of people; (18) Harlot or bitter woman.

Also see *Trap*.

(1) Job 18:9-10; (Ps. 38:12; Matt. 22:15-18); Ps. 69:22; (2) Isa. 8:14; 29:21; (3) 2 Cor. 2:10-11; (4) Prov. 7:10, 23; 1 Tim. 6:9; (5) Eccles. 9:12; Luke 21:34b-35; (6) 1 Cor. 7:35 (KJV); (7) 1 Tim. 3:7; (8) 2 Tim. 2:24-26; (9) Ps. 106:36; (10) Ps. 91:3; 119:110; 140:5; 141:9; (11) Ps. 124:7-8; (12) Ps. 142:3; (13) Prov. 6:1-2; (14) Prov. 12:13; 18:7; (15) Prov. 13:14; 14:27; (16) Prov. 22:24-25; (17) Prov. 29:25; (18) Prov. 7:10,23; Eccles. 7:26.

Sneakers: (1) In the Spirit; (2) By faith.

(1) 1 Kings 18:46; (2) Heb. 12:1.

Sneeze: (1) Sudden irritant; (2) Heart exposure (what comes out in the sneeze).

(1) Dan. 2:12; 3:13,19; (2) Matt. 12:34; 15:18-19.

Sniper: (1) Words against you in secret; (2) Unexpected words against; (3) Intercessor; (4) The devil lining up to tempt you; (5) You are unaware that the enemy is focused on you to destroy you.

Also see *Assassin*, *Contract Killer*, and *Rifle*.

(1-2) Ps. 11:2; 64:3-4; (3) Neh. 4:9; (4) Luke 22:31; (5) Prov. 7:23.

Snorkeling: (1) Exploring things of the Spirit.

(1) 2 Kings 6:17; Matt. 7:7; Rom. 8:14.

Snow: (1) Pure (white); (2) Robe of righteousness (Snow on the earth is like a robe of righteousness on an earthen vessel); (3) Glory; (4) Refreshing; (5) God's Word; (6) Sin (Leprosy is the bodily equivalent of sin); (7) Inappropriate honor (snow in summer); (8) Timely message.

Also see *Snowballs* and *Snowman*.

(1) Job 9:30 (KJV); Ps. 51:7; Isa. 1:18; Lam. 4:7; (2) Matt. 28:3; (Job 37:6; 2 Cor. 4:7); (3) Dan. 7:9; (Mark 9:3; 2 Pet. 1:17); Rev. 1:14; (4) Prov. 25:13;(5) Isa. 55:10-11; (6) Exod. 4:6; Num. 12:10; 2 Kings 5:27; (7) Prov. 26:1; (8) Prov. 25:13.

Snowball(s): (1) Godly words without impact; (2) Words lacking power; (3) Words without love; (4) Empty words; (5) Playful words; (6) Cold words; (7) Escalating issue (grows bigger as it is rolled); (8) Out of control (something snowballing).

Also see *Snow* and *Snowman.*
(1) 1 Sam. 3:19; (2) 1 Cor. 2:4; (3) Matt. 24:12; (4) Eph. 5:6; (5) Gen. 26:8 (KJV); (6) Matt. 12:34; 24:12: (7) 1 Sam. 14:13-16; Pr. 17:14; Acts 4:17-20; 12:24; 19:20; (8) Job 1:13-20.

Snowman: (1) Cold-hearted person; (2) Righteous person.
(1) Matt. 24:12; (2) Ps. 51:7,10.

Snowshoes: (1) Gospel ministry; (2) Shoes of peace; (3) Walking a righteous path.
Also see *Snow.*
(1) Eph. 6:15.

Soap: (1) Confession and repentance; (2) Cleansing; (3) Regular application of the Word of God.
(1-2) 1 John 1:9; (2-3) John 13:10.

Soccer: See *Football Game* and *Sport.*

Socks: (1) Little things that affect your walk; (2) Daily choice; (3) May speak about your past or your future walk; (4) Things that are held close to you (personal); (5) Clothing your feet to determine your path; (6) Preparation; (7) Walking in the flesh (no socks); (8) Unprepared (no socks); (9) Disorderly (odd socks); (10) The Gospel; (11) The old way of doing things (old socks).
Consider the color of the socks.
Also see *Feet, Shoes, Sole, Toes,* and *Walk.*
(1) John 11:9-10; 12:35; 1 John 1:6-7; (2) Josh. 24:15; (3) John 6:66; 7:1; (4) Acts 9:31; (5) John 8:12; 21:18; (6) Eph. 6:15; (7) 2 Cor. 10:3; (8) Eph. 6:15; (9) 2 Thess. 3:6,11; (10) Eph. 6:15; (11) John 8:4-5.

Socket: (1) Leverage; (2) Support or strength; (3) Foundation.
(1-2) Gen. 32:25; (3) Exod. 26:19,21; Song 5:15 (KJV).

Soda: (1) The Holy Spirit (as a well of springing water); (2) Gaining spiritual insight.
Also see *Effervescence.*
(1) John 4:14; (2) Prov. 16:22.

Sofa: (1) Comfort; (2) God (as comfort); (3) Complacent.
Also see *Armchair, Couch,* and *Seat.*
(1-2) 2 Cor. 1:3; (3) Luke 12:18-19.

Software: (1) The human spirit; (2) The Holy Spirit.
Also see *Computer, Hard Drive, Hardware,* and *Laptop.*
(1) Gen. 2:7; John 6:63; (2) Col. 2:9.

Soil: (1) A heart or hearts.
Also see *Earth.*
(1) Matt. 13:19; Mark 4:15; Luke 8:15.

Soldier: (1) Spiritual warrior; (2) Spiritual warfare; (3) May speak of a battle in the mind; (4) Bringing your thoughts into line with God's Word in preparation for battle; (5) Angel; (6) Christ.
See *Battle* and *Weapon*.
(1) Judg. 6:12; (2) Eph. 6:12-18; (3) 2 Cor. 10:3-5; (4) 1 Pet. 1:13; (5) Dan. 10:13; (6) Josh. 5:13-15.

Sole (Foot): (1) Dominion; (2) Promise; (3) Step out in faith; (4) Resting place; (5) Lower extremity; (6) Dwelling place (home).
(1-2) Deut. 11:24; Josh. 1:3; 1 Kings 5:3; Mal. 4:3; (3) Josh. 3:13; (4) Gen. 8:9; Deut. 28:65; (5) 2 Sam. 14:25; Job 2:7; Isa. 1:6; (6) Ezek. 43:7.

Solid: (1) Strong; (2) True/Truth; (3) Foundation.
(1) Gal. 2:9; (2) 1 Tim. 3:15; (3) Matt. 7:25; Luke 6:48.

Someone Giving Directions: (1) An angel.
(1) Matt. 1:20; 2:13,19-20; Acts 10:3-6.

Somersault: (1) Moving in the Spirit; (2) Celebration; (3) Excitement; (4) Returning to past (backflip).
(1) 2 Sam. 6:16,20-23; (cf. Matt. 12:31); (2-3) 1 Sam. 18:6; Jer. 31:13; (4) Acts 7:39.

Son: (1) Jesus Christ; (2) Mature believer; (3) Your future; (4) Natural son; (5) The meaning of your son's name (see Name and Place Dictionary); (6) Promise; (7) Strength; (8) Resurrection/Revival; (9) Aspect of your personality.
(1) John 3:16; (2) Heb. 2:10; Rom. 8:14; (3) Job 21:8; (6) Gal. 4:22-23; (7) Deut. 21:17; (8) Luke 20:36; Rom. 1:4; (9) As seen in your children; John 8:44.

Son-in-Law: (1) Believer not free in the Spirit (bound by law). Also see *Brother-in-Law* and *Father-in-Law*.
(1) 2 Cor. 3:17; Heb. 2:10; Tit. 3:9-10.

Sore: See *Spot*.

Sorrow: (1) Repentance to life (godly sorrow); (2) Self-pity for being caught leads to death (worldly sorrow).
(1-2) 2 Cor. 7:10.

Soup: (1) Simple teaching of the Word; (2) Fleshly sell-out.
(1) Heb. 5:12-14; (2) Gen. 25:29-34.

Sour: (1) Not ripe; (2) Complaint (sour grapes); (3) Harlotry; (4) Rebellion; (5) Bitter.
(1) Isa. 18:5; (2) Ezek. 18:2; (3-4) Hos. 4:18 (NKJV & KJV); (5) Heb. 12:15.

South: (1) Place away from God; (2) Place of restoration; (3) Place of testing (source of hot wind); (4) Going back into the world (heading south); (5) Consider aspects in your own environment relating to south.
Also see *Down*, *North*, and *Steps (Going Down)*.

(1) Ps. 48:2; 75:6; (2) Ps. 126:4 (Streams in the south fill suddenly after storms); (3) Song 4:16 (the south wind in Israel is hot because it comes off the equator; in the southern hemisphere, the north wind will be hot); (4) Gen. 12:9-10; Num. 14:3-4; Josh. 15:4.

Sow (verb): (1) Speaking or preaching the Word of God; (2) What is sown to the flesh will reap flesh, what is sown to the Spirit will reap Spirit: (3) What you are putting into your life (investment); (4) Righteousness.

Also see *Investment*, *Plant*, and *Seed*.

(1) Matt. 13:3-4, 18-19; Mark 4:14; (2-3) Gal. 6:8; (4) James 3:18.

Sower: (1) God; (2) Jesus Christ; (3) Minister; (4) Believer; (5) Devil; (6) Person (good or evil).

(1) Matt. 13:3,19,24; (2) Matt. 13:37; (3-4) 1 Cor. 9:11; 2 Cor. 9:6; James 3:18; (5) Matt. 13:39; (6) Gal. 6:7-8.

Spa: (1) Refreshing in the Holy Spirit; (2) Refreshing Holy Spirit-led ministry.

(1) 1 Sam. 16:23; (2) 1 Cor. 16:17-18.

Space: (1) Eternity; (2) The heavenlies.

Also see *Spaceship* and *Space Suit*.

(1) Isa. 57:15; (2) Gen. 1:14-15.

Spaceship: (1) Rapture; (2) Heavenly encounter.

Also see *Starship Enterprise*.

(1-2) 2 Kings 2:11.

Space Suit: (1) In the Spirit; (2) Armor of God.

Also see *Astronaut* and *Space*.

(1-2) Eph. 6:11-18.

Spade: (1) Turning new ground; (2) New season in God; (3) Warning to remove the hardness of heart; (4) Open your heart; (5) Time to seek God (as in, "digging deep"); (6) Seed time; (7) Applying the Word of God to your heart (digging deep); (8) The Word of God.

Also see *Digging* and *Shovel*.

(1) Isa. 42:9; 43:19; (2) Song 2:11; (3-4) Jer. 4:3-4 (5) Gen. 26:18; Hos. 10:12; (6) Gen. 8:22; Hos. 10:12; (7) Luke 6:48; (8) Matt. 13:21; Mark 4:17 (unearthed by the Word); 2 Cor. 4:7; Heb. 4:12.

Spark(s): (1) Fiery dart; (2) A little word that ignites a fire of controversy; (3) Conflict; (4) Trouble or labor; (5) Troublemaker; (6) The human spirit; (7) The beginning of judgment; (8) Self-destruction; (9) Anguish, torment, or sorrow; (10) Electrician; (11) The glory of God.

(1-2) Job 41:19; Eph. 6:16; James 3:5-6; (3) Exod. 11:7b; Lev. 10:10; 11:47a; Acts 15:39; (4-6) Job 5:7; (6) Job 18:5 (KJV); (7) Isa. 1:31; (8-9) Isa. 50:11; (10) Slang term for electrician; (11) Isa. 24:15 (KJV).

Sparrow: (1) Believer; (2) Cared for by God; (3) Someone who finds security in God's Presence; (4) Feelings of insignificance; (5) Alone, lonely, or loner; (6) Not at rest (flitting sparrow).

Also see *Birds*.

(1-2) Matt. 10:29, 31; (3) Ps. 84:3; (4) Matt. 10:29; Luke 12:6-7; (5) Ps. 102:7: (6) Prov. 26:2.

Spear: (1) Threat; (2) Word with piercing momentum; (2) Someone trying to nail you; (3) God's piercing Word.

(1) 1 Sam. 17:7-10; 19:10-11; (2) Ps. 57:4 (teeth = spears); (Prov. 30:14 [teeth & Eph. 6:17]); 1 Sam. 17:7,43-44; 1 Sam. 19:10-11; (3) Luke 2:35.

Speed: (1) Accelerating to destiny; (2) Carried in the Spirit; (3) Indicates power; (4) Indicative of a powerful ministry; (5) Soon (ASAP); (6) Quickly; (7) Without restraint; (8) Without delay; (9) At once (immediately); (10) Expulsion; (11) A salutation (greeting/farewell) of blessing a person with joyful health and happiness (Godspeed).

Also see *Speeding (Auto)*, *Time*, and *Urgency*.

(1) Exod. 12:11; Josh. 4:10; 1 Sam. 17:48; (2-4) 1 Kings 18:46; Acts 8:39-40; (5) Acts 17:15; (6) Gen. 24:12 (KJV); Luke 18:8; (7) Joel 3:4; Isa. 5:26; (8-9) Eccles. 8:11; Zech. 8:21; (10) Exod. 12:33; (11) 2 John 1:10-11 (KJV).

Speedboat: (1) Accelerating the ministry (accelerating to destiny); (2) Powerful ministry; (3) Quickly or suddenly.

Also see *Boat*, *Ship*, and *Speed*.

(1) Gen. 41:14; 45:13b; (2) Isa. 5:26-30a; (3) Job 9:26.

Speed (Drug): (1) Offense; (2) Trying to jump ahead of the timing of God; (3) Counterfeit spirit.

Also see *Drug-Taking* and *Needle*.

(1) Isa. 28:16b; (2) 2 Sam. 18:19-23, 29-30; (3) John 6:63.

Speeding (Auto): (1) Trying to jump ahead of the timing of God.

Also see *Speed*.

(1) 2 Sam. 18:19-23, 29-30.

Spew: See *Vomit*.

Spice: (1) Fragrant anointing; (2) Fragrant prayer; (3) Romance; (4) Desire; (5) Oil; (6) Enliven (spice up); (7) Praise; (8) Heart (bed of spices); (9) Praise and adoration.

(1) Exod. 25:6; 30:23-25; Mark 16:1; (2) Exod. 30:34-37 (cf. Ps. 141:2a; Rev. 8:3-4); Exod. 35:8, 28; (3-4) Song 4:16; Prov. 7:17; (5) In the 1700-1800s, spice was the commodity all the nations sought after; today oil has taken its place; (6) As in "The team played woefully; we need to spice it up a bit in the next half" or "They need to spice up their love life"; (7) Song 4:16; (8) Song 6:2; (9) Song 8:14 (mountain of spices).

Spider: (1) An issue or stronghold; (2) An issue that raises fear or has the potential to be messy to deal with; (3) Threat (with a danger of entanglement); (4) Deceiver (web = lies); (5) One who casts spells; (6) False trust; (7) Tenacious; (8) One from whom it is difficult to disentangle or extricate oneself; (9) A clever one; (10) Conflict; (11) A very big spider may mean death; (12) Death or danger (black widow); (13) Red (or red-backed) spider means sin; (14) Red spider can be the early stages of pregnancy (medical imaging); (15) Killing a red spider may refer to an abortion; (16) Influential deceiver (long-legged spider); (17) Long-standing issue (long-legged spider); (18) If bitten by a spider, it means venomous words against you; (19) Curse (yellow spider); (20) Spirit of fear (flying spider); (21) Conflict in the heavenlies (flying spider); (22) Religious spirit (white spider); (23) Evil spirit; (24) Predatory person/organization/church/issue (huntsman spider); (25) Condemning/blaming husband with words (black widow spider).
Also see *Bite/Bitten* and *Snake*.
(1) 2 Cor. 10:4-5; (2) (3) Acts 4:17,21,29; 1 Pet. 2:23; (4) Isa. 59:4-5; (5) 1 Kings 19:2; (6) Job 8:14-15; (7) Prov. 30:28; (8) Gen. 31:27; (9) Prov. 30:28; (13) Isa. 59:5-6; (16) Prov. 30:28 (as in Jezebel); (17) Mark 5:25; (18) 1 Kings 21:9-10, 13; (19) See *Yellow*; (20) 2 Tim. 1:7; (21) Eph. 6:12; (22) Matt. 23:27; (23) 1 Tim. 3:6; 2 Tim. 2:26; (24) Ps. 91:3; 124:7; Hos. 9:8; (25) Prov. 21:9.

Spiked Drink(s): (1) Manipulation; (2) Spellbound.
(1-2) Gen. 19:31-35; (2) Prov. 20:1.

Spine: (1) Spirit (center of being).
(1) Mic. 2:7; Eph. 3:16.

Spinning: (1) About to collapse; (2) Drunk; (3) Lacking faith (trying to make it happen) (4) Not putting the Kingdom first; (5) Out of control (driven by circumstance); (6) Lying; (7) Laying a trap (spinning thread).
Also see *Whirlwind*.
(1) Isa. 24:20; (2) Ps. 107:27; (3-4) Matt. 6:28-30; Luke 12:27-28; (5) James 1:6; (6) As in "He's spinning you a yarn"; (7) Isa. 59:5-6; Mark 12:13.

Spiral: (1) Ascending in the Spirit (spiral ascent).
(1) Isa. 40:31; Gen. 28:12; John 1:51.

Spirit of Poverty: (1) Withholding when things are tight and there is a call to bless; (2) Self-survival mentality; (3) Robbing your own blessing.
Also see *Pigeon*.
(1-3) Prov. 3:27-28; 11:24-25; (cf. 1 Kings 17:10-14; Matt: 14:15-21; 15:32-38).

Spit/Spittle: (1) Word of God; (2) Anointing; (3) Insult; (4) Offense.
(1-2) John 9:6; (3-4) Matt. 26:67; 27:30.

Splinter: (1) Something that gets under your flesh and is irritating you; (2) Fleshly Christian who gets under your skin.
(1) Job 2:7; 3:1; (2) Gen. 13:11; Matt.15:23.

Sponge: (1) Thirsting for God (thirsty heart); (2) Cleansing; (3) Soaking; (4) All word, no Spirit (watering plants using a sponge).
Also see *Hose*.
(1) Ps. 42:2; John 19:28; (2) John 13:3-4; (3) Joel 2:28; (4) Ps. 33:31b.

Spoon: (1) Heart; (2) A measure or amount; (3) Feeding (serving up); (4) Stirring (good or evil); (5) Someone who is used for a short time (plastic spoon); (6) Superficially or temporarily receiving (plastic spoon).
(1) Exod. 25:29; Num. 4:7 (Here the Hebrew word for spoon, *kaph*, describes a concave vessel); (2) Num. 7:14,20,26ff; (3) 1 Kings 17:11; (4) Luke 23:5; Acts 6:12; 13:50; (5) Matt. 11:7-10; (6) John 6:66; Acts 8:13.

Sport: (1) Moving in faith; (2) Spiritual warfare.
Also see *Ball, Bat, Cricket, Football Game, Sports Store, Umpire*, and *Winning*.
(1) Heb. 12:1; (2) Eph. 6:12.

Sports Store: (1) Church; (2) Place where the anointing is released.
(1-2) As the place of equipping the saints to run the race of faith; Eph. 4:11-12; Heb. 12:1-2.

Spot: (1) Moral blemish; (2) Defilement; (3) Irresponsible; (4) Blemish (sin); (5) Without godly fear; (6) Stain; (7) Works of the flesh; (8) Holding something back (not wholly given to God).
(1) Eph. 5:27; (2) Jude 1:23 (cf. KJV & NKJV); (3) 1 Tim. 6:14; (4) Heb. 9:14;1 Pet. 1:19; 2 Pet. 2:13-14; (5-6) Jude 1:12; (7) Jude 1:23 (KJV); (8) Exod. 12:5 (the Hebrew word for "without blemish" means "entirely or whole").

Spotlight: (1) Bringing things from darkness into light (revealing issues/sin); (2) Salvation; (3) Your time to perform; (4) High profile; (5) All eyes are on you; (6) Caught unawares; (7) Suddenly exposed.
Also see *Light* and *Stage*.
(1) Rom. 13:12; 1 Cor. 4:5; 1 John 1:5-7; (2) John 1:9; 2 Cor. 4:6; Eph. 5:8;1 Pet. 2:9; (3-4) Acts 9:3; (5) 1 Sam. 9:20b; 17:48; (6-7) Acts 9:3.

Spray: (1) Holy Spirit (Breath of God); (2) Evidence of a storm (enemy resistance); (3) Angry or emotional words.
Also see *Anointing* and *Perfume*.
(1) Gen.1:2; Job 33:4; John 3:8; Rev. 1:15; (2) Matt. 14:24; (3) 1 Sam. 20:30; Prov. 18:4.

Spring (noun): (1) Bouncing back or returning; (2) Comfort; (3) Young and enthusiastic (spring lamb); (4) Launching out.
(1) Ps. 78:34; Luke 4:14; (2) Job 7:13; Ps. 119:82; (3) Luke 1:41; (4) 2 Sam.11:1a.

Spring (season): (1) Time to act; (2) Fruitfulness; (3) Time to fight spiritually; (4) Summer (harvest) at hand; (5) Jesus's return at hand.
(1-2) Song 2:10-13; (3) 2 Sam. 11:1; 1 Kings 20:22; (4-5) Luke 21:29-30.

Spring Up: There are positive and negative aspects (+): (1) Spiritual enlivening/awakening; (2) Holy Spirit overflowing; (3) Grow; (4) A new thing; (5) Healing; (6) Truth; (-): (7) Lack of heart; (8) Choked by weeds; (9) Root of bitterness.
(1) Gen. 26:19 (KJV); 35:1-3; Isa. 45:8; Mark 4:8, 27; Luke 8:8; Acts 3:8; Heb. 11:11-12 (KJV); (2) Num. 21:17; John 4:14; (3) Job 38:27; Heb. 7:14 (KJV); (4) Isa. 42:9; 43:19; (5) Isa. 58:8; (6) Ps. 85:11; (7) Matt. 13:5; Mark 4:5; Luke 8:6; (8) Matt. 13:7,26; Luke 8:7; (9) Heb. 12:15.

Sprinkle: (1) Cleansing; (2) Purification of the flesh; (3) Sanctification; (4) Forgiveness; (5) Covenant; (6) Salvation; (7) Clear conscience; (8) Call to exercise confident faith.
Also see *Shower*, *Rain*, and *Water*.
(1) Heb. 10:22; (2-3) Ezek. 36:25; Heb. 9:13; (3-4) Heb. 9:19-22; (5-6) Isa. 52:15; Heb.12:24; (7-8) Heb. 10:22; 11:28.

Sprout: (1) Resurrection; (2) New life; (3) Hope.
(1-3) Job 14:7-9.

Spud Bag: See *Beanbag*.

Spud Gun: (1) Words without power and effect.
(1) 1 Sam. 3:19b (this is the opposite).

Spy: (1) Prophet; (2) Seeing in the Spirit; (3) Gathering intelligence about the enemy.
Also see *Staring*, *U2*, and *View*.
(1-3) 2 Kings 6:8-12.

Square: (1) Unspiritual (not of God); (2) Legalism; (3) Religious; (4) Not changing; (5) Global; (6) All-encompassing (complete coverage); (7) Regulated or regulation.
Also see *Circle*, *Round*, and *Wheel*.
(1) Compare: Ezek. 1:20; Heb. 9:14 (in the sense that the eternal Spirit is never-ending like a circle); (2-3) Lev. 19:9; 23:22 (this is grace); Lev. 19:27; 21:5; (4) In the sense that a round object is capable of rolling whereas a square one is not; (5) Isa. 11:12; Rev. 7:1; as in "the four corners of the globe"; (6) Ezek. 7:2; (7) A square has regular sides.

Squash (Racket Ball): (1) Indirect communication.
Also see *Ball*, *Bat*, and *Sport*.
(1) Prov. 16:13.

Squid: (1) Spineless (not standing up for important issues).
Also see *Octopus*.
(1) Ps. 5:5; 106:23.

Stable (Horse): (1) House of an unbeliever/living as the unsaved; (2) Living in the world/flesh.
Also see *Barn*.
(1-2) Deut. 17:16; Isa. 31:1.

Staff: (1) The Word of God; (2) Strength or support; (3) Pledge; (4) Bread (The staff, *matteh* in Hebrew, was used to walk, i.e., support life; therefore, figuratively it also meant "bread"); (5) Bearer of fruit; (6) Tool of discipline/judgment; (7) Shaft of an arrow or spear; (8) Authority or rule; (9) Care and comfort; (10) Person, church, or nation; (11) Tool or talent for the purposes of God; (12) Signifies readiness for journey (staff in hand); (13) May indicate agedness (i.e., need of support).

Also see *Rod* and *Sticks*.

(1) Exod. 14:16 (cf. Heb. 4:12); 1 Sam. 17:40,43,45 (cf. 2 Cor. 10:3-5); 2 Sam. 23:21; Mark 6:8; Heb. 11:21; (2) Exod. 21:19; Isa 36:6; Ps. 23:4; (3) Gen. 38:18,25; (4) Lev. 26:26 (KJV); Ps. 105:16 (KJV); Ezek. 5:16 (KJV); 14:13 (KJV); (5) Num. 13:23; 17:8; (6) Num. 22:27; Isa. 10:5; (7) 1 Sam. 17:7; (8) 2 Kings 4:29,31; Isa. 14:5; (9) Ps. 23:4; (10) Isa. 36:6 (whoever you lean on); (11) Exod. 4:2; 2 Kings 4:29; (12) Exod. 12:11; (13) Zech. 8:4.

Stage (Theater): (1) In the public eye; (2) Success; (3) Given a public profile (in the arena/under the spotlight); (4) Façade (being staged).

Also see *Pulpit* and *Spotlight*.

(1) Luke 1:80; (2) Josh. 1:8; (3) Gen. 37:9; 42:6; Luke 1:80; (4) Matt. 2:4,8.

Stain: (1) Offense; (2) Contempt; (3) Pollute; (4) Anger; (5) Sin.

(1) Matt. 15:11-12 (defile = unclean, pollute, make common); Jer. 16:18; (2-3) Isa. 23:9; (4) Isa. 63:3; (5) Zech. 3:3-4.

Stained Glass (Window): (1) Religious spirit; (2) Seeing the promises of God in the glory (refers to seeing through multi-colored glass).

(1) John 12:42-46 (having a tainted view of things); (2) Gen. 9:12-13; 37:3; Rev. 4:3.

Stairs: See *Steps*.

Stakes (Tent Pegs): (1) Certainty; (2) Expansion (strengthening or moving stakes).

(1) Isa. 33:20; (2) Isa. 54:2-3.

Stalled Vehicle: (1) Ministry in limbo; (2) On hold; (3) Doing things your way, not God's way; (4) Stumbling; (5) Heart preparation (test); (6) Awaiting the timing of God; (7) Fear; (8) Not seeing in the Spirit (wrong perception); (9) A call to exercise faith/ spiritual authority; (10) Something getting in the way, such as: (11) Religion; (12) Greater pressing needs; (13) Opposition; (14) Obstructed by the devil; (15) Problems in family relationships; (16) Emotional issues overriding obedience; (17) Loss of heart.

(1) 1 Kings 19:4; (2) Isa. 49:2; (3-4) 2 Sam. 6:3-10; (cf. 1 Chron. 15:11-13); (5) Gen. 42:16; (6) John 11:6; Isa. 49:2; (7) 1 Kings 19:2-3; (8) 1 Kings 19:9-10; (9) Exod. 14:13-16; (10) Any of the following: (11) Luke 11:52; (12) Rom. 15:22; (13) Mark 6:48; Gal. 5:7-12; (14) Neh. 4:1-18; 1 Thess. 2:18; (15) 1 Pet. 3:7; (16) Gen. 24:55-56; (17) Neh. 4:10-12.

Stamp: See *Postage Stamp*.

Stand/ing: (1) Ready to serve; (2) Standing one's ground in God's might; (3) Standing in faith; (4) Honoring; (5) Spiritual warfare; (6) Uprightness of spirit; (7) Being aligned with/rubbing shoulders with (positive or negative).

Also see *Laying Down* and *Upright.*

(1) Zech. 6:5 (KJV); (2) Eph. 6:13 (This is seen as the third of three progressive steps. [Sit > Walk > Stand]); (3) 2 Cor. 1:24b; (4) Acts 7:55-56; (5) Eph. 6:13; (6) Ps. 51:10 (KJV); (7) Ps. 1:1 (this verse shows the second of three progressively negative steps away from godliness. [Walking > Standing > Sitting]).

Star(s): (1) Believers or children of God; (2) Angels; (3) Satan; (4) Jesus Christ; (5) Evil spirits (fallen angels); (6) Someone who is a righteous and wise soul winner; (7) Revival (seeing lots of stars); (8) Fame (stardom); (9) Glorious birth; (10) Appointed time; (11) Revelation; (12) Falling Christians (falling stars); (13) Revival; (14) Promise.

Also see *Shooting Star* and *Sun.*

(1) Gen. 15:5-6; Phil. 2:15; (2) Ps. 33:6; Rev. 1:20; (3) Isa. 14:12 (lucifer = day star); (4) Rev. 22:16 (the bright and morning star); (5) Rev. 12:4; (6) Dan. 12:3; (7) Gen. 15:5-6; (8) Rev. 22:16; Matt. 14:1; (9) Matt. 2:2,10-11; Luke 2:8-16; (10) Gen. 1:14-18; Esther 4:14; (11) Gen. 22:17; (12) Exod. 32:13; Gal. 3:7; (13-14) Gen. 15:5.

Staring: (1) Seeing in the Spirit; (2) Prophesying; (3) Seer; (4) Love; (5) May be a sign of an idolatrous heart; (6) Fleeting riches (staring at worldly goods); (7) Turning or looking to the world.

(1) Num. 24:3-4; Mark 10:21; Acts 13:9-10; (2) Ezek. 6:2; 13:17; 20:46; 21:2; (3) 1 Sam. 9:9; (4) Jer. 24:6; (5) Ezek. 14:4; (6) Prov. 23:4-5; (7) Jer. 42:15,17.

Starship Enterprise: (1) Pioneering heavenly realities.

(1) Josh. 3:4b; mission: "Boldly go where no man has gone before."

Station Wagon: (1) Family vehicle.

(1) Gen. 46:5.

Statue: (1) Memorial; (2) Person/event of past significance; (3) Someone once alive, but now dead; (4) Idol; (5) Pride (idolizing self); (6) Looking back at the world (pillar of salt); (7) Idol.

(1-2) Josh. 4:7; (3) 1 Sam. 25:37; (4) Dan. 3:1,18; (5) 2 Sam. 18:18; (6) Gen. 19:26; (7) Deut. 4:16; Dan. 3:1,5.

Statue of Liberty: (1) Freedom; (2) Spiritual deliverance.

(1-2) Isa. 61:1; Luke 4:18; 2 Cor. 3:17.

Staying Somewhere: (1) Place of rest and refreshment; (2) Settling down (dwelling) instead of sojourning (pilgrimage); (3) Stopping short of God's intended destiny.

(1) Luke 24:29; (2) Heb. 11:9-10; (3) Num. 13:31.

Steak: See *Meat.*

Steal/Stealing: (1) The devil (thief); (2) Taking from or replacing God's Word; (3) Capturing hearts; (4) Deception; (5) Secretly leave (to "steal away"); (6) Take secretly; (7) Shame; (8) Adultery; (9) Hypocrisy; (10) Need to work; (11) Idolatry; (12) Taking the Lord's name in vain; (13) Earthly treasures (heart centered on earthly cares); (14) Not tithing to the work of God; (15) Not releasing sin at the cross (you carrying something Jesus owns [paid for by the blood]); (16) Doing your own thing on borrowed time (you are a love-slave owned by God).
Also see *Robbery* and *Thief.*
(1) John 10:10; (2) Deut.4:2; Prov. 30:6; Jer. 23:30; Rev. 22:19; (3) 2 Sam. 15:6; (4) Matt. 28:13; Gen. 31:20 (the word *unawares* means "to steal the mind of, deceive, outwit"); (5) Gen. 31:20; (6) Gen. 40:15; 2 Chron. 22:11; (7) 2 Sam. 19:3; (8) Prov. 9:17-18; (9) Rom. 2:21; (10) Eph. 4:28; (11) Gen. 31:19; (12) Prov. 30:9; (13) Matt. 6:19-21; (14) Mal. 3:8; (15-16) 1 Cor. 6:20; Gal. 2:20.

Steam: (1) Anger; (2) Power or powerful; (3) Venting.
(1) Isa. 64:2,5; as in "He was letting off steam"; (2) Job 41:20-22, 31-32; (3) As in "letting off steam."

Steel: (1) Strong; (2) Powerful; (3) Strength of humanity; (4) Human strength.
Also see *Bow* and *Iron.*
(1-4) 2 Sam. 22:35 (KJV); Job 20:24; Ps.18:34.

Steering: (1) In control; (2) Leading; (3) The person steering is often God or the Holy Spirit (known noble character); (4) It may be wrong for us to be steering (i.e., not letting go); (5) If someone of questionable character is steering, it may mean that you are being manipulated, driven, or led.
(1) 1 Kings 19:19; John 21:18; (2) Ps, 23:2-3; (3) Ps. 5:8; 23:2-3; 31:3; John 14:6; 21:18; (4) Prov. 12:15; 14:12; 16:25; 21:2; John 21:18; (5) Prov. 7:25.

Stepping: (1) Moving into your inheritance (stepping through); (2) Overcoming (stepping through); (3) Boldness or courage (stepping out); (4) Stages of growth or development (stepping stones).
Also see *Footsteps* and *Walking.*
(1) Josh. 3:13; (2) Num. 13:30; 1 John 4:4; (3) Acts 4:31; (4) 2 Cor. 3:18.

Stepping Stones: (1) Progressive revelation; (2) Walking on water.
(1) Josh. 1:3; (2) Matt. 14:28.

Steps (Going Down): (1) Stairway to death/hell; (2) Going away from God; (3) Self-indulgence; (4) Being seduced away from God; (5) Loss of heart; (6) Condemned (thrown down stairs/steps); (7) Becoming progressively more ungodly (steps becoming further apart as you go down); (8) Bringing Heaven to earth.
Also see *South* and *Steps (Going Up).*
(1) 1 Sam. 20:3; Prov. 5:5; (2) Ps. 44:18; 73:2; (3) Luke 12:16-21; (4) Prov. 7:25-27; (5) Judg. 20:42-43; (6) 2 Chron. 36:3; Isa. 54:17; Matt. 12:41-42; 2 Pet. 2:6; (7) Ps. 1:1; Prov. 5:3-5; Song 2:15; (8) Matt. 6:10.

Steps (Going Up): (1) Stairway to Heaven/God; (2) Jesus Christ; (3) Flesh; (4) Established by God; (5) Discipleship (effort required); (6) God may be bringing you to a place of being mindful of the things of the Spirit; (7) Growing in the Spirit; (8) Praise; (9) Going from faith to faith/glory to glory; (10) A church.
Also see *Angels Ascending, Footsteps, Ladder, Lift, Steps (Going Down)*, and *Walking*.
(1-2) Gen. 28:12; John 1:51; (3) Exod. 20:26; (cf. 1 Kings 10:19-20 (six steps) with Ezek. 40:22 [seven steps]); (4) Ps. 37:23; (5) Matt. 5:1-2; (6-7) Isa. 40:31; Eph. 2:6; (8) Ps. 68:4 (AMP); (9) Rom. 1:17; 2 Cor. 3:18; (10) Matt. 16:18-19; John 1:51 (as the Body of Christ); Eph. 3:10.

Step-Sister: (1) Church on another level (positive or negative); (2) Church merger/transfer growth; (3) Fellow believer from another church.
Also see *Sister.*
(1) Rev. 3:8-10; (2) Judg. 21:21; Acts 15:22; (3) Acts 10:34-35.

Stereo: (1) Witness of the Spirit; (2) Witness; (3) Word (double-edged sword); (4) Encountering revelation.
See *Radio.*
(1) Mark 16:20; Rom. 8:16; (2) Matt. 18:16; (3) Heb. 4:12; (4) 2 Cor. 12:1-4.

Sticks: (1) Discipline; (2) The Word of God; (3) An individual or group of people; (4) United (sticks bunched or tied together); (5) Turning the Word of God to their advantage (spinning sticks); (6) Firewood.
(1) Prov. 13:24; (2) 1 Sam. 17:40,43 (here the staff is called a "stick"); Exod. 14:16 (here the rod or staff (Hebrew: *matteh*) divides); (3-4) Ezek. 37:16-22; (5) 1 Tim. 6:3-5; 2 Pet. 2:1; 3:16; (6) 1 Kings 17:10,12; Acts 28:3.

Stilts: (1) Making yourself look more spiritual (higher); (2) Claiming to be more than you really are spiritually; (3) Elevating self; (4) Spiritual giant.
(1) 1 Sam. 15:17,21; (2) 1 Sam. 9:2; 2 Chron. 26:16; Acts 8:9; (3) Acts 8:9,19-20; (4) 1 Sam. 17:43-51.

Sting: (1) Painful consequences; (2) Deadly consequences; (3) Sin; (4) Hurt; (5) Rebuke; (6) Criticism.
Also see *Bees.*
(1) Prov. 23:32; (2-3) 1 Cor. 15:55-56; (4) Rev. 9:10; (5) Ezek. 5:15 (NIV); as in "He gave them a stinging rebuke"; (6) Ps. 64:3-4.

Stingray: (1) Spirit of death.
(1) 1 Cor. 15:55-56.

Stink: See *Odor* and *Smell.*

Stirred/Troubled Waters: (1) Stirring in one's heart; (2) Disturb/Agitate; (3) Revelation (whirlpool); (4) Healing (whirlpool); (5) Dark night of the soul.
(1-2) Jonah 2:3-7; John 6:16-21; (3-4) John 5:4,7; (5) Ps. 42:7; Jon. 2:3.

Stolen: See *Steal/Stealing* and *Thief*.

Stomach: See *Belly*.

Stone(s): (1) Heart; (2) Words; (3) Believers; (4) People; (5) Jesus Christ or God; (6) Flesh; (7) Strong enough to build on; (8) Hardened heart or dead; (9) Blockage of heart (well); (10) Witness; (11) Memorial; (12) Law; (13) Death or dead; (14) Stumbling offense; (15) Judgment (throwing stones).

Also see *Brick*, *Foundation*, *Precious Stones*, and *Stony*.

(1) Prov. 3:3; 2 Cor. 3:3; (2) 1 Sam. 17:40,49; Matt. 16:17-19; (3) Eph. 2:20; 1 Pet. 2:5-8; (4) Matt. 24:2; Luke 19:40, 43-44; John 2:6; Eccles. 3:5; (5) Gen. 28:11-18; John 1:51 (Jacob's actions symbolize the death [sleep] and resurrection [pillar]); Gen. 49:24; Dan. 2:34-35; (6) Ezek. 11:19; 36:26; (7) John 1:42; (8) 1 Sam. 25:37-38; Job 41:24; Ezek. 11:19; 36:26; Zech. 7:12 (KJV); (9) Gen. 29:2-3, 8-10; (10) Gen. 31:46-49; Josh. 24:26-27; (11) Josh. 4:7-9; (12) Josh. 8:32; (13) John 8:59; 10:31; (14) Isa. 8:14; (15) Lev. 20:27; John 8:59; 10:31.

Stone(s) (A Stone's Throw): (1) The distance a voice heard.

(1) Luke 22:41.

Stone(s) (Cut & Uncut Stone): (1) Spirit ordained (uncut stone); (2) Human works (cut stone); (3) Idolatry (cut stone).

(1-2) Josh. 8:31; Isa. 37:19; Lam. 3:9; (3) Dan. 5:4,23.

Stone(s) (Falling on a Stone): (1) Brokenness.

(1) Matt. 21:44.

Stone(s) (Stone Falling Upon): (1) Crushing; (2) Grinding; (3) Judgment.

(1-3) Matt. 21:44.

Stone(s) (Throwing/Slinging Stones): (1) Words.

(1) Judg. 20:16; 2 Sam. 16:6,13.

Stone(s) (White Stone): (1) Pure heart; (2) New name.

(1-2) Rev. 2:17.

Stoney: (1) Hardened heart; (2) No depth; (3) No heart experience; (4) Wilt under pressure; (5) Offended in affliction and persecution.

(1) Ezek.11:19; Zech. 7:11-12; (2-5) Matt. 13:5-6; Mark 4:5-6, 16-17.

Store: See *Shop* and *Warehouse*.

Store Clerk: (1) Pastor; (2) Hired shepherd.

Also see *Salesman*.

(1) Matt. 18:12-13 (keeping account of the stock); (2) John 10:12-13.

Stork: (1) Timing of God (sensitive to the seasons); (2) Revival (mass immigration); (3) Settled in righteousness.

Also see *Birds* and *Fir Tree*.

(1-2) Jer. 8:7; (3) Ps. 104:17.

Storm: (1) Trouble; (2) Test; (3) Adversity; (4) Judgment; (5) Purging or separating; (6) Words against you (opposition); (7) Spiritual opposition.
(1) Ps. 107:25-26,28; (2) Mark 4:37,40; Luke 8:23-25; (3) Isa. 25:4; (4) Ps. 83:14-15; Isa. 28:2; 29:6; Jer. 23:19-20; 25:32; Ezek. 13:13; (5) Job 21:18; (6) Ps. 55:3,8; (7) Mark 4:35-37.

Storm Clouds: Forecasting and foreseeing of imminent: (1) Trouble; (2) Test; (3) Adversity; (4) Opposition; (5) Judgment.
Also see *Storm* for Scriptures.

Stove: See *Oven*.

Straight: (1) Of God; (2) Faithful spiritual progress; (3) Trusting God; (4) Prepared or open hearts; (5) Without deviation or detour; (6) Upright in spirit; (7) Resolve to go ahead; (8) Not turning aside; (9) Righteous; (10) Obedient.
Also see *Upright*.
(1) James 1:17; (2) Prov. 3:5-6; John 1:23; (3) Prov. 3:5-6 ("He shall direct your paths" = "make straight your paths"); (4) Isa. 40:3-4; Matt. 3:3; Mark 1:3; John 1:23; (5) Acts 16:11; 21:1; (6) Luke 13:11-13; (7) Heb. 12:12-13; (8) 1 Sam. 6:12; Prov. 4:25; (9) Ezek. 1:7; (10) Ezek. 1:12.

Straitjacket: (1) Unable to do anything about the situation (helpless); (2) Unable to do anything in your own strength; (3) Under control; (4) Disarmed or wounded; (5) No threat; (6) Controlling spirit; (7) Loss of strength and influence; (8) Wild and out of control; (9) Fool.
Also see *Arms*.
(1) Lam. 1:14; (2) Judg. 15:12-14; Dan. 3:21,23-27; Eph. 6:10-11; (3-4) 2 Sam. 23:21; 1 Kings 22:34; (5) Judg. 15:12-14; (6) 1 Kings 21:7; Eccles. 7:26; (7) 1 Kings 13:4; (8) Mark 5:3-5; (9) Prov. 7:22b; 14:16-17a; 20:3.

Strange: (1) Foreign; (2) Unrecognized/not known/disguised; (3) Not of God; (4) Not home; (5) Worldly; (6) Profane; (7) False; (8) Wronged; (9) Offensive; (10) Liar; (11) Non-believing; (12) Unusual; (13) Homosexuality.
Also see *Foreign*, *Stranger*, and *Unfamiliar*.
(1) Gen. 35:2,4 (KJV); Exod. 2:22; Ps. 137:4 (KJV); (2) Gen. 42:7 Josh. 24:23 (KJV); Ps. 114:1; Acts 17:20; (3) Gen. 35:2,4 (KJV); Exod. 30:9; Lev. 10:1; Heb. 13:9; (4) Exod. 2:22; Heb. 11:9-10 (KJV); (5) Exod. 22:21; Deut. 32:12; Josh. 24:20 (KJV); (6) Lev. 10:1 (cf. KJV & NKJV); (7) Deut. 32:16; (8) Job 19:3 (cf. KJV & NKJV); (9) Job 19:17 (cf. KJV & NKJV); (10) Ps. 144:7,11; (11) Prov. 2:16-17; 6:23-24; 22:14; 27:13; (12) 1 Pet. 4:4, 12; (13) Jude 1:7.

Stranger: (1) Non-believer (not of the household of faith); (2) Not belonging; (3) Christ (If Christ appears as a stranger, it is either a test, as per the Scripture below, or a serious warning because it says you do not know Him); (4) Angel; (5) Sojourner or pilgrim; (6) Not of the family (alien); (7) Not at home; (8) An outcast; (9) One without their own provision; (10) Not yourself; (11) Not known or not knowing; (12) Not from the "in crowd."
Also see *Aliens, Foreign, Foreigner*, and *Strange*.
(1) Gen. 17:12 (KJV); Exod. 12:42-43,48 (KJV); 29:33 (KJV); Lev. 22:25 (KJV); Deut. 17:15 (KJV); Ps. 18:45 (KJV); Ps. 54:3; Prov. 2:16-17 (KJV); 6:1; 11:15; 27:13; Isa. 1:7; Luke 17:18 (KJV); Eph. 2:19; (2) Gen. 15:13; (3) Matt. 25:38,40,45; (4) Heb. 13:2; (5) Gen. 17:8; 23:4 (KJV); 28:4; 36:7; 37:1; Lev. 25:23; Exod. 6:4; Heb. 11:13; 1 Pet. 2:11; (6) Gen. 31:15; Exod. 18:3; Job 19:15; Ps. 69:8; Matt. 17:25; (7-8) Exod. 2:22; Ps. 119:19; (9) Lev. 19:10; 23:22; (10) Prov. 27:2; (11) Luke 24:18; John 10:5; (12) Matt. 25:35-36.

Strangle/d: (1) Having your spiritual life choked out of you; (2) Python spirit; (3) The cares of the world choking faith; (4) Stopping the flow of the Holy Spirit.
Also see *Choke/ing, Kill/Killing, Murder*, and *Python*.
(1) Job 7:15; (2) Acts 16:16-18; (3) Matt. 13:22; (4) 1 Thess. 5:19.

Strawberries: (1) Romance; (2) Love and friendship; (3) Good fruit; (4) Temptation.
Also see *Berries*.
(1) Song 2:3b; (2) As a "heart-shaped" fruit with a sweet fragrance; (3) Matt. 7:17; (4) Gen. 3:6.

Stream: (1) A believer or church; (2) Outpouring of the Word or Spirit; (3) Place of refreshing; (4) Revival (streams in the desert); (5) Righteousness; (6) A flow of testing words; (7) Fickle person (changing stream); (8) Overwhelmed (overflowing stream); (9) Judgment (stream of fire).
Also see *Brook, Creek, River*, and *Water*.
(1) Song 4:12-15; Isa. 66:12; (2) Ps. 46:4; 78:16,20; (3) Ps. 126:4; (4) Isa. 35:6; (5) Amos 5:24; (6) Luke 6:48-49; (7) Job 6:15; (8) Ps. 124:4; (9) Isa. 30:28,33; Dan. 7:10.

Street: (1) Exposed; (2) Bring out into the open (make public); (3) Public announcement or proclamation; (4) Well-known; (5) A person's path of life; (6) What lies ahead; (7) Gathering place; (8) Call to trust God (straight street); (9) Pure and without agenda (gold and transparent); (10) Destructive path (broad street); (11) The street may be a measure of a city's morality, prosperity, or spiritual condition; (12) The world (the street is contrasted with the house with the scarlet cord [the Church]); (13) The place of dirt (sin); (14) Uncared for (out on the street); (15) The place of busyness/diligence; (16) Place to be walked over.
Also see *Road, Walk, Path*, and *Highway*.
(1) Matt. 6:5; (2) 2 Sam. 21:12; Esther 6:9 (KJV); Prov. 1:20 (KJV); Eccles. 12:4; Song 3:2; Isa. 15:3; Mark 6:56; Acts 5:15; 12:10; (3) 2 Sam. 1:20; Neh. 8:3 (KJV); Esther 6:11 (KJV);

Prov. 1:20-21 (KJV); Eccles. 12:5; Isa. 42:2; Jer. 11:6; Matt. 6:2; 12:19; Luke 10:10-11; (4) Luke 13:25b-26; (5) Prov. 7:8; 26:13; (6) Ps. 119:105; Prov. 4:18; Isa. 42:16 (God's path is lit); (7) Neh. 8:1 (KJV); Job 29:7; Luke 14:21; (8) Prov. 3:5-6; Acts 9:11-15; (9) Rev. 21:21; (10) Song 3:2; Matt. 7:13-14; (11) Gen. 19:2; Judg. 19:15-27; Ps. 55:11; 144:13-14; Isa. 59:14; Jer. 5:1; 7:17; (12) Josh. 2:19; Prov. 7:12; (13) 2 Sam. 22:43; Ps. 18:42; Isa. 10:6; (14) Job 31:32; Jer. 14:16; as in "on the streets"; (15) Prov. 22:13; 26:13; (16) Isa. 51:23.

Street Directory: (1) Lost; (2) Seeking directions; (3) Guidance; (4) Wanting to know the way; (5) Where someone is at.
(1-5) Exod. 33:13; Ps. 25:4; Jer. 42:3; Acts 16:17.

Street Light: See *Light Pole*.

Strength: (1) God; (2) Spiritual power; (3) Boldness; (4) Strength of heart, soul, or spirit; (5) Firstborn.
Also see *Hill* and *Power*.
(1) 1 Sam. 15:29; (2) Judg. 16:6,19-20; Luke 1:80; (3) Ps. 138:3; (4) Ps. 27:14; 31:24; 73:26; 138:3; Luke 1:80; Eph. 3:16; (5) Gen. 49:3; Deut. 21:17; Ps. 78:51; 105:36.

Stretcher: (1) Casualty of spiritual warfare (because of ignorance).
(1) 1 Sam. 31:3.

Stretching: (1) Enlarging; (2) Exaggeration; (3) Preparing for ministry (stretching muscles); (4) Extending one's area of influence; (5) Exercising (or exerting) spiritual or physical power and dominion over (often forcibly); (6) Covering; (7) Waking up spiritually; (8) Being taken to the next spiritual level; (9) Reaching out (hand); (10) Embracing (hand); (11) Assisting (hand); (12) Exercising faith; (13) Displaying dominion; (14) Judgment (hand); (15) Forcibly; (16) Reaching out to (entreating); (17) Performing signs and wonders (exercising power); (18) Identifying with (body to body); (19) Entreating God (or a false god); (20) Defiance; (21) Expressing mercy or grace; (22) Haughtiness (necks).
Also see *Taller*.
(1) Isa. 54:2; (2) As in exaggerating the size of a fish with your hands; (3) Luke 1:80; (4) Isa. 8:8; (5) Exod. 14:16,21,26-27; 15:12; Deut. 4:34; 5:15; 9:29; Josh. 8:18-19; 1 Sam. 24:6; 26:9,11; 2 Sam. 24:16; 1 Kings 8:42 (directed by prayer); Isa. 8:8; 23:11; (6) Exod. 25:20; 1 Kings 6:27; (7) Song 5:2; Isa. 50:4; Zech. 4:1; (8) Rom. 1:17; 2 Cor. 3:18; (9) Matt. 12:13; 2 Cor. 10:14 (KJV); (10) Matt. 12:49; (11) Matt. 14:30-31; (12) Mark 3:5; (13) Acts 4:30; (14) Exod. 3:20; 6:6b; 7:5, 19; 8:5-6; 2 Kings 21:13 (measured and wanting); Isa. 5:25; 9:12,17,21; 10:4; (15) Exod. 6:6b; (16) Prov. 1:24; Rom. 10:21; (17) Deut. 7:19; Acts 4:30; (18) 1 Kings 17:21; 2 Kings 4:34-35; (19) Job 11:13; Ps. 44:20; 68:31; 88:9; 143:6; (20) Job 15:25; (21) Prov. 31:20; (22) Isa. 3:16.

Stripes: (1) Healing; (2) Iniquity; (3) Discipline; (4) Peace; (5) Purified; (6) Speaks of the bearing of one's cross (wearing stripes); (7) Speaks of double-mindedness (wearing stripes).

Also see individual colors.
(1) Isa. 53:5; 1 Pet. 2:24; (2-3) 2 Sam. 7:14; Ps. 89:32; (4) Isa. 53:5; (5) Lev. 8:15; (6) Col. 1:24; Matt. 16:24; (7) James 1:8; 4:8.

Stroke: (1) Bad blood; (2) Family relational problem; (3) Attack of the enemy; (4) Judgment.
(1) Judg. 5:26-27; (2) Isa. 1:5; (3) 2 Kings 4:17-37; (4) Jer. 30:23.

Stroller: See *Pram*.

Stuffed Toy: (1) Not real/false (not truth); (2) False comfort; (3) Looking for comfort; (4) Harmless/innocent or looks harmless/innocent.
(1) Matt. 7:15; (2) Ps. 69:20; Zech. 10:2; (3) 2 Cor. 1:3-4; (4) Matt. 10:16; Acts 28:5.

Stumble: See *Falling*.

Stump: (1) A person cut down; (2) Judgment; (3) Humbling.
(1-3) Dan. 4:15-26.

Subdividing Land: (1) Moving into your inheritance.
(1) Josh. 1:6.

Submarine: (1) Not openly shown or not public; (2) Underground church; (3) Church in the Spirit; (4) Spiritual vessel not yet revealed; (5) The Spirit (submarine searching underwater).
(1) John 8:59; 12:36; (2) Acts 8:1,3-4; (3) 1 Cor. 12:13; (4) John 14:22; 17:6; Rom. 16:25-26; (5) Prov. 20:27; Rom. 8:27.

Substitute: (1) Appointment; (2) Replacement.
(1) Gen. 4:25; (2) 1 Sam. 16:1.

Sucking: (1) Dependence; (2) Drawing from or being sustained by; (3) Nurturing and nursing (baby); (4) Emptying; (5) Sapping the life out of (parasite); (6) Providence; (7) Youngest and immature (baby); (8) Innocent; (9) Feeding (blood); (10) Milk-fed (baby); (11) Consolation; (12) Comfort;
Also see *Leech*.
(1) Deut. 32:13; 1 Sam. 1:23; (2) Deut. 32:13; Job 39:30; Isa. 60:16; (3) Num. 11:12; Matt. 24:19 (KJV); (4) Ezek. 23:34; (5) Prov. 30:15; (6) Deut. 33:19 (KJV); (7) Num. 11:12; Deut. 32:25; 1 Sam. 15:3; (8) 1 Sam. 7:9; Isa. 11:8; (9) Job 39:30; (10) 1 Sam. 1:23; 1 Kings 3:21 (KJV); (11) Isa. 66:11; (12) Isa. 66:12-13.

Sue/Suing: (1) Exercising your legal right spiritually over what has been stolen from you; (2) Claiming the wealth of the world; (3) Harboring unforgiveness (being sued); (4) A threat of real litigation.
(1) Prov. 6:30-31; (2) Exod. 3:22; 12:35-36; (3) Matt. 5:23-26; 18:32-35; Luke 12:58.

Sugar: See *Honey*.

Suicide: (1) Warning of pending suicidal thoughts; (2) Oppression and/or depression; (3) Hopelessness; (4) Spirit of heaviness; (5) Self-hatred; (6) Wanting to give up; (7) Self-pity; (8) Twisted form of revenge (getting back at someone).

(1) See below; (2) 1 Kings 19:4; Jon. 4:3,8; (3) Num. 11:15; 1 Sam. 31:3-5; (4) Isa. 61:3; (5) 1 John 3:15; (6) 1 Kings 19:4; (7) 1 Kings 19:4; (8) Num. 35:31; Deut. 21:9 (trying to make them guilty).

The Bible appears to set forth three stages in the life of one contemplating suicide: (1) Impossiblity, loss, or failure; (2) Emotions dominating over sound decision making; (3) Lack of social support. If these seem evident, seek professional assistance immediately.

Suit: (1) Business; (2) Pastor; (3) Desire for prominence (expensive suit); (4) Pretense; (5) Renewed authority (best suit); (6) Mocking (stunning suit); (7) Angels (glorious suit); (8) Rottenness and decay (moth-eaten); (9) Garment of Christ (perfumed). The suit color may also be a major indicator of its meaning.

Also see *Clothing* and individual colors.

(1) Ezek. 27:20-21,24a; (3-4) Mark 12:38-40 (look for the other witnesses in this passage before proclaiming this interpretation); (5) Luke 15:22; (6) Luke 23:11; (7) Luke 24:4; (8) Job 13:28; (9) Ps. 45:8.

Suitcase: (1) Travel; (2) Departure; (3) Preparedness; (4) Baggage; (5) Giving you a burden (someone giving you a suitcase); (6) Helping with your burdens (someone carrying your suitcase); (7) Heart preparing to move on (packing suitcase); (8) Itinerant ministry.

Also see *Bag*, *Cruise Ship*, and *Holiday*.

(1) Josh. 9:3-6; (2-3) 1 Kings 10:2, 10; (4) Isa. 46:1-2; Jon. 1:5; (5) Luke 11:46; (6) Gal. 6:2; (7) Gen. 6:13; 1 Kings 17:3; (8) Acts 13:3-4.

Summer: (1) Harvest time (end of summer); (2) The prelude to the Second Coming of Christ; (3) Preparation time; (4) Time of drought (and heat); (5) Fruitfulness; (6) The end.

Also see *Drought*, *Fig*, and *Winter.*

(1) Prov. 10:5; Isa. 16:9b; 18:5-6; Jer. 8:20; Dan. 2:35; John 4:35; (2) Matt. 24:32-34; Mark 13:26-28; Luke 21:30; (3) Prov. 10:5; 30:25; (4) Ps. 32:4; (5) 2 Sam. 16:1-2; Isa. 28:4; Jer. 40:10; 48:32b; Mic. 7:1; (6) Amos 8:1-2; Jer. 8:20.

Sun: (1) Glory of God; (2) Father; (3) Jesus Christ.

(1) Ps. 19:1-6; 84:11; (2) Gen. 37:9-10; (3) Ps. 19:4b-6; Mal. 4:2a; Acts 26:13-15; Rev. 1:16-17.

Sun (Setting): (1) Setting sun means the Glory is departing; (2) End of an issue; (3) Time to settle accounts; (4) Followed by dark activity; (5) Death.

(1) Judg. 19:14-28; 1 Kings 22:36; 2 Chron. 18:34; (2) Exod. 17:12; Josh. 10:13; Eph. 4:26; (3) Deut. 24:13,15; Josh. 10:27; Judg. 14:18; Ps. 50:1; Eph. 4:26; (4) Ps. 104:19-20; John 13:30; (5) Gen. 28:11; Sleep parallels death in Scripture (e.g., John 11:11-13); Dan. 6:14; Daniel's experience in the lion's den pre-pictures Jesus's death, hell, and resurrection experience.

Sun (Rising): (1) New revelation; (2) Beginning or new beginning; (3) Eve of revival; (4) Resurrection.

(1) Gen. 32:31; (2-3) Matt. 28:1, 7-8; (4) Matt. 28:1,7.

Sunburn: (1) The judgment of God; (2) Sin brought to the light; (3) Coming down out of the glory (only if the experience is positive).

Also see *Burn* and *Burnt*.

Ezek. 16:41; Rev. 18:8; (cf. John 5:22; Mal. 4:2); (2) John 3:20-21; (3) Exod. 34:29; Rev. 1:15; 2:18.

Sunscreen: (1) The Blood of Christ; (2) Protection.

See Sunburn

(1) Ex. 12:23; Rom. 5:9; (2) 1 Sam. 17:45; Ps. 91:1.

Sunday: (1) One; (2) God; (3) Resurrection; (4) New Beginnings; (5) Rest.

Also see *Day* and *Seven* (The secular world sees Sunday as the seventh day of the week).

(1-2) Gen. 1:1; (3-4) Matt. 28:1,6; (5) Exod. 23:12.

Sunflowers: (1) Disciples (They follow the sun [Son] and are full of seeds [Word]).

(1) Mal. 4:2; Matt. 8:23, (cf. Luke 8:11).

Sunglasses: (1) Christ's perspective; (2) Spiritual outlook; (3) Coping with God's glory; (4) Self-image issues (especially if sunglasses are worn inside); (5) Not able to handle the glory.

Also see *Sun.*

(1) Ps. 19:4b-5a; Mal. 4:2; (2) Num. 12:6-8; 1 Cor. 13:12; (3) 2 Cor. 3:7-8; (4) 1 Pet. 3:3; (5) Exod. 34:33,35.

Suntan: (1) The glory of God (bronze suntan).

(1) Exod. 34:29; Rev. 1:15; 2:18.

Superhero: (1) Christ; (2) The Holy Spirit; (3) You empowered by the Holy Spirit (you as the superhero); (4) Powerful man or woman of God; (5) Demonic spirit (enemies); (6) Superman can be an antichrist (instead of Christ).

Also see *Famous Person.*

(1) Luke 24:19, 51; (2-3) Acts 10:38; (4) Acts 7:22; 2 Cor. 12:12; (5) Luke 4:6; 10:19; (6) 2 Thess. 2:9.

Supermarket: See *Shop.*

Supervisor: (1) The Holy Spirit; (2) Leader.

(1) John 14:26; Acts 16:6-7; (2) Acts 6:3.

Supper: (1) Marriage Supper of the Lamb (Great Feast); (2) Covenant meal; (3) Intimate fellowship; (4) Last Supper; (5) Remembrance of Jesus's death; (6) Celebration; (7) Call to heart fellowship with Christ.

Also see *Table.*

(1) Luke 14:16; Rev. 19:9a,17; (2) Luke 22:20; (3) John 12:2; 21:20; Rev. 3:20; (4) John 13:2,4; (5) 1 Cor. 11:20; (6) Mark 6:21; (7) Rev. 3:20.

Surf: (1) Wave of the Holy Spirit; (2) Flow of the Holy Spirit.

(1-2) 1 Kings 18:12; Isa. 44:3; Isa. 59:19 (Consider here that the comma is in the wrong place); Mark 1:8; Acts 2:17.

Surfer: (1) Prophet (waiting on the wave of the Spirit); (2) Worship leader (surfing the anointing); (3) Moving in the Spirit (operating in the gifts).
Also see *Surf*, *Surfing*, and *Waves*.
(1) Isa. 40:31; Hab. 2:1-2; (2) 1 Sam. 10:5-6; Matt. 14:29-30; (3) Rom. 5:15 (NIV).

Surfing: (1) Flowing in the Holy Spirit (standing surfer); (2) Negatively surfing the World Wide Web (surfer lying down, not upright).
Also see *Surf*, *Surfer*, and *Waves*.
(1) Acts 11:28; Rev. 11:11; (2) Ps. 51:10 (KJV).

Swallow (bird): (1) Type of true believer (heavenly being). Seen in the bird's attributes: (2) Brings up her young in God's courts; (3) Non-landing; (4) Non-stop prayer (chattering); (5) Aware of the times (seasons).
(2) Ps. 84:3; (3) Prov. 26:2 (cf. Heb. 11:9-10); (4) Isa. 38:14 (cf. 1 Thess. 5:17); (5) Jer. 8:7 (cf. 1 Thess. 5:1-2).

Swallow (verb): (1) Allow or embrace; (2) Engulf; (3) Consumed; (4) Caught and Killed; (5) Destroy; (6) Steal; (7) Smothered; (8) Partake; (9) Speed (swallow up the ground); (10) Devour; (11) Oppression; (12) Reproach; (13) Kill; (14) Abuse; (15) Envelope.
Also see *Drink*, *Eat*, and *Mouth*.
(1) Matt. 23:24; (2) Ezek. 36:3; 1 Cor. 15:54; (3) Num. 16:30, 32, 34; Deut. 11:6; Eccles. 10:12; Isa. 28:7; Lam. 2:5; (4) 2 Sam. 17:16; (5) 2 Sam. 20:19-20; (6) Job 5:5; (7) Job 6:3; (8) Job 20:18; (9) Job 39:24; (10) Ps. 21:9; (11) Ps. 56:1; (12) Ps. 57:3; (13) Ps. 124:3; Prov. 1:12; (14) Amos 8:4; (15) Jon. 1:17.

Swamp: (1) No flow of the Spirit; (2) No output; (3) Quenching the Spirit; (4) Stagnant water; (5) Bogged down.
(1) Matt. 13:58; Acts 10:38; (2) Mark 4:24; (3) 1 Thess. 5:19; (4) Exod. 15:23; (5) Ps. 69:2,14; Heb. 12:1.

Swan: (1) Gracefulness; (2) Love (two swans); (2) Sun; (3) Moon; (4) Unclean spirit.
(1-4) Historical, cultural, and mythological associations; (4) Lev. 11:18.

Swearing (Cussing): (1) Bitter water; (2) Speaking words of death; (3) Denial of Christ; (4) Putting a curse on someone or self; (5) To lose spiritual strength; (6) Corruption; (7) Ungodly discontent; (8) Covetousness; (9) Verbal violence; (10) Disputes; (11) Pride; (12) Jealousy; (13) Hatred; (14) Spirit of murder; (15) Frustration.
(1) Num. 5:18b; James 3:9-12; (2) Prov. 18:21; Mark 15:11-15; (3) Matt. 26:74-75; (4) Matt. 26:74; (cf. Matt. 27:23, Acts 5:30; Gal. 3:13); (5-6) Eph. 4:26,27,29,30; (7) Phil. 4:11; 3 John 1:10; (8) Heb. 13:5; (9) Luke 3:14; (10) Jude 1:8-9; (11) Prov. 21:24; 1 Tim. 6:3-6; (12) Prov. 6:34-35; (13-14) Mark 15:11-15; 1 John 3:15; (15) 3 John 1:10.

Sweat/ing: (1) Human works or self-effort; (2) Sin; (3) Anguish and distress (sweating blood); (4) Worry; (5) Poverty mindset.

(1) Gen. 3:19; Ezek. 44:18; (2) Gen. 3:17-19; (3) Luke 22:44; (4) As in "Don't sweat it"; (4-5) 2 Sam. 9:6-7; Matt. 6:31-33, 34; Luke 10:38-42.

Sweeping: (1) Cleaning out; (2) Searching; (3) Drastic reform; (4) Judgment.

Also see *Broom.*

(1-2) Luke 15:8; (3) As in "sweeping changes"; (4) As in, "getting rid of sin and filth"; Gen. 18:23 (NIV).

Sweetcorn: (1) Words of victory; (2) Standing spiritual army (field of corn); (3) Bible teaching.

See *Popcorn.*

(1) Ps. 119:103; 141:6; (2) Judg. 15:5; Ezek. 37:10; Dan. 11:7. (cf. Ps. 1:3; Isa. 53:2); (3) Isa. 50:4-5.

Sweets: See *Candy.*

Swelling: (1) Flattery; (2) Sign of corruption or defilement; (3) Iniquity; (4) Poison or venomous; (5) Conceit.

Also see *Taller* and *Yeast.*

(1) 2 Pet. 2:18; Jude 1:16 (empty words); (2) Num. 5:21-22,27; Deut. 8:4; (3) Isa. 30:13; (4) Acts 28:6; (5) 2 Cor. 12:20 (compare KJV & NKJV).

Swimming: (1) Moving in the Spirit; (2) River of Life; (3) Bringing to the surface; (4) Deep (suggests that the water is deep); (5) Having to let go and trust God; (6) Advancing in own strength; (7) Overcome with sorrow or grief.

Also see *Deep.*

(1-2) Ezek. 47:5; Isa. 25:11; (3) 2 Kings 6:6; (4) Ps. 42:7 (deep within); Ezek. 47:5; (5) Ezek. 47:5 (having to break reliance on the earth beneath your feet); (6) John 21:7 (cf. John 21:3,18); (7) Ps. 6:6-7.

Swimming Pool: (1) Immersed in God (in pool); (2) Ready for baptism; (3) Purification or cleansing; (4) Church; (5) Church without love (pool with ice in it).

Also see *Swimming.*

(1-3) Acts 8:38b-39a; Heb.10:22b; John 9:7; (4) John 5:2; (5) Matt. 24:12.

Swine: See *Pig.*

Swing: (1) Moved by circumstance/opposition; (2) Change of mind; (3) Doubt; (4) Double-mindedness.

Also see *Shaking.*

(1) Matt. 11:7; 14:30; Luke 7:24; (2) 2 Thess. 2:2; (3) James 1:6; (4) James 1:8.

Swiss: See *Switzerland* in Name and Place Dictionary.

Sword: (1) Word of God; (2) Words; (3) Divides and separates; (4) Live by it, die by it; (5) Two-edged; (6) Tongue; (7) Judgment.

Also see *Knife* and *Tongue.*

(1) Eph. 6:17; Heb. 4:12; (2) Ps. 55:21; 64:3a; (3) Matt. 10:34-35; Rom. 8:35; Heb. 4:12; (4) Matt. 26:52; Rev. 13:10; (5) Rev. 1:16; 2:12; (6) Rev. 1:16; 2:16; (7) 1 Chron. 21:16; Ezek. 21:3-5, 9-17; Rom. 13:1-4; Rev. 19:15.

Syringe: (1) Inoculation; (2) Antidote (injection of life); (3) As they are used to inject into a vein, they speak of spiritual life or death (dependent on the contents). Also see *Drug Taking* and *Needle.*
(1) Prov. 4:23; (2) Job 33:4; 2 Cor. 3:6; (3) Lev. 17:11a.

T

Table: (1) Communion or fellowship; (2) Alignment with someone; (3) In relationship; (4) Communion with God; (5) The King's or Father's provision; (6) Commerce or trade; (7) A writing place; (8) The heart; (9) Union with Christ; (10) Planning place; (11) Negotiation leading to agreement and treaty or contract signing; (12) Decision-making; (13) Serving the Body of Christ; (14) Indicative of your sphere of influence (big/small table).
Also see *Glass Table, Kitchen, Meal, Sitting,* and *Under the Table.*
(1) 1 Cor. 10:20-21; (2) 1 Sam. 20:34; Luke 22:21; (3) John 12:2; 13:28; (4) 1 Cor. 10:20-21; (5) 2 Sam. 9:7-11; 19:28; Ps. 23:5; 78:19; Matt. 15:26-27; Luke 22:30; (6) Matt. 21:12; Mark 11:15; John 2:15; (7) 2 Cor. 3:3; (8) Lev. 24:6 (pure table); 2 Cor. 3:3; (9) John 13:28; (10) Dan. 11:27; (11) As in "Both parties came to the table"; (12) John 13:27,30; (13) Acts 6:2; (14) 1 Kings 10:5.

Table (Glass): (1) Transparency of communion; (2) Seeing through to the heart; (3) Fragile relationship.
(1) 1 Cor. 10:21; (2) 2 Cor. 3:3 (KJV); (3) 1 Sam. 19:7-10; 20:32-34.

Table (Under the Table): (1) Deception; (2) Bribe; (3) Taxation.
(1) Prov. 23:7 (The heart is below the surface); (2) 1 Sam. 8:3; 12:3; Job 15:34; Ps. 26:10; Amos 5:12.

Table Tennis: See *Tennis/Court.*

Tail: (1) Subservient; (2) Second place; (3) Beneath; (4) Disobedience; (5) Cursed; (6) Troublemaker; (7) False prophet; (8) Powerful sting; (9) Influence or allegiance; (10) Past issue; (11) Spirit of poverty; (12) Slave to the system.
Also see *Head.*
(1-3) Deut. 28:13; (4) Deut. 28:44; (5) Gen. 3:14 (A snake is all tail!); (6) Isa. 7:4 (KJV); (7) Isa. 9:14-15; (8) Rev. 9:10,19; (9) Rev. 12:3-4; (10) Deut. 28:13; Rev. 12:4; (11-12) Deut. 28:44.

Tall: (1) Leader (tall person); (2) Authority (tall person); (3) Champion; (4) Proud or arrogant.
Also see *Length, Little, Short, Taller,* and *Tower* for *Tall Building.*

(1-2) 1 Sam. 9:2; (3) 1 Sam. 17:4; (4) Isa. 2:12; Jer. 48:29.

Taller: If something is taller than it was originally, it may mean that: (1) Its influence is increasing; (2) It is getting stronger; (3) It is taking more leadership; (4) It is becoming proud.

(1) Exod. 34:24; (2) Exod. 1:9; Ps. 119:32; (3) 1 Sam. 9:2; (4) 1 Sam. 15:17.

Tandem Bicycle: (1) Kindred spirits; (2) Working together.

Also see *Bicycle*.

(1-2) Phil. 1:27; 2:19-20.

Tank (Army): (1) Powerful ministry; (2) Impacting ministry; (3) Powerful deliverance ministry (breaks open enemy strongholds); (4) Spiritual warfare; (5) Heavy or weighty words.

(1-2) 1 Sam. 2:10; Deut. 20:1; Joel 2:5; Nah. 2:3; (3) Matt. 17:18; (4) Eph. 6:11; (5) Eccles. 8:4; Luke 4:32.

Tap: (1) Open portal; (2) Holy Spirit ministry; (3) Jesus.

Also see *Well*.

(1) Gen. 7:11b-12; (2-3) John 7:37-39.

Tape Measure: (1) Fitting preparation; (2) Being measured for service; (3) Small change of heart needed to enter in (small distance); (4) Expansion preparation.

Also see *Measure/measuring*.

(1) 1 Sam. 2:19; (2) Gen. 37:3; (3) Mark 12:34; (4) Isa. 54:2.

Tapestry: See *Fabric*.

Tar: (1) Atonement; (2) Protection against sinking; (3) Judgment; (4) Works of people.

Also see *Bricks* and *Salt*.

(1) Gen. 6:14 (The word *pitch* used here is the Hebrew word for "atonement"); (2) Exod. 2:3; (3) Gen. 14:10; Isa. 34:9; (4) Gen.11:3.

Target: (1) Place of vulnerability.

Also see *Goal* and see *Target* in the Name and Place Dictionary.

(1) 2 Kings 6:9.

Tasmanian Devil: (1) Evil spirit that attacks children; (2) Manifests in outbursts of anger; (3) Devil/demon.

(1-2) 1 Kings 4:32-33. These characteristics are seen in the size of the creature and its ferocity as well as experience; (3) Isa. 14:16; Matt. 17:18.

Tassels: (1) Mind of God (His laws, commandments).

Also see *Bookmark*.

(1) Num. 15:38-39.

Tasting: (1) Experiencing; (2) Testing and trying; (3) Partaking; (4) Strengthening; (5) Discerning; (6) Heart revelation; (7) Unchanged (bad taste); (8) Humbling (not eating).

Also see *Sweet*, *Sour*, and *Bitter*.

(1) Matt. 16:28; Luke 9:27; John 8:52; 1 Pet. 2:3; (2) Job 34:3; Matt. 27:34; John 2:9; (3) Luke 14:24; Heb. 6:4-5; (4) 1 Sam. 14:29; (5) Job 6:30; (6) Ps. 34:8; 119:103-104; Prov. 24:13-14; (7) Jer. 48:11; (8) John 3:7.

Tattoo: (1) Tough; (2) Identity or Identifying mark; (3) Fleshly person; (4) Fugitive; (5) Vagabond; (6) Message; (7) The placement of a tattoo is important to its interpretation, e.g., a tattooed leg would mean corrupted strength; a tattooed face would mean a defiled or poisoned heart. (8) If the tattoo has recognizable figures or numbers within it, these of course will carry deep significance and must be interpreted individually.
Also see *Biker/Bikie* and *Scar.*
(1) Ps. 22:16; (2-5) Gen. 4:14-15; (6) Song 8:6; Isa. 49:16.

Tax: See *IRS.*

Taxi: See *Cab.*

Tea Bag: (1) Healing.
(1) Rev. 22:2.

Teacher: (1) The Holy Spirit; (2) Mature disciple of Christ; (3) Fleshly (false, academic, money-hungry, demonic) teacher; (4) Nature; (5) Revelation; (6) Jesus; (7) Known teacher.
(1) Luke 12:12; John 14:26; 1 Cor. 2:13; 1 John 2:27; (2) Rom. 12:7; Eph. 4:11; Col. 1:28; 3:16; 1 Tim. 2:24; 2 Tim. 3:2; Heb. 5:12; (3) 2 Tim. 4:3; Tit. 1:11; 2 Pet. 2:1; Rev. 2:20; (4) 1 Kings 4:30-33; 1 Cor. 11:14; (5) Gal. 1:12; (6) Eph. 4:20-21; (7) Acts 13:1.

Team: (1) Family; (2) Church; (3) Business; (4) Christian (disciple); (5) Spiritual opposition.
(1) Eph. 5:22-27; (2) Eph. 4:16; (3) Neh. 4:6; (4) Mark 9:40; Rom. 8:31; (5) Eph. 6:12.

Tear (verb): (1) Loss; (2) Judgment; (3) Persecution; (4) Personal attack; (5) Separation; (6) Destruction; (7) Division; (8) Painful parting; (9) Violence.
(1) 1 Sam. 15:27-28; (2) 1 Kings 13:26; Isa. 5:25 (KJV); (3) Ps. 7:1-2; (4) Ps. 35:15 (NKJV); (5) 1 Sam. 6:10-12; (6) 2 Kings 2:24; Jer. 50:23; Ezek. 30:16; Acts 1:18; (7) Dan. 11:4; John 19:23; (8) 1 Sam. 6:10-12; (9) Acts 27:41.

Tear(s) (noun): (1) Sadness or sorrow; (2) Grief (loss of expectation); (3) Trouble; (4) Affliction; (5) Joy; (6) Pain; (7) Repentance; (8) Unbridled expression of the heart; (9) Heartless emotion (crocodile tears).
Also see *Crying* and *Sorrow.*
(1) John 16:20; Rev. 21:4; (2) Ps. 6:7; 31:9; (3) Ps. 31:9; (4) Ps. 88:9; (5) Ps. 126:5; John 16:20; 2 Tim. 1:4; (6) John 16:20; Rev. 21:4; (7) Heb. 12:17; (8) Matt. 26:75; Luke 19:41; John 11:35; (9) Zech. 7:5; Luke 7:32; Heb. 12:17.

Tea Towel: (1) Servanthood.
(1) John 13:4.

Teddy Bear: (1) Family-friendly false prophet; (2) Antichrist spirit that preys on immature believers; (3) False comforter; (4) Being comforted by a religious spirit (white teddy bear); (5) Childhood comforter.

(1-3) 2 Tim. 3:5-7; 2 Pet. 2:1-2; (4) Matt. 23:27; John 11:19,31; (5) 1 Thess. 2:11.

Teenager: (1) Folly; (2) Rebellious; (3) Mocking; (4) Consider your perception of teenager(s).

Also see *Gang, Skinhead, Youth,* and *Younger.*

(1) Prov. 22:15; (2) Prov. 30:11; (3) 2 Kings 2:23.

Teeth: (1) Believer or congregation; (2) Words; (3) Wisdom; (4) Pride of appearance; (5) Maturity; (6) Unfaithful person (bad tooth); (7) Not the upfront person (bad teeth); (8) Biting; (9) Fierce (as in baring the fangs); (10) Instrument of judgment; (11) Decision making or discernment; (12) Mocking; (13) Lies (false teeth); (14) Predator (sharp teeth); (15) Power.

Also see *Braces, Cheek, Lips, Losing Teeth* (directly below), *Mouth, Tongue, Toothache, Toothbrush,* and *Toothpaste.*

(1) Song 4:2; 6:6; (sheep); (2) Prov. 30:14; Ps. 35:16; 57:4; Jer. 2:16; (4) (5) Heb. 5:14; (6) Prov. 25:19; (7) Isa. 53:2-3; (8) (9-10) Isa. 41:15; Hab. 1:8 (fierce = sharp); (11) Isa. 41:15 (judgment carries the meaning of decision-making); (12) Ps. 35:16; (13) Ps 57:4; 59:12; (14) Job 16:9; Ps. 57:4; (15) Dan. 7:7; Joel 1:6.

Teeth (Losing Teeth): (1) Losing face; (2) Shame; (3) Loss of words or lost for words; (4) Judgment of God (broken teeth); (5) Unfaithful or ungodly person (broken tooth); (6) Humbled (loss of pride); (7) Legalistic retribution; (8) Losing sheep; (9) Poor self-image; (10) Embarrassed to speak; (11) Hidden self-image problems (missing bottom teeth); (12) Hidden disability (missing bottom teeth); (13) Disarmed/no power (no teeth).

Also see *Arrows* and *Teeth.*

(1-3) Lam. 3:16; Eph. 5:12; Ps. 58:3-7; (4) Ps. 3:7; 58:6; (5) Ps. 3:7; Prov. 25:19; (6) Ezek. 28:17; (7) Exod. 21:24; Matt. 5:38; (8) Song 6:6; (9) Isa. 41:14; (10) Exod. 6:30; (11) Nah. 2:10; (12) Prov. 25:19; (13) Dan. 7:7; Joel 1:6.

Teeth (New Teeth): (1) Dignity; (2) Glory.

(1) Lam. 3:16 (opposite of this); (2) Isa. 60:1.

Telephone: (1) Communication; (2) Heart/spirit (spiritual receiver); (3) Communication with God in prayer; (4) Heart sensitive to the Spirit of God (touchscreen cell phone); (5) The old avenue of hearing (old phone); (6) Gossip; (7) Not in prayer (misplaced phone).

(1) Gen. 23:8 (KJV); (2) Matt. 11:15; (3) Ps. 4:1; 17:6; 18:6; 1 Cor. 14:2; (4) Matt. 12:28; Luke 11:30; (5) Isa. 48:6; Heb. 12:25; (6) Prov. 6:19; 26:22; Eccles. 10:20. 2 Thess. 3:11; 1 Tim. 5:13; 1 Pet. 4:15; (7) Matt. 26:40.

Telephone (Faulty Telephone): (1) Communication barrier; (2) Communication problems; (3) Hardened heart.

(1) John 8:43; (2) Eccles. 9:16; Jer. 22:5; (3) Heb. 3:15; 4:7b.

Telephone Message: (1) Message from God.
(1) Matt. 10:27.

Telescope: (1) Distant in space or time; (2) Long-term promise; (3) About to see visions of Heaven; (4) Turning to righteousness; (5) Prophet or seer; (6) Viewed from the second heaven (telescopic sight).
Also see *Sniper* and *Staring*.
(1-2) Gen. 3:15; Gal. 4:4; Gen. 15:5; (3) Ezek. 1:1; Dan. 4:13; Acts 26:19; (4) Dan. 12:3; (5) 1 Sam. 9:9; (6) Ps. 14:2; 53:2 [The first heaven is the sky (see Deut. 4:19), the third heaven is God's dwelling place (see 2 Cor. 12:2), and the second heaven the spirit realm (see Eph. 6:12)].

Television: (1) Vision/destiny; (2) Message; (3) News (media headlines good or bad); (4) Gift of reception (prophet); (5) Receiving visions and dreams; (6) Idol/idolatry; (7) Tuning/search/searching for God; (8) Mind-"set"; (9) Letting the world in; (10) Looking to the world.
Also see *Radio* and *Stereo*.
(1) Num. 24:4; Dan. 4:13; (2) Num. 12:6; (3) 2 Sam. 18:26; 1 King 14:6; Matt. 4:23-24; (4-5) Num. 12:6; (6) Dan. 3:5b; Rev. 16:2b; (7) Num. 23:3; (8) As in "what you are watching"; (9-10) Isa. 31:1 (Egypt is the world); 1 John 2:16.

Television (Asleep in Front of Television): (1) Watchlessness or prayerlessness; (2) Spiritually insensitive; (3) Dulled by idolatry; (4) Not aware of idolatry in our lives.
Also see *Asleep* and *Sleeping*.
(1-2) Isa. 56:10-11; (3-4) Matt. 13:15.

Teller: (1) Author or authority.
(1) Heb. 12:2.

Temple: (1) Human body (individually); (2) Church body (corporately); (3) God's heavenly temple.
(1) 1 Cor. 6:19; (2) 2 Cor. 6:16; (3) Rev. 11:19.

Ten: (1) Complete; (2) Completion of order/cycle; (3) Full.
(1-2) Gen. 16:3 (waiting); Gen. 31:7,41 (deceit); Exod. 7–12 (plagues/judgment); Exod. 20:2-17 (instruction); Num. 14:22 (rebellion); Matt. 25:1 (bride); Matt. 25:20, 28 (talents/investment); Luke 15:8 (riches/redemption); 17:12-17 (cleansing); Rev. 2:10 (tribulation/testing); (3) Num. 7:14ff.

Tennis/Tennis Court: (1) Verbal conflict; (2) Spiritual warfare.
Also see *Ball*.
(1-2) Matt. 4:1-10.

Ten-Pin Bowling: (1) Preaching with authority; (2) Impacting word (strike).
(1-2) 1 Sam. 3:19; Mark 1:39; (2) Ps. 107:20; Matt. 8:16; Luke 8:29.

Ten Thousand: (1) Seems to express the maximum possible in earthly terms; (2) Extreme; (3) The world.
(1) Lev. 26:8 (enemies); Matt. 18:24 (debt); 1 Cor. 4:15 (instructors); 1 Cor. 14:19 (words); Jude 1:14 (saints); (3) Lev.26:8; Deut. 32:30.

Tent: (1) Human body; (2) Temporary church; (3) Earthly dwelling place (contrasted with heavenly home).
(1) 2 Pet. 1:13-14 (NKJV); (2) Exod. 33:7-8; Num. 10:11-12; (3) Heb. 11:9-10; (cf. John 14:2).

Termites: (1) Heretic; (2) Undermining words (white-anting); (3) Unseen and destructive; (4) Little unseen sins that bring down the house; (5) Cancer.
(1) 2 Tim. 2:17; Tit. 3:10-11; (2-3) Acts 15:24; Tit. 1:11; (4) Gal. 5:9; (5) 2 Tim. 2:17.

Terrorism: (1) Schemes of the devil.
Also see *Terrorist*.
(1) John 10:10; 2 Cor. 2:11.

Terrorist: (1) Children of the devil; (2) Distorter of the Gospel; (3) False believers; (4) Plotting in the shadows (5) Pending surprise attack.
Also see *Terrorism*.
(1-3) John 8:44; Acts 13:10; 1 John 3:10; (4) Prov. 6:14; (5) 1 Sam. 30:3.

Testicles: See *Genitals*.

Theater: See *Stage (Theater)*.

Theft: See *Thief*.

Theme Park: (1) Representation of a believer's life; (2) Scenario or episode in one's life; (3) Entertainment; (4) Excitement; (5) The Kingdom of God.
(1) Deut. 32:13a; Rev. 20:12; (2) 2 Cor. 11:26; (3) Exod. 32:6b; Luke 8:14; 2 Tim. 3:4; (4) Ps. 68:4; (5) Mark 10:14.

Thick: (1) Fat; (2) Insensitive to God; (3) Insensitive; (4) Dull or insensitive heart.
Also see *Fat* and *Thin*.
(1-2) Deut. 32:15; (3) As in "thick-skinned"; (4) Matt. 15:16 (Understanding relates to heart receptivity, Matt. 13:19).

Thief: (1) Warning; (2) Potential to have something—possession, virtue, spiritual gift, etc.—stolen; (3) The devil; (4) Destroyer; (5) Murderer; (6) Non-believer; (7) Doubt; (8) Sevenfold return (thief caught); (9) Dangerous partnership; (10) Shame; (11) Scorn; (12) Cursed; (13) A heart centered on earthly treasures; (14) Evil heart; (15) Profiteer in church; (16) Sign of prayerlessness; (17) Mocker; (18) Not caring; (19) Without warning; (20) Adulterer.
Also see *Robbery* and *Steal*.
(1-5) John 10:1,10; (5) Job 24:14; (6) Ps. 50:17-18; 1 Cor. 6:9-10; (7) James 1:6; (8) Prov. 6:30-31; (9) Prov. 29:24; Isa. 1:23; (10) Jer. 2:26; (11) Jer. 48:27; (12) Zech. 5:3-4; (13) Matt. 6:19-21; (14) Matt. 15:19; Mark 7:21-22; (15) Matt. 21:12-13;

(16) Matt. 24:43; Rev. 16:15; (17) Matt. 27:44; (18) John 12:6; (19) 1 Thess. 5:2-4; 2 Pet. 3:10; Rev. 3:3; 16:15; (20) 2 Sam. 12:4,7-9; Prov. 6:26-32.

Thigh: (1) Oath; (2) Strength.
Also see *Leg* and *Shin*.
(1) Gen. 24:2-3; 47:29; (2) Ps. 147:10.

Thin: (1) Famine; (2) Fine; (3) Lean.
Also see *Emaciated*, *Fat*, and *Skinny*.
(1) Gen. 41:6-7,27; (2) Exod. 39:3; Lev. 13:30; 1 Kings 7:29 (KJV); (3) Isa. 17:4.

Thirsty: (1) Desire for God; (2) Desire for eternal fulfillment; (3) Dry and barren believer; (4) Desire to be filled; (5) In a wilderness; (6) It appears that thirst generally relates to a need for the Spirit whereas hunger relates to the Word.
Also see *Hunger* and *Throat*.
(1-3) Ps. 42:1-2; 69:3; (cf. Ps. 69:21; John 19:28); John 7:37-39; (4) Matt. 5:6; (5) Neh. 9:15; (6) Neh. 9:15; John 6:35; 7:38-39.

Thirteen: (1) Rebellion; (2) Sin; (3) Apostasy; (4) Defection; (5) Corruption; (6) Backsliding.
(1) Gen. 14:4; (2) The "sixth" prime number (1, 3, 5, 7, 11, 13); (3-6) Gen. 10:8, Nimrod thirteenth generation from Adam (beginning of Babylon); Gen 16:12, of Ishmael it was foretold he would be *"a wild man, his hand against every man"*; Gen. 17:25, Ishmael (son of the flesh) was circumcised at thirteen years of age; 1 Kings 7:1, Solomon was thirteen years building his own house, compared to seven building the Temple (1 Kings 6:38).

Thirty: (1) Right timing/moment to reign or minister; (2) 3 x 10 = 30 as such it carries the meaning of perfection or fullness [3] of Divine order [10] which marks the right moment.
(1-2) Gen. 41:46; 2 Sam. 5:4; Luke 3:23.

Thistle: See *Thorn*.

Thorns: (1) Sin; (2) Curse; (3) Deceitfulness of wealth/cares of the world; (4) Evil men; (5) Choker of the Word/Life; (6) Hedged in; (7) Fleshly weakness; (8) Face judgment.
Also see *Tree*.
(1-2) Gen. 3:17-18; (cf. Gen. 22:13; John 19:2); (3) Matt. 13:22; (4) Matt. 13:25 (false grain); Luke 6:44-45; (5) Luke 8:14; (6) Hos. 2:6; (7) 2 Cor. 12:7,9; (8) Heb. 6:8.

Thousand: (1) Ever increasing (or more); (2) Amplification of the number; (3) Literal thousands; (4) Day; (5) Ankles (1,000); (6) Knees (2,000); (7) Waist (3,000); (8) Must swim (4,000); (9) Ever-increasing grace (5,000); (10) Nation/clan.
You may also use the meaning of the numbers 1-17 to interpret these thousands (with the exception of ten thousand, which is listed above).

If the number involves a figure such as 34,000, consider 30 (if there is an entry for the tens) and 4, i.e., ever increasing dominion after the fullness of waiting.

You might also consider 3 and 4; in this case, a possible meaning would be "ever increasing fullness of dominion." If the number is a product (two numbers multiplied) or a sum (two numbers added) consider each number that make up these equations, e.g., 66,000 = 6 x 11 x 1,000 = ever increasing disorganization/disintegration of humanity. Another example might be 19,000 = 10 + 9 x 1,000 = complete judgment forever or ever increasing and complete fruitfulness. Allow the witness of the Spirit and the context of the incident/event to confirm which interpretation is more likely.
(1) Gen. 20:16 (Ever increasing redemption); Exod. 20:6, 34:7 (ever increasing mercy); (2) Exod. 32:28 (a full complement of humanity); (4) Ps. 90:4; 2 Pet. 3:8; (5) Ezek. 47:3; (7) Ezek. 47:4; (8) Ezek. 47:4; (9) Ezek. 47:5; (9) Matt. 14:21; John 6:10; (10) Isa. 60:22; (Hebrew for "thousand" same as "clan").

Thread (Scarlet Thread): (1) The story of redemption throughout God's Word; (2) Word of God; (3) The blood of Jesus; (4) Thin or fine line; (5) Love.
(1-2) Song 4:3a; (3-4) Josh. 2:18-19 (speaks of the blood of Christ); (5) Song 4:3a.

Three: (1) God/The Godhead (2) Complete; (3) Resurrection; (4) Perfect; (5) Divine fullness; (6) The Holy Spirit; (7) Three items may = three days or three years; (8) Witness; (9) Father, Son, and Holy Spirit; (10) Spirit, soul, and body; (11) Third heaven; (12) Counsel of God; (13) Separation spirit and flesh (Moses wanted to go three days into wilderness; Jacob, three days separation from Laban's sheep).
Also see *Hundred* (i.e., 300), *Three-Story Building*, and *Two*.
(1) Isa.6:3; Matt. 28:19; 1 John 5:7; (2) Exod. 5:3 (complete separation); Mark 14:30, 66-72 (complete denial); John 21:15-17 (complete confession); (3) Gen. 1:13; Josh. 1:11; Matt. 12:39-40; (4) Luke 13:32; (5) Eph. 3:19 (Father); 4:13 (Son), Col. 2:9 (Holy Spirit); (6) Matt. 28:19; (7) Gen. 40:10,12,16,18; 41:1; (8) Deut. 19:15; Matt. 18:16; (9) Matt. 28:19; 1 John 5:7 (KJV); (10) 1 Thess. 5:23; (11) 2 Cor. 12:2; (12) Gen. 18:1-17; (13) Exod. 5:3; Gen. 30:36; 1 Sam. 30:12; Rev. 11:11.

Three-Story Building: (1) Fullness of the Spirit; (2) Maturity in Christ; (3) Illustration of the first, second, and third heaven (which heaven [1-3] relates to the level in the building you are on).
Also see *House*, *Individual Numbers*, and *Three*.
(1-3) Col. 2:9-10; 1 John 5:8; Rev. 12:11; (cf. Gen. 6:16); 2 Cor. 12:2.

.357 Magnum: (1) Powerful words; (2) Threat; (3) Fear.
Also see *Bow* and *Bullets*.
(1) 1 Sam. 17:43-44; (2-3) 1 Sam. 17:7.

300mm Lens: (1) Vision of Glory.
(1) Judg. 7:16-22; Gen. 5:22.

Three Thousand: (1) Best/choicest/leaders of the nation.
(1) (Isa. 60:22; Matt. 22:14); Exod. 32:28; Josh. 7:8; Judg. 15:11; 16:27; 1 Sam. 13:2; 24:2.

Throat: (1) Passage to the heart; (2) Open grave; (3) Infers that one's words reflect the state of the heart; (4) Threat of death (knife to throat); (5) Without God or missing God (thirsty or dry throat); (6) Heart unforgiveness (grabbed by the throat); (7) Threat.
Also see *Jugular Vein, Neck, Thirsty, Throat (Cut)*, and *Tongue*.
(1-3) Ps. 5:9; Rom. 3:13; (4) Prov. 23:2; (5) Ps. 69:3 (cf. John 19:28); (6-7) Matt. 18:28.

Throat (Cut): (1) Death; (2) Ruthlessly killing someone with words; (3) Threat; (4) Warning; (5) Stop (as in "kill" what you are doing).
Also see *Decapitation, Kill/Killing, Murder, Neck, Jugular Vein*, and *Throat*.
(1) Isa. 1:11; (2) Ps. 57:4; (3-5) Prov. 23:2.

Thrombosis: (1) Lack of circulation; (2) Sitting down too long; (3) Lazy in the Lord; (4) Slowing the flow and hindering the walk.
Also see *Walking*.
(1) Prov. 6:9-11; 24:33-34; (2-3) 1 Cor. 15:58; 2 Thess. 3:8; (4) Ps. 44:18.

Throne: (1) Authority; (2) Judgment; (3) Heaven; (4) Seat; (5) Christ's Glory; (6) Dominion; (7) The place of grace (mercy seat); (8) The place from which God rules.
(1) Luke 1:32-33; (2) Matt. 19:28; Luke 22:30; Rev. 20:4, 11-12; (3-4) Matt. 5:34; 23:22; Acts 7:49; (5) Matt. 25:31; (6) Col. 1:16; (7) Heb. 4:16; (8) Heb. 12:2; Rev. 1:4; 3:21; 4:2-5; 7:10; 19:4.

Throwing: (1) Launching Words; (2) Speaking; (3) Danger; (4) To pull down (throw down); (5) Condemning (thrown down).
Also see *Ball* and *Steps (Going Down)*.
(1-2) 1 Sam. 17:40-49; 2 Sam. 16:13; (3) 1 Sam. 18:11; (4) Jer. 1:10; (5) 2 Chron. 36:3.

Thumb: (1) Leverage; (2) Power; (3) Works; (4) Controlled by.
(1-2) Judg. 1:6-7; (3) Exod. 29:20 (consecrated for service); Lev. 8:23-24; 14:14,17,25,28; (4) As in "under the thumb."

Thumbnail: (1) Miniature version of larger unfolding scene; (2) Embryonic view of the future; (3) Thumbnail sketch.
Also see *Nails (Finger)*.
(1-2) Gen. 1:12; (3) See *Plan(s)*.

Thunder: (1) Voice of God; (2) Judgment; (3) Power; (4) Powerful voices.
(1) Job 37:4-5; John 12:28-30; (2) 1 Sam. 2:10; Rev. 6:1ff; (3) Job 26:14; (4) Rev. 10:4.

Thursday: (1) Five; (2) Grace or favor.
Also see *Day* and *Four* (The secular world sees Thursday as the fourth day of the week).
(1) Gen. 1:22-23; (2) Gen. 43:34; 45:11; Lev. 26:8.

Tick (noun): (1) Hidden parasite; (2) Life-sapping parasite.
Also see *Parasite*.
(1-2) Prov. 30:15a.

Tick (verb): (1) Approval of God; (2) Approval; (3) Correct; (4) Pass; (5) Right.
Also see *Mark*.

(1) Acts 2:22 (KJV); 2 Tim. 2:15; (2) Rom. 14:18; (3-4) Phil. 3:14, 17; (5) Luke 10:28.

Ticket: (1) Your ministry calling; (2); Salvation; (3) Entry authority; (4) Entry to the promises of God (the Kingdom); (5) The Holy Spirit; (6) Something you have bought into; (7) Opening yourself up to something.
Also see *Buying* and *Queue*.
(1) Matt. 10:1; Luke 6:13; (2) Gen. 7:13; (3) Num. 14:24; (4) John 3:5; (5) 2 Cor. 1:22 (guarantee of entry); Rom. 8:16; (6-7) Prov. 18:17.

Tidal Wave: See *Tide*, *Tsunami*, and *Waves*.

Tide: (1) Public opinion (the pull of the world); (2) Flood of sin (high tide); (3) The Church's influence; (4) Flow of the Spirit leaving (tide going out); (5) Eve of destruction or revival (tide really out).
Also see *Flood*, *Moon*, and *Tsunami*.
(1) Matt. 16:14; John 7:12; as in, "the tide of public opinion"; (2) Josh. 3:15b; Isa. 59:19b; (3) 1 Cor. 11:7; Mal. 4:2; Eph. 5:23 (sun = Jesus, moon = Church, moon reflects the sun's glory); (4-5) Amos 8:11; Isa. 35:1.

Tie (noun): (1) Business; (2) Formal.
(1) Prov. 6:20-21; (2) As in "black tie."

Tie (verb): (1) Secured; (2) Fastened; (3) Lead.
(1) Matt. 21:2; Mark 11:2; Luke 19:30; (2) Exod. 39:31; 1 Sam. 6:7; 2 Kings 7:10; (3) Prov. 6:21-22.

Tiger: (1) Strong evil force; (2) satan; (3) Vicious religious spirit (white tiger).
Also see *Lion*.
(1) Mic. 3:1-3; (2) Mark 1:13; (3) Mic. 3:1-3.

Tightrope: (1) Walking a fine line; (2) In jeopardy of falling; (3) On a risky path; (4) Balance required; (5) Spiritually focused.
(1-2) Gen. 4:7; Ps. 56:13; Prov. 10:8; 11:5; (3) Num. 22:32; (4) Job 31:6; Prov. 11:1; 20:23; (5) Matt. 14:29-30.

Tiles: (1) Heart as a foundation (floor tiles); (2) Heart (shower tiles).
Also see *Stepping Stones*.
(1) Matt. 7:25; Luke 6:48; (2) Eccles. 12:6-7.

Time: (1) Life (as in "life-time"); (2) An on-the-hour time (e.g., 6:00 a.m.) may refer to the meaning of the numbers 1 to 12. (3) Appreciate the timing of God; (4) Eve of Christ's return; (5 minutes to 12); (5) Time or part times may refer to years.
Also see individual numbers, *Before and After*, *Clock*, *Early*, *Late*, *Measure*, *Time Running Out*, *Timetable*, and *Urgency*.
(1) Gen. 18:10; Acts 17:26; James 4:14; 1 Pet. 4:2; (3) Acts 2:1; Gal. 4:4; Eph. 1:10; (4) Phil 4:5b; (5) Dan. 7:25b.

Time Running Out: (1) Endtimes; (2) Christ's return; (3) The brevity of life.
Also see *Urgency*.

(1) 1 Cor. 7:29; (2) 1 Cor. 7:29; Phil. 4:5; (3) Ps. 89:47-48.

Timetable: (1) Timing of God.

Also see *Clock*, *Diary (Personal)*, *Diary (Work)*, *Time*, and *Watch*.

(1) Esther 4:14b; Gal. 4:4; Eph. 1:10.

Tin: (1) Impurity; (2) Hypocrisy; (3) Refining.

Also see *Pewter*.

(1-2) Isa. 1:25 (KJV); Ezek. 22:18, 20; (3) Num. 31:22-23.

Tin Man: (1) Heartless man.

(1) Ezek. 11:19; Matt. 24:12.

Tire: (1) Where the rubber meets the road (where our faith is outworked); (2) The type of tires may indicate the nature of a ministry (i.e. chunky off-road tires may mean powerful, non-conventional ministry); (3) Fitting tires may be preparation for ministry; (4) Screeching tires may indicate: (a) In a hurry; (b) Powerful; (c) Immaturity; (d) Attention-seeking.

Also see *Automobile*, *Flat Tire*, *Four-Wheel Drive*, *Tire (No Tread)* (directly below), and *Wheels*.

(1) Matt. 7:21; Luke 11:2b (KJV); Phil. 2:12 (obedience); (2) Ps. 18:33; (3) Eph. 6:15; (4a) Exod. 14:9; (4b) 1 Kings 18:46; (4c) Prov. 20:29; (4d) Prov. 25:27b; Jer. 9:23-24.

Tire (No Tread): (1) Unsafe ministry; (2) Worn out (spiritually tired); (3) Careless ministry.

(1) 1 Tim. 1:19-20; 2 Pet. 2:14-15; (2) Exod. 18:18 (not delegating); (3) Ps. 73:2.

Tissues: (1) Mourning or grieving; (2) Cleansing; (3) Repentance.

(1) Matt. 5:4; (2) Num. 8:7; Rev. 19:14; (3) Matt. 5:4; 2 Cor. 7:9-10.

T-Junction: (1) Decision; (2) Choice between God and the world (T-junction); (3) Lukewarm (standing at the intersection: indecision).

Also see *Crossroads* and *Road*.

(1) Josh. 24:15; Matt. 25:33; (2) Josh 24:15; (3) Rev. 3:16.

Toad: (1) Poisonous individual.

Also see *Frog*.

(1) Rom. 3:13; James 3:8.

Toast (Bread): (1) Speaking in anger; (2) Getting angry about words; (3) If you are a regular toast eater, just see entries under *Bread*.

(1) 1 Sam. 17:28; Ezek. 5:13 ("you're toast"); (2) Judg. 9:30; Neh. 5:6; Prov. 15:1.

Toe(s): (1) The walk of the person; (2) Smallest division of a kingdom/body/church; (3) Spiritual offspring (smallest members); (4) Six toes symbolizes the ultimate of humanity's dominion; (6) Straining to reach or see (tippy-toes); (7) Secretly and quietly (tip-toe); (8) Dominant nation or superpower (big toe); (9) Leader or king; (10) Drive; (11) New spiritual vitality (running on toes).

Also see *Feet*, *Shoe*, and *Toe(s) (Big Toe)*.

(1) Exod. 29:20; Lev. 8:23; 14:14; (2) Dan. 2:41; (3) 1 Cor. 12:23-26; (4) 2 Sam. 21:20; (6) Luke 19:3; (7) 2 Tim. 3:6; Jude 1:4; (8-9) Dan. 2:41; (10) Judg. 1:6-7; (11) 1 Kings 18:46.

Toe(s) (Big Toe): (1) Power and dominion; (2) Drive and influence; (3) Leverage; (4) Leadership.

Also see *Toes* and *Thumb*.

(1-3) Judg. 1:6-7.

Toilet: (1) Spiritual cleansing or detoxing; (2) Deliverance; (3) Confession and repentance; (4) Personal repentance; (5) Secret lust or sin; (6) Secret issues; (7) Dealing with sin apart from sexual immorality (outside toilet); (8) Heart (toilet cistern).

Also see *Bathroom* and *Dung*.

(1) Ps. 51:2; Mic. 7:19; Heb. 9:14; 1 John 1:7b; (2) Jer. 4:14; Ezek. 37:23; Tit. 3:5; (3) 1 John 1:9; (4) Ps. 22:14; (5-6) 2 Sam. 12:12; Ps. 64:4; Jer. 23:24; John 7:4; Eph. 5:12; (7) 1 Cor. 6:18; (8) Matt. 23:25,27.

Toilet Paper: (1) Spiritual cleansing; (2) Putting off misdeeds of the body.

(1) Ps. 51:2; 1 John 1:9; (2) Rom. 8:13.

Tomorrow: (1) Future.

(1) James 4:14.

Tongue: (1) Words; (2) Spiritual language; (3) Confession; (4) Potential for good or evil (death and life); (5) Fire; (6) International languages; (7) Pain (gnawing the tongue); (8) Lying; (9) Flattery; (10) Justified/righteous (silver); (11) Perverse/crooked (cut out); (12) Health; (13) Wise; (14) Tree of life; (15) Wicked; (16) Need for control; (17) Soft; (18) Anger; (19) Deceit.

Also see *Lips, Mouth, Teeth,* and *Throat*.

(1) Rom. 3:13; 14:11; (2) 1 Cor. 12:10; 13:1; 14:2,4,14; (3) Phil. 2:11; (4) Prov. 18:21; James 3:5,10; (5) James 3:6; (6) Rev. 5:9; 7:9; 9:11; 10:11; (7) Rev. 16:10; (8) Prov. 6:17; 12:19; 21:6; 26:28; (9) Prov. 6:24; 28:23; (10) Prov. 10:20; (11) Prov. 10:31; 17:20; (12) Prov. 12:18; (13) Prov. 15:2; (14) Prov. 15:4; (15) Prov. 17:4; (16) Prov. 21:23; (17) Prov. 25:15; (18) Prov. 25:23;

(19) Rom. 3:13.

Tool(s): (1) Gifts of the Spirit; (2) Works of people; (3) Work of the flesh; (4) A work in progress; (5) Work needed; (6) Repairing; (7) Work of God (without tools); (8) Work of self-righteousness; (9) Ministry gift.

(1) 1 Cor. 12:11; (2-3) Exod. 20:25; Deut. 27:5; 1 Kings 6:7; Isa. 44:12; (3) Exod. 32:3-4 (cf. Gal. 5:19-20); (4) Neh. 4:17; (5) Jer. 18:3-4; 48:11; 2 Tim. 2:19-21; (6) 2 Kings 12:12; 2 Chron. 24:4,12; (7) Exod. 20:25; Deut. 27:5; Dan. 2:34,45; (8) Exod. 20:25; (cf. Eph. 2:8-9); (9) Eph. 4:11-12.

Tool Box: (1) Something that can be used against you; (2) Problem solver; (3) Maintenance.

(1) Mark 12:13; Luke 20:20-26; (2) Ruth 4:6; (3) 1 Chron. 26:27; Ps. 16:5.

Toothache: (1) Hurting believer; (2) Devouring words; (3) Painful messenger.
Also see *Teeth*.
(1) Song 4:2; 6:6; (tooth = sheep); (2) Prov. 30:14; (3) Prov. 10:26.

Toothbrush: (1) The Word of God; (2) Pride of appearance (self-image); (3) Self-enhancement; (4) Tainted Bible (dirty toothbrush); (5) Ministry (as the vehicle delivering God's Word); (6) The means of delivering God's Word (dream, prophecy, natural event, incident, etc.).
Also see *Comb* and *Teeth*.
(1) Song 4:2; 6:6 (tooth = sheep = believers); (cf. Ps. 119:9); John 15:3; Eph. 5:26; (that which cleans believers is the Word of God); (2-3) 2 Sam. 14:25-26; (4) 2 Cor. 2:17 (KJV); 2 Pet. 2:3 (KJV); (5-6) Ps. 119:9; John 15:3; Eph. 5:26.

Tooth Decay: (1) Sin; (2) Sinful words.
Also see *Teeth* and *Toothbrush*.
(1) Ps. 3:7; (2) Prov. 30:14.

Toothpaste: (1) The blood of Jesus; (1) The Word of God.
Also see *Teeth* and *Toothbrush*.
(1) 1 John 1:7; (2) Ps. 119:9; John 15:3.

Torch: (1) The Holy Spirit; (2) The human spirit; (3) The Word of God; (4) The Gospel of Christ (the glory of God); (5) A guide (pointing the way); (6) Deliverance and guidance; (7) Humanity's light (self-sufficiency); (8) Exposing something hidden (shining light onto something).
Also see *Beacon*, *Lampstand*, *Light*, *Lighthouse*, and *Spotlight*.
(1) Judg. 7:20 (cf. 2 Cor. 4:7); Matt. 25:3-4; (2) Job 18:5; Ps. 18:28; Prov. 20:27; (3) Ps.119:105; (4) 2 Cor. 4:4,6; (5) Rom. 2:19-20; (6) John 5:35; Acts 12:7; (7) Isa. 50:11; (8) Job 12:22; 28:11; 33:30.

Tornado: (1) The devil; (2) Judgment against sin; (3) Unstoppable; (4) Trials and calamity; (5) Spirit of death.
Also see *Storm*, *Dust Storm*, *Whirlpool*, *Whirlwind*, and *Wind*.
(1) John 10:10; (2) Jer. 30:23; Zech. 9:14; (3) Dan. 11:40; (4) Acts 27:4; (5) Ps. 103:15-16; Prov. 10:25; Zech. 7:14.

Torpedo: See *Bomb*, *Propeller*, and *Missile*.

Tortoise: (1) Sluggish church; (2) Traditional religion; (3) Counterfeit gospel (false rock).
Also see *Turtle*.
(1-2) Rev. 3:1-2; (3) Gal. 1:6-7.

Touchdown: See *Goal*, *Hole in One*, and *Winning*.

Tour Guide: (1) Anointed international ministry (international ministry led by the Spirit); (2) Angel.

Also see *Tourist*.

(1) Acts 16:6-9; (2) Exod. 23:23; Zech. 1:9; Luke 1:19.

Tourist and Tourist Bus: (1) Searching from church to church; (2) Leisurely spiritual journey; (3) Looking for signs; (4) Ineffective mission; (5) Pleasure-seeker; (6) Learning the ropes; (7) Sight-seeing, but really going nowhere (non-productive); (8) Someone just passing through; (9) Sojourner.

Also see *Bus* and *Tour Guide*.

(1) 2 Kings 2:1-5; (2) Rev. 3:16; (3) Matt. 12:39; (4) Acts 13:13; (5) James 4:3; (6) Luke 8:1; (7) John 3:3, 5; (8) John 6:66; (9) Gen. 12:10; Acts 7:6.

Towel: (1) Servant ministry; (2) Ministry; (3) Cleansing (as in cleaning the water off after a shower); (4) Drying; (5) Cover; (6) Giving up.

(1-5) John 13:4-5-16; Acts 3:19; (6) As in "throwing in the towel."

Tower: (1) People's attempts to make a name for themselves; (2) Pride; (3) Christ; (4) The Church/Kingdom of God; (5) Salvation; (6) Refuge; (7) Security/ shelter/defense; (8) Watchtower (a prophet's place of prayer); (9) Place of the watchman (prophet); (10) Judgment (tower falling); (11) Spiritually strong person; (12) Jerusalem (Zion).

Also see *Brick*, *Tall*, and *Tornado*.

(1) Gen. 11:4; (2) Ezek. 30:6 (KJV); Isa. 3:16a; (3) Ps. 18:2; 144:1-2; Prov. 18:10; Isa. 5:2; (4) Luke 14:26-33; (5) 2 Sam. 22:51; Ps. 18:2; (6) 2 Sam. 22:3; (7) Judg. 8:9,17; 9:46,49,51-53; 2 Chron. 14:7; 26:9-10,15; Ps. 61:3; (8) 2 Kings 5:24-26; Hab. 2:1; (9) 2 Kings 17:9; 18:8; 2 Chron. 20:24; (10) Isa. 30:25; Luke 13:4; (11) Jer. 6:27; (12) Mic. 4:8; Matt. 21:33; Mark 12:1.

Towing (Being Towed): (1) Not in the main vehicle; (2) Along for the ride; (3) The one without strength; (4) Being brought into line.

Towing (Doing the Towing): (5) Helping a broken ministry; (6) The powerhouse; (7) The one with strength; (8) Showing the way.

Also see *Pulling*, *Tow Truck*, and *Trailer (Goods)*.

(1-4) 1 Kings 19:19; (5) Gal. 6:2; (6-8) Ps. 23:1-2; Isa. 40:11.

Town: See *City*.

Tow Truck: (1) Five-fold ministry gift; (2) Strong ministry helping others; (3) Apostolic ministry.

(1) Eph. 4:11-12; (2) Acts 18:26; (3) Acts 5:12; 2 Cor. 12:12.

Toxic Vapors: (1) Demonic strongholds.

Also see *Smoke*.

(1) Rev. 9:2-3.

Toys: (1) Playing games; (2) Childishness; (3) Childlikeness; (4) Spoilt (many toys); (5) Toying with; (6) Idolatry; (7) Immature ministry (toy car).

(1) Matt. 15:8; (2) 1 Cor. 13:11; (3) Matt. 18:2-4; (4) Ps. 78:29; Isa. 3:16-23; (5) Judg. 16:6-7, 10-11, 13, 15; (6) Exod. 32:6; 1 Cor. 10:7; (7) Matt. 9:33; Acts 13:13.

Tracksuit Pants: (1) Faith step (choosing track pants); (2) Preparing for the race of faith; (3) Call to walk by faith; (4) Being clothed with strength; (5) Youth ministry or fitness industry.
(1) Rom. 13:14; (2-3) 2 Cor. 5:7; Heb. 12:1; (4) Ps. 147:10; (5) 1 John 2:14.

Tractor: (1) Powerful; (2) Strength (parallels the ox as a strong servant); (3) Powerful harvest multiplier (plows in hope); (4) Powerful ministry/minister; (5) Earning potential; (6) Preparing the harvest; (7) Working the harvest; (8) Business interests/excuses; (9) Idol; (10) Business sowing into the Kingdom; (11) Breaking new ground.
(1-2) Ps. 144:14; Prov. 14:4; (3) 1 Cor. 9:9-10; (4) 1 Cor. 9:9; 1 Tim. 5:17-18; (5) Job 24:3; Deut. 24:6; (the ox is someone's potential to earn or sustain themselves); (6) 1 Kings 19:19; (7) Ruth 2:3; (8) Luke 14:19; John 2:14; (9) Ps. 106:19-20; (10) 1 Kings 10:2; 1 Sam. 25:18; Acts 16:14-15; (11) Hos. 10:12.

Tradesman: See *Workman*.

Traffic: (1) Different walks of life (lanes of traffic); (2) Different ministries being busy; (3) Playing leap-frog in traffic means playing with life and death. This could point to having sexual relations without understanding the consequences.
Also see *Automobile*, *Bus*, and *Truck*.
(1) Prov. 14:12; Matt. 7:13-14; (2) Dan. 12:4; Eph. 4:11; 1 Cor. 12:28; (3) Deut. 30:15-16, 19.

Traffic Jam: (1) Ministries in gridlock; (2) Unable to move because those up front are going nowhere.
(1) 1 Sam. 17:4-11, 23-24; (2) 1 Sam. 14:2; Matt. 23:13.

Traffic Lights: (1) Waiting on God; (2) Guidance; (3) Timing of God; (4) Danger/stop (red light); (5) Warning (amber light); (6) Go into the world and preach the Gospel (green light).
(1) Ps. 27:14; John 8:12; (2) Exod. 13:21b; Neh. 9:19b; Ps. 43:3; (3) Gal. 4:4; (4) Rev. 6:4; (5-6) See *Amber* and *Green*.

Trail Bike: (1) Independent ministry; (2) Pioneering spirit.
Also see *Motorcycle*.
(1-2) Ps. 18:33; Hab. 3:19.

Trailer (Boat): (1) Dependence on another ministry (not free to minister in your own right).
(1) Acts 15:40.

Trailer (Caravan): (1) Temporary home; (2) Itinerant ministry; (3) Mobile; (4) Holiday; (5) Contract work.
(1) 2 Cor. 5:1; 2 Pet. 1:14; (2-3) Gen. 13:18; Heb. 11:9.

Trailer (Goods): (1) Burden (extra baggage you are carrying); (2) Something/one in tow; (3) Followers; (4) May represent a family, congregation, or ministry group; (5) Without leadership (no auto pulling the trailer); (6) Under the influence of the vehicle doing the towing.
(1) Isa. 46:1; Matt. 11:28; (2) See *Towing*; (3-4) Matt. 8:19,23; 10:38; (5) Matt. 9:36b; 1 Pet. 2:25; (6) 2 Pet. 2:19.

Train: (1) Ministry with clout; (2) Large (continuous) ministry; (3) Vehicle to destiny; (4) The Church; (5) Vehicle of the flesh (ministry with an agenda, i.e., "rail-roading"); (6) Lucrative endeavor or money; (7) Nothing gets in its way; (8) Trying to stop the course of a train can be dangerous.
Also see *Freight, Railway Station, Railroad Platform, Railroad Tracks*, and *Train (Ride-On Model)*.
(1) Acts 5:12; (2) Acts 2:42; (3) Jer. 29:11; (4) Acts 2:42; (5) John 3:8; (6) As in "gravy train"; (7-8) 1 Kings 19:1-3.

Train (Ride-On Model): (1) Church playing games; (2) Not spiritually effective (going around in circles); (3) Taking people for a ride; (4) Spiritually immature; (5) Small church.
Also see *Train*.
(1-2) Rev. 3:1; (3) Acts 5:37; (4) 1 Cor. 13:11; (5) Acts 2:46.

Train (Freight): See *Freight*.

Train (off the Rails): (1) (any of the above) derailed; (2) Individual or church not on track for God's destiny.
(1) Job 12:24; Ps. 107:40; (2) Isa. 53:6.

Train Running Without Rails: (1) Holy Spirit led ministry.
(1) John 3:8.

Trample/d: (1) Taking authority over the enemy; (2) Sharing revelation with unbelievers; (3) Anger.
(1) Ps. 91:13; (cf. Luke 10:19); (2) Matt. 7:6; (3) Isa. 63:3.

Trampoline: (1) In the Spirit; (2) Launching in the Spirit.
(1-2) Isa. 40:31.

Transmission: (1) Spirit (good or evil).
(1) Mark 1:12; Luke 8:29; (Acts 27:15,17; cf. John 3:8).

Transparent (Crystal): (1) River of life (water); (2) Glory of God (light); (3) Spirit; (4) Sea of glass before the throne; (5) Honest and open (revealing one's heart).
(1) Rev. 22:1; (2) Rev. 21:11; (3) Ezek. 1:22; (4) Rev. 4:6; (5) John 1:47.

Transparent: (1) The revealing of one's heart.
(1) John 1:47; Acts 1:24.

Trap: (1) Warning of danger; (2) Deceit and deception; (3) Sudden destruction; (4) Stronghold; (5) Sign of backsliding; (6) Sin.

Also see *Snare*.

(1) 2 Kings 6:9; 2 Cor. 2:11; 2 Tim. 2:26; (2) Jer. 5:26-27; (3) Eccles. 9:12; (4) Prov. 11:6; 12:13; (5) Josh. 23:13; (6) Prov. 5:22.

Trash: See *Garbage, Garbage Truck, Rubbish,* and *Rubbish Bag/Bin.*

Treasure: (1) Heart; (2) The Holy Spirit; (3) God's people; (4) God's (Heaven's) provision or storehouse; (5) Godly wisdom, understanding, and knowledge; (6) Spiritual gifts; (7) Suffering reproach for Christ; (8) Earthly wealth; (9) Foolishness (bragging or showing all your treasure); (10) Intricate secrets; (11) May indicate a righteous or wise person; (12) May come with trouble; (13) Beware gaining it by lying; (14) Fear of the Lord; (15) Wickedness.

Also see *Precious Stones*.

(1) Matt. 6:21; Luke 2:19; (2) (1 Cor. 2:4-5; 2 Cor. 4:7); (3) Exod. 19:5; Ps. 135:4; (4) Deut. 28:12a; Ps. 135:7; Isa. 45:3; Jer. 10:13; (5) Prov. 2:3-5; 8:21; Col. 2:3; (6) Prov. 8:10-11; 2:3-4; 20:15; 24:4; (cf. 1 Cor. 12:8); (7) Heb. 11:25-26; (8) James 5:3; (9) 2 Kings 20:15-18; (10) Job 38:22; (11) Prov. 15:6; 21:20; (12) Prov. 15:16; (13) Prov. 21:6; (14) Isa. 33:6b; (15) Prov. 10:2; Mic. 6:10.

Tree: (1) Person; (2) Righteous believer; (3) Jesus Christ; (4) Country or nation; (5) The cross; (6) Life; (7) The Kingdom; (8) Family; (9) Company (of people); (10) If planted by a stream, it means prosperity; (11) Hanging on a tree means judgment or cursed; (12) Beside still waters means peace/rest; (13) Under a green tree can mean idolatry or spiritual adultery; (14) Cursed (stuck in a tree); (15) Believer choked by cares of world/riches (tree of thorns); (16) People trusting in people, not in God (stunted tree).

Also see *Big Tree, Bush, Evergreen, Thorns,* and individual tree names.

(1-2) Ps. 1:3; Isa. 7:2; 61:3; Jer. 17:8; (3) See *Big Tree*; (4) 1 Kings 4:33; Ps. 29:5; (5) 1 Pet. 2:24; Acts 5:30; 10:39; Gal. 3:13; (6) Rev. 2:7; 22:2,14; (7) Luke 13:18-19; (8) John 15:5 (cf. John 1:12); Rom. 11:17; as in "family tree"; (9) Isa. 7:2; 24:13; 65:22; (10) Num. 24:6; Ps. 1:3; (11) Esther 2:23; Gal. 3:13; (12) Ps. 23:2; (13) Jer. 3:6; (14) Gal. 3:13; (15) Matt. 13:22; (16) Jer. 17:5-6.

Tree (Big Tree): (1) Jesus; (2) Church or leader; (3) Corporation; (4) Business or country leader; (5) Kingdom of God; (6) Longevity; (7) Pride and arrogance (tall tree); (8) Flourishing prosperity (tall tree); (9) Believer with strong foundation.

Also see *Oak* and *Tree*.

(1) Isa. 11:1; Jer. 23:5; 33:15-16; (2) Ps. 37:35; Luke 13:18-19; (3) As in, a hierarchy; (4) Dan. 4:10-11, 20-22; (5) Matt. 13:31-32; (6) Gen. 21:33; (7) Ezek. 31:3-10; (8) Ps. 92:12; (9) Isa. 61:3 (NIV).

Tree House: (1) Cursed individual; (2) You in Christ; (3) You in the Kingdom.

Also see *House* and *Tree*.

(1) Gal. 3:13; (2) Eph. 1:1; (3) Matt. 12:28; 13:31-32.

Tree Uprooted/Cut Down: (1) Warning of judgment; (2) Collapse of a ministry; (3) Not ordained of God; (4) Death or destruction.

(1) Dan. 4:14-15, 24-26; Luke 13:6-9; Matt. 3:10; (2) Dan. 4:14-15; (3) Matt. 15:13; (4) Luke 13:6-9.

Trellis: (1) Supportive framework; (2) The Word of God; (3) God.
Also see *Scaffold*.
(1) John 15:5; 1 Thess. 5:14; (2) Job 4:4; Ps. 119:28; (3) Isa. 40:31 (the word *wait* can mean "to entwine").

Trench: (1) Heart; (2) Depression; (3) Path for the Holy Spirit; (4) Pathway of the mind (soul-tie [godly or ungodly]).
Also see *Gutter(s)*, *Pipe*, *Plowing*, and *Plumber*.
(1) Matt. 13:19; Mark 4:15; (cf. Gen. 2:7; 2 Cor. 4:7); (2) Ps. 42:5; (3) John 1:33; Acts 9:17; (4) Ps. 119:59; Isa. 55:7.

Trench Coat: (1) Someone stuck in a rut; (2) Stronghold (dug in); (3) Stronghold of depression.
Also see *Coat*.
(1) Ps. 40:2; 69:2; (2) 2 Chron. 11:11a; Ps. 89:40; 2 Cor. 10:4-5; (3) Ps. 43:5; Gal. 5:1.

Triangle: (1) Divine order; (2) Godhead; (3) Threesome.
(1-3) Matt. 28:19; 1 John 5:7-8.

Tribal: See *Indigenous*.

Trick: (1) Deception; (2) Mock or fool; (3) Self-glory (doing tricks to draw attention to oneself); (4) Moving in the gifts of the Holy Spirit; (5) Test; (6) Counterfeit signs and wonders.
(1) Prov. 10:23; 14:8b; Gal. 3:1; (2) Gal. 6:7-8; (3) Prov. 25:27b; 27:2; (4) Acts 10:44-45; Heb. 2:4; (5) Mark 12:13; (6) Exod. 7:11-12; Acts 8:9.

Trimming: (1) Short-cutting; (2) Fine-tuning; (3) Beautifying; (4) Cutting away that which is superfluous; (5) Trimming or not trimming may be a sign of allegiance, an oath, or respect; (6) Disciplining (as in pruning).
Also see *Pruning*.
(1, 3) Jer. 2:33 (KJV); (2) Matt. 25:7; (4) Acts 27:32; (5) 2 Sam. 19:24; (6) John 15:2.

Trip (noun): See *Cruise Ship*, *Holiday*, *Suitcase*, and *Tourist*.

Trip (verb): (1) Temptation (cause to sin).
Also see *Falling* and *Losing Footing*.
(1) Gen. 3:4-5; Matt. 4:6.

Tripod: (1) Stable; (2) God.
(1) Eccles. 4:12; (2) Matt. 28:19.

Trophy: (1) Victory; (2) Pride; (3) Self-glory; (4) The empty tomb (victory in Christ); (5) Heavenly rewards.
(1) 1 Sam. 17:54; (2) 1 Sam. 15:8,17; Prov. 20:29; (3) Prov. 25:27; Jer. 9:23-24; Matt. 6:2; Rom. 1:23; 1 Cor. 3:21a; 2 Cor. 12:6; 1 Thess. 2:6a; 1 Pet. 1:24a; (4) 1 Cor. 15:57; (5) Luke 6:23.

Trousers: See *Clothing*.

Truck/Semi: (1) Powerful ministry; (2) Big ministry; (3) Deliverance ministry; (4) Leadership; (5) Business (freight truck); (6) Intimidation (relating to size: truck vs. car). Also see *Automobile, Bulldozer, Earthmover, Road Grader*, and *Utility (Ute/Truck)*. (1) 1 Kings 10:2; 1 Sam. 14:6,22; Acts 4:33; 6:8; (2) 2 Cor. 11:28; (3) Zech. 3:9b; as in the removal of sin and iniquity; (4) Acts 13:43; (5) 1 Kings 10:15; (6) 1 Sam. 17:4-11; Isa. 37:10-11.

Trumpet: (1) Warning or alarm; (2) Gathering; (3) Gathering the elect; (4) Rapturous gathering; (5) Voice of God/Word of God; (6) Announcement/self-glory/pronouncing own goodness; (7) Judgment; (8) Battle signal; (9) Memorial; (10) Jubilee; (11) Tongues (an unknown tongue).
Also see *Shofar* and *Thunder*.
(1) Num. 10:9; Jer. 4:19b; Amos 3:6; (2) Exod. 20:18-20; (3) Matt. 24:31; (4) 1 Cor. 15:52; 1 Thess. 4:16; (5) Exod. 19:16,19; 1 Cor. 14:8; Rev. 1:10; 4:1; (6) Matt. 6:2; (7) Josh. 6:4; Rev. 8:2; (8) Num. 10:9; 31:6; 1 Cor. 14:8; (9) Lev. 23:24; (10) Lev. 25:9; (11) Rev. 4:1; 1 Cor. 14:8,10.

Tsunami: (1) Upheaval; (2) Destruction/judgment; (3) Carried away; (4) Holy Spirit outpouring/revival.
Also see *Wave*.
(1-3) Isa. 28:2-3; 59:19b; (4) Isa 59:19; Acts 2:17.

Tuesday: (1) Three; (2) Double Blessing; (3) Resurrection.
Also see *Day* and *Two* (the secular world sees Tuesday as the second day of the week).
(1-2) Gen. 1: 9-13 (Note v. 10, 12); (3) Matt. 20:19.

Tumor: (1) Judgment; (2) Corruption; (3) Self-destructive thoughts/words (brain tumor); (4) Literal tumor.
Also see *Cancer*.
(1) 1 Sam. 5:6; (2-3) 2 Cor. 10:5; 2 Tim. 2:16-17.

Tunnel: (1) Passage through; (2) Transition; (3) Way in or way out; (4) Entrance to your heart; (5) Way to the light (as in "light at the end of the tunnel"); (6) What is going on inside of you; (7) Throat; (8) Going through dark times; (9) Uncertainty.
Also see *Cave*.
(1) 2 Sam. 5:8 (NKJV); (2) Exod. 14:22; Num. 22:24; (3-4) 2 Sam. 5:8; Ezek. 8:8; (5) Ps. 56:13; Isa. 9:2; Matt. 4:16; (6) 1 Pet. 3:4; (7) Ps. 5:9; (8-9) Matt. 4:16; Mark 15:33.

Turbulent: (1) Unsettling; (2) Rough; (3) Test or trial.
(1-2) Isa. 57:20; Matt. 14:25-26; (3) Josh. 3:15b; Mark 6:48.

Turkey: (1) Thanksgiving; (2) Christmas; (3) Contemptuously rich; (4) Foolish; (5) Pleasure seeker; (6) Preparation for slaughter; (7) Waxen fat and forsaking God.

(1) Ps. 107:22; 116:17; (2) Esther 5:4; (3) Prov. 30:8-9; Luke 12:19-20; 16:19 (cf. v. 21) (4) Eccles. 9:12; (5) James 5:5 (being fattened); (6) James 5:5; Jer. 12:3; (7) Deut. 32:15; Prov. 27:7.

Turning: (1) Altered course or change (of direction); (2) Denying or turning away; (3) Attacking you; (4) Repentance; (5) Moving into the Spirit; (6) Moving into the flesh (natural); (7) Coming to God; (8) To change the heart attitude; (9) To acknowledge or make your focus (turning to someone); (10) Unexpected opportunity (as in turning for the better); (11) Changing from sorrow to joy or vice versa; (12) Turning for the worse. Also see *Corner*, *Dancing*, and *U-Turn*.
(1) Matt. 2:22b; Luke 1:17; Acts 13:46; (2) Matt. 5:42; (3) Matt. 7:6; (4) Luke 17:4; Acts 3:26; (5) Matt. 9:22; 16:23; Luke 2:45; 7:9; 9:55; 23:28; John 1:38; 16:20; 20:16; (6) John 21:20-21; (7) Luke 1:16; 17:15; Acts 11:21; (8) Luke 1:17; Acts 7:39; 13:8; (9) Luke 7:44; (10) Luke 21:12-13; (11) John 16:20; Acts 2:20; (12) 1 Kings 17:18.

Turnstile: (1) Entry point; (2) Restricted entry (the narrow way).
(1) Acts 13:2; (2) Matt. 7:13.

Turtle: (1) Religious spirit (hardened hearts [shell]); (2) Traditional church (old covering); (3) Primarily concerned about protection/security; (4) Shy (not evangelistic); (5) Snake-like head (poisonous thinking); (6) Ducking for cover; (7) Believer; (8) Slow to change; (9) Withdrawn.
Also see *Shells* and *Tortoise*.
(1) Matt. 23:4; John 12:37-40; (2) Matt. 15:1-3; Mark 7:5; (3) 1 Thess. 5:3; (4) Joel 2:10 (cf. Gen. 15:5); (5) Rom. 3:13; (6) Matt. 26:56; Mark 14:50; (7) Isa. 28:16; (8) Jer. 48:11; (9) Gal. 2:12.

Tuxedo: (1) Special occasion; (2) Position of honor; (3) Ready for marriage supper; (4) Cleansed from sin.
(1) Gen. 41:14; (2) Luke 15:22; (3) Matt. 22:11-12; Rev. 19:9; (4) Zech. 3:4.

Tweezers: (1) Sensitivity; (2) Accuracy; (3) Carefully.
(1) 2 Sam. 18:5; (2) Matt. 7:5; (3) Luke 10:34; 1 Cor. 12:25.

Twelve: (1) Perfect government or rule; (2) Divine organization; (3) Apostolic fullness; (4) Literally twelve; (5) Turning point; (6) Israel.
(1-2) Gen. 49:28; Exod. 28:21 (twelve sons of Jacob); Exod. 24:4 (twelve pillars); Josh. 4:3,9 (twelve stones); Josh. 3:12-13 (twelve priests bearing the ark); Job 38:32 (sun and moon made to rule the day and night. To do this they pass through the twelve signs of the zodiac. Hebrew: *mazzaroth* completing 360 degrees); Luke 6:13 (twelve apostles); John 11:9 (twelve hours in a day); twelve months in a year; Rev. 21:10-21 (New Jerusalem (perfection of rule) twelve gates, twelve pearls, twelve angels, twelve foundations, twelve precious stones, twelve fruits); Exod. 15:27 (twelve wells at Elim); (3) Exod. 24:4; Matt. 10:2-5; 19:28; (5) Twelve hours of light; Jesus at age twelve enters temple; girl twelve years old brought to life; woman with issue of blood had it twelve years; twelve months in year; twelfth letter of Hebrew alphabet center letter; (6) Matt. 19:28.

Twenty: (1) Expectancy; (2) Waiting; (3) Accountability; (4) Responsibility; (5) Service; (6) Literally twenty.
(1-2) Gen. 31:38,41; (Jacob waited twenty years to get his inheritance); Judg. 15:20; 16:31; (Israel waited for deliverance through Samson); 1 Sam. 7:2; (the Ark waited twenty years at Kirjath-jearim); twenty dreams recorded in Scripture; (3-5) Exod. 30:14; (Israel numbered from age twenty years and upward); Num. 1:3,18-24; (warfare at twenty years); 1 Chron. 23:24,27; (Levites served from age twenty years).

Twenty-One: (1) The product of 3 x 7, it therefore means fullness or the completion [3] of spiritual perfection [7]; (2) Expecting God (20 + 1); (3) Serving God (20 + 1).
(1) Exod. 12:18; (2-3) Dan. 10:13; Hag. 2:1.

Twenty-Two: Carries the meaning of double eleven. (1) Disorganization; (2) Disintegration; (especially in regard to the Word of God); (3) Expecting testimony (20 + 2); (4) Expecting separation or division (20 + 2).
(1-2) 1 Kings 14:20; 1 Kings 16:29.

Twenty-Four: (1) Governmental perfection; (2) Elder.
(1) Josh. 4:2-9,20; 1 Kings 19:19; Rev. 4:4; (2) Rev. 4:4,10; 5:8.

Twenty-Five: (1) Being brought to account by the grace of God; (2) Expecting grace or mercy (20+5).
(1-2) See *Twenty* and *Five*.

Twenty-Six: (1) Being brought to account because of the flesh.
(1) See *Twenty* and *Six*.

Twenty-Eight: (1) Awaiting or expecting a new beginning.
(1) See *Twenty* and *Eight*.

Twig: (1) Young and tender Christian; (2) The position of a twig on a plant may indicate its standing (e.g., high twig is royalty/leadership).
(1) Ezek. 17:4,22.

Twins: (1) Contention; (2) Double-mindedness; (3) Unity/union; (4) Symmetry; (5) Double portion; (6) Double blessing; (7) A repeat experience.
The sex of the twins is important to their interpretation.
Also see *Baby*, *Boy*, *Girl*, and *Two*.
(1-2) Gen. 25:24,27-28; Gen. 38:27 (the product of contention and different intent); (3-4) Song 4:2,5; 6:6; (5) Dan. 1:13; (6) Prov. 20:7; (1) Gen. 12:13; 20:2; Ps. 85:8.

Twirl/ing: (1) Ascending in the Spirit.
See also *Somersault*.
(1) Ezek. 1:19-20.

Twister: See *Tornado*.

Two: (1) Witness; (2) Testimony; (3) Division or separation; (4) Difference; (5) Association or agreement; (6) Reward: multiplication (7) Support; (8) Warmth; (9) Doubt (double-mindedness); (10) Death (precedes three [resurrection]); (11) Second heaven (spiritual realm); (12) Repeated situation.

Also see *Twins*.

(1) Matt. 18:16; (2) John 8:17; (3) Gen. 1:6-8; (4) Gen. 13:6-7; Exod. 8:23; Matt. 24:40-41; (5) Amos 3:3; (6) Eccles. 4:9; (7) Eccles. 4:10, 12; (8) Eccles. 4:11; (9) Matt. 14:30-31; 21:21; Mark 11:23; James 1:8; 4:8; (10) Gen. 1:6-8 (no blessing); (11) Eph. 6:12 (cf. 2 Cor. 12:2); (12) Mark 14:72.

Two Hundred: (1) Insufficient or insufficiency; (2) Double blessing/harvest (hundredfold x two).

Also see *Hundred*.

(1) Josh. 7:21; (cf. Ps. 49:7-9; Mark 8:36-37) (insufficiency of money); Judg. 17:4-6; (insufficiency of religion); 2 Sam. 14:26; 18:9 (insufficiency of beauty); John 6:7 (KJV); (2) Matt. 13:23.

Tyre: See *Tire*.

U

Uber: (1) Cost-effective ministry/option to your destination; (2) Ministry you see available and coming.

See *Automobile*, *Hire Car*, and *Taxi/Cab*.

(1) 1 Sam. 9:6-10; Matt. 17:27; (2) Acts 9:12; 10:5.

UFO: (1) Spiritual principality; (2) Deceiving spirits; (3) Counterfeit portals.

Also see *Alien* and *Spaceship*.

(1) Eph. 6:12; (2) Gal. 1:8; (3) 2 Cor. 11:3.

Ugly: (1) Ungodliness; (2) Sin; (3) Without the Spirit (no life).

Also see *Beautiful*.

(1) 1 Sam. 16:13; (2) Isa. 64:6; (3) Gen. 41:3.

Umbilical Cord: (1) Soul-tie.

(1) Gen. 44:30.

Umbrella: (1) Covering; (2) Protection; (3) Authority structure; (4) Shield.

(1-2) Gen. 19:8b; Jon. 4:6; (3) Matt. 8:9; (4) Eph. 6:16.

Umpire: (1) God; (2) Authority.

(1) 1 Cor. 5:13; (2) Exod. 2:14; Deut. 21:2; 1 Chron. 17:10.

Uncertainty: (1) Double-mindedness; (2) Doubt (not operating in faith); (3) A call to draw near to God and humble the heart; (4) May indicate a person is avoiding the question; (5) Inner battle between flesh and spirit; (6) Awaiting confirmation or more revelation; (7) Time to look to God not circumstance.

(1-2) James 1:6-8; (3) James 4:8; (4) John 9:25; (5) Rom. 6:16; (6) Gen. 24:21; (7) Gen. 27:21; 1 Sam. 17:10-11.

Uncle: (1) Married Christian brother; (2) Actual uncle; (3) A relative who takes advantage of you; (4) An uncle could speak about his character, name, position, or profession.
(1-3) Gen. 28:2; 29:25.

Uncooked: (1) Not ready for consumption; (2) Raw.
(1-2) Exod. 12:9; Acts 10:10; Heb. 5:12-14.

Under: (1) Inferior position; (2) In subjection to; (3) Influenced by; (4) Hidden; (5) In the shade; (6) In the shadow of; (7) Idolatry (green tree); (8) Spiritual adultery; (9) Protection and safety; (10) Living safely/prosperously; (11) Annoyance (under the skin); (12) Authority structure.
Also see *Above and Below*.
(1) Deut. 28:13; (2) 2 Sam. 12:31; (3) Luke 6:40; (4) Judg. 3:16; (5) Song 2:3; (6) Ps. 91:1; (7) Deut. 12:2; (8) Jer. 2:20; 3:6,13; (8) Ps. 91:1-4; (9) 1 Kings 4:25; Mic. 4:4; Zech. 3:10; (10) Neh. 4:1; Esther 5:9; (11) Matt. 8:9.

Underarm: See *Body Odor* and *Hairy*.

Underground: (1) Undercover (under authority); (2) Secretive or hidden; (3) Inside the heart; (4) Buried; (5) No hope (trapped underground).
Also see *Burying*, *Cave*, *Tunnel*, and *Under*.
(1) Exod. 33:22; Matt. 8:9; (2) Josh. 10:16; 1 Kings 18:13; (3) Song 2:14; (4) Gen. 23:19; (5) Josh. 10:18.

Under the Hood: See *Auto Engine* and *Engine*.

Undertow: (1) Undercurrent; (2) Dissension; (3) Hidden pull (on hearts); (4) Lose position (pull down); (5) Destruction (pull down); (6) Division; (7) Sedition.
(1, 3) 2 Sam. 15:4-6; (2) Acts 23:10; (4) Isa. 22:19; Jer. 1:10; (5) Jer. 18:7; (6) Acts 13:8; (7) Num. 12:1-2; Gal. 5:19-20.

Underwater: (1) Death of the flesh; (2) Baptism; (3) Death or dead; (4) Cleaning the conscience; (5) Overwhelmed; (6) Going under (opposite of "keeping my head above water"); (7) In the Deep; (8) In the Spirit; (9) Sunk; (10) Not operating in faith.
Also see *Deep*, *Drowning*, and *Water*.
(1) Gen. 6:17; 2 Pet. 3:6; (2) Acts 8:38-39; 1 Cor. 10:1-2; (3) Job 26:5 (KJV); Rom. 6:3; (4) 1 Pet. 3:21; (5-6) Ps. 61:2; 77:3; 124:4; 142:3; 143:4; (7) Ps. 42:7; (8) Ezek. 47:5; (9) Exod. 15:5; Ps. 69:14; Jon. 2:3; (10) Matt. 14:30.

Underwear: (1) Spiritually vulnerable; (2) Coming to or from nakedness; (3) Not ready (ill-dressed); (4) Revealing someone's true spiritual state; (5) Not yet clothed with Christ; (6) Stripped of upper garments; (7) The bare essentials; (8) Shamed; (9) Deeply grieved; (10) Sexual perversion; (11) Self-atonement; (12) Uncovered wickedness; (13) What you are wearing on the inside; (14) Unrighteousness (dirty underwear).

Also see *Breast*, *Genitals*, *Nakedness*, and *Pants*.

(1-4) Mark 14:51-52; John 21:7; (5) Rom. 13:14; Gal. 3:27; (6-7) John 21:7; (8) 2 Sam. 13:18-19; (9) Gen. 37:34; (10) Lev. 18:6-23; (11) Gen. 3:7; (12) Ezek. 16:57 (NKJV); (13) Eph. 3:16; (14) Isa. 64:6.

Undone: (1) Perishing (without protection); (2) Incomplete (not finished); (3) Revealed; (4) Without strength; (5) Destroyed or cut off; (6) Neglecting; (7) Loose or release.

(1) Num. 21:29; (2) Josh. 11:15; (3-5) Isa. 6:5; (6) Matt. 23:23; Luke 11:42; (7) Isa. 58:6.

Unfamiliar: (1) Not recognized; (2) Not known; (3) Dead to the world; (4) Spiritually insensitive.

Also see *Foreign*, *Foreigner*, *Strange*, and *Woman (Foreign Woman)*.

(1-2) Matt. 25:12; Acts 17:23; (3) 2 Cor. 6:9; (4) Matt. 17:12.

Unicorn: (1) God/Jesus; (2) Strength.

(1) Num. 23:22 (KJV); (2) Ps. 18:2; 89:17.

Unicycle: (1) Going it alone; (2) Moving in your own strength; (3) Without God.

Also see *Bicycle* and *Clown*.

(1) Gen. 2:18; Exod. 18:14; (2) Num. 14:42; Job 18:7; (3) Eph. 2:12.

Uniform: (1) Recognized authority. (2) Members; (3) All the same.

(1) Rom. 13:3-4. (2-3) Rom. 12:16; 1 Cor. 12:12; Phil. 2:2.

Unite: See *Bound*, *Cleave*, and *Marriage*.

University: (1) Education; (2) Study; (3) Intellect or human wisdom; (4) Degree or qualification; (5) Human authority; (6) Human wisdom; (7) Natural person; (8) School of the Spirit (higher learning).

(1-2) Acts 22:3; 2 Tim. 2:15; (3) 1 Cor. 1:19-20-25; James 3:13-18; (4) John 7:15; Acts 7:22; (5-6) John 7:15-17; 1 Cor. 2:1-5; (7) 1 Cor. 2:14; (8) John 14:26.

Unprepared: (1) Prayerlessness; (2) Danger of falling into temptation; (3) Not willing to pay the price; (4) Need for a fresh anointing of the Holy Spirit; (5) Not praying in the Holy Spirit; (6) Not understanding the sign of the times.

Also see *Watch*.

(1) Matt. 24:42; 26:41; Luke 12:35-40; 21:36; 22:40; Eph. 6:18; Rev. 3:3; (2) Matt. 26:41; Mark 14:38; (3) Matt. 22:11-14; (4) Matt. 25:1-13; (5) Jude 1:19-20; (6) Matt. 16:3; Mark 13:33; 1 Pet. 4:7.

Unrecognized: (1) In the Spirit.

(1) Luke 24:16, 31; John 20:14; 1 Cor. 2:14.

Unseen Accomplice: (1) The Holy Spirit.

(1) John 16:13; 11:51.

Unstable: (1) Double-minded; (2) Heart trained in covetous practices; (3) Prone to fall back into sin; (4) Unlearned in the ways of God and likely to twist things to suit themselves; (5) Shall not excel.

(1) James 1:8; (2-3) 2 Pet. 2:14; (4) 2 Pet. 3:16; (5) Gen. 49:4.

Up: (1) God; (2) Heaven; (3) Spiritual ascension; (4) Approval or success; (5) Pride; (6) Positive; (7) Operating in faith (as in "nowhere to look but up"); (8) Spiritually strengthened.

Also see *Down, North*, and *Uphill*.

(1) Gen. 14:22; (2) Gen. 28:12; Deut. 4:19; (3) Isa. 2:3a; (4) As in "thumbs up"; (5) Matt. 4:5-6 (appealing to "the pride of life"); (6) Ps. 24:7; (7) Heb. 12:2; (8) Ps. 110:7.

Upgrade: (1) Moving to another spiritual level; (2) Passing through death (spiritual promotion).

Also see *Computer*.

(1) 2 Cor. 3:18; (2) 2 Kings 2:11.

Uphill: (1) Spiritual ascension; (2) Battling, as in "an uphill battle."

(1) Ps. 122:1; Isa. 2:3a; Mic. 4:1; (2) 1 Sam. 14:13.

Upper Room: (1) Spiritual place; (2) Heaven; (3) Spiritual thinking.

Also see *Upstairs*.

(1) Acts 1:13; 2:1-4; (2) John 14:2; (3) Isa. 55:9; Matt. 6:20.

Upright: (1) Righteous; (2) Standing in faith; (3) Truth; (4) Leadership; (5) Not in bondage; (6) Good; (7) Honest conduct; (8) God; (9) Integrity; (10) Understanding (spiritually in tune); (11) Blessed.

Also see *Crooked, Curved, Down, Straight, Standing*, and *Tall*.

(1) Prov. 11:6; (2) 2 Cor. 1:24b; (3) Eccles. 12:10; (4) Gen. 37:7; (5) Lev. 26:13; (6) 1 Sam. 29:6; (7) Ps. 37:14; (8) Ps. 92:15; (9) Ps. 11:3; (10) Prov. 15:21; (11) Ps. 112:2; Prov. 11:11.

Uproot/ed: (1) Judgment; (2) Idolatry; (3) Sin; (4) Deceitful and lying tongue; (5) Self-righteous, greedy, or rebellious heart; (6) The role of the prophet (to uproot sin).

Also see *Root*.

(1) Deut. 29:28; Zeph. 2:4; (2-3) 1 Kings 14:15-16; 2 Chron. 7:19-20; (3) Prov. 2:22; (4) Ps. 52:2-5; (5) Jude 1:11-12; (6) Jer. 1:10; Matt. 3:10; Luke 3:9.

Upside Down: (1) Overturned.

Also see *Somersault*.

(1) Acts 17:6.

Upstairs: (1) Heaven; (2) Presence of God; (3) Leading to spiritual blessing; (4) Going into heavenly places; (5) God's plans; (6) Thoughts; (7) Mind or thoughts; (8) Place of prayer or renewal (rest).

Also see *Upper Room*.

(1) Gen. 28:12; (2) Exod. 34:2; (Gen. 49:33; Matt. 22:32); (3) Eph. 1:3; (4) Eph. 1:20; (5) Mark 14:15; Luke 1:76; Rom. 9:17; Col. 3:1; Heb. 8:5; (6) 1 Pet. 1:13; 2 Pet. 3:1-2; (7) 2 Cor. 10:5; Col. 2:18; (8) Mark 6:46; Luke 9:28-29.

Urgency: (1) Time running out; (2) Flesh (pushes whereas the Spirit leads); (3) Provocation; (4) Persecution (The devil's time is short and therefore he persecutes); (5) Rage; (6) Lacking foundation (Beware of being urged or rushed into something).
Also see *Hurry*, *Speed*, *Time*, and *Time Running Out*.
(1) 1 Cor. 7:29; Rev. 12:12-13; (2) Judg. 16:16; 2 Kings 2:17; (3) Luke 11:53-54. (4) Exod. 14:8-9; Rev. 12:12-13; (5) Dan. 3:19, 22; (6) Isa. 28:16.

Urination: (1) Insult or offense; (2) Offense needing to be dealt with; (3) Acts and words of defilement; (4) Foolishness; (5) Rubbish or refuse; (6) Cleansing (disposing of sin); (7) Unbelief; (8) Judgment; (9) Sin; (10) Disrespect (on someone); (11) Foul spirit; (12) Territorial spirit (as an animal marking its territory).
Also see *Dung*, *Feces*, *Rubbish*, and *Sewage*.
All KJV: (1-4) 1 Sam. 25:16, 21-22; 2 Kings 18:27 (urination literally: water of the feet); Isa. 36:12; (4) 1 Sam. 25:34; 1 Kings 14:10; (urination on your provider/protection); (5) 1 Kings 14:10; (6) 1 Kings 16:11-13; (7) 1 Kings 21:21; 2 Kings 9:8; (8) 2 Kings 18:27; (9) Deut. 28:20; Phil. 3:8; (11) Rev. 18:2; (12) Amos 4:10.

USB: (1) Memories; (2) Thoughts.
Also see *Computer* and *Hard Drive*.
(1-2) Neh. 4:14; 1 Cor. 15:2; 2 Cor. 10:5.

U-Turn: (1) Repentance; (2) Return to idolatry; (3) Disobedience; (4) Changing your mind; (5) Going back on your word; (6) Drawn back to the world; (7) Double-minded.
(1) Luke 17:4; Acts 26:20b; (2) Josh. 23:12-13; (3) Job 23:12; (4) Matt. 21:29; (5) Matt. 26:33-35, 70-74; (6) Gen. 19:26; 2 Kings 5:20; (7) Luke 9:62.

Utility (Ute/Truck): (1) Working vehicle (i.e., business).
(1) Esther 3:9; Eccles. 5:3.

U2: (1) Secrets; (2) Heart secrets revealed; (3) Spiritual insight; (4) Prophetic ministry.
Also see *Spy*.
(1-2) Luke 10:21; 1 Cor. 4:5; 1 Pet. 3:4; (3-4) 1 Sam. 9:9; Isa. 45:2-3.

V

Vacuum Cleaner: (1) Deep cleansing work of the Holy Spirit; (2) Deliverance ministry (casting out unclean spirits).
(1) 1 Cor. 6:11; Tit. 3:5; (2) Matt. 12:28; Luke 11:14.

Vagina: See *Genitals*.

Valley: (1) Depression; (2) Hopelessness; (3) Discouragement; (4) Trouble; (5) Fear; (6) Separation; (7) The enemy's domain; (8) Mourning or grief; (9) Shadow of death or death; (10) Weeping; (11) Hell; (12) Pride or haughtiness (limiting spiritual vision); (13) Salt; (14) Humble person (to be exalted); (15) Fruitfulness; (16) Decision; (17) Tribulation; (18) Trial; (19) Hidden (in the secret place).
Also see *Hills*.
(1) By physical association; Isa. 7:19; (2) Ps. 23:4a; (3) Num. 32:9; (4) Josh. 7:24-25 (*Achor* = trouble); (5-6) 1 Sam. 17:3; (7) Judg. 1:19,34; (8) Ezek. 7:16; Zech. 12:11; (9) Ps. 23:4a; Isa. 57:5; (10) Ps. 84:6 (*Baca* = weeping); (11) Prov. 30:17 (see *Raven*); (12) Isa. 22:1,5; (13) 2 Sam. 8:13; 2 Kings 14:7; (14) Isa. 40:4; Luke 3:5; (15) Song 6:11; Isa. 65:10; (16-18) Joel 3:14; (19) Song 2:1,16.

Vampire: (1) Totally sold out to the devil; (2) Resurrection of something from the past (an issue) that sucks the life out of you; (3) Powerful evil spirit (principality) that seeks to take the life out of you; (4) Spirit behind chronic fatigue syndrome.
Also see *Bats (Animals)*.
(1) Num. 23:24b; 1 Pet.5:8; Jer. 46:10b; (2) 2 Sam. 14:21; 15:6; (cf. Lev. 17:11a); (3) Isa. 2:20; Eph. 1:21; 6:12; (4) 1 Sam. 26:12; Isa. 61:3

Van: (1) Commercial vehicle; (2) Business outlook; (3) Courier; (4) Delivery/deliverer.
Also see *Automobile*, *Trailer*, and *Utility*.
(1-4) Gen. 45:27; 1 Sam. 6:7-8; Joel 3:5; Amos 2:13.

Vase: (1) Flesh; (2) Person/people (as human vessel[s]). (1-2) Mark 14:3; John 2:6-7.

Vegetables: (1) Weak; (2) Insufficient sermon; (3) Immature; (4) Avoiding offense; (5) Legalistic food laws; (6) Spiritual health (incorporating wisdom, knowledge, dreams, and visions); (6) Doing nothing ("vegging out"); (7) The Word of God (that which is sown).
(1) Rom. 14:2; (2-3) 1 Cor. 3:2; Heb. 5:12-14; (4) Rom. 14:15-21; (5) 1 Tim. 4:3; (6) Dan. 1:12,15-17 (NKJV); (7) Dan. 1:12 (vegetables = that which is sown); Luke 8:11.

Veil: (1) Spiritual blindness; (2) Deception; (3) Flesh; (4) Heart (behind the veil); (5) Secret (as in "secret place"); (6) Covering; (7) Eternity/Heaven (behind the veil); (8) Authority (on head: marriage veil).
Also see *Curtain*.
(1) 2 Cor. 3:13-14; (2) 2 Cor. 4:4; (3) Matt. 27:50-51; 2 Cor. 3:15; Heb. 10:20; (4) Heb. 6:19 (heart of the temple [cf. 1 Cor. 6:19]); Heb. 9:3; (5) Gen. 24:65; Heb. 9:3; (6) Exod. 35:12; 34:33; 39:34; 40:3; (7) The root of the Hebrew word *olam* means "to be veiled from sight"; (8) 1 Cor. 11:10.

Velvet: (1) Royal; (2) Rich and sumptuous.
(1-2) Esther 1:6a; as in "royal velvet."

Vending Machine: (1) Convenience (hearing what you want to hear); (2) Accessibility; (3) God (as accessed by prayer); (4) Wrong concept of God (quick fix).
Also see *Junk Food*.

(1) Mark 14:11; 2 Tim. 4:3; (2) John 6:5b; (3) Phil. 4:6; (4) James 4:3.

Venom: (1) Poisonous words.

(1) Job 6:4; 20:16; Ps. 58:3-7; 140:3; Rom. 3:13; James 3:8.

Venus Fly Trap: (1) Authority over evil spirits; (2) Spiritual warfare; (3) Witch (partaking of demons).

Also see *Fly* and *Fly Spray*.

(1) Luke 10:19; (2) Matt. 16:19; 18:18; (3) 1 Cor. 10:21.

Verandah: (1) Covering; (2) Hidden; (3) Protected.

Also see *Porch*.

(1-2) Matt. 26:71-72; Gen. 19:8; (3) Gen. 19:8.

Vessels: (1) The human body; (2) The human heart; (3) An instrument of God; (4) The Church or a nation.

(1-3) 2 Cor. 4:7; (4) Isa. 40:15; Jer. 18:6; 2 Cor. 6:16 (corporate temple).

Veterinarian: (1) Christ; (2) Pastoral leadership; (3) Leader working with unsaved people and on domestic issues.

Also see *Doctor* and individual animal types: *Cat, Dog*, etc.

(1) 1 Pet. 5:4; (2) 1 Pet. 5:2; (3) 1 Cor. 15:32 (cf. Acts 19:29-31).

Videoing: See *Filming*.

View: (1) Prophetic office; (2) Oversee (shepherd); (3) Watchman; (4) Reconnoiter; (5) Choosing; (6) Assess and plan.

Also see *Spy*.

(1) 1 Sam. 9:9; 2 Kings 2:7,15; (2) Acts 20:28; Heb. 13:17; 1 Pet. 5:2; (3) 2 Sam. 18:24; Ezek. 3:17; (4) Josh. 2:1; 7:2; (5) Ezra 8:15; (6) Neh. 2:13,15.

Vine: (1) Christ and His Church; (2) Life (A vine in relationship with God is prosperous, a vine in rebellion is unfruitful); (3) Israel; (4) Wife; (5) A vine speaks of fruit not works; (6) Peace (under a vine); (7) Poison (wild vine); (8) Reaping of godless wicked (vine of the earth).

Also see *Grapes*.

(1) John 15:1,4-5; (2) Gen. 40:9-11; 49:22 (NIV); 2 Chron. 26:10 (also see vs. 4-5); Ps. 78:47; (3) Ps. 80:8-11; Isa. 5:2; Jer. 2:21; Hos. 10:1; Joel 1:7; (4) Ps. 128:3; (5) Gen. 40:9-11; Ezek. 15:2; (6) 1 Kings 4:25; 2 Kings 18:31; Mic. 4:4; Zech. 3:10; (7) 2 Kings 4:39; (8) Rev. 14:18.

Vinegar: (1) Sour/Bitterness; (2) Fruit of the vine; (3) Soliciting a negative reaction (vinegar on soda); (4) It is evident from both Jesus's and Judas's responses that bitterness is a choice.

(1) Ps. 69:21; Matt. 27:34, 48; Mark 15:36; Luke 23:36; (Exod. 12:8; John 13:26-30); (2) Num. 6:3; John 19:29-30 (cf. Mark 14:25); (3) Prov. 25:20; (4) cf. Matt. 27:34; John 13:26-30.

Vineyard: (1) Kingdom of Heaven; (2) Israel; (3) Place of glory.

Also see *Fruit Tree.*

(1) Matt. 20:1-8; (2) Isa. 5:1-7; (3) John 2:11.

Violin: (1) Instrument of love; (2) Heart (violin case); (3) Worship.

Also see *Music* and *Musical Instrument.*

(1) Ps. 18:1; (2) Eph. 5:19; (3) John 4:24; Phil 3:3.

Viper: (1) Small issue with potential for calamity; (2) Venomous words from son/daughter/children.

Also see *Snake.*

(1) Acts 28:3-6; (2) Prov. 30:14.

Virgin: (1) Church; (2) Pure; (3) Kingdom of Heaven; (4) Unmarried; (5) Jerusalem; (6) Israel.

(1-2) 2 Cor. 11:2; (3) Matt. 25:1-12; (4) 1 Cor. 7:25,28,34; (5) Isa. 62:5; Jer. 14:17; Lam. 2:13; (6) Amos 5:2.

Visit/ors: (1) Impartation (visitation); (2) Taking someone and their words in; (3) Brief ministry; (4) Angelic visitation; (5) Audience with God.

(1-2) Gen. 21:1; (3) Acts 10:33; (4) Gen. 19:1-2; Heb. 13:2; (5) Gen. 18:1-3.

Vitamins: (1) Spiritually healthy; (2) Strengthening in the Holy Spirit; (3) Communion.

(1-2) 1 Sam. 30:6b; 1 Tim. 4:8; Jude 1:20; (3) John 6:35,48,68.

Voice: (1) God (voice of father); (2) The Word of God; (3) Powerful witness; (4) Still small voice; (5) God (trumpet voice); (6) Evil or demon (disturbing voice).

(1) 1 Sam. 3:4-9; Ps. 29:3-4; (2) (Acts 9:4-5; John 1:1); (3) Luke 3:4; (4) 1 Kings 19:12; Ps. 46:10a; (5) Exod. 19:16,19; (6) Mark 1:26; 9:26.

Volcano: (1) Wrath of God; (2) Judgment; (3) Person who erupts; (4) Pressure within; (5) Unresolved anger; (6) Sudden destruction.

Also see *Lava.*

(1) Ezek. 22:20; Nah. 1:2b,5-6; (2) Isa. 5:24-25; Mic. 1:4,5a; (3-4) Ps. 39:3; (5) Ps. 4:4; (6) 1 Thess. 5:3.

Vomit: (1) Backsliding fool; (2) Expulsion or purging; (3) Empty promises; (4) Greed; (5) To go astray morally or spiritually; (6) Erring with wine; (7) Coughed up; (8) Self-destruction (drowning in vomit); (9) Lukewarm (God vomiting); (10) Rejection of something or someone; (11) Revival or resurrection.

Also see *Belch*, *Drunk*, and *Purge.*

(1) Prov. 26:11; 2 Pet. 2:22; (2) Lev. 18:25; (3) Prov. 23:6-8; (4) Prov. 25:16; (5) Isa. 19:14; Jer. 48:26; (6) Isa. 28:7-8; (7) Jon. 2:10; (8) (9-10) Rev. 3:16; (11) Jon. 2:10-3:1.

Voting: (1) Decision on who leads you; (2) A call to put that which is in the heart into action.

(1-2) Josh. 24:15.

Vulture: (1) Keen-eyed; (2) Bird of the wilderness; (3) Sign of death; (4) Demons taking souls to hell.

(1) Job 28:7; (2) Isa. 34:15; (3) Matt. 24:28; Luke 17:37; (4) Lev. 11:13-14.

W

Wages: (1) Harvest (reaping) wages; (2) Death; (3) Unrighteousness (greed); (4) Deception (changed wages); (5) Rewards.

(1) John 4:36; (2) Rom. 6:23; (3) 2 Pet. 2:15; Jude 1:11; (4) Gen. 31:7; Prov. 11:18; (6) Prov. 31:31 (NIV).

Waist: (1) Truth; (2) Your spirit; (3) Half committed.

(1) Eph. 6:14; (2) Dan. 7:15; (3) Ezek. 47:4.

Waiter: (1) Faithful servant of God; (2) Filled and ready for service.

Also see *Waiting.*

(1-2) Luke 12:35-42.

Waiting: (1) Awaiting ministry; (2) Preparation time; (3) Awaiting God's timing; (4) A need to spend time with God.

Also see *Waiter.*

(1-2) Luke 1:80; (3) Isa. 49:2. (4) Ps. 27:14; Isa. 40:31.

Walking: (1) Living by faith; (2) In step with the Spirit; (3) Our pre-Christian lifestyle (worldly living); (4) Taking up God's ways; (5) Endurance; (6) Advancement (positive or negative); (7) Progress or forward movement; (8) Natural reasoning; (9) Brotherly hatred (walking in darkness).

Also see *Footsteps* and *Stepping.*

(1) Rom. 4:12; 6:4b; 2 Cor. 5:7; Gal. 2:14; (2) Rom. 8:1,4,14; Gal. 5:25; (3) Eph. 2:2; 1 Pet. 4:3; (4) Isa. 2:3; (5) Isa. 40:31; (6) Ps. 1:1; Eph. 5:2; (7) 1 John 1:7; (8) Eph. 4:17; (9) 1 John 2:11.

Walking together: (1) Agreement.

(1) Amos 3:3; Ps. 1:1.

Wall(s): (1) Protection; (2) Strength; (3) Barrier or blockade or blockage; (4) Partition; (5) Hardened hearts; (6) God; (7) Barrier to the things of the Spirit (no windows); (8) Security; (9) Body or flesh (wooden wall); (10) Phobia; (11) Protected or forced path (walls either side); (12) Boundary; (13) Defensive fortification; (14) Place from which words launched (vulnerability: close to the wall); (15) Vantage point; (16) Hiding or hidden; (17) A rich person's status and protection; (18) Salvation; (19) The believer; (20) Recluse.

Also see *Bricks, Fence, Hedge,* and *House.*

(1) 1 Sam. 25:16,21; (2) 2 Chron. 32:5; Neh. 4:10; Prov. 18:11; Isa. 25:4; (3) Gen. 49:22; Num. 13:28; 2 Sam. 22:30; Isa. 5:5; Heb. 11:30; (4) Eph. 2:14; (5) Ps. 62:3; Eccles. 10:8;

(6) Ps. 18:2; 144:2 (cf. Deut. 28:52); (7) 2 Kings 2:10; (8) Num. 13:28; (9) 1 Kings 6:15 (The walls symbolize our earthly bodies) (cf. 1 Cor. 6:19); (10) Prov. 29:25; (11) Exod. 14:22,29; Num. 22:24; (12) Num. 35:4; (13) Deut. 3:5; (14) 2 Sam. 11:20-24 (See *Arrows*); (15) 2 Sam. 18:24; (16) Ezek. 8:7-12; (17) Prov. 18:11; (18) Isa. 60:18; (19) Jer. 1:18; 15:20; (20) Prov. 18:1 (AMP) as in "putting walls up."

Wall(s) (Falling or Fallen Wall): (1) Judgment; (2) Loss of protection; (3) Spiritually unguarded; (4) Disgraced, naked, or vulnerable; (5) Spiritually lazy; (6) Spiritually undisciplined; (7) Revealing of the heart; (8) Rape (Forceful breaking down of a wall); (9) Breakthrough.
(1) 1 Kings 20:30; (Gen. 15:16; Josh. 6:4-5); 2 Kings 14:13; Neh. 2:13; Jer. 1:15; Ezek. 13:14; (2) 2 Kings 25:10; Isa. 5:5; (3) Neh. 1:3-8; Jer. 39:8; Ezek. 38:11-12; (4) Neh. 2:17; Ps. 62:3; (5) Prov. 24:30-33; (6) Prov. 25:28; (7) Ezek. 13:14; (8) Ezek. 26:12; (9) 1 Chron. 14:11.

Wall(s) (Measuring an Internal Wall): (1) Dividing between soul and spirit; (2) Rightly dividing the Word of truth; (3) Call for personal introspection.
(1) Heb. 4:12; (2) 2 Tim. 2:15; (3) 1 Cor. 11:28.

Wall(s) (Repairing a Wall): (1) Renewing relationship with God; (2) Rebuilding; (3) Favor of God; (4) Diligence.
(1) 2 Chron. 33:12-16 (note v. 14); Ps. 51:17-18; (2-3) Neh. 2:5,8; 6:16; (4) Neh. 4:6.

Wallet/Billfold: (1) Heart (as the place where values stored); (2) Identity; (3) Money or finances; (4) Credit; (5) Security; (6) Two masters; (7) Greed; (8) Faith; (9) Forgetting the house of God (wallet with holes).
Also see *Money*.
(1) Matt. 6:21,24; (4) Eccles. 7:12; (5) Matt. 6:21; (6) John 12:6; (7) Mark 6:8 (no money in purse); Luke 9:3; (8) Hag. 1:6.

Wallpaper: (1) Build-up of heart issues (several layers); (2) Allowing issues to build up over time (several layers of wallpaper); (3) Façade that covers sin (dirty or faulty walls).
(1-2) Gen. 6:5; Neh. 13:6-8; John 13:10 (need for regular cleansing); Rom. 7:17; (3) Matt. 23:27.

Walrus: (1) If attacking you is an evil spirit (walrus is a pinniped [winged-feet] creature).
Also see *Dolphin*, *Dugong*, and *Whale*.
(1) Matt. 8:28; 1 Pet. 5:8 (walrus's roar).

Wardrobe: See *Cupboard*.

Warehouse: (1) Heaven; (2) Place of equipping; (3) Place of abundant supply; (4) Unconventional church; (5) Underground church. (6) Stopping the flow of the Spirit (mothballing the Spirit).
(1) Phil. 4:19; (2) 2 Chron. 2:9; (3) 1 Chron. 29:16; (4) Mal. 3:10a; (5) 1 Sam. 22:1-2. (6) 1 Thess. 5:19; Acts 7:51.

War Heroes/Museum: (1) Heroes of faith.

Also see *Museum.*

(1) Heb. 11.

Warrior: See *Soldier.*

Wash/ing: (1) Being born again (whole body wash); (2) Washing in the Word of God (part of body being washed); (3) Confession of sin; (4) Bible study and application; (5) Being born again or need to be born again (clothes washing); (6) Renewal; (7) Idiom: "something coming out in the wash."

Also see *Washbasin, Washcloth,* and *Washing Machine.*

(1-2) John 3:5; 13:10; Tit. 3:5; (3) 1 John 1:9; (4) John 15:3; 17:17; Eph. 5:26; (5) Joel 2:13; Matt. 23:25-28; Mark 7:21-23; 11:39-40; (6) Tit. 3:5; (7) Acts 22:16; Titus 3:5.

Washbasin: (1) Heart; (2) The Word of God; (3) Cleansing.

(1) Matt. 23:27; 2 Cor. 4:7; (2) Exod. 30:18-19; Eph. 5:26 (that which holds the water of the Word); (3) John 13:10; Isa. 1:16.

Washcloth: (1) Cleansing; (2) Servanthood.

Also see *Towel.*

(1-2) John 13:4-5.

Washing Line: See *Clothesline.*

Washing Machine: (1) Need for regeneration; (2) Wanting to be right (clean/white) with God; (3) Wanting clean clothes (robes of salvation and righteousness); (4) Holy Spirit ministry used in cleaning others.

(1) Tit. 3:5; (2-3) Isa. 61:10; (4) Isa. 61:1,10.

Wasp: (1) Evil spirits; (2) Used in God's clearance of enemy forces; (3) Sting/ing; (4) Painful scourge.

Also see *Bees.*

(1-2) Exod. 23:28; Deut. 7:20; Josh. 24:12; (3-4) Taken from the Hebrew word used in these passages and its root.

Watch (Timepiece): (1) Time; (2) Deadline (time's running out); (3) Timing of God; (4) Not wanting to be there (time to leave); (5) Glory that comes from waiting on God (gold watch); (6) Life; (7) Death (time to die); (8) Glorious calling (selecting a gold watch).

Also see *Time* and *Clock.*

(1) Mark 13:33; (2) 1 Cor. 7:29; Eph. 5:15-16; Col. 4:5; Rev. 12:12; (3) Esther 4:14; John 7:30; Gal. 4:4; (4) John 6:24; (5) Exod. 34:29; (6-7) Eccles. 3:2; John 7:6,8; (8) Esther 4:14; 2 Thess. 2:14; 1 Pet. 5:10.

Water: (1) The Holy Spirit (flowing water); (2) The Word of God (still water); (3) Cleansing; (4) Heart; (5) Desire for God (thirsting); (6) Prayers; (7) Peoples; (8) Peace (still waters); (9) Calm (still water); (10) In the Spirit (in the water); (11) Deliverer (someone drawn out of water); (12) Spiritually dead believers (stinky water); (13) Judgment (stinky water); (14) Emotions (as in "stirred up"); (15) Unstable.

Also see *Clear Water, Deep, Glass of Water, Water (Dirty Water), Watering,* and *Underwater.*

(1) Lev. 14:6 (*running water* means "living water" in the Hebrew); John 7:37-39; (2) Eph. 5:26; (3) John 13:5-10; (4) Lam. 2:19 (cf. Prov. 18:4; Luke 6:45b); (4) Ps. 42:1-2; 63:1; 69:21; John 19:28; Note that in Exodus 17:3-6, the people thirsted and water came forth by striking the Lord who "stood before the Rock." Their natural thirst was to lead them to a spiritual revelation that God was the satisfier of the soul; (5) Ps. 126:5; Jer. 31:9; 50:4; (6) Rev. 17:15; (7) Ps. 23:2; Mark 4:39; (8) Ps. 107:29; (9) Ezek. 32:14; (10) Exod. 2:10; (11) Exod.15:23-24; (12-13) Exod. 7:18; Rev. 3:1; (14) Jer. 51:55; Matt. 14:30; Luke 8:24; (15) Gen. 49:4.

Water (Dirty Water): (1) Causing strife (muddying the waters); (2) Tainted words; (3) Sowing poisonous words (murmuring); (4) Having not applied Christ (salt) to the heart (source) of an issue; (5) Personal fleshly issues muddying the flow of God's Spirit; (6) Instability; (7) Deceitfulness (8) Lies; (9) Adding to the Word (tainted truth); (10) Wickedness; (11) Unappealing.
Also see *Clear Water, Flood, River, Water,* and *Underwater.*
(1) Isa. 57:20; Ezek. 32:2; 34:18-19; (2-3) Num. 20:24; Prov. 18:4; (4) Exod. 15:23-25; 2 Kings 2:19,21; Prov. 18:4; James 3:10-11; (5) 2 Cor. 4:7; (6) Job 8:11; (7-8) Ps. 62:4 (mouth saying one thing, heart another); Ps. 78:36-37; 101:7; 120:2; Prov. 14:25; (9) Prov. 30:5-6; 2 Cor. 2:17; (10) Isa. 57:20; (11) 2 Kings 5:12.

Water (Hot): (1) A heart on fire for God; (2) Angry words; (3) Finding oneself in trouble.
(1) Jer. 20:9; (Lam. 2:19; Matt. 24:12); (2) Ps. 79:5; Eph. 5:26; (3) As in "I found myself in hot water about..."

Waterfall: (1) Outpouring of the Spirit; (2) Baptism in the Holy Spirit.
Also see *Fountain.*
(1) Ps. 42:7; Prov. 1:23; Isa. 32:15a; 44:3; Ezek. 39:29; Joel 2:28-29; Acts 2:17-18; (2) Acts 10:45.

Watering: (1) Speaking under the anointing; (2) Sharing the Gospel (cleaning); (3) Speaking.
(1) John 6:63; 7:38-39; (2) Eph. 5:26; (3) Prov. 18:4.

Watermelon: (1) Word of God.
(1) Eph. 5:26.

Water Meter: (1) The human agency (church, pastor, father) by which the Word and Spirit of God is measured out; (2) The human heart; (3) Measuring the anointing.
Also see *Meter.*
(1) John 3:34; Eph. 5:26; (2) 2 Tim. 2:15; Heb. 4:12; (3) John 12:3; Acts 4:8; 6:5.

Water Pipe: (1) Holy Spirit minister or ministry; (2) Christ; (3) Mouth; (4) The avenue to breaking strongholds (through the water shaft).

(1-2) John 7:37-39; (3) Matt. 12:34; Luke 6:45; (4) 2 Sam. 5:6-9; 1 Chron. 11:6-9; (*Jebus* means "trodden down." Notice how the Jebusites put David down: 2 Sam. 5:6).

Water Pump: (1) Heart; (2) Sensitivity (understanding) to the Spirit of God; (3) Thirst for the Spirit of God; (4) Minister or ministry; (5) Full Gospel church.
(1) John 7:38; (2) Prov. 20:5; (3) Ps. 42:1; (3) John 7:37-39; 2 Tim. 4:2; (4) Matt. 28:18-20; Eph. 1:22-23; Col. 1:18

Waterslide: (1) Flowing in the anointing; (2) Bringing things from Heaven to earth in the Spirit.
(1-2) Ezek. 47:5.

Waves: (1) Strong and emotive words or great voice; (2) Outpouring of the Holy Spirit (big wave); (3) Opposition; (4) Double-minded Christian; (5) Change of mind (given to change); (6) Complainers, grumblers, mockers; (7) Tests; (8) Circumstance; (9) Death; (10) Pride; (11) False/dangerous spirit (dumpers); (12) Heart in turmoil.
See *Beach*, *Deep*, and *Water*.
(1) Ps. 65:7; 42:7; 51:15; 93:3-4; Jer. 51:42,55; Jon. 2:3; (Gen. 7:17; John 12:48); (9) Isa. 59:19: "...*When the enemy comes in, like a flood the Spirit of the Lord shall lift up a standard against him*"; (2) Matt. 14:24; (3-4) James 1:6-8; (5) Jude 1:13,16; (6) Matt. 8:24; Mark 4:37; (7) Matt. 14:24; (8) 2 Sam. 22:5; (9) Job 38:11; (11) 1 Kings 22:22; Mic. 2:11 (Dumpers only let you down hard); (12) As a body of water stirred; Ps. 42:7; Prov. 20:5; Lam. 2:19.

Wax: (1) Melted away; (2) Seal.
Also see *Candle*.
(1) Ps. 22:14; 68:2; 97:5; Mic. 1:4; (2) 1 Kings 21:8.

Weapon: (1) Words or cutting words; (2) Spiritual weapons: obedience, faith, the Word of God, prayer, truth, righteousness, the name of Jesus, the Gospel of peace, salvation.
Also see *Arrows*, *Guns*, and *Hands*.
(1) Eccles. 9:17-18; Isa. 54:17; (2) 2 Cor. 10:4-5; Eph. 6:10-18.

Wear/ing: (1) The heart shown outwardly; (2) Outward/ly; (3) Superficial/ly; (4) Praise; (5) Joy; (6) Honor bestowed upon; (7) Prepared or ready; (8) Pride (when showy); (9) Modesty or humility (when conservative); (10) Welcome.
Also see *Clothing*, *Hat*, *Robe*, and *Skirt*.
(2) Isa. 61:10; 1 Pet. 3:3-5; (2) 1 Pet. 3:3; (3) Luke 21:5; (4-5) Isa. 61:3; (6) Dan. 5:29; (7) Rev. 21:2; (8-9); 1 Tim. 2:9; (10) As in a Hawaiian lei.

Weasel: (1) Someone who reneges on their word; (2) Unclean animal. (1) As in "He weaseled his way out of it"; (2) Lev. 11:29.

Weaving/Woven: (1) Union (close connection); (2) Interlocking (strong and robust); (3) Creating; (4) Planning (good or evil); (5) Skilled work; (6) Expensive; (7) Trap.
(1) Ps. 133:1; Eph. 4:3; (2) Exod. 39:22,27; (3-4) Isa. 59:5; (5) Exod. 35:35; (6) John 19:23; (7) Isa. 59:5.

Web: (1) Predator's trap; (2) Deception; (3) Schemes of iniquity; (4) False trust; (5) Place of old (end of an era [old wineskin]); (6) Not spiritually active (abandoned house); (7) Ensnared by the Internet; (8) Old issue; (9) Ensnarement of soul/mind (web in hair); (10) Diagnosed terminal condition.
Also see *Spider*, *Net*, and *Trap*.
(1-3) Isa. 59:5-6; (4) Job 8:14; (5) Matt. 9:17; (6) Isa. 58:12; Hag. 1:4b; (7) Ps. 91:3; 124:7; (8) Job 8:14; Jer. 8:5; 50:33; (9) Ps. 142:3; Jer. 5:26; (10) Jud. 15:14; Esther 5:14; 7:9; Acts 12:5-11.

Wedding: See *Marriage*.

Wedding Dress: (1) Standing in righteousness (white dress).
(1) Rev. 19:8.

Wednesday: (1) Four; (2) Dominion or rule.
Also see *Day* and *Three* (the secular world sees Wednesday as the third day of the week).
(1-2) Gen. 1:18-19.

Weeds: (1) Curse; (2) Quick growing and energy-soaking issues/individuals that block out the light; (3) Enemy plant; (4) People that choke others; (5) The result of the enemy's words; (6) Sin.
(1) Gen. 3:18; (2-3) Matt. 13:25; (4) Matt. 13:7; (5) Matt. 13:25 (sowing = words); (6) Gal. 6:8.

Weed Whacker/Weed Eater/Whipper Snipper: (1) Harvesting time; (2) Sorting good from bad; (3) Harvest angel; (4) Spirit of death (grim reaper).
(1-2) Matt. 13:28-30; (3) Matt. 13:39-42; (4) Ps. 103:14-15; Isa. 51:12; 1 Pet. 1:24-25.

Weevils: (1) Hidden destruction of the Word of God.
Also see *Wheat* and *Termites*.
(1) 2 Cor. 2:17a.

Weighing: (1) Thinking something through (weighing up); (2) Judging a prophetic word.
Also see *Scales (Weight)* and *Weight*.
(1) 2 Tim. 2:15; (2) 1 Cor. 14:29; 1 Thess. 5:20-21.

Weight: (1) Glory; (2) Power; (3) Sin (that which holds us back); (4) Hearts/spirits and actions are weighed; (5) Measured; (6) More important (weightier); (7) Responsibility.
Also see *Balances*, *Heavy*, *Weighing*, and *Weight Loss*.
(1) 2 Cor. 4:17; (2) 2 Cor. 10:10; (3) Heb. 12:1; (4) 1 Sam. 2:3; Ps. 58:2; Prov. 16:2; Isa. 26:7; Dan. 5:27; (5) Job 6:2; 31:6; (6) Matt. 23:23; (7) As in "feeling the weight of responsibility."

Weightlifting: (1) Building your faith; (2) Burden-bearing; (3) Taking on someone's sin or burden (spotting weights for someone); (4) Sinning; (5) Taking on more than you can handle.

(1) Jude 1:20; (2) Matt. 11:30; (3) Matt. 11:30; Heb. 12:1; (4) Heb. 12:1; (5) Matt. 11:28; 17:16-17.

Weight Loss: (1) Sin dealt with; (2) Loss of glory/anointing; (3) Loss of importance. Also see *Fat, Scales (Weight), Weighing*, and *Weight.*

(1) Heb. 12:1; (2) 2 Cor. 4:17; (3) As in "Weightier matters are more important."

Welding: (1) Joining (strong bond); (2) Manufacturing/fabricating; (3) Repairing. Also see *Steel.*

(1) Exod.28:7; 1 Chron. 22:3 (KJV); (2) 2 Kings 15:35; (3) Neh. 3:6.

Well: (1) God; (2) Heart; (3) God's Word; (4) Jesus Christ; (5) Salvation or eternal life; (6) The Holy Spirit. Also see *Fountain.*

(1) Gen. 21:27-32 (well of covenant); Gen. 49:22; Num. 21:16-17 (They sang to the well!; (2 Sam. 17:17-19; Col. 3:3); (2) Prov. 5:15; 18:4; John 7:37-38; (3) Gen. 29:2 (flock watered from this well); (4-5) Isa. 12:2-3; (6) John 7:37-38.

Stopped-Up Well: (1) Things dumped on the spirit to spoil it; (2) Attempt to stop salvation.

(1-2) Gen 26:15,18; 2 Kings 3:19,25.

West: (1) Glory departing; (2) Departure from God or God departing; (3) Place of sunset; (4) A setting down or end; (5) From the west may mean ungodly/unbeliever; (6) Consider aspects in your own environment relating to west. Also see *East.*

(1-2) The sun sets in the west. A setting sun ushers in night (ungodliness); John 9:4; 12:30; (3) Isa. 59:19; (4) Ps. 103:12; Matt. 8:11; (4) Dan. 8:5; John 3:2 (by night).

Wet: See *Water.*

Wet Suit: (1) An anointing/mantle (having put on Christ); (2) Protected by the Holy Spirit (wet suit); (3) The old self (coming out of sea and taking off the wet suit). Also see *Surfing* and *Waves.*

(1) Exod. 29:7; Lev. 8:12; 1 Sam. 10:1; 2 Kings 2:8; (cf. Gal. 3:27; 2 Cor.3:18 (AMP)); (2) 2 Kings 2:13-14; Isa. 61:1-2; (3) Col. 2:11-12; (Here a black wet suit may represent putting off the old self).

Whale: (1) Prophetic ministry (leader who is sensitive to the Spirit); (2) Great fish; (3) Big fish; (4) Influential believer; (5) The prophetic mantle (Jonah was encompassed by the whale and then sent to the nations).

(1) As the whale is an extremely sensitive creature communicating over long distances, so is the prophet sensitive to the Spirit; (2-3) Matt. 12:40 (cf. KJ & NKJ); (4) As believers are as fish, a big fish is seen as one of significance; (5) Jonah 1:17–3:2.

Wheat: (1) The Word of God; (2) Believers; (3) Believers that lay down their lives (death to self); (4) Purified hearts (threshed/sifted); (5) Related to the main harvest (favor of God); (6) Fruitfulness and provision.

Also see *Barley*, *Chaff*, and *Seed*.
(1) Matt. 13:20; Mark 4:14; (2) Matt. 3:12 (contrasted with chaff); Matt. 13:25,29-30 (contrasted with tares); Luke 3:17; (3) John 12:24-25; (4) 1 Chron. 21:20; Luke 22:31; (5) Exod. 34:22; Ruth 2:23 (wheat harvest followed barley harvest); 1 Sam. 6:13; (6) Deut. 8:8; 32:14; 2 Sam. 17:28; Ps. 81:16; 147:14; Song 7:2.

Wheel(s): (1) Holy Spirit; (2) Spirit; (3) Progress; (4) Movable; (5) Repeat; (6) Roll; (7) Transport; (8) Heavy spirit (stone wheel).
Also see *Automobile*, *Bicycle*, *Circle*, *Rollerblades*, and *Scooter*.
(1) (Job 33:4; Jer. 18:3); Heb. 9:14 (eternal = never ending); (2) Eccles. 12:6; Ezek.1:20; (3) Exod. 14:25; (4) 1 Kings 7:30-33; (5-6) The Hebrew for "wheel" is *ghalghal*; (7) Gen. 45:27; (8) Isa. 61:3.

Wheelbarrow: (1) Carrying burdens; (2) Sinful journey; (3) Deliverance; (4) Vessel of sin; (5) Carrying sinful burdens; (6) Walking in the flesh.
(1) Jer. 17:22; Matt. 11:28; (2) 1 Kings 15:26; Isa. 30:1 (NIV); (3) Zech. 3:9 (as in removing sin); (4) Luke 11:39; (5) Luke 11:46; (6) Gal. 5:16-21; Ps. 38:4.

Wheelchair: (1) Incapacitated/infirmity; (2) Not walking by faith; (3) Dependence (on the person pushing the chair); (4) Healing (coming out of the chair); (5) Wholeness (coming out of the chair).
Also see *Polio*.
(1) 2 Sam. 4:4; (2) 2 Cor. 5:7; (3) Acts 3:2; (4) Matt. 21:14; Acts 3:6-8; (5) Acts 4:10.

Whip: (1) Harsh chastisement, discipline, or punishment; (2) Correction; (3) Purging; (4) Authority (cracking the whip); (5) Being driven rather than led.
Also see *Cowboy*.
(1) 1 Kings 12:11, 14; 2 Chron. 10:11; (2) Prov. 26:3; (3) Prov. 20:30; Isa. 53:5; (4) John 2:15,18 (NIV); (5) cf. Ps. 23:2-3.

Whipper Snipper: See *Weed Whacker*.

Whirlpool: (1) Being drawn or sucked into something; (2) Path to hell; (3) Troubled heart.
Also see *Tornado*.
(1) Prov. 7:22-23; 9:13-18; (2) Ezek. 31:14b; Matt. 8:32; (3) Ps. 46:3; 77:16; Isa. 57:20.

Whirlwind: Open Heaven bringing: (1) Rapture; (2) Revelation (hearing the Word of God); (3) Resurrection; (4) Destruction; (5) Judgment; (6) About to have a heavenly encounter.
Also see *Dust Storm* and *Tornado*.
(1) 2 Kings 2:1,11; (2) Job 38:1; Ezek. 1:4ff; (3) Job 40:6–42:10; (4) Prov. 1:27; Jer. 23:19; (5) Isa. 66:15; Jer. 30:23; (6) 2 Kings 2:1ff; Job 38:1; Ez. 1:4ff.

Whispering: (1) Voice of the Holy Spirit; (2) Secret; (3) Plotting against; (4) Sowing strife (division); (5) Familiar spirit sowing deception; (6) No strength or spiritually dying.
Also see *Lips*.

(1) 1 Kings 19:12; (2) 2 Sam. 12:19; (3) Ps. 41:7; (4) Prov. 16:28; Rom. 1:29-30; 2 Cor. 12:20; (5) Isa. 29:4; (6) Gen. 21:16-17; 1 Sam. 30:11-13.

White: (1) Righteous; (2) Pure/holy(garments); (3) Believer; (4) Clean/washed/purified; (5) Angel; (6) Worthy; (7) Portrayed innocence/purity/righteousness; (8) Ready for harvest; (9) Sin (skin); (10) Glory (cloud); (11) Glory (whiter than white); (12) Tasteless (white of an egg); (13) Conquer/ing (horse); (14) Light.
(1) Rev. 19:8; (2) Lam. 4:7; Dan. 7:9; Matt. 17:2; Rev. 3:5; (3) Rev. 4:4; 6:11; 7:9; (4) Ps. 51:7; Isa. 1:18; Dan. 11:35; 12:10; Rev. 7:14; (5) Matt. 28:2-3; Mark 16:5; John 20:12; Rev. 15:6; (6) Rev. 3:4; (7) Gen. 40:16; Matt. 23:27 (outward white/inward black); (8) John 4:35; (9) Num. 12:10-11; 2 Kings 5:27; Joel 1:7; (10) 2 Chron. 5:12-14; (11) Mark 9:3; Rev. 14:14; (12) Job 6:6;
(13) Rev. 6:2; 19:11; (14) Mark 9:3; Luke 9:29; Rev. 1:14; 3:18 (glory is the opposite of shame).

White (Off-White): (1) Not quite right; (2) False righteousness; (3) Not right with God.
(1-3) Isa. 64:6a; 2 Cor. 11:14-15; 2 Tim. 3:4b-5.

White Ants: (1) Undermining words; (2) Cancer; (3) Two-faced person.
(1) Matt. 12:32; Acts 6:11-13; (2) 2 Tim. 2:17 (KJV); (3) James 1:8; Luke 23:8-11.

White Man: See *Black Man*, *Foreigner*, and *Caucasian*.

White Water Rafting: (1) Moving in the Holy Spirit, flowing between rocks of revelation (exhilarating ride); (2) Not comfortable moving in the Holy Spirit (scary ride).
(1) Rom. 8:14; Ezek. 47:1-5; (2) (Acts 23:11; 27:41-44).

Widow: (1) Casting off the faith; (2) Naturally or spiritually without a husband; (3) Spiritual grief; (4) Cared for by God; (5) Gather gleanings; (6) Trusting in God; (7) Their oppression is a sign of ungodliness; (8) Their abuse will be judged by God; (9) Widowhood may be a sign of judgment; (10) Reproach; (11) Place from which God can become our Husband; (12) Spirit of death (black widow).
Also see *Woman*.
(1) Eph. 5:23-25; 1 Tim. 5:11-12; (2) Exod. 22:22,24; 2 Sam. 20:3; (3) Isa. 54:6; (4) Deut. 10:18; Ps. 68:5; 146:9; Prov. 15:25; (5) Deut. 24:19-21; (6) 1 Kings 17:9-15; 1 Tim. 5:5; (7) Ps. 94:6; Isa. 1:16-17,23; 10:2; (8) Isa. 1:23-25; (9) Isa. 9:17; 47:8-10; (10-11) Isa. 54:4-6; (12) Isa. 59:5.

Wife: (1) The Church (Bride of Christ); (2) Actual wife; (3) Israel; (4) Business; (5) Husband's spirit; (6) Holy Spirit; (7) Your spirit man.
(1) Eph. 5:23-25; Rev. 19:7; (3) Jer. 3:1,20; (4) 2 Cor. 6:14; (5) As in "married to the business"; 5) Gen. 26:7 (Isaac lying about his wife is a picture of not being one with his heart); 1 Cor. 6:17; (6) John 3:5; Rom. 8:22,26; (7) 1 Cor. 2:11; Gal. 6:1; 1 Pet. 3:4-5.

Wig: (1) False anointing/authority; (2) Without the Spirit; (3) Pretending to be something you are not; (4) High up in the hierarchy ("big wig"); (5) Pending court case (judge-type wigs).
(1) 2 Sam. 14:26; 15:10; (2) Judg. 16:19-20; (3) 1 Sam. 28:8; Rom. 1:21-22; (4-5) Acts 23:2-5.

Wilderness: See *Desert*.

Wildfire/Bushfire: (1) Judgment; (2) Encounter with God; (3) Words that have gotten out of control (gossip, slander, lies, false promises, etc.); (4) Battle.
(1) Matt. 13:40; 2 Pet. 3:7; (2) Exod. 3:2; (3) James 3:6; (4) Jud. 1:8; 9:52; Jer. 32:29; 37:8.

Willow: (1) Sadness; (2) Weeping.
(1-2) Ps. 137:1-2.

Wind: (1) Holy Spirit; (2) Affliction/adversity/trouble (windy); (3) False teaching; (4) Evil spirits; (5) Resurrection (second wind); (6) Voices of opposition.
Also see *Dark Clouds* and *Storm*.
(1) John 3:8; Acts 2:2-4; (2) Matt. 7:25; 8:25-26; (3) Eph. 4:14; (4) Dan. 7:2-3; Matt. 14:24; Eph. 4:14 (These are behind false teaching); (5) Gen. 8:1; Judg. 15:19; Luke 8:55; (6) John 6:18,41-42.

Wind Chimes: (1) Spirit of God moving; (2) Spontaneous worship.
(1-2) John 3:8.

Winding Road: (1) Inability to see what's ahead; (2) Difficult path ahead; (3) Sin or evil; (4) Self-reliance (not trusting God); (5) Double-minded; (6) Unstable; (7) Loss of peace.
Also see *Country Road, Crooked, Road*, and *Up and Down*.
(1) James 1:6 (without the eyes of faith); (2) Lam. 3:9; (3) Prov. 2:15; (4) Prov. 3:5-6 (NKJV alternative rending); (5-6) James 1:6-8; (7) Isa. 59:8.

Window: (1) Prophetic gifting (seeing through window); (2) Entrance to the soul; (3) Insight/revelation; (4) Escape; (5) Opportunity; (6) Thief; (7) Prophecy; (8) Lacking spiritual discernment (small window/s); (9) Spiritual discernment (large window); (10) Trying to get a spiritual breakthrough (trying to break window); (11) Broken heart or shattered hope (smashed window).
Also see *Lookout, Open Window*, and *Shutting Window*.
(1) 1 Sam. 9:9 (seer); Prov. 7:6; Isa. 6:1; (2) Matt. 6:22-23; (3) Gen. 26:8; 2 Sam. 6:16; Prov. 7:6-7; Song 2:9; (4) Josh. 2:15; 1 Sam. 19:12; (5) As in "window of opportunity"; (6) Joel 2:9; (7) 1 Sam. 9:9; (8) Prov. 7:7; John 4:11; Luke 12:56; 1 Cor. 2:14; (9) 1 Cor. 2:14; 12:10; (10) Exod. 19:21,24; (11) Ps. 69:20; Prov. 15:13; 27:19.

Window (Open Window): (1) Momentary opportunity; (2) Prayer/worship; (3) Investigation; (4) Calling for you to see in the Spirit (prophetic ministry); (5) Flow of the Spirit (air flow/fresh air); (6) Revelation; (2 Kings 13:17).

Also see *Shutting Window* (directly below).

(1) 2 Kings 13:17; (2) Dan. 6:10; (3) Gen. 8:6-9; (4) 1 Sam. 9:9; (5) Job 33:4.

Window (Shutting Window): (1) Opportunity closing; (2) Closing off the Spirit; (3) Shutting out the prophetic; (4) Closing the windows of Heaven.

(1) Heb. 11:15; (2) Ezek. 3:24; Acts 4:18-20; (3) Num. 11:27-28; 23:13; Isa. 30:10; (4) Gen. 8:2; Mal. 3:10.

Windows of Heaven: (1) Abundance; (2) The delivery of a promise from Heaven; (3) Blessing; (4) Revelation.

Also see *Open Heaven*.

(1-2) Gen. 7:11b-12; 2 Kings 7:2, 18-19; Mal. 3:10; (3) Mal. 3:10; (4) Matt. 3:16.

Window Shopping: (1) Desire of the heart; (2) Not yet entering in; (3) Meditating on the things of God.

(1) Ps. 10:3; 37:4; (2) John 3:3 (cf. John 3:5); (3) Gen. 24:63.

Window Wiper: (1) Jesus cleansing your spiritual sight (arm of the Lord); (2) Clearing your vision; (3) Better focus on your destiny.

(1-2) Eph. 1:18; (3) Matt. 20:16; 22:14.

Windscreen/Windshield: (1) Window of Heaven; (2) Ministry destiny; (3) Shield of the Spirit; (4) Foretelling the future (what's ahead of you).

(1) Gen. 8:2; (2) 2 Kings 2:9-15; (3) Deflecting wind and insects it could be a shield of the Spirit; (4) 1 Kings 18:44; Dan. 2:29.

Wine: (1) Holy Spirit; (2) Joy; (3) Communion; (4) Resurrection; (5) Prosperity/ Plenty; (6) Loud/Violent/Mocker; (7) Blessing; (8) Beguiled/Deceived; (9) Heavy-hearted/wanting to forget; (10) Blood; (11) Cup of wrath for fornication with the world; (12) Under the influence of the religious whore; (13) Substitute for God.

Also see *Bread*.

(1) Matt. 9:17; John 2:3-4; Eph. 5:18; (2) Ps. 4:7; 104:15; Eccles. 10:19; Isa. 16:10; (3) Gen. 14:18; (4) Gen. 40:10-13; (5) Deut. 33:28; Ps. 4:7; Prov. 3:10; Hos. 2:8; (6) Ps. 78:65; Prov. 4:17; 20:1; 23:29-35; (7) Prov. 9:2,5; (8) Gen. 9:21; 19:32-35; 27:25; Isa. 28:7; Hos. 3:1; 4:11; (9) Prov. 31:4-7; (10) Gen. 49:11; (11) Ps. 75:8; Rev. 14:8,10; 16:19; 18:3; (12) Rev. 17:2; (13) Ps. 42:2; 63:1; 69:21; Song 1:2; John 19:28.

Wine Skins: See *Bottles*.

Wing(s): (1) Carried by the Spirit; (2) Covering; (3) Protection/trust; (4) Intimacy (under wings); (5) Warmth; (6) Hidden/refuge; (7) Worship and service; (8) Heavenly; (9) Heavenly beings (good or bad); (10) Escape; (11) Joy (under wings); (12) Glory; (13) Lifted; (14) Riches that quickly disappear; (15) Come under the dominion of (stretched out); (16) Healing; (17) Spiritual judgment (plane wings on fire); (18) Angel imparting the fire of God (bird wings on fire); (19) Spirit; (20) Spirit realm; (21) Great authority (big wings).

Also see *Angel(s)*, *Bird(s)*, and *Feather(s)*.

(1) Exod. 19:4; Deut. 32:11; Ps. 18:10; 139:9; Isa. 40:31; Rev. 12:14; (2) Exod. 25:20; 37:9; (3) Ruth 2:12; Ps. 36:7; 61:4; 91:4; (4) 1 Kings 8:6-7; (3-5) Matt. 23:37; Luke 13:34; (6) Ps. 17:8; 57:1; (7) Isa. 6:2; Rev. 4:8; (8-9) Eccles. 10:20; Ezek. 1:4ff, 10:5ff; Dan. 7:4ff; (10) Ps. 55:6-8; Jer. 48:9; (11) Ps. 63:7; (12) Ps. 68:13; (13) Zech. 5:9; (14) Prov. 23:5; (15) Isa. 8:8; Jer. 48:40; 49:22; Ezek. 17:3; (16) Mal. 4:2; (17) Lev. 1:17; (18) Isa. 6:6; (19-20) Ps. 104:4; Heb.1:7; Rev. 8:13; 14:6; (21) Ezek. 17:3,7; Rev. 12:14.

Wing Nut: (1) Tightening things up spiritually (tightening); (2) Putting something together; (3) Letting things slide spiritually (loosening and falling away).
(1-3) 1 Pet. 1:13; 2 Thess. 2:3.

Wink/ing: (1) Deception; (2) Wickedness; (3) Impending trouble.
(1) Ps. 35:19-20; (2) Prov. 6:12-13; (3) Prov. 10:10.

Winning: (1) Divine favor and blessing; (2) Victory; (3) Salvation; (4) Finishing the race; (5) Financial blessing (winning money).
(1) Deut. 28:6 ("going out" and "coming in" are references to going to and returning from battle); Ps. 41:11; (2) 1 Chron. 26:27; (3) Prov. 11:30b; (4) 1 Cor. 9:24; 2 Tim. 4:7; Heb. 12:1; (5) Prov. 10:22; Eph. 2:7.

Winter: (1) Death; (2) Hardship/tribulation; (3) Little light (no revelation of Christ); (4) Difficulty in progress; (5) Time of rain; (6) Time of pruning; (7) Time of hibernation/rest; (8) Time of planning and preparation; (9) Unbelief.
See also *Cold.*
(1) Song 2:11-14 (represents death to resurrection); (2) Mark 13:18-19; (3) John 10:22-24; (4) Acts 27:12; 2 Tim. 4:21; (5) Song 2:11; (6) John 15:2; (7) Isa. 18:6; Acts 27:12; 28:11; (8) 1 Kings 20:22-26; (9) John 10:22-26.

Wipe: (1) Cleanse; (2) Rub out/forget; (3) Replace; (4) Dry; (5) Judgment; (6) Comfort (as in wiping away tears).
(1) 2 Kings 21:13; Luke 7:38,44; John 11:2; 12:3; (2) Neh. 13:14; Prov. 6:33; 30:20; (3) Isa. 25:8; Rev. 21:4; (4) John 13:5; (5) Luke 10:11; (6) Rev. 7:17; 21:4.

Wire/Wiring: (1) Communication (telephone cord); (2) Snare; (3) Test or trap (trip wire); (4) Bomb (colored wires); (5) Conductor of power; (6) Someone as a connection or connector; (7) Thinking; (8) Thought pattern; (9) Renewing the belief system (rewiring).
Also see *Barbed Wire, Electric Cable, Fence,* and *Printed Circuit Board.*
(1) Matt. 13:43b; (2-3) Heb. 12:1; (4) 1 Thess. 5:3; (5) Job 37:3; (6) 1 Cor. 1:10; 6:17; (7) Isa.59:7. Rom.12:2; (8) Col. 3:1; (9) Rom. 12:2.

Witch: (1) Demonic powers (a devil); (2) Manipulator and controller; (3) Spell-caster; (4) Deception; (5) Manipulating church.
These people enter the spirit realm outside of Christ (the Door) and, therefore, are an abomination to God.
Also see *Witchcraft, Witch Doctor,* and *Woman—Ungodly.*

(1-5) Exod. 22:18; 1 Sam. 28:3-25; Rev. 2:20.

Witchcraft: (1) Rebellion; (2) Illegitimate authority (= rebellion); (3) Manipulation and control; (4) Use of familiar spirits and spells; (5) Practice magic; (6) Work of the flesh; (7) Drug use.

Also see *Witch*.

(1) 1 Sam. 15:23; (2) 2 Kings 9:22 (cf.1 Kings 21:7); (3) 2 Kings 9:22; 1 Kings 21:7,10,15; (4) 2 Chron. 33:6; (5) Mic. 5:12 (soothsayers practiced magic); (6) Gal. 5:19-20; (7) Rev. 9:21 (The word *sorceries* is the Greek *pharmakeia,* from which we get the word *pharmacy*).

Witch Doctor: (1) Counterfeit healer; (2) Demonic powers; (3) One under the influence of familiar spirits; (4) Opposed to God/resisters of truth.

(1-4) Exod. 7:11,22; 8:7; Deut. 18:9-12; Acts 13:8-11.

Wolf: (1) satan; (2) Unregenerate predators; (3) Predatory ministers; (4) False prophets; (5) Those who ruthlessly destroy people for selfish gain; (6) Sexual or financial predator; (7) Fierce; (8) Deception; (9) Independent spirit (lone wolf).

(1) John 10:10-12; (2) Matt. 10:16; Luke 10:3; (3) 2 Pet. 2:15 (greed); Jude 1:11 (greed); (4) Matt. 7:15; Acts 20:29; (5) Ezek. 22:27; (6) Judg. 16:4-5; (7) Hab. 1:8; (8) Matt. 7:15; (9) Gen. 49:27; Prov. 18:1; John 13:2,21.

Woman: (1) Church; (2) The Holy Spirit; (3) Israel; (4) Spiritual mother; (5) Angel; (6) Literally a woman (possibly you).

The interpretation depends on your assessment of the person. How do you see that person?

Woman (Godly Woman): (2) The Holy Spirit; (5) An angel; (7) A godly example; (8) Wisdom; (9) Justice (legal system).

Woman (Foreign Woman): (1) Ungodly church/person; (2) The Holy Spirit (you do not know her); (3) Church or person from overseas/different denomination; (4) Seductive woman; (5) Idolatrous woman; (6) Corrupt woman; (7) Someone leading you astray; (8) Worldly church (Egyptian woman); (9) Unclean spirit.

Also see *Foreign*, *Foreigner*, and *Woman*.

(1) Rev. 3:1-3; (2) See *Woman*; (3) John 4:9; Acts 16:9; (4-7) 1 Kings 11:1a,4; Prov. 5:3-10; (8) See *Egypt* and *Woman*; (9) Prov. 7:26-27.

Woman (Ungodly Woman): (10) Demonic powers; (11) Jezebel Spirit (controlling or in purple); (12) Religious spirit (seducing followers); (13) Sinful church; (14) Babylon (sexually seductive); (15) Spirit of death (black widow); (16) Independent spirit; (17) Fleshly or unattractive church (woman with facial hair). (18) Spirit of the world (uncouth woman).

Also see *Black*, *Woman (Foreign Woman)*, *Jezebel*, *Red*, *Widow*, and for an enticing married woman in red, see *Harlot*. Finally, also see individual names in Name and Place Dictionary.

(1) Eph. 5:25; (2) (Gen. 8:9; Matt. 3:16); Matt. 23:37; John 3:5; Rom. 8:14,22,26a (giving birth); Eph. 5:31-32; (3) Jer. 3:20; (4) 1 Tim. 5:2; Tit. 2:3-4; (7) 1 Pet. 3:5-6; (8) Prov. 9:1; 14:1; (9) As in blindfolded woman with scales in her hand; (11) Rev. 2:20; 17:4; (12) Prov. 7:10-27; (13) 2 Cor. 6:16; 7:1; (14) Rev. 17:5; (15) Isa. 59:5; (16) 1 Sam. 20:30; Ezek. 36:17; 1 Cor. 11:6a; 1 Pet. 3:5; (17) Gen. 25:25; Eph. 5:23; (18) 1 Cor. 2:12; 7:33.

Womb: (1) Heart or spirit; (2) Foundation; (3) Place of conception; (4) The place of faith; (5) The place from which one is sent out; (6) Fruit (offspring); (7) Place of unseen preparation.
(1) John 3:3-4; Heb. 11:11; (2) Jer. 1:5; Matt. 1:18; 13:23; John 18:37; (3) Luke 1:31; 2:21; Rom. 4:19-20; (4) Rom. 4:19-20; 1 John 5:4; (5) Gen. 25:23; Gal. 1:15; (6) Gen. 30:2; Deut. 7:13; Ps. 127:3; (7) Isa. 49:5; Ps. 139:15-16 (NKJV).

Wombat: (1) Underground church/person (not openly acknowledged); (2) Subterranean Christian (focused on earthly things); (3) Someone more active in the night than in the day; (4) Someone prone to be killed spiritually by others (hit by cars).
(1) John 7:10; (2) Matt. 6:19-21; John 3:19; 8:12; 12:35,46; (3) John 13:30; (4) Matt. 16:6,11-12; Luke 5:21; 7:39; 11:53-54.

Wood: (1) Fleshly works (earthly effort); (2) Coming from self rather than from the Spirit; (3) Dishonor; (4) Talebearer (gossip); (5) Contention; (6) Humanity.
Also see *Tree*.
(1-2) 1 Cor. 3:12-13,15; (3) 2 Tim. 2:20; (4) Prov. 26:20; (5) Prov. 26:21; (6) Exod. 25:10; as the ark of the covenant is wood covered with gold and symbolises the humanity of Christ.

Woods: (1) Beginning of freedom, but not yet fully secured; (2) Group of people.
Also see *Forest*.
(1) As in "We're not yet out of the woods"; (2) Isa. 7:2.

Wooden Sword: (1) Carnal words; (2) Fighting in the flesh; (1) Naïve presumption; (4) Play fighting or training.
(1) 1 Cor. 3:12-15; Eph. 6:17; (2-3) 1 Cor. 3:12-15; Heb. 4:12; (4) 1 Sam. 17:42-43 (NKJV).

Wool: (1) Godly garment rather than human-made garment; (2) Glory; (3) Righteousness; (4) Fleece (test).
Also see *Clothes*, *Cotton*, *Snow*, and *White*.
(1) Lev. 19:19b; Deut. 22:11; (2) Dan. 7:9; Rev. 1:14; (3) Isa. 1:18; (4) Judg. 6:37.

Woolworths: See Name and Place Dictionary.

Work: (1) Work for God (faith in action); (2) Self-effort (as opposed to faith); (3) Flesh (as opposed to fruit of the Spirit).
(1) 1 Cor. 15:58; Gal. 5:6 (the key); 1 Thess. 1:3; James 2:14,17-18,20,26; (2) Ps. 127:1a; Gal. 2:16; Heb. 6:1; (3) Gal. 5:19-21.

Workman: (1) Believers in the harvest; (2) Healing angel (working on the house); (3) Jesus (fixing the body/temple); (4) Person of the flesh.
Also see *Builder*.
(1) Matt. 9:38; 2 Cor. 8:23; (2) Job 33:23-24; (3) Matt. 12:13; (4) Gal. 2:16.

World War III: (1) Contention/arguments in the home.
(1) Prov. 21:19; 27:15.

Worm(s): (1) Old self (person of the flesh); (2) Stinking flesh; (3) Having no backbone or spineless (lacking spiritual fortitude); (4) Disobedience/transgression; (5) Decay/rottenness/corruption; (6) Despised and reproached; (7) The Gospel (as bait); (8) Opening up something that is complicated and may lead to chaos; (9) Bitterness (worms in wood).
(1) Isa. 41:14; (2) Exod. 16:20,24; Isa. 66:24; (3) Isa. 41:14; Mic. 7:17; (4) Exod. 16:20; Isa. 66:24; (5) Deut. 28:39; Job 7:5; 17:14; (6) Ps. 22:6; (7) Matt. 4:19; (8) As in "opening a can of worms"; (9) Prov. 5:4; Rev. 8:11.

Worship: (1) A life (sacrifice); (2) Service; (3) Activating the Kingdom of Heaven (releasing the Lordship of Christ into a situation); (4) Divine warfare.
(1) Gen. 22:5, 10; (2) Matt. 4:10 (whatever you worship you serve); (3-4) 2 Chron. 20:21-22; Ps. 22:3; 2 Cor. 10:4.

Wound/ed: (1) Damaged conscience; (2) Wounded heart/spirit; (3) Heart pierced by words; (4) Sin; (5) Judgment; (6) Hurts; (7) Troubled; (8) Grief; (9) Adultery; (10) Addict (innumerable wounds); (11) Friendly correction; (12) Victory over the enemy.
Also see *Healing*.
(1) Gen. 4:23; Job 24:12; Ps. 38:4-8; 1 Cor. 8:12; (2) Ps. 109:22; 147:3; Prov. 18:14; 20:30; (3) 1 Sam. 31:3; Ps. 64:7-8; Prov. 18:8; 26:22; (4) Ps. 38:4-5; 68:21; Isa. 1:6, 18; 53:5; Jer. 6:7; 30:14; 1 Cor. 8:12; (5) Jer. 51:52; Ezek. 28:23; (6) Jer. 10:19; (7) Ps. 38:4-8; (8) Jer. 6:7; 10:19; 30:12; Nah. 3:19; (9) Prov. 6:32-33; 7:26; (10) Prov. 23:29-30; (11) Prov. 27:6; (12) Isa. 51:9.

Wrap/ping: (1) Caring for; (2) Respect; (3) Preserving; (4) Nurturing; (5) Hiding or keeping secret; (6) Protecting; (7) Wrapping something may change its function; (8) Wrapping strengthens; (9) Be deeply enmeshed; (10) Preparing a gift.
(1-3) Matt. 27:59; Mark 15:46; Luke 23:53; (3) 1 Sam. 21:9; (4) Luke 2:7; (5) Gen. 38:14; (6) 1 Kings 19:13; (7) 2 Kings 2:8; (8) Job 40:17; (9) Jon. 2:5; (10) Matt. 2:11.

Wrecking Ball: (1) Heavy-handedness; (2) Demolish or demolition.
(1) 1 Kings 12:13-14,19; (2) 2 Cor. 10:4.

Wrecking Yard: (1) Dysfunctional ministries/people; (2) Has-been ministries/business/organization/relationship; (3) Washed-up ministries/business/organization/relationship; (4) Ministry/business/organization/individual that destroys lives.
(1) Gen. 9:21-25; (2) 1 Sam. 15:28; (3) Ezek. 37:1ff; (4) Gen. 33:18–34:31; Judg. 16:4-21; Rev. 2:14-15.

Wrestling: (1) Spiritual warfare; (2) Coming to the point of admission/submission; (3) Internal battle between flesh and spirit; (4) Strong-man.
(1) Eph. 6:12; (2-3) Gen. 32:24-28; (4) Luke 11:21-22.

Wrinkles: (1) Hardship; (2) Sign of age and decay; (3) Holy (without wrinkles); (4) Sin (as the opposite of holiness).
Also see *Folding* and *Shadow*.
(1) Job 16:8; (2) Eph. 5:27; (3-4) Eph. 5:27.

Wrist: (1) Relationship (particularly within the Body of Christ); (2) Broken relationship (broken wrist).
Also see *Ankle*.
(1-2) Eph. 4:16; Col. 2:19.

Writing: (1) The Word of God; (2) Correspondence; (3) Contract; (4) Journaling; (5) Destiny Vision; (6) A call to write; (7) Law.
(1) 2 Tim. 3:16; 2 Pet. 1:21; (2) Gal. 6:11; (3) Gen. 26:28; Dan. 11:6; (4) 1 Chron. 16:4; Ezra 6:2; (5-6) Hab. 2:2-3; (7) Luke 10:26.

Writing on the Wall: (1) Sign of pending judgment; (2) Negative self-talk; (3) Confirmation of bad news.
See also *Graffiti*.
Dan. 5:5,25-28; (2) Prov. 23:7a; Isa. 26:3; (3) Matt. 26:34, 75; John 13:26.

X

X-Box: (1) Playing games; (2) No heart for the things of God.
(1) Matt. 11:16-17; (2) X = No, and box = heart.

X- Ray: (1) Spiritual insight; (2) Actual X-ray required.
(1) Mark 1:10; John 1:32-33; 11:33, 14:17; Acts 2:17.

Y

Yacht: (1) Holy Spirit ministry.
Also see *Boat*, *Cruise Ship*, and *Houseboat*.
(1) John 3:8.

Yard (Back): (1) Private; (2) Personal; (3) Closed; (4) Exit; (5) Works; (6) Past; (7) Return to idolatry; (8) Disobedience; (9) Your family.
Also see *Garden* and *Yard (Front)*.
(1-2) (Matt. 24:3; John 18:1); Luke 8:17; (3) Song 4:12; (4) 2 Kings 9:27; 25:4; (5) Gen. 2:15; 3:23; (6) Ruth 1:15-16; 2 Sam. 12:23; (7) Josh. 23:12-13 (KJV); (8) Job 23:12; (9) As in "You first need to deal with issues in your own backyard."

Yard (Front): (1) Public; (2) Widely known; (3) Open; (4) Entry; (5) Expectancy; (6) Faith; (7) Future; (8) Obedience.

Also see *Garden* and *Yard (Back)*.

(1-2) John 18:20; (4) 2 Chron. 3:4; (5) Judg. 11:34; (8) As in "coming in the right way."

Year: (1) A year may equal a time; (2) A year may equal a day.

Also see *Time* and individual numbers.

(1) Dan. 7:25; (2) Num. 14:34; Ezek. 4:6.

Yeast: (1) Pride; (2) Sin; (3) That which grows when heated/pressured/persecuted; (4) Teaching that puffs up/corrupts; (5) Hypocrisy/treading on others/legalism; (6) Skepticism and rationalism (denial of the supernatural); (7) Sensualism and materialism; (8) The Kingdom of Heaven; (9) Imposed legalism; (10) Unclean or unholy; (11) Causes double-mindedness; (12) Concentrating on knowledge.

Also see *Salt*.

(1) That which corrupts by puffing up; 1 Cor. 5:6; (2) 1 Cor. 5:6-8; (3) Matt. 13:33; (4) Matt. 16:6, 12; Mark 8:15; Gal. 5:9; (5) Luke 12:1 (leaven of Pharisees); (6) Matt. 16:6 (leaven of Sadducees); (7) Mark 8:15 (leaven of Herod); (8) Matt. 13:33; (9) Matt. 16:6-11; (10) Lev. 10:12; 1 Cor. 5:7; (11) Matt. 16:11-12; (12) 1 Cor. 8:1.

Yellow: (1) Welcoming (ribbon); (2) Fearful or cowardly; (3) Spirit of fear; (4) Sin (unclean); (5) Glory of God; (6) Attention-seeking (self-glory); (7) Judgment; (8) Curse/plague.

Also see *Gold*.

(1-3) Present-day cultural associations; (4) Lev. 13:30-36 (Yellow hair associated with leprosy. Leprosy is bodily equivalent to sin, leprosy is cleansed, but never healed); (5) Ps. 68:13-14; 1 Pet. 1:7 (association between gold and glory); Isa. 60:9 (association between gold and glory); (6) Prov. 25:27b; 27:2; Isa. 42:8; 48:11b; Jer. 9:23-24a; Matt. 6:2; John 8:50; Acts 12:23; 2 Cor. 12:5-6; (7) Rev. 9:17; (8) Dan. 9:11 (cursed for sin); Lev. 13:30 (Leprosy is a type of sin).

Yesterday: (1) The past.

(1) Ps. 90:4.

Y-Junction: See *T-Junction*.

Yoke: (1) Legalistic bondage; (2) Oppression; (3) Joined with; (4) Burden (heavy or light); (5) Under the control of; (6) Harnessed power; (7) Service; (8) Half an acre.

Also see *Bound* and *Egg*.

(1) Acts 15:10; Gal. 5:1; (2) Lev. 26:13; Deut. 28:48; 1 Kings 12:4; (3) 2 Cor. 6:14; (4) Isa. 9:4; 10:27; 14:25; 58:6; Matt. 11:29-30; (5) Gen. 27:40; (6) Job 1:3; 42:12; (7) Jer. 27:2,7; 1 Tim. 6:1; (8) 1 Sam. 14:14.

Younger: If in an incident/event a person appears younger than they currently are, possible meanings include:

(1) You are looking at the spiritual person who is having youth renewed like the eagle; (2) This is the person of the future; (3) Can symbolize purity and humility; (4) Submissiveness (see 1 Pet. 5:5); (5) Spiritual dominion; (6) Immaturity; (7) You may be conversely looking at a person's past, where that person was independent, selfish, and living a life apart from the Father; (8) This is a person ruled by the lust of the eyes and the flesh; (9) Religious zealot; (10) Someone you haven't known long (If there are two and one younger you may not have known the younger person as long, i.e., it is a younger relationship).

Also see *Child/ren* and *Youth*.

(1) Ps. 103:5; (2) Acts 7:19 (where the babies were the future men of Israel); 2 Cor. 4:16; (3) Luke 22:26; John 12:14; (4) 1 Pet. 5:5; (5) Rom. 9:12; (6) 1 Cor. 13:11; (7) Luke 15:12-13; (8) Eccles. 11:9; John 21:18; (9) Acts 7:58; (10) Acts 7:58.

Youth: (1) Redeemed individual; (2) Young person.

Also see *Teenager* and *Younger*.

(1) Job 33:23-25; Ps. 103:3-5.

Youth Hostel: (1) Vibrant young church.

Also see *Backpacker's Hostel*.

(1) 1 John 2:13-14.

Yo-yo: (1) Something/issue that goes away and comes back again; (2) Idle hands.

(1) Prov. 26:11; (2) Eccles. 10:18.

Z

Zebra: (1) Africa; (2) Double-mindedness (black and white); (3) Lukewarm and in the world (horse: not black, not white).

Also see *Horse*.

(1) Country of origin; (2) Matt. 5:36-37; (3) Rev. 3:16.

Zeppelin: See *Blimp*.

Zipper: (1) Opening or opportunity; (2) Not open (stuck zipper); (3) Undone (exposed, revealed, or shamed); (4) Door of your heart; (5) Window of Heaven; (6) Teeth (mouth: keep it "zipped").

Also see *Curtain*, *Door*, *Genitals*, and *Veil*.

(1-2) Col. 4:3; (3) Isa. 6:5; (4) Acts 16:14; (5) Luke 17:21; Rev. 4:1; (6) Job 41:14; Prov. 25:19; Prov. 30:14.

Zombie: (1) A Christian who claims to be alive, but who is without true spiritual life; (2) Someone unable to think for themselves; (3) Someone bewitched and controlled by another.

(1) Rev. 3:1; (2-3) Gal. 3:1.

Zoo: (1) Mix of types/races; (2) Caged/frustrated; (3) On display; (4) Out of your environment; (5) Out of control; (6) The world.
(5) As in "the place is a zoo"; (6) 1 John 2:16.

THE NAME AND PLACE DICTIONARY

Aaron: (1) Elevated; (2) Stately; (3) Christ as High Priest; (4) High priest; (5) Spokesperson; (6) Intercessor.
(1-2) Name meaning; (3) Heb. 5:1-4; (4) Exod. 28:1-4; (5) Exod. 4:14; (6) Heb. 7:25-26.

Abba: (1) Father; (2) Papa.
(1) Mark 14:36.

Abbott: (1) Head priest of an abbey.

Abb/y/ey: (1) Her father rejoices.

Abel: (1) Vanity; (2) A meadow; (3) True believer; (4) Shepherd; (5) Martyr.
(3-5) Gen. 4:1-8; Heb. 12:24.

Abigail: (1) Father of exultation; (2) Her father rejoices. (1) 1 Sam. 25:14.

Abraham: (1) God the Father; (2) Father of many nations; (3) Friend of God; (4) Patriarch.
(1) Gen 22:2ff; (2) Gen 17:4-5; (3) James 2:23; cf. James 4:4; (4) Heb. 7:4.

Absalom: (1) Peaceful father; (2) Bodily perfection and outward beauty, but wicked heart; (3) Treasonous heart-stealer; (4) Infidelity.
(1) Name meaning; (2) 2 Sam. 14:25-26; (3-4) 2 Sam. 15:2-6.

Achan: (1) Misfortune or trouble; (2) A person who enriches themselves from God's work; (3) Remover of protection; (4) Thief; (5) Deceiver.
(1) Name meaning; (2-4) Josh. 7:1, 11; (5) Josh. 7:4-8.

Adam: (1) Red; (2) Earth colored (of the earth); (3) Human; (4) Humankind (5) Sin; (6) Christ.
(1-2) Name meaning; (3-4) One of four Hebrew words for "human"; 1 Cor. 15:22; (5) Gen. 3; (6) 1 Cor. 15:45.

Adan: See *Aidan*.

Adelaide: (1) Dignified; (2) Aristocrat; (3) May also carry the person's assessment of the city or a person by this name.

Adele: (1) Dignified aristocrat.

Adeline: (1) Amiable; (2) Pleasant.

Adrian: (1) Dark; (2) Dark-skinned.

Adullam: (1) Justice of the people; (2) Shelter.

Agnes: (1) Spotless and pure; (2) Chaste.

Aidan: (1) Fervent; (2) Fiery.

Akubra: (1) Lit. "head covering"; (2) Aussie drover's (one who drives cattle/sheep) hat.

Alabama: (1) Cleaners of thickets; (2) Thicket clearers.

Alamo: (1) Poplar tree.

Alan: (1) (Celtic) Good-looking; (2) (Gaelic) Rock; (3) (French) Noble.

Alana: See *Alan*.

Alba: (1) Dawn.

Albert/o: (1) Shining nobleman.

Alby: See *Albert*.

Alcatraz: (1) Pelican; (2) Prison.

Alexander: (1) Protector; (2) Defender of people.

Alex/Alexi/Alexia: See *Alexander*.

Alf: (1) (German) Noble and ready to fight; (2) (Swedish) Advised by elves.

Alfonso: (1) Noble and ready to fight.

Alfred: (1) Advised by elves (evil spirits).

Alice: (1) Dignified aristocrat.

Alicia: See *Alice*.

Alita: (1) Having wings.

Allison: (1) Honorable; (2) God-like fame.

Almund: (1) One who defends the temple.

Almunda: (1) Worships the Virgin Mary.

Althea: (1) Faultless.

Alvaro: (1) Guard of all; (2) Guards the truth.

Alvin: (1) Noble friend.

Amado: (1) Beloved.

Amalia: (1) Work; (2) Diligent.

Amanda: (1) Worthy of love.

Amato: See *Amado*.

Amerigo: See *Henry*.

Amos: (1) Courageous; (2) Carried; (3) A prophet of judgment. (3) Amos 1:1-3.

Amparo: (1) Protection; (2) Shelter.

Amy: (1) One who is dearly loved.

Ananias: (1) Liar; (2) Greed-driven deception; (3) Messenger. (1-2) Acts 5:3; (3) Acts 9:17.

Anarhlia: (1) Drink of water (as possible variant of nahla).

Andre: See *Andrew*.

Andrea: (1) Womanly.

Andrew: (1) Masculine; (2) Man; (3) Of a man; in Scripture the name is associated with; (4) Evangelism (It was Andrew who gathered Simon-Peter). (4) John 1:40-41.

Angelo: (1) Messenger; (2) Angel.

Angus: (1) Unique choice; (2) Only option.

Ani: (1) Good-looking.

Anita: See *Hannah*.

Ann: (1) Favored graciously.

Annabel/la: (1) Favored graciously; (2) Full of grace and beauty.

Annunziata/o: (1) Announces news; (2) Proclaims.

Anthea: (1) Flower lady.

Anthony: (1) Invaluable.

Antoinette: (1) Invaluable.

Anton: (1) Invaluable.

April: (1) To open; (2) When the buds open.

Ari: (1) (Greek) Great thinker; (2) (Norse) Strength of an eagle.

Ariel/e: (1) Lion of God.

Arizona: (1) Place of the small spring.

Arlene: (1) A sworn promise; (2) Oath.

Arnold: (1) Strength of an eagle.

(1) Isa. 40:31.

Art: See *Arthur.*

Arthur: (1) Having the strength of a bear.

Asa: (1) One who heals.

Asher: (1) Joyful.

Ashley: (1) Grove of ash trees.

Ashlyn: (1) Grove of ash trees.

Ashton: (1) A farm of ash trees.

Aspen: (1) The poplar or aspen tree.

Atlanta: (1) Mighty huntress.

Audrey: (1) Has strength.

August: (1) (English) Born in the eighth month; (2) (Latin) Grand and magnificent (venerable).

Aurelio: (1) Golden; (2) Gilded.

Austin: (1) Renowned.

Austen: (1) Grand and magnificent.

Aymeric: (1) Diligent ruler.

Azam: (1) Greatest; (2) Biggest.

Balder: (1) Without hair.

Bali: (1) Jewel of the east.

Baltimore: (1) Settlement of the big house.

Bani: (1) Constructed.

Barack: (1) Blessed.

Barak: (1) Lightning flash.

Barbara: (1) Stranger; (2) Foreigner.

Barret: (1) Having the power of a bear.

Barrett: (1) At the head; (2) Chief.

Barry: (1) Lives near the border; (2) Having the strength of a bear; (3) Excellent marksman.

Bart: (1) Son of the furrows; (2) Son of the ridges; (3) Son of the plowman.

Barton: (1) Lives on a barley farm.

Baruch: (1) Exalted; (2) Blessed.

Bea: See *Beatrice*.

Beatrice: (1) One who brings joy.

Beena: (1) Comprehends; (2) Discerns.

Belinda: (1) One who comes with wisdom.

Benedict: (1) Blessed.

Benit/a/o: (1) Blessed; (2) Happy.

Benjamin: (1) Son of my right hand; (2) Son of my strength.

Ber: (1) A bear.

Bernadette: (1) As brave as a bear; (2) Burn a debt (play on words).

Bernice: (1) She brings victory.

Bernie/Bernard: (1) As brave as a bear.

Berri: (1) Bend in the river.

Bess: (1) My God is bountiful.

Betty: See *Elizabeth*.

Bethany: (1) House of dates.

Bethel: (1) House of God.

Bevan: (1) Young soldier.

Beverley: (1) Field where beavers live.

Beulah: (1) Married; (2) Joined in marriage.

Biju: (1) Victory; (2) Jewels.

Bill: See *William*.

Bina/h: (1) Comprehends; (2) Discerning.

Bing: (1) Cauldron-shaped hollow.

Blake: (1) Dark; (2) Dark-skinned.

Blair: (1) Child of the field; (2) From the plain.

Blaise: (1) One who lisps or speaks imperfectly.

Blayze: (1) Flaming fire.

Bo: (1) Pleasing appearance; (2) Respected; (3) Having the strength of a bow; (4) Cherished.

Boaz: (1) Fleetness; (2) In His strength.

Bob: (1) One whose fame shines brightly.

Bobby: (1) One whose fame shines brightly.

Boca Raton: (1) Mouth of the mouse; (2) Place where pirates hid.

Bolton: (1) From the main house on the farm.

Bondi: (1) The place of breaking water.

Bonnie: (1) Beautiful; (2) Good.

Boston: (1) Town by the woods.

Bosworth: (1) Lives near the cattle yards.

Boyle: (1) Money-making.

Brad: (1) Broad.

Bradley: (1) Large clearing; (2) Broad meadow.

Brazil: (1) Strength; (2) Conflict.

Brenda: (1) A sword or swordsman.

Brendon: (1) Lives by the beacon.

Brenton: (1) A steep hill.

Brett: (1) Old English tradition; (2) British; (3) Not changing; (4) Government.

Brewer: (1) Beer maker. Also see *Brewery* and *Drugs*.

Brian: (1) Strength; (2) Hill; (3) May represent Jesus as the arm or strength of God. Also see *Hill* and *Strength* in Metaphor Dictionary.
(3) 2 Kings 9:24 & John 12:38.

Bridget: (1) Has strength.

Brock: (1) Lives beside the stream.

Bronwyn: (1) Fair-breasted; (2) May represent the Holy Spirit.

Brooke: (1) Lives beside the stream.

Bruce: (1) Forest.

Bruno: (1) Brown.

Brunswick: (1) Bruno's village.

Bryce: (1) (Celtic) Quick; (2) Watchful; (3) Aspiring; (4) (Scottish) Marked with freckles.

Bubba: (1) Good fellow.

Buick: (1) (Irish) Outlying farm; (2) (Dutch) Fat man.

Burn: (1) Lives near the stream.

Cain: (1) Murderer; (2) Carnal believer; (3) Man of the flesh; (4) Self-righteous believer; (5) Sin at the door; (6) Religious.
(1-6) Gen. 4:1-16; Heb. 11:4.

Cairns: (1) Mound of rocks.

Caitlin: (1) Pure; (2) Spotless.

Caleb: (1) Dog; (2) Bold; (3) Impetuous.

Callum: (1) Dove-like.

Campbell: (1) Crooked mouth; (2) Bent mouth.

Camden: (1) Winding valley.

Cameron: (1) Has a bent nose; (2) From the place where the stream bends.

Camilla: (1) Temple attendant.

Canada: (1) Village; (2) Settlement.

Canberra: (1) Field for meeting; (2) Capital (place of decision-making).

Candace: (1) Radiant.

Cape Canaveral: (1) Cane break; (2) Place of rocket launches.

Cara: (1) One who is loved.

Carlo/s: (1) Manly; (2) Masculine.

Carlton: (1) Land between two creeks.

Carol: (1) Womanly; (2) Manly.

Carolyn: (1) Feminine; (2) Womanly; (3) May relate a woman's point of view; (4) Female influence in your life.

Carolina/e: (1) Womanly.

Carmel: (1) Fruitful pasture; (2) Place of victory.
(2) 1 Kings 18:20-40.

Carmen: (1) Crimson color.

Casey: (1) Attentive or alert; (2) Fragrant spice; (3) Small stream.

Cassandra: (1) She confuses.

Cassi: See *Cassandra*.

Catherine: (1) Spotless; (2) Pure.
(1-2) Eph. 5:27.

Cavan: (1) Born good-looking.

Ceduna: (1) A place to sit down and rest.

Chad: (1) Warrior.

Chandler: (1) Produces candles.

Chantal: (1) Nun who birthed an order to care for the sick; (2) Place of stones; (3) To sing.

Charles: (1) Manly; (2) Masculine.

Charlotte: (1) Man.

Chelsea: (1) Place to land on a river.

Cheryl: (1) One who is loved.

Chevy: (1) Skillful with horses; (2) Mounted soldier.

Chicago: (1) Onion place; (2) Bears (football team).

Chloe: (1) Lush green and blooming.

Christine: (1) One who believes in Christ.

Christopher: (1) Carries the Anointed One.

Christy: (1) One who believes in Christ.

Chrysler: (1) Veil; (2) Weaver of veils.

Chuck: See *Charles*.

Cienega: (1) Marsh; (2) Swamp.

Cilla: (1) Old; (2) Lived long.

Cinderella: (1) From cinders or ashes.

Cindi/a: (1) To illuminate.

Cindy: (1) Lofty; (2) From the mount.

Cindylou: (1) Fight from the ashes.

Clare: (1) Bright and clear.

Clarence: (1) Shining sword.

Clark/Clarke: (1) Keeper of records; (2) Scholarly.

Claude: (1) Crippled; (2) Lame.

Claudia: See *Claude*.

Cleveland: (1) Area full of cliffs.

Clinton: (1) Village on a hill.

Col: (1) Dove-like.

Colby: (1) Lives in the dark town.

Cole: (1) (Latin) Farms cabbages; (2) (Greek) Victory over the people; (3) (Irish) Immature cub.

Colin: (1) Victory of the people; (2) Vigorous masculine child.

Colleen: (1) A girl child; (2) Young woman.

Collette: (1) Victory of the people.

Colorado: (1) Reddish.

Con: See *Constantine*.

Concha: (1) Becoming pregnant.

Connecticut: (1) The long river; (2) Beside the long tidal river.

Connie: (1) Determined and wise; (2) Not changing or constant (Constance).

Constance: (1) Unchanging, constant; (2) Certainty.

Constantine: (1) Unchanging, constant; (2) Certainty.

Conway: (1) (Irish) Plains hound; (2) (Welsh) Consecrated water.

Copenhagen: (1) Merchants' harbor.

Cora: See *Coralea*.

Coral: (1) Sea coral; (2) Salmon colored.

Coralea: (1) Young lady; (2) Virgin.

Coralee: See *Coralea*.

Corby: (1) Raven; (2) Blackbird.

Corbyn: See *Corby*.

Corcoran: (1) Having a reddish complexion.

Cordel: (1) Maker of rope.

Cordelia: (1) Jewel from the sea.

Coree: (1) Hollow or depression.

Corey: (1) (Irish) A rounded depression or hill; (2) (Scottish) Pool appearing to boil; (3) (English) Chosen one.

Corvette: (1) A fast, lightly armed warship, smaller than a destroyer, often armed for anti-submarine operations.

Cornelius: (1) Horn-shaped; (2) Animal horns.

Corrin: (1) A spear-bearer.

Corrinne: (1) Young lady; (2) Virgin.

Corry: (1) A round hill.

Costa: (1) Unchanging; (2) Constant.

Courtney: (1) Lives at the court.

Craig: (1) Rock; (2) Cliff or crag; (3) Steep rocky outcrop.

Croydon: (1) Saffron valley; (2) Spice valley.

Crystal: (1) Clear and sparkling gem.

Cunningham: (1) Milk bucket hamlet.

Cyndy: (1) Lofty; (2) From the mount.

Dakota: (1) Ally; (2) Friend.

Dale: (1) A valley.

Dallas: (1) From the waterfall.

(1) Ps. 42:7.

Damon: (1) Overcomes; (2) Tames.

Damian: (1) Overcomes; (2) Tames.

Daniel: (1) God is judge.

Danielle: See *Daniel*.

Dannika: (1) Star of the morning.

Danny: (1) Judging (evaluating).

Daphne: (1) Victory.

Darlene: (1) Darling; (2) Loved.

Darren: (1) Great; (2) Tiny; (3) Stony hill.

Darryl: (1) One who is loved.

Darryn: (1) Little and great.

Darwin: (1) Close friend.

David: (1) Dearly loved one; (2) Beloved; (3) Jesus (as the Beloved).

(3) Eph. 1:6.

Dawn: (1) Sunrise.

Dayna: (1) Judged by God.

Dayton: (1) From the sunlit village.

Dean: (1) From the sandhills.

(1) Matt. 7:26-27.

Deborah: (1) Honey bee; (2) Religious spirit.

Debbie: See *Deborah*.

December: (1) Ten/th; (2) Tenth month from March, the beginning of first month of ancient Roman calendar.

Declan: (1) Man of prayer; (2) Saint of Ireland.

Deiter: (1) People's army.

Deitrich: (1) One who rules the people.

Deja: (1) Ahead of time; (2) Before.

Dejon: See *Deja*.

Delany: (1) Challenger; (2) Son of the competitor.

Delilah: (1) Wanted; (2) Desired.

(2) Judg. 16.

Dell: (1) (English) A valley; (2) (German) Dignified aristocrat.

Delma: (1) Belonging to the sea.

Del Sur: (1) Of the south.

Demi: (1) Half of a whole.

Demiah: See *Demi*.

Demicah: (1) Overcomes.

Demingo: (1) Of the Lord.

Denise: (1) Follower of the wine god.

Dennis: (1) Follower of the wine god.

Denver: (1) Green or grassy valley.

Deion: (1) Plunderer.

Deon: (1) (m) The wine harvest god; (2) (f) The moon.

Derek: (1) One who rules the people; (2) The way. (2) Ps. 103:7.

Dermot/t: (1) Content; (2) Free from jealousy.

Detroit: (1) Strait; (2) Also see Automobile (auto capital).

Dharma: (1) Justice and duty.

Dianne: (1) Godly; (2) Divine.

Dick: (1) Powerful ruler; (2) Strong.

Diego: (1) See *James*.

Dierdre/Diedre: (1) Full of grief.

Dinah: (1) Judged as innocent.

Dixie: (1) Strong; (2) Powerful ruler.

Dixy: (1) Upright structure; (2) Wall; (3) Embankment.

Dolores: (1) Sorrowful.

Dominic: (1) Of the Lord.

Donald: (1) Rules over everything.

Donegal: (1) Stranger's fortress.

Donna: (1) Respected woman.

Doreen: (1) Changeable disposition; (2) Melancholy; (3) Good-looking.

Doris: (1) Gift; (2) Present.

Dorothy: (1) A gift from God.

Douglas: (1) Lives near the dark waters; (2) Dark or blood waters.

Drew: (1) Manly; (2) Masculine (i.e., man/kind); (3) Carrier; (4) Vigorous.

Duane: (1) Dark-skinned; (2) Black.

Dudley: (1) From the people's field.

Duncan: (1) Dark fighter; (2) Brown fighter.

Dusten: (1) Courageous soldier.

Dustin: (1) Quarry for brown rock.

Dutch: (1) From Germany.

Dwayne: (1) A song; (2) Little and dark.

Dwight: (1) White.

Dylan: (1) Son of the sea.

Dymock: (1) Swine enclosure.

Dymphna: (1) Poet; (2) Minstrel.

Dympna: (1) Suitable for the task.

Dyna: (1) Having authority.

Earl: (1) Aristocrat; (2) Earl. The fourth rank of nobility (prince, duke, marquis, earl).

Earn: (1) Falcon or eagle.

Edinburgh: (1) Secure; (2) Wealthy and content.

Edith: (1) Gives richly.

Edna: (1) Wealthy advisor.

Edward: (1) Affluent (rich) protector.

Edwin: (1) Wealthy companion.

Egor: (1) Farmer.

Eileen: (1) Of the light.

Elaine: (1) Of the light.

Eleazar: (1) Helper; (2) Whom God aids.

Eli: (1) My God; (2) Uplifted.

Elijah: (1) My God is Jehovah; (2) Preparatory prophet; (3) The Prophets.

Elim: (1) Palm Trees; (2) Oaks.

Eliot/t: (1) The Lord is God.

Elise: (1) Dignified aristocrat.

Elisha: (1) God is Savior; (2) To whom God is salvation.

Elizabeth: (1) To whom God is the oath; (2) My God is bountiful.

Ellen: (1) Of the light.

Ellie: (1) Of the light.

Elliot: (1) An old man from Wales.

Elliott: (1) The Lord is God.

Eloise: (1) Well-known in battle.

El Paso: (1) Passage.

Elton: (1) From the village given by elves.

Elvin: (1) Loved by everyone.

Emi: See *Emily*.

Emilio: (1) One who flatters.

Emily: (1) One who works hard.

Emma: (1) Great; (2) Universal.

Encino: (1) Oak.

England: (1) Angel-land; (2) The people who dwell by the narrow water.

Enoch: (1) Teaching; (2) Instructed; (3) Dedicated; (4) Experienced.

Enrica: (1) Commands the household.

Enrikos: (1) Commands the household.

Enya: (1) Kernel; (2) Seed.

Enyo: (1) Destroyer of cities.

Enz/o/io: (1) Commands the household.

Eric: (1) Will rule forever.

Erielle: (1) Lion of God.

Erin: (1) Peace; (2) From Ireland.

Esau: (1) Hairy; (2) Man of the flesh.
(1-2) Gen. 25:25, 34; Rom. 9:13; Heb. 12:16-17.

Estelle: (1) Star.

Esther: (1) Star.

Ethan: (1) Firmness.

Eugene: (1) Of good birth.

Eunice: (1) Joyfully triumphant; (2) Conquering well.

Eva: (1) Life-giving.

Evans: (1) Young soldier.
(1) 1 John 2:14.

Eve: (1) Life; (2) Life-giving; (3) Womankind; (4) Mother; (5) Deceived; (6) Church.
(1-2) Name meaning; (3) As Eve was the first woman she may be representative of women; (4) <u>Gen. 3:20</u>; (5) 1 Tim. 2:14; (6) Adam and Eve can symbolize Christ and the Church.

Evin: (1) God has favored.

Ezekiel: (1) Whom God will strengthen.

Ezra: (1) Help; (2) Gives assistance.

Fabio: (1) A bean farmer.

Fatima: (1) Fascinating; (2) Weaned; (3) Daughter of the prophet.

Fausto: (1) Favoring.

Fay: (1) A fairy; (2) Demon.

February: (1) To purify by sacrifice.

Felicity: (1) Lucky; (2) Happy.

Ferdinand/o: (1) Bold travel; (2) Daring adventure.

Fernando: (1) One who dares adventure.

Ferrari: (1) Blacksmith; (2) Iron; (3) Recognized as fast, powerful, and expensive autos.

Findon: (1) Lit. "heap-hill"; (2) Church hill.

Fiona: (1) Fair complexioned.

Flabio: (1) Golden-haired.

Fletch/Fletcher: (1) One who makes arrows.

Fleur: (1) A flower.

Flint: (1) Hard stone that sparks when hit.

Florence: (1) Blooming.

Florida: (1) Blooming; (2) Flowering.
(2) Song 2:12-13; Matt. 24:32.

Floyd: (1) (Irish) God's will; (2) (Celtic) Grey-haired.

Fogerty: (1) Banished.

Fons/Fonsie/zie: (1) Noble and ready to fight.

Ford: (1) Shallow river crossing.

Forest: (1) One who guards the woods.

Forrest: (1) Tree-covered land.

Forrester: (1) One who guards the woods.

Fran/Francis: (1) From France; (2) A javelin; (3) Free.

Frank: (1) A javelin; (2) Free; (3) From France.

Franklin: (1) A landholder of free birth.

Fred: (1) Peace-making ruler.

Freda: See *Fred*.

Freeman: (1) At liberty.

Fremantle: (1) A poor man's thin coat.

Fremont: (1) Great guardian.

Fresno: (1) Ash tree.

Gabby: (1) See *Gabriel*.

Gabriel: (1) God-given strength.

Gad: (1) Fortunate; (2) Favorable.

Gail: (1) Full of joy; (2) Delighted.

Gareth: (1) Gentle; (2) Compassionate.

Garth: (1) Gardener.

Gary: (1) Spear-carrier; (2) Spear.

Gavin: (1) Hawk used in battle.

Gemima: (1) One of two; (2) A twin.

Gemini: (1) One of two; (2) A twin.

Gemma: (1) Precious stone.

Gena: (1) (French) White spirit; (2) (Russian) Of good birth.

Genna: (1) Springtime.

Geoff/rey: (1) Full of peace; (2) Has the peace of God.

George: (1) Farmer; (2) Ground-breaker; (3) Harvest worker.

Gerrald: (1) Commands with a spear.

Gerrard: (1) Strength like a spear.

Gideon: (1) One who cuts down; (2) May symbolize a great work done by a few. (1) Judg. 6:25; (2) Judg. 7:7.

Gilbert: (1) Bright pledge/promise; (2) Intelligent boy.

Gilchrist: (1) One who serves Christ.

Gilead: (1) Hill of witness.

Gillian: (1) Youthful.

Giovani: (1) God has favored.

Gisele/Giselle: (1) Promise.

Gladys: (1) Crippled.

Glen: (1) Lives in the valley.

Glenda: (1) Lives in the valley.

Glenelg: (1) In and out of a valley (viewed as a palindrome).

Glenice: (1) Lives in the valley.

Glynn: (1) Lives in the valley.

Godfrey: (1) The peace of God.

Godwin: (1) Friend of God.

Gold Coast: (1) Glorious living; (2) Money (expense or wealth); (3) Ritzy (up-market); (4) The world.

Goldie: (1) Finances; (2) Precious metal.

Goliath: (1) Exile; (2) Soothsayer; (3) Giant.
(1-3) 1 Sam. 17:4,23.

Gomez: (1) Adult male.

Goran: (1) Farmer.

Gordon: (1) From the wetlands; (2) Marshy field.

Grace: (1) Favor; (2) Esteem; (3) Mercy; (4) Gift.
(1-4) John 1:14.

Graham: (1) From the gravelly farm.

Grant: (1) Bestow or give.

Greg/Gregory: (1) Watchful; (2) Alert; (3) Vigilant.

Gretel: (1) Pearl; (2) Sea jewel.

Grosvenor: (1) Mighty hunter.

Guenter: (1) Fighter; (2) Warrior.

Guido: (1) Escort; (2) Pilot.

Guiseppe: (1) My God will increase.

Guild: (1) Association of craftsmen.

Gunter: (1) Fighter; (2) Warrior.

Gus: (1) Sword or club of the Goths.

Guy: (1) (Celtic) Well-reasoned; (2) (Teutonic) Fighter; (3) Warrior.

Gwen: (1) Fair complexion; (2) White spirit.

Hal: (1) Ruler of the house.

Halifax: (1) Sacred field.

Ham: (1) Warm or hot/heat; (2) Burnt; (3) Dark.
(1) Gen. 9:18.

Hamish: (1) Replacement; (2) See James/Jacob.

Hank: (1) Commands the household.

Hannah: (1) Favored graciously; (2) Experienced anguish to break through to birth the promise in the Spirit.
(2) 1 Sam. 1:10-17; Rom. 8:26; Eph. 5:18.

Hans/el: (1) God has favored.

Harley: (1) Field of hares; (2) Doctor/specialist (Harley St.).

Harold: (1) Military commander.

Harris: (1) Son of the commander of the household.

Harry: (1) Commands the household; (2) Military commander.

Harvey: (1) Soldier; (2) Warrior.

Hawaii: (1) From the breath of God came the water of life.

Hayley: (1) Field of hay.

Hazel: (1) Under God's protection.

Heath: (1) Moorland; (2) Wilderness.

Heather: (1) Purple flowering shrub.

Heidi: (1) Dignified aristocrat.

Helen: (1) Of the light.

Henderson: (1) Son of the commander of the household.

Hendon: (1) Valley frequented by hinds.

Henry: (1) Commands the household; (2) Home ruler; (3) Home power.

Herbert: (1) Glorious soldier.

Hilary: (1) Joy; (2) Happiness.

Hilda: (1) Warrior; (2) Battle.

Hilton: (1) Lives at the farm on the hill.

Hobart: (1) Exalted brightness.

Holden: (1) Benevolent; (2) Courteous.

Holly: (1) Small woody plant with red berries; (2) Sacred.

Homer: (1) Security; (2) Held as a pledge; (3) Earnest down payment. (3) 2 Cor. 1:22.

Honda: (1) One from the base of the fields.

Honolulu: (1) Place of shelter; (2) Sheltered bay.

Horace: (1) Keeps account of time.

Houston: (1) Village on a hill.

Howard: (1) The chief watchman.

Hudson: (1) The hooded man's son.

Hugh: (1) Intelligent; (2) Clever.

Hume: (1) The river island.

Humphrey: (1) Guards the household.

Hyde: (1) Prepares hides.

Ian: (1) God has favored.

Illinois: (1) Tribe of superior men.

Imani: (1) Follower; (2) One who believes.

Imogen: (1) Daughter; (2) Girl child.

Impala: (1) Medium-sized African antelope.

Imran: (1) One who entertains guests.

India: (1) River; (2) Body of water.

Indiana: (1) Land of Indians.

Ingrid: (1) Beautiful one.

Innsbruck: (1) Bridge over the inn.

Iona: (1) (Greek) Amethyst; (2) (Aust. Aborigine) Flame.

Iowa: (1) Sleepy ones; (2) This is the place; (3) The beautiful land.

Iran: (1) Mountain.

Iraq: (1) The bank; (2) Between the rivers (from meaning of Mesopotamia).

Ireland: (1) Fat land; (2) Land of abundance.

Irene: (1) Peace; (2) At peace.

Iris: (1) Rainbow; (2) Message from God.

Irwin: (1) One who enjoys the ocean.

Isaac: (1) Laughter; (2) Promise.

Isabel: (1) My God is bountiful.

Isaiah: (1) Salvation of Jehovah; (2) Jehovah is Helper.

Ishmael: (1) Whom God hears; (2) Born of the flesh.
(1) Gen. 16:11; (2) Rom. 9:7-9.

Israel: (1) Prince with God (sitting in heavenly places); (2) Struggles with God; (3) Compared to Jacob, Israel is the spiritual man; (4) Compared to Judah, Israel is the backslidden church.

Issachar: (1) He is hired; (2) One who works for wages.

Italy: (1) Calf land.

Jabez: (1) Causing pain.

Jacinta: (1) Fragrant bell-shaped flowers.

Jack: (1) (English) God has favored; (2) (American) See *Jacob*.

Jackie/Jacquie: See *Jacob*.

Jackson: (1) Son of God's gift.

Jacob: (1) Man of the flesh; (2) The old man; (3) Grabber/swindler; (4) Opponent of the spiritual man; (5) Deceiver; (6) Spineless; (7) Worm. (1-4) Gen. 32:28; (5) Gen. 27:36, 31:20; (6-7) Isa. 41:14.

Jamaal: (1) Beautiful; (2) Good-looking.

Jamahl: (1) Beautiful.

Jameel/a: (1) Beautiful.

James: (1) Replacement; (2) See *Jacob*.

Jamie: (1) See *Jacob*.

Jamin: (1) Right arm; (2) Strength.

Jan: (1) God has favored.

Jana: (1) God has favored.

Jane: (1) God has favored.

Janel: (1) Winner; (2) Champion.

Janelle: (1) God has favored.

Janet: (1) God has favored.

Janine: (1) God has favored.

Jannette: (1) God has favored.

Janson: (1) God has favored.

Janssen: (1) Son of God's gift.

January: (1) Beginning; (2) Entrance; (3) Passage; (4) Named after Janus, Roman god of gates and doorways.

Japan: (1) Land of the rising sun.

Japheth: (1) Extension; (2) Expanded; (3) Open.

Jarad: (1) Descending.

Jar/rad/red/rod: (1) (English) Strength like a spear; (2) (Hebrew) Descending.

Jason: (1) Healer.

Jasmine: (1) Fragrant shrub.

Jean: (1) God has favored.

Jeanette: (1) God has been gracious.

Jed: (1) Loved by God.

Jeffery: (1) Full of peace.

Jemimah: (1) Small dove; (2) Affectionate.

Jenna: (1) Tiny bird.

Jennifer: (1) Fair and smooth skinned; (2) White spirit.

Jeremiah: (1) Esteemed by God; (2) Uplifted by God.

Jeremy: (1) Esteemed by God; (2) Uplifted by God.

Jericho: (1) Moon city.

Jeriel: (1) God notices.

Jerusalem: (1) City of wholeness; (2) City of peace; (3) Hub of the kingdom.

Jess: (1) He exists.

Jesse: (1) God is.

Jessica: (1) God exists; (2) God sees.

Jesus: (1) The Lord is deliverance; (2) Savior.

Jezebel: (1) Unmarried (lit. "not at home"); (2) Controlling and manipulative spirit; (3) The spirit behind false or religious church.

Jill: (1) Youthful.

Jim: See *James*.

Joab: (1) God is my Father.

Joan: (1) God has favored; (2) The grace of God.

Joash: (1) On fire for God.

Job: (1) A desert; (2) One persecuted.

Jody: (1) God gives the ability to increase.

Jody-ann: (1) Celebrated.

Joe: (1) He (God) shall add; (2) May God increase.

Joel: (1) The Lord is God; (2) Jehovah is might.

John: (1) God has favored; (2) The grace of God; (3) Love.

Jonah: (1) Dove. See *Dove* in Metaphor Dictionary.

Jonathan: (1) A gift from God.

Jones: (1) Son of one God has favored.

Joni: (1) God has favored.

Joram: (1) The Lord is lifted up.

Jordan: (1) Descender; (2) Going down; (3) Death.

Joseph: (1) He (God) shall add; (2) May God increase; (3) God exceeds.

Joshua: (1) Jehovah is salvation; (2) Jesus.

Josiah: (1) Whom Jehovah heals; (2) The fire of the Lord.

Josilin: (1) Joy.

Josy/Josi: (1) God adds.

Joy: (1) Happy.

Joyce: (1) Joy.

Juan: (1) God has favored.

Juanita: (1) God has favored.

Judah: (1) Praise.

Judas: (1) A Jew from Judea.

Judith: (1) Praised; (2) Youthful; (3) From Judea.

Judson: (1) Celebrated.

Judy: (1) Celebrated.

Julia/Julie: (1) Young; (2) Youthful.

Julian: (1) Young; (2) Youthful.

Julie-anne: (1) Young; (2) Youthful; (3) Young by God's grace.

Juliette: (1) Young; (2) Youthful.

July: (1) Young; (2) Youthful.

June: (1) Protector of women; (2) Guardian.

Justin: (1) Unbiased; (2) Upright.

Kalisha: (1) Spotless; (2) Pure.

Kansas: (1) People of the south wind.
(1) Song. 4:16; Luke 12:55; Acts 27:13.

Kara: (1) Small marsupial; (2) Possum.

Karen: (1) Spotless; (2) Pure.

Karl: (1) Masculine; (2) Manly.

Karralee: (1) Spotless or pure-haven.

Kasey: (1) Attentive; (2) Alert.

Kasie: See *Kasey*.

Kate: (1) Spotless; (2) Pure.

Katherine: (1) Spotless; (2) Pure; (3) The Church.
(1-3) Eph. 5:27.

Kay: (1) Spotless; (2) Pure.

Kaylene: (1) Cares for the keys.

K.C.: (1) Courageous; (2) Brave.

Keith: (1) From the woodlands.

Keiler: (1) Maker of wooden pegs/wedges.

Keimer: Described by Ben Franklin as an: (1) Odd fish.

Keisha: (1) Great happiness.

Kelly: (1) Fighter; (2) Warrior.

Kelsie: (1) From island of ships.

Kemp/e: (1) Fighter; (2) Warrior.

Kenneth: (1) Handsome.

Kentucky: (1) Meadowland; (2) Land of tomorrow.

Kevin: (1) Born good-looking.

Kerry: (1) Dark; (2) Dark-skinned.

Kim: See *Kimberley*.

Kimberley: (1) From a royal town.

Kira: See *Jacob*.

Kirk: (1) Lives near the church.

Kirrily: (1) Leaf or bark of a gum tree.

Kirrin: See *Kyrin*.

Kirsten: (1) Christ follower.

Kirsty: (1) Christ follower.

K-Mart: From meaning of the founder's name, Kresge: (1) Love; (2) Fish (believer); (3) Merchandising/greedy (business or church).

Korah: (1) Baldness; (2) Worship; (3) Rebellion.

Kristan: (1) One who believes in Christ.

Kristen: (1) Consecrated by anointing.

Krystal: (1) Sparking clear quartz gemstone.

Kurt: (1) Candid counselor.

Kyle: (1) Where the water narrows.

Kylie: (1) Boomerang; (2) Something that has to go ("take off" overseas) and return to be appreciated.

Kym: (1) Chief; (2) Ruler.

Kyrin: (1) Dark-skinned.

La Brea: (1) Tar; (2) Tar pits.

Lachlan: (1) Hostile; (2) War-like.

Lachlann: (1) Comes from Scandinavia (Denmark, Norway, or Sweden).

Lalor: (1) One with leprosy.

Lana: (1) Calmly floating.

Lancaster: (1) Castle on the Lune (pure) River.

Lance: (1) An attendant; (2) One who serves.

Lara: (1) Shining ones; (2) Full of joy.

Larissa: (1) Full of joy; (2) Laughing.

Las Cruces: (1) The crosses.

Las Vegas: (1) Meadows; (2) Gambling.

Latoya: (1) Achieved victory; (2) Triumphed.

Laura: (1) Victory.

Lauren: (1) Victory.

Laurence: (1) Victory.

Lavinia: (1) Cleansed; (2) Made pure.

Lazarus: (1) Whom God aids; (2) Protected by God.

Leane: (1) Favored willow tree.

Leann: (1) Young and beautiful.

Leanna: (1) Bound like a vine-covered tree.

Leanne: (1) Luminous; (2) Full of beauty.

Leah: (1) Weary; (2) Tired.

Lee: (1) On the sheltered side.

Leif: (1) Relative; (2) Descendant; (3) Heir.

Leisel: (1) Dedicated to God.

Leith: (1) Grassy land; (2) Broad.

Lenny: (1) Like a lion.

Leon/a: (1) Lion cub.

Leonard: (1) Lion-like.

Leroy: (1) Kingly; (2) Royal.

Lesley: (1) Lives by the grey fort/castle.

Lester: (1) Camp of the legion.

Levi: (1) United; (2) Joined; (3) Union.

Lewis: (1) Famed in battle.

Liam: (1) Determined to guard. See *William*.

Libby: (1) My God is bountiful.

Lillian: (1) Lily.

Lima: (1) Goddess of the entrance.

Linda: (1) Beautiful; (2) One who comes with wisdom; (3) Could be from Germanic *lindi*, which means "serpent" or "dragon."

Lindley: (1) From the peaceful field.

Lindsay: (1) Island of linden trees.

Linley: (1) Pool of water in a field.

Lionel: (1) Lion cub.

Lisa: (1) My God is bountiful.

Lissie/Lissy: (1) My God is bountiful.

Liz: (1) My God is bountiful.

Lobethal: (1) Valley of praise.

Lois: (1) At liberty.

Lola: (1) Womanly.

London: (1) The moon's stronghold; (2) Church stronghold.

Lorenzo: (1) Victory; (2) Faith; (3) From the island of the bay trees.

Lorraine: (1) Known for war exploits.

Lorna: (1) From the place of the bay (laurel) trees; (2) Victory (laurel wreath).

Lorne: (1) Desolate; (2) Deserted.

Los Angeles: (1) The angels.

Los Gatos: (1) The cats.

Los Nietos: (1) The grandchildren.

Lou: (1) Famed in battle.

Louise: (1) Famed in battle.

Luba: (1) Delightfully affectionate.

Luca: (1) To illuminate.

Lucas: (1) Of the light.

Lucien: (1) To illuminate.

Lucille: (1) To illuminate.

Lucinda: (1) To illuminate.

Lucretia: (1) Gain; (2) Profit.

Lucy: (1) To illuminate.

Luigi: (1) Well-known in battle.

Luisa: (1) Famed in battle.

Luke: (1) Of the light.

Lulu: (1) Famed in battle.

Lynda: See *Linda*.

Lynne: (1) Water cascade or the pool beneath.

Mac: (1) The son of.

Macadam: (1) Son of the red earth.

Maddison: (1) (English) Child of courage; (2) (Hebrew) Gift of God.

Madeleine: (1) From the place of the tower.

Madison: (1) Child of courage.

Madonna: (1) My lady; (2) Religious church (Mary and child).

Magill: (1) Son of the lowlander; (2) Son of the foreigner.

Makala: (1) The myrtle tree.

Malachi: (1) Messenger of Jehovah.

Malcolm: (1) Dove servant.

Mandy: (1) Worthy of love.

Manel: (1) God is with us.

Mannum: (1) Unknown; (2) Camping ground.

Manoah: (1) Relaxed; (2) Tranquil place.

Manuel: (1) God is with us.

Mara: (1) Bitter.

Marcell/o: (1) Small hammer.

March: (1) Lives at the border; (2) The god of war; (3) March was originally the beginning of the year and marked the return to war.

Marcy: (1) A large hammer.

Marduk: (1) Chief god, champion against chaos.

Margaret: (1) Pearl; (2) Sea jewel.

Maria/h: (1) Beloved one.

Marilyn: (1) Descended from Mary.

Mario: (1) Hostile; (2) Warlike.

Marion: (1) Sea of bitterness; (2) Rebelliousness; (3) Beloved one.

Marjorie: (1) Pearl; (2) Sea jewel.

Mark: (1) A hammer.
(1) Jer. 23:29.

Marlane: (1) From the place of the tower.

Marlene: (1) Beloved one from Magdala (tower).

Marlon: (1) Small hawk or falcon.

Marlow: (1) Hill by the sea.

Marshall: (1) One who manages another's property.

Martin: (1) Hostile; (2) Warlike.

Marty: See *Martin*.

Marvel: (1) Miraculous.

Mary: (1) Beloved one.

Marylou: (1) Beloved one who is famed as a warrior.

Massachusetts: (1) At the range of hills; (2) At or about the great hill.

Makita: (1) Pet form of Matilda; (2) Sweet.

Matilda: (1) Strong battle maiden; (2) Stamina to fight.

Matsushita: (1) Below the pine.

Matthew: (1) Gift from God.

Maureen: (1) Beloved one.

Maurice: (1) One who has dark skin.

Maverick: (1) Self-confident; (2) Self-sufficient.

Max: (1) Most of all; (2) Greatest; (3) From maximum.

May: (1) (Old English) Grandmother; (2) Growth or increase.

McAllister: (1) Son of the one who protects men.

McArthur: (1) Son of a fearless father.

McBride: (1) Son of one who has strength.

McCallum: (1) Son of the dove.

McCauley: (1) Son of ancestors.

McCloud: (1) Unattractive man's son.

McCoy: (1) Bright; (2) Intelligent.

McCrea: (1) Son of mercy.

McDonald: (1) Son who rules over everything.

McDougall: (1) Lives near the dark waters.

McDuff: (1) Blackman's son.

McGuire: (1) Fair son.

McKenzie: (1) Good-looking.

McKinley: (1) Son of the wise chief.

McLaine: (1) Son of a lion.

McLean: (1) Son of a lion.

McMahon: (1) Son of a bear.

McMurray: (1) Son of the sea lord.

McSorley: (1) Son of summer seafarer.

Megan: (1) Pearl; (2) Sea jewel.

Mel: (1) Chief.

Melanie: (1) Dark; (2) Dark-skinned.

Melbourne: (1) From the mill by the stream.

Melissa: (1) As sweet as honey; (2) Honey.

Merlin: (1) Hill by the sea.

Mervyn: (1) Seafarer; (2) One who enjoys the sea.

Mexico: (1) In the navel of the moon; (2) The rabbit's navel.

Miami: (1) People of the peninsula.

Michael: (1) Who is like God! (2) Who is like God? (3) Chief angel.

Michelle: See *Michael*.

Michigan: (1) Great or large lake.

Midian: (1) Judgment.

Miles: (1) (English) Tender (benevolent); (2) (Latin) Member of the army (soldier).

Millar: (1) Mill manager.

Miller: (1) Grinds grain at the mill.

Millicent: (1) Diligent; (2) Hard-working.

Milwaukee: (1) A rich beautiful land; (2) Fine land.

Minnesota: (1) Water that reflects the sky; (2) Sky-tinted water.

Miranda: (1) Fantastic; (2) Wonderful.

Miriam: (1) One who opposes authority.

Mississippi: (1) Large river; (2) Father of waters.

Missouri: (1) People with the dugout canoes; (2) Town of large canoes.

Mitsubishi: (1) Three water chestnuts.

Mitchell: (1) Who is like God! (2) Who is like God?

Mahogany: (1) Wealthy; (2) Powerful.

Molly: (1) Beloved one.

Mona: (1) (Greek) Alone; (2) (Irish) Honorable, noble.

Monaro: (1) High plateau or high plain.

Monica: (1) Advisor.

Montana: (1) Mountain.

Montecito: (1) Little woods.

Montreal: (1) Imperial mountain.

Monty: (1) A mountain.

Monro: (1) At the mouth of the river.

Monroe: (1) Red-colored marshland.

Moor/e: (1) One who has dark skin.

Mordecai: (1) Worshiper of Marduk/Merodach.

Moriah: (1) God educates.

Morocco: (1) Land of the setting sun; (2) Fortified.

Morris: (1) Son of dark skin.

Moses: (1) Delivered from water; (2) Drawn out of the water; (3) The Law.

Muncie: (1) People of the stony country.

Munro/e: (1) Red-colored marshlands.

Murial: (1) Perfume; (2) Aromatic ointment.

Muriel: (1) Ocean sparkle.

Murray: (1) Of the ocean.

Mustafa: (1) Chosen as king.

Mustang: (1) Wild and untamed.

Myer/s: (1) Illuminates.

Myra/n: (1) Aromatic ointment; (2) Perfume.

Nabal: (1) Fool.
(1) 1 Sam. 25:25; Ps. 14:1.

Nadia: (1) Hope.

Nadine: (1) Hope.

Nahbi: (1) Hidden.
(1) Num. 13:14.

Nahum: (1) Comforter.

Nancy: (1) Favored graciously.

Naomi: (1) Pleasant; (2) Delightful.

Naphtali: (1) My wrestling.
(1) Gen. 30:8.

Narelle: (1) Small one.

Natalie: (1) Born on Christmas Day.

Natanya: (1) Gift of God; (2) What God gave.

Natasha: (1) Born on Christmas Day.

Nathan: (1) Gift.
(1) 2 Sam. 7:2.

Nathaniel: (1) Gift of God; (2) God has given.

Nazareth: (1) Branch.

Neah: (1) Of a slope.

Nebai: (1) Fruitful.

Nebo: (1) A lofty pace; (2) Could relate to pride; (3) Place where Moses died. (1) Deut. 32:49.

Nebraska: (1) Flat or spreading water.

Nehemiah: (1) God comforts.

Nelly: (1) Of the light.

Nelson: (1) Son of Neil; (2) Champion; (3) Winner.

Neo: (1) Chosen one; (2) New. (1) As in, *The Matrix;* Matt. 22:14.

Neil: (1) Winner; (2) Champion; (3) Cloud.

Nestle: (1) Bird's nest.

Nevada: (1) Snow-covered.

Neville: (1) From the new settlement.

New Zealand: (1) New zeal-land; (2) Land of the long white cloud.

Nick: (1) Victory; (2) Triumph.

Nicolas: (1) Victory of the people; (2) Conqueror of the people. (2) Acts 6:5.

Nicole: (1) Victory of the people.

Nigel: (1) Champion; (2) Winner.

Nike: (1) Victory.

Nikita: (1) Victory of the people.

Nintendo: (1) Entrusted to Heaven's store.

Noah: (1) Comfort; (2) Rest.

Nolly: (1) The olive tree.

Noni: (1) Highly esteemed; (2) Honored.

Nora: (1) Esteemed; (2) Honored.

Noreen: (1) Law; (2) Regulation.

Norelle: (1) Comes from the north.

Norm/an: (1) Man from the north.

Norr/ie/y: (1) Man from the north.

North Dakota: (1) Allies.

Norton: (1) Northern farm.

Norwood: (1) Northern forest.

November: (1) Nine.

Nun: (1) Fish.

Oakley: (1) Field of the oak tree.

O'Brien: (1) Son of a strong man.

October: (1) Eight/h; (2) Eighth month from March, the beginning of ancient Roman calendar.

Odette: (1) Prosperous.

Odin: (1) The chief god.

Ohio: (1) Beautiful river; (2) Great river.

Oklahoma: (1) Red people.

Olaf: (1) Relic; (2) Inherited from forbears.

Olive: (1) The fruit of the olive.

Oliver: (1) The olive tree.

Olivia: (1) Fruit of the olive tree.

Onkaparinga: (1) The women's river.

Onslow/e: (1) Hill of a zealous man.

Ony: (1) An eagle.

Oprah: (1) A young deer.
(1) Ps. 42:1.

Orlando: (1) Well known in the land.

Orson: (1) Young bear.

Osborn/e: (1) One who fights for the gods.

Oscar: (1) Spear of the gods.

Oshea: (1) Son from the fairy palace.

Osmar: (1) Glory from God.

Osmund: (1) Security of God.

Ossie: (1) One who fights for God.

Oswald: (1) The power of God.

Oswego: (1) The outpouring.

Oswin: (1) Friend of God.

Owen: (1) Of good birth.

Pacoima: (1) Running water.
(1) John 7:38.

Paige: (1) Attendant.

Pamela: (1) Sweetness of honey.

Parkhurst: (1) Dweller in the park house.

Parkins/on: (1) Son of stone.

Pasquale: (1) Born at Easter.

Patrice: (1) Noble; (2) Aristocrat.

Patricia: (1) Noble; (2) Aristocratic.

Patrick: (1) Noble; (2) Aristocratic.

Paul: (1) Small; (2) Little; (3) Humble.

Paris: (1) One who loves.

Paterson: (1) Father's son.

Payne: (1) Rural; (2) Villager; (3) Homely.

Pedro: See *Peter*.

Peggy: (1) Pearl.

Pennington: (1) Lit. "Penny town"; (2) i.e., Poorville.

Penny: (1) Plant with large, handsome flowers.

Penrith: (1) Main river crossing.

Percival: See *Percy*.

Percy: (1) Penetrates the valley.

Perri: (1) The tree bearing pears.

Perry: (1) (French) Rock; (2) (Latin) Roaming, traveling, wanderer; (3) (French) The tree bearing pears.

Persian: (1) Independent (as in cat).

Perth: (1) Shrubbery with prickles or spines.

Peta: (1) See *Peter*; (2) Golden-colored eagle.

Peter: (1) A rock; (2) A stone.

Petronella: See *Peter*.

Philadelphia: (1) Brotherly love.

Philip: (1) One who loves horses; (2) Lover of Egypt (turning to the world). (2) Isa. 31:1,3.

Phoebe: (1) Radiant; (2) Glowing.

Phoenix: (1) Red as blood; (2) Mythological bird that was resurrected.

Phylis: (1) A leafy green branch.

Pierre: See *Peter*.

Pino: (1) My God will increase.

Pirie: (1) The son of Peter; (2) Dweller by the pear tree.

Pittsburgh: (1) Former steel producer; (2) Pirates (baseball team).

Polly: (1) Beloved one.

Porsche: (1) Portion or offering.

Port: (1) A door; (2) Doorkeeper.

Priscilla: (1) Old; (2) Lived long.

Prospect: (1) Positive future.

Pryor: (1) Officer in a monastic order.

Quade: (1) Powerful ruler.

Quaide: (1) Powerful fighter.

Quanesha: (1) Energetic or vivacious; (2) Woman.

Queens (NY): See *Queen* in Metaphor Dictionary.

Queensland: See *Queen* in Metaphor Dictionary.

Quigley: (1) Wild or unruly hair.

Quigly: (1) Of mother's side.

Quimby: (1) Lady's estate.

Quincy: (1) Fifth born.

Quinten: (1) Fifth born.

Quong: (1) A bright light.

Rachel: (1) Ewe; (2) Female sheep; (3) May represent one's wife; (4) Christ (as the Lamb).
(2-3) 2 Sam. 12:3,7-9.

Raelene: (1) A female sheep.

Rafael: See *Raphael*.

Rahab: (1) Broad; (2) Violence; (3) Proud; (4) Free; (5) Prostitute.
(1) Josh. 2:1; (2) Ps. 87:4.

Ralph: (1) Consults with wolves.

Randall: (1) Shield wolf; (2) Courage and strength.

Randy: (1) Shield wolf; (2) Courage and strength.

Raphael: (1) Healed by God.
(1) 1 Chron. 26:7.

Raul: (1) Consults with wolves.

Ray-anne: (1) Friendly.

Raylena: (1) Ewe.

Raylene: (1) Deer by the cascades.

Raymond: (1) Mighty and wise protector.

Rea/h: (1) Poppy (graceful and delicate flower).

Reannan: (1) Favored graciously.

Rebecca: (1) Tied to; (2) Noose; (3) Secured.

Redondo: (1) Round.

Reese: (1) Keen; (2) Fervent; (3) Fiery.

Reg: (1) Judges with strength.

Regan: (1) Royal descendant.

Reinhart: (1) Judges with strength.

Renee: (1) Born again.
(1) John 3:3.

Reuben: (1) Behold a son.

Rex: (1) A king.

Rhea: (1) Flowing stream.

Rhett: (1) Fervent; (2) Keen.

Rhonda: (1) Majestic; (2) Noisy.

Rhyanna: (1) A nymph or demon.

Rhys: (1) Fervent; (2) Keen.

Ria/h: (1) The river mouth; (2) The river.

Richard: (1) Strong; (2) Powerful ruler.

Richmond: (1) Powerful guardian.

Rick: See *Richard*.

Riddley: (1) Marshy land where reeds grow.

Ridley: (1) Red-colored fields.

Riki: See *Richard*.

Riley: (1) Courageous; (2) Field of rye.

Rita: (1) Pearl; (2) Sea jewel.

Robert: (1) One whose fame shines brightly.

Robin: (1) One whose fame shines brightly.

Rochelle: (1) Rock.

Rod: (1) See *Rodney*; (2) Word of God (as the Rod in Moses's hand).

Rodney: (1) Reedy island.

Roebuck: (1) Small deer.

Roger: (1) Famous spearman.
(1) 1 Chron. 11:11.

Rohan: (1) Horse country; (2) Having red hair; (3) Fragrant wood.

Roland: (1) Well-known in the land; (2) lit. "Famous land."

Roma: (1) From Rome, Italy; (2) May be a symbol of the religious church.

Romeo: (1) A Roman pilgrim.

Ronald: (1) Judges with strength.
(1) Ps. 54:1.

Rosalind: (1) Wisdom and strength.

Ross: (1) From the cape or peninsula.

Rowan: (1) Red.

Roweena: (1) Well-known friend.

Rowland: See *Roland*.

Roxanne: (1) Sunrise; (2) A bright light.

Roy: (1) Having red hair.

Rundle: (1) Spacious or roomy valley.

Rush: (1) Having red or fox-colored hair.

Russell: (1) A fox; (2) Red-haired.
(1) Luke 13:31-32; (2) Gen. 25:25.

Ruth: (1) Companion; (2) Friend.

Ryan: (1) Royal descendant.

Rylie: See *Riley*.

Salem: (1) Peace; (2) At peace.

Salisbury: (1) Fortress or stronghold near a pond.

Sally: (1) Princess.

Samantha: (1) God heard.

Samsung: (1) Three stars.

Samuel: (1) God has heard; (2) God hears.

San Francisco: (1) Saint Francis of Assisi.

San Diego: (1) Saint James.

Sandra: (1) Protector; (2) Defender of man.

Sangre de Cristo Mountains: (1) The blood of Christ mountains.

San Pedro: (1) Saint Peter.

Santa Fe: (1) Holy faith.

Sarah: (1) Princess.

Sasha: (1) Protector; (2) Defender of men.

Saul: (1) Asked for; (2) Demanded.

Savannah: (1) Wide grasslands.

Sawyer: (1) Wood cutter.

Scott: (1) From Scotland; (2) Tattooed (from the blue faces of the Picts).

Sean: (1) God has favored.

Sears: (1) Carpenter.

Seaton: (1) Sea town.

Sebastian: (1) Revered or respected.

September: (1) Seven/th; (2) Seventh month from March which used to be the beginning of Roman calendar.

Sergio: (1) Assistant; (2) Aide.

Shalem: (1) Whole; (2) Peace.

Shane: (1) God has favored; (2) The grace of God.

Shanghai: (1) Lit. "Above sea"; (2) Heaven's river.

Shani: (1) Wonderful.

Shanna: See *Shannon*.

Shannon: (1) Small, but wise.

Shantelle: See *Chantal*.

Sharna/y: (1) Flat plain.

Sharpay: (1) Sand skin.

Sharon: (1) Flat plain.

Shaun: (1) God has favored.

Sheila: (1) Sight-impaired; (2) Blind.

Shelley: (1) From the field on the ridge.

Shemus: (1) Replacement; (2) See James.

Sherilyn: (1) One who is loved.

Shireen: (1) Sweet.

Shirley: (1) Sunlit meadow.

Shivon: (1) God has favored.

Shivonne: (1) Bowman/archer.

Shona/h: (1) God has favored.

Sibyl: (1) Fortune teller; (2) Sage.

Siegfried: (1) Peace from victory.

Silvana/o: (1) From the woodland.

Silvia: (1) From the woodland.

Silvio: (1) Made of silver.

Simeon: (1) Hearing; (2) Obedience.

Simon: (1) One who hears; (2) Reed (moved by the wind of circumstance).

Simone: See *Simon*.

Simmonds: See *Simon*.

Simpson: See *Simon*.

Singapore: (1) Lion city.

Siobhan: (1) God is gracious; (2) God has favored.

Slobodan: (1) Freedom.

Smith: (1) Iron worker; (2) Blacksmith; (3) Works.

Sommara: (1) One who calls a group together.

Sonya: (1) One who is wise.

Sony: (1) Sound.

Sophie/a: (1) One who is wise.

Spalding: (1) From a divided meadow.

Spencer: (1) Custodian of the provisions.

Sporting Team Names:

Aussie Rules Football

Adelaide Crows: See *Raven* in Metaphor Dictionary.

Brisbane Lions: See *Lion* in Metaphor Dictionary.

Carlton Blues: See *Blue* in Metaphor Dictionary.

Collingwood Magpies: See *Raven* and *Black and White* in Metaphor Dictionary.

Essendon Bombers: See *Aeroplane* and *Bomb* in Metaphor Dictionary.

Footscray Bulldogs: See *Dog* in Metaphor Dictionary.

Fremantle Dockers: See *Fremantle* in Metaphor Dictionary.

Melbourne Demons: See *Demon* in Metaphor Dictionary.

North Melbourne Kangaroos: See *Kangaroo* in Metaphor Dictionary.

Port Adelaide Power: See *Power* in Metaphor Dictionary.

Richmond Tigers: See *Tiger* in Metaphor Dictionary.

Sydney Swans: See *Sydney* in Name and Place Dictionary and *Swan* in Metaphor Dictionary.

St. Kilda Saints: (1) Fellow believers; (2) Deceased fellow believers.

West Coast Eagles: See *Coast*, *Eagle*, and *West* in Metaphor Dictionary.

Hawthorn Hawks: See *Hawk* in Metaphor Dictionary .

Baseball

Anaheim Angels: See *Angels* in Metaphor Dictionary.

Cleveland Indians: See *Indigenous* in Metaphor Dictionary.

Detroit Tigers: See *Tiger* in Metaphor Dictionary.

Houston Astros: See *Astronaut* and *Flying* in Metaphor Dictionary.

Los Angeles Dodgers: See *Jacob*.

Milwaukee Brewers: See *Brewer* in Metaphor Dictionary.

Minnesota Twins: See *Thomas* in Name and Place Dictionary and *Two* in Metaphor Dictionary.

Montreal Expos: See *Carnival* in Metaphor Dictionary.

New York Mets: See *City* in Metaphor Dictionary.

Pittsburgh Pirates: See *Thief* in Metaphor Dictionary.

San Francisco Giants: See *Giant* in Metaphor Dictionary.

Basketball

Atlanta Hawks: See *Hawk* in Metaphor Dictionary.

Denver Nuggets: See *Gold* in Metaphor Dictionary.

Detroit Pistons: See *Cog* and *Automobile* in Metaphor Dictionary.

Indiana Pacers: See *Horse* in Metaphor Dictionary.

Los Angeles Clippers: See *Sail* and *Ship* in Metaphor Dictionary.

Los Angeles Lakers: See *Lake* in Metaphor Dictionary.

New Jersey Nets: See *Net* in Metaphor Dictionary.

New York Knickerbockers: See *York*.

Seattle Supersonics: See *Aeroplane*, *Flying*, and *Speed* in Metaphor Dictionary.

Utah Jazz: See *Jazz* in Metaphor Dictionary.

Football

Arizona Cardinals: See *Priest* in Metaphor Dictionary.

Baltimore Ravens: See *Raven* in Metaphor Dictionary.

Chicago Bears: See *Bear* in Metaphor Dictionary.

Green Bay Packers: See *Gift*, *Industry*, and *Moving House* in Metaphor Dictionary.

Philadelphia Eagles: See *Eagles* in Metaphor Dictionary.

Kansas City Chiefs: See *Chief* in Metaphor Dictionary.

Ice Hockey

Anaheim Mighty Ducks: See *Duck* in Metaphor Dictionary.

Boston Bruins: See *Boston* in Name and Place Dictionary and *Bear* (*Bruin* is Dutch for "brown") in Metaphor Dictionary.

Calgary Flames: See *Flame* in Metaphor Dictionary.

Detroit Red Wings: See combinations of entries under *Red* and *Wings* in Metaphor Dictionary.

New Jersey Devils: See *Demon* in Metaphor Dictionary.

New York Rangers: See *Police* in Metaphor Dictionary.

Sri Lanka: (1) Resplendent land.

Stacey: (1) Restored to life.

Stanley: (1) From the rocky meadow.

Stavros: (1) The cross.

Stefani: See *Stephen*.

Stella: (1) A star.

Stephanie: See *Stephen*.

Stephen: (1) Crowned with a laurel wreath; (2) Victorious; (3) May represent faith; (4) May represent Christ.
(3) Acts 6:5, 8; 1 John 5:4.

Steven: (1) See *Stephen*.

Stuart: (1) A caretaker of royal property.

Susan: (1) Lily.

Suzuki: (1) Bell tree.

Switzerland: (1) Neutral; (2) Banking.
(1) Isa. 62:6; (2) Ob. 1:3; Jer. 17:3.

Sydney: (1) Wide meadow; (2) Wide island; (3) From the French town St. Denis near Paris.

Sylvester: (1) From the woodland.

Tabor: (1) Height; (2) Broken.

Tahiti: (1) Facing the sunrise; (2) East.

Tahlia: (1) (Hebrew) Small, gentle sheep; (2) (Greek) Blossoming or blooming.

Takahashi: (1) High bridge.

Talya: (1) Heaven dew; (2) Light rain.

Tamara: (1) A palm tree.

Tameka: (1) One of two; (2) A twin.

Tammy: (1) Palm tree.

Tampa: (1) Stick of fire.

Tamsin: (1) One of twins.

Tandy: (1) Masculine; (2) Male.

Tanicha: (1) Symbol.

Tanja: (1) Angel; (2) Messenger from God.

Tanya: (1) Fairy queen; (2) Queen.

Tara: (1) Rocky crag or hill; (2) Tower; (3) King's meeting place.

Target (Shop-Mart): (1) Targeted (vulnerable); (2) Goal.

Tarzana: (1) Tarzan.

Taylor: (1) Worker in cloth.

Teak: (1) Writer of poems.

Ted: (1) Affluent protector.

Teegan: (1) Attractive woman.

Teresa: See *Theresa*.

Terri: (1) One who harvests.

Terry: (1) Glossy; (2) Smooth.

Tess: (1) One who harvests.

Tessa: (1) Fourth born.

Tessie/Tessy: (1) One who harvests.

Texas: (1) Friendship; (2) Ally.

Thailand: (1) Land of the free.

Thampy: (1) Second son.

Theadora: (1) A gift from God.

Thelma: (1) Nurturing.

Theo: (1) God.

Theodore: (1) A gift from God.

Theresa: (1) One who harvests.

Thomas: (1) One of two; (2) A twin; (3) Doubt; (4) From which the surnames Thompson, Tomkin, and Tomlin come.

Thor: (1) The god of thunder.

Thorp: (1) One who looks after the fires.

Thorpe: (1) Lives in the small village.

Tiara: (1) Semi-circular crown.

Tiffany: (1) God is appearing.

Timothy: (1) Gives honor to God; (2) God-honoring.

Tina: (1) Small.

Tobias: (1) The Lord is good.

Toby: (1) The Lord is good.

Todd: (1) Fox hunter.

Tokyo: (1) Expressing hope.

Tom: See *Thomas*.

Toni/y: (1) Invaluable.

Topeka: (1) A good place to grow potatoes.

Toronto: (1) Place where trees stand in the water; (2) Meeting place.

Toula: (1) Light of God.

Toya: (1) Achieved victory; (2) Triumphed.

Toyota: (1) Lucky; (2) Eight.

Tracey: (1) One who harvests.

Travis: (1) Road junction.

Trent: (1) Fast flowing stream.

Trevor: (1) From the large village.

Tri: (1) Third child.

Troy: (1) (Irish) Foot soldier; (2) (French) Having curly hair; (3) From Troyes, France.

Truc: (1) Bamboo.

Trudy: (1) Having strength.

Tucker: (1) One who sews tucks in fabric.

Tujunga: (1) Mountain range.

Tyler: (1) Tiler of roofs; (2) Can be a reference to Christ as covering.

Tyrone: (1) Land of the youthful soldier.

Tyson: (1) Flaming torch.

Ulrich: (1) King of the wolves.

Una: (1) Number one; (2) Unity.

Ur: (1) Light; (2) Flaming fire.

Uri: (1) The Lord is my light.

Ursula: (1) A bear.

Utah: (1) High up; (2) Land of the sun; (3) People of the mountains.

Valentine: (1) Brave and strong.

Valerie: (1) Brave; (2) Courageous.

Valiant: (1) Brave and strong.

Valmai: (1) Hawthorn blossom; (2) May.

Valyermo: (1) Desert valley.

Vancouver: (1) Cow ford; (i.e., from the place where cows cross the river).

Vanessa: (1) A butterfly.

Vashti: (1) Good-looking.

Vasilis/Vasilii: (1) Kingly; (2) Royal.

Vaughan: (1) Small.

Vera: (1) Faith; (2) Belief.

Verity: (1) Truth.

Vermont: (1) Green mountain.

Veronica: (1) True image.

Vesna: (1) Messenger.

Vick: (1) One who looks after the fires.

Vicki: (1) Achieved victory or triumph.

Victoria: (1) Achieved victory or triumph.

Vietnam: (1) Great south.

Vincent: (1) Conqueror.

Violet: (1) Small blue-purple flower.

Virgil: (1) One who carries the staff.

Virginia: (1) Chaste; (2) Pure.

Vivien: (1) Lively; (2) Spritely.

Volker: (1) Protector of the people.

Vulcan: (1) The god of fire, metalwork, and craftwork.

Waikerie: (1) Many wings; (2) Things that fly.

Wakelin: (1) Foreigner.

Wallace: (1) Foreigner; (2) Stranger.

Wallie: See *Wallace*.

Wally: See *Walter*.

Walter: (1) Powerful fighter.

Wanda: (1) To wander.

Warren: (1) Guardian of wildlife.

Washington: (1) (English) Lives at the farm of the discerning; (2) (Teutonic) Spritely; (3) Active; (4) Capital (place of decision-making).

Wayne: (1) Maker of wagons.

Wendle: (1) A wanderer.

Wendy: (1) Friend.

Wesley: (1) Western field.

Westcott: (1) Cottage to the west.

Whitaker: (1) A white field.

Whitmore: (1) White grassy fields.

Whitney: (1) A white island.

Whittany: (1) White island.

Whoopie: (1) Enthusiastic merrymaking.

Whyalla: (1) Place with deep water.

Wilfred: (1) Steadfast tranquility.

William: (1) Your will acting as a guard of the thoughts of your mind (lit. "will-helmet"); (2) Strong-willed; (3) Determined to guard; (4) Speaks of choice.

Wilson: (1) Determined to guard; (2) See *William*.

Windsor: (1) Where the river bends.

Winifred: (1) Made peace; (2) Rewarded.

Winona: (1) First-born daughter.

Winston: (1) Wine's town.

Wisconsin: (1) Gathering of waters.

Wolfgang: (1) Wolf who moves forward.

Woolworths: (1) Sheep enclosure; (2) Sheep farm.

Wyoming: (1) Extensive plains; (2) Mountains and valleys alternating.

Yago: See *Jacob*.

Yale: (1) Fertile high ground.

Yamada: (1) Mountain rice field.

Yamamoto: (1) Base of the mountain.

Yan: (1) God has favored.

Yana: (1) (Slavic) God has favored; (2) (American Indian) A bear.

Yasmin: (1) Fragrant shrub.

Yisrael: (1) Rules with God.

York: (1) From the area of the yew trees; (2) Boar settlement.

Yorke/Yorkie: (1) Wild pig farm.

Yeshua: (1) God is Savior.

Yukimura: (1) Snowy village.

Yvonne: (1) Bowman or archer.

Zac: (1) Remember; (2) Past.

Zachary: (1) God has remembered.

Zam Zam: (1) Well of Mecca; (2) Spring of Islam.

Zane: (1) God has favored.

Zara: (1) Daybreak.

Zebulun: (1) Dwelling.

Zechariah: (1) The Lord has remembered.

Zedekiah: (1) God is impartial; (2) Justice of Jehovah.

Zeeb: (1) A wolf.

Zeena: (1) A woman; (2) Feminine.

Zephaniah: (1) Hidden by God.

Zoe: (1) Spiritual Life.

Zoran: (1) Daybreak; (2) Dawn.

Zorka: (1) Star of the morning.

Appendix

GETTING RIGHT WITH GOD

If I am not a Christian, what must I do to get right with God?

God loves you and has been trying to get your attention through the dreams and visions He has given you. If you now want to get right with Him, then you need to take the following steps:

1. Admit your insensitivity to His communication (the Bible calls this *having a hardened heart*).

2. Recognize and admit that in your life you have done wrong (the Bible calls this *sin*).

3. Turn away from doing your own thing and be prepared to let God lead you.

4. Understand that when Jesus Christ died upon the cross, He died as the penalty for your sin. He took your punishment. Jesus willingly laid down His life so that you could come into a relationship with God. This

privilege is based solely on your faith in the worth of Jesus's blood shed for you. Jesus is the sinless and eternal Son of God. (Jesus was raised from the dead after three days as proof of God's acceptance of Jesus's blood as payment for your sin).

5. With this knowledge, now ask God with all of your heart for forgiveness for all your sins. By faith as you pray this prayer, your sin is placed upon Christ, and in return God has brought you into right standing with Himself. You are now born again and have eternal life. Hallelujah!

6. If you prayed that prayer, you have been cleansed from your sin and now need the Holy Spirit to fill you so that you have the power to live the Christian life. Simply ask Jesus to fill you with His Spirit right now.

Congratulations! You have just made the most important decision of your life! Where do you go from here?

- Get to know God by reading the Bible daily. (The Gospel of Mark in the New Testament is a great place to start.)

- Set aside a time to speak with God in prayer on a daily basis.

- Ask Him to lead you to a Spirit-filled church that you may be strengthened and encouraged by the faith of other believers.

ABOUT THE AUTHORS

ADAM F. THOMPSON

Adam has a remarkable grace to interpret dreams, move in the word of knowledge, and demonstrate the prophetic. Supernatural signs and manifestations regularly accompany his ministry as he desires to see Jesus "magnified" through the moving of the Holy Spirit. He has ministered extensively in America, Pakistan, India, Africa, Indonesia, Papua New Guinea, Malaysia, and the Philippines in crusades, feeding programs, and pastors' conferences. Adam has been instrumental in planting the "Field of Dreams" Church in South Australia.

ADRIAN BEALE

Adrian has an ability to release the Spirit of Understanding so that congregations are awakened and enlivened to new levels of revelation. He loves to open Old Covenant passages to bring out relevant kingdom truth and also interpret the voice of the Spirit in dreams, visions, and supernatural phenomena whilst cementing his audiences on the Word of God. He has ministered extensively in the USA, Canada, New Zealand, and Australia. He is the co-author of the best-selling book, *The Divinity Code to Understanding your Dreams and Visions* and author of *The Mystic Awakening* and *The Lost Kingdom*.

Printed in Great Britain
by Amazon

59627214R00255

THE DIABETES CODE COOKBOOK

DR. JASON FUNG
RECIPES BY ALISON MACLEAN

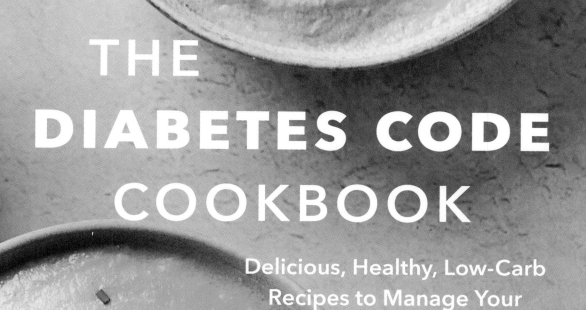

THE
DIABETES CODE
COOKBOOK

Delicious, Healthy, Low-Carb
Recipes to Manage Your
Insulin and Prevent and
Reverse Type 2 Diabetes

GREYSTONE BOOKS
VANCOUVER/BERKELEY

Greystone Books Ltd.
greystonebooks.com

Cataloguing data available from Library and Archives Canada
ISBN 978-1-77164-791-5 (cloth)
ISBN 978-1-77164-792-2 (epub)

Editing by Lucy Kenward
Copy editing by Arlene Prunkl
Proofreading by Stefania Alexandru
Index by Gillian Watts

Jacket and interior design by Jessica Sullivan
Photography (cover/interior recipes) by Gabriel Cabrera
Food styling by Bri Beaudoin, assisted by Sophie Mackenzie
Ancillary photos by Shutterstock: Viktor.G (p. 24), Nopparat Promtha (p. 44), Jiri Hera (p. 66), Ihor Berkyta (p. 86), AmyLv (chickpeas p. 110), xpixel (walnuts p. 110), New Africa (p. 128), Bozena Fulawka (p. 148), joker1991 (p. 168); by iStock: dkidpix (oil drips cover, p. 69)

Printed in China on FSC® certified paper at 1010 Printing Asia Ltd. The FSC® label means that materials used for the product have been responsibly sourced.

Greystone Books gratefully acknowledges the Musqueam, Squamish, and Tsleil-Waututh peoples on whose land our office is located.

Greystone Books thanks the Canada Council for the Arts, the British Columbia Arts Council, the Province of British Columbia through the Book Publishing Tax Credit, and the Government of Canada for supporting our publishing activities.

Canadä

*For Hannah and Charlie,
discerning eaters and kind critics.
And for Russ, who tells me
everything I make is delicious.*
AM

CONTENTS

PREFACE

In recent decades, an epidemic of type 2 diabetes has closely followed an epidemic of obesity, with many health implications. Type 2 diabetes significantly increases the risk of most types of chronic disease, including heart disease, strokes, some types of cancer, blindness, amputation, kidney disease, nerve damage, and infections. But it doesn't have to be this way.

Although most people, and even some medical professionals, believe that type 2 diabetes is a chronic and irreversible disease, this perception is largely unfounded. Most health-care providers accept that weight loss will significantly improve or even reverse this disease and all its accompanying conditions. The key, then, is to adjust our dietary habits to facilitate this weight loss and improve our health. To that end, we've developed new, delicious recipes to make it easier to implement the teachings of *The Diabetes Code*.

You will not find calorie counts or carbohydrate counts or nutritional breakdown information about these recipes, and some readers may wonder why. This is because I want people to focus on what good food is: natural, unprocessed, and wholesome. Some of these foods may be higher or lower in calories, and some may be higher or lower in carbs, but that doesn't mean they cannot be enjoyed. After all, many cultures have eaten high-calorie, high-carb traditional foods for a long time without developing type 2 diabetes.

The key is to savor natural, unprocessed foods and to eat until you are full. Eating until you are satiated allows you to avoid eating constantly. The timeless advice of grandmothers to children looking for a bedtime snack? "You should have eaten more at dinner." That was great advice.

Enjoy!

Best,

JASON FUNG

INTRODUCTION

By the year 2040, one in every ten adults worldwide will have type 2 diabetes, a disease typically considered to be chronic and progressive. This idea that type 2 diabetes continually gets worse until you eventually require insulin injections is actually just a great big lie—which is excellent news for anyone who has been diagnosed with pre-diabetes or type 2 diabetes.

Imagine you have a friend who is diagnosed with type 2 diabetes, meaning that the level of glucose in their blood is above normal levels. They work hard to lose fifty pounds, which enables them to stop taking glucose-lowering medications because their blood glucose levels are now normal. It seems perfectly obvious that the type 2 diabetes reversed because your friend lost all that weight. And that's the point: *type 2 diabetes is a reversible disease.*

Obesity and type 2 diabetes are closely related, and generally, increased weight increases the risk of disease, though the correlation is not perfect. Most of the medications used to treat type 2 diabetes do not cause weight loss. Quite the contrary. Insulin, for example, is notorious for causing *weight gain*. Since weight loss is the key to reversing type 2 diabetes, medications don't help. Medications improve the blood glucose levels but not the underlying cause of diabetes. We only *pretend* that they do, which is the reason some doctors think type 2 diabetes is a chronic and progressive disease.

There is a tendency to paint type 2 diabetes as an inevitable part of modern life, but this is not true. *Only* diet and lifestyle changes—*not* medications—will reverse this disease, simply because type 2 diabetes is largely a dietary disease. And the most important determinant is weight loss. The same principles that reverse type 2 diabetes also prevent it.

THE EPIDEMIC OF DIABETES

Diabetes mellitus is the name for a group of metabolic disorders characterized by chronically high blood glucose, or hyperglycemia. The prefix *hyper* means "excessive," and the suffix *emia* means "in the blood," so this term literally means "excessive glucose in the blood."

There are four broad categories of diabetes mellitus: type 1, type 2, gestational diabetes (high blood glucose associated with pregnancy), and "other specific types." Type 2 diabetes is by far the most common. Gestational diabetes, by definition, is not a chronic disease, though it is a risk factor for developing type 2 diabetes in the future.

Type 1 diabetes is an autoimmune disease, meaning that the body's own immune system damages the islet cells within the pancreas that secrete the hormone insulin, and it often affects children. In contrast, type 2 diabetes has historically afflicted older adults, but the prevalence is rising quickly in children worldwide, mirroring the increase in childhood obesity. Overall, type 2 diabetes accounts for 90 to 95 percent of diabetes cases globally. It typically develops gradually, over many years, and progresses in an orderly manner from normal to pre-diabetes to full-blown type 2 diabetes.

Fundamentally, type 1 and type 2 diabetes are polar opposites: the first characterized by very low insulin levels and the second by very high ones. Yet, curiously, current drug treatments for both types seek to lower blood glucose by increasing insulin, even though the high level of blood glucose is only the *symptom* of the disease and not the disease itself. Insulin helps type 1 diabetes because that disease's underlying core problem is a lack of insulin in the body naturally. However, the underlying core problem of type 2 diabetes is insulin resistance, which remains virtually untreated with standard medications.

The problem of type 2 diabetes is not trivial. In the U.S., 14.3 percent of adults have type 2 diabetes and 38 percent of the population has pre-diabetes, totaling 52.3 percent. This means that for the first time in history, there are more people with the disease than without. Pre-diabetes and diabetes are the new normal. Worse, the prevalence of type 2 diabetes has increased only in the last forty years, making it clear that this epidemic is not some genetic disease or part of the normal aging process. It is a lifestyle issue. So, how does type 2 diabetes develop?

Type 2 diabetes is caused by too much sugar

All foods are composed of three main constituents, called macronutrients. These are proteins, fats, and carbohydrates, and they are all handled differently by the digestive system. After we eat, foods are broken down for easier absorption. Proteins are broken down into amino acids. Fats are broken down into fatty acids. Carbohydrates, composed of chains of sugars, are broken down into smaller sugars, including glucose. Amino acids, fatty acids, and glucose are carried throughout the body in the bloodstream.

When you eat sugar, your body secretes the hormone insulin to help move the sugar into your cells, where it's used for energy. If you don't burn off that sugar sufficiently through physical activity, over decades your cells become completely filled and cannot handle any more. And when insulin cannot force any more sugar into your overflowing cells, that excess sugar spills out, back into the blood. Sugar travels in your blood as glucose, and having too much of it—known as high blood glucose—is a primary symptom of type 2 diabetes.

Imagine your body as a big sugar bowl. At birth, the bowl is empty. Over several decades, if you overeat sugar and refined carbohydrates, the bowl gradually fills up. Once the bowl is full, when you next eat, sugar is forced in but spills over the sides of the bowl.

The high blood glucose is only part of the issue. When there's too much glucose in the blood, insulin does not appear to be doing its usual job of moving the sugar into the cells. We say that the body has become insulin resistant. But it's not truly insulin's fault. The primary problem is that the cells are already overflowing with glucose. Not only is there too much glucose in the blood, there's too much glucose in all of the cells. Type 2 diabetes is simply the overflow phenomenon of too much glucose in the *entire body*.

In response to excess glucose in the blood, the body secretes even more insulin to "overcome" this resistance to it. This forces more glucose into the overflowing cells to keep blood levels normal. This works, but the effect is only temporary. The problem of excess sugar has not been addressed; it has only been moved from the blood to the cells, making insulin resistance worse. At some point, even with more insulin the body cannot force any more glucose into the cells.

What happens if the excess glucose is not removed from the body? First, more and more insulin is produced to force more and more glucose into the cells. But this *hyperinsulinemia* only creates even more insulin resistance and becomes a vicious cycle. When the insulin levels are finally unable to keep pace with the rising "resistance," blood glucose spikes. That's when the diagnosis of type 2 diabetes is made.

Your doctor may prescribe a medication such as insulin injections to lower the blood glucose. *But insulin does not rid the body of that excess glucose.* Instead, it continues to take the glucose out of the blood and ram it back into the body. It gets shipped out to all the other organs—the kidneys, the nerves, the eyes, and the heart. The underlying problem, of course, is unchanged.

The bowl is still overflowing with sugar. Insulin has simply moved the glucose from the blood, where you can detect it, into the body, where you can't. The next time you eat, sugar spills out into the blood again, and you inject insulin to cram it back into your body's cells. It's the same overflow phenomenon all over again.

As more insulin forces more glucose into the already filled cell, more insulin resistance develops. *More insulin creates more insulin resistance.* Once you've exceeded what your body

DIABETES IS GETTING WORSE!

Metformin Metformin
DPP4 Metformin
DPP4
Sulphonylurea Insulin More
Insulin Even
more
Insulin

TIME

can produce naturally, insulin medications can take over. At first, you need only a single medication (e.g., metformin), but eventually it becomes two (e.g., metformin and DPP4) and then three (e.g., metformin, DPP4, and sulphonylurea), and the doses will become larger. And here's the thing: if you are taking more and more medications to keep your blood glucose at the same level, your diabetes is actually getting worse!

The symptom (high blood glucose) got better with insulin, but the *disease* (diabetes) got worse. The medications can only hide the blood glucose by cramming it into the already engorged cells. The diabetes *looks* better but actually it is worse.

When excessive glucose piles up in the body over ten or twenty years, every cell in the body *just starts to rot*, which is precisely why type 2 diabetes, unlike virtually every other disease, affects every single organ. Your eyes rot, and you go blind. Your kidneys rot, and you need dialysis. Your heart rots, and you get heart attacks and heart failure. Your brain rots, and you get Alzheimer's disease. Your liver rots, and you get fatty liver disease and cirrhosis. Your legs rot, and you get diabetic foot ulcers. Your nerves rot, and you get diabetic neuropathy. No part of your body is spared.

At its very core, type 2 diabetes can be understood as a disease caused by too much of the hormone insulin, which is produced by eating too much sugar. Insulin is like the key that fits into the lock on each cell to let the glucose in. Framing the problem this way is incredibly powerful because the solution becomes immediately obvious. If insulin levels are too high, we must lower them. How? By reducing our dietary intake of sugar, particularly added sugars and refined carbohydrates.

Type 2 diabetes is also a disease of energy storage

Glucose provides energy for working tissue, and the excess is stored in the liver. Amino acids are used to produce proteins, such as those in muscle, skin, and connective tissue, but the excess is converted to glucose in the liver since amino acids cannot be stored directly. Once your immediate energy needs have been met, insulin gives the signal to store any remaining food energy for later use.

Your body stores food energy in two forms: glycogen and body fat. Excess glucose—whether derived from protein or from carbohydrates—is strung together in long chains to form the molecule glycogen and stored in the liver. It can be converted to and from glucose easily and released into the bloodstream for use by any cell in the body.

The liver can stockpile only a limited amount of glycogen, and once it is full the excess glucose is turned into fat by a process called *de novo lipogenesis* (DNL). *De novo* means "from new" and *lipogenesis* means "making new fat," so this term means literally "to make new fat." Insulin turns excess glucose into new fat molecules that can be exported out of the liver to longer-term fat-storage cells called adipocytes.

The word *fasting* describes any period of time when we are not eating, when our body relies on its stored energy: glycogen and fat. When we eat, our insulin level rises, signaling the body to stop burning sugar and fat and to start storing it instead.

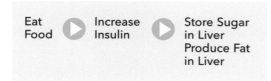

Several hours after a meal, blood glucose drops and insulin levels begin to fall. To provide energy, the liver starts to break down the stored glycogen into its component glucose molecules and releases them into general circulation in the blood. This is merely the glycogen-storage process in reverse. This happens most nights, assuming you don't eat at night.

Glycogen is easily available but in limited supply. During a short-term fast (twenty-four to thirty-six hours), glycogen will provide all the glucose necessary for normal body functioning. When glycogen runs out, as during a prolonged fast, fat is burned for energy. This is merely the fat-storage process in reverse.

This energy storage and release process happens every day. Normally this well-designed, balanced system keeps itself in check. We eat, insulin goes up, and we store energy as glycogen and fat. We fast, insulin goes down, and we use our stored glycogen and fat. As long as feeding (insulin high) is balanced with fasting (insulin low), no overall fat is gained. If high insulin persists, however, then the body receives a constant signal to store food energy as body fat.

Type 2 diabetes is reversible and preventable without medications

When insulin levels stay too high for too long, the liver produces more new fat via DNL than can be exported, and the fat accumulates in the liver. This is often the first sign of hyperinsulinemia/insulin resistance.

Eventually, fat accumulates in other organs too, including the muscles and pancreas. As the pancreas becomes clogged with fat, it is unable to produce the high levels of insulin required to keep blood glucose levels relatively normal, and the diagnosis of type 2 diabetes is made.

Excessive insulin drives ectopic fat production and organ infiltration. This is driven in turn by excessive dietary consumption of sugar, primarily glucose and fructose. Basically, *type 2 diabetes is a disease entirely caused by too much sugar.*

Once we understand that type 2 diabetes is simply too much sugar in the body, the solution becomes obvious. Get rid of the sugar. Don't hide it away. Get rid of it. There are really only two ways to accomplish this.

1 Don't put sugar in.
2 Burn it off.

It's no different than an overflowing sink. Either stop putting more water in, or drain some out.

STEP 1: **Don't put sugar in**

The first step is to eliminate all sugar and refined carbohydrates from your diet. Added sugars have no nutritional value and can be safely withheld. Complex carbohydrates are simply long chains of sugars. Highly refined carbohydrates such as flour are quickly digested into glucose. The optimal strategy is to limit or eliminate breads, pastas, white rice, and potatoes and other starchy vegetables.

Another strategy to avoid consuming sugar is to maintain a moderate—not high—intake of protein. When it is digested, dietary protein such as meat breaks down into amino acids. Adequate protein is required for good health, but excess amino acids cannot be stored in the body and so they are converted into glucose by the liver. Therefore, eating too much protein also adds sugar to the body. Avoid highly processed, concentrated protein sources such as protein shakes, protein bars, and protein powders.

And what about dietary fat? Natural fats such as those found in avocados, nuts, and olive oil—major components of the Mediterranean diet—have a minimal effect on blood glucose or insulin and are well known to have healthy effects on both heart disease and diabetes. Eggs and butter are also excellent sources of natural fats and dietary cholesterol, with no harmful health effects. Eating dietary fat does not lead to type 2 diabetes or heart disease. In fact, it may be beneficial because it does not add sugar to the body.

To avoid putting sugar in, stick to whole, natural, unprocessed foods. Eat a diet low in refined carbohydrates, moderate in protein, and high in natural fats.

STEP 2: **Burn it off**

Physical exercise can certainly help type 2 diabetes, but it is a far less powerful solution than fasting, the simplest and surest method to force your body to burn sugar.

Fasting is merely the flip side of eating: if you are not eating, you are fasting. When you eat, your body *stores* food energy. When you fast, your body *burns* food energy. Glucose is the most easily accessible source of food energy, so longer periods of fasting burn off more stored sugar.

While fasting may sound severe, it is literally the oldest dietary therapy known and practiced throughout human history without problems. If you are taking prescription medications, you should seek the advice of a physician. But the bottom line is this:

If you don't eat, will your blood glucose come down? Of course.

If you don't eat, will you lose weight? Of course.

So, what's the problem? None that I can see.

To burn off sugar, a popular strategy is to fast for twenty-four hours, two to three times per week. Another popular fasting regime is to fast for sixteen hours, five to six times per week.

That's it. That's all we need to do. The best part? It's all natural and completely free. No drugs. No surgery. No cost. Type 2 diabetes is a dietary disease, and dietary solutions are the answer. Step 1 is what to eat. Step 2 is when to eat.

Fasting is only one part of the solution. Knowing the right foods to eat is important too. Here are our three top food "rules" for reducing blood glucose, reducing insulin, and reversing type 2 diabetes.

RULE #1: **Eliminate all added sugars and avoid fructose completely**

The most important rule is to eliminate all added sugars from your diet. Recall that insulin resistance is the result of a fatty liver becoming overfilled and unable to accept more glucose. The most important determinant of a fatty liver is the fructose contained in sucrose (table sugar) and high-fructose corn syrup. Table sugar is 50 percent glucose and 50 percent fructose. High-fructose corn syrup contains 55 percent fructose.

Every single cell in the body can help disperse glucose, but the liver is the only organ that can metabolize fructose. Thus, fructose is many times more likely to cause a fatty liver than glucose. Pure fructose is not commonly available but may be found in some processed foods. Don't be fooled: maltose, dextrose, molasses, hydrolyzed starch, honey, invert sugar, cane sugar, glucose-fructose, high-fructose corn syrup, brown sugar, corn sweetener, rice/corn/cane/maple/malt/golden/palm syrup, and agave nectar are all names for different types of sugar. They have no nutritional value and can be safely withheld.

Some obvious foods to eliminate are sugar-sweetened beverages, including sodas, iced tea, sports drinks, mixed alcoholic drinks, juices, smoothies, flavored coffee drinks, and "enhanced" water. These liquids are loaded with sugar. Cookies, cakes, muffins, cupcakes, ice cream, and most desserts are other obvious sources.

Virtually all processed foods contain added sugars for the simple reason that they enhance flavor and texture at virtually no cost. Check the labels on meat products, where sugar is often added to the sauce or during processing. Sugar is often hidden in condiments (ketchup, relish), spaghetti/tomato sauces, flavored yogurts, salad dressings, barbecue sauces, applesauce, and spice mixes. Cereals and granola bars are usually very high in sugar too. And ask about your restaurant meals; sugar is often included in savory dishes because it's a cheap way to make all foods taste better.

What about fruit? There is no chemical difference between the fructose contained naturally in fruit and the fructose contained within sucrose. As with anything, the dose makes the poison. My best advice is to avoid eating excessive amounts of fruit, especially as many modern varieties are now available year-round and have been bred to be sweeter than in the past. Dried fruits are usually high in sugar, and for that reason dates, raisins, dried cranberries, and fruit leathers are probably best avoided.

What about artificial sweeteners? I advise patients to avoid all sweeteners, whether they contain calories or not. While it may seem logical that replacing sugar with non-caloric sweeteners is helpful, the empirical evidence is that it is not. If non-caloric sweeteners could truly reduce diabetes and obesity, then we would not have an epidemic on our hands. We would have simply replaced sugar with sweeteners and the diabetes epidemic should have died away. But it has not. When was the last time somebody told you, "I switched to sweeteners and my diabetes went away?" We have used these chemicals extensively in our food supply for decades and the empirical evidence is clear: artificial sweeteners are no better than sugar. Avoid them all.

So, what can you do about dessert? A small plate of nuts and cheeses makes for a very satisfying end to a meal, without the burden of added sugars. Most nuts are full of healthful monounsaturated fats, have few or no carbohydrates, and are high in fiber, which increases their potential health benefits. Many studies show an association between increased nut consumption and better health, including reduced risk of heart disease and diabetes. But as with any food, moderation is the key to health.

And what is left to drink?

Water

The best drink is really just plain or sparkling water. Adding slices of lemon, lime, or orange is a refreshing twist. Infusing water by adding fruits (e.g., strawberries), herbs (e.g., mint), or vegetables (e.g., cucumber) and leaving it overnight is a great way to give it flavor. Use a home carbonation machine like a SodaStream to make your own sparkling water. Several other drinks are also delicious and do not raise insulin (see below).

Tea

After water, tea is the most popular beverage in the world. Black tea accounts for almost 75 percent of the tea consumed globally. The harvested leaves are fully fermented, giving the tea its characteristic black color. Black tea tends to be higher in caffeine than other varieties. Oolong tea is semi-fermented, meaning that it undergoes a shorter period of fermentation.

Green tea is unfermented. Green tea is naturally much lower in caffeine than coffee, and polyphenols in green tea may boost metabolism, which can improve fat burning. Furthermore, drinking green tea has been linked to increased fat oxidation during exercise, increased resting energy expenditure, and a lower risk of various types of cancer. Green tea is a particularly rich source of catechins, which are believed to protect against metabolic diseases.

Herbal teas are infusions of herbs, spices, or other plant matter in hot water. These are not true teas because they do not contain tea leaves. Nevertheless, they make excellent drinks without added sugars.

Coffee

Because of its high caffeine content, coffee is sometimes considered unhealthy. However, recent research suggests that both the caffeinated and decaffeinated versions appear to protect against type 2 diabetes. In a 2009 review, every daily cup of coffee lowered the risk of diabetes by 7 percent—even up to six cups per day (for a reduced risk of 42 percent). Coffee may also guard against Alzheimer's disease, Parkinson's disease, liver cirrhosis, and liver cancer. While these studies are not proof of benefit, they do suggest that coffee may not be as harmful as we had imagined. (But remember to skip the sugar!)

Bone broth

Virtually every culture's culinary traditions include nutritious and delicious bone broth—bones simmered with vegetables, herbs, and spices for flavoring. The long simmering time (four to forty-eight hours) releases most of the bones' minerals, gelatin, and nutrients. The addition of a small amount of vinegar during cooking helps leach some of the stored minerals. Bone broths are very high in amino acids such as proline, arginine, and glycine, as well as minerals such as calcium, magnesium, and phosphorus.

RULE #2: Eat a diet low in refined carbohydrates and high in natural fats

Complex carbohydrates are not intrinsically bad foods. Many traditional societies ate diets heavy in whole, unrefined carbohydrates—such as sweet potatoes—and thrived. The refining process is the major problem. When carbohydrates such as wheat, rice, and corn are refined—by being ground, bleached, and processed—they are even more quickly digested into glucose. Removing the natural fats and protein and leaving behind a pure carbohydrate is not natural, and our bodies have not evolved to handle the insulin response to these foods.

Since refined carbohydrates, of all the food groups, cause the highest rise in insulin levels, it is logical to eat less of them. Reduce or avoid refined wheat products such as bread, pasta, waffles, muffins, cupcakes, and donuts. Limit processed corn products, such as popcorn, corn chips, and tortillas, and refined potato products, particularly french fries and potato chips. And eat white rice, which is also a refined carbohydrate, in small amounts. Even many whole-wheat and whole-grain products are highly refined. Some great alternatives to refined grains are seeds and legumes.

Quinoa

Technically a seed but often used as a grain, quinoa has been referred to as "the mother of all grains." It was grown originally by the Inca in South America but is now widely available in three varieties: red, white, and black. Quinoa is high in fiber, protein, and vitamins. In addition, it has a low glycemic index and contains plenty of antioxidants, such as quercetin and kaempferol, that are believed to be anti-inflammatory.

Chia seeds

These ancient seeds are native to South and Central America and have been dated to the Aztecs and Mayans. Their name is derived from the ancient Mayan word for strength. Chia seeds, regardless of color, are high in fiber, vitamins, minerals, omega 3, proteins, and antioxidants.

Beans

Dried beans and peas are a versatile, fiber-rich carbohydrate staple of many traditional diets and an extremely good source of protein. They come in a wide range of colors, flavors, and textures, from green lentils to black-eyed peas, and red kidney beans to dark brown chickpeas. Canned beans are also great, but be sure to rinse them well before using.

Olive oil

The Mediterranean diet, widely acknowledged as a healthy diet, is high in oleic acid, one of the monounsaturated fats contained in olive oil. Olive oil also contains large amounts of antioxidants, including polyphenols and oleocanthal, which has anti-inflammatory properties. It is purported to reduce inflammation, lower cholesterol, decrease blood clotting, and reduce blood pressure. Together, these potential properties may reduce the overall risk of cardiovascular disease, including heart attacks and strokes.

There are different methods of extracting olive oil, and these differences are reflected in the grading. To obtain the oil, ripe olive fruit is crushed into a paste and then cold pressed. Extra-virgin olive oil is extracted using these mechanical means only and is certainly the best choice. Other grades of olive oil rely on chemical methods and/or high heat to extract the oil and neutralize bad tastes and should be avoided. Be aware that "pure olive oil" often denotes these refined oils.

Avocados

A healthy and delicious addition to any diet, avocados are high in vitamins and particularly high in potassium. Avocados are unique among fruits for being very low in carbohydrates and high in the monounsaturated fat oleic acid. Furthermore, they are very high in both soluble and insoluble fiber.

Nuts

Long shunned for their high fat content, nuts are now recognized for these healthy fats, and they are naturally high in fiber and low in carbohydrates. They may be enjoyed raw or toasted, but avoid those with added sugars, like honey-toasted nuts. Walnuts, in particular, are high in omega-3 fatty acids, which may be beneficial for heart health. Nut milks without added sugars are also delicious.

Full-fat dairy products

Milk, cream, yogurt, butter, and cheese are delicious and can be enjoyed without concern about fattening effects. A review of twenty-nine randomized control trials showed neither a fat-gaining nor fat-reducing effect from their consumption. Full-fat dairy is associated with a 62 percent lower risk of type 2 diabetes. Choose whole-fat dairy products, and raw or organic if you prefer. All milks, including sheep's and goat's milks, are healthy.

Eggs

A natural whole food, previously shunned because of cholesterol concerns, eggs can be enjoyed in a variety of ways. Egg whites are high in protein, and yolks contain many vitamins and minerals including choline and selenium. Eggs are particularly good sources of lutein and zeaxanthin, antioxidants that may help protect against eye problems such as macular degeneration and cataracts. The

cholesterol in eggs may change the cholesterol particles in your blood to the larger, less
harmful particles. Indeed, large epidemiolog-
ical studies have failed to link increased egg
consumption to increased heart disease. Most
of all, eat eggs because they are delicious,
whole, unprocessed foods.

REPLACE REFINED carbohydrates with natural fats such as fatty fish, olive oil, avocados,
and nuts. The natural saturated fats found in
beef, pork, bacon, butter, cream, and coconuts
are also healthy fats. Eggs are an excellent
choice, as is most seafood.

Not all fats are benign, however. The
industrially processed, highly refined seed oils
that are high in omega-6 fat are *not* recom-
mended because they can cause inflammation
and adversely affect human health. These
oils include sunflower, corn, canola, safflower,
and vegetable oils. In particular, do not use
these vegetable oils at high heat because they
release harmful chemicals called aldehydes
when heated. Stay away from deep-fried foods
and all hydrogenated (trans) fats.

The diet I recommend has been called a
low-carbohydrate, high (healthy)-fat (LCHF)
diet. It is designed to keep blood glucose low,
decrease insulin, and therefore burn more fat.
The result? Weight loss and an improvement
in diabetes.

RULE #3: Just eat real food

There are good fats and bad fats. There are
good carbohydrates and bad carbohydrates.
What is the key distinguishing factor? Refining
and processing.

Our bodies have had millennia to adapt
to foods in their natural state. So some traditional societies, such as people living in the far
north, may eat an almost purely meat diet. And
others, such as people living on the Japanese
island of Okinawa, can eat a high-carbohy-
drate diet. Because these foods are not refined
or processed and because they contain little
or no sugar, neither group has traditionally
had trouble with high blood glucose, obesity,
or type 2 diabetes. When traditional societies
eating traditional diets begin to eat highly processed foods and sugar, however, obesity and
type 2 diabetes follow closely behind.

The most important rule of all is to *just eat
real food*. If the food you are eating looks like it
does when you see it in nature, it is probably
good for you.

What if that's not enough?

Avoiding fructose, eating an LCHF diet, and
consuming real food are a great start, but type
2 diabetes can take decades to develop, so the
vicious cycle of hyperinsulinemia and insulin resistance can continue despite following
all of the dietary "rules." What if these simple
dietary changes are not enough?

Like many solutions, the answer is not new. It's the oldest dietary intervention known to humans, its natural cleansing power has been harnessed by virtually all religions in the world, it's free, and it can be done anywhere. What are we talking about? The power of fasting.

Fasting, the voluntary abstinence from food, has been known to cure diabetes for close to one hundred years. But the focus on dietary therapies for diabetes shifted with the momentous discovery of insulin. While insulin was indeed a miraculous cure for type 1 diabetes, it was no panacea for type 2 diabetes. Interest in fasting disappeared as doctors focused on what would be their treatment mantra for the next century: drugs, drugs, and more drugs. When doctors say there is no cure for type 2 diabetes, what they mean is that there is no *drug* cure.

We've long known that bariatric surgery can reverse type 2 diabetes by inducing a sudden, severe caloric deficit, which drops insulin levels. Basically, *bariatrics is surgically enforced fasting*. But surgery is not the only way to create a sudden, severe caloric deprivation. We can simply stop eating. This is the time-tested, ancient healing tradition of fasting. Remember that at its core, type 2 diabetes means there is too much sugar in the body.

Essentially, fasting stops sugar from going in and helps burn it off. It is the most powerful natural therapy available for type 2 diabetes.

Intermittent fasting is not caloric restriction

Continuous mild calorie restriction is not at all the same as *intermittent*, severe restriction. Consider that jumping off a foot-high wall a thousand times is far different from jumping off a thousand-foot-high wall once. The difference between the two is literally the difference between life and death. Similarly, reducing three hundred calories per day over seven days (constant caloric restriction) is not the same as reducing twenty-one hundred calories over a single day (intermittent fasting). Each scenario provokes profoundly different hormonal responses. The difference between the two is literally the difference between success and failure at reversing type 2 diabetes.

Continuously restricting calories causes a compensatory increase in hunger and a decrease in the body's metabolic rate. This effect often derails weight-loss efforts and ultimately ends in failure. Intermittent fasting succeeds because it produces beneficial hormonal changes that chronic caloric deprivation does not. During fasting, your body reduces hunger levels and maintains its metabolic rate by switching to an alternative fuel source, your own body fat.

This reduces both high insulin levels and insulin resistance, which also depends upon the *persistence* of those elevated levels. Intermittent fasting prevents the development of insulin resistance by creating extended periods of low insulin that maintain the body's sensitivity to insulin. When you eat all the time, even if those meals and snacks don't contain a lot of calories, insulin goes up. When you don't eat, insulin stays low. This is the key to reversing pre-diabetes and type 2 diabetes.

Intermittent fasting maintains basal metabolism

The secret to long-term weight loss is to maintain your basal metabolism—the energy needed to keep the heart pumping, the lungs breathing, the brain thinking, the kidneys detoxing, etc. Fasting triggers numerous hormonal adaptations that do *not* happen with simple caloric reduction. Insulin drops sharply, preventing insulin resistance. But other hormones increase during fasting. Noradrenalin rises, keeping metabolism high. Growth hormone, or somatotropin, rises, maintaining lean mass.

Fasting works because it keeps basal metabolism high. Why? It's a survival mechanism. Imagine we are cave dwellers in the Stone Age. It's winter and food is scarce. If our bodies were to go into "starvation mode," we would not have the energy to go out and find food. Each day the situation would become worse and eventually we would die. The human species would have become extinct long ago if our bodies slowed down every time we didn't eat for a few hours.

During fasting, the body opens up its ample supply of stored food: body fat! Basal metabolism stays high, and instead of using food as our fuel, we use our stored food (or body fat). After all, that's precisely why we store and carry it in the first place. Now we have enough energy to go out and hunt some woolly mammoths.

During fasting, we first burn glycogen stored in the liver. When that is finished, we use body fat. Oh, and hey, good news: there's plenty of fat stored here. Burn, baby, burn. And since there is plenty of fuel, there is no reason for basal metabolism to drop. That's the difference between long-term weight loss and a lifetime of despair. That's the knife edge between success and failure. Essentially, fasting provides beneficial hormonal changes that are entirely prevented by the constant intake of food, even when the calories in that food are reduced. It is the *intermittency* of the fasting that makes it so much more effective.

Which is better, fasting or low carb? Or both?

Both intermittent fasting and low-carbohydrate, healthy-fat (LCHF) diets effectively reduce insulin, and thus can cause weight loss and reverse type 2 diabetes.

Fasting lowers insulin maximally, so it is quite simply the quickest and most efficient method. Fasting allows us to naturally empty the sugar from our body's cells (the sugar bowl). Once the cells are empty, any incoming sugar will no longer spill out into the blood, and we will no longer meet the criteria for diabetes. We will have reversed the disease.

The more we eat ultra-processed, insulin-stimulating food, the more we need to fast to bring those insulin levels back down. And *nothing* beats fasting for bringing down insulin. But should we fast or follow a LCHF diet? It's not a question of either/or. We can incorporate *both* fasting and a LCHF diet for maximal benefits.

FASTING FACTS AND FAQS FOR TYPE 2 DIABETES

Certain general principles apply to fasting with type 2 diabetes. How long it takes to reverse the disease depends on the intensity of the fasting regimen and the length of time you've had the disease. More intensive fasting will give quicker results, but if you have had type 2 diabetes for twenty years, it is unlikely to reverse in several months. It will take longer, though the exact time differs from patient to patient.

The basics of fasting

If you are taking medications, then you must speak with your physician before starting a fast. Diabetic medications are prescribed based on your current diet. If you change your diet without adjusting your medications, then you risk triggering hypoglycemic reactions, which are extremely dangerous. You may feel shaky, sweaty, or nauseated. In more severe cases, you could lose consciousness or even die. Carefully monitoring and adjusting your medications is essential.

If you are taking medication for diabetes—and again, talk to your physician first—then it's important to monitor your blood glucose frequently with a standard home monitor. Check your blood sugar at least twice a day and ideally up to four times a day on both fasting and non-fasting days. If you are not taking medication, this is not necessary. Blood glucose may drop slightly but should remain in the normal range. Your physician can explain how to reduce or hold diabetic medications, and especially insulin, during fasting days.

If you have repeated low blood sugar results, you may be overmedicated, so check with your physician to adjust them. If your blood sugars become extremely low, though, you must take some sugar or juice to bring your sugars back to normal, even if it means stopping your fast for that day. The long-term goal is to successfully reduce and then stop all medications and still be able to maintain your sugars in the normal range.

You should also check your blood pressure regularly, preferably weekly. Be sure to discuss routine blood work, including electrolyte measurement, with your physician. Should you feel unwell for any reason, stop your fast immediately and seek medical advice.

For the fasts I recommend, non-caloric drinks such as black coffee, clear broth, water, and tea are permitted to help suppress appetite and prevent dehydration. Fasting has no standard duration or interval; fasts can range from twelve hours to three months or more, with weekly, monthly, or annual intervals between them. Intermittent fasting involves fasting for shorter periods on a regular, more frequent basis. The three most common fasting periods I recommend are sixteen hours, twenty-four hours, and thirty-six hours. A thirty-hour fast can provide a stepping-stone between twenty-four and thirty-six hours.

- A daily sixteen-hour fast means you eat your meals within an eight-hour window. So if you begin your fast at 7:00 p.m., for example, you don't eat anything until 11:00 a.m. the following day. You consume two or three meals from that point on and resume your fast at 7:00 p.m. that evening.

- For a twenty-four-hour fast, you fast from, for example, dinner at 7:00 p.m. on the first day until dinner at 7:00 p.m. the next day.

- For a thirty-six-hour fast, you fast from, for example, dinner at 7:00 p.m. on the first day until breakfast at 7:00 a.m. two days later.

Longer fasting periods produce lower insulin levels, greater weight loss, and greater blood sugar reduction in people with diabetes. In the clinic, I typically recommend a twenty-four-hour or thirty-six-hour fast, two or three times per week (see Sample Meal Plans, pages 189–191).

Ready to give it a try but still have questions? Here are answers to some of the most common ones.

Fasting FAQs

What can I consume on fasting days?
All calorie-containing foods and beverages are withheld during fasting. However, you must stay well hydrated throughout your fast. Water—still or sparkling—is always a good choice. Aim to drink eight cups (two liters) of water daily. You may add a squeeze of lemon or lime for flavor. Try diluted apple cider vinegar (just dilute according to taste), which may help with your blood sugars. Tea and coffee—without milk, sugar, or other additions—are fine. Homemade bone broth (pages 46–49), made from beef, pork, chicken, or fish bones and a good pinch of salt, is also a good choice for fasting days. Vegetable broth is a suitable alternative, although bone broth contains more nutrients. Avoid canned broths and

bouillon cubes, which are full of artificial flavors and monosodium glutamate. Any form of sugar, artificial flavors, or sweeteners is prohibited during a fast.

I take medications with food. What can I do while fasting?
Certain medications may cause problems on an empty stomach. For example, Aspirin can cause stomach upset or even ulcers. Iron supplements may cause nausea and vomiting. Metformin may cause nausea or diarrhea. Always discuss your medications with your physician before starting a fast.

My blood glucose is spiking early in the morning. What should I do?
Nothing. Just before awakening (around 4:00 a.m.), the body secretes higher levels of certain hormones to prepare for the upcoming day. One of them, called glucagon, helps move glucose from storage into the blood so it's ready to use as energy. This dawn phenomenon (DP), or dawn effect, is created by the circadian rhythm. In nondiabetic situations the DP is a normal occurrence, but most people miss it because the magnitude of the rise is very small.

In about 75 percent of type 2 diabetics, however, the DP shows up as a noticeable spike in blood glucose levels early in the morning. The severity varies widely and occurs whether patients are being treated with insulin or not. This happens because the enlarged fatty liver

wants desperately to deflate itself. As soon as it gets the signal, sugar comes whooshing out of the liver and into the blood. The same phenomenon exists during extended fasts. Insulin drops, so the liver releases some of its stored sugar and fat. This is natural and it is not a bad thing. It just means that you have more work to do to burn off all the stored sugar in your body. If high blood glucose persists throughout the day, let your doctor know.

What can I do if I get hungry while fasting?
This is probably the number one concern of fasters everywhere. People assume they'll be overwhelmed with hunger and unable to control themselves. The truth is that hunger does not persist; it comes in waves. If you're experiencing hunger, understand that it will soon pass. Staying busy during a fasting day can help you resist the desire to eat. As your body becomes accustomed to fasting, it becomes more efficient at burning its stores of fat, and your hunger will decrease. During longer fasts, many people notice that their hunger has completely disappeared by the second or third day.

Can I exercise while fasting?
Absolutely. There is no reason to stop your exercise routine. All types of exercise, including resistance (weights) and cardio, are encouraged. There is a common misperception that eating is necessary to supply energy

to the working body. That's not true. Your body carries ample sources of energy. During longer fasting periods, muscles use fatty acids directly for energy. In fact, because your adrenalin levels will be higher during fasting, it is an ideal time to exercise. The rise in growth hormone that comes with fasting may also promote muscle growth.

Will fasting make me tired?

Probably not. In my experience, the opposite is true. Many people find they have more energy during a fast—probably because of increased adrenalin levels. Basal metabolism does not fall during fasting; it rises. You'll find you can perform all the normal activities of daily living while fasting. Persistent or excessive fatigue is not a normal part of fasting. If you experience those, you should stop fasting immediately and seek medical advice.

Will fasting make me confused or forgetful?

You should not experience any decrease in memory or concentration during your fast. The ancient Greeks believed that fasting significantly improved cognitive abilities, helping the great thinkers attain more clarity and mental acuity. Over the long term, fasting may improve memory. One theory is that fasting activates a form of cellular cleansing called *autophagy* that may help prevent age-associated memory loss.

If I get dizzy, what can I do?

If you're experiencing dizziness, you're most probably becoming dehydrated. Be sure to drink plenty of fluids and add extra salt to your broth or mineral water to help retain the fluids longer. Another possibility is that your blood pressure is too low, particularly if you're taking medications for hypertension. Speak to your physician about adjusting your medications. Persistent dizziness, nausea, or vomiting are not normal with intermittent or continuous fasting. If you experience any of these symptoms persistently, you should stop fasting and seek medical advice.

If I get muscle cramps, what can I do?

Low magnesium levels, which are particularly common in people with diabetes, may cause muscle cramps. To address this, you may take an over-the-counter magnesium supplement or soak in Epsom salts, which are magnesium salts. Add one cup (250 milliliters) to a warm bath and soak in it for half an hour. The magnesium will be absorbed through your skin.

If I get a headache, what can I do?

Try increasing your salt intake by adding an extra pinch or two to your bone broth or mineral water. Headaches are quite common the first few times you try a fast. It is believed that they're caused by the transition from a relatively high-salt diet to very low salt intake on fasting days. They are usually temporary, and as you become accustomed to fasting, this problem often resolves itself. If you have any concerns about your headaches, speak to a physician.

If I experience constipation, what can I do?

It is not uncommon to experience constipation at the start of a fast. Increasing your intake of fiber, fruits, and vegetables during the non-fasting period may help. Metamucil can also be taken to increase fiber and stool bulk. If the problem continues, ask your doctor to consider prescribing a laxative.

How should I break my fast?

Be careful to break your fast gently by starting with a handful of nuts or a small salad. Over-eating right after fasting may lead to stomach discomfort or heartburn. While not serious, these conditions can be quite uncomfortable. Avoid lying down immediately after a meal; instead, try to stay upright for at least half an hour. If you experience heartburn at night, placing wooden blocks under the legs at the head of your bed to raise it may help. If none of these solutions work for you, consult your physician.

I'm not losing weight. What's wrong?

If one of the goals of your fast is to lose weight, persist and be patient. The amount of weight loss varies tremendously from person to person. The longer you have struggled with obesity, the more difficult you'll find it to lose weight. Certain medications may make it hard to lose weight. And you'll probably eventually experience a weight-loss plateau. Changing your fasting or dietary regimen, or both, may help. Some patients fast for longer, going from a twenty-four-hour fast to a thirty-six-hour or even forty-eight-hour fasting period. Some people try eating only once a day, every day. Others try a continuous fast for an entire week. Or you could make the fast stricter, say, by shifting from a bone-broth fast to a water-only fast. Changing the fasting protocol is often what's required to break through a plateau, but consult with your physician to determine what might be right for you.

Tips for Success

In the Fasting Method program, we help hundreds of people of all ages and with varying health conditions fast successfully every year. Here are some tips that may help you.

1 **Drink water:** Start each morning with a glass of water.

2 **Stay busy:** Work, chores, exercise, and hobbies will keep your mind off food. It helps to choose a busy day at work when you're planning to fast.

3 **Drink coffee:** Coffee is a mild appetite suppressant. Also try green tea, black tea, and bone broth.

4 **Ride the waves:** Hunger comes in waves; it is not continuous. Be patient and distract yourself.

5 **Don't tell everybody you're fasting:** People may try to discourage you if they don't understand the benefits.

6 **Give yourself thirty days:** It takes time for your body to get used to fasting. Don't be discouraged if you experience a setback. It will get easier.

7 **Follow a nutritious diet on non-fasting days:** Intermittent fasting is not an excuse to eat whatever you like on non-fasting days. Stick to a nutritious diet that is low in sugars and refined carbohydrates.

8 **Don't binge:** After a fast, pretend it never happened. Eat normally, as if you had never fasted.

9 **Fit fasting into your life!** This is the last and most important tip. Arrange your fasting schedule so that it works with your lifestyle and do not limit yourself socially because you're fasting. There will be times during which it's impossible to fast: vacations, holidays, and weddings, for example. Do not try to force fasting into these celebrations. These occasions are times to relax and enjoy yourself. Afterward, just resume your regular fasting schedule. While changing your diet may seem daunting, know that by making the decision to do so you've already taken the first step to better health.

RECIPES

The recipes in this book emphasize healthy fats in their natural form and de-emphasize refined carbohydrates, particularly sugar, and highly processed foods. Instead, the ingredients and techniques reflect international cuisines, embracing traditional and newer approaches to make satisfying, savory meals. No recipe here is exacting or difficult to prepare. Throughout, you will find suggestions for ingredient substitutions so you can truly make your eating plan your own.

Having a well-stocked pantry is key to enabling your culinary creativity. It doesn't need to be extensive—or expensive! Here are some pantry staples to keep on hand.

PANTRY

Coffee and Tea
Coffee and black tea are mild appetite suppressants. During fasting periods, don't add too much dairy. Never add sweetener of any kind.

- Coffee: caffeinated and decaffeinated
- Tea: black, green, oolong, herbal

Condiments
Packaged condiments often contain added sugar. Be on the lookout for any ingredients ending in "-ose" as they may be sugars in disguise. Check balsamic vinegar labels, in particular, for added sugar.

- Chili paste: harissa and sambal oelek
- Curry paste: yellow, green, and red
- Dijon mustard

- Hot sauce
- Miso paste
- Tahini (sesame paste)
- Tamari soy sauce
- Vinegar: apple cider, red and white wine, rice wine, sherry

Dairy
Full-fat dairy is the best choice. Choose cow, sheep, or goat dairy; all are healthy. Avoid packaged fruit yogurts, even those labeled as sugar-free, which may contain artificial sweeteners.

- Butter
- Cheese
- Cream
- Milk
- Yogurt

Oils
Choose extra-virgin olive oil for its minimal processing. Avoid processed vegetable oils including corn, safflower, and canola.

- Coconut oil
- Extra-virgin olive oil
- Ghee (clarified butter)
- Toasted sesame oil
- Walnut oil

Protein (Animal)
Choose fattier cuts of meat and fish for their healthy fats. Eggs are high in protein and rich in nutrients. If you have eggs, you have a meal on hand.

- Beef
- Eggs
- Fish and shellfish
- Lamb
- Pork
- Poultry

Protein (Plant)

Beans, nuts, and seeds are naturally high in fiber and low in carbohydrates. Nuts and seeds contain healthy fats. Rinse canned beans well before using.

BEANS

- Borlotti beans
- Butter beans
- Cannellini beans
- Chickpeas
- Kidney beans
- Lentils
- Navy beans

NUTS

- Almonds
- Brazil nuts
- Cashews
- Walnuts

SEEDS

- Chia
- Quinoa
- Sesame

Spices

Dried spices and herbs lose their flavor quickly. Buy in small quantities and use within three months, if possible.

- Black pepper
- Cayenne pepper
- Chili flakes and chili powder
- Chipotle powder
- Cinnamon, whole
- Cumin, ground and whole seeds
- Curry powder
- Herbes de Provence (dried basil, lavender, rosemary, fennel, thyme, tarragon)
- Nutmeg, whole
- Turmeric

Vegetables

Eat a wide variety of vegetables but avoid white potatoes because of their high starch, which tends to raise blood glucose. Fresh or frozen veggies are the best choices, although canned tomatoes are always good to have on hand.

- Arugula
- Avocado
- Broccoli
- Brussels sprouts
- Cabbage
- Carrots
- Cauliflower
- Citrus: lemons, limes
- Garlic
- Green beans
- Kale
- Leeks
- Onions
- Spinach
- Squash
- Swiss chard
- Tomatoes

Wheat-free Flours

These alternatives to wheat flour thicken soups and stews and provide a binding agent for other recipes, e.g., Socca Pancake (page 34). Although these are better for you than wheat flour, limit consumption. Use occasionally, not daily.

- Almond flour
- Arrowroot starch
- Chickpea flour
- Coconut flour

A DOZEN EGGS

DEVILLED EGGS WITH BACON CRUMBLE

Once a staple of picnics and hors d'oeuvres, devilled eggs have fallen out of fashion. But whenever we serve them, people go crazy for them! Traditionally, devilled eggs are made with a spicy red seasoning such as cayenne pepper or paprika. In this recipe, there is some heat, but it's pungency from the mustard powder. If you don't have mustard powder, substitute prepared mustard such as Dijon.

MAKES 12 DEVILLED EGG HALVES

6 eggs
6 rashers bacon
2 Tbsp butter, softened
2 tsp mustard powder
Salt and pepper

1 Carefully immerse eggs in saucepan of boiling water. Set a timer for 8 minutes to hard-boil eggs.

2 While eggs are cooking, put bacon in a cold frying pan. Turn heat on to medium and place pan on heat. Cook bacon for about 5 minutes on each side until it's well done but not burnt. Drain on paper towels. Allow to cool, then crumble with your fingers or chop with a knife.

3 Peel eggs under cold running water. Halve eggs, and carefully scoop out yolks, leaving whites intact. Beat yolks with butter, mustard powder, and salt and pepper. Spoon devilled yolks back into egg-white centers. Don't worry about artful swirls; this is home cooking. Sprinkle bacon crumbles over eggs.

4 To serve, arrange eggs on a platter. (Some platters are specially designed with divots for devilled eggs.)

HARD-BOILED EGGS WITH PESTO

This dish is really an excuse to share a versatile pesto recipe and a good idea. The pesto is mellow in flavor, which makes it perfect drizzled over just about any dish that's otherwise unadorned. The good idea? If you're going to hard-boil one egg, why not four or six so you have some on hand? Serve these eggs with vegetables or salad to make a light meal.

MAKES 6 EGGS AND ABOUT ⅓ CUP/80 ML PESTO

6 cloves garlic

1 bunch basil, cilantro, or flat-leaf parsley

6 large eggs

⅓ cup/80 mL olive oil, divided

2 oz/55 g Parmesan cheese

Salt and pepper

1 Put garlic in a medium saucepan. Cover with cold water, bring to a boil, and drain. Repeat, then set garlic aside. Half fill the saucepan with water, set it over high heat, and bring to a boil. Ready a bowl of ice water. Drop basil into boiling water for 10 seconds, then remove it with tongs and plunge it in ice water. Remove and drain on a tea towel.

2 Carefully immerse eggs in the saucepan of hot water. Bring water back to a boil and set a timer for 8 minutes.

3 While eggs are cooking, drop 3 garlic cloves into a food processor, followed by basil and a spoonful of olive oil. Grate Parmesan into food processor. Season with salt and pepper. Whir it all up to make a smooth paste, then add remaining olive oil in a slow stream while processor is running. Taste and adjust seasoning. Add another garlic clove or two, if you like. If pesto seems too thick, add a spoonful or two of warm water.

4 Peel the eggs you'll use now under cold running water; refrigerate the rest for up to 5 days.

5 To serve, cut the eggs in half and drizzle with pesto. Leftover pesto will keep refrigerated in a covered glass jar for up to a week.

ANGEL CLOUD EGGS

Fanciful and visually appealing, these eggs in their own white nests are an easy solution when you need to prepare several eggs at once. Baked eggs are a boon for a brunch cook; they're much easier and less finicky than poached or fried eggs. This recipe doubles easily.

MAKES 4 SERVINGS

4 large eggs
4 oz/112 g Parmesan cheese
4 slices cooked bacon
Salt and pepper
Fresh herbs (optional)

1 Separate egg whites and yolks, slipping yolks into individual little bowls and whites into one bowl. Grate cheese. Chop the bacon to a fine crumble. Mince fresh herbs, if using. Preheat oven to 425°F/220°C. Line a baking sheet with baking parchment.

2 Using a stand mixer with the whisk attachment, a hand blender, or several athletic turns of a whisk, beat the egg whites with a pinch of salt until stiff peaks form. Fold in the cheese and bacon.

3 Form egg whites into four nests on the parchment paper. Make a deep indentation in the middle of each nest and bake nests for 6–8 minutes until firm.

4 Carefully slip an egg yolk into each of the indentations. Top with minced herbs, if using, and a few grinds of pepper. If dark pepper flecks displease you, a pinch of white pepper will do instead. Bake cloud eggs for another 3–5 minutes or until yolks are cooked as you like them.

5 To serve, place eggs on individual plates.

EGGS BAKED IN PROSCIUTTO CUPS

This preparation is so simple you'll wonder why you haven't always eaten your "bacon" and eggs this way. If you like hot sauce with eggs, Aleppo pepper or chili flakes are optional; adapt this recipe to the flavors you prefer. For a fresh lift, add some chopped herbs such as basil, thyme, or tarragon. Have ready a 6-cup large muffin tin or double the recipe to make an even dozen—any extras will keep refrigerated for a couple of days.

MAKES 6 SERVINGS

1 Tbsp olive oil

12 slices prosciutto

6 large eggs

Aleppo pepper or chili flakes (optional)

Salt and pepper

Chopped fresh herbs (optional)

1 Preheat oven to 375°F/190°C. Lightly grease a muffin tin with olive oil.

2 Line each muffin cup with 2 slices of prosciutto arranged in a crisscross pattern. You're trying to completely cover the inside of each cup so the egg doesn't stick to the pan.

3 Crack an egg into each prosciutto cup. Season with Aleppo pepper or chili flakes, if using, and salt and pepper.

4 Bake for 15–18 minutes or until egg whites are opaque and prosciutto edges have browned.

5 To serve, place on individual plates and scatter herbs on top, if using. Leftovers will keep well refrigerated in an airtight container for 5 days. Serve at room temperature or rewarm briefly in a microwave oven.

OEUFS EN COCOTTE

A *cocotte* is the French word for a small casserole or a term of endearment that means "little hen." Somewhat less playfully, this dish is also known as baked eggs and adapts beautifully no matter how soft or well cooked you like your eggs and which flavorings you add. Try diced cooked vegetables, grated cheese, chopped bacon or smoked salmon, and vary your choice of fresh herb and creamy base. Serve with a simple green salad, such as Herb Salad (page 70).

MAKES 4 SERVINGS

1 Tbsp butter, softened

4 slices ham

Handful of fresh tarragon, chives, or flat-leaf parsley

¼ cup/60 mL spreadable cheese such as Boursin, sour cream, or crème fraîche

4 eggs

Salt and pepper

1 Butter four small ramekins and place in a gratin or other oven-safe dish. Slice ham into thin slivers. Mince fresh herbs; you'll need about 4 teaspoonfuls. Preheat oven to 425°F/220°C. Boil a kettle of water.

2 In each ramekin, place a tablespoon of Boursin (or sour cream or crème fraîche). Top with slivers of ham. Crack an egg into each ramekin, then season with salt and pepper.

3 Place dish with ramekins into oven. Carefully pour boiling water into dish until it comes halfway up the sides of the ramekins. Bake for 12–15 minutes or until egg yolks are cooked to your preference.

4 To serve, sprinkle each baked egg with herbs and transfer the hot ramekins to individual plates. Serve immediately—and warn people the dishes are still hot!

OLIVE OIL–FRIED EGGS

Olive oil may be rich in oleic acid, which has anti-inflammatory properties, but that's not the reason to use it here. It's the star just because it's delicious! Make sure you use your favorite oil for this recipe. A hint of spice and a bed of greens complement the creamy olive oil and egg yolks. Please don't overcook the yolks; they should blend with the olive oil for full effect.

MAKES 4 SERVINGS

4 large handfuls tender lettuce (Boston, mâche, or arugula)

4 Tbsp olive oil, divided

4 eggs

4 pinches of chili flakes

Salt and pepper

1 Wash and dry lettuce thoroughly. Heat a heavy skillet with a lid over medium-high heat. When pan is hot, add 2 tablespoons of olive oil and swirl it around to warm. Crack eggs into pan, season with salt and pepper and chili flakes. Cook until whites have set and edges are browning. Cover and cook eggs for another 2 minutes to finish whites.

2 While eggs are cooking, distribute handfuls of lettuce among four individual plates. To serve, top lettuce with an egg, spoon olive oil over each serving, and season with another round of salt and pepper.

FRIED EGG
ON
SOCCA PANCAKE

MAKES 4 SERVINGS

1 onion
1 bunch flat-leaf parsley
5 Tbsp olive oil, divided
1 Tbsp butter
1 cup/250 mL chickpea
    flour
4 eggs
Salt and pepper

1 Slice onion into thin half-moons. Chop parsley. Line a baking sheet with paper towel.

2 To cook onions, heat a heavy skillet over medium-high heat. Add 1 tablespoon of olive oil and the butter. Heat until mixture foams, then stir onions into skillet and cook, undisturbed, for 10 minutes or until they start to brown. Reduce heat if onions start to singe; you want a slow-cooked golden result. Stir onions again, season with salt and pepper, and cook for another 10 minutes, undisturbed. Taste an onion; if it's soft and delicious, turn off heat. If not, stir and cook for another 5–10 minutes, undisturbed, until onions are tender. Remove onions and reserve.

3 While onions are cooking, make socca batter. In a small bowl, whisk 1 cup/250 mL warm water into chickpea flour. Stir in 2 tablespoons of olive oil and a pinch of salt. Set aside for up to 5 minutes to thicken slightly. If batter becomes too thick, stir in another ¼ cup/60 mL warm water and a spoonful of olive oil.

A source of protein and fiber, chickpeas are gluten-free and substantial—a good choice when you crave something hearty. In this recipe, chickpea flour is the main ingredient in a dense "pancake" base for slow-cooked onions and fried eggs. If you're a kitchen experimenter, try a teaspoon of cumin, cayenne, or curry powder in the socca batter.

4 In the skillet used to cook onions, heat a tablespoon of olive oil on medium heat. Ladle in ¼ cup/60 mL socca batter and cook for 3 minutes or until underside is golden. Flip and cook for another 2 minutes. Set aside on the baking sheet. Sprinkle with salt while pancake is still warm. Repeat to make 6–8 cooked pancakes.

5 Heat a nonstick frying pan over medium-high heat. Add 1 tablespoon of olive oil. Crack eggs into pan. Season with salt and pepper. Cook until whites set. Cover and cook eggs for another 2 minutes to finish whites. Or flip eggs and fry them over easy.

6 To serve, put a socca pancake on each plate, top with onions, and crown with a fried egg. Sprinkle with parsley and serve.

FRITTATA

A frittata is a baked omelet, but instead of folding the fillings into an egg envelope, you incorporate them evenly throughout. It's a simple, versatile meal that makes it easy to break your fast whatever the time of day. Add your favorite ingredients and eat it cold, warm, or hot—it's difficult to get a frittata wrong unless you overcook it. Note to chef: Set an oven timer!

10 eggs

1 small onion

2 cloves garlic

1 large bunch spinach

2/3 cup/160 mL sundried tomatoes in oil

1 Tbsp olive oil

Pinch of herbes de Provence

8 oz/225 g crumbled feta, divided

Pinch of chili flakes

1/2 cup/125 mL whole milk

Salt and pepper

1 Crack eggs into a bowl. Dice onion. Mince garlic. Roughly chop spinach leaves. Thinly slice sundried tomatoes. Preheat oven to 425°F/220°C. Lightly oil a baking dish or casserole.

2 In a skillet, warm olive oil over medium heat. Add onion and garlic. Cook for 5–7 minutes or until onion is translucent and soft. Remove from heat and season with salt and pepper. Scatter onions and garlic evenly in prepared baking dish.

3 Reduce heat to medium-low. Add spinach to skillet and cook for about 3 minutes or until spinach wilts. Drain any excess liquid from spinach. Add spinach to baking dish and sprinkle with herbes de Provence. Scatter sundried tomatoes and three-quarters of the feta cheese evenly on top of spinach. Sprinkle with chili flakes, salt and pepper.

4 Whisk eggs with milk to combine. Pour over vegetables and cheese in baking dish, ensuring that everything is covered by the egg. Bake for 30–35 minutes or until frittata is puffy and brown on top.

5 To serve, sprinkle with remaining feta cheese and cut into wedges.

SOFTLY FOLDED EGGS WITH CHÈVRE

Pillowy eggs yielding to creamy melting cheese; this is food for when you need to be gentle on yourself or the people you're cooking for. Folding the eggs results in something between scrambled eggs and an omelet—just be careful not to overcook them. A simple arugula salad dressed with olive oil and lemon juice makes a perfect accompaniment.

MAKES 4 SERVINGS

8 eggs
½ lb/225 g chèvre or other creamy goat cheese
3 sprigs dill
2 Tbsp butter
Salt and pepper

1 Beat eggs with salt and pepper, just to incorporate whites and yolks. Don't overbeat. Crumble or break up goat cheese into small pieces. Snip dill with kitchen scissors.

2 Heat a medium skillet over medium-high heat. Add butter. After butter foams up and subsides, pour eggs into skillet. With a wooden spoon, pull eggs in from edges toward the center of the pan. Don't stir the eggs or break them up; allow folds to form. After about 3 minutes, eggs will be cooked on the underside but still shiny on the surface.

3 Sprinkle cheese evenly over eggs. Cook for a minute or two more until cheese is melting. Season with salt and pepper.

4 To serve, spoon eggs out onto four individual plates. Sprinkle with dill and serve.

OMELET WITH FONTINA AND HAM

An omelet is a simple and versatile mealtime solution. No pro chef-style flipping is required and any combination of cheese, cooked meats, or veggies can be a delicious filling. Fontina cheese is mild and melts very easily, resulting in a luxurious, creamy omelet.

MAKES 4 SERVINGS

8 eggs
½ lb/225 g fontina cheese
½ lb/225 g ham
1 bunch chives
8 tsp butter, divided
Salt and pepper

1   Beat eggs with ¼ cup/60 mL water. Season with salt and pepper. Grate cheese. Cut ham into slivers or small cubes. Chop chives.

2   Melt 2 teaspoons of butter in a small nonstick sauté pan over medium-high heat. Pour in a quarter of the egg mixture and tilt pan to completely cover surface. Use a wooden spoon to pull edges of omelet into the center, allowing uncooked eggs to run to the edges and cook.

3   When underside of omelet is set and top is still runny, spoon a quarter of the cheese and a quarter of the ham down the center. Season with salt and pepper. Use a spatula to fold over a third of the omelet. Hold pan over a plate and gently roll omelet onto the plate.

4   Repeat to make three more omelets. Serve omelets warm with chives sprinkled over top.

POACHED EGG ON CAULIFLOWER CRUST

Cauliflower is a veggie chameleon. It's a convincing and less starchy stand-in for rice, mashed potato, and, as we're using it here, pizza crust. Mastering this technique will give you so many options. Use cauliflower crust as a platform for shaved Parmesan and tomato sauce, or spicy spinach with roasted pine nuts, or a variation of bacon and eggs—like this one!

MAKES 4 SERVINGS

2½ lb/1 kg cauliflower

½ lb/225 g Cheddar, Gruyère, or mozzarella cheese

5 large eggs, divided

Salt and pepper

4 slices prosciutto (optional)

1 Break cauliflower into florets and pulse in a food processor very briefly until it looks like rice grains. Don't make cauliflower paste! Grate cheese. Preheat oven to 400°F/200°C. Line a baking sheet with parchment paper.

2 Heat a large heavy skillet over high heat. Sauté cauliflower, stirring constantly, for 5–7 minutes. You're trying to dry-roast as much moisture as possible from the cauliflower. Allow to cool, then squeeze and drain cauliflower grains through cheesecloth or a clean tea towel.

3 Combine drained cauliflower with cheese, 1 egg, salt and pepper. Form mixture into four discs on the baking sheet. Bake for 17–20 minutes until edges are crisp and brown.

4 Bring two small pots or a medium saucepan of water to a boil. Turn down heat, make a whirlpool with a wooden spoon, and crack 4 eggs, one at a time, gently sliding each of them into the water (2 to each pot if using small pots). Set a timer for 5 minutes. When eggs are poached, carefully remove to a plate.

5 To serve, place each cauliflower crust on a plate and top with a slice of prosciutto, if using, and a poached egg. Season eggs with salt and pepper.

FULL ENGLISH BREAKFAST

This hearty dish is a good way to break your fast if you're planning any activity that demands a good fuel-up. A traditional full breakfast emphasizes protein; this one adds juicy grilled tomato and quick-cooked spinach for balance. Get two frying pans going: a nonstick for the eggs and a large heavy stainless-steel or cast-iron pan to brown the meats and veggies.

2 medium tomatoes

¼ lb/112 g button or little cremini mushrooms

1 large bunch spinach (not baby leaves)

8 rashers or slices bacon

8 mild sausages

4 large eggs

2 tsp olive oil

Salt and pepper

1 Slice tomatoes in half. With a damp paper towel or mushroom brush, clean any dirt from mushrooms and cut into quarters. Rinse spinach and dry leaves gently with a tea towel or paper towel.

2 Set heavy frying pan over medium-high heat and add bacon before the pan heats. After bacon has been cooking for 3 minutes or its fat has started to render, cut sausages in half lengthwise and add them, cut side down. Cook for another 5 minutes, then turn sausages.

3 Push meats to the side and add mushrooms. Cook for 2–3 minutes until mushrooms release their liquid. Season with salt and pepper. Push mushrooms to the side and add tomatoes, cut side down. Turn heat down to medium-low.

4 Warm 1 teaspoon of olive oil in a nonstick frying pan over medium heat. Crack eggs into the warming oil. Cook for 2 minutes or until egg whites start to set. Season with salt and pepper. Cover and cook until yolks are as firm as you like. Turn tomatoes, rounded side down. Season tomatoes with salt and pepper.

5 When eggs are ready, slide one onto each plate. Add remaining olive oil to the nonstick frying pan, turn up heat, and pile spinach into the pan. Stir spinach and season with salt and pepper.

6 To serve, divide bacon, sausages, mushrooms, and tomatoes among the plates. Give spinach one last stir and dollop a spoonful onto each plate.

HUEVOS RANCHEROS

Spicy and fresh, this variation on a classic hearty Mexican breakfast dish encourages you to make a homemade *pico de gallo* sauce, aka salsa. To save time, it's okay to use commercially prepared salsa, but please read the label, as many jarred salsas contain sugar. Feel free to adjust the quantity of jalapeño, chipotle peppers in adobo, and cilantro. You control the zest and zing!

MAKES 4 SERVINGS

1 small onion

1 red bell pepper

2 medium tomatoes or 1 small can (14 fl oz/ 398 mL) diced tomatoes

2 cloves garlic

1 jalapeño pepper

1 can (14 fl oz/398 mL) black beans

1 avocado

1 lime

1 bunch cilantro

2 Tbsp olive oil

1 Tbsp chipotle peppers in adobo

4 eggs

Salt and pepper

Hot sauce (optional, for serving)

1. Chop onion. Dice red pepper and tomatoes. Finely chop garlic and jalapeño. Drain and rinse black beans. Slice avocado. Cut lime into quarters. Chop cilantro leaves and stems.

2. Heat a large skillet over medium-high. Add the olive oil. Fry onion and bell pepper for 5 minutes or until softened and aromatic. Stir in tomatoes, garlic, jalapeño, and chilies in adobo. Add ½ cup/125 mL water or juice from canned tomatoes. Season with salt and pepper. Simmer for 5 minutes. Stir in black beans.

3. Make four indentations in salsa. Slide eggs into indentations, cover, and cook for 5 minutes.

4. To serve, spoon eggs and salsa into wide, shallow bowls. Garnish with avocado slices and chopped cilantro. Serve with hot sauce, if using, and lime wedges.

SOUP'S ON

BASIC BROTHS

BEEF BONE BROTH

It isn't always easy to find beef bones on display in grocery stores. But ask at the butcher's counter; there will often be bones cut and frozen or ready to be freshly cut for you. Don't be put off by how long it takes to make this broth. You can leave it simmering away while you do other things at home. You'll be so happy to sip the delicious results, particularly during fasting!

MAKES ABOUT 2 QUARTS/2 L

2 carrots
2 stalks celery
1 onion
4 cloves garlic
3½ lb/1.5 kg beef bones
2 bay leaves
2 Tbsp apple cider vinegar
Salt and pepper

1 Chop carrots, celery, and onion. Crush garlic.

2 Place carrots, celery, onion, garlic, and beef bones in a large stockpot and season generously with salt and pepper. Add enough cold water to cover, then toss in bay leaves and pour in apple cider vinegar. Bring to a boil, then reduce heat to low, and simmer, uncovered, for at least 10 hours, adding more cold water as necessary to keep the bones covered.

3 Strain broth through a fine-mesh sieve into a clean saucepan and discard the solids. Return broth to the stockpot, taste, and adjust seasoning.

4 Serve immediately, or refrigerate and reheat in a microwave oven or over low heat, covered.

TRADITIONAL CHICKEN BROTH

This broth is in the style of old-school chicken soup: rich, savory, and good for what ails you. It makes a perfect base for soup and a delicious clear broth to keep hunger at bay while you're fasting. For a delicious change, use three whole star anise in place of fresh herbs, and add a tablespoon of tamari to serve.

MAKES ABOUT 3 QUARTS/3 L

1 onion

2 carrots

2 stalks celery

2 cloves garlic

5½ lb/2.5 kg raw chicken bones—wings, back, feet, neck

2 bay leaves

4 sprigs fresh thyme

1 small bunch flat-leaf parsley

1 Tbsp tamari, for serving

Salt and pepper

1 Chop onion, carrots, and celery. Crush garlic. Preheat oven to 450°F/230°C.

2 Place bones in large roasting pan and roast for 45 minutes. Transfer the bones to a large stockpot. Deglaze the roasting pan with water, using a wooden spoon to scrape up the brown bits. Pour pan juices over the bones in the stockpot.

3 To the stockpot, add onions, carrots, celery, garlic, bay leaves, thyme, and parsley, and season generously with salt and pepper. Add enough cold water to cover by 1 inch/2.5 cm. Bring to a boil over high heat, then reduce heat to low, and simmer, uncovered, for 2 hours, skimming off any foam that collects on the surface. Add water if necessary to keep bones submerged.

4 Strain broth through a fine-mesh sieve into a clean saucepan and discard the solids. Return broth to the stockpot, taste, and adjust seasoning. Stir in tamari.

5 Serve immediately, or refrigerate and reheat in a microwave oven or over low heat, covered.

BEEF AND CHICKEN BONE BROTH

Use any combination of beef and chicken bones to make this broth; just make sure they weigh 6 pounds (2.7 kilograms) in total.

2 onions

3 carrots

3 stalks celery

6 cloves garlic

4 lb/1.8 kg chicken bones—
    wings, necks, backs

2 lb/900 g beef bones—
    shins or ribs

1 bunch parsley

1 bunch thyme

2 bay leaves

Salt and pepper

1 Chop onions, carrots, and celery. Crush garlic.

2 Place bones in a large stockpot and season generously with salt and pepper. Add enough cold water to cover by 2 inches/ 5 cm. Bring to a boil, then reduce heat to low and simmer for 1 hour. Skim off any foam that forms on the surface.

3 Add onions, carrots, celery, garlic, parsley, thyme, and bay leaves. Simmer for another 6 hours, continuing to skim any foam from the surface. Add water if necessary to keep bones submerged. Strain broth through a fine-mesh sieve into a clean saucepan and discard the solids.

4 Return broth to the stockpot, taste, and adjust seasonings with salt and pepper.

5 Serve hot broth right away, or keep refrigerated in an airtight container for up to 2 weeks or frozen for up to 4 weeks.

SHRIMP BROTH

This recipe makes a good alternative to fish broth, and it is often easier to acquire shrimp shells than raw fish bones and heads. When you eat shrimp, just toss the shells into a freezer bag and make a broth when you have a good stockpile.

3 cloves garlic

3 sprigs fresh thyme

2 Tbsp olive oil

Shells of 36-48 shrimp (from about 2 lb/900 g shrimp)

1 bay leaf

Salt and pepper

1 Chop garlic. Pick thyme leaves from stalks; discard stalks.

2 In a stockpot, warm olive oil over medium heat. Stir in shrimp shells, garlic, and thyme. Cook, stirring constantly, for about 5 minutes or until aromatic but not browning. Adjust heat if necessary.

3 Add enough cold water to cover the shells, and toss in bay leaf. Bring to a boil, then reduce heat immediately to low and simmer broth for 30 minutes.

4 Strain broth through a fine-mesh sieve into a clean saucepan and discard the solids. Return broth to the stockpot and season with salt and pepper. Taste broth; if it seems too weak, simmer until desired flavor is achieved.

5 Serve immediately, or refrigerate and reheat in a microwave oven or over low heat, covered.

GAZPACHO

This chilled, uncooked soup is bliss on a hot day. It's also surprisingly satisfying and energizing, given that it doesn't contain protein. Served in glasses with a meal, it's like a salad and a beverage in one! The sherry vinegar is a nod to gazpacho's culinary roots in Spanish cuisine, but feel free to use lemon juice instead.

MAKES 4 SMALL SERVINGS

1 cucumber, peeled

6 medium tomatoes (about 2 lb/900 g)

1 red, orange, or yellow bell pepper

1 shallot

2 cloves garlic

1 lemon

Chives, for garnish

1 Tbsp sherry vinegar

4 Tbsp olive oil

Salt and pepper

1 Have ready a large glass bowl or other nonreactive bowl. Peel and cut cucumber into small dice, reserving 4 tablespoons for garnish. Cut 5 tomatoes into wedges. Cut remaining tomato into small dice; combine with cucumber for garnish in a small bowl. Chop bell pepper. Mince shallot and garlic. Juice lemon. Snip chives.

2 Add sherry vinegar to diced cucumber-tomato garnish and refrigerate until ready to serve.

3 In a large bowl, combine remaining cucumber dice, tomato wedges, bell pepper, shallot, and garlic with 1 tablespoon of lemon juice. Season with salt and pepper, cover, and leave at room temperature for 1 hour to allow flavors to mingle.

4 Puree tomato-pepper mixture briefly in a blender, 6–8 pulses. With motor running, slowly drizzle in olive oil and puree until gazpacho has liquified. Season with salt and pepper. Taste and add more lemon juice if you'd like a brighter flavor. Pour into a pitcher or glass bowl and refrigerate for at least 1 hour and up to 24 hours.

5 To serve, divide among four individual bowls, glasses, or shot glasses. Garnish with cucumber-tomato salsa and a sprinkling of chives.

SPICY PUMPKIN SOUP

This quick and easy soup comes together almost entirely with pantry ingredients. Hokkaido pumpkin is also known as red kuri squash. It's a small squash with thick skin and tender flesh, well suited to roasting whole, so there's no need to peel or attempt to cube it while it's raw. Acorn or other thick-skinned squash makes an acceptable substitute.

MAKES 4-6 SERVINGS

1 Hokkaido pumpkin or acorn squash (about 3 lb/1.3 kg)

1 onion

4 cloves garlic

1-inch/2.5-cm piece fresh ginger

3-4 Tbsp olive oil, divided

1 Tbsp Thai green curry paste

2 cups/500 mL vegetable stock

1 can (14 fl oz/400 mL) coconut milk

Salt and pepper

1 Cut pumpkin in half, scoop out seeds, and discard (or toss with a tablespoon of olive oil and a light sprinkling of salt, and roast on a separate baking sheet at the same time as you roast the pumpkin flesh). Dice onion. Mince garlic and ginger. Preheat oven to 425°F/220°C.

2 Place pumpkin halves in a roasting pan, flesh side up. Drizzle with 2 tablespoons of olive oil and season with salt and pepper. Roast pumpkin for 30 minutes or until flesh is very soft and pulls away from skin easily. Let cool for about 10 minutes, then spoon flesh into a bowl.

3 In a large soup pot, warm remaining tablespoon of olive oil over medium heat. Cook onion, garlic, and ginger for 5–7 minutes or until onion is translucent and garlic and ginger are fragrant. Season with salt and pepper. Add curry paste and pumpkin and stir to combine.

4 Add vegetable stock and simmer for about 10 minutes. If you have an immersion blender, blend soup in the pot. If not, transfer to a blender in batches. Be careful—soup is hot! Puree and return soup to pot.

5 Stir in coconut milk and season with salt and pepper. Ladle into bowls to serve. If you roasted seeds, use them to garnish soup.

TOMATO SOUP WITH PARM CRISPS

This richer-than-usual take on tomato soup is perfect when fresh field tomatoes are in season, but it works with drained canned whole tomatoes too. Pair the soup with either—or both!—of the "parm" garnishes: prosciutto (aka Parma ham) or Parmesan (aka Parmigiano-Reggiano) crisps.

MAKES 4 SERVINGS

2 lb/900 g fresh tomatoes or 2 cans (19 fl oz/540 mL) whole tomatoes

4 cloves garlic

1 yellow onion

3 Tbsp olive oil, divided

1 quart/1 L Chicken Broth (page 47) or store-bought stock

½ cup/125 mL 35% cream

Salt and pepper

4 oz/112 g Parmesan cheese (optional)

4 slices prosciutto (about 2 oz/55 g, optional)

1 Halve tomatoes. Mince garlic. Dice onion. Coarsely grate Parmesan cheese or cut prosciutto into slivers, if using. Preheat oven to 350°F/180°C. Line two baking sheets with parchment paper and a plate with paper towel.

2 Skip this step if using canned tomatoes. Spread tomatoes on one baking sheet, drizzle with 2 tablespoons of olive oil, and toss to coat. Sprinkle with garlic and season with salt and pepper. Roast for 45–55 minutes or until tomatoes have started to caramelize.

3 On second baking sheet, make 8 mounds of grated Parmesan, if using, and scatter prosciutto loosely, if using. Bake with the tomatoes during the last 15 minutes they are roasting.

4 Remove both baking sheets from oven. With a thin spatula, carefully transfer Parmesan crisps to a cooling rack (they break easily). Drain prosciutto crisps on the lined plate.

5 In a heavy-bottomed soup pot, heat remaining tablespoon of olive oil over medium heat. Add onion and cook for 8–10 minutes until translucent and very soft, almost disappearing. Add roasted or canned tomatoes with their juice, and chicken broth. Simmer for 15–20 minutes to allow flavors to mingle.

6 Transfer soup, in batches, to a blender and blend to a silky puree. Return soup to the pot, stir in cream, and heat just until wisps of steam rise. Don't boil it! Taste and adjust seasoning.

7 Serve in individual bowls, on its own or garnished with floating Parmesan crisps and/or prosciutto crisps.

CALLALOO (CARIBBEAN SPINACH SOUP)

If you are lucky enough to find fresh callaloo leaves, this soup will be authentically West Indian. But spinach is an acceptable alternative as long as you don't use baby spinach, which is too tender and mild to stand up to the bold, hot flavors in this recipe. Our version emphasizes vegetables, but feel free to add some cooked crab meat or shredded chicken for a heartier meal.

MAKES 4 SERVINGS

1 yellow onion

3 cloves garlic

4 green onions

1 Scotch bonnet or other hot chili pepper (optional)

1 butternut squash

1 lb/450 g fresh or frozen, thawed okra

2 big bunches callaloo or dark green spinach

2 Tbsp olive or coconut oil

1 tsp allspice

3 sprigs thyme

3 cups/750 mL Chicken Broth (page 47) or store-bought stock

2 cups/500 mL coconut milk

Salt and pepper

1 Dice onion. Finely chop garlic and green onions. Mince chili pepper. Peel, seed, and dice squash. Slice okra. Chop callaloo (or spinach) leaves and stalks.

2 Heat a soup pot over medium-high. Add olive or coconut oil. Stir in onion and garlic and sauté for 60 seconds. Add green onions, chili pepper, if using, allspice, and thyme. Cook, stirring, until aromatic, about 2 minutes. Season with salt and pepper.

3 Add squash and okra. Cook for 3–5 minutes, allowing vegetables to brown but not singe. Season with salt and pepper. Add callaloo or spinach, stock, and coconut milk. Stir and bring to a simmer (little bubbles). Cover and cook for 45 minutes until squash is tender and soup has thickened.

4 To serve, ladle soup into four individual bowls.

MINESTRONE

Also known as fridge-clearing soup, this classic recipe can be made with whatever bits and pieces you have on hand—except broccoli or cauliflower, whose flavors are too dominant once cooked and cooled. As a nod to its Italian culinary roots, this minestrone recipe calls for cannellini beans, but use your favorite bean. Kidney or navy beans both work well.

MAKES 6–8 SERVINGS

1 onion

1 carrot

2 stalks celery

2 zucchini (about 1 lb/ 450 g)

½ lb/225 g green beans

1 lb/450 g Savoy (or green) cabbage

2 cups/500 mL cooked or canned cannellini beans

½ cup/125 mL olive oil, plus extra for serving

2 Tbsp butter

6 cups/1.5 L Chicken Broth (page 47) or Beef Bone Broth (page 46) or store-bought stock

2 cups/500 mL fresh or canned plum tomatoes, juice reserved

Salt and pepper

1 Parmesan cheese rind (optional)

½ cup/45 g grated Parmesan cheese, for serving

1 Chop onion. Dice carrot, celery, and zucchini. Slice green beans. Shred (or very finely cut) Savoy cabbage. If using canned or jarred cannellini beans, rinse them well.

2 Heat olive oil and butter in a soup pot over medium-high. When butter foams, add onion and reduce heat. Cook, stirring occasionally, for 20 minutes or until onion is golden and soft.

3 Add carrots and celery. Cook, stirring for 3–5 minutes or until softened. Add zucchini, green beans, and cabbage. Season with salt and pepper.

4 Add broth and tomatoes with their juice. Add Parmesan rind, if using. Bring soup to a simmer, cover, and allow to bubble gently for about an hour. Stir in cannellini beans and simmer for a further 15 minutes or up to 30 minutes for a thicker soup.

5 When vegetables are tender and soup is deliciously aromatic, remove Parmesan rind.

6 Serve in individual bowls with a sprinkling of grated cheese and a drizzle of olive oil.

MUSHROOM AND WILD RICE SOUP

This soup is a meal in a bowl. Mushrooms provide deep flavor in this recipe, especially if you use several kinds, and they are enhanced by the liberal addition of cream. To save time, cook the wild rice—a high-protein, gluten-free grass indigenous to North America—while you chop the aromatic ingredients.

MAKES 4 SERVINGS

1 onion

3 stalks celery

1 lb/450 g mushrooms, any kind or a combination

3 cloves garlic

1 cup/250 mL wild rice

1 Tbsp olive oil

2 sprigs thyme

1 cup/250 mL white wine

4 cups/1 L Chicken Broth (page 47) or store-bought stock

1 cup/250 mL 18% cream

1 Tbsp Dijon mustard

Salt and pepper

1 Dice onion and celery. Chop mushrooms. Mince garlic.

2 Bring 4 cups/1 L salted water to a boil, add wild rice, and turn heat down to simmer. Cover and cook for 40–45 minutes or until rice starts to split and is tender. Drain through a fine-mesh sieve and set aside.

3 In a soup pot over medium-high heat, warm olive oil. Add onions and celery. Season with salt and pepper, and cook, stirring, for about 5 minutes or until vegetables have softened. Add mushrooms and cook until they release their liquid, 3–5 minutes. Stir in garlic and thyme sprigs and stir for 30 seconds until garlic is fragrant. Don't let the garlic singe. Season with salt and pepper.

4 Pour in wine and cook until it has reduced by half, 7–10 minutes. Add broth and cooked wild rice. Simmer, partially covered, for 20 minutes. Add cream, simmer for another 10 minutes, and remove from heat.

5 Stir in Dijon, taste, and season again if you wish. To serve, ladle into four bowls.

ITALIAN WHITE BEAN SOUP

Save leftover Parmesan rinds in the freezer until you're ready to make this soup. I prefer to use dried beans because you can infuse them with more flavor as you rehydrate them. Be mindful not to oversalt when seasoning; there is already salt in the bacon and the Parmesan rinds.

BEANS

¾ cup/155 g dried navy or cannellini beans (or 14 fl oz/398 mL can)

1 bay leaf

1 Tbsp olive oil

Pinch of red pepper flakes or smoked paprika

Salt and pepper

SOUP

1 medium onion

3 cloves garlic

6 oz/170 g bacon

1 large bunch spinach

2 Tbsp olive oil

1 Tbsp tomato paste

1 can (14 fl oz/398 mL) diced tomatoes

1 tsp paprika

1 tsp herbes de Provence

2 cups/500 mL vegetable stock

Squeeze of lemon juice

2 Parmesan cheese rinds

Salt and pepper

1. If using dried beans, soak them in about 3 cups of fresh water with a generous pinch of salt for at least 8 hours. Put the soaking water and beans into a soup pot, add the bay leaf, olive oil, red pepper flakes or paprika, and pepper, and set the pot on high heat. When the water boils, reduce heat to medium to keep it at a simmer for about 45 minutes or until beans are tender but still firm. Drain water and discard bay leaf.

2. Dice onion. Mince garlic. Chop bacon into cubes. Roughly chop spinach.

3. Place bacon in a cold saucepan over medium heat; cook the bacon until browned. Remove from pan, leaving 1–2 tablespoons of rendered fat in pan. Add oil, onion, and garlic, and cook over medium heat until onion is translucent and garlic is fragrant, 5–7 minutes. Season with pepper, and stir in beans, tomato paste, tomatoes, paprika, herbes de Provence, and Parmesan rinds. Stir until combined, and simmer for a few minutes so some of the liquid from the vegetables cooks off.

4. Add vegetable stock, and an additional cup of water to pot. Turn heat to medium-high and bring to a boil, then reduce heat and simmer, uncovered, for about 30 minutes or until broth is slightly thickened. Season with salt and pepper.

5. To serve, remove from heat and stir in spinach and bacon. Add a squeeze of lemon juice, ladle into six individual bowls, and serve.

CALDO VERDE (PORTUGUESE KALE SOUP)

In its traditional form, caldo verde is a thick soup based on potato stock. This version uses rich, savory chicken broth and goes lighter on the starch. Instead, liberal use of olive oil during cooking and as a finishing touch makes this meal in a bowl silky and substantial. In Lisbon, you would add a dash or two (or six!) of piri piri hot sauce, but any hot sauce will do.

MAKES 4 SERVINGS

1 large or 2 small onions

3 cloves garlic

½ lb/225 g lacinato kale

3 Tbsp olive oil

2 sprigs thyme

5 cups/1.2 L Chicken Broth (page 47) or store-bought stock

½ lb/225 g fresh chorizo sausage

Piri piri or other hot sauce (optional)

Salt and pepper

1 Chop onions. Finely chop garlic. Strip kale from stems, discard stems, and slice kale into very fine ribbons.

2 In a large soup pot, warm olive oil over medium-high heat. Tip in onions and garlic. Cook, stirring for 3–5 minutes or until onions are translucent but not brown. Adjust heat as necessary to avoid burning garlic. Season with salt and pepper.

3 Stir in kale ribbons and thyme sprigs. Season with salt and pepper, bearing in mind the chorizo sausage may be quite salty. Pour in chicken broth, bring to a simmer, cover, and cook for 8–10 minutes until kale is very tender. Turn off heat.

4 While kale is cooking, heat a grill pan or heavy skillet over medium-high. Sear sausages, then turn down heat and cook them through, turning frequently to avoid charring. When sausages are cooked, slice them in quarters lengthwise. Chop into neat little pieces.

5 Remove and discard thyme sprigs from kale, add chorizo, and stir to combine. To serve, ladle hot soup into individual bowls. Serve with extra olive oil and hot sauce on the side, if using.

SPLIT PEA SOUP WITH SMOKED PORK CHOP

Pea soup is often made so thick that it resembles porridge. This simple recipe goes a little lighter on the split peas but remains hearty and satisfying. If you can't find a smoked pork chop, use chopped ham and a leftover ham bone if you have one.

MAKES 8-10 SERVINGS

1½ lb/700 g yellow or green dried split peas

2 stalks celery

2 carrots

1 onion

2 Tbsp olive oil

2 tsp chili flakes

1 tsp dried thyme

2 bay leaves

1 smoked pork chop on the bone or ½ lb/225 g cooked ham

Salt and pepper

1 ham bone (optional)

1. Rinse and pick any debris from the split peas. Dice celery, carrots, and onion.

2. In a large soup pot, bring 3 quarts/3 L of water and the split peas to a boil. Turn off heat, skim off any foam, cover, and let sit for 1 hour.

3. While beans soak, heat olive oil in a skillet over medium heat. Add the celery, carrots, onion, chili flakes, and thyme. Season with salt and pepper. Cook until vegetables have softened but not browned, about 8 minutes.

4. Return soaked split peas to heat and bring back to a boil. Skim off any foam, then add vegetable-herb mixture, bay leaves, and smoked pork or ham and ham bone, if using. Turn down heat and simmer for 1½ to 2 hours or until split peas have softened completely and soup has thickened. Remove bay leaves and pork or ham and bones.

5. Shred meat and return it to soup. Taste and season with salt and pepper before ladling into individual bowls. Leftover soup will keep in an airtight container, covered and refrigerated, for up to 3 days.

MULLIGATAWNY SOUP

Aromatic, golden colored, and warming, mulligatawny soup is a feast for the senses. Be sure to use chicken thighs rather than breast meat for their assertive taste and fat content, which grounds the other complex flavors in this dish. This soup is a good make-ahead choice; it will keep, covered and refrigerated, for three days.

MAKES 6 SERVINGS

1 onion

2 carrots

2 stalks celery

3 cloves garlic

1-inch/2.5-cm piece fresh ginger

1 small red chili pepper

¼ cup/60 mL olive oil

1 Tbsp yellow curry powder

1 tsp ground cumin

1 tsp ground cinnamon

½ tsp ground turmeric

¼ tsp ground cardamom

2 cups/500 mL Chicken Broth (page 47) or store-bought stock

1½ lb/700 g skinless, boneless chicken thighs

¼ cup/48 g red lentils

Salt and pepper

1 Finely chop onion, carrots, and celery. Mince garlic and ginger. Split chili, remove seeds, and slice chili as fine as your knife skills permit.

2 In a heavy-bottomed soup pot set over medium heat, warm olive oil. Stir in curry powder, cumin, cinnamon, turmeric, and cardamom, allowing spices to warm and bloom for about 1 minute. Add onion, carrots, and celery. Cook, stirring, for about 5 minutes, or until slightly softened but not mushy. Stir in garlic, ginger, and chili. Season with salt and pepper.

3 Pour in chicken broth and 2 cups/500 mL water. Add chicken thighs and bring liquid to a simmer. Partially cover and cook for about 20 minutes or until chicken has cooked through. Cut into a piece to check. When chicken is cooked, remove it to a platter and set aside to cool.

4 Add lentils to soup pot. Simmer for 25–30 minutes or until lentils are tender. Shred meat from chicken thighs and stir back into soup. Taste and adjust seasoning with salt and pepper.

5 Ladle into individual bowls and serve hot.

SCOTCH BROTH

Scottish cooks make this traditional soup with mutton neck and stewing lamb, so add the lamb bones from leftover cooked lamb if you have them. They also use a lot of ground black pepper and might finish the soup with a dash of Scotch whisky. Use either ingredient according to your taste! Pot barley, a whole grain, is a usual addition but omit it if you prefer to avoid all grains.

MAKES 6-8 SERVINGS

1 lb/450 g cooked lamb or 1½ lb/700 g uncooked boneless lamb

1 leek

1 onion

2 carrots

2 stalks celery

2 cloves garlic

1 small yellow turnip

2-3 Tbsp olive oil, divided

12 cups/3 L Beef Bone Broth (page 46) or store-bought stock

¼ cup/60 mL pot barley

Salt and pepper

Lamb bones (optional)

Dash of Scotch whisky (optional)

1   Cube lamb, whether it's cooked or uncooked. Trim tough green ends from leek, then chop white and green parts. Chop onion, carrots, and celery. Mince garlic. Cube turnip.

2   If using uncooked lamb, heat 1 tablespoon of olive oil in a large heavy-bottomed pot over medium-high. Sear lamb on all sides, about 10 minutes. Season with salt and pepper. Cover lamb with 4 cups/1 L of broth. Bring to a boil, then turn down heat to low and simmer for 30 minutes. (If using cooked lamb, skip this step.)

3   Heat 2 tablespoons of olive oil in a large heavy-bottomed pot over medium-high. Add leek, onion, carrots, and celery, turn down heat to medium-low, and cook for 15–20 minutes or until vegetables are reduced and very soft.

4   Add garlic and turnip and stir in cubed lamb and pot barley. Add lamb bones, if using. Cover with 12 cups/3 L beef broth (or 8 cups/2 L beef broth + the 4 cups/1 L you used to cook the lamb). Simmer for 45–55 minutes or until all ingredients are very soft. Remove and discard bones, if using.

5   Season liberally with salt and pepper, add Scotch whisky, if using, and ladle into bowls.

TOM KHA

This Thai-inspired soup combines richness and freshness through the magic of coconut milk. It's always a good idea to have a can or two of coconut milk in your pantry, to fortify soups and stews and unite flavors. Be sure to use only fresh, plump lemongrass stalks in this recipe. If they appear papery or dry, leave them out!

1-inch/2.5-cm piece fresh ginger

2 stalks lemongrass

3 limes

1½ lb/700 g boneless chicken thighs or extra-firm tofu

½ lb/225 g shiitake or oyster mushrooms

6 sprigs cilantro, for serving

6 cups/1.5 L Chicken Broth (page 47) or store-bought stock

2 cups/500 mL coconut milk

2 Tbsp fish sauce

Salt and pepper

Chili oil, for serving

1 Grate ginger. Bruise lemongrass with the blunt edge of a knife and cut into pieces. Zest 2 limes and juice one of them. Cut the unzested lime into wedges. Cut chicken or tofu into 1-inch/2.5-cm cubes. Roughly chop mushrooms. Pick leaves from cilantro stalks.

2 In a medium soup pot over medium-high heat, combine ginger, lemongrass, lime zest, lime juice, and chicken broth. Bring mixture to a boil, turn down heat, and simmer for 15 minutes. Strain through a fine-mesh sieve, discarding solids. Return broth to soup pot.

3 Add chicken (or tofu) and return to a boil. Turn down heat immediately, add mushrooms, and simmer for 15–20 minutes or until chicken is cooked through. If you are using tofu, this step will take 10–15 minutes.

4 Stir in coconut milk and fish sauce just until heated through. To serve, ladle into bowls and garnish with chili oil and cilantro.

SALAD
DAYS

STAPLE DRESSINGS

Add one part of your favorite acid, such as lemon juice or vinegar, to three parts oil to make a delicious salad dressing—no formal recipe required! Some cooks just pour the ingredients directly onto their salads, but we prefer salad dressing emulsified so it clings better to the salad leaves. Combine the ingredients in a pitcher, or shake them in a jar, or whisk them together in the bottom of a large bowl before piling the salad on top and tossing to coat.

DIJON VINAIGRETTE

2 Tbsp white wine vinegar

1 Tbsp Dijon mustard

6 Tbsp olive oil

Salt and pepper

Chopped fresh herbs to taste (optional)

CITRUS SESAME VINAIGRETTE

2 Tbsp fresh orange, lime, or lemon juice (or a combination)

1 Tbsp white wine vinegar

1 tsp roasted sesame oil

6 Tbsp olive oil

Salt and pepper

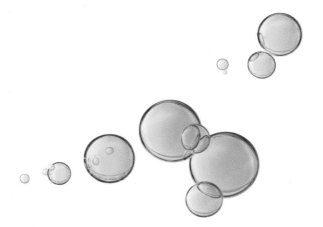

CRÈME FRAÎCHE

½ cup/125 mL crème fraîche or sour cream

2 Tbsp olive oil

2 Tbsp apple cider vinegar

1 tsp celery seed

Salt and pepper

CREAMY YOGURT GARLIC DRESSING

1 clove garlic, grated

1 Tbsp fresh lemon juice

2 Tbsp plain full-fat yogurt

6 Tbsp olive oil

Salt and pepper

HERB SALAD

This salad celebrates the flavors of tender greens and fresh herbs. Try to use at least three different greens and two herbs to ensure variety; a mesclun mix or other store-bought combinations are also good options. But no iceberg lettuce in this salad, please! Use the best-quality olive oil and vinegar that your budget allows.

MAKES 4–6 SERVINGS

6 large handfuls salad greens, such as arugula, lamb's lettuce, frisée, romaine, radicchio, escarole, oak-leaf lettuce

2 bunches herbs, such as parsley, basil, savory, chervil, tarragon, sorrel

2 Tbsp white or red wine vinegar

6 Tbsp olive oil

Salt and pepper

1 Wash salad greens and herbs gently but thoroughly and dry leaves well in a salad spinner or with tea towels or paper towel. Tear greens into bite-sized pieces. Chop herbs roughly, including stems.

2 In a large wooden or glass bowl, combine salad greens with herbs. Pour vinegar over top, followed by olive oil. Season with salt and pepper. With your hands, toss the salad to coat all of the leaves.

3 Serve this delicate salad right away before the leaves begin to wilt in the dressing.

CRUSHED CUCUMBER SALAD WITH SESAME

It's important to smash the cucumbers for this recipe—breaking them in places and leaving them crunchy in others—so they can absorb the delicious soy dressing. If you can find them, use the little cucumbers with very thin skin that are available in many grocery stores now.

MAKES 4 GENEROUS SERVINGS

2 lb/900 g cucumbers, English or Persian

2 Tbsp sesame seeds

1 clove garlic

1-inch/2.5-cm piece fresh ginger

3 tsp rice vinegar

2 tsp toasted sesame oil

1 tsp tamari

Salt

1 Set cucumbers on a large chopping board. With the bottom of a heavy frying pan, a rolling pin, or the flat side of a cleaver, lightly and swiftly smash cucumbers so they break apart. Cut smashed cucumbers into large pieces, salt lightly, and put into a fine-mesh sieve set over a bowl. Refrigerate for 10 minutes or up to 30 minutes. Toast sesame seeds in a dry nonstick skillet for 3 minutes or until light brown. Mince garlic and ginger.

2 To serve, rinse and drain liquid from cucumbers. In a large bowl, stir together garlic, ginger, rice vinegar, sesame oil, and tamari. Add cucumbers and toss well. Sprinkle with toasted sesame seeds and serve immediately in individual bowls.

FENNEL AND ORANGE WITH GREENS

Segmenting oranges can be a bit tricky, but this recipe is otherwise very easy. If you are anxious about cutting the oranges over a bowl, use a cutting board with a drip groove so none of the precious juice is lost. Allowing the onion to macerate in the citrus dressing will mellow its sharp taste. If you're a fan of raw onion, go ahead and skip this step.

MAKES 4 SERVINGS

2 navel oranges
1 fennel bulb
½ red onion
1 bunch flat-leaf parsley
1 Tbsp olive oil
1 Tbsp grainy mustard
4 large handfuls arugula
Salt and pepper

1 With a sharp paring knife, peel oranges. Holding each orange over a bowl to catch the juice, slide the knife between the membrane and the flesh to cut out orange segments. Discard pith and membrane. Put orange segments in a large glass or wooden bowl. Reserve the orange juice. Slice fennel into slender half-moons. Slice onion into paper-thin half-moons. Chop parsley leaves and stems roughly.

2 In a small bowl, combine olive oil, mustard, and orange juice, and whisk to combine. Add a teaspoonful or two of olive oil (to thicken) or water (to thin) to desired consistency. Season with salt and pepper.

3 Add fennel and onion to the bowl with orange segments. Toss with dressing and leave to macerate for 30 minutes at room temperature.

4 To serve, distribute arugula among plates. Top with fennel-orange salad and a sprinkling of parsley.

SPICY QUINOA WITH TOMATOES AND PINE NUTS

This risotto-like recipe makes a substantial and satisfying meal with the addition of feta cheese. Taste and adjust the amount of harissa based on how much spice you like and how spicy your harissa is. If you use Le Phare du Cap Bon brand in this recipe, it makes a relatively mild dish. Do not skip the fresh herbs at the end.

MAKES 4–6 SERVINGS

1 medium onion

3 cloves garlic

1½ cups/375 mL quinoa

8 oz/225 g feta cheese

¾ cup/100 g pine nuts (or slivered almonds), reserve some for garnish

1 bunch flat-leaf parsley, reserve some for garnish

1 bunch mint, reserve some for garnish

2 Tbsp olive oil

½ tsp ground coriander

¼ tsp sweet paprika

1 tsp harissa (or more, if you like it spicier)

4 strips of lemon peel

1 can (19 fl oz/540 mL) diced tomatoes

1 cup/250 mL vegetable broth

Salt and pepper

1 Dice onion. Mince garlic. Rinse quinoa in a fine-mesh sieve. Cube feta. Toast pine nuts in a dry skillet until fragrant, about 3 minutes. Finely chop herbs.

2 In a saucepan, warm olive oil over medium heat. Add onion and garlic and cook until onion is translucent and garlic is fragrant, 5–7 minutes. Season with salt, pepper, coriander, and paprika, then stir in harissa, lemon peel, and quinoa.

3 Cook quinoa until it begins to toast, then add canned tomatoes and vegetable broth. Increase heat to medium-high and bring liquid to an active simmer (small bubbles will form). Simmer for 20 minutes or until quinoa is cooked but not mushy. Stir often. Adjust seasoning with salt and pepper.

4 Remove saucepan from heat. Remove lemon peel and stir in feta, toasted pine nuts, and fresh herbs. Serve immediately, garnished with more pine nuts and herbs.

GRILLED TOMATO AND ZUCCHINI SALAD WITH MOZZARELLA

Make this salad in late summer when tomatoes and zucchini are at their peak. The vegetables can be grilled or roasted in a grill pan on the stovetop or in the oven if you don't have access to an outdoor grill. We recommend using burrata, which is fresh mozzarella with cream at its center. If you can find fresh mozzarella or burrata made with buffalo milk, these are even creamier and richer than their relatives made with cow's milk.

MAKES 6 SERVINGS

1 lb/450 g ripe tomatoes on the vine

1 large zucchini (or 2 small)

½ red bell pepper

½ red onion

1 bunch basil

4½ oz/125 g fresh mozzarella (ideally, burrata!)

6 Tbsp olive oil, divided

1 Tbsp white wine vinegar

1 clove garlic

1 tsp Dijon mustard

⅓ cup/45 g pine nuts or thinly sliced almonds

Salt and pepper

1   Quarter tomatoes. Slice zucchini lengthwise and into batons about 1 inch/2.5 cm long. Chop bell pepper into bite-sized wedges. Thinly slice onion. Pick basil leaves and chop, discarding stalks. Tear mozzarella into bite-sized pieces with your hands. Preheat oven or grill to 400°F/200°C.

2   Toss tomatoes, zucchini, and bell pepper with 2 tablespoons of olive oil and salt and pepper. If baking, transfer vegetables to a roasting dish and roast for 25 minutes. If using a grill, carefully place the vegetables directly on the grill for about 10 minutes, then flip for another 10 minutes or until they start to caramelize and brown. Remove from heat and allow to cool to room temperature. Drain any excess liquid from the vegetables.

3   In a small food processor or blender, blend 4 tablespoons of olive oil, vinegar, basil leaves, garlic, Dijon, and salt and pepper until smooth. Pour the dressing over the onions, stir, and allow to marinate for about 30 minutes.

4   Toast pine nuts or almonds in a dry skillet over medium heat for about 2 minutes, tossing so they brown evenly and watching carefully that they don't burn.

5   To serve, put roasted vegetables in a large serving bowl, add mozzarella, salad dressing, nuts, and onion and toss gently. Season with salt and pepper to taste. Divide among individual plates.

AVOCADO WITH TUNA SALAD

Serving tuna salad in delicious edible avocado "bowls" is very pleasing, but if you prefer a more elegant presentation, you could serve the tuna alongside sliced avocado or atop avocado chunks. This meal contains plenty of healthy fat and protein to keep you feeling satisfied for hours. If it seems too light, serve over simply dressed arugula or baby spinach, sprinkled with chopped almonds.

MAKES 4 SERVINGS

2 stalks celery

¼ red onion

6 sprigs flat-leaf parsley

2 cans (each 6 oz/170 g) tuna, packed in oil or water

⅓ cup/80 mL full-fat sour cream

2 large perfectly ripe avocados

Salt and pepper

Lemon wedges, for serving

1 Mince celery, onion, and parsley. You should have approximately 2 tablespoons of each, minced. If your tuna is water packed, drain it.

2 In a bowl large enough to easily combine the ingredients, flake tuna with a fork. Lightly fold in sour cream, celery, onion, and parsley. Don't be rough—you don't want to make tuna paste! Season with salt and pepper. You can refrigerate tuna salad, covered, for up to 24 hours before serving.

3 To serve, halve avocados and remove pits. Scoop tuna salad into avocado centers, spritz with lemon juice, and serve with a lemon wedge on the side.

CHOPPED LOBSTER SALAD ON GREENS

This indulgent recipe makes the most of lobster's naturally sweet, briny flavor by enhancing it with Mediterranean ingredients, including olive oil, lemon juice, basil, and capers. Frozen canned lobster often goes on sale. When it does, stock your freezer.

1 lb/450 g cooked lobster meat (frozen is fine)

1 lemon

2 stalks celery

2 sprigs basil

6 Tbsp fruity olive oil

1 Tbsp capers

5 large handfuls sturdy salad greens, such as spinach, arugula, baby kale

Salt and pepper

1 If using frozen lobster, thaw in the refrigerator for 24 hours. Discard any bits of shell from lobster meat. Zest, then juice lemon. Chop celery. Finely chop basil leaves and stems.

2 Combine 1 tablespoon of lemon juice with olive oil and salt and pepper. Stir in celery, basil, and capers. Taste and adjust seasoning, then gently stir in lobster meat.

3 To serve, toss greens with lemon juice to taste—1–2 teaspoons should be plenty—and divide among four plates. Top with lobster salad and sprinkle with lemon zest.

CURRIED CHICKEN SALAD WITH ARUGULA

This pretty and appetizing one-dish meal comes together in less than thirty minutes and is a handy standby for summer when you don't always want to cook. You can poach the chicken in the morning or evening when it's cooler and make the dressing in advance too. Refrigerate both, separately, for up to three days.

MAKES 4 SERVINGS

1 Granny Smith or other tart apple

½ lemon

2 carrots

1 bunch cilantro

¼ cup/35 g roasted cashews or almonds

2 Tbsp olive oil, divided

1 lb/450 g boneless chicken breasts

2 tsp curry powder or to taste

1 cup/250 mL plain Greek yogurt

4 large handfuls arugula

Salt and pepper

1 Dice apple. Squeeze lemon over apple to prevent browning. Shred or grate carrots. Chop cilantro. Finely chop nuts.

2 In a shallow skillet with a lid, warm 1 tablespoon of olive oil over medium heat. Season chicken with salt and pepper, then sear for about 2 minutes per side or until nicely golden. Add water to cover chicken. Bring to a boil, then turn down heat, cover, and simmer for 15–18 minutes or until internal temperature of chicken is 160°F/71°C. Remove from heat and allow chicken to cool in its poaching liquid. When cool, remove from liquid and cut into bite-sized pieces.

3 Combine curry powder with yogurt, the remaining olive oil, and a squeeze of lemon juice. Season with salt and pepper.

4 To serve, arrange arugula on four individual plates. Gently stir chicken, apple, and carrots into curried yogurt. Spoon salad over arugula and top with chopped nuts.

FRISÉE SALAD WITH POACHED EGGS AND LARDONS

This traditional French bistro offering isn't nearly as fancy sounding if you call it bacon-and-egg salad. But that's what it is! Frisée lettuce has a sturdy, curly texture that can support the bacon lardons without collapsing, which allows for a generous amount of bacon in this recipe.

1 large shallot
4 heads frisée lettuce
4 slices thick-cut bacon
¼ cup/60 mL red wine vinegar
2 Tbsp white vinegar or lemon juice
4 eggs
Salt and pepper

1 Dice shallot. Tear frisée into bite-sized pieces. Cut bacon into thin strips. Line a plate with paper towel.

2 In a saucepan over medium heat, cook bacon strips for 6–8 minutes or until browned and fat has rendered. Add shallots and cook for 5 minutes or until they start to turn transparent. Remove pan from heat. Add red wine vinegar, stirring to incorporate.

3 Fill a saucepan two-thirds full of water and white vinegar or lemon juice, and bring to a gentle simmer. Crack eggs one at a time into a ladle or a small bowl, and very gently slide eggs into simmering water. Use a spoon to gently guide whites so eggs stay together as much as possible. Cook for 5–8 minutes until whites are completely set. With a slotted spoon, remove eggs and set aside on paper towel.

4 In a large salad bowl, toss frisée with red wine vinegar and bacon dressing until coated.

5 To serve, divide dressed greens among four bowls and top with a poached egg. Season with salt and pepper and serve immediately.

QUICK PICKLE

Making quick pickles will give you a sense of culinary arts mastery, and it's so easy! You'll need a couple of large, wide-mouthed glass preserving jars. Because you aren't truly canning preserves, you don't need to go through the rigmarole of sterilizing and boiling the filled jars. A good wash in hot soapy water and a thorough rinse will suffice. If you use a combination of vegetables, the result will be like an Italian *giardiniera*.

1 lb/450 g firm vegetables (any combination of carrots, green beans, red onion, asparagus, cucumber, broccoli, or your favorites)

4 cloves garlic

8 sprigs thyme or dill (or 4 sprigs of each)

1 Tbsp black peppercorns

1 cup/250 mL apple cider vinegar or white wine vinegar

1 Tbsp coarse salt

2 mason jars with lids (1 pint/500 mL each)

1. Peel and trim vegetables, if necessary, and cut into long, slender pieces. Cut onion into concentric circles and separate into rings. Smash garlic cloves.

2. Divide vegetables, herbs, peppercorns, and garlic equally between glass jars.

3. In a small saucepan, bring 2 cups/500 mL water, vinegar, and salt to a boil, just until the salt dissolves.

4. Pour hot vinegar mixture over vegetables. Allow vinegar to cool, then screw on lids and refrigerate for at least 24 hours. Quick pickles will keep for up to 2 weeks, covered and refrigerated.

MASON-JAR MIRACLES

A smart make-ahead strategy, these layered salads can be built in mason jars or any other nonreactive container with a lid. The salad doesn't get tossed in the dressing until you're ready to eat, so the ingredients stay fresh and crunchy and the flavors remain distinct. Put a couple of tablespoons of a Staple Salad Dressing (pages 68–69) in the bottom of each container, add the rest of the ingredients, and you're set. Refrigerate for up to three days until ready to serve.

EACH RECIPE MAKES
4 MASON JARS OF SALAD

TBA

1 lb/450 g grape or cherry tomatoes

2 avocados

1 lime

1 head Belgian endive

4 eggs

4 large handfuls baby spinach

2 Tbsp sesame seeds

PBJ

¾ lb/350 g jicama

½ cup/55 g walnuts or almonds

1 can (19 fl oz/540 mL) cannellini beans

1 bunch flat-leaf parsley

1 head radicchio

4 large handfuls arugula

TBA (TOMATO, BELGIAN ENDIVE, AVOCADO)

1 Halve tomatoes. Halve avocado, scoop out flesh, and chop into bite-sized pieces. Squeeze lime over avocado to prevent browning. Slice endive into ribbons.

2 In a small saucepan, cover eggs with cold water and bring to a boil over high heat. Boil for 5 minutes. Immediately remove eggs from heat, drain, and gently roll on countertop to crack shells. Peel eggs under cold running water and set aside. When cool, chop eggs.

3 Layer ingredients in mason jar in this order: dressing, tomatoes, avocado, endive, egg, spinach, sesame seeds. To serve, toss in the jar and eat.

PBJ (PARSLEY, BEANS, JICAMA)

1 Peel and cut jicama into small cubes. Chop nuts. Drain and rinse cannellini beans. Chop parsley leaves and stems. Slice radicchio.

2 Layer ingredients in mason jar in this order: dressing, jicama, nuts, cannellini, parsley, radicchio, arugula. To serve, simply toss in the jar and eat.

EACH RECIPE MAKES

4 MASON JARS OF SALAD

TLC

8 radishes

1 English cucumber

3 carrots

4 large handfuls red leaf lettuce

1 lb/450 g slender green beans

3 cans (each 6 oz/170 g) tuna packed in olive oil

BRB

4 oz/112 g Beemster aged gouda or other semi-soft cheese

8 radishes

2 heads frisée lettuce

1 head lamb's lettuce or other very tender green

4 slices bacon

TLC (TUNA, LETTUCE, CUCUMBER)

1 Slice radishes very thinly. Cube cucumber. Grate carrots. Tear lettuce into bite-sized pieces. Trim green beans and cut into bite-sized pieces.

2 Fill a large bowl with ice water. Bring a small saucepan of salted water to a boil, add beans, and blanch for about 4 minutes or until tender-crisp. Plunge into ice water to stop cooking, then drain.

3 Layer ingredients in mason jar in this order: dressing, radishes, cucumber, carrots, beans, tuna, lettuce. To serve, simply toss in the jar and eat.

BRB (BEEMSTER, RADISHES, BACON)

1 Grate cheese. Slice radishes thinly. Chop frisée lettuce. Tear lamb's lettuce into bite-sized pieces. Line a plate with paper towel.

2 Fry bacon in a skillet over low heat for 12–15 minutes. Drain on paper towel and crumble when cool.

3 Layer ingredients in mason jar in this order: dressing, radishes, cheese, frisée, bacon, lamb's lettuce. To serve, simply toss in the jar and eat.

VEGETABLE SIDES

CAULIFLOWER RICE

Small pieces of grated cauliflower—cauliflower rice—are a great low-carb alternative to starches like rice, potatoes, and bread. Remember to use cauliflower rice right away because, like many other crucifers such as cabbage, broccoli, kale, and bok choi, cauliflower becomes stronger tasting in storage. If you want to store it, cook the cauliflower rice and freeze it for up to one month.

MAKES 4-6 SERVINGS, DEPENDING ON SIZE OF CAULIFLOWER

1 head cauliflower
1 Tbsp olive oil, butter, or broth (pages 46–49)
Salt and pepper

1 Using a box grater or the grating blade of a food processor, grate cauliflower into small pieces. Discard the tough core.

2 Heat olive oil, butter, or broth in a wide heavy-bottomed skillet over medium-high. Stir cauliflower into skillet and cook, stirring every so often, for 5–7 minutes or until cauliflower is translucent. Season with salt and pepper.

3 To serve, layer a bed of cauliflower rice on individual plates and top with your favorite stir-fry, stew, chili, roasted fish, or any creamy, saucy dish. Or add it to a stir-fry as you would rice.

PUREED TURNIP AND PARSNIP

Turnip has a stronger flavor than its sweeter relative, the parsnip. Together, they make a delicious puree to serve on the side of a sauced main dish, and each is equally good pureed on its own for a single flavor note.

MAKES 6 SERVINGS

2½ lb/1 kg turnip and/or parsnip

1 shallot

1 clove garlic

4 sprigs flat-leaf parsley, for garnish

3 Tbsp butter

1 Tbsp olive oil

Salt and pepper

1 Cube turnip and/or parsnip. Mince shallot. Mince garlic. Chop parsley leaves.

2 Melt butter in a heavy-bottomed skillet with a lid over medium heat. Add turnip and/or parsnip, shallot, and garlic. Cook, stirring every so often, for 5 minutes. Season with salt.

3 Add enough water to just cover vegetables and bring to a boil. Turn down heat to a simmer (little bubbles) and cook until root veggies are soft, 10–15 minutes. Turn off heat, drain vegetables, and allow excess moisture to evaporate.

4 Transfer vegetable mixture to a blender or food processor, add olive oil, and puree to a very fine texture. If you don't mind a few delicious lumps, simply mash vegetables in a large bowl. Taste and season with salt and pepper.

5 To serve, transfer mashed or pureed vegetables to a serving dish and serve immediately or at room temperature. This puree is best consumed the day you make it.

CREAMED SPINACH

Creamy, garlicky, and rich, this classic side dish goes well with any roasted meat, poultry, or fish. It's always a crowd pleaser. Luckily, this recipe doubles or triples very easily and you can make it up to two days before you plan to serve it. Refrigerate, covered, in a baking dish, then reheat at 320°F/160°C for 30 minutes. If the sauce seems too thick, just add a spoonful or two of water.

MAKES 4 SERVINGS

1 shallot
2 cloves garlic
1 lb/450 g frozen spinach
1 Tbsp butter
1 cup/250 mL 35% cream
Pinch of ground nutmeg
Salt and pepper

1 Mince shallot. Mince garlic. Thaw spinach at room temperature or place frozen spinach in a steamer basket over a pot of boiling water for 5 minutes. In either case, drain spinach very well.

2 In a skillet, melt butter over medium-low heat. Cook shallot and garlic for 2–4 minutes, or until translucent but not browning. Stir in spinach. Season with nutmeg and salt and pepper.

3 Add cream, increase heat, and simmer spinach in cream for 3–5 minutes or until slightly thickened. This shouldn't be too wet; watch and stir patiently.

4 To serve, taste and adjust seasonings, then divide among plates. Serve hot.

BUTTERED SAVOY CABBAGE

Many people associate cabbage with the strong aroma and flavor it develops when steamed, boiled, or braised. If you don't favor that strong cabbage-y taste, cook it in a good dollop of olive oil, butter, or duck fat (delicious!) first. Here we use beautiful, crinkly Savoy cabbage and pair it with caraway seeds, but omit the caraway if you aren't a fan.

MAKES 6–8 SERVINGS

1 large head Savoy cabbage
1 shallot
1 Tbsp butter
Salt and pepper
1 tsp caraway seeds (optional)

1 Slice cabbage into fine ribbons. Finely chop shallot.

2 In a heavy-bottomed skillet with a lid, melt butter over medium heat. Tip cabbage ribbons and shallots into butter. Cook, stirring constantly, for 5–7 minutes or until cabbage has started to soften and shallots are translucent. Add caraway, if using, and season with salt and pepper.

3 Add a large spoonful of water to cabbage, cover, and steam very briefly until the cabbage has softened but isn't disintegrating, about 2 minutes.

4 Serve cabbage hot.

LEMONY MINTED PEAS

Frozen peas get a bad rap, but peas are at their sweetest, most tender best when frozen at the peak of harvest. Unlike fresh peas, they don't need shelling, and unlike canned peas, they retain a little burst of resistance when you bite into them. It's convention to serve peas with mint, and in this recipe, we use fresh mint, lemon zest, and butter to make peas that taste like springtime on a plate.

MAKES 4 SERVINGS

1 lb/450 g frozen tiny peas
1 lemon
4-6 sprigs fresh mint
2 Tbsp butter
Salt and pepper

1 Thaw peas in the fridge at room temperature or by blanching them in hot water. Zest, then juice lemon. Pick leaves from mint, stack, and slice them into narrow ribbons.

2 In a medium saucepan, bring about 4 cups/1 L of water to a boil. Salt boiling water lightly. Turn down heat and allow peas to simmer for 2 minutes. Drain peas.

3 Melt butter in the same saucepan over low heat. Add 1 tablespoon of lemon juice, then stir peas into butter-lemon mixture. Remove from heat and stir in mint.

4 To serve, scoop peas into a serving dish and sprinkle with lemon zest. Serve immediately.

STIR-FRIED GREEN BEANS WITH SNOW PEAS

Crunchy, spicy, and satisfying, this side dish is made using a cooking method that is somewhere between an Asian dry-fry and a French sauté. How much garlic you add, and whether you serve the vegetables with sriracha sauce or not, is up to you. But why not go big and bold with these flavors? A few curls of lemon zest are another good way to finish this dish, if spicy isn't your thing.

MAKES 4-6 SERVINGS

½ lb/225 g snow peas
1 lb/450 g green beans
1-2 cloves garlic
¼ cup/60 mL ghee
1 tsp toasted sesame oil
Salt and pepper
Sriracha sauce for serving
(optional)

1 Trim strings from snow peas and cut stem ends from green beans. Mince garlic. Have ready a large bowl of ice water and two clean, dry tea towels.

2 Bring a large pot of salted water to a rolling, vigorous boil. Blanch green beans for 3–5 minutes or until they are still firm in the center. Bite into a bean to test for doneness. Add snow peas for 60 seconds. Drain, then immerse beans and peas in ice water. Drain again, pat dry with tea towel, then spread out beans and snow peas on second tea towel to dry completely. (If they are not dry, they will spatter dangerously in the oil in the next step.)

3 Heat ghee in a heavy-bottomed sauté pan over high heat. When oil is searing hot, add beans and peas and sauté for 1 minute. The skins will begin to blister and blacken. Add garlic and continue to sauté for another minute. Season with salt and pepper.

4 Finish with a drizzle of toasted sesame oil and some dots of sriracha, if using. To serve, transfer to individual plates or a serving platter and serve blazing hot.

PANFRIED KALE WITH CHILI

This is a gutsy preparation with big bold flavors that you control by deciding how much garlic and heat you want. It's important to use lacinato kale, the very dark-green kale with frilled edges also known as dinosaur kale, because its assertive flavor stands up to the garlic, chili, and olive oil. The paler green, smoother varieties of kale have a more delicate flavor and texture that may get lost. This side dish is particularly good with Roasted Flattened Chicken (page 161).

MAKES 4 SERVINGS

½ lb/225 g lacinato kale

1 large or 2 small cloves garlic

1 or 2 bird's eye chilies

1 Tbsp assertive olive oil, plus more for serving

Salt and pepper

1 Strip kale from its stems and cut leaves into narrow strips (julienne). Mince garlic. Split chilies and remove seeds.

2 Warm olive oil in a wide heavy-bottomed skillet over medium-high heat. Add kale and sauté for 4–6 minutes or until dark and glossy and wilted. Stir in garlic and bird's eye chilies and continue to cook, stirring constantly, for 2 minutes.

3 To serve, transfer to a serving dish, season with salt and pepper, and drizzle with olive oil, if you like. Serve hot.

ASPARAGUS STIR-FRY

Once a harbinger of spring, asparagus is now available for more of the year because it can be grown indoors, in greenhouses and hydroponic gardens. The very green taste still evokes spring, even if you're eating asparagus in February! It's perfectly acceptable to steam asparagus, but adding olive oil, garlic, and lemon zest in this recipe lifts it into a more interesting and satisfying side dish.

MAKES 4 SERVINGS

1 lb/450 g asparagus
1 lemon
1 clove garlic
2 Tbsp olive oil
Salt and pepper

1 Snap tough ends from asparagus and cut stalks on the diagonal into 2-inch/5-cm pieces. Zest, then juice lemon. Mince garlic.

2 In a heavy-bottomed frying pan, warm olive oil over medium-high heat. Add asparagus and let it cook without moving for about a minute, to brown the underside. Add garlic, season with salt and pepper, and continue to cook, stirring, for another 4–5 minutes or until asparagus is done to your liking.

3 Stir in 1 tablespoon of lemon zest and 1 tablespoon of lemon juice.

4 Serve as soon as possible, either hot or at room temperature, as cooked asparagus doesn't keep well.

OPEN SESAME BROCCOLI

Broccoli has its own strong, distinctive flavor and it also absorbs the flavors of whatever is cooked with it. It can easily stand up to the gutsy ginger and sesame in this preparation. We've doubled down on the sesame, using both sesame oil and sesame seeds. Crunchy, tasty, and good for you!

MAKES 4 SERVINGS

1 large head broccoli

2-inch/5-cm piece fresh ginger

2 Tbsp toasted sesame oil

2 Tbsp tamari

4 Tbsp sesame seeds

Salt and pepper

1 Cut broccoli into florets with some stem still attached. Cut stalk into slender discs. Finely chop ginger. Preheat oven to 425°F/220°C. Line a baking sheet with parchment paper.

2 In a bowl, toss broccoli with sesame oil and tamari. Arrange broccoli in a single layer on baking sheet, season lightly with salt and pepper, and roast for 20 minutes. Turn broccoli florets and cook for a further 5–8 minutes or until deep brown in places and still tender-crisp.

3 While broccoli is roasting, heat a small nonstick pan over medium heat. Add sesame seeds and dry-roast for 2–3 minutes or until light brown. Be careful—sesame seeds burn easily.

4 To serve, spoon broccoli into a large serving dish and shower generously with toasted sesame seeds. Serve immediately.

BAKED BUTTERNUT SQUASH

The natural sweetness of squash makes it a perfect contrast to spicy flavors such as cayenne, chili, jalapeño, and other hot peppers. Butternut squash, like its name, is rich and tender, perfect for baking and then mashing or slicing. Peeling squash before it's been cooked is a tedious chore; this recipe doesn't require you to peel the squash before you roast it.

MAKES 6 SERVINGS

1 butternut squash
2 Tbsp butter
Salt and pepper
1 Tbsp olive oil (optional)

1. Halve squash lengthwise and scoop out the seeds as well as any loose strings. Melt butter. Preheat oven to 400°F/200°C. Line a roasting pan or baking sheet with parchment paper.

2. Place squash cut side up in roasting pan or on baking sheet. Brush with melted butter. Season with plenty of salt and pepper, then bake for 45–55 minutes until squash is tender and the top has browned. Test for doneness with the point of a sharp knife.

3. To serve, scoop squash out of its skin and mash with a little olive oil, if using. Or leave the skin on and cut into slices or wedges.

RAINBOW BEETS WITH CHÈVRE

Rainbow beets or candy cane (Chioggia) beets are gorgeous in this dish, but go ahead and use purple beets if you can't find the colorful variants. No matter what they look like, beets are a great choice from the root vegetable family. They pack vitamins, minerals, and fiber to keep you feeling satisfied. The creamy goat cheese in this recipe helps with that too.

MAKES 4 SERVINGS

8 small or medium rainbow, candy cane, or dark purple beets

½ cup/55 g walnut halves or pieces

1 Tbsp apple cider vinegar

3 Tbsp olive oil

4 oz/112 g creamy goat cheese, such as chèvre

Salt and pepper

1 Scrub beets. Preheat oven to 350°F/180°C.

2 Place beets in a baking dish just large enough to hold them without crowding. Cover tightly with aluminum foil and roast for 90 minutes or until fork tender. Allow to cool enough to handle, then rub the skins off and cut beets into large chunks.

3 While beets are roasting, toast walnuts in a heavy-bottomed skillet over medium heat, stirring from time to time, for about 3 minutes or until nuts are fragrant but not blackened. Chop nuts.

4 To serve, scoop beets onto a platter or into a shallow bowl and douse with apple cider vinegar and olive oil. Season with salt and pepper. Distribute nuts and pieces of chèvre evenly over beets. Serve warm.

PAN-ROASTED FENNEL WITH PARMESAN

Fennel has a fresh taste that's faintly reminiscent of licorice and pairs well with any fish. If you prefer, you can roast the fennel in the oven at 400°F/200°C for 35 to 40 minutes, adding the Parmesan for the last 5 minutes. Or omit the Parmesan completely if you do not want the richness or flavor of the cheese.

MAKES 4-6 SERVINGS

3 fennel bulbs

4 Tbsp olive oil

Salt and pepper

½ cup/45 g grated, shredded, or shaved Parmesan cheese (optional)

1 Halve fennel bulbs, then cut into 6 or 8 wedges.

2 In a large heavy sauté pan, warm olive oil over medium-high heat. Add fennel wedges in a single layer and cook, undisturbed, for 10–12 minutes, or until fennel begins to color but not burn. Turn fennel and cook for another 8–10 minutes. Turn down heat if fennel is browning too quickly.

3 Season fennel liberally with salt and pepper, cover partially, and allow to soften completely, 5–7 minutes. Test for doneness with the tip of a sharp knife.

4 To serve, transfer fennel to a platter, sprinkle Parmesan over top, if using, and serve hot or at room temperature.

CAULIFLOWER STEAKS WITH CHEESE

Cauliflower is transformed when it's dry-roasted at high temperature: its flavor deepens and mellows and it becomes a delicious foundation for a meal. Here we use strong cheeses that would work well with beef, but you could substitute any melting cheese, such as mild fontina or mozzarella, if you prefer. Gruyère is also a classic pairing. Think "cheese fondue," and you won't go wrong.

MAKES 4 SERVINGS

1 head cauliflower

1 lemon

4 oz/112 g aged Cheddar or tangy blue cheese

1 clove garlic

¼ cup/60 mL olive oil

1 tsp cayenne powder or Espelette pepper

Salt and pepper

Hot sauce, for serving (optional)

1　Slice cauliflower into 4 thick slices. You will need to sacrifice both ends, which won't be large enough to constitute "steaks" (turn them into Cauliflower Rice, page 88). Zest and juice lemon. Grate Cheddar or crumble blue cheese. Mince garlic. Preheat oven to 425°F/220°C. Line a baking sheet with parchment paper or aluminum foil.

2　In a small bowl, combine 1 tablespoon of lemon zest, 1 tablespoon of lemon juice, garlic, olive oil, cayenne or Espelette pepper, and salt and pepper. Put cauliflower steaks on baking sheet and brush tops generously with half of the olive oil mixture. Bake for 15 minutes or until cauliflower turns dark brown and starts to smell nutty.

3　Remove from oven, turn cauliflower over, brush with remaining olive oil mixture, and return to oven for another 12–15 minutes. Cauliflower will be very dark brown, but don't allow the edges to blacken.

4　Remove cauliflower from oven, sprinkle with cheese, and return to oven for just long enough to melt cheese, 2–3 minutes.

5　Serve warm, with hot sauce on the side if you're feeding spicy food lovers.

STUFFED TOMATOES WITH GOAT CHEESE

These tomatoes are a wonderful side dish for any simply prepared meat, particularly chicken. Take note: the cheese filling will be melted and soft when you first take these out of the oven. Be patient for a minute or two, to give the filling a chance to firm up. Not only will the tomatoes be easier to serve, you'll avoid searing the roof of your mouth!

MAKES 4 SERVINGS

2 onions

½ cup/55 g walnut pieces

8 roma (plum) tomatoes

1 bunch flat-leaf parsley

1 Tbsp olive oil

4 oz/112 g fresh goat cheese

1 tsp white wine vinegar

Salt and pepper

1 Thinly slice onions. Roughly chop walnuts. Halve tomatoes and remove pulp with a spoon. Chop parsley leaves.

2 In a skillet over medium heat, warm olive oil. Cook onions, stirring often so they don't burn, until they turn golden brown, 35–40 minutes. Remove from heat, set aside to cool, and season with salt and pepper.

3 In a bowl, stir together goat cheese, onions, walnuts, and vinegar.

4 Preheat oven to 350°F/180°C. Arrange tomato halves cut side up in a baking dish. Spoon cheese filling carefully into cavity of the tomatoes, being careful not to overfill. Bake tomatoes for 30 minutes or until lightly browned on top. Remove from oven and allow to cool almost to room temperature so cheese filling sets.

5 To serve, arrange tomatoes on a platter and sprinkle with parsley.

Crudités with Pesto
(page 108)

Steamed vegetables aren't technically crudités, which means "raw vegetables" in French. But it's a good idea to blanch or steam some vegetables, particularly cruciferous ones such as cauliflower and broccoli, because it makes them easier to digest and brings out their naturally delicious flavors. The suggested dips are creamy or thick, so they adhere well to the veggies. The dips and veggies will keep, covered and refrigerated, for three days.

CRUDITÉS WITH FOUR DIPS

EACH DIP MAKES ABOUT ½ CUP/125 ML

VEGETABLE SUGGESTIONS:

Belgian endive, leaves separated

Bell peppers (red or yellow), sliced lengthwise into strips

Broccoli, blanched for 3 minutes

Carrots, cut into sticks

Cauliflower, blanched for 3 minutes

Celery, cut into sticks

Jicama, cut into sticks

Zucchini, cut into sticks

AIOLI

2 cloves garlic

1 Tbsp lemon juice

½ cup/125 mL mayonnaise

Big pinch of Espelette or cayenne pepper

Salt and pepper

BLUE CHEESE DIP

4 oz/112 g tangy blue cheese

¼ cup/60 mL sour cream

¼ cup/60 mL mayonnaise

1 Tbsp lemon juice

Salt and pepper

ONE: AIOLI

1 Mince garlic and combine with lemon juice. Allow to infuse for 5 minutes.

2 In a small bowl, stir garlic-lemon mixture into mayonnaise. Add a generous pinch of Espelette or cayenne pepper. Season with salt and pepper.

3 Serve immediately or cover and refrigerate for up to 3 days.

TWO: BLUE CHEESE DIP

1 Crumble blue cheese.

2 In a small bowl, stir blue cheese gently into sour cream and mayonnaise. Stir in lemon juice. Season with salt and pepper.

3 Serve immediately or cover and refrigerate for up to 3 days.

PESTO

1 bunch basil, parsley,
   cilantro, or a
   combination
1 clove garlic
3 Tbsp lemon juice, divided
1 Tbsp pine nuts
2 Tbsp olive oil
Salt and pepper

TZATZIKI

1 English cucumber or
   4 little Turkish
   cucumbers
1 bunch fresh dill
4 sprigs fresh mint
1 clove garlic
1 Tbsp lemon juice
1 cup/250 mL plain
   full-fat yogurt
Salt and pepper

THREE: PESTO

1 Chop fresh herbs. Mince garlic.

2 In a food processor, pulse herbs with garlic and 1 tablespoon
   of lemon juice. Pulse in pine nuts until crumbly—don't create
   nut butter! With the motor running at a constant speed, pour
   in olive oil slowly, followed by remaining lemon juice, until
   pesto reaches desired consistency. Season with salt and pepper.

3 Serve immediately or cover and refrigerate for up to 3 days.

FOUR: TZATZIKI

1 Grate cucumber. Roughly chop dill and mint, including stems.
   Mince garlic and stir into lemon juice.

2 Place cucumber in a fine-mesh sieve, salt lightly, and leave
   for 10 minutes to drain. Push cucumber with the back of a
   wooden spoon to get out as much liquid as possible.

3 In a small bowl, stir grated cucumber into yogurt. Add dill and
   mint, and garlic-lemon mixture. Season with salt and pepper.

4 Cover and refrigerate for at least 1 hour and up to 3 days.

GOLDEN CURRIED VEGETABLES

You may want to cut the vegetables into different shapes for more visual appeal, but this rich yellow curry looks appetizing whatever shape the veggies take. This dish is wonderful with a Socca Pancake (page 34) on the side. If serving with socca pancakes, allow one per person and use half the chickpeas called for in the curry.

MAKES 6 SERVINGS

1 onion

2 cloves garlic

1 lb/450 g butternut squash

1 lb/450 g cauliflower

1 yellow or green zucchini

1 bird's eye chili

6 sprigs cilantro or flat-leaf parsley

4 large handfuls spinach

1 can (14 fl oz/398 mL) chickpeas

2 Tbsp olive oil or ghee

5 Tbsp yellow curry paste

1 can (14 fl oz/398 mL) coconut cream

Salt and pepper

1 Dice onion. Mince garlic. Peel squash and cut into bite-sized chunks. Break cauliflower into bite-sized florets. Slice zucchini lengthwise, then into chunky half-moons. Slice bird's eye chili into slivers. Roughly chop cilantro or parsley. Rinse spinach. Drain and rinse chickpeas.

2 In a large heavy-bottomed skillet over medium heat, warm olive oil or ghee. Add onions and garlic. Cook, stirring, for about 5 minutes or until onions start to color. Add squash, cauliflower, zucchini, and chili. Give everything a good stir. Season with salt and pepper.

3 Pile in spinach, cilantro or parsley, and chickpeas. In a glass measuring cup or bowl, combine curry paste with 2 cups/ 500 mL warm water. Stir mixture into veggies. Cover and cook for 10–12 minutes or until the vegetables are tender. If curry seems dry, add a little more water. If it seems too liquid, leave uncovered and reduce to your preferred consistency.

4 When vegetables are tender, stir in coconut cream just enough to warm and incorporate it. Serve immediately or refrigerate overnight and reheat. The flavor of this curry, like most stews and soups, improves if it has a chance to mellow.

5 To serve, ladle into bowls.

PLANT
PROTEIN

WALNUT CRUMBLE

This easy-to-make topping adds crunch, depth, and richness—not to mention a nice little protein and fiber hit—to round out any vegetable-based recipe. Nutritional yeast gives this savory crumble a flavor that suggests cheese but it doesn't get gooey! Sprinkle it over cooked vegetables or salads.

MAKES 1 CUP/250 ML

1 cup/110 g walnut pieces
1 Tbsp olive oil or melted coconut oil
2 tsp nutritional yeast
2 Tbsp flaxseed
Salt and pepper

1 Preheat oven to 400°F/200°C. Lightly oil a baking sheet.

2 Combine walnut pieces with olive or coconut oil. Season with salt and pepper. Arrange in a single layer on baking sheet and roast for 5–7 minutes, stirring after a couple of minutes so nuts don't burn. Allow walnuts to cool completely on baking sheet.

3 In a large bowl, toss nutritional yeast and flaxseed with crisp walnuts. Taste and adjust seasoning if you like. Leftover crumble will keep refrigerated in a covered glass container for up to a week.

*See photo
on page 114*

Along with some crunchy veggies, a small mound of this hummus makes a meal in itself. Or prepare it as an additional dip to accompany Crudités (page 107) or Seed Crackers (page 115). It's easy, portable, and hearty, with healthy fat from the olive oil and tahini (sesame seed paste) and plenty of fiber from the chickpeas.

HUMMUS

MAKES ABOUT 2 CUPS/500 ML

1 can (19 fl oz/540 mL)
    chickpeas
2 cloves garlic
1 lemon
2 Tbsp tahini
½ tsp ground cumin
1 Tbsp olive oil
Salt and pepper
1 tsp Espelette pepper,
    for serving (optional)

1   Drain and rinse chickpeas. Mince garlic. Zest, then juice lemon.

2   In a food processor fitted with blade attachment, combine chickpeas, garlic, 2 tablespoons of lemon juice, tahini, and cumin until smooth and silky. This will take a couple of minutes. Thin with more water or lemon juice, a teaspoon at a time, until hummus is the consistency you prefer. Season with salt and pepper.

3   To serve, spoon hummus into a bowl or rimmed plate. Sprinkle with lemon zest and Espelette pepper, if using, and drizzle with olive oil.

*Seed Crackers
with Hummus* (page 113)

These crackers are crisp, slightly salty, and satisfying. Try them to round out a soup, salad, or raw veggie platter with some protein. What they don't have is starch or refined carbohydrates, which makes them a perfect staple to have on hand instead of commercially prepared crackers.

SEED CRACKERS

MAKES 20–24 CRACKERS, DEPENDING ON SIZE

¼ cup/60 mL coconut oil

½ cup/125 mL whole raw sunflower seeds

½ cup/125 mL whole raw flaxseed, plus 2 Tbsp ground flaxseed

¼ cup/60 mL raw chia seeds

¼ cup/60 mL raw sesame seeds

Salt and pepper

1 Melt coconut oil in a small saucepan over low heat. Preheat oven to 350°F/180°C. Lightly oil a rimmed baking sheet or line with parchment paper.

2 In a bowl, combine sunflower, flax, chia, and sesame seeds with melted coconut oil and 1 cup/250 mL of boiling water. Use a spatula to move cracker dough to baking sheet, pressing it out into a rough rectangle. Press dough flat with your hands until about ¼ inch/6 mm thick. Season with salt and pepper. Bake for 25 minutes.

3 Remove cracker from oven. Loosen with a metal spatula and flip. Return to oven to bake for another 10–15 minutes or until light brown. Turn off heat and leave cracker to cool in oven for an hour.

4 When cool, break into pieces. Sprinkle lightly with more salt, if you like, before serving.

ROASTED TOFU

Tofu's mild flavor and various textures make it endlessly versatile. Tofu Scramble (page 126) highlights one popular way to prepare tofu, and oven roasting is another method that adapts well to many flavors. In place of the olive oil in this recipe, try chili-garlic oil, toasted sesame oil, or lemon basil–infused oil. In place of the fish sauce, try tamari sauce, rice wine vinegar with some miso paste stirred into it, or hot sauce. Play around with the balance of hot and sour to find a combo you like!

MAKES 4 SERVINGS

1½ blocks (20 oz/560 g) firm tofu

2 cloves garlic

1 lemon

2 Tbsp fish sauce

¼ cup/60 mL olive oil (or flavored oil)

Salt and pepper

1 Drain tofu on a double thickness of paper towel. Lay a sheet of paper towel on top and press down lightly for a few seconds. Slice tofu across the short side into roughly ½-inch/1-cm slices. Mince garlic. Juice lemon (you will need 1 tablespoon of fresh lemon juice). Preheat oven to 450°F/230°C. Lightly oil a baking sheet or line with parchment paper.

2 Arrange tofu slices in a single layer on baking sheet. In a small bowl, combine garlic, lemon juice, fish sauce, and olive oil. Using a pastry brush, paint the sauce generously over tofu. Season with salt and pepper. Roast tofu for 15–18 minutes.

3 Remove baking sheet from oven, flip tofu slices, and paint with remaining sauce. Roast for a further 8–10 minutes, or until tofu has slightly crusted edges and is warm all the way through.

4 To serve, drizzle with any sauce that has collected in the baking sheet and serve hot or at room temperature. Cover and refrigerate any leftover roasted tofu for up to 3 days.

BUTTERED
BUTTER BEANS

Fun fact about butter beans: they're nothing other than mature lima beans. That's right, the much-loathed bean of many childhood dinners is the pale green baby version of this rich, aptly named buttery bean. Possibly you like them better now? This preparation will work with any white bean, including navy, cannellini, or kidney beans.

1 cup/170 g dried butter beans or 1 can (19 fl oz/540 mL)

1 sprig rosemary or large pinch of herbes de Provence

2 Tbsp butter

1 Tbsp olive oil

Salt and pepper

1 For dried beans, boil for 2 minutes in enough water to cover. Turn off heat and allow beans to soak for 2 hours. Then rinse, drain, and cover with fresh water. Bring to a boil, turn down heat, and simmer for 60–90 minutes. Test beans after 30 minutes. When they become tender, add a teaspoon of salt. Continue to simmer until beans are yielding and soft but not mushy. Drain.

2 If you're using fresh rosemary, pick the leaves and finely chop. If you're using canned beans, rinse and drain them.

3 Melt butter in a pot over medium heat. Add rosemary or herbes de Provence to taste. Stir in beans, crushing some of them with a wooden spoon as you continue to stir until beans are heated through.

4 To serve, divide beans among individual bowls, drizzle with olive oil, and season with salt and pepper.

CHICKPEAS WITH BITTER GREENS

Chickpeas have a mild, slightly nutty flavor that is balanced nicely by bitter greens. If you can find them, dandelion greens make a wonderful change. They are seasonal greens, so we always snap them up when they're available. Asian greens such as bok choi will also work well in this warm salad.

½ cup/55 g slivered almonds

2 carrots

1 lemon

8-10 large handfuls bitter greens (escarole, chicory, and/or frisée)

1 bunch flat-leaf parsley

1 can (14 fl oz/398 mL) chickpeas

7 Tbsp olive oil, divided

½ tsp sweet paprika

2 Tbsp Dijon mustard

Salt and pepper

1 In a dry skillet over medium heat, toast slivered almonds until browned, being careful not to burn them. Grate carrots. Juice lemon. Tear greens into bite-sized pieces. Roughly chop parsley. Rinse chickpeas and drain, then pat dry with paper towel. Preheat oven to 425°F/220°C.

2 Toss chickpeas with 2 tablespoons of olive oil, salt and pepper, and paprika. Arrange in a single layer on a baking sheet and roast for 20 minutes or until crispy on the outside. Set aside to cool.

3 In a small bowl, whisk together the lemon juice, Dijon, 4 tablespoons olive oil, and salt and pepper.

4 In a large pot or Dutch oven, heat remaining olive oil on medium-high until shimmering. Add bitter greens and toss just until wilted. Remove from heat and allow to cool.

5 In a big salad bowl, toss together bitter greens, parsley, chickpeas, carrots, almonds, and vinaigrette. Serve immediately.

CRANBERRY BEAN STEW

Cranberry beans are also known as borlotti beans. They are meaty, reddish-brown beans with the virtues of high fiber, plant protein, and low cost. As with most beans, use canned if that's more convenient for you, but fresh beans have a nuttier flavor and you can control the sodium by deciding how much salt to add during cooking.

MAKES 4 SERVINGS

1 cup/170 g dried cranberry beans or 1 can (19 fl oz/540 mL)

1 onion

3 cloves garlic

1 carrot

1 stalk celery

1 yellow or green zucchini

2 Tbsp olive oil, divided

2 sprigs fresh sage, rosemary, or oregano

1 cup/250 mL Chicken Broth (page 47) or store-bought stock

Salt and pepper

1 For dried beans, boil for 2 minutes in enough water to cover. Turn off heat and allow beans to soak for 2 hours. Then rinse, drain, and cover with fresh water. Bring to a boil, turn down heat, and simmer for 60–90 minutes. Test beans after 30 minutes. When they become tender, add a teaspoon of salt. Continue to simmer until beans are yielding and soft but not mushy. Drain.

2 Dice onion. Mince garlic. Chop carrot, celery, and zucchini.

3 In a large heavy-bottomed skillet or Dutch oven, heat 1 tablespoon of olive oil. Add onion, garlic, and carrot. Cook, stirring often, for about 10 minutes or until carrot has started to soften. Add celery and zucchini and cook for another 5 minutes. Add herb sprigs and broth. Taste and season with salt and pepper.

4 Bring to a boil, turn down heat, and simmer, partially covered, for 30 minutes or until vegetables have softened to your liking. Stir in cooked beans and heat for 3–5 minutes just until they are warm. Remove herb sprigs.

5 Serve hot in bowls with a drizzle of olive oil on each serving.

MEDITERRANEAN BAKED BROAD BEANS

This recipe is wonderful as part of a tapas-style meal of several small shared plates. It's a make-ahead recipe that's delicious served hot or cold and will keep well if refrigerated for up to three days. Allow it to warm to room temperature before eating.

MAKES 4 SERVINGS

2 carrots

2 stalks celery

1 leek

1 bunch flat-leaf parsley

1 can (28 fl oz/796 mL) broad beans

½ cup/125 mL olive oil, divided

2 cups/500 mL vegetable broth

1 Tbsp herbes de Provence

1 can (14 fl oz/398 mL) diced tomatoes

Salt and pepper

1 Dice carrots and celery. Remove and discard dark green leaves from leek, cut in half lengthwise, and chop, discarding tough end. Roughly chop parsley. Rinse and drain beans. Preheat oven to 300°F/150°C.

2 Add 1 tablespoon of olive oil to a large skillet over medium-high heat. Add carrots, celery, and leek. Cook, stirring occasionally, until leek is translucent and vegetables start to sweat and steam, about 7 minutes. Season generously with salt and pepper. Cook for another minute, then remove from heat.

3 In a saucepan, heat broth until wisps of steam rise, but don't allow it to boil.

4 Transfer vegetables to a wide, shallow baking dish. Add beans, half of the parsley, and canned tomatoes, and stir. Pour vegetable broth, herbes de Provence, and remaining olive oil over the mixture.

5 Place baking dish in the oven, and cook uncovered for about 3 hours or until liquid is quite thick. It will thicken more as it cools. Stir in remaining parsley and serve.

BEANS, GREENS, AND TOMATOES WITH BROWN BUTTER

Browned butter is an easy "secret" ingredient to enrich and add depth of flavor any time you would use olive oil. You can mix it with a little Dijon mustard and fresh lemon juice to make a dressing, or just spoon it over the simplest ingredients. Once you've tried brown butter, you'll use it all the time as a finishing touch for vegetables. Try it on steamed kale or broccoli; it's transformational! Leftover brown butter will keep refrigerated in an airtight container for weeks, as does ghee or clarified butter.

MAKES 4 SERVINGS

1 can (19 fl oz/540 mL) cannellini beans

2 cups/500 mL grape or cherry tomatoes

6 large handfuls arugula, chard, dandelion, or beet greens

½ cup/112 g (1 stick) salted butter

Salt and pepper

1 Rinse and drain beans. Halve tomatoes. Rinse greens and spin or pat dry.

2 In a small heavy-bottomed pot, warm butter over medium-low heat. Butter will bubble up, but don't let it overflow. Skim foam every so often and swirl butter to brown evenly. Milk solids will fall to the bottom, foam will rise to the top, and the liquid in between will turn dark brown. This process takes 5–8 minutes, depending on the butter you're using. Skim any remaining foam from the top.

3 To serve, divide greens among four bowls or plates. Distribute tomatoes and beans over greens. Spoon two or three table-spoons of the liquid brown butter over each serving. Season with more salt, if you like, and pepper. Serve immediately, before butter cools.

TOFU SCRAMBLE
*See recipe
on page 126*

*See photo
on pages 124–5*

This scramble is not so much a
stand-in for eggs as proof of tofu's
versatility. Firm tofu is mild and
absorbent with a springy texture,
and it adapts well to different
flavors. A few suggestions are
below. Always cook the vegetables
first, adding tofu for a few minutes
just to heat it through. Leave tofu
too long and you'll have a rubbery,
watery scramble.

TOFU SCRAMBLE

MAKES 4 SERVINGS

1 lb/450 g firm tofu
1 large or 2 small shallots
1 large bunch spinach
¼ lb/112 g mushrooms
2 sprigs fresh tarragon or
   1 tsp dried
1–2 Tbsp olive oil
Salt and pepper

1 Drain tofu on a double thickness of paper towel. Lay a sheet
of paper towel on top and press down lightly for a few seconds
to press out and absorb any moisture. Break up tofu with a
fork into bite-sized chunks—or whatever size you like. Mince
shallots. Roughly chop spinach. Slice mushrooms. Pick leaves
from fresh tarragon, if using, and chop.

2 In a large wide skillet, heat 1 tablespoon of olive oil. Sauté
shallots for 3–5 minutes until translucent but not browning.
Stir in spinach and mushrooms. Cook, stirring for another
3 minutes or until mushrooms have released their water and
it has evaporated.

3 Add another drizzle of olive oil if mixture is drying out. Stir
in tofu with tarragon. Continue to stir for 2–3 minutes or
until tofu is heated through. Season with salt and pepper.

4 To serve, divide among individual plates and serve hot.

**Here are some alternatives to spinach, mushrooms,
and tarragon:**
- Diced red bell pepper, diced fresh tomatoes, and chili powder
- Frozen peas, chickpeas, and curry powder
- Sliced baby bok choi, grated fresh ginger, and tamari

RED AND WHITE BEAN CHILI

This meatless recipe is classic and versatile. Add another can of tomatoes, adjust the seasoning, and you have bean soup. Add a small handful of quinoa to make it more like a stew. If you prefer less heat, omit the chilies in adobo. Like it spicy? Use all of them! This chili works well over Cauliflower Rice (page 88). Serve with any or all of the classic accompaniments suggested below.

MAKES 4 SERVINGS

1 yellow onion
1 red bell pepper
3 cloves garlic
2–4 chilies in adobo (optional)
1 can (14 fl oz/398 mL) cannellini beans
1 can (14 fl oz/398 mL) red kidney beans
2 Tbsp olive oil
2 Tbsp tomato paste
1 Tbsp chili powder
1 tsp ground cumin
1 tsp ground coriander
1 can (19 fl oz/540 mL) diced tomatoes
Salt and pepper
Grated cheese, sour cream, hot sauce, fresh cilantro, guacamole, avocado slices, for serving

1 Dice onion. Chop bell pepper. Mince garlic. Finely chop chilies in adobo, if using. Rinse and drain cannellini and kidney beans.

2 In a large heavy-bottomed pot, warm olive oil over medium heat. Stir in onion, bell pepper, garlic, and chilies, if using. Continue to cook, stirring occasionally, until onion is translucent and has softened and browned, about 5 minutes. Stir in tomato paste and cook for about 30 seconds.

3 Add cannellini and kidney beans with chili powder, cumin, and coriander. Stir in tomatoes with their liquid. Season with salt and pepper.

4 Bring to a boil, then turn down heat, and simmer, uncovered, for 45 minutes. If chili seems too dry, add water by the half cup (125 mL) until desired consistency is reached.

5 To serve, divide into bowls and top with grated cheese, sour cream, hot sauce, chopped cilantro, guacamole, and/or avocado slices.

FISH & SHELLFISH

POACHED WHITEFISH WITH GREMOLATA

Traditional gremolata is made without olive oil, but here it helps to create more of a sauce-like consistency that's easier to spoon over the fish. Sole or cod work well in this recipe, but any sturdy whitefish will benefit from the oven-poaching method, which prevents the fish from drying out and makes a scrumptious sauce.

MAKES 8 SERVINGS

1 lemon

8 sprigs flat-leaf parsley

1 clove garlic

1 leek

½ cup/113 g butter

1 cup/250 mL dry white wine

8 fillets whitefish (total weight 4 lb/1.8 kg)

2 Tbsp olive oil

Salt and pepper

1. Zest and juice lemon. Finely chop parsley. Finely grate garlic. Remove and discard dark green leaves from leek. Halve leek lengthwise and slice thinly, discarding the tough end. Preheat oven to 300°F/150°C.

2. In a wide saucepan, add butter and cook leeks on medium heat until they begin to sweat and turn translucent. Season with salt and pepper. Add wine and bring the liquid to a simmer, then remove from heat.

3. Arrange fish fillets in a single layer in a baking dish. Pour in white wine, melted butter, and leeks. Add lemon juice, saving 1 tablespoon for the gremolata. The liquid should come at least halfway up the sides of the fish. If it doesn't, add a bit more wine or water. Cover dish with aluminum foil and place in the oven for 17–20 minutes, or until the thickest part of the fish easily flakes apart with a fork.

4. Make gremolata while fish is poaching. In a bowl, stir together parsley, garlic, lemon zest, reserved lemon juice, and olive oil. Season with salt and pepper.

5. To serve, transfer fish from poaching liquid to a serving platter. Spoon gremolata over fish and serve immediately.

SPEEDY SHEET-PAN FISH SUPPER

If you usually think of chicken for a sheet-pan meal, we suggest you expand the possibilities to include fish. Firm whitefish fillets work well in most one-dish recipes, especially those where you'd use chicken breasts, and fish cooks more quickly than chicken. Make sure the fillets are roughly the same thickness, 1½–2 inches (2.5–4 cm).

MAKES 4 SERVINGS

1 red onion

1 lb/450 g slender green beans

4 Tbsp mayonnaise

4 tsp Dijon mustard

4 fillets (each 6 oz/170 g) haddock, cod, halibut, or swordfish

⅓ cup/30 g sliced almonds

1 lb/450 g cherry or grape tomatoes

2 Tbsp olive oil

Salt and pepper

1 Line a rimmed baking sheet with parchment paper. Cut onion into large chunks. Trim green beans. In a small bowl, combine mayonnaise and Dijon. Preheat oven to 500°F/260°C.

2 Place fish fillets on baking sheet with plenty of space between them. With paper towel, pat fish dry. Brush mayonnaise-mustard mixture over each fillet. Sprinkle with sliced almonds. Season with salt and pepper.

3 In a large bowl, toss green beans, onion, and tomatoes in olive oil to coat. Distribute vegetables around and between fish fillets. Season with salt and pepper. Roast for 10–12 minutes, checking fish after 8 minutes and moving vegetables around so they don't burn. Fish is ready when it flakes easily with a fork.

4 To serve, divide fish and vegetables among individual plates. Serve immediately.

COD WITH BRAZIL NUT CRUST

The spicy nut topping in this recipe is a good choice instead of batter for oven-fried fish. Brazil nuts are among the healthiest nuts, with plenty of healthy natural fats, fiber, and other nutrients. In a food processor, along with sesame seeds, they whir up into a buttery crust in no time. You can make the topping with olive oil instead of butter, but the butter adds a noticeably rich and lovely flavor.

MAKES 4 SERVINGS

⅓ cup/75 g butter

1 cup/135 g Brazil nuts

¼ cup/60 mL sesame seeds

1 Tbsp chickpea flour

1 tsp hot paprika, Cajun seasoning, or chili powder, plus more to taste

4 fillets cod, halibut, or any meaty whitefish (total weight 24 oz/700 g)

Salt and pepper

Lemon wedges, for serving

1 Melt and cool butter. Preheat oven to 450°F/230°C. Lightly oil a baking dish large enough to fit the fish in a single layer.

2 Add Brazil nuts and sesame seeds to a food processor with a spoonful of melted butter. Whir briefly to break up nuts. Add remaining melted butter, chickpea flour, and salt and pepper. Whir again to make a coarse crumble. Don't overprocess; be careful not to make nut butter! Add hot paprika or other spice and stir. Taste and add more spice if you want more heat.

3 Slide fish into oven and bake for 5 minutes. Remove and pat nut mixture equally and evenly over fish fillets. Bake for a further 7–10 minutes or until fish flakes easily.

4 Allow fish to rest for 10 minutes to firm up crust. Serve warm with lemon wedges.

MASALA SALMON

MAKES 4 SERVINGS

Garam masala is a delicious mixture of spices, herbs, and chilies associated with Indian cuisine. It's a warming, aromatic, slightly sweet spice blend that goes wonderfully with just about anything you may be eating. It makes an unexpected finishing seasoning; just use it as you would a final sprinkling of salt. Be bold and make your own garam masala with this easy recipe.

GARAM MASALA

1-inch/2.5-cm piece cinnamon stick

1 bay leaf

¼ cup/60 mL coriander seeds

¼ cup/60 mL cumin seeds

1 Tbsp green cardamom pods

1 Tbsp black peppercorns

2 tsp whole cloves

1 dried chili pepper

½ tsp grated nutmeg

Pinch of ground mace

MASALA SALMON

2 Tbsp butter

4 fillets salmon (total weight 24 oz/700 g), skin on if you prefer

4 Tbsp Garam Masala (above) or store-bought

Salt and pepper

GARAM MASALA

1 In a dry skillet over medium-high heat, toast cinnamon, bay leaf, coriander seeds, cumin seeds, cardamom pods, black peppercorns, cloves, and chili for 2–3 minutes or until spices are fragrant and starting to brown.

2 Scrape toasted spices into a spice grinder or clean (!) coffee grinder. Add nutmeg and mace. Grind to a fine powder. Garam masala will keep in an airtight glass container for up to 3 months, but it's better used as soon as possible so spices retain their aroma.

MASALA SALMON

1 Melt and cool butter. Preheat oven to 450°F/230°C. With melted butter, lightly brush a baking dish large enough to hold the salmon fillets in a single layer.

2 Place salmon fillets in baking dish, skin side down, if skin on. Brush with remaining melted butter and season with salt and pepper. Bake for 5 minutes, remove, and sprinkle each fillet with a tablespoon of garam masala. Return to oven and bake for a further 5–7 minutes until center of each salmon fillet is still deep pink.

3 To serve, plate while salmon is still warm.

SALMON WITH ANTIPASTO TOPPING

The big, briny Mediterranean flavors in this quick and easy antipasto amplify the rich taste of salmon. If you're cooking for those who don't enjoy brined food, simply omit the antipasto and finish the salmon with a drizzle of vinaigrette and some lemon zest. If crisping up the salmon skin feels too fussy, don't worry about doing it; the salmon will still be delicious.

MAKES 4 SERVINGS

1 jar (6 oz/170 mL) artichoke hearts in olive oil

6 oz/170 mL pickled mushrooms

6 oz/170 mL black or green olives, not canned

1 lemon

4 anchovies

2 Tbsp capers

⅓ cup/80 mL Dijon Vinaigrette (page 68)

2 Tbsp olive oil, divided

4 fillets salmon (total weight 2 lb/900 g), skin on

Salt and pepper

1 Drain and coarsely chop artichoke hearts, pickled mushrooms, and olives. Zest and juice lemon. Chop anchovies.

2 In a nonreactive bowl, toss vegetables, anchovies, capers, and Dijon vinaigrette with 1 tablespoon of olive oil and 1 tablespoon of lemon juice. Set aside to allow flavors to blend while you cook the salmon.

3 Turn on oven broiler. Line a baking sheet with parchment or a silicone pad. Brush salmon with 1 tablespoon of olive oil and season with salt and pepper. Arrange fish on baking sheet and broil for 8–10 minutes, depending on the thickness. Salmon should still be translucent pink in the middle, not opaque.

4 Transfer salmon to individual plates, leaving salmon skins on baking sheet. Return baking sheet to oven to crisp up skins, about 3 minutes. Remove from oven and slice finely.

5 To serve, spoon antipasto over the individual salmon fillets, then scatter crisp salmon skin and lemon zest over top.

SALMON GRAVLAX

Curing salmon at home takes time—three days, in fact—but yields a tender, mild result that's perfect with eggs or atop a sturdy winter salad. Chopped gravlax, folded with dill and some sour cream and served on whole Belgian endive leaves, also makes a beautiful light meal or first course. Gravlax (or *gravadlax*) recipes usually contain granulated sugar. Here, the sugar in a small amount of orange juice does the trick.

MAKES APPROXIMATELY 1½ LB/700 G GRAVLAX

1½ lb/700 g fillets salmon, skin on

1 lemon, plus thin slices for serving

1 bunch dill, plus more for serving

1 tsp juniper berries

2 Tbsp freshly squeezed orange juice

3 Tbsp coarse salt

1 tsp ground white pepper

Sour cream, for serving

1 Pat salmon dry. Zest lemon. Finely chop dill. Line a baking dish with enough plastic wrap to completely envelop and seal the salmon.

2 With a pestle and mortar, combine juniper berries, orange juice, lemon zest, dill, salt, and white pepper. If you don't have a pestle and mortar, grind juniper berries coarsely in a spice grinder or clean (!) coffee grinder first, then combine with orange juice, lemon zest, dill, salt, and white pepper.

3 Arrange salmon in baking dish, skin side down. Rub juniper cure all over salmon. Wrap salmon tightly in plastic, then cover with a small wooden board or plate. Set a couple of cans from your cupboard on top to provide weight.

4 Refrigerate salmon for 24 hours, then turn it over, replace board or plate and cans, and return to refrigerator. Repeat twice more, for a total of 3 days' curing time.

5 To serve salmon, unwrap plastic and brush off and discard excess cure, pat dry, and cut into paper-thin slices. Arrange on a platter with fresh dill, thin slices of lemon, and sour cream.

OLIVE OIL–POACHED TUNA WITH CAPER SALSA

Poaching is a handy technique to keep food moist. If the temperature is low enough and you don't lose track of time, it's difficult to overcook whatever you're poaching. This recipe uses sushi-grade tuna, and you certainly don't want it to be dry and chewy. Don't lose track of time! With its elegant—but optional—caper salsa topping, this dish is dinner-party worthy.

MAKES 4 SERVINGS

CAPER SALSA

4 sprigs flat-leaf parsley
1 clove garlic
½ cup/90 g black olives
2 Tbsp capers
2 tsp red wine vinegar
⅓ cup/80 mL olive oil
Salt and pepper

OLIVE OIL–POACHED TUNA

2 cloves garlic
6 whole black peppercorns
4 sushi-grade tuna steaks (total weight 24 oz/700 g)
3 cups/750 mL olive oil
Salt and pepper
Caper Salsa, for serving (optional)

CAPER SALSA

1 Roughly chop parsley and garlic. Pit and roughly chop olives.

2 Add parsley, garlic, olives, capers, vinegar, and olive oil to a food processor. Season with salt and pepper. Pulse processor to emulsify vinegar and oil. Salsa will keep refrigerated in an airtight container for up to 5 days.

OLIVE OIL-POACHED TUNA

1 Crush garlic. Crack peppercorns coarsely in a spice grinder or with a mortar and pestle. Allow tuna to come to room temperature for 20–30 minutes so steaks are not cold at their center. Season tuna liberally with salt and pepper.

2 In a deep sauté pan large enough to hold tuna steaks in a single layer, warm olive oil over medium heat to 130°F/55°C. Turn down heat to low. Add crushed garlic and peppercorns. Carefully place tuna steaks in oil.

3 Poach tuna for 5 minutes, then turn and baste with oil. Remove from heat and allow fish to cook in warm oil for another 10 minutes. Tuna is ready when the surface is white but the center is still rosy.

4 Serve at room temperature with a spoonful of Caper Salsa, if using, or poaching liquid drizzled over top.

MIXED G(R)ILL

Some of these ocean treasures don't have gills, but who can resist a good foodie pun? This is the simplest possible preparation for fish and shellfish, its appeal relying on variety and quality. If your budget doesn't stretch to sea scallops, use more squid. If sablefish is too rich, use cod. What's important is that the fish you choose is fresh as can be. Frozen shellfish is fine, if that's what's available and affordable.

MAKES 6 SERVINGS

1 lemon

1 bunch dill

½ lb/225 g baby squid

½ lb/225 g sablefish, mackerel, or sea bream fillets

½ lb/225 g cod, haddock, or sea bass fillets

½ lb/225 g sea scallops or shrimp, shelled

2 Tbsp olive oil, divided

Salt and pepper

1 Quarter lemon. Chop dill. Cut tentacles off squid and reserve. Cut squid bodies in half lengthwise. Have ready a platter with a cover.

2 Heat a heavy solid (no holes) grill pan on an outdoor grill or indoor stovetop over medium-high. Warm 1 tablespoon of olive oil. Add lemon quarters, fish fillets, and squid tentacles. Season with salt and pepper. Cook briskly for 2–3 minutes, then turn. Add scallops and squid bodies. Continue to grill for another 2–3 minutes, removing fish as it's ready, keeping it warm on a platter.

3 When all of the fish and shellfish is ready to serve, pour any pan juices over the platter. Squeeze cooked lemon quarters over seafood, drizzle with remaining olive oil, and sprinkle with dill to taste.

4 Serve immediately or at room temperature. This dish doesn't keep well, so best to enjoy it on the day it's made.

SCALLOPS WITH LEMON BUTTER

Elegant and easy to prepare, large sea scallops need careful handling only to avoid overcooking. Otherwise, they are simply delicious, classic fare. Use the heaviest skillet you have and ensure the scallops are well dried before you sear them in butter and olive oil for a few minutes, which is all they require to be firm, sweet, and perfectly cooked.

MAKES 4 SERVINGS

1 lb/450 g sea scallops

1 clove garlic

1 lemon

1 Tbsp butter

3 Tbsp olive oil, divided

⅓ cup/80 mL dry white wine

1 cup/250 mL Chicken Broth (page 47) or store-bought stock

1 Tbsp Dijon mustard

Salt and pepper

1 Pat scallops dry with paper towel. Mince garlic. Zest and then juice lemon. Preheat oven to 200°F/95°C.

2 In a heavy-bottomed skillet large enough to fit scallops in a single layer, melt butter in 2 tablespoons of olive oil over medium heat. Add scallops and season with salt and pepper. Cook without moving scallops for 3 minutes, then turn to cook the other sides. Season again with salt and pepper. Baste frequently with pan sauce for another 1–2 minutes. Transfer to an oven-safe platter, tent loosely with aluminum foil, and keep warm in the oven.

3 To the skillet, add remaining olive oil and garlic. Stir garlic for 1 minute until fragrant, taking care not to burn it or the pan sauce will taste bitter. Pour in wine and cook until reduced by half. Add broth, lemon zest, and 2 tablespoons of lemon juice. Cook for 8–10 minutes or until sauce has reduced by half. Remove from heat and whisk in Dijon.

4 To serve, divide scallops among four individual plates and drizzle with lemon-butter sauce.

SCALLOP CEVICHE

As with the Salmon Gravlax (page 138), citrus juice cures rich sea scallops in this recipe. Allow an hour or two for the citrus to do its work, and be sure to use the freshest scallops you can find. Jalapeños add sharp, spicy notes, and creamy avocado and crunchy cucumber provide wonderful textural contrast. Make the scallop mixture separately from the cucumber relish, combining them at the last minute when you're ready to serve. If you use an English cucumber, the skin is thin and tender enough that you don't need to peel it.

MAKES 4 SMALL SERVINGS

12 sea scallops

3 limes

4 plum tomatoes

1 English cucumber

4 sprigs cilantro

1 avocado

3 jalapeño peppers

1 clove garlic

Salt and pepper

1 Pat scallops dry with paper towel and halve them horizontally. Zest 1 lime and juice all 3 limes. Dice tomatoes. Peel cucumber, if you wish, and dice. Chop cilantro stems and leaves. Cube avocado. Seed and mince jalapeños. Mince garlic.

2 In a small bowl, combine tomatoes, cucumber, cilantro, and 1 teaspoon of lime juice. Season with salt and pepper. Cover and refrigerate while you prepare scallops.

3 In another bowl, combine scallops, avocado, jalapeño, garlic, lime zest, and remaining lime juice. Season with salt and pepper. Cover and refrigerate for at least 1 and up to 2 hours.

4 To serve, spoon a quarter of the relish onto each plate and top with a quarter of the scallop ceviche.

MUSSELS IN CURRY CREAM

Known in France as *moules mouclade*, these tasty shellfish take very well to a little curry powder and cream. This recipe works equally well with coconut cream or dairy; use whichever you prefer. Please discard any mussels that don't close when tapped gently before cooking or open fully during cooking—these are indicators the mussel isn't fresh enough to eat.

MAKES 4 SERVINGS

4 lb/1.8 kg mussels in their shells

2 shallots

3 cloves garlic

½ cup/125 mL dry white wine

4 Tbsp butter

1 tsp curry powder

¾ cup/180 mL 35% cream, crème fraîche, or coconut cream

Salt and pepper

1 Scrub and debeard mussels. Tap them to confirm they close up tight. Discard any that do not. Mince shallots. Mince garlic.

2 In a large pot with a lid, bring white wine and 2 tablespoons of cold water to a boil. Tip in mussels, cover, and cook for 3–5 minutes. Shake the pan every so often to cook mussels evenly. Remove from heat and discard any unopened mussels. Drain mussels in a colander over a bowl to catch cooking liquid. Wipe out pan, being sure to clean away any grit settled at the bottom.

3 In same pan, melt butter over medium-low heat. Add shallots, garlic, and curry powder. Cook for 3 minutes or until shallots are translucent. Don't allow vegetables to color. Pour reserved cooking liquid back into pan. Bring to boil, then turn down heat, stir in cream, and simmer for 2 minutes. Taste and adjust seasoning with salt and pepper. Remove from heat.

4 Still off the heat, tip mussels back into curry cream sauce to warm them through. Serve right away, with spoons to catch every drop of the delicious sauce.

SPICY GARLIC SHRIMP

Eating these spicy shrimp can get a little messy, so it may not be your first choice of dishes to serve to new acquaintances. On the other hand, it's fun and informal to eat with your fingers, and this recipe could be the perfect icebreaker! Have little finger bowls of warm water with slices of floating lemon for anyone who would prefer not to lick their fingers at the table. Serve with a simple green salad.

MAKES 4 SERVINGS

4 cloves garlic

1 lemon

2 bird's eye chilies

4 sprigs flat-leaf parsley

2 Tbsp olive oil

1 Tbsp butter

2 lb/900 g large shrimp with shells, easy-peel are fine

Salt and pepper

1. Mince garlic. Juice half the lemon and slice the other half for finger bowls. Very finely slice chilies. Chop parsley leaves.

2. Warm olive oil and butter over medium heat in a large heavy-bottomed skillet. Stir in two-thirds of the garlic and the chilies. Stir for 1 minute, just until fragrant. Be careful not to burn the garlic.

3. Add shrimp and sauté for 3–5 minutes, depending on size. Shrimp will become opaque and tails will curl into a C-shape when they're ready. Season with salt and pepper. Baste often with buttery, garlicky, spicy pan juices.

4. Serve on a platter, garnished with chopped parsley. Don't forget a bowl for shells and individual finger bowls for your guests.

LOUISIANA GUMBO

Let's get ahead of purists by calling out what isn't authentic about this gumbo: it isn't thickened with a traditional flour-based roux. But that's okay! Here, we use chickpea flour and okra to thicken the stew. If you can find some andouille sausage, you'll enjoy this spicy, slightly unconventional version that's close to the original. Try it over Cauliflower Rice (page 88).

MAKES 6 SERVINGS

1 stalk celery

1 onion

1 red bell pepper

2 cloves garlic

1 lb/450 g spicy sausage

1 lb/450 g medium shrimp

⅓ cup/80 mL plus 1 Tbsp rendered bacon fat or olive oil, divided

¼ cup/60 mL chickpea flour

4 cups/1 L Chicken Broth (page 47) or store-bought stock

1 Tbsp Cajun seasoning

1 bay leaf

½ lb/225 g frozen chopped or sliced okra

1 can (14 fl oz/398 mL) crushed tomatoes

Salt and pepper

Hot sauce, for serving

1 Chop celery, onion, and bell pepper. Mince garlic. Slice sausages. Remove shells and tails from shrimp.

2 Heat ⅓ cup/80 mL bacon fat or olive oil in a large heavy-bottomed pot over medium heat. Whisk in chickpea flour. Cook this roux, whisking often, for 25–30 minutes or until flour paste has turned deep brown. Season with salt and pepper.

3 While roux is cooking, heat 1 tablespoon of bacon fat or olive oil in a wide skillet over medium-high. Stir in Cajun seasoning, bay leaf, celery, onion, bell pepper, and garlic. Cook, stirring, until vegetables have softened, 7–10 minutes. Remove veggies to a bowl and add sausages. Brown sausages for 3 minutes on each side. Remove sausages to same bowl. Add shrimp to skillet and fry quickly for 2 minutes.

4 Warm broth to a simmer. Whisk 1 cup/250 mL of broth into the roux until smooth. Then add remaining broth, stirring to ensure no lumps form. Heat until the mixture begins to bubble throughout.

5 Add okra, browned vegetables, sausage, and shrimp to bubbling roux. Stir in tomatoes. Taste and adjust seasoning with salt and pepper and Cajun spices. Cook for 30 minutes at a steady simmer.

6 Divide into bowls and serve with plenty of hot sauce.

POULTRY

ASIAN CHICKEN LETTUCE WRAPS

These lettuce wraps are fresh and bright, with an umami kick from fish sauce that is difficult to identify but makes such a difference. Look for fish sauce in any major grocery store or find it in an Asian specialty market. You can easily substitute the ground chicken with ground pork, ground beef, or a mixture of the two.

MAKES 6-8 LETTUCE WRAPS

1 small red onion
½ cucumber
2 cloves garlic
1 bunch cilantro
1 bunch mint
1 lime
2 Tbsp rice wine vinegar
1 tsp olive oil
1 lb/450 g ground chicken
½ tsp chili flakes
2 tsp fish sauce
6-8 Boston lettuce leaves
Salt and pepper

1. Thinly slice red onion into half-moons. Cut cucumber into matchsticks (julienne). Peel and grate garlic. Roughly chop cilantro and mint. Cut lime into wedges.

2. In a shallow bowl, stir the onion with the rice wine vinegar, and season with salt. Allow to marinate for at least 20 minutes, then toss in the cucumber.

3. While onion and cucumber are marinating, heat olive oil in a skillet over medium-high. Add ground chicken, garlic, salt and pepper, and chili flakes. Turn down heat to medium and stir until chicken is cooked through, about 12 minutes. Remove from heat, stir in fish sauce, and set aside to cool.

4. To assemble lettuce wraps, arrange lettuce leaves on a plate. Spoon some onion and cucumber mixture into the curve of each lettuce leaf, as if you were filling a bowl. Spoon ground meat on top. Sprinkle with chopped herbs and add a generous squeeze of lime juice.

5. To eat, roll the lettuce around the filling with your fingers, trying your best to seal up the ends. Fun and delicious—please pass the napkins!

CHICKEN WINGS WITH HOT SAUCE

If you're not a fan of spicy food, the hot-sauce bath at the end of cooking these wings is optional. You could serve it as a dip instead of coating the crispy wings. Crudités with Dips (page 107) makes a perfect accompaniment for an informal finger-food meal, especially the Blue Cheese Dip. Both the wings and the sauce recipes double easily, as do the dips with the crudités.

MAKES 4 SERVINGS

2 lb/900 g chicken wings
⅓ cup/80 mL hot sauce
1 Tbsp butter
1 tsp Worcestershire sauce
1 tsp white wine vinegar
Salt and pepper

1 If chicken wings are attached, separate them into drumettes and wingettes. Line a baking sheet with paper towel.

2 Bring a large pot of salted water to a boil. Add chicken wings and turn down heat to a simmer. Parboil wings for 10 minutes. Drain wings in a colander, then spread them out on baking sheet. Allow any remaining moisture to evaporate and wings to cool, about 15 minutes. Pat dry thoroughly with paper towel before cooking.

3 Preheat oven to 450°F/230°C. When wings are completely dry, arrange them in a single layer on the unlined baking sheet. Bake for 10–12 minutes. Turn wings when undersides are nicely brown and bake for another 10–12 minutes or until wings are brown and crisp.

4 While wings are baking, combine butter, hot sauce, Worcestershire sauce, vinegar, and salt and pepper in a small saucepan over medium heat. Stir until butter melts, then remove from heat.

5 In a large bowl, toss wings with hot sauce. Serve hot or at room temperature.

RED WINE VINEGAR-BRAISED CHICKEN THIGHS

This classic preparation is akin to *coq au vin*, but with red wine vinegar in place of the red wine. The onions are allowed to cook slowly to bring out their natural sugar, which is balanced by the red wine vinegar sauce. Be patient as you soften the onions and brown the chicken; the delicious cooked pieces you scrape up when you deglaze the pan give the finished dish deep flavor.

MAKES 4 SERVINGS

½ small onion

½ lb/225 g pancetta

2 cloves garlic

2 Tbsp olive oil

2 lb/900 g chicken thighs, skin on and bones in

¾ cup/180 mL red wine vinegar

1 cup/250 mL Chicken Broth (page 47) or store-bought stock

1 bay leaf

Salt and pepper

1 Slice onion into very thin half-moons (you should have about ½ cup/125 mL onion). Dice pancetta. Slice garlic.

2 In a large heavy-bottomed pot, warm olive oil over medium heat. Fry pancetta with onion gently until onion is soft and brown, 20–25 minutes. Remove and reserve.

3 Season chicken generously with salt and pepper. Brown chicken, skin side down, for 12–15 minutes, turning after 7 minutes to cook undersides. Stir in garlic for a few seconds. Remove chicken and garlic and reserve with onion and pancetta.

4 Deglaze pot with red wine vinegar, using a wooden spoon to lift brown bits (fond). Add chicken broth, bay leaf, onion, pancetta, chicken, and garlic. Bring to a boil, turn down heat to a simmer, and cook for 30–35 minutes until chicken is tender.

5 To serve, divide chicken among individual plates and spoon pan juices over top.

CHICKEN THIGHS WITH SPROUTS AND SQUASH

A classic combination of dark chicken meat with sturdy, satisfying vegetables. Many chicken sheet-pan or tray-bake recipes call for honey, maple syrup, or brown sugar for sweetening, but added sugar isn't necessary! Brussels sprouts and butternut squash caramelize lightly in the high roasting temperature at the beginning of this recipe, then cook to a flavorful deep brown by the time you're ready to serve.

MAKES 4–6 SERVINGS

1 lb/450 g Brussels sprouts

1 lb/450 g butternut squash

1 onion

4 cloves garlic

1 lemon

4 Tbsp olive oil, divided

2 Tbsp apple cider vinegar

1 tsp cayenne pepper

2 tsp paprika

8 chicken thighs, skin on and bones in

Salt and pepper

1 Trim and halve Brussels sprouts. Peel and chop squash into chunks. Cut onion into wedges. Mince garlic. Slice lemon thinly. Preheat oven to 450°F/230°C. Using 1 tablespoon of the olive oil, brush a roasting pan large enough to hold (just about) everything in one layer.

2 In a large bowl, combine sprouts, squash, onion, garlic, and lemon slices with 1 tablespoon of olive oil. Season with salt and pepper. Transfer to roasting pan and roast veggies in oven for 10 minutes.

3 While vegetables are roasting, combine remaining olive oil with apple cider vinegar, cayenne, paprika, and salt and pepper. Coat chicken with olive oil–vinegar mixture. Turn down the oven to 400°F/200°C. Place chicken atop veggies and roast for a further 35–40 minutes until juices run clear when chicken is pierced close to the bone.

4 To serve, divide chicken and vegetables among individual plates and spoon pan juices over top.

CHICKEN WITH FORTY CLOVES OF GARLIC

Forty cloves seems like a lot of garlic, yes. But this classic French recipe makes a rich and savory sauce that is not too pungent or overwhelming. Although many cooks leave the garlic skins on, it's better to remove them to avoid weird floating wisps in the sauce and make the garlic easier to mash. There's no need for precision in counting: use anywhere from forty to one hundred garlic cloves without adverse effect. An enameled cast-iron pot is perfect for this dish, if you have one.

MAKES 4–6 SERVINGS

3 heads garlic

4 sprigs tarragon

4 chicken legs with thighs attached (total weight 4 lb/1.8 kg)

2 Tbsp olive oil

½ cup/125 mL white vermouth

1 cup/250 mL Chicken Broth (page 47) or store-bought stock

Salt and pepper

1 Use the bottom of a little pot or frying pan to lightly and sharply break open garlic heads. Use the flat side of a large knife to crush garlic lightly, splitting the skin and making it easy to peel. Peel garlic. Chop tarragon leaves.

2 Season chicken with salt and pepper. Warm olive oil in a heavy-bottomed oven-safe pot over medium heat. Brown chicken for 12–15 minutes, flipping chicken after 7 minutes to brown undersides. Transfer chicken to a platter to rest.

3 Add garlic cloves to pan juices and cook, stirring, for 5–7 minutes or until golden brown. Transfer about one-third of the garlic to platter with chicken.

4 Stir vermouth into pot, stirring up brown bits. Add chicken broth and bring to boil. Turn down heat to a simmer. Mash garlic into sauce. Return reserved chicken and garlic to pot and baste with pan sauce.

5 Preheat oven to 350°F/180°C. Place the pot in the oven, cover, and bake for 25–30 minutes or until a meat thermometer inserted in the thigh reads 165°F/74°C.

6 To serve, divide chicken among individual plates, spoon pan juices over top, and sprinkle with tarragon.

CHICKEN FRICASSEE

Chef and cookbook author Julia Child described a fricassee as "something between a sauté and a stew." The chicken is cooked first in fat, sometimes but not always browned, then braised. Really, the distinction isn't crucial for us home cooks. We do like the idea of leaving this dish blond for its lighter appearance and flavor. If you agree, be careful not to allow the vegetables or chicken to brown when you are parcooking. If you prefer deep browning, go for it.

MAKES 4 SERVINGS

1 onion

3 lb/1.3 kg chicken pieces, skin on and bones in

2 Tbsp olive oil

1 Tbsp butter

1 cup/250 mL crisp white wine

2 cups/500 mL Chicken Broth (page 47) or store-bought stock

4 sprigs tarragon

1 bay leaf

½ cup/125 mL 35% cream

Salt and pepper

1 Dice onion. Season chicken with salt and pepper. Warm olive oil and butter in a heavy-bottomed oven-safe pot over medium-low heat. Sauté onion for 10 minutes or until it is translucent and soft. Watch carefully to prevent browning and reduce heat, if necessary. Transfer cooked onion to a platter and reserve.

2 In the same pot, gently sauté chicken in batches, 10–12 minutes for each batch. You don't want to crowd the chicken or it will steam and become rubbery. Transfer cooked chicken to the platter with the onions.

3 Add wine to the pot, increase heat to medium, and cook for 5–7 minutes or until wine has reduced by half. Add chicken broth, tarragon, and bay leaf. Return onion and chicken to pot and simmer uncovered for 30–35 minutes, watching carefully to ensure liquid doesn't boil. When chicken is tender, remove to a serving platter. Remove and discard chicken skin, if you wish. Remove bay leaf and tarragon from pot.

4 Add cream to the pot and simmer for a couple of minutes to thicken sauce slightly. To serve, ladle cream sauce over the chicken.

PIRI PIRI CHICKEN
*See recipe
on page 160*

*See photo
on pages 158–9*

Make your own piri piri sauce. The traditional Portuguese preparation would use port, which is high in sugar, as are most fortified wines. Using Scotch whisky gives depth to the basting sauce without adding sugar. Of course, you can buy commercially prepared piri piri sauce and thin it with lemon juice and olive oil. That's not as much fun, though. This chicken dish is perfect served with a simple tomato and cucumber salad sprinkled with chopped flat-leaf parsley.

PIRI PIRI CHICKEN

MAKES 4 SERVINGS

2 lemons

6 cloves garlic, divided

1 tsp oregano

1 tsp smoked paprika

8 chicken thighs, skin on and bones in

6 dried piri piri chilies or 3 fresh bird's eye chilies

3 Tbsp butter

2 Tbsp olive oil

4 Tbsp Scotch whisky

Salt and pepper

1. Juice lemons, reserving squeezed halves. Chop 3 garlic cloves.

2. In a large bowl, combine juice of 1 lemon, lemon halves, 3 cloves of chopped garlic, oregano, and paprika. Season chicken with salt and pepper, add to the marinade, cover, and refrigerate for 30 minutes and up to 2 hours.

3. In a food processor, pulse remaining garlic with chilies to form a chunky paste. In a small heavy-bottomed saucepan, warm butter with olive oil. Add chili paste and stir for a minute or two until fragrant. Add juice of 1 lemon and whisky. Season with salt and pepper. Stir well. Allow sauce to simmer (frequent small bubbles) for 5 minutes to reduce slightly and to cook off the alcohol.

4. Heat a grill pan or outdoor grill to medium-high. Remove chicken thighs from marinade and grill, turning and basting frequently with piri piri sauce, for 25–35 minutes or until juices run clear when chicken is pierced with the tip of a knife.

5. Allow cooked chicken to rest at room temperature for at least 30 minutes before serving. The piri piri flavor becomes more pronounced as the temperature of the chicken drops.

6. To serve, divide chicken among individual plates.

ROASTED FLATTENED CHICKEN

You may have noticed a proliferation of packaged flat whole chickens in your local grocery or butcher shop. Also known as *spatchcocked* or *butterflied*, chickens split down the middle and opened up this way cook more quickly and evenly. Food writer Melissa Clark has introduced *splayed* chicken, which opens up the leg joints while preserving the breast cavity to fill with flavorings such as the lemon used here. Splayed chicken cooks quickly and stays moist and juicy.

MAKES 4 SERVINGS

1 whole chicken (total weight 4 lb/1.8 kg)
1 lemon
1 Tbsp olive oil
1 Tbsp butter
Salt and pepper

1 To splay chicken, place it on a work surface. Cut the skin connecting the legs to the body. Push down on chicken thighs to dislocate leg joints. You'll feel them pop out. Good work! Halve lemon. Preheat oven to 450°F/230°C. Brush a roasting pan or baking dish with olive oil.

2 Place chicken flat in roasting pan or baking dish. Squeeze juice from lemon halves into cavity, then add squeezed lemon halves. Using your hands, rub butter all over chicken skin. Season chicken inside and out with salt and pepper. Make sure legs are resting flat.

3 Roast chicken, basting every 10 minutes or so with pan juices, for 45–50 minutes or until a meat thermometer inserted in the thigh reads 165°F/74°C. Allow chicken to rest for 5 minutes before carving.

4 To serve, remove chicken breasts and slice. Remove legs and separate into thighs and drumsticks. Arrange chicken on a platter, spoon pan juices over top, and serve.

STIR-FRIED CHICKEN AND VEGGIES

The cornstarch in most stir-fry recipes just makes the sauce shiny and slightly thicker. That's it. You don't need it to make a speedy, yummy one-pot meal. Change up the vegetables in this recipe according to your preference and the contents of your fridge. Just be sure to cut the veggies small enough that they cook in a couple of minutes. Serve this dish with Cauliflower Rice (page 88).

MAKES 4 SERVINGS

3 cloves garlic

1-inch/2.5-cm piece fresh ginger

2 green onions

1 lb/450 g skinless, boneless chicken breast

½ lb/225 g mushrooms

2 carrots

2 stalks celery

1 tsp chili oil

4 Tbsp tamari

2 Tbsp ghee

½ cup/73 g cashew or peanut pieces

1 Tbsp toasted sesame oil

1 Mince garlic. Grate ginger. Slice green onions, separating whites from green tops. Slice chicken into thin strips. Slice mushrooms. Slice carrots on the bias as thinly as you can. Slice celery.

2 In a small bowl, combine chili oil, garlic, ginger, the white parts of the onion, tamari, and ½ cup/125 mL cold water. Set this sauce aside.

3 Heat ghee in a wok or wide-bottomed skillet over medium-high. Stir-fry chicken for 5 minutes. Remove and reserve. Stir-fry cashew or peanut pieces for 1 minute. Reserve separately from chicken.

4 Add sesame oil to wok or skillet. Stir-fry vegetables for 5 minutes. Add reserved stir-fry sauce, then return chicken to wok or skillet. Cook, stirring, for 5 minutes or until vegetables are tender-crisp.

5 To serve, divide among individual bowls and top with cashews or peanuts and green onions. Serve immediately.

TURKEY SCALLOPINI

Turkey cutlets are generally white meat, which means they cook quickly and take well to other flavors. You can use turkey in place of veal or chicken for any scallopini recipe. The relative leanness of these baked crunchy cutlets makes for a good culinary pairing with rich Creamed Spinach (page 90) or a simple spinach salad.

MAKES 4-6 SERVINGS

1 egg

¼ cup/60 mL almond flour

½ cup/45 g grated Parmesan cheese

2 tsp dried Italian seasoning or dried oregano

1 Tbsp olive oil

4-6 turkey cutlets (total weight 1-1½ lb/ 450-700 g)

Salt and pepper

1 In a bowl large enough to dip cutlets, beat egg with 1 tablespoon of cold water. In another bowl large enough to dip cutlets, combine almond flour, Parmesan, Italian seasoning or oregano, and salt and pepper. Preheat oven to 375°F/190°C. Lightly oil a baking sheet with olive oil.

2 One at a time, dip turkey cutlets in egg wash, then in seasoned flour mixture. Arrange in a single layer on baking sheet. Sprinkle another spoonful of seasoned flour on each cutlet, if there is any left over.

3 Bake for 10 minutes, then flip and bake for another 8 minutes or until cutlets are no longer pink in the middle. Use a sharp knife to cut into one and check.

4 Serve hot or at room temperature. Best eaten the day you make them.

TURKEY MEATBALLS

The addition of zucchini to these meatballs is not a stealthy approach to get you to eat more vegetables; it's a tactic to keep the ground turkey from drying out. Turkey is wonderfully flavorful but it tends to be lean. Zucchini's moisture, sealed in with some butter, keeps these meatballs tender and juicy. Serve with your favorite tomato sauce.

MAKES 20-24 MEATBALLS

1 onion

1 clove garlic

2 sprigs flat-leaf parsley

1 zucchini

1 Tbsp butter

2 lb/900 g ground turkey

1 Tbsp coconut flour or almond flour

Salt and pepper

1 Finely chop onion. Mince garlic. Finely chop parsley. Shred zucchini. Melt butter. Preheat oven to 400°F/200°C. Line a rimmed baking sheet with parchment paper.

2 In a large bowl, gently combine turkey with onion, garlic, parsley, zucchini, nut flour, and melted butter. Season with salt and pepper.

3 Gently but quickly roll turkey into walnut-sized balls, arranging them in a single layer on baking sheet. Bake meatballs for 25–30 minutes or until internal temperature is 165°F/74°C.

4 To serve, divide meatballs among individual plates. Leftover cooked meatballs will keep, covered and refrigerated, for 2 days. Steaming is the best method for reheating.

TURKEY BREAST STUFFED WITH GRUYÈRE

This preparation is elegant enough for special occasions but easy enough that you could make it on any weekend throughout the year. Don't worry too much about perfectly rolling and tying the turkey. You can help to secure it with wooden skewers, presoaked in warm water for 30 minutes. If you're worried about visual appeal, check out online videos on ways to tie a roast.

MAKES 6–8 SERVINGS

1 onion

4 large handfuls spinach

½ lb/225 g Gruyère

1 Tbsp butter

3 lb/1.3 kg skinless, boneless turkey breast

1 Tbsp olive oil

Pinch of ground nutmeg

Salt and pepper

1 Mince onion. Chop spinach. Grate Gruyère. Melt butter. Cut horizontally most of the way through turkey, then open the halves like a book. With the bottom of a heavy skillet or a rolling pin, and using wax paper, pound turkey to ½-inch/1-cm thickness. Have ready some kitchen twine and wooden skewers. Preheat oven to 400°F/200°C.

2 In a large skillet, warm olive oil over medium-high heat. Cook onion for 3–5 minutes or until translucent and softened. Add spinach by the handful, cooking it down before adding more. When all spinach has wilted, season with nutmeg and salt and pepper.

3 Spread spinach mixture evenly over butterflied turkey, leaving a 1-inch/2.5-cm border on all sides. Sprinkle cheese over spinach. Roll turkey as tightly as you can, then tie with kitchen twine and secure with wooden skewers. Brush turkey with melted butter. Season with salt and pepper.

4 Place turkey roll in roasting pan or baking dish and roast for 20 minutes. Turn down the oven to 325°F/163°C and continue to roast for 20 minutes more. Turkey should reach an internal temperature of 165°F/74°C. Remove from oven, tent loosely with aluminum foil, and allow to rest for 10 minutes.

5 To serve, carve into thick slices (thinner slices may fall apart) and arrange on plates.

BISON BURGERS

These burgers are fabulous with a ripe red tomato salad. If bison meat isn't available to you, ground beef will also work. But do try bison if you can get it. The taste is wonderful, much like an intense version of beef. Because bison are usually raised without growth hormones or antibiotics, you benefit from the absence of these unwanted additives. This mix also makes yummy meatballs.

MAKES 4 BURGERS

1 small onion

2 sprigs sage

2 Tbsp olive oil, divided, plus more to dress arugula

1¼ lb/565 g ground bison (buffalo)

Salt and pepper

⅓ cup/80 mL mayonnaise, for serving (optional)

1 Tbsp hot sauce, for serving (optional)

4 handfuls peppery arugula (optional)

1 Dice onion. Pick sage leaves and slice; discard stalks.

2 Heat 1 tablespoon of olive oil in a heavy skillet over medium heat. Sauté onion for 10–12 minutes or until deep brown and starting to caramelize. Transfer onion to a plate and allow to cool completely.

3 In a large bowl, combine bison, onion, sage, and salt and pepper. Use your fingertips to gently combine burger ingredients. Don't compress or overwork the meat or burgers will be tough.

4 In the skillet used to sauté onions or a grill pan, heat 1 tablespoon of olive oil. Cook burgers for 7 minutes, then flip and cook for 5 minutes for medium-rare. Remove from heat, tent loosely with aluminum foil, and allow to rest for 5–10 minutes.

5 In a small bowl, stir together mayonnaise and hot sauce, if using.

6 To serve, mound some arugula, if using, on plates. Drizzle with olive oil and season with salt and pepper. Top with burgers. Dollop burgers with spicy mayo and serve.

CLASSIC BOWL O' RED

People get passionate about what should or should *not* be included in their chili—or as chili con carne is known in Texas, bowl o' red. Cubed or ground beef? Kidney beans or black beans or no beans? Chili flakes or chili powder or both? My beloved gave me the tip to use strong brewed coffee in chili . . . and to leave the canned tomatoes for making spaghetti sauce. I tried chili with coffee and *sans* tomatoes, and I love it. Is this a new classic? Top with your favorite accompaniments.

MAKES 4 SERVINGS

2 onions

4 cloves garlic

1 red bell pepper

3 whole chipotles in adobo

1 can (19 oz/540 g) red kidney beans

2-3 Tbsp olive oil

3 Tbsp tomato paste

1 lb/450 g ground beef

2 Tbsp chipotle chili powder or Mexican chili powder

1 Tbsp ground cumin

2 cups/500 mL Beef Bone Broth (page 46) or good-quality store-bought stock

1 cup/250 mL brewed strong coffee

Salt and pepper

continued overleaf...

1 Dice onions. Chop garlic. Seed and chop bell pepper. Chop chipotle chilies, reserving their adobo sauce. Drain and rinse kidney beans, discarding liquid.

2 In a large heavy-bottomed pot, warm 2 tablespoons of olive oil over medium heat. Cook onions, garlic, and bell pepper, stirring frequently for 5–7 minutes or until onions are translucent and peppers have softened. Season with salt and pepper. Stir in tomato paste, chilies, and reserved adobo sauce. Cook for about 30 seconds. Transfer vegetables to a bowl and reserve.

3 Increase heat to medium-high, and in the same pot add another tablespoon of olive oil if necessary. Stir in beef, breaking it up as it cooks. Make sure heat is high enough to brown the beef, not steam it. After 10–12 minutes, or when beef is nicely browned, add chili powder and cumin. Stir to toast spices briefly. Season with salt and pepper.

continued overleaf...

Grated cheese,
for serving (optional)

Sliced green onions,
for serving (optional)

Chopped cilantro,
for serving (optional)

Hot sauce, for serving
(optional)

Sour cream or crème
fraîche, for serving
(optional)

4 Turn down heat to medium-low. Return vegetables to pot with beef broth and coffee. Simmer, partially covered, for 30 minutes. Add kidney beans. Taste and adjust seasoning. Cook gently for another 15 minutes. If you want to thin chili, add boiling water a quarter-cup at a time. For thicker chili, cook for longer. Try not to allow the chili to boil as it will lose flavor.

5 To serve, divide chili among individual bowls and allow guests to top with their preferred accompaniments. Traditional choices include grated cheese, sliced green onions, chopped cilantro, hot sauce, and sour cream or crème fraîche—but feel free to get creative.

SPICY ORANGE BEEF

As this dish cooks, heady aromas of garlic, ginger, and orange zest waft around your kitchen and throughout your home. It smells so good that you may be able to entice people to help you in the kitchen—or at least promise to do the dishes afterward. Asparagus Stir-fry (page 96) is a great sidekick for this recipe.

MAKES 4-6 SERVINGS

2 cloves garlic

2-inch/5-cm piece fresh ginger

1 small red chili

3 green onions

1 small navel orange

1½ lb/700 g flank steak

¼ cup/60 mL tamari

1 Tbsp rice wine vinegar

2 Tbsp arrowroot starch

2 Tbsp coconut oil

Salt and pepper

1 Mince garlic. Grate ginger. Slice chili. Slice green onions, separating green and white parts. Zest and juice orange.

2 Slice steak thinly and toss slices in a glass bowl with tamari and vinegar. Allow to marinate for 15 minutes. Drain and discard marinade. Sprinkle steak slices with arrowroot starch to coat, and season with salt and pepper.

3 Heat coconut oil in a large wok or heavy-bottomed skillet over medium-high. Stir-fry beef for 3–5 minutes or until it's done to your preference. Transfer to a plate and set aside.

4 To the skillet, add garlic, ginger, chili, and the white parts of the onion. Sauté for 60–90 seconds. Pour in ¼ cup/60 mL fresh orange juice and 2 teaspoons of orange zest. Allow sauce to bubble and thicken for a couple of minutes, then remove from heat. Add steak to sauce and stir briefly and gently.

5 To serve, divide among individual bowls and top with green onions and a light sprinkle of orange zest.

FLANK STEAK WITH ROQUEFORT SAUCE

Flank steak is a hardworking, muscular cut of beef. It's lean, flavorful, and has a satisfying chewiness. Roquefort is a sharp and rich sheep's milk blue cheese, with acidity to perfectly offset the steak. Roquefort is lively but if you prefer a creamier, deeper flavor, go for a creamy Danish blue or the almighty Stilton.

MAKES 6-8 SERVINGS

¼ cup/60 mL red wine vinegar

¼ cup/60 mL olive oil

2 Tbsp tamari

2 lb/900 g flank steak

4 oz/112 g Roquefort or sharp Danish blue cheese

⅓ cup/80 mL buttermilk

Salt and pepper

1 In a small bowl, combine vinegar, olive oil, tamari, and pepper. Put steak in shallow glass dish large enough to hold it flat and pour marinade over top. Cover with plastic wrap and allow to marinate for 30 minutes at room temperature.

2 Heat grill pan over medium-high. Remove steak from marinade, pat dry, and season with salt and pepper. Discard marinade. Grill steak for 6 minutes, then turn and grill for 4 minutes on second side for medium-rare. Tent loosely with aluminum foil and allow to rest for 10 minutes.

3 While steak is resting, crumble blue cheese into a small bowl. Add buttermilk and, using a fork, roughly mash cheese with the buttermilk, leaving some discernible cheese crumbles.

4 To serve, slice steak thinly, divide among plates, and spoon blue cheese sauce over top.

HOT TIP ROAST BEEF

This is more of a method than a recipe, but you'll turn to it again and again once you've tried it. It's a great strategy to turn an economical cut of meat into a juicy and tender indulgence, and with such minimal effort you'll have time to do other things. Pair this roast beef with Panfried Kale with Chili (page 95) or Open Sesame Broccoli (page 98).

MAKES 6-8 SERVINGS

3-4 lb/1.3-1.8 kg sirloin tip or eye of round beef roast

Salt and pepper

1 Preheat oven to 500°F/260°C.

2 Season meat generously with salt and pepper, then place in a roasting pan and put in the oven. Turn down the oven temperature right away to 475°F/245°C. Roast for 7 minutes per pound, or 21–28 minutes. Turn off heat and leave roast in oven for 2½ hours. *Do not open the oven door even once.*

3 Remove roast from oven, tent loosely with aluminum foil, and allow to rest for 10 minutes.

4 To serve, slice thinly. Leftover roast beef will keep wrapped in foil and refrigerated for 5 days.

ROAST LEG OF LAMB

Creamed Spinach (page 90) is a classic pairing with lamb. You could also try roasting some root vegetables at the same time as the lamb. Parsnips, carrots, white turnip, or rutabaga cut into coarse chunks, tossed in olive oil, seasoned with salt and pepper, and roasted for an hour—that's it. Done like dinner! Add any leftover roasted lamb to curries or strew it over salads.

3 cloves garlic
6 sprigs rosemary
1 lemon
2 Tbsp olive oil, divided
4–4½ lb/1.8-2 kg leg of lamb with bone
Salt and pepper

1 Chop garlic. From 2 rosemary sprigs, pick and chop leaves. Zest and juice lemon. Preheat oven to 400°F/200°C. Lightly oil a roasting pan.

2 With a mortar and pestle, or with a few pulses in a food processor, combine garlic, chopped rosemary, lemon zest, 1 tablespoon of olive oil, and 1 tablespoon of lemon juice.

3 Place whole rosemary sprigs in roasting pan. Place lamb atop rosemary. Season lamb with salt and pepper, then use your hands to rub garlic-rosemary mixture all over. Roast lamb for 75 minutes for medium-rare or 90 minutes for medium. Remove from oven and tent loosely with aluminum foil. Allow meat to rest for at least 15 minutes and up to 30 minutes before carving and serving.

4 To serve, carve lamb into individual portions. Leftover cooked lamb will keep refrigerated in an airtight container for up to 5 days.

LAMB PATTIES WITH SUMAC YOGURT SAUCE

Sumac is a tart spice made by grinding the red berries of several varieties of sumac. Look for it in a well-stocked spice aisle, in a Middle Eastern or Persian supermarket, or even online. If it's impossible to track down, substitute lemon zest for an extra lemony yogurt sauce.

MAKES 4 SERVINGS

1 lemon
15–20 mint leaves
2 shallots
1 lb/450 g ground lamb
1 cup/250 mL plain full-fat yogurt
1 tsp ground sumac
Salt and pepper

1 Zest and juice lemon. Finely chop mint leaves. Dice shallots. Preheat oven to 375°F/190°C.

2 In a bowl, combine ground lamb with lemon zest, mint leaves, and shallots. Season with salt and pepper. Scoop 2 tablespoons of the mixture into your hands, roll into a ball, and place in a shallow baking pan. Repeat with remaining meat mixture. With your fingers or with a fork, press meatballs slightly to make a thick patty. Bake for about 15 minutes or until just barely pink in the middle.

3 While patties are baking, in a bowl combine yogurt with sumac, 1 tablespoon of lemon juice, and salt and pepper.

4 To serve, arrange cooked lamb patties on a serving platter. Top each with a dollop of yogurt sauce. Spoon remaining sauce into a serving dish so people can help themselves to more.

LAMB MOUSSAKA

1 onion

5 cloves garlic

1 medium eggplant

½ cauliflower

1 lemon

6 Tbsp olive oil, divided

1 lb/450 g ground lamb

1 Tbsp dried oregano

2 tsp ground cinnamon

1 Tbsp tomato paste

¼ cup/60 mL dry white wine

1 can (14 fl oz/398 mL) whole tomatoes

1 cup/250 mL coconut cream

2 Tbsp almond flour

Salt and pepper

1 Chop onion. Mince garlic. Slice eggplant into rounds. Break cauliflower into florets. Juice half of lemon. Preheat oven to 400°F/200°C. Lightly oil a rimmed baking sheet and an ovenproof casserole or dish.

2 Arrange eggplant rounds in a single layer on baking sheet. Brush tops with olive oil and season with salt and pepper. Roast for 15 minutes, then turn, brush again with olive oil, and roast for a further 10–15 minutes. The centers should be dark brownish green, no longer the pale green of raw eggplant. When eggplant is cooked, remove from oven and reserve. Leave the oven on.

3 While eggplant is roasting, steam cauliflower. Fill a pot with about 1 inch/2.5 cm of water, set a steaming basket on top (or use a covered steamer), and steam cauliflower florets for 8–10 minutes or until tender. Remove from heat, cover, and set aside.

4 While eggplant and cauliflower are cooking, make meat filling. Warm 2 tablespoons of olive oil in a large heavy-bottomed skillet over medium-high heat. Add onion and sauté for 5–7 minutes or until softened and translucent. Add garlic and stir for 1 minute or until fragrant. Transfer vegetables to a bowl and reserve.

Ingredient assembly and preparation are important for this recipe. The whole dish comes together in just over an hour, if you're well organized. A more leisurely approach could take closer to two hours, which may be a good distraction for days when you're breaking your fast at dinner-time. The cauliflower-based creamy topping is more delicious than traditional béchamel topping—really!

5 Add lamb to skillet and brown until no pink meat is visible. Season with salt and pepper. Return onion and garlic to skillet. Stir in oregano, cinnamon, and tomato paste. Add wine and allow to reduce slightly. Add tomatoes and simmer sauce for 8–10 minutes or until most of the liquid has cooked off.

6 While meat sauce simmers, make cauliflower cream topping. In a blender or food processor, combine coconut cream, 1 tablespoon of lemon juice, and salt and pepper. In a small bowl, add ¼ cup/60 mL of warm water to almond flour. Mix with a fork and add to blender. Blend briefly or process with a couple of pulses. Tip cauliflower into blender and blend thoroughly to make a smooth sauce.

7 Arrange a single layer of cooked eggplant in bottom of an ovenproof dish. Top with half of the meat sauce. Add another layer of eggplant and sauce, repeating until you have used them all. Top with creamy cauliflower sauce. Bake for 35–40 minutes.

8 To serve, allow moussaka to rest for 20 minutes, then cut into individual portions. Leftover moussaka will keep, covered and refrigerated, for 2 days.

SAUSAGE AND LENTIL STEW

A quick and hearty stew for cold days. The foundation is a simple mirepoix: a roughly equal mix of carrots, celery, and leek, which can serve as a flavorful base for all kinds of dishes. If you like to be super efficient in the kitchen, chop double the amount of mirepoix and freeze the extra to have on hand for quick soups and stews.

MAKES 4 SERVINGS

2 carrots

2 stalks celery

1 leek

1 lb/450 g mild Italian sausage

1 bunch flat-leaf parsley

1 Tbsp olive oil

1 Tbsp tomato paste

Pinch of chili flakes

Pinch of herbes de Provence

1 can (14 fl oz/398 mL) diced tomatoes

1 cup/190 g brown or green lentils

2½ cups/625 mL Chicken Broth (page 47) or store-bought stock

Salt and pepper

1. Dice carrots and celery. Remove and discard dark green leaves and tough end from leek. Halve leek lengthwise and slice thinly. Chop sausage into ½-inch/1-cm pieces. Roughly chop parsley.

2. Add olive oil to a large saucepan and heat over medium-high. Add carrots, celery, and leek and give a quick stir. Cook, stirring occasionally, until leek is translucent and vegetables start to sweat and steam, about 5 minutes. Season generously with salt and pepper and cook for another minute.

3. Add tomato paste, chili flakes, herbes de Provence, chopped sausage, canned tomatoes, and lentils. Simmer until lentils have absorbed most of the liquid, about 15 minutes. Add broth and simmer, uncovered, for about 15 minutes or until lentils are soft and stew has thickened to your desired consistency.

4. To serve, season with salt and pepper to taste, and stir in about two-thirds of the parsley. Ladle into bowls and sprinkle with remaining parsley.

STUFFED PORK TENDERLOIN

Mediterranean flavors sing in this easy-to-prepare tenderloin recipe. Because the pork available in grocery stores is usually very lean and can become dry when cooked, we need to add some fat for taste and moisture. Feta to the rescue! Also, be careful not to overcook the pork. Gone are the days when meat had to be gray to be safe. Now, we cook to a lower internal temperature and allow the meat to rest for 5 minutes so it is tender and juicy when served.

MAKES 4–6 SERVINGS

1½ lb/700 g pork
   tenderloin

2 cloves garlic

2 sprigs basil

¼ cup/60 mL sundried
   tomatoes in oil
   (6-8 pieces)

¾ cup/180 mL creamy feta
   (approximately 3 oz)

1 lemon

3 Tbsp olive oil, divided

1 tsp red pepper flakes

1 Tbsp Dijon mustard

Salt and pepper

1 Cut most of the way through the tenderloin, then open up the halves like a book. Mince garlic. Chop basil stems and leaves. Chop sundried tomatoes. Crumble or chop feta. Zest and juice lemon. Have some kitchen twine at hand. Preheat oven to 425°F/220°C.

2 In a small bowl, combine 1 tablespoon of olive oil with garlic, basil, sundried tomatoes, feta, and 1 teaspoon of lemon zest. Season with salt and pepper. Set this filling aside.

3 In another small bowl, combine 2 tablespoons of olive oil, red pepper flakes, Dijon, and 1 tablespoon of lemon juice. Season with salt and pepper. Set this coating aside.

4 Spread filling over tenderloin, leaving a border around the edge. Roll meat around filling, squeezing gently to adhere edges. Don't worry if some filling falls out or edges don't seal. Tie with kitchen twine, if you wish.

5 Place tenderloin in roasting pan and brush all over with Dijon coating. Cook for 15 minutes at 425°F/220°C, then turn down the oven temperature to 350°F/180°C and continue to cook for another 25–30 minutes or until the internal temperature measured with a meat thermometer is 145°F/63°C.

6 To serve, allow pork to rest for 5 minutes before slicing thickly.

PORTUGUESE PORK AND CLAMS

If you haven't tried this wonderful Portuguese stew known as *carne de porco à Alentejana*, it's time to expand your cooking horizons. Although it may seem unusual to some of us, the combination of pork and bivalves is authentically Portuguese. The Buttered Butter Beans (page 117) make a nice accompaniment. Use light, crisp Portuguese white wine, *vinho verde*, if you can.

MAKES 4 SERVINGS

1 lb/450 g pork shoulder or loin

1 onion

4 cloves garlic

1 lemon

4 sprigs flat-leaf parsley

¼ cup/60 mL olive oil

1 Tbsp mild or spicy smoked paprika

½ cup/125 mL vinho verde or other crisp white wine

1½ lb/700 g small clams in shells

Salt and pepper

1 Cut pork into bite-sized cubes. Chop onion and garlic. Zest and juice lemon.

2 In a large pot with a lid, warm olive oil over medium-high heat. Add pork and brown well on all sides, 15–18 minutes. Season with paprika and salt and pepper.

3 Add onions and sauté for 5–7 minutes or until softened and browning. Add garlic and sauté for 1 minute or until fragrant. Add white wine. Cook for 5 minutes or until wine has reduced slightly. Add 1 cup/250 mL of cold water, bring to boil, then turn down heat, cover, and simmer for 1 hour. Stir occasionally and add water if necessary.

4 When the pork is tender, add clams, 2 tablespoons of lemon juice, and salt and pepper. Cover and steam clams for 8–10 minutes or until they have opened. Discard any shells that do not open.

5 Serve in individual bowls, garnished with lemon zest and parsley.

VENISON HUNTER STEW

Finding fresh wild or farmed venison isn't always easy, but this basic stew works equally well with beef chuck. If you are using venison, the eight-hour marinating stage is important; you can forgo it for beef.

2 lb/900 g venison or beef chuck

4 slices bacon

1 onion

3 carrots

1 parsnip

4 oz/112 g button or cremini mushrooms

2 sprigs rosemary

1 bay leaf

2 cups/500 mL dry red wine

1 cup/250 mL Beef Bone Broth (page 46) or store-bought stock

1 Tbsp tomato paste

Salt and pepper

1 Cube venison or beef. Chop bacon. Chop onion. Slice carrots and parsnip. Stem and halve mushrooms.

2 If using venison, put meat, onion, carrots, parsnip, rosemary sprigs, and bay leaf into a nonreactive bowl. Pour red wine and beef broth over meat and veggies. Cover and refrigerate for 8 hours. (Omit this step if using beef.)

3 Drain and reserve marinade. In a large heavy-bottomed Dutch oven or pot with a lid, cook bacon for 5 minutes or until fat has rendered. Remove and reserve bacon. Stir in venison (or beef) and vegetables. Add tomato paste and stir for 2 minutes to cook out some of the rawness. Season with salt and pepper.

4 Pour wine and broth marinade, including bay leaf and rosemary, into pot and bring to a boil. Reduce heat to simmer. Add mushrooms. Simmer, partially covered, for 60–75 minutes or until meat is tender. Don't allow stew to return to a boil or it will become tasteless.

5 To serve, remove bay leaf and rosemary and spoon into individual bowls. Leftovers will keep, covered and refrigerated, for up to 3 days. Reheat very gently.

ACKNOWLEDGMENTS

Special thanks from Alison Maclean to Dr. Jason Fung, whose talent and skill in medical arts and clear explanations in *The Diabetes Code* convinced my dad to give up sugar in all its forms, permanently reversing his type 2 diabetes.

The following avid cooks, testers, guinea pigs, and food adventurers made invaluable contributions to the recipes in *The Diabetes Code Cookbook*. Thanks especially to Julia, for your wondrous work and creativity *dans la cuisine*.

Julia Chanter
Moira French
Charlie Johnston
David Johnston
Hannah Johnston
Scott Lewis
Drummond Maclean
Sandra Maclean
Diane Morch
John Morch
Marilou Roth
Russ Seton

APPENDIX

16-HOUR FAST, 6 DAYS/WEEK

MEALTIME	MONDAY	TUESDAY	WEDNESDAY	THURSDAY	FRIDAY	SATURDAY	SUNDAY
BREAKFAST 7:00 a.m.							Frittata
LUNCH 12:00 p.m.	Mulligatawny Soup	Avocado with Tuna Salad Tomato Soup	Omelet with Fontina and Ham Herb Salad	Mason-jar Miracle	Seed Crackers Hummus Rainbow Beets with Chèvre	Eggs Baked in Prosciutto Cups	Crudités with Dip Chicken Wings with Hot Sauce
DINNER 7:00 p.m.	Cod with Brazil Nut Crust Asparagus Stir-fry	Red Wine Vinegar-braised Chicken Thighs Beans and Greens with Brown Butter	Mussels in Curry Cream Frisée Salad with Poached Eggs and Lardons	Red and White Bean Chili	Sheet-pan Fish Supper	Chicken Thighs with Sprouts and Squash	Hot Tip Roast Beef Stuffed Tomatoes with Goat Cheese Open Sesame Broccoli

24-HOUR FAST, 3 DAYS/WEEK

MEALTIME	MONDAY	TUESDAY	WEDNESDAY	THURSDAY	FRIDAY	SATURDAY	SUNDAY
BREAKFAST 7:00 a.m.	Softly Folded Eggs with Chèvre		Olive Oil–Fried Eggs Herb Salad		Angel Cloud Eggs		Full English Breakfast
LUNCH 12:00 pm	Curried Chicken Salad with Arugula		Spicy Quinoa with Tomatoes and Pine Nuts		Mason-jar Miracle Salad		Italian White Bean Soup
DINNER 7:00 p.m.	Salmon Gravlax Grilled Tomato and Zucchini Salad	Louisiana Gumbo	Masala Salmon Baked Butternut Squash	Chicken Fricassee Pureed Turnip and Parsnip	Turkey Meatballs Creamed Spinach	Bison Burgers Golden Curried Vegetables	Roast Leg of Lamb Panfried Kale with Chili

24-HOUR FAST, 3 DAYS/WEEK

MEALTIME	MONDAY	TUESDAY	WEDNESDAY	THURSDAY	FRIDAY	SATURDAY	SUNDAY
BREAKFAST 7:00 a.m.	Fried Egg on Socca Pancake		Frisée Salad with Poached Eggs and Lardons Softly Folded Eggs with Chèvre		Tofu Scramble Stuffed Tomatoes with Goat Cheese		Omelet with Fontina and Ham
LUNCH 12:00 p.m.	Spicy Garlic Shrimp Buttered Savoy Cabbage	Poached Egg on Cauliflower Crust	Bison Burgers Beans, Greens, and Tomatoes with Brown Butter	Asian Chicken Lettuce Wraps	Mulligatawny Soup	Turkey Breast Stuffed with Gruyère Panfried Kale with Chili	Roasted Flattened Chicken Baked Butternut Squash Lemony Minted Peas
DINNER 7:00 p.m.		Stir-fried Chicken and Veggies		Olive Oil–Poached Tuna with Caper Salsa Mediterranean Baked Broad Beans		Portuguese Pork with Clams Pan-roasted Fennel with Parmesan	

30-HOUR FAST, 3 DAYS/WEEK

MEALTIME	MONDAY	TUESDAY	WEDNESDAY	THURSDAY	FRIDAY	SATURDAY	SUNDAY
BREAKFAST 7:00 a.m.	Huevos Rancheros		Oeufs en Cocotte Herb Salad		Eggs Baked in Prosciutto Cups		Devilled Eggs with Bacon Crumble Tomato Soup with Parm Crisps
LUNCH 12:00 p.m.	Chickpeas with Bitter Greens Roasted Tofu		Tom Kha Crudités with Dip		Mason-jar Miracle		Chicken with Forty Cloves of Garlic Creamed Spinach
DINNER 7:00 p.m.		Mixed G(r)ill Open Sesame Broccoli		Lamb Patties with Sumac Yogurt Sauce Spicy Quinoa with Tomatoes and Pine Nuts		Hot Tip Roast Beef Pureed Turnip and Parsnip Asparagus Stir-fry	

36-HOUR FAST, 3 DAYS/WEEK

MEALTIME	MONDAY	TUESDAY	WEDNESDAY	THURSDAY	FRIDAY	SATURDAY	SUNDAY
BREAKFAST 7:00 a.m.	Hard-boiled Eggs with Pesto Salmon Gravlax		Poached Egg on Cauliflower Crust		Angel Cloud Eggs		Omelet with Fontina and Ham
LUNCH 12:00 p.m.	Italian White Bean Soup		Cauliflower Steak with Cheese		Caldo Verde		Curried Chicken Salad with Arugula
DINNER 7:00 p.m.	Sheet-pan Fish Supper Lemony Minted Peas		Stuffed Pork Tenderloin Fennel and Orange with Greens		Spicy Orange Beef Open Sesame Broccoli Cauliflower Rice		Lamb Moussaka Buttered Savoy Cabbage

INDEX